This book is dedicated to the
memory of *Halloween*'s Godfather.

Moustapha Akkad
1930 - 2005

TAKING SHAPE II: **THE LOST HALLOWEEN SEQUELS**

# TAKING SHAPE II

## THE LOST HALLOWEEN SEQUELS

Dustin McNeill
Travis Mullins

Introduction by
Anthony Masi

Edited by
Natalie Tomaszewski

# TABLE OF CONTENTS

# Introduction
## by Anthony Masi

Producer - Halloween 25 Years of Terror

When Dustin McNeill and Travis Mullins released *Taking Shape: Developing Halloween from Script to Scream*, I thought, "*Holy Haddonfield! Someone finally did it!*" Over the years I had known of many writers working on various tell-all books about the *Halloween* franchise, but none of them ever made it to print. It frustrated me because I knew from my years spent studying the franchise that there was an ocean of behind-the-scenes information that *Halloween* fans would find captivating. When I randomly saw an online ad for their glorious coffee-table sized book, I hit the "*Buy Now*" button faster than Bob reached for Lynda's blouse.

There is something mysteriously addicting about the relationship between Michael Myers, Dr. Loomis, and Laurie Strode that has kept fans hyper-engaged since 1978. We are so engaged, in fact, that we've made fan films, written fan fiction, organized *Halloween*-themed conventions, plastered our bodies with Myers tattoos, cosplayed as the characters, visited the filming locations, designed various forms of artwork, gotten hitched at *Halloween*-themed weddings, and created endless independent and officially-licensed merchandise that would make George Lucas envious. *Star Wars* may have the largest fan base in the mainstream world, but it's *Halloween* that rules the horror underground.

I was therefore honored and thrilled when the authors approached me to write the foreword for *Taking Shape II*, and I attribute their generous request to my front-row seat to watching the *Halloween* phenomenon explode over the years. Let me explain.

I first saw *Halloween* as a pre-teenage boy when it premiered on network television in 1981. The story of the boogeyman stalking teenagers fascinated me, and I couldn't get enough with each new installment that came out in the ensuing years. During those two decades of pure fandom, I never thought I would ever have anything to actually do with the franchise, but life has this miraculous way of bowling you over with beautiful surprises. Today, I am writing this foreword in the wake of running the most popular *Halloween* fansite for six years, working for Trancas International Films for seven years, creating the first *Halloween*-themed convention, and ultimately writing and producing the definitive documentary on the series. It seems that all I've done is watch the franchise gain in popularity since I was barely a teenager, and due to the multiple hats I've worn throughout the years, I've been given some unique and privileged insights into its success.

In 1998, I wanted to learn html programming and decided to design my first website. Since I had also been amassing a large collection of *Halloween* movie memorabilia from around the world, I thought the website could be a fun way to showcase all of my posters, press kits, figurines, novels, etc., that I had collected over the years. I named the site *The Myers Museum*.

As my collection grew and my programming skills improved, the website began attracting a slew of *Halloween* fans that started demanding more frequent updates. I became obsessed with *The Myers Museum*, updating it daily via an America Online dial-up connection from my little apartment in Lake Hiawatha, New Jersey. The website was a one-stop hub for *Halloween* fans where they could find news, contests, fan-fiction, photo galleries, trivia questions, games, reviews, and also the *OHMB* (the *Official Halloween Message Board*), which became the web's main discussion grounds for all-things *Halloween*. In one short year I met so many people whom I still keep in touch with today, and I established myself as an avid *Halloween* memorabilia collector, and obviously, super-fan.

In 1999, I moved to San Diego and eventually attended my first West Coast horror convention at the Pasadena Convention Center where I got to meet Dick Warlock, Pamela Susan Shoop, Daniel Farrands, and Danielle Harris. They were all so friendly as they answered all of our questions and took pictures with us, and I just kept thinking to myself that every *Halloween* fan should be having this amazing and immersive experience. Later, as my friend snapped a photo of me with my arm around Pamela (in my cherished *Halloween 4* t-shirt), I remember thinking how amazing this convention would have been if *all* of the guests were from the *Halloween* series. Right there, the idea flashed before my eyes of a themed event where nothing but *Halloween* celebrities, activities, and merchandise filled the convention floor.

But while my friends thought it was a great idea and encouraged me to pursue it, my inexperience at organizing such an event led to me to believe it would just be too big of a mountain to climb. And so, the idea of a *Halloween* convention remained a pipedream. But not for long.

In 2002, I received an email from Brian Martin and Bruce Dierbeck that, in retrospect, changed the course of my life forever. Brian and Bruce were the webmasters of the official *Halloween* website (*HalloweenMovies.com*, which I'll call *HM.com* from here on out), and were emailing me about the upcoming premiere of *Halloween: Resurrection* in Century City (Los Angeles). Since they both lived out of state and neither were able to attend the premiere, they needed someone local to attend and help them cover it for *HM.com*. Having known about my fansite and that I lived in San Diego, they thought I would be the perfect person to help them out. I jumped at the chance, and even offered to run a contest on *The Myers Museum* to give out free tickets to fans. Brian and Bruce ran it past the powers-that-be at Trancas, and they ultimately gave me permission to raffle off ten pairs of tickets.

The contest received hundreds of replies in less than 24 hours. To select the ten winners, all I did was go into the submissions folder and scroll my cursor up and down to randomly click on ten emails. I called people all around the country handing out tickets to the premiere, and boy did I make a bunch of people really happy that day. At that time, I figured this would be the closest I'd ever get to being a part of the *Halloween* franchise, but my journey was only just beginning.

The very first ticket winner was Paul Swearingen, who called me the day after the premiere. He thanked me profusely and then said, *"You know, I was thinking last night how fun it would be to host a convention that focused on the* Halloween *films."* I told him I had been thinking about that exact idea for years, and then said, *"Let's do it together!"* I remember thinking, *"What am I saying? This guy is a complete stranger, what if he's a nutcase?"* But I was just so excited that I might have actually found a partner to produce the *Halloween* convention with me that I couldn't help myself. We brainstormed hosting the event in a ballroom in a hotel somewhere in South Pasadena where we could screen the *Halloween* films and get as many actors, producers, writers, and directors as possible to attend and mingle with fans. We figured we could draw five hundred people or so to attend, and that's only if we were lucky.

Paul and I started putting things in motion very quickly. He contacted the Hilton Hotel in South Pasadena (where *Halloween* and *Halloween II* were filmed) and they seemed interested in hosting the event. Paul also contacted the city's town hall to see if they would help us with

publicity, and they, too, liked the idea. I then pitched the concept of a *Halloween* convention to the members of the *OHMB* to get an interest check, and everyone responded with resounding approval. With all this enthusiasm in the air and someone to work with me, I figured it was finally time to attempt the climb up this giant mountain.

We met with the hotel manager, signed their contract (well, I did), began selling tickets on *The Myers Museum*, and mailed physical invitations to as many cast and crew from the *Halloween* films as possible to make an appearance. One of those invitees was the great Moustapha Akkad, the executive producer of all the *Halloween* films and owner of Trancas International Films. About a week after mailing his invitation, we received a letter from his office saying that Moustapha would indeed appear, and that he was excited to celebrate the franchise and do a Q&A with the attendees. With his involvement, we were euphoric and unstoppable. *This. Event. Was. Happening!*

I had a full-time job in 2003, but all of my free time was spent organizing the convention, which was to take place on Halloween weekend that same year. I would eventually learn that this wasn't just any mountain I was climbing, it was Mount fucking Everest! Processing ticket sales, finding sponsors, organizing all of the activities, obtaining permits, buying insurance, dealing with hotel requirements, designing and shipping merchandise, responding to daily inquiries, booking guests, updating the website, handling the accounting, doing press, etc., not to mention all the drama between the different personalities involved from certain guests to the convention crew, it was an insane amount of work and frustration, and I bore the brunt of it. Had I known at the onset how difficult and stressful it was going to be, *I can tell you now that I wouldn't have done it.* It wasn't until the event was over that I learned to appreciate my naïveté in that situation.

During this crazy time, I came home from work one day to the following message on my answering machine: *"Hi Tony, my name is Christi, I'm the office manager at Trancas Films, and we'd like to know if you would run our website for us? You came highly recommended. Please call me back."* I was absolutely elated. I played the message at least a dozen times. Of course I was interested, but why were they calling me? What happened to Brian and Bruce? I called Christi back and she explained that the guys chose to pass their webmaster torch to someone else and they recommended me to fill their shoes. She said that since I stepped in to help Trancas with the *Halloween: Resurrection* premiere, and since I was organizing the upcoming convention, that Moustapha felt comfortable with their recommendation. *"Yes! A thousand times yes!"* I said, *"And thank you so much!"*

A few days later I was driving up to Los Angeles to meet with Moustapha and his son, Malek, in their Century City high-rise office building, ready to officially slash my way into the *Halloween* universe. During our interview in Malek's office, Moustapha asked me, *"What is it that makes the fans love* Halloween *so much?"* *"I honestly don't know,"* I said, *"but I do know how to keep them engaged."* Malek loaded up my website on his computer and clicked on a few links while I talked about the various sections, trying to impress him and his dad with my knowledge and excitement for the franchise. I remember Malek saying something complimentary about the site's animated autumn leaves that filled his computer screen. After we discussed pay, Malek said, *"Well, it looks like you're our new guy,"* and welcomed me aboard with a handshake. Moustapha smiled and said, *"Believe me, my son knows much more about the* Halloween*s than me, so he will take it from here. Thank you, Tony."*

When I became the webmaster of *HM.com*, I closed *The Myers Museum* and eagerly transitioned into my new adventure of running the official *Halloween* website. One of the first things I did was promote my precious *Halloween Returns To Haddonfield* 25th anniversary convention, and ticket sales increased to the point where I had to sign another contract with a second hotel. Realizing that a small ballroom was not going to be a large enough space to host the event, Paul and I eventually moved it to the Pasadena Convention Center – the very venue I was standing in when I originally got the idea to create an all-*Halloween* event.

When the weekend of the convention finally arrived, it was nothing short of blissful. It brimmed with so much magic and excitement that I could write an entire book about what unfolded over the course of those two very special days. During the Q&As with the *Halloween* actors, directors, producers, and writers, fans wanted to know every little detail about all eight movies, with so much of their focus being on the storylines in the films. Would there ever be a sequel to *Halloween III*? Why was there an alternate cut to *Halloween: The Curse of Michael Myers*? Would Jamie Lloyd ever return to the series? When one fan suggested that Charles Cyphers reprise his role as Sheriff Brackett in *Halloween 9,* the audience responded with thunderous applause that made Moustapha take notice. I was sitting on the stage right next to him and saw his reaction up-close; it definitely resonated, and I could see that he was seriously considering the idea.

What I witnessed at the convention were 2,500 fans celebrating their unconditional love for the *Halloween* series, and it was palpable. As I walked past the long lines of fans waiting to meet the special guests, I saw people crying and watched friendships forming. When attendees returned from the Haddonfield Bus Tour (we bussed fans up and down the streets of South Pasadena to see *Halloween*'s filming locations), they were elated and smiling from ear to ear. Even a cast member from the original *Halloween* pulled me aside to say, *"I've done a lot of events, but this one by far had the most heart in it."*

The smartest thing we did was film the entire convention experience from beginning to end with multiple cameras. Before Trancas hired me, the reason behind filming everything was to create a DVD to sell on *The Myers Museum* for the fans who were unable to attend the convention. However, once I had joined Trancas, the idea eventually morphed into producing the first feature-length documentary that would tell the incredible story of the entire *Halloween* franchise and its impact on the horror genre. We called it *Halloween: 25 Years of Terror* (*H25* from here on out), and it was eventually distributed by Anchor Bay Entertainment in 2006. We held a DVD signing at Dark Delicacies (a horror bookstore in Burbank, California) and hundreds of fans lined up around the block. In two hours, the store's entire stock of DVDs sold out, and *H25* would go on to become one of Anchor Bay's best-selling titles. The reason for its success was obvious: this was the first time the door had been opened to behind-the-scenes information about the *Halloween* series in such a grand and comprehensive way.

**ABOVE**: Anthony Masi hosting the Producers Panel with Irwin Yablans and Moustapha Akkad at the Halloween Returns To Haddonfield 25th Anniversary Convention in 2003.

**ABOVE**: Charles Cyphers cuts the Silver Anniversary cake during the VIP Party at the convention. (L to R): Malek Akkad, Daniel Farrands, Don Shanks, Brad Loree, Cliff Emmich, Chris Durand, Brian Andrews, Tom Morga, Lance Warlock, Dick Warlock, Anthony Masi, and Jim Winburn.

When Malek asked me to help organize the 30th anniversary convention, I respectfully turned the opportunity down because I couldn't imagine what satisfaction could be derived from conquering Mount Everest twice. To this day, the *Halloween*-only convention experience is replicated every five years and I've attended all of them. They've certainly gotten bigger and more lucrative, and that's been very rewarding to see.

During my seven years at Trancas, I didn't have to actually visit the office to perform my webmaster duties, but I was there often because *H25* took three years to make. Our director lived in another country, so I had to oversee all of the documentary's post-production tasks completely by myself. At the same time I also produced several other projects for Trancas, so it worked out that I was there regularly.

Whenever I actually saw Moustapha, I'd ask him, *"What's new in* Halloween *land?"* and every now and then he would share something with me. One day he said, *"Tony, I don't know what to do,"* then went on to say that Busta Rhymes was in the office the day before and they had a long talk about his potential return for *Halloween 9* (to this day I've been bummed for having missed bumping into Busta by one lousy day). When I asked Moustapha what the problem was, he said, *"Busta wasn't happy with his performance in the last movie, and he is concerned about being in another one."* He said they talked about the potential storyline of Freddie (Busta's character) tracking down Myers to confront and finally kill him. "*Oh no, Moustapha,*" I thought, "*please don't do that!*" But instead I said, "*Would you really kill Michael?*" And Moustapha said in a loud voice, "*Michael never dies!*" After that, I thought to myself, "*It's the end of the road for you, Freddie.*"

Another time, I was at my desk job in San Diego when my cell rang. It said "Trancas" on the screen so I got up and hurried outside to take the call. I thought it was Christi because she would call frequently, but this time it was Moustapha himself calling me directly. I remember thinking, "*Oh shit, what's wrong? What did I do?*" Luckily, he only wanted a favor. "*I need your help, Tony,*" he said. "*Can you please put up a poll on the website to see how the fans feel about doing a Myers vs Pinhead movie?*" "*Myers vs Pinhead?*" I asked. "*Well yeah, the* Freddy vs Jason *movie made a lot of money and Miramax has this idea to do something similar, and they are pressuring me. But you know, Tony, I don't see it.*" I couldn't help myself and blurted out, "*Neither do I. It's a bad idea!*" "*This Pinhead,*" he said, "*he does not mix well in the real world of Michael Myers, and I want to do a poll to prove to Miramax that the fans won't like this idea. I just think it stinks.*"

That night, I launched the poll on the website and, like the wise producer he was, Moustapha was right. The fans voted in droves and while it wasn't by any means a landslide (I believe it was actually a surprising 65% No against 35% Yes), and since I never heard a word about the Myers vs Pinhead mash-up again, I always liked to think that I helped Moustapha give the fans a voice to collectively band together and avoid a *Halloween* disaster.

I had to go to Miramax Films for something one day, and I spoke with an executive who said the studio was definitely interested in making *Halloween 9* despite the poor box office performance of *Halloween: Resurrection*, but the story had to be top-notch before anyone took a step forward. The executive said they had heard dozens of pitches, and when one writer eventually pitched a story about the U.S. Army harnessing Michael's blood to create a super-Army, they were convinced the series could finally be out of ideas.

Another time, I had brought a friend (also a *Halloween* fan) who was visiting from Canada with me to the office when Christi answered a call. My friend and I could tell from what Christi was saying on her end that they were indeed going to remake *Halloween* with Rob Zombie, and when she hung up I tried to drag it out of her as my friend just smiled the whole time. Christi put up a good fight, but eventually spilled the beans and confirmed that it was officially happening. She begged us, "*Please don't say anything to anyone!*" We all just laughed about it, and my friend and I held to our promise of secrecy.

My worst memory of my time at Trancas was the day Moustapha Akkad died in 2005. I will never forget the look on Christi's face when she gave me the news. I was supposed to meet with Malek at their Century City office on that fateful morning, and as I walked in I noticed that all the lights were out. Christi was quietly sitting at her desk holding the phone, which she was just hanging up. Since she was obviously alone in the office I immediately assumed that Malek forgot about our meeting because he was guilty of doing that once before, and that the look of concern on Christi's face was going to be followed with, *"So sorry, Tony, but Malek isn't here."* I made light of things and said with a smile, *"Oh no, don't tell me Malek forgot... again!"* Christi responded in a serious tone, *"Moustapha and his daughter were in a terrorist attack, a bombing."* Her eyes were wide as she spoke, and her words horrified me. Christi told me they were being treated in a hospital in Amman, Jordan, and that she thought they were going to die, and then she started crying. I remember saying things to try and comfort her, but then we both got silent and just sat in the office for a long time in near shock. Sixty people died that day due to bombings from an Al-Qaeda attack on three hotels, and Moustapha and his daughter, Rima Al Akkad Monla, were among the victims. They were apparently in town for a wedding and were attending a reception at the hotel when the bomb went off.

Since I was running *HM.com*, I immediately converted the website into a tribute page for Moustapha and Rima, where I posted every single email that poured in from heartbroken fans and *Halloween* alumni, and sat in front of my computer for days making sure every sentiment got posted. I won't lie, I was in tears the entire time out of pain, but also out of pressure. I felt a responsibility to make sure the website was perfect, it was the least I could do for a man whom I admired so much, and who generously included me in his *Halloween* family. But my thoughts were also with Malek, and since the website would probably be one of the first places news outlets would go for updates, I wanted Malek to know that I had things covered, and for him to just not have to worry about giving me any direction. Malek called me about a week later and thanked me for how I handled everything and it was one of the few times in my life when I was at a loss for words. My heart broke for him, and I just reassured him that I would continue to help in any way that I could. I eventually designed the full-page tribute to Moustapha that appeared in *Variety* magazine, and I also helped Malek organize a beautiful memorial service for his father at the Writers Guild of America in Beverly Hills, which took place in early January 2006.

Looking back, I loved working for Trancas International Films and I am so grateful to Moustapha and Malek for the opportunities they gave me. My time at Trancas ended in 2009, and because I had such an immersive foundation in *Halloween* land, I developed valuable skills which allowed me to go on to produce many other projects in a career I'm very proud of through my company, MasiMedia.

So here we are over four decades since John Carpenter and Debra Hill made their $325,000 movie blockbuster, and we're still watching and talking about *Halloween* and its sequels. One could argue the series is currently in its prime, and its rising success has surely surprised even the harshest critics who thought *Halloween: Resurrection* was the death knell of the franchise. Hell, we've even watched "I'll-never-make-another-*Halloween*" John Carpenter push himself so far away from the series with such resistance that he's finally circled back around again to help more movies get made forty years later.

When I read *Taking Shape*, I was delighted to discover that Dustin and Travis had the same revelation that I did after studying the franchise, which was that the *Halloween* films are brimming with textured and thoughtful stories that went above and beyond what most slasher films were doing, and that's the very reason that supplemental documentaries and tell-all books are so necessary for this series. All these years later, I'm still joyfully connecting dots that I didn't know were there, whether they were intentional or not. Throughout my years running the *Halloween* websites, organizing the convention, and producing *H25*, all I did was see fans and experts examining, dissecting, and interpreting everything in every *Halloween* movie. It never gets old and there is always something exciting to talk about when it comes to the saga of the boogeyman and his reign of terror in Haddonfield. And with new fans discovering the franchise with each new sequel, the momentum has only gotten stronger.

After sitting in my front-row seat all these years, I've concluded that there are two key ingredients that keep breathing life into the series.

The first ingredient is something Moustapha realized after *Halloween III* tanked at the box office. He understood that the character of Michael Myers – more specifically, the mask – would continue to make the franchise successful. Not John Carpenter, not Jamie Lee Curtis, not the music, not the actors that played Michael, nothing else but the white rubber mask itself. *The mask was the boogeyman*. Therefore, Moustapha's main priority was making sure that Michael lived to wear his infamous mask again for as many sequels as possible.

The second ingredient is the more important one, and it's <u>story</u>. Ignorantly, snooty movie critics have insulted the slasher genre for years by saying, *"They're all the same, it's always just a bunch of teenagers getting killed,"* yet any die-hard slasher fan knows that it goes much deeper than that. In movies, story is everything, and that's true for all movie genres, including the ones where teenagers get murdered every ten minutes. A good friend of mine, who was a famous magician, once said: *"The human heart cries out for magic,"* and a good story is, at its core, a magical experience; it teaches us something and mesmerizes us, and in turn we'll *feel* something, even if people are screaming and blood is spraying everywhere. The reason why the *Halloween* series has so many story arcs and characters and has changed directions multiple times is very simple: *it's because the filmmakers are pulling out all the stops to tell stories that move us.* And in order to do that, they over-develop many storylines and, hopefully, they end up producing the best ones.

This is why the book you're holding in your hands is so special. For the first time in history, Dustin McNeill and Travis Mullins have pulled back the curtain to reveal twenty-four "lost" sequel ideas for the *Halloween* universe that were pondered and nurtured, and for various reasons didn't make it to the big screen. This isn't fan fiction, rather, these are actual storylines that were developed by professional writers alongside the producers of the franchise. These lost sequels have lived in the background, peering back at us from the shadows like silent predators wanting to strike, waiting patiently for the day they could finally spring forth and unleash their terror upon us. And it is my absolute pleasure to introduce them to you.

It's now time for you to whip up a frothy Stomach Pounder, get comfy, and dig into these alternate visions from Haddonfield.

Anthony Masi

Los Angeles, California

October 2020

# A Word From the Authors

Well, here we are again. Truthfully, we had never planned on doing another *Taking Shape*. The book you're now holding began as an appendix in the first book. That soon grew into its own chapter, which quickly evolved into several chapters. We realized we had a problem when the lost sequel chapters began to overtake the actual sequel chapters. Twas then we knew we had the makings of a second book.

*Halloween* fans are a passionate bunch and, given that, some of these unmade takes may well prove divisive. We have tried to remain diplomatic, allowing the screenwriters to share their valid perspectives on, at times, such varied stories. Fans tend to have strict criteria for what does and does not belong in a *Halloween* sequel. That said, art is subjective and open to interpretation. By shedding light on these unmade films, we hope to do justice to the series creators, the creative process, and the writers themselves.

We should be upfront about something - these aren't *all* the lost sequels. Chronicling them all would be impossible - there's just too many! Rather, this book examines twenty-four lost projects we were able to cover in reasonable detail, most often by connecting with the talents behind them. We were quite selective in choosing which scripts to cover - no fan fics or spec works by unproven talent. If you finish this book and want to read some of these stories, the vast majority have been available online for years, some leaked by the writers themselves.

Having ourselves fallen down the deep rabbit hole of lost sequels, we wouldn't encourage anyone to read this book in one or even two sittings. Take frequent breaks, drink lots of water, and give yourself time to process it all. If you start to confuse the details of these these unmade projects, feel free to consult the summary guide on page 584.

It should be said the majority of *Taking Shape II* was written before it was announced that the eleventh follow-up - *Halloween Kills* - had been delayed to October 2021. We hope our book might serve as some consolation and make the wait a little easier to bear. Like you, we're eager to see what's next in store for the franchise we hold so dear.

Photo courtesy Andy Mathieu (IG: myersfiendclub)

# Prologue:
# Fear and Loathing in Haddonfield

In the forty years since John Carpenter's 1978 classic was released, the *Halloween* franchise has reigned as one of the most enduring horror sagas of all time. The eleven-film series – soon to welcome two more sequels – has accumulated over $750 million at the worldwide box office while also becoming the highest-grossing horror franchise in North America. That's quite a feat, too, when you consider that original film and its most humble of beginnings. Fans have long poured over each installment, which depict the various misadventures of screen slasher Michael Myers as he battles familial relations, Druidic cults, reality television, and even Rob Zombie, before coming full circle with 2018's *Halloween*. But what of the many sequels that *didn't* reach the screen? Now, that's surely a topic worth examining.

The tale of the "lost" *Halloween* sequels begins with its fourth installment. As we'll come to find, there's a reason that entry holds this distinction, spawning from a rather precarious situation – the result of conflicting producers and disappointing endeavors. But we're getting ahead of ourselves here. Before we can dive into these lost treasures, we must first acknowledge the inherent difficulty in producing a decent follow-up to *Halloween* – a film that, by most accounts, was never intended to have a sequel, let alone thirteen. It's true that neither John Carpenter nor Debra Hill had ever planned on *Halloween* becoming a franchise. (Nor did they set out to christen the birth of a new sub-genre of horror film.) How could they have known they were making a seminal motion picture – the specter of which would forever loom over their entire careers? Had they even the slightest inkling of these things, they might've not made *Halloween*.

Unlike the franchise it would lead to, development on the first film was an organic process between genial collaborators. The initial spark began with producer Irwin Yablans in 1977 as he mulled potential subjects for his next production. He quickly settled on producing a horror film, the plot of which would revolve around a killer that targets babysitters in a quiet suburban community. Titled *The Babysitter Murders*, Yablans pitched this premise to writer/director John Carpenter, whose *Assault on Precinct 13* had just been released through Yablans' Compass International Pictures. Carpenter liked the idea and agreed to write, direct, and score the production for $10,000. He also negotiated a deal for his then-girlfriend Debra Hill to co-write and produce alongside him.

Yablans next pitched *The Babysitter Murders* to business partner Moustapha Akkad, who, at the time, was busy prepping his own directorial effort overseas – a Libyan historical epic titled *Lion of the Desert*. While initially hesitant to invest in the production, he was eventually persuaded by Yablans to fund the project for a mere $300,000 – a fraction of what he was accustomed to spending with his great epics. Though Akkad remained overseas for most of the film's production, he would later take a much more hands-on role in developing future sequels. He would forego executive producer billing on the original film, opting for a "Presented By" credit instead.

By all accounts, the screenplay for the project came together with relative ease in a matter of weeks. Carpenter and Hill began by creating a basic outline together. They then expanded that outline into a full script by separately focusing on individual plot elements. Their story would open on six-year-old Michael Myers, who brutally murders his teenage sister on Halloween night with a large kitchen knife, motivation unknown. The boy falls into a catatonic daze and is immediately moved to a sanitarium. Over time, his psychiatrist – Dr. Sam Loomis – grows convinced that Michael isn't mentally ill but rather pure evil and incredibly dangerous. Fifteen years later, the now adult Michael escapes custody just before Halloween. Donning a featureless white mask, he now becomes "The Shape" and begins to stalk teenage babysitter Laurie Strode and her peers. By night's end, Laurie's friends will all be dead. She'll be saved from the Shape's attack at the last moment by Dr. Loomis, though the slasher will ultimately escape into the night.

In retrospect, it's odd just how unremarkable the creation of this original *Halloween* was – especially given the creative clashes that would unfurl on nearly every one of its sequels. For example, as readers likely know, practically every filmmaker involved in *Halloween 6* had a different opinion on how the story should proceed. Its production involved feuding producers, endless rewrites, studio intervention, last-minute reshoots, and a lawsuit. That's in addition to the revolving door of writers and directors that defined its development. None of this happened on the original *Halloween* and there's a perfectly good reason why it didn't. With his contract,

Carpenter negotiated that he would have complete control over the film – and so he did. Yablans did provide some helpful notes which Carpenter voluntarily incorporated. One of these was to condense the film's action to a single night to save on budget. Another was to re-title the project from *The Babysitter Murders* to *Halloween*.

*Halloween*'s production proceeded just as uneventfully as its development had. Newcomer Jamie Lee Curtis was cast as Laurie Strode and veteran actor Donald Pleasence as Dr. Loomis. Aspiring filmmaker Nick Castle would perform the role of the adult Shape. Filming took place across three weeks in the spring of 1978. The filmmakers chose locations throughout South Pasadena, California to represent the fictional town of Haddonfield, Illinois. Cinematographer Dean Cundey gave the film a unique look by using the new Panavision camera system to simulate the killer's point-of-view. Production designer Tommy Lee Wallace would fashion the Shape's iconic white visage from a Captain Kirk mask by Don Post Studios. In addition to co-writing and directing, Carpenter also stepped up to score the film in post-production. His theme music would hauntingly blend synthesized chords with a staccato piano rhythm to create an unforgettable melody. These elements and more would combine to create *Halloween* as we know it.

The film arrived in just four theaters in Kansas City, Missouri on October 25, 1978, operating under a regional release strategy – typical for the era. Within two weeks, the film was playing on roughly two-hundred screens, mostly throughout New York and Los Angeles. While garnering some dismissive reviews, the majority of audiences and critics seemed quick to recognize *Halloween* as a masterwork of the genre. Carpenter was frequently compared to Alfred Hitchcock by way of *Psycho*, which was lofty praise. Even the most ardent anti-horror critics seemed in favor of the movie. This included Chicago columnists Gene Siskel and Roger Ebert, both of whom would become well-known opponents of modern horror, especially slashers.

The film also took home several awards soon after release. Carpenter was presented with a special Silver Plaque award at the 1978 Chicago Film Festival for his work on this and *Assault on Precinct 13*. Other accolades included the New Generation Award from the Los Angeles Film Critics Association, and the Critics Award at the prestigious Avoriaz Fantastic Film Festival in Portes du Soleil, France. (Though losing to *The Wicker Man*, the film was also nominated for Best Horror Film at the 1979 Saturn Awards.) *Halloween* would go on to age incredibly well over the years. In 2006, the film was chosen for preservation in the United States National Film Registry by the Library of Congress for being "culturally, historically, or aesthetically significant."

*Halloween* wasn't just a critical darling upon release but a commercial one as well. The film would gross an impressive $5 million in its first month of limited release before expanding to more screens throughout the country. That *Halloween* played beyond fall 1978 and well into winter and spring of 1979 spoke volumes of its strong word-of-mouth with audiences. As Compass International Pictures' own self-congratulatory advertising boasted, "Everyday is Halloween when you're doing this kind of business!" That would certainly explain its successful re-releases in October of 1979 and 1980. The film's commercial appeal was not limited to its homeland either, becoming an international hit in Denmark, Italy, and West Germany among other territories – despite Halloween not being a recognized holiday outside of North America. Foreign releases would reflect this lack of familiarity, adding additional titles such as *The Night of the Masks*, *The Night of the Witches*, and even *The Night of the Creeps*, in France, Italy, and Belgium, respectively.

"Halloween may not have been an international holiday, but we might be making it one," Irwin Yablans proudly declared to *Starburst* in 1979. "I've appropriated an American tradition!" Indeed, several countries such as Germany and Italy would begin adopting elements of the holiday, purportedly fueled by exposure to Western pop culture. Altogether, *Halloween* would go on to gross a reported $70 million worldwide, making it among the most successful independent productions of all time. The film would find further success on television with NBC buying broadcast rights for an astounding $3 million in 1980.

With a meager budget of $325,000 and a gross many times that, *Halloween* had demonstrated an extremely viable formula for filmmakers looking to make a quick buck. This resulted in a number of ripoffs and imitators, the most well-known and successful being 1980's *Friday the 13th* and its numerous sequels. (You might also consider *Prom Night, The Prowler, Absurd, Blood Rage, Offerings,* and *Final Exam* – among many others.) The Australian producers of 1979's *Snapshot* were so eager to cash in on *Halloween*'s popularity that they re-titled their film *The Day After Halloween* for release in the United States. (That was despite the fact that *Snapshot* had nothing to do with Halloween nor was it even a slasher film.) In lieu of big budgets, strong casts, and well-written screenplays, these imitators often turned to graphic violence to shock their audiences and build reputations. While this was an undeniable side effect of *Halloween*'s success, it was counter to the values that had made it scary in the first place.

"Imitation is the highest form of flattery," John Carpenter told *Starlog* in 1985. "So, in a way, I'm very flattered. But I don't think the motives of the people who imitate *Halloween* are such that I should be flattered. They just want to make big bucks. That's not why you make a film. You should make a film because you want to make a good film."

Compared to its sequels, the creation of the original *Halloween* had been a smooth ride. As already mentioned, Carpenter retained full creative control, which left little room for strife or disagreement. With such a low budget, there was also less pressure to deliver a huge commercial hit. Even a modest box office success would likely yield a return on investment. Then again, no one yet knew what *Halloween*'s true potential was. None of these factors would apply on the sequels that followed. The investments would be greater as would be the expectations. And Carpenter would be the first and last director to have complete creative control on a *Halloween*.

Regardless of how you may feel about it, there is simply no romanticizing the origins of 1981's *Halloween II*. John Carpenter and Debra Hill had been vocal about not wanting to return for a sequel in any capacity. They did so largely (and admittedly) to recoup profits they felt were still owed to them from the original *Halloween*. While the pair agreed to once again co-write and co-produce, neither was willing to fill the director's chair. For that, Carpenter chose Rick Rosenthal, an up-and-coming director from the American Film Institute (AFI) who had yet to helm a full-length feature. Unlike its predecessor, the creation of *Halloween II* would be rife with creative differences at all stages of production. And not just your garden-variety spats, mind you, but deep disagreements on the most fundamental aspects of the project. *Halloween II* didn't just generate conflict among its creators – it was born from it.

# "We were literally forced into making a sequel because of business considerations."

- John Carpenter, Halloween Audio Commentary

Though not released until October 1981, Irwin Yablans first conceived of a potential follow-up in 1979 as *Halloween*'s box office success was still ongoing. He secured a verbal agreement from Carpenter to partner on two upcoming productions for Compass International – *The Fog* and *Halloween II*. Yablans made the mistake of discussing his plans with AVCO Embassy head Bob Rehme, who quickly went behind Yablans' back to sign Carpenter to a two-picture deal for *The Fog* and *Escape from New York*. This infuriated Yablans, who immediately sued both Rehme and Carpenter. The suit was settled out of court and allowed Carpenter to make *The Fog* for AVCO so long as he agreed to make *Halloween II* for Compass immediately after. With this, Carpenter and Yablans were no longer affable colleagues but bitter business partners. *Halloween*'s writer/director would later sue its executive producer over claims of missed profit-sharing payments. Yablans would vent on their soured relationship in his 2012 autobiography: "It still disturbs me when I think of the ingratitude displayed by Carpenter, after having literally changed his life."

In 1980, Italian movie mogul Dino De Laurentiis reached out to Yablans with a lucrative offer to buy the production rights to *Halloween II* which, shockingly, Yablans agreed to sell. On the bright side, this deal earned Compass millions of dollars before a script for *Halloween II* was even written. On the down side, it excluded the company from the untold millions the film would later earn at the box office. It also prevented Yablans from having any direct input or control over *Halloween*'s first sequel. He would still retain an executive producer credit, though it would be in name only. Yablans would later decry his deal with Dino De Laurentiis as one of the biggest mistakes of his entire career. For his part, De Laurentiis would secure a distribution arrangement with Universal Pictures and oversee Carpenter and Hill's work on *Halloween II*.

It should be noted that, barring issues with Yablans, the chief reason Carpenter and Hill were reluctant to pursue the project was their belief that a story as simple as *Halloween* didn't lend itself to a sequel. Keep in mind, sequels were relatively uncommon during this period. In particular, horror sequels were only just starting to gain momentum, with *Jaws 2*, *Omen II,* and *Exorcist II* all released the same year as *Halloween*. For Carpenter and Hill, their mission would be to produce a follow-up that not only bested their competition but would also be worthy of their original and the critics' adoration for it – all the while not truly wanting to repeat themselves. For them, it would prove challenging in tracking the progression of Laurie, Loomis, and the Shape – a challenge that would also present with each succeeding sequel.

The filmmakers initially considered several different directions for the sequel. Prior to selling the rights, Yablans teased that the Shape might follow Laurie off to college. Likewise, Carpenter and Hill alternately formulated an idea where Laurie might now be living in a highrise apartment building. The Shape would appear once again to terrorize her on Halloween night with Dr. Loomis not far behind. While briefly considered, neither of these ideas were developed into a full screenplay. "It would have been absolutely ludicrous to [set] the film several years later," Debra Hill informed *Twilight Zone*, "Where has the Shape been? He hasn't spoken a word since he was six years old, he's not schooled … so where has he been all that time? We figured that people would least expect us to do it with a five-minute overlap."

As written, *Halloween II* picks up directly from its predecessor with the Shape having vanished into the night. Laurie Strode is taken to nearby Haddonfield Memorial Hospital for treatment while Loomis continues the search for his escaped patient. The wounded Shape follows Laurie to the hospital and begins slashing through staff in an effort to reach her. Elsewhere, Loomis learns the startling secret behind his patient's latest fixation – Michael and Laurie are siblings! With this, he rushes to Haddonfield Memorial only to find Laurie under attack from her estranged brother. A bloody confrontation ensues with Loomis appearing to kill himself and the Shape in a massive explosion. While severely traumatized, Laurie survives the night.

Not everyone was a fan of this new approach, to put it mildly. Among the project's earliest detractors was *Halloween* production designer Tommy Lee Wallace, whom Carpenter and Hill had initially invited to helm the sequel. (Early reports indicate David Lynch was once attached as well.) Like Rosenthal, *Halloween II* would've marked Wallace's directorial debut and a tremendous opportunity. He was excited for the gig – until he read Carpenter and Hill's screenplay. Feeling that audiences would expect *Halloween II* to adhere to popular horror trends, Carpenter elected to pack the sequel with blood splatter and gore – elements that were largely absent from the original *Halloween* but present in imitators such as *Friday the 13th*. This marked a noticeable change in tone from the first film. For Wallace, this was a deal-breaker.

"The most vivid thing I remember about the *Halloween II* script was the Shape punching a hypodermic needle through someone's eyeball," Wallace said in his *Taking Shape* interview. "I hated that so bad. It felt like a huge sell-out to me. I will say that I've noticed in recent interviews that John also feels like he sold out, but he was doing what he felt he had to do. And let's face it, *Halloween II* was a profitable venture for both him and Debra."

Even co-writer and producer Debra Hill seemed against this direction, which was not at all how she originally envisioned the sequel. "If you remember, there was no blood in *Halloween*," she told *The Indianapolis News*. "Everything since then has been blood and guts. We want *Halloween II* to end the trend. […] *Halloween II* is a continuation of the same night. It will be another emotional roller coaster without any visceral images. We can leave that up to the imagination of the audience."

The decision to pattern *Halloween* after the very films it had inspired marked an unfortunate turning point. Carpenter's original *Halloween* was an undeniable trailblazer that had led the genre into a new era. That leadership would effectively end on *Halloween II*, which would opt to follow genre trends rather than create them. This would happen again on subsequent entries, most notably with *Halloween H20* (drawing on *Scream*), *Halloween: Resurrection* (echoing *The Blair Witch Project*, even if unintentionally), and Rob Zombie's *Halloween* (the remake bandwagon.) Tommy Lee Wallace wasn't alone in his opposition to this new direction. Rosenthal himself was no fan of splatter. Neither were Moustapha Akkad or Irwin Yablans – not that Yablans could voice that opinion. Given the legal sparring that begat *Halloween II*, Carpenter and Hill ensured their former collaborator was not allowed on-set nor afforded any control over the sequel.

*Halloween II* was shot across roughly six weeks in the spring of 1981, double the length of filming on Carpenter's original. While the $2.5 million budget was almost nine times that of the original film, it was among the most cheaply-produced box office hits of the year. Unfortunately, the sequel's backstage drama extended beyond its early development and well into post-production. There existed a growing concern amongst producers that *Halloween II* wasn't shaping up to par. They felt the sequel needed additional work and that Rosenthal might not be the one to oversee it. This concern was bolstered by negative feedback collected during the test screening process. To remedy this, Carpenter himself assumed control of the film, re-cutting key sequences while altogether deleting others. He also returned to the director's chair for several days of additional photography, which upped the bloodletting and kill count. These changes radically altered the film's chronology, tone, and pacing much to Rosenthal's frustration. Being a new filmmaker and an outsider to the Carpenter camp, he lacked the political pull to oppose these changes. "I was pretty pissed," the director told *Cinefantastique* upon the film's release.

"It was tough for John to be a director and not be directing. And it was tough for me to be a director and have another director producing. And Debra, who had worked only with John, found it tough to work with a first-time director."

- Rick Rosenthal, Cinefantastique

"Rick was challenged by the fact that he didn't want to direct *Halloween II* in the shadow of John Carpenter," Dean Cundey recalled in his *Taking Shape* interview. "He wanted to add his own storytelling touches to it. […] It wasn't always easy trying to support Rick while also supporting John and Debra, all the while trying to make a film that was worthy of the original *Halloween*."

"There were an awful lot of producers who wanted a shot at crafting the film," Rosenthal later told *Fangoria*. "Dino De Laurentiis had one idea of how the film should be paced, and John and Debra had another idea. I had a third idea, but I was the one who counted the least. I was the least experienced and had the least power. In the end, the cut of *Halloween II* that was released was certainly not mine. […] Sequences were stripped out that I liked and other scenes were put in that would not have been my choice had I been the producer."

To make matters worse, Carpenter would soon come to regret some of his own choices on the production, later lambasting the sequel as "an abomination and a horrible movie" on *Cinema Showcase* in 1984. In clarifying his remarks, Carpenter blamed his own script for the movie's most serious failings. He would continue to criticize his *Halloween II* contributions in subsequent years, particularly the decision to make Michael and Laurie siblings. Many others have signaled their agreement, arguing that this sudden change in direction demystifies the Shape by assigning him a motivation. Why go this route in the first place then? Carpenter cites an unfortunate combination of alcohol and writer's block. Love it or hate it, the sibling twist does seem at odds with the spirit of the original *Halloween*.

Resentful writers, an inexperienced director, and opinionated producers. You might think this a sure recipe for disaster but by most accounts, *Halloween II* was not a bad sequel. The 1981 follow-up was a worthwhile thriller in its own right. Many would argue it re-defined the franchise in a way that would carry it forward across the next three decades. In 2018, *Variety*'s Matthew Chernov ranked it the second-best *Halloween* behind the original, hailing it a "superlative sequel" that "looks and feels like it was shot simultaneously with its predecessor." The following year, *Rolling Stone* ranked the film sixth on their list of the twenty best horror sequels. Not by any means was the film a commercial failure, either. Unlike the original's slow burn success, *Halloween II* was an immediate hit, debuting atop the domestic box office with $7.4 million and maintaining that spot the following weekend. Upon opening, the sequel set two box office records – the highest debut for an R-rated film and the highest debut for a slasher film. The follow-up would earn over $25 million at the domestic box office, making it the second-highest grossing horror film of 1981 behind *An American Werewolf in London*. When we adjust for inflation, *Halloween II* stands as the highest-grossing franchise follow-up until the Rob Zombie remake in 2007.

Given *Halloween II*'s box office performance, both Dino De Laurentiis and Universal Pictures were eager to sign on for *Halloween III*. Unsurprisingly, Carpenter and Hill were again less eager to return, even telling reporters they had no plans for a third film. They had genuinely intended for *Halloween II* to be the last word on the Michael Myers storyline, which is why both the Shape and Dr. Loomis perish in its fiery finale. The pair remained steadfast in their refusal to resurrect the dead slasher. They would consider returning, however, if they would be permitted to develop a new storyline unrelated to the first two films. Universal and De Laurentiis agreed and *Halloween III* entered into development not long after the release of *Halloween II*. Carpenter and Hill's roles would be even more scaled back this time around, serving only as producers.

Both Moustapha Akkad and Irwin Yablans were vehemently opposed to the idea of a *Halloween* that didn't continue in the tradition of the original film. Neither were consulted on the new direction, however, given that Compass International had sold *Halloween III*'s production rights to Dino De Laurentiis along with those of *Halloween II*. Compass would eventually transition to a subsidiary of Moustapha Akkad's Trancas International Pictures, who would never again relinquish their stake in the franchise.

Carpenter initially developed *Halloween III* with the understanding that filmmaker Joe Dante would be directing it. Dante had expressed enthusiasm for the project and suggested they turn to famed British screenwriter Nigel Kneale to pen the script. The pair met with Kneale and, despite finding him to be a curmudgeonly old man, invited him to write *Halloween III*. The scribe accepted their invite despite not liking either of the first two *Halloween* movies and feeling his installment would surely be the best. Soon after this, Dante departed the project for another opportunity. In desperate need of a new director, Carpenter turned to friend and colleague Tommy Lee Wallace, who had been production designer on the original *Halloween*. Wallace enthusiastically signed on to direct *Halloween III*.

While writing *Halloween II* had been a laborious chore for John Carpenter, it was produced with relative autonomy. The same cannot be said for *Halloween III*, which endured a much-complicated road to the screen. Nigel Kneale was given enormous creative freedom in composing his first draft. His only direction had been to create a story that brought witchcraft into the computer age. He would draw heavily upon the traditions and mythologies of his homeland, particularly those he learned growing up on the Isle of Man. While Carpenter and Wallace liked Kneale's original draft, they did have notes on changes they wished to see incorporated into a second draft. Kneale was strongly opposed to these changes, however, and refused to modify his draft. This led Carpenter to perform an uncredited re-write of Kneale's work. Despite liking some of his colleague's changes, Wallace was still unhappy with the script and did his own credited re-write. In the end, *Halloween III*'s shooting script was so far removed from Kneale's original draft that the screenwriter demanded his name be taken off it. Since Carpenter's work had been uncredited, this left Wallace as the only screenwriter on the project. The project took on a subtitle under their watch to become *Halloween III: Season of the Witch*.

*Halloween III*'s story begins a week before the titular holiday with a deranged old man being hospitalized for his bizarre behavior. Incoherent and clutching a rubber mask, he's soon killed in his bed by a robot assassin, who self-immolates after the murder. His daughter, Ellie Grimbridge, teams up with his physician, Dr. Dan Challis, to investigate further. Their search leads them to the small town of Santa Mira, California, home of the Silver Shamrock Novelty Company. It's here they uncover a diabolical plot by company boss Conal Cochran to murder millions of children on Halloween night. Cochran, an immortal warlock in disguise, has designed the company's masks to murder the wearer upon broadcast of special signal scheduled for Halloween evening. Challis manages to escape the Silver Shamrock factory, which is guarded by an army of deadly robot henchmen, but Ellie is captured and killed. Rushing to the nearest gas station, Challis phones authorities to demand they take Silver Shamrock's in-progress broadcast off the air immediately. One by one, the major networks switch off the signal – except for the final channel. Challis shouts into the phone as we cut to black, the final station still broadcasting.

Aside from Nigel Kneale jumping ship early on, *Halloween III*'s production went relatively smoothly. Budgeted at $2.5 million, the film would lens in April and May of 1982. There was one hiccup in post-production, however. Universal execs were vocally unhappy with the film's ending, which they felt was a downer. They requested that Carpenter have it changed so that audiences knew for sure Dr. Challis had managed to foil Cochran's evil scheme. Carpenter felt this decision was best left to director Tommy Lee Wallace, who considered Universal's request but ultimately stuck with the original ending. This sudden respect for the director's vision was in sharp contrast to Carpenter's approach on *Halloween II*. Why treat Wallace any differently than Rosenthal? Two reasons. First, *Halloween III* told an entirely new story using characters Carpenter wasn't already vested in. He therefore had no preconceived notions of how the film should come together. Second, he was quite familiar with Wallace's cinematic sensibilities as a longtime collaborator. He might not have had "final cut" on *Halloween III*, but he had Carpenter's trust.

"I feel for Rick in the position he found himself in," Wallace said in his *Taking Shape* interview. "The problem is that he wasn't family, if you will. I was family and I was very much a known quantity. John and Debra knew they could completely trust me to get in the groove. Had I directed *Halloween II*, it would've felt like a John Carpenter-directed movie. That's because I had a lot of experience working with him. I knew the way he thought and what he would've done to a notable degree. Rick didn't have any of that going for him and he suffered because of it. […] He was in a rough spot, but it was absolutely unique to that position and that time and that situation. I didn't have that experience on *Halloween III* because we're different people with different histories."

# "Halloween III has a certain guaranteed box office, but we have a lot to lose professionally if the picture's no good."

- Debra Hill, The Baltimore Sun

*Halloween III*'s filmmakers were aware of the risk they were taking in abandoning the Michael Myers storyline, but they were woefully unprepared for the tsunami of negative reactions that greeted the film, both from audiences and from critics. "How could a *Halloween* movie minus the Shape be anything but shapeless?" asked Eleanor Ringel of *The Atlanta Constitution*. "It satisfies no one – neither the laughers nor the shriekers." Viewers weren't just disappointed at the Shape's absence – some were actually confused by it. Roger Ebert erroneously wrote in his review that *Halloween III* picked up where *Halloween II* had ended, apparently mistaking the self-immolating android for Michael Myers who also burned to death in the previous film. Ebert was further confused as to why a lab technician spent so much time sifting through the dead Shape's ashes throughout the film. (It's okay if you need to put the book down to face palm over that.)

Season of the Witch arrived in theaters on October 22, 1982. It debuted with $6.3 million, which was just below its predecessor's opening – despite the fact *Halloween III* was playing on slightly more screens. Whereas *Halloween II* continued its impressive performance well into November, *Halloween III* saw a sharp falloff in ticket sales early on. This likely owed to dismal reviews and poor word-of-mouth, both things that had driven the success of the original *Halloween*. The threequel would end its box office run with just $14.4 million. While it didn't lose money for anyone, it had fallen far short of its potential. To make matters worse, *Friday the 13th Part III* had managed to gross twice what *Halloween III* had on a smaller budget just two months earlier. Adding insult to injury, the Jason Voorhees-led sequel also surpassed *Halloween II*'s opening weekend record for a slasher film. It was now crystal clear – audiences wanted slashers.

In retrospect, it was Universal Pictures who most fatally erred with *Halloween III* by not adequately communicating to audiences that it was telling the first chapter a new story. This essentially doomed the sequel to failure. Moviegoers turned out expecting to see Laurie, Loomis, and the Shape – despite the fact that they had been wholly absent from the film's marketing campaign. The only indication Universal gave that *Halloween III* was a fresh start involved a small "All New!" tag printed on certain posters advertising the film's theatrical release. This was grossly insufficient, however, as all first-run movies are technically "All New!" (Universal also bizarrely marketed the R-rated film to young children, who could gain free admission to their famed Studio Tour if they completed coloring sheets of the Silver Shamrock masks.) Given the studio's botched marketing job, we'll likely never know if *Halloween* could've succeeded as an anthology series on its own merits.

"It hurt so badly when the film came out," Wallace further said in *Taking Shape*. "I was crushed. When you're in the position I was in, you feel as though you let everyone down. There was shame involved and all sorts of other horrible feelings." The experience was so disheartening for Debra Hill that she swore off the entire genre, telling *The Baltimore Sun* soon after *Halloween III*'s release, "I don't want to make another horror picture for a long time." True to her word, she didn't produce another horror film until the 2005 remake of *The Fog*.

The irony and tragedy of *Halloween III*'s release is that it's actually a good film – if not a great one. The story is chock full of mystery and intrigue, unfurling slowly as a tightly scripted thriller would. Tom Atkins further cements his status as a cult horror icon and Dan O'Herlihy steals every scene he's in. Fortunately, time has been very kind. New generations have expressed a strong appreciation for the sequel, most armed with the foreknowledge that it doesn't take place anywhere near Haddonfield. In 2018, *Variety*'s Matthew Chernov dubbed it "the lovable black sheep of the series" before ranking it the third overall best *Halloween* movie. *Empire* magazine even named *Halloween III* one of the fifty greatest movie sequels of all time in 2010, the only series entry to make the list. As Wallace now regularly tells *Halloween III* apologists, "You don't have to defend it anymore. It's finally found its audience. If anyone ever puts it down, just cock your head and say, "*Didn't you get the memo? This is a good movie!*"

So this is where we start off – with the Shape dead and his creators intent on leaving him that way. Prior to *Halloween III*'s release, John Carpenter had been the infallible guiding voice of the franchise who no one dared question. That infallibility was now over given the third film's poor reception. Everyone suddenly had their own opinion as to what was best for the series. This brings us right to the doorstep of *Halloween 4*, which is where our book truly begins.

# LOCK YOUR DOORS....

# BOLT YOUR WINDOWS...

# AND TURN OUT THE LIGHTS...

(... except maybe one for reading.)

# IT'S TIME FOR

# THE LOST HALLOWEEN SEQUELS!

# HALLOWEEN 4

Try as you might,
you can't ban the Boogeyman.

**Screenplay by**
**Dennis Etchison**

While *Halloween III*'s reputation has improved considerably over the years, there is simply no denying that its original release badly damaged the overall brand. The threequel had intentionally steered the franchise away from its slasher roots – a confounding move given the slasher boom happening throughout Hollywood. *Halloween*'s filmmakers willingly abandoned Michael Myers at a time when other studios were desperate to establish slashers with even half as much box office appeal. It is incredibly telling that Universal Pictures declined to pursue a fourth installment, instead turning attention to other horror properties. The studio also declined to bid for an ownership stake when the franchise rights hit the auction block several years later. (No major studio put in a bid for the series, which is almost unfathomable in retrospect.)

The release of *Halloween III* concluded the two-sequel deal Compass International had made with Dino De Laurentiis. Production rights to future sequels now reverted back to the original five partners: John Carpenter, Debra Hill, Moustapha Akkad, Joseph Wolf, and Irwin Yablans. Having been a silent partner on the last two films, Yablans was ready to step up and help guide the series forward. The same was true for Akkad, who had his own misgivings about the previous sequels. In essence, the producers were ready to breathe new life into the franchise in order to prevent the complete ruination of the *Halloween* brand. Yablans wasted no time in stating his intentions publicly. "*Halloween 4* will get made somehow, somewhere, and in the not-too-distant future," he told *The Hollywood Reporter* in December 1982.

Carpenter and Hill felt differently and strongly preferred to let the Shape rest in peace. Both were adamant in their public and private comments about wanting to step away from *Halloween* to pursue other projects – and so they did. The following summer, Tommy Lee Wallace confirmed to *Starburst* that Yablans and Akkad had indeed been trying to coax Carpenter and Hill back, though both remained opposed. "The people behind the studio desks will be prepared to back an idea as long as there is money in it," Wallace said. "There is talk of *Halloween 4*, but I'm not interested and neither do John and Debra want to be closely involved."

Despite disappointment in his own sequel's performance, Wallace maintained that the anthology idea was still a worthwhile pursuit. He further relayed to *Starburst*, "There are a great number of stories that could still be told about the Halloween phenomenon. You could have *Halloween 20* feasibly and still be coming up with a scary story as long as you worked alongside the guidelines set down by *The Twilight Zone* or *Night Gallery* and weren't confined to the same characters." To this end, *Season of the Witch* scribe Nigel Kneale publicly admitted to having an idea for a fourth film that might've involved ghosts. The writer quickly dismissed the concept, however, after deeming it too similar to 1982's *Poltergeist*.

"After *Halloween III*, we couldn't agree on how to proceed," Irwin Yablans told *The Los Angeles Times*. "We had become rich and comfortable, and suddenly everyone was an artist."

For John Carpenter, success did not come easy following *Halloween*. 1982 had been a particularly bruising year with both *Halloween III* and *The Thing* failing to find success with audiences. While both films have since aged terrifically, they were huge disappointments upon initial release. The filmmaker followed these with 1983's *Christine*, a modest commercial and critical win. Next came 1984's *Starman*, which barely grossed its production budget, and 1986's *Big Trouble in Little China*, which bombed horribly upon release. Hill's career suffered along a similar trajectory. After a modest hit with 1983's *The Dead Zone*, she produced back-to-back bombs with 1985's *Clue* and *Head Office*. Yet heading into 1986, both Carpenter and Hill remained steadfast in their refusal to return to *Halloween*.

"We really have no place to go with the story," Hill told *The New York Times* in 1985. "If we're going to invest a year of our lives in a movie, we want to do something original. Doing *Halloween II* and *III* gave us the financial freedom to say no to *Halloween 4*."

From 1982 to 1986, Yablans and Akkad tried unsuccessfully to re-team with Carpenter and Hill on a fourth movie. In retrospect, it's no surprise these efforts failed to gain traction. Both creatives still deeply resented Yablans, who in turn resented them for resenting him. Given the five-way power split, there could be no movement on a new *Halloween* until all parties were in agreement. The situation was further complicated in 1986 when Moustapha Akkad sued Yablans for withholding millions of dollars in contractually-guaranteed royalty payments on *Halloween*. Yablans blamed this entirely on the accounting practices of business partner Joseph Wolf, which he equated to embezzlement. As a result of this, Yablans took over Wolf's share of the franchise and the lawsuit was painfully settled out of court. The partners now numbered four.

By year's end, Yablans and Akkad had grown impatient waiting for Carpenter and Hill to return to the series. The franchise was now languishing without a new sequel. This was made worse by the fact that subsequent slasher franchises like *Friday the 13th* and *A Nightmare on Elm Street* were flourishing at the box office with each new sequel. Every year without a new *Halloween* meant missing out on untold millions. This eventually led Yablans and Akkad to threaten their former collaborators with a lawsuit if they continued to block their efforts to make *Halloween 4*.

"This is the nature of business in America," Carpenter told *Fangoria*. "The partners threatened me by saying, '*If you don't do something with this property, we're going to sue you for preventing us from using an asset.*' I had been claiming for years that I wouldn't have anything more to do with the *Halloween* films. But I would always get suckered in at the last minute. The partners would say, '*Your name will be on it. Everybody will associate it with you. Don't you want it to be good?*' It was like a curse."

Threat of legal action aside, there was another incentive for Carpenter to return to the franchise. He had recently been offered a multi-picture deal by Cannon Film Group predicated on the condition that one of those films be a new *Halloween* sequel. Cannon had recently signed a similar deal with horror maestro Tobe Hooper, which yielded films such as *Lifeforce*, *Invaders from Mars* and – most notably – *Texas Chainsaw Massacre 2* – itself a sequel to Hooper's own 1974 shocker. Naturally, Cannon was only too eager to add another movie monster to its growing catalog. Given this opportunity, Carpenter reluctantly agreed to oversee *Halloween 4* in a producorial role with Hill also returning to co-produce. Carpenter's involvement on the new sequel would be the most limited of any *Halloween* yet. While he had co-written, directed, and scored the original, he had only returned to co-write and co-score its first sequel. His efforts on *Halloween III* were even less, performing an uncredited re-write and co-scoring once again. On *Halloween 4*, his commitment would be only to supervise the creation of the screenplay by a writer of his choosing.

"[The audience] wants to see another slasher movie," Carpenter told *Fangoria*. "But I don't want to pander to the slasher audience. So, if I decide to create the story for *Halloween 4*, I would want it to be more stylish, like [the original] *Halloween*."

For the task of writing *Halloween 4*, Carpenter hired esteemed science-fiction and horror author Dennis Etchison. A multi-award-winning scribe, the late Etchison had penned numerous novels, articles, essays, short stories, and plays across a career spanning more than sixty years. Stephen King hailed Etchison "the most original living horror writer in America" and later invited him to consult on his 1981 book *Danse Macabre*, a non-fiction study of horror in popular culture. (King cites *Halloween* as one of his favorite movies, so you know his opinion is sound.) Of course, Etchison was no stranger to the world of *Halloween*. He'd previously written the official novelizations for *Halloween II* and *Halloween III* under the pen name Jack Martin. Prior to those, he'd also penned the novelization for John Carpenter's *The Fog* under his own name. While Etchison had written numerous screenplays before signing onto *Halloween 4*, none had yet been produced. *Halloween 4* was poised to become his screenwriting debut.

While the creative sensibilities of the four partners differed to varying extents, there was one crucial aspect that everyone seemed in agreement on – it was time to bring back Michael Myers. By returning to the series, *Halloween*'s creators hoped they could at least manage his resurrection in a unique and meaningful way. Carpenter would personally supervise the writing of the Etchison script, offering guidance and suggestions where needed. In total, Etchison would produce three drafts of his proposed sequel with the final dated January 2, 1987. This new story would, by design, mark a bold departure from the standard slasher formula of the first two movies.

## THE STORY

Set ten years after the original, Etchison's *Halloween 4* finds Haddonfield still paralyzed with fear of the long dead killer Michael Myers. Local parents have mounted an aggressive anti-Halloween crusade in the decade since the infamous murders, banning everything from trick-or-treating to scary movies. This has all been to the angst and frustration of the younger generation, which includes Tommy Doyle and Lindsey Wallace, the two children Laurie Strode babysat that fateful night. Now a rebellious teen, Tommy is angry over the town's constant obsession with Michael Myers. Lindsey feels much the same, but keeps quiet to appease her overbearing mother. Even the memory of Halloween is forbidden, which has forced Lindsey to psychologically bury the trauma of that long ago night. The town is counting on this year being another quiet and uneventful All Hallows' Eve. Even so, Sheriff Brackett and Detective Hunt (former deputy) have called in police reinforcements from Warren County to ensure as much.

Unfortunately, the town's worst fears are soon realized when the Shape makes an inexplicable return from beyond the grave. He first resurfaces at a pumpkin patch just outside town (such patches are a no-go inside Haddonfield) where he murders the teenaged D'Arcy, one of Lindsey's schoolmates. D'Arcy becomes trapped when a large pumpkin mound topples onto her. As she struggles to free herself, the Shape erupts up through the avalanche of orange, angrily slashing his blade through the pumpkins and through D'Arcy. The reborn Shape then returns to his house at 45 Lampkin Lane to await nightfall.

Elsewhere, Haddonfield's citizenry heatedly debate the Halloween ban. Parents are infuriated that the proprietor of the Lost River Drive-In, located just outside town, has chosen to commemorate Halloween with a horror movie marathon. In covering this controversy, WWAR reporter Robert Mundy prepares a retrospective on the 1978 murders – further angering the locals. Unable to track down Laurie Strode, Mundy visits Smith's Grove Sanitarium hoping to gain insight on Michael's time there. He meets with hospital administrator Dr. Stern, who allows him to read through portions of Michael's psychiatric history. Mundy learns that Micahel was widely feared as a "dark god" within the hospital, known by his peers as "the Lord of the Dead." As night falls on Haddonfield, the Shape begins to kill again in a bloody trek across town.

The screenplay climaxes at the Lost River Drive-In with the full cast present: Lindsey, Tommy, Brackett, Hunt, Mundy, Dr. Stern, and a handful of youths. The Shape manages to slaughter *the entire drive-in audience* by going car to car. (The muffled screams of his victims are indistinguishable from the horror movies up on the screen.) Alerted to the massacre, Brackett and his Warren County reinforcements arrive and open fire on the slasher, though he doesn't die. The bullets somehow make him even stronger and he grows to over twelve-feet tall. This high-caliber hailstorm eventually strikes a gas tank, turning the outdoor theater into an inferno. When the smoke and fire clears, the giant-sized Shape is nowhere to be found. Lindsey and Tommy leave the fear-gripped Haddonfield together, convinced their troubles will not follow them.

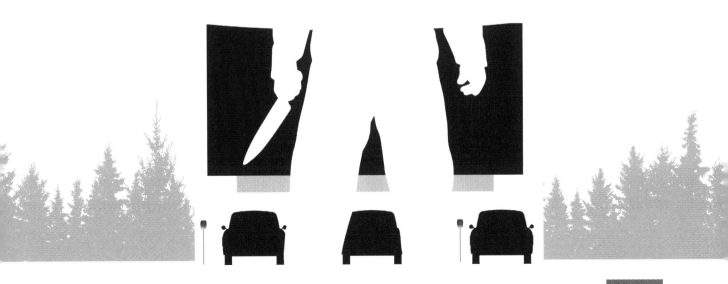

## THE PAST RETURNS

If nothing else, Dennis Etchison's *Halloween 4* is profoundly unlike any other film in the franchise, made or unmade. From its first pages, we gather that the author feels no obligation to the rules or tropes as established across the first two movies. In fact, his *Halloween 4* doesn't appear to follow any rules at all and therein lies a problem. The characters and situations are interesting enough, but the concepts at play are nebulously defined at best. By the script's final page, we've no idea how the Shape managed to return or how the heroes managed to vanquish him. We're also shown a *twelve-foot-tall Shape* with literally no explanation as to how he grew so large. This is all in sharp contrast to director Dwight Little's approach on the actual *Halloween 4*, which was firmly grounded in reality. As an overtly supernatural slasher film, Etchison's *Halloween 4* is a beast of a different nature that leaves the reader with many, many questions.

That's not to say Etchison tries to distance his story from the first two movies. *Not at all.* He actually seeks to closely align his sequel with previous entries wherever possible. That includes seizing on second-tier characters from *Halloween* and *Halloween II* to populate his story. Lindsey Wallace and Tommy Doyle, while supporting players in *Halloween*, now feature quite prominently. Reporter Robert Mundy, a very minor part from *Halloween II*, receives a much meatier role this time around. Remember the three boys who goad each other into entering the Myers house in *Halloween*? They're back as well, now young adults. (That's right – Etchison brought back Lonnie Elam long before David Gordon Green and company did in *Halloween Kills*.) The author takes a similar approach to story details and locations. In one scene, Lindsey receives high marks for her essay on fate and free will – a clear nod to the classroom scene in Carpenter's original. The Lost River Drive-In, which was only briefly mentioned in *Halloween II*, becomes a major setting in the final act. (The Shop and Bag "out by the mall" also features.) Etchison even tips his hat to *Halloween III* with children gleefully singing the "Silver Shamrock" jingle.

Another unique quality of the Etchison script is that it never fully commits to a main character. The first two *Halloween*s cut back and forth between Laurie Strode and Dr. Loomis. The actual *Halloween 4* followed along a similar path. Yet this version of the fourth installment strays from that formula, instead featuring a diverse character ensemble throughout its story. The narrative focus never stays on one group for too long before moving onto the next. While Tommy and Lindsey initially appear to be the main leads, it's worth noting we spend an almost equal amount of time with Brackett, Hunt, Mundy, and Lindsey's parents. If there's a drawback to this approach, it's that the sudden promotion of so many background characters makes this feel like leftovers. It also makes the regrettable absence of both Laurie and Loomis even more noticeable. (For reasons unknown, the third and final draft of the Etchison script drops Sheriff Brackett from the story, re-assigning his role to Hunt instead. This results in a notably weaker connection to the original film.)

The one wholly original character worth mentioning is Lia, one of Lindsey's classmates. Though not part of D'Arcy's group, she's not a true friend to Lindsey, either. She'll happily accept homework help but would rather not be seen with Lindsey while walking to school. More concerned with her own affairs, she battles commitment issues with her on-again, off-again boyfriend Shaun, thus making her this story's archetypal "normal" girl. (Not too bitchy. Not too repressed. Think Rachel Carruthers.) Lia does prove herself useful in giving Lindsey a ride to the drive-in to search for Tommy, though this doesn't bode well for either girl. (Especially Lia. The Shape drags her into a parked car and stabs her to death.)

A surprisingly minor character in the story is the Shape himself, who seldom appears until the finale. The reborn slasher does feature into an opening nightmare sequence, but he doesn't actually kill anyone until halfway through the script. Speaking of kills, this *Halloween 4* appears to have the lowest body count of any franchise entry up until the finale in which it soars to arguably the highest body count of any slasher *ever* – more than a hundred murdered in a massive set-piece. That's not to say the earlier deaths would've been short on the red stuff. One notable kill involves Lia's boyfriend Shaun, who meets his end while physically engaged with another girl at the drug store where he works. His date warmly embraces him, failing to notice the Bowie knife plunged into his back. Shaun's subsequent thrusts aren't of passion, but rather the Shape's repeated attempts to dislodge his blade. Once doing so, he slits the unwitting girl's throat.

It's wild to note just how different this *Halloween 4* is from the film that was eventually made. They're practically opposites. In this script, Haddonfield has passed an ordinance officially banning the celebration of Halloween. In the 1988 film, we see no such opposition to the holiday with kids out trick-or-treating as normal. In the Etchison script, both Michael Myers and Dr. Loomis are said to have died in *Halloween II*'s fiery ending. In the 1988 film, both characters are shown to have survived the hospital blaze. The 1988 film's Shape is depicted as a flesh-and-blood killer. Not so in the Etchison script, which veers deep into supernatural territory. This draft also reveals that Laurie Strode is still alive, albeit long gone from Haddonfield. The actual *Halloween 4* alternately tells that she died in a car accident.

Fans of sanguinary spectacle would've found much to appreciate in this *Halloween 4*, which is chock full of horrifying and surreal imagery. One early nightmare sequence depicts a panicked Mrs. Wallace returning home on Halloween night to find a knife-wielding child on her staircase. ("The little girl raises the knife higher [...] until she breaks open. Splitting down the middle to reveal the Shape, dressed in black, crawling up out of her skin to stand there tall on the stairs, the knife now in his hand.") If that wasn't frightening enough, the walls and furniture of her home begin to bleed as though alive. A terrified Mrs. Wallace runs outside to find a gushing river of blood where the street once was.

## THE... GHOST OF MICHAEL MYERS?

Etchison's *Halloween 4* immediately establishes the Shape's return by cleverly restaging *Halloween*'s iconic opening shot, the first of several such Panaglide moments written into the script. As we approach the Myers house via the killer's point-of-view, we're to notice that it now appears abandoned and decrepit. We enter through the backdoor, pass through the kitchen, and head upstairs to one of the bedrooms. Here we see the Shape suiting up for Halloween – not unlike how Batman does before a night of crime fighting. Etchison's script seems to reason that a new Shape deserves a new look. The character's outfit now includes a t-shirt and coat, both black, along with the familiar white mask. It's unclear where this particular mask originated from as his original burned like a marshmallow in *Halloween II*'s fiery ending. Then again, it's also unclear as to how the Shape has returned *at all*.

Of *Halloween II*'s finale at Haddonfield Memorial, Detective Hunt comments, "There wasn't anything left. It was all mixed up with Dr. Loomis after he blew 'em both sky high. They never could tell which was which. Nobody could have lived through that fire." Despite factually knowing the Shape perished in that night's blaze, Hunt remains uneasy heading into Halloween 1988: "He's back. I can feel it. I don't know how, but I feel like Michael Myers is trying to come home one more time."

While visually similar, this is *not* the same Shape we came to know across the first two films. This take on the character has uncanny new powers and abilities. As the town's fear grows stronger, so does he. This makes for a more unstoppable slasher than we've ever seen before. At one point, a mischievous teen throws a rock through the front window of the Myers house. Picking it up, the Shape single-handedly crushes the rock to dust. He can also withstand far greater injury (having a chunk of his skull blown off is but an inconvenience) and can regenerate lost body parts. Midway through the script, the Shape loses two fingers to a dog, which grow back later in the story.

In an unusual twist, this *Halloween 4* tries to distinguish between Michael Myers and the Shape, which gets pretty confusing. Etchison hints that they're not necessarily one and the same as previously thought. Per this story, Michael Myers very much died at the end of *Halloween II* but the evil of the Shape somehow lives on. While they may be separate entities, they do share a spirit or consciousness. The Shape returns to the Myers house and responds when called "Michael." (Non-verbally, of course.) According to Hunt, he's still in search of Laurie Strode and won't stop killing until he finds her. Maybe Michael Myers referred to the slasher's physical form, which burned up in *Halloween II*, and the Shape now describes his reborn form? The logic isn't *at all* clear, but Carpenter has acknowledged as much in interviews about the abandoned sequel.

"It was an excellent script, but it didn't include Michael Myers. The premise was that the adults' fear caused the Shape to reappear. He was created by the dark side of the adults in Haddonfield, by their fear of life and of something different."

- John Carpenter, Fangoria

## HALLOWEEN NO MORE

The most central theme of Etchison's *Halloween 4* involves the banning of Halloween, which permeates nearly every scene. It's like a slasher-themed riff on *Footloose* but with a ban on trick-or-treating instead of dancing. No one is more vocal (or obnoxious) about this than Mrs. Wallace, who angrily accuses Sheriff Brackett of not doing enough to quash the holiday. Brackett somberly reminds her that he lost his only child to Michael Myers before promising there'll be no Halloween in Haddonfield ever again. Some of the town's more level-headed minds decry the ban as unnecessary, but they're ignored by the angry mob. Miss Oldfield, a teacher at Haddonfield High, tells the parents, "Let's bury our dead and get on with living. You've kept the hysteria alive and you're passing it on to the children. Some of them weren't even born then!"

The overbearing Mrs. Wallace may mean well, but she almost comes across as a secondary villain. She's psychologically conditioned her daughter to have no memory of that horrible night ten years ago. Lindsey is strictly forbidden from speaking about it or even referencing it. (She's not even allowed to pass by the Myers house and must take an unnecessarily long route to school to avoid it.) Not surprisingly, she's also forbidden from associating with Tommy Doyle as he would surely dredge up unwanted memories. Lindsey doesn't agree with her mother's anti-Halloween crusade, but stays mum as a way to maintain peace in her tense household.

Whereas Lindsey tolerates her mother's war on Halloween, Tommy does not. Now a young man, he's fed up with the town's paranoid obsession. Tommy suspects that the parents of Haddonfield have kept the spirit of Michael Myers alive as a way to control their children, a theory that appears to have some merit. Unable to convince anyone of this, however, he starts to lash out at those around him. In one scene, Detective Hunt mistakenly arrests Tommy for a crime he did not commit. Rather than simply assert his innocence, he steals Hunt's gun and turns it on him before escaping with it. Tommy later uses this gun on the Shape, whom he spends the entire story swearing is dead and never coming back. (He also claims to have watched Michael Myers burn to death in 1978, which another character rightly calls bullshit on.) Tommy's self-righteous claims of Michael being dead eventually ring false, which makes him a huge asshole in the scheme of things. Witness his anger in the following tirade to Lindsey early in the story.

**Tommy:** *"The boogeyman is dead! We know that – if only you'll remember. Our parents don't believe it. But we don't have to be afraid anymore. Think, Lindsey! And they won't be able to make you sick. It's the adults who're afraid. They want to keep us that way, too. To control us. So we won't grow up to be like Michael Myers. It's them!"*

This resurrected-by-fear approach feels quite reminiscent of Freddy Krueger and *A Nightmare on Elm Street*. In both this story and *Elm Street*, parental efforts to repress an evil entity backfire miserably, resulting in said evil only growing stronger. There's a line by the dream demon in *Freddy vs Jason* that well encapsulates the Shape's return in the Etchison script. If the silent slasher could speak, he may well have said it himself: "From the very beginning, it was the children who gave me my power. When I was alive, I might have been a little naughty, but after they killed me, I became something much, much worse. The stuff nightmares are made of. The children still feared me, and their fear gave me the power […] and that's when the fun really began... until they figured out a way to forget about me, to erase me completely. Being dead wasn't a problem. But being forgotten? Now, *that's* a bitch!"

In a humorous touch, Etchison likens Halloween-related paraphernalia to street drugs. Certain businesses still sell costumes and candy in spite of the official ban, but such illegal merch is kept behind the counter and out of public view. Etchison later provides interesting commentary on the state of the horror genre during a city council meeting where angry parents rally in support of the holiday's continued ban. They decry not only the Halloween marathon planned for the Lost River Drive-In, but horror movies in general. "They played good pictures [in my youth]," Mrs. Wallace complains. "Not sex and violence and craziness!" The Lost River owner snaps back, "Yeah, like Fifty-Foot Women and Blobs and Dracula rising from the grave. (*mockingly*) Those were great art pictures!"

This is a rather cheeky exchange not only when you consider the critical lambasting that slasher films received in the 1980s but also John Carpenter and Debra Hill's own reluctance to return to *Halloween*. When another irate parent claims that film standards have indeed changed, the Lost River owner queries of when the last time the man actually went to see a movie. ("If you people hadn't stopped going, maybe movies would be the way you like them today.")

## LOOMIS THE MONSTER

One of this *Halloween 4*'s more interesting sequences takes us inside Smith's Grove Sanitarium. (Recall that we never actually went inside Smith's Grove in *Halloween* – only outside of it.) It's here that reporter Robert Mundy hopes to score an on-camera interview for a news story on the anniversary of the 1978 killings. He quickly finds that the previous administrator, Dr. Rogers, has since retired. The new head honcho is Dr. Marion Stern, who we come to realize is the same Marion from *Halloween* and *Halloween II*. (Etchison might've possibly erred by giving the character a new last name and title. Nurse Marion Chambers is now Dr. Marion Stern.)

Marion tells the reporter that it was the late Dr. Loomis' sick obsession with Michael Myers that ultimately destroyed him. Per her account, he was gripped by a fierce paranoia that eventually infected the entire institution. Loomis then spiraled into madness under the delusion that his patient was not a man but superhuman evil. To illustrate her point, Marion plays an unsettling videotape of a therapy session between Loomis and Michael. This moment would've afforded Donald Pleasence a brief but memorable cameo. As the tape begins, Loomis greets his patient in a gentle tone. It soon turns ugly, however.

*"For three years, we've been doing this. I'm losing my patience, Mikey. It's true. But I'm not going to give up. You think you can wear me down? You won't win, you know. I'm going to see this through to the end, no matter how long it takes. (LOOMIS turns to the camera.) You can turn that thing off now. He's not going to say anything. Waste of time. (But the tape does not stop. LOOMIS approaches the BOY, becoming angry.)*

*"You think you're fooling everybody, don't you? Well, I know your game. I've seen it played by experts. And it won't work! You're not fooling me. I know who you are, what you are!"*

*(SHOUTING, ENRAGED) "Mikey -- that's a name for a human boy! And you're not that, are you? Your name must be, let's see, does your kind even have a name? What do they call you in the place where you came from? What's the proper name for evil these days? Answer me, by God, or I'll..." (Loomis raises his fist to strike Michael)*

This scene is interesting for going against the traditional narrative of Loomis as the shining hero who can do no wrong. Etchison charges that Loomis might not have been the selfless savior the later films made him out to be and that – just maybe – he was a monster in his own right. The image of Loomis raising his hand to strike a child, even a young Michael Myers, is a disturbing one. This unhinged take brings to mind a similar depiction in 1989's *Halloween 5*. In discussing her colleague to Robert Mundy, Marion makes a most interesting comment: "Eventually, Loomis decided that the child was the incarnation of some pagan Druidic cult." This remark references *Halloween*'s official novelization by Richard Curtis while simultaneously foretelling the plot of 1995's *Halloween 6*.

## INFERNO AT THE LOST RIVER DRIVE-IN

*Halloween 4*'s finale takes place at the Lost River Drive-in, which has dedicated its three screens to an all-night horror movie marathon. Among the films mentioned as playing are *Re-Animator, The Texas Chain Saw Massacre, Christine, Psycho, Psycho II, Psycho III,* and *The Fog.* (That last fright flick is liberally referenced throughout the screenplay, which is no surprise given that it was written/directed by John Carpenter and novelized by Etchison himself.) The constant barrage of screams from this lineup help to muffle the actual screams of the Shape's victims as he murders the entire drive-in audience. This sequence would've likely given him the largest body count of any slasher *ever*. Etchison describes the scene as such: "Acres of cars. Silent. Dead. A graveyard of vehicles beneath the projector beam, where a million moths flutter in the light."

The screenwriter also uses the drive-in as an opportunity to poke fun at a fellow horror franchise. At one point in the night, we would notice a nondescript *Friday the 13th* sequel playing on the main screen. This makes for an interesting juxtaposition as the cinema slashers kill side by side, Jason on the big screen and Michael in the audience. The script reads, "A shadow falls across Jason Voorhees as something passes in front of the projector – a shape. *The Shape.* Now superimposed over Jason, the Shape cocks its head in curiosity. Then the film burns through and the screen goes white."

The ensemble cast eventually descend upon the Lost River Drive-In, initially unaware that it's become a giant automotive graveyard. This includes Lonnie Elam and his friends, who arrive wearing knock-off Michael Myers masks as part of a planned prank. Sheriff Brackett and his trigger-happy backup arrive soon after and are alarmed to find thirteen white-masked individuals roaming the drive-in. They soon learn that the pranksters only number twelve, meaning one of these imposters isn't an imposter. The true Shape gives himself away, however, by turning his head when Marion calls out to him. Smiling, she motions toward him. "Michael. Don't be frightened. I'm here to help you. Come back with me to Smith's Grove. It's your home. It's where you belong. Nobody can hurt you there. Take my hand." Here, the Shape delivers a "powerful blow" to Marion, knocking the doctor off her feet. Detective Hunt uses this moment to confront the Shape, which goes badly. Firing his shotgun into the slasher's chest has little effect. The Shape breaks Hunt's weapon in half before smashing his face in. Tommy also fires upon his masked nemesis, blasting away part of his skull. This barely slows him down.

As Lindsey and Tommy take cover, the Warren County reinforcements open fire on the Shape from all directions. This has an unintended effect, however. ("Suddenly – the Shape starts to GROW as if feeding off the bullets and becoming stronger with each shot! The Shape swells to eight... ten... twelve feet tall!") One of the deputies' bullets strikes a gas tank, causing the vehicle to explode into a giant fireball. This sets off a chain reaction of car explosions, engulfing the giant-sized Shape in fire and turning the drive-in into an inferno. Everyone manages to escape the blaze except Hunt, who was already dead. When the massive fire clears the following morning, the Shape is nowhere to be found.

The visual of terrified police surrounded by Shape lookalikes recalls a similar moment from the actual *Halloween 4* when Loomis and Sheriff Meeker pick up Jamie and Rachel. Furthermore, the bizarre concept of an oversized Shape strangely echoes Nigel Kneale's originally-planned finale for *Halloween III*. That unused ending saw Conal Cochran also growing to a monstrous size, towering above Dr. Challis in the factory warehouse. Might this have been a direct reference to Kneale's original ending? That we may never know, but Etchison did have access to earlier drafts of the *Halloween III* script as evidenced by his official novelization of the film.

The screenplay's final scene is as strange as a twelve-foot-tall Shape. Tommy and Lindsey escape the blaze – without telling anyone – and hide in a random barn outside town. While in romantic embrace, they decide to leave Haddonfield and start a new life elsewhere – *despite the fact that their grieving parents believe they died in the fire*. (The script mentions the Doyles and Wallaces sobbing outside the smoldering drive-in.) It's unclear why both Tommy and Lindsey would be so quick to leave behind their distraught families. Yes, Mrs. Wallace was awful, but Mr.

Wallace was a good man. We never hear of the Doyles, but how bad could they be? Then again, the sudden thought of Tommy and Lindsey as a couple is also strange as we only see them interact *twice* before this finale. These two chats are terribly awkward and devoid of sparks or chemistry.

A more fitting conclusion might've seen Tommy at least commenting on the Shape's inexplicable return. (Something along the lines of, "Guess I was wrong. He *was* back. My bad.") After all, he spends the entire story angrily telling everyone how dead the boogeyman is – only for the boogeyman to reappear and start killing people. It's also a little surprising how Lindsey isn't throwing this in his face given that *scores of their friends were just murdered at the drive-in!!* In fact, any kind of post-game discussion from any character on what the actual hell just happened would be helpful in processing this story's events.

## WHY IT WASN'T MADE

You'd think a *Halloween* sequel blessed by John Carpenter would be an easy sell. For a moment in time, that may have been the case as reports indicate *Halloween 4* was initially expected to begin filming in April 1987. One of the earliest frontrunners for the director's chair was none other than Joe Dante, whom Carpenter had originally approached for the third film. While Dante never officially signed onto the project, he did meet with Etchison to discuss their visions for the project. Keep in mind, Etchison had written not one but three drafts of his story. Surely, there must've been fanfare for this direction? Not quite. Development would soon come to a screeching halt.

In short, this *Halloween 4* was killed by Irwin Yablans and Moustapha Akkad, both of whom felt a supernatural approach was the wrong direction to pursue. Not even the glowing endorsement of Carpenter and Hill could sway their opinion, either. Feeling that Etchison's script was too cerebral for mainstream audiences, Akkad instead advocated for something more like the first two films. Not surprisingly, Carpenter and Hill were strongly opposed. Carpenter lamented that he was once again being asked to make the same film over and over again. If inferior sequels were going to be produced, he wanted nothing to do with them.

Frustrated by their experiences, Carpenter and Hill soon decided they wanted out of the *Halloween* business altogether. They put their collective stake in the franchise up for sale, thus ending their contractual oversight once and for all. The lucky recipient of their shares? None other than Moustapha Akkad himself. With this, the rights holders of *Halloween* now numbered two: Akkad and Yablans. This might've proven a winning arrangement, but Yablans had become disillusioned with filmmaking given the expensive and tumultuous lawsuits he had been embroiled in related to *Halloween*. These legal battles were not with rivals or strangers, but with men he respected and considered longtime friends. As already mentioned, Akkad had rightly sued Compass for millions in withheld profit payments related to *Halloween*. As company president, Yablans was on the hook for these missed sums. He wholly blamed his company's indefensible accounting on pal and lawyer Joseph Wolf. In settling with Akkad, both Compass and Yablans took a major financial hit. Yablans soon sued Wolf in order to recoup his own losses.

At any rate, Yablans was ready to retire from filmmaking. "The messy affair was over," he wrote in his autobiography. "But it left me disgusted with the industry. Making movies is fun and can be creative, but the business of making movies is often ugly."

The partners now numbered one. For the first time in series history, Moustapha Akkad could exert total control over future installments. The producer immediately sought to correct what he viewed as the mistakes of the previous sequels by returning to the style of the original. Dennis Etchison's script did not fit into that plan. Sadly, the screenwriter wouldn't learn of his involvement's dissolution until after Carpenter and Hill had already sold their rights.

With no *Halloween* in the works from him, Carpenter would pass on the deal offered by Cannon Films. Instead, he would partner with Alive Films to helm the original features *Prince of Darkness* and *They Live*. Of selling his stake in *Halloween* to Akkad, he told *Fangoria*, "It was like a great weight had been lifted from my shoulders. I could finally stop feeling guilty about being responsible for the outcome. I told the producers, '*Don't put my name on it. Don't even credit it 'Based on characters created by John Carpenter and Debra Hill*.' But they're trying to attach my name to it anyway. I suppose they will, at least in terms of the music."

# "It was a philosophical type of Halloween, but it was too intellectual for the producers."

- John Carpenter, Fangoria

# interview:
# DENNIS ETCHISON
Writer - Halloween 4 (The Etchison Draft)

Interviewed by Michael Ryan Assip

**How did you and John Carpenter first meet?**

One day out of the blue, I got a call from somebody at John's office, Pumpkin Pie Productions, who said, '*John Carpenter would like to meet with you.*' Well, that was good news because I was a great fan of his. And I said, '*Sure,*' and I went in the next day and met him and Debra Hill. Debra took me into another room and sat me down and said they needed a novelization for *The Fog*. Somebody else had written one but she didn't like it and they weren't going to use it. She said, '*He [the other writer] had a reporter having sex with ghosts on the beach! It's terrible. We don't have much time, and we need someone to do it, and someone recommended you.*'

**What was the writing process like for novelizing *The Fog*?**

I'm very visual when I write, and I didn't want to visualize it in a way that was different from the film. At some point in the next few days, Tommy Wallace, I think, showed me a couple of reels of it, the opening, so I could get the flavor and the look of it. And then I got a copy of the script and I studied that. The deal with Bantam Books was that they needed it in exactly six weeks, and I said, '*Okay, I can do that.*' And I sat myself down — I was working on a manual typewriter at the time — and I figured, '*I'll do a draft and then I'll mark it up and then I'll re-type it once, and if I do a certain number of pages a day, like thirteen, I can get it done by that date.*' So I signed and started and I finished it six weeks to the day.

**And how was it that your involvement in the *Halloween* films came into play?**

*The Fog* went through eight printings. It did well. John asked if I'd like to novelize *Halloween II* and then *Halloween III,* and so I did those. At some point after *Halloween III,* on Christmas Eve, I got a call from John, and he said, '*Debra and I would like you to write the script for Halloween 4*' And I said, '*That's wonderful!*' A few minutes later, Debra called and said the same exact thing. And I was just ecstatic. I started meeting with John and we talked about what would be in it. We agreed that it should start ten years after *Halloween,* and the story would concern the two little kids Laurie Strode was babysitting, who were now teenagers, and still living across the street from each other.

**Tommy and Lindsey?**

Right, Tommy Doyle and Lindsey Wallace. The idea is that the town, after all those terrible murders ten years earlier, has banned Halloween. They don't recognize it as a holiday; they don't allow masks and costumes or candy. And you know Hunt, the deputy from the first two films?

**Totally! Hunter von Leer.**

Hunt is now the sheriff. And ten years of repression and suppression have boiled to the surface and there are some hints that *HE'S BACK*! So I foresaw on the poster the words, '*The night he came home…again!*' And I had this set piece in mind where Michael Myers comes bursting up out of a big lot full of pumpkins. Erupting out of this orange mound. I thought that would be a nice shot to use on the poster.

The
Night
He
Came
Home...
AGAIN!

**What was your writing process for *Halloween 4*?**

I did three drafts of it. For the last draft, I went over to John's house and we sat down cross-legged on the floor opposite each other. He gave me a Xerox copy of the script, and he had one in his lap, and he took out two Carter's Marks-A-Lot pens and we started reading through it. And he would say, '*All right, take out that line there, you don't need it. Okay. And on this page, you need a couple lines to explain why they're going over there,*' and other small but not unimportant things like that.

At one point there was a speech — they have a town meeting and everyone is up in arms about whether they should have Halloween or not. And the guy who runs the local drive-in, the Lost River, which is the name of a real drive-in… John grew up in Bowling Green, Kentucky and he said there was a real Lost River Drive-In, and Haddonfield was also based on a town in Illinois where Debra had grown up. So there is this town meeting where everyone is arguing, and the guy who runs the drive-in says, '*You can't ban a night of Halloween movies! I'm trying to make a living here! Kids wanna see horror movies!*' '*Well, maybe they shouldn't,*' some people are saying. '*Maybe it's better if they don't see them.*' So the whole idea was repression versus acknowledging the bad things in the world.

And then we got to one speech in there where someone sort of explains the meaning of all this, and John said, '*Take this out, or two-thirds of it.*' And he started blacking out some lines. I said, '*Well, I kind of like that speech. It sums up the meaning of the whole thing.*' And John said, '*Yeah, but you don't need it, because a couple of pages earlier you have a shot of their faces, and we'll be able to see that.*' So you see, I thought *I* was visual, but he is even *more* visual. He was thinking about what the shots would be. So he taught me to be even more concise than I already was. He taught me to take out explicit things that don't need to be stated because the camera's gonna show them. So the final draft of the script came out to be even leaner.

**Once you came to that draft of the script, what happened?**

A few weeks later, I stopped by Debra Hill's office to pick up a copy of the final re-typing of the script. She had a tall stack of them in front of her and said, '*We're sending these out to the investors.*' And then, sometime later, I got a call from her, saying, '*I just wanted to tell you, John and I have sold our interest in the* Halloween *franchise and unfortunately your script was not part of the deal.*' Who knows why. Apparently the partners hired something like ten other writers to work on it after me, and I lost a Writer's Guild arbitration over the final credits, even though I was the first writer on the project. So my name's not on the picture.

**What inspired you to take the sequel in this direction?**

I was not allowed to read horror comics as a kid, so I had an unusual interest in them, and in science fiction movies like *The Thing*, the original Howard Hawks version. I was not allowed to go because my mother said, '*Oh, I hear it's very scary. Too scary for you.*' So naturally I grew up with a great interest in scary movies. The more you repress something, or try to repress it, like sex among teenagers, the hotter they get, right? So for *Halloween 4*, the town is trying to deny all this, but it's actually bringing him [the Shape] back into being. I don't want to go on forever about this, but may I read you a page I found in the *Halloween II* novelization?

**Please!**

Here's a page I wrote near the end of the *Halloween II* novel and it sort of sums up everything. It's on page 218 in the paperback…

> "*And so it was now, one more re-run on the Late, Late, Very Late Show on Halloween night in this particular town, acting out the last reels of its relentless stalking of the heart of the American dream. It was always so. Variations of figures like it had come again and again to towns exactly like this all across the country and would continue to come in endless variety and profusion whenever the days grew short and the horror of an unburied past returned to haunt the long night of the human soul. They would come to movie theaters and TV screens over and over in untiring replays for as long as people turned away and pretended it was not really there; that very refusal gave it unopposed entrance to their most inner lives. Nothing ever stopped its coming and nothing ever would stop it, not for as long as people deferred the issue of its existence to the realm of fantasy fiction, that elaborate system of popular mythology which provided the essence of its beachhead. For now, it came on and on.*"

**Wow! All kinds of chills!**

I think originally, when I met with the guy John had in mind to direct *Halloween 4*… It was going to be Joe Dante, and I met with him at the old Schwab's Drugstore in Hollywood. It's not there anymore, but it's where Lana Turner was discovered in the 1940s. We [Joe and I] met and we sat and talked about what we might do with *Halloween 4*. I took out *Halloween II* and read the paragraph that I just read to you. And when I was finished he looked at me and said, '*Would you consider that a digression?*' And I said, '*Well, uh, no. I thought it summed it all up.*' So I don't know the reasons, but Joe did not direct *Halloween 4*. Just as I don't really know why my script for *Halloween 4* was not used.

**What was it like to work with John Carpenter?**

He's the last honest man. A straight arrow. I've seen him a few times over the years since, and I did an interview with him that was published, and he is the best guy I've ever known and worked with in Hollywood. He is 100% honest, loyal, and true. He doesn't lie. He doesn't cheat people. His goal is to make good films. And on the set of some of his films — I was on the set one day for *Halloween III*, and on the shoot of *Prince of Darkness* a couple of days — and I would have lunch with the crew, and they'd all say, '*Oh, I'd work with J.C. anytime!*' They called him J.C. on the set. '*I could be making three times as much on another show, but I'd rather work with J.C. He never yells. He never chews anybody out in front of the crew. It's a pleasure to work for him.*' I watched him direct scenes, and he even gave me some tips about directing, because he knew that's what I'd always wanted to do. He's a prince of a man.

**What are your thoughts on the fans of the *Halloween* film series?**

In the last six months, I've met several people who have made me aware that there is a fan group, a cult around the *Halloween* films and around movie novelizations. And I always figured, compared to the books with my name on them, those movie novelizations…well, I did not do them as hack work, I took them seriously…but of all my books, those would be the least that are me because they're not my stories, they're Carpenter's stories, and Cronenberg's in the case of *Videodrome*. So I did the very best I could with what I was given.

But I discovered that there are these people who say — two people in the last six months — *'Halloween III is my favorite book. It's my favorite novel of all time.'* I can't believe it. I teach a writing class sometimes, and I was standing outside during the break one afternoon and a guy who was a guest of one of the kids in the class came over to me and started quoting from memory an entire paragraph from *Halloween III.* And I kept nodding and saying *'Uh-huh, yeah.'* He had memorized this whole long paragraph, and he kept going, and I kept saying, *'I know, I know.'* And when he was finished I said, *'Well, I wrote that, you know."* And he said, *'What? What? You wrote that? You're Jack Martin? You wrote Halloween III?"*

**What else do you want the world to know about your *Halloween 4?***

It ends up with an enormous climax. Tommy and Lindsey go on the run into the countryside, away from Haddonfield. Lindsey hasn't been able to remember anything that happened in 1978. She has no memory of it; it's blacked out of her mind. And her mother wants it that way. Tommy, on the other hand — they both saw shrinks for a while when they were kids, and Tommy is beginning to get some flashes of it and begins to understand what's happening. Whenever he tries to call Lindsey from across the street the mother never accepts the calls. *'Don't call here again, Tommy Doyle!'* Because it will remind Lindsey of what happened. But they're bonded together because of what they went through, and they're grown up now and they kind of like each other. But she's not allowed to see him. Anyway, it ends up with this tremendous bloody scene at the packed drive-in at midnight. It's really incredible. And the Shape is there and he's stalking and killing people right and left. Tommy and Lindsey get away. They wake up in a farmhouse outside of town, in the country somewhere, and she has had a dream that starts to bring it all together for her…In short, it's not just a slasher movie. The story has a philosophy behind it.

WWAR-TV CHANNEL **10**

**ROBERT MUNDY**
reporter

418 555-6701
Haddonfield, Illinois

*the number ONE STATION in the area!*

Dr. Stern

(421) 555-1401

# Halloween Banned!

## • Town Council Passes New Ordinance.

HADDONFIELD - Caving to immense pressure by parent and church groups, local authorities voted unanimously to enact an official ban on the celebration of the Halloween holiday.

This ordinance extends to decorations, costumes, displays, and gatherings both public and private. Those who choose to defy this new rule could face fines of up to $2,000 per violation. Officials also announced that Haddonfield will be under a strict curfew lasting the entire week of October 31, though no exact time has yet been specified.

The ban is set to automatically renew each year going forward until officially deauthorized by the council, meaning it may be decades before Halloween returns to Haddonfield, if it ever does.

Parents protesting at the Haddonfield city hall

# HALLOWEEN 4

Evil arrives in the Windy City.

**Screenplay by**
**Marc Allyn Medina**
**& Daniel Kenney**

To put *Halloween 4*'s complicated development into context, it should be noted that for any sequel to have been produced during this time, all rights holders would need to be in agreement. No one filmmaker could move forward on a new installment without the approval of the others. This in mind, a cursory exploration of '80s pop culture will show that the *Halloween* franchise took a serious backseat to *Friday the 13th* and *A Nightmare on Elm Street*, both of which were booming with yearly sequels, merchandise and other cross-promotional materials. Part of the reason for *Halloween* being eclipsed by its contemporaries was that with so many rights holders getting all to agree on something was a difficult task. If even one of the parties held out in any form, a sequel could not be produced. (It's honestly amazing there was ever an Atari game!)

It was this type of dealing that ultimately led John Carpenter to exit the series. His suggestion of creating a more supernatural *Halloween* was thoroughly dismissed by Akkad. The producer asserted that Carpenter's general reluctance to helm another film was hindering his fellow rights holders from capitalizing on a jointly-owned commercial asset. In buying out his partners, Akkad ensured he would never again struggle with this issue. For the first time in series' history, he would now exert total control over future installments. Given his faith in the brand, it seemed a task he was prepared to take on – and all that would come afterward is most surely credited to his efforts.

Without major studio backing, Akkad would be financing the next production through himself and other channels. Not long after securing the franchise rights, Trancas International launched an open call for screenwriters to pitch their own take on *Halloween 4*. In a sense, the franchise was going back to its indie roots as the opportunity was open to both guild and non-guild writers. (This being an ingenious cost-saving measure.) The only stipulation given to potential screenwriters was that they needed to do what Dennis Etchison's script had not – revive Michael Myers as a true flesh-and-blood killer.

Hundreds of hopeful scribes answered the open submission. Few received callbacks from Trancas and even fewer had their scripts purchased. One draft that had been considered, however, was composed by the writing team of Daniel Kenney and Marc Allyn Medina. Dated October 1987, this *Halloween 4* has never been publicly acknowledged. True to the call, neither Kenney nor Medina were Writer's Guild members. In fact, Medina had a most colorful background as the lead singer of Perfect Stranger, a short-lived new wave act that enjoyed some success on the LA music scene.

In the 1980s, Perfect Stranger boasted members like Robert Trujillo and Angelo Barbera, performing regularly at local hot spots like the Whisky a Go Go and Madame Wong's West. These efforts would culminate in a 1990 cassette titled *The Politics of Passion*. It was during this endeavor that Medina met Daniel Kenney, a friend of the band's bassist. Having known of the open call for *Halloween* scripts, Kenney proposed that the two fashion their own concept for consideration. Interestingly, their take - which was developed over several months - would resurrect not only Michael Myers but also Laurie Strode.

## THE STORY

The Kenney/Medina draft opens with a pre-title recap and continuation of *Halloween II*'s ending. We learn that both Dr. Loomis and the Shape survived that film's operating room explosion, albeit with serious injuries. A newscaster explains that Michael suffered third-degree burns over ninety percent of his body and is not expected to live. Loomis, however, received only first and second-degree burns over thirty-five percent of his body. Both are flown via choppers to an emergency burn center in nearby Chicago. Medics fail to notice the worn-out safety cable on Michael's stretcher, which snaps entirely over Lake Michigan. This sends the burned slasher plunging into the waters below. His body is never recovered. We're then shown a montage of Laurie Strode spending quite some time in a psychiatric hospital, often crying as seasons pass. The final pre-title shot is of Michael's neglected gravesite in Haddonfield. The headstone reads 1957 – 1978.

This *Halloween 4* then jumps ahead ten years to find Laurie Strode – now Laurie Jamison – leading a reasonably happy life in Chicago with husband Terrence and six-year-old daughter Stephie. As the editor of *Real People Magazine,* Laurie is "an '80s modern young businesswoman" with a high-rise office and a BMW 325i convertible. She, Terrence, and Stephie live in an upscale neighborhood with Terrence's teenage sister Heather visiting from California this week. In the days leading up to Halloween, Laurie is preparing a high-profile cover story on a rock star for an upcoming issue. She seemingly has it all – yet she's plagued by nightmares and panic attacks. Inexplicable feelings of dread and unease inhibit her peace of mind on a regular basis. This is due to having subconsciously repressed the memories of the first two films. Laurie meets regularly with her psychiatrist – the burn-scarred Dr. Loomis – who helps her work through these feelings. He dictates into a tape recorder:

> *"Michael Myers burned to death on October 31, 1978, but not before leaving an open wound within Laurie Strode. These dreams not only plague her sleep but threaten to interfere with her waking hours. One day soon she will remember. My only prayer is when this happens.... I will be there."*

At a psychotherapy conference, Loomis interacts with colleague Robert Newman, who suggests that Laurie's memory lapse may render her a prime candidate for hypnotherapy. On Halloween morning, Loomis performs just this, hoping that Laurie may remember her past trauma so that she may finally conquer it. Eventually, she does regain her memory of that tragic Halloween night, along with the fact her own brother was the killer. Laurie emerges from this session deeply disturbed and fearful that Michael will return to kill again.

Loomis also fears his former patient's return, though he conceals these worries from Laurie. Unbeknownst to both, he already has returned, though how remains a mystery. Prior to the hypnotherapy session, the Shape murders the rock star from Laurie's cover story (and a groupie) before stealing the rocker's Porsche 928S, which he uses to stalk his sister throughout Chicago. The vehicle's tinted windows allow him to pull right alongside Laurie without her even knowing it. While cruising outside town, the slasher notices a parked squad car. Finding the local sheriff snoozing inside, he slashes the lawman's throat. The Shape then crashes his car into pedestrians queued outside a movie theater, killing thirteen people in one fell swoop.

Laurie and Loomis soon learn the shocking truth about the returned killer, each in their own way. While developing family photos taken the day before, Laurie notices a strange blurred figure in the background. Several enlargements later, she recognizes the Shape's trademark white mask in the background – *meaning he's already been to her home*. This sequence is intercut with Loomis exhuming Michael's grave. The casket within is shown to be empty. With the sun setting on Halloween night, both Laurie and Loomis separately race to the Jamison residence where the Shape is already stalking Stephie and her teenage Aunt Heather.

The Shape quickly murders Heather by jamming her hand down a garbage disposal, which "devours her arm with the efficiency of a buzz saw." He then chases a terrified Stephie throughout the home in a deadly game of cat-and-mouse. She's very nearly caught when the Shape hears Laurie's BMW screeching into the driveway. Entering the house, Laurie finds Terrence stabbed to the wall, his feet dangling off the floor à la Bob in *Halloween*. Mother and daughter reunite and attempt to escape. Meanwhile, Loomis is speeding toward Laurie's home in a commandeered coroner's van. Upon entering her neighborhood, he tries slowing down but finds the brake lines have been cut. He slams into a series of utility poles, knocking out power to the area. Some of these downed cables land in Laurie's backyard, one notably in her pool.

Laurie battles her brother while also protecting Stephie, inflicting much damage upon her opponent. She strikes him across the face with an iron poker several times, *even lodging it in his skull.* She also runs him down with her BMW. The climactic chase ends with mother and daughter trapped in their backyard. Laurie charges the Shape once more, this time with a steel-pronged rake, and knocks him into the pool. An injured Loomis arrives just in time to see the slasher trying to pull himself out of the pool with a downed power cable. The scene then cuts to across town where utility workers are beginning to restore power to the neighborhood. This electrocutes the water-treading Shape, who catches fire before exploding. Laurie, Stephie, and Loomis embrace. The script ends back at Michael's grave, now amended to read "1957 – 1988." The camera zooms in as a new inscription is burned into the tombstone. It reads, "For in that sleep of death, what dreams may come…" - Edgar Allen Poe.

SCRIPT: "*Michael convulses violently. His eyes glow bright yellow then white hot, yet he continues toward Dr. Loomis. Michael's eyes darkened, black smoke pours through the eyeholes of the white mask. Suddenly shooting flames with the intensity of two flame throwers. Then in one enormous explosion, Michael's entire body explodes.*"

## THE MTV HALLOWEEN

Of all the unused *Halloween 4* scripts, the Kenney/Medina version most evokes the decade in which it was written. This is essentially what *Halloween* would've been had MTV produced it back when the channel actually played music videos. Virtually everything from John Carpenter's original is updated for the '80s. The screenwriters trade out sleepy suburban Haddonfield for bustling downtown Chicago. Laurie previously rode shotgun in Annie's Chevrolet Monte Carlo, but now sits in the driver's seat of a BMW. The Shape has also upgraded his ride from a Ford LTD Station Wagon to a Porsche. Laurie now sports "modern fashion and hair" as rock music blares throughout her home. This script is so ridiculously '80s that if its pages could somehow spring to life and snort blow, they probably would. (This all makes for an interesting contrast to the actual *Halloween 4*, which largely eschewed the trends of the era for a timeless feel. *Halloween 5*, however...)

This change in style feels evocative of other rock-heavy, pop culture-infused slasher sequels of the time. (Think *Slumber Party Massacre II* or *A Nightmare on Elm Street 4*.) In a unique departure, this *Halloween 4* was poised to have a major celebrity cameo with the aforementioned rock star character, which was to have been played by a real-life figure to be cast at a later date. Though ultimately murdered by the Shape, we would first get a glimpse of the rocker's larger-than-life mansion by way of a Panaglide shot depicting the killer's point-of-view. This sequence would be chock full of images you don't typically see in a *Halloween* movie: a six-car garage, a grand marble fireplace, gold records, rows of guitar amps, and a big screen television tuned to MTV.

The screenwriters twice veer their sequel into hyper-meta territory to interesting effect. Early in this *Halloween 4*, Laurie and Terrence take in a movie at home – Alfred Hitchcock's *Psycho*. This scene depicts Jamie Lee Curtis' Laurie watching the infamous shower scene in which the character played by her real-life mother, Janet Leigh, is brutally murdered. The script frames this contextualization of existing art within new art as being "a connection critics will surely pick up on." Within the story, Laurie and Terrence watching *Psycho*'s shower scene is intercut with the Shape murdering the rock star's groupie in the shower.

A far more meta moment unfolds immediately after. Having murdered the rock star, the Shape takes his Porsche for a joyride at 160 miles-per-hour. Throwing subtlety to the wind, the car's license plate reads "1MANIAC" (the title of the rocker's latest hit). He then drives the sports car into patrons queued outside a theater showing *Halloween 4*, which is just about as meta as you can possibly get. It's as if the Shape is literally murdering people outside the very theater where viewers would be watching the film. This vehicular assault kills thirteen movie-goers in all. Oddly enough, their deaths may have been accidental. The script notes that the Shape "gears down for the turn, hits water, and slides into movie line pedestrians." (Those who took issue with Michael being able to drive in *Halloween* would've had a field day with him being able to drive stick in this proposed sequel.)

The Kenney/Medina script may sound like a far cry from Carpenter's original *Halloween*, but it maintains a close connection to both it and *Halloween II*. The screenwriters frequently reference the past and liberally utilize flashbacks to both films. While the overtly '80s aesthetic may sound jarring, the script is also peppered with Panaglide shots in an effort to recreate Dean Cundey's memorable cinematography. This *Halloween 4* is clearly trying new things while also maintaining a healthy respect for where the series has already been.

## FAMILIAR STRANGERS

Much like the actual *Halloween 4*, this proposed sequel brings back Dr. Loomis, though he doesn't have nearly as much to do here. (He does, however, get to fully recite his "purely and simply evil" speech while speaking to a colleague.) The screenwriters tease out his return in present day, opting for an effective build-up before the reveal. We hear his voice throughout Laurie's first therapy session, but the focus remains on her. The scene ends with the camera pulling back for a full view of the character. ("Though he has had extensive plastic surgery, the right side of his face is scarred as are his gloved hands. Laurie knows not of the connection with her past.") It is incredibly satisfying to have Laurie and Loomis interacting in this way as patient and doctor. The characters were strangers throughout *Halloween* and *Halloween II*, sharing the screen only briefly in the finales of both films. Here they're shown to have a warm therapeutic relationship.

Among this story's more interesting new characters is that of Laurie's husband – Terrence Jamison. In contrast to her later appearances, the Kenney/Medina draft offers us something rare by depicting Laurie Strode as happily married. Described as a Jack Nicholson type, Terrence is a surgeon by trade, and a character that might've benefited from further development had this script gone forward. As Laurie's husband, we're left wondering how much, if anything, he knows about the buried trauma of her past. Surely, he's met Laurie's adoptive parents and *surely* they've told him of that October night a decade ago? She doesn't hide her therapy sessions from him, either. Like *Halloween H20*'s Will Brennan, Terrence is frequently there to comfort Laurie's anxiety and nightmares. Yet in this first draft, we're never given any indication that Terrence knows anything about his wife's bloody past. Sadly, he also "exits" the picture (off-screen) before any kind of realization can occur.

Long before she parented Karen, John, or even Jamie Lloyd – Laurie Strode was mother to Stephanie "Stephie" Jamison, a spunky six-year-old with a yet uncorrupted enthusiasm for Halloween. While she spends much of the story acting her age (skipping through the house in bunny pajamas and singing made-up songs about Fruit Loops), it's awfully difficult not to draw comparisons between her and the final film's Jamie. Both recognize the Shape as "the boogeyman" and both have Golden Retrievers as pets. (Clancey in this script, Sundae in the actual *Halloween 4*.) This script features a wonderfully tense chase sequence between Stephie and her murderous uncle. The slasher terrorizes the girl throughout her own home, right past the dead bodies of her father and aunt. By script's end, Stephie's witnessed so much horror that she may well go mute and start having spaz-out nightmares. Better reserve a room at the Masterson clinic.

## THE FIRST RETURN OF LAURIE STRODE

When last we saw her in *Halloween II*, Laurie Strode wasn't exactly at the height of her game. Recall that our heroine spent much of that first sequel in a hospital bed wavering between delirium and catatonia – a characterization that disappointed even the actress who played her. This *Halloween 4* takes one of the second film's biggest weaknesses and transforms it into a fascinating plot point. Per this new story, Laurie wasn't just chilling throughout *Halloween*'s first sequel – she was in the early stages of a mental breakdown. Her brief time at Haddonfield Memorial was followed by a lengthy admission to a psychiatric facility. As we find her in present day, Laurie has absolutely no memory of October 31, 1978. Her mind appears to have blocked off such painful memories in an unconscious act of self-preservation. In the decade since, we find that Dr. Loomis has taken on a paternal role as Laurie's therapist. Why would he feel so obligated to aid in her recovery? It's possible he feels responsible for the horrors she endured that fateful October night.

In the present day of this *Halloween 4*, we find Laurie leading a fairly wonderful life. Happily married with a young daughter, she enjoys a thriving career while living in an upper middle-class home. Despite all this, she's far from carefree. Laurie suffers from increasingly worsening anxiety, which manifests itself through panic attacks and nightmares. Loomis knows well the cause of these ailments, even if Laurie herself does not. In truth, he thought she would've surely remembered the events of that terrible night by now. Hoping to alleviate her symptoms, Loomis uses guided hypnotherapy to help Laurie remember her past. She wakes from this treatment far more disturbed than before. Her previously generalized fear now has a face and a name. And it just so happens to have recently returned.

Laurie's nightmare sequences in the script are surreal and positively Kafkaesque. The screenwriters recycle a visual from *Halloween II* ("The thick red blood drips on the glossy black floor.") and turn it into a recurring motif. This was, of course, the splattering of Mrs. Alves' blood as she lay dying on the stretcher. Why is this tiny sliver of a memory significant? In the context of that sequel, it was the sound that woke Laurie from the dream-memory of visiting her brother at Smith's Grove. The visual and sound of the blood dripping is therefore associated with the pain of remembering long forgotten experiences. (Nevermind that Mrs. Alves was murdered some distance away from Laurie's hospital room at Haddonfield Memorial. With all due respect to the writers, this scene in *Halloween II* is confusing given the hospital's layout. Props to Kenney and Medina trying to strengthen this tenuous connection.)

As photographer, Laurie participates in a *Real People* photoshoot. The shoot's set consists of models surrounded by dozens of faceless black mannequins, an eerie inversion of the Shape's white mask. This image ingrains itself in Laurie's mind, causing her to have a nightmare of the same visual that night. She wakes with overwhelming dread and anxiety. ("Always in these dreams I feel I am being watched. I don't know why, I don't know by whom or what, but I am definitely being watched. I toss and turn. I wake up feeling violated in some way.") A dive into the nightmare-plagued mind of *Halloween*'s iconic heroine would surely make for a fascinating part of any sequel story. It would also offer ample opportunity for new and unique scares.

The plot device of Laurie having selective amnesia and being unable to remember her trauma isn't exactly out of left field. We caught a glimpse of this in *Halloween II* when she suddenly recalls the repressed memory of her true lineage. This is clearly how Laurie's mind works. When something becomes too painful to think about, she simply buries it deep within her subconscious. As we see in this story, that's not a great thing to do with such memories as they affect her emotional well-being regardless. Still, you have to wonder how Laurie *doesn't* know about the events of the first two films. Did she never watch the news again? Did no one tell her? Does Laurie not wonder what happened to Annie or Lynda? How did she finish high school and advance onto college? And how exactly did Loomis become her therapist? These questions might have been answered with further story development.

One winning aspect of this *Halloween 4* is that Laurie finally saves herself in the end, which is a welcome change. In *Halloween*, she was very nearly killed by the Shape until Dr. Loomis rushed in to save her, somewhat undermining her credibility as a final girl. The exact same thing happened again in *Halloween II*. Yet in the Kenney/Medina draft, Laurie's victory is entirely her own. In an almost humorous flip of the "Loomis saves the day" trope, the doctor contributes almost nothing to the ending save for accidentally ramming his vehicle into some power lines. (This sets up Michael's eventual demise.) Injured from the accident, Loomis arrives just in time to see the Shape electrocuted, having been knocked into the pool by Laurie's unrelenting assault. It is altogether refreshing to see Laurie once again being the resourceful fighter rather than a mere damsel in distress.

While this script finds Laurie in a much happier place at its start than *Halloween H20* or *Halloween 2018*, it leaves her quite broken. She's only just re-discovered the trauma of her past when forced to confront the exact same threat once more. This *Halloween 4* ends with Laurie's husband and young sister-in-law murdered and her six-year-old daughter traumatized for life. Her next therapy session with Dr. Loomis is bound to be an interesting one. A pity that it happens long after the final script page.

## DEAD MAN WALKING

This *Halloween 4*'s approach to the Shape differs considerably from the actual film series. As in the Etchison draft, we're assured that Michael Myers truly died following the explosive ending of *Halloween II*. Not only was over ninety percent of his body severely burned in that film, but this story's opening sees him tied to a stretcher and dropped into Lake Michigan. Dr. Loomis even claims to have seen his former patient buried in Haddonfield Cemetery, though we're not sure how true this is. (This comment could've merely been Loomis' way of easing Laurie's fears). Given that the Shape survives being shot, falling off a balcony, being set on fire, and dumped into Lake Michigan (tied to a stretcher, at that) – it's safe to assume there's something supernatural going on here. In fact, Loomis pretty much admits as such.

In another similarity to the Etchison script, the Kenney/Medina draft offers no concrete explanation as to how the dead slasher returns to life. We simply find him back in action sporting a new white mask. At just seventy-eight pages, this is the shortest unproduced draft (barring treatments) covered in this book and, as a first draft, it's not the most detailed. It's entirely possible that Michael's body was never actually recovered from Lake Michigan, which would explain his empty gravesite. Yet Loomis seemingly believes Michael *is* buried in Haddonfield Cemetery, which is why he later tries to exhume his body. Was Loomis not informed of the helicopter fiasco? The screenplay never clarifies whether Michael escaped his watery grave in Lake Michigan or his actual grave in Haddonfield Cemetery.

When contemplating the Shape's unlikely return, Loomis considers a supernatural explanation tied to the festival of Samhain. His dialogue here feels eerily similar to lines spoken by Conal Cochran in *Halloween III*.

### Loomis in the Kenney/Medina draft of Halloween 4:

*She is Michael Myers' sole surviving blood relative. I can't help but fear that one day he may return to fulfill an ancient prophecy. [...] I know what I'm suggesting cannot be explained in scientific terms. According to ancient mythology, the medieval Druids separated their year into two equal segments. The first, from May 1st, was presided over by "the Lord of the Sun." The second, from November 1st, was presided over by "the Lord of the Dead." Samhain. During this transformation of seasons, there's a time when the natural world and the world beyond are one. This provides an opportunity for the spirits of the dead to come dance on the hill with the other demon fairies and a time when "the Lord of the Dead" can interfere with the lives of men.... violently. October 31st is the festival of Samhain. [...] As with all great legends, they sometimes contain truths. And that truth may live in the soul of Michael Myers.*

### Conal Cochran in Halloween III:

*The barriers would be down, you see, between the real and the unreal, and the dead might be looking in...to sit by our fires of turf. Halloween...the festival of Samhain!*

In keeping with the MTV-aesthetic of this alternate *Halloween 4*, the Shape gets a makeover from the neck down. This means we never once see him wearing his trademark coveralls, which were also missing from the Etchison draft. (Oh – and this screenplay doesn't call him "the Shape" as John Carpenter and Debra Hill did. Here he's known as "the Silhouette.") The slasher's first murders, the groupie and the rock star, unfold at the latter's extravagant mansion. Here, Michael raids the musician's wardrobe for new duds. He emerges from the walk-in closet wearing black leather pants, black boots, a leather jacket, and black driving gloves. (In a visual similarity, Loomis also wears black gloves to cover his burned hands.) It would seem this makeover gives the Shape somewhat of a mental boost. Kenney and Medina write that "the Silhouette" spots the Porsche keys, tosses them in the air, and catches them confidently before peeling out of the driveway. (This is both wildly irreverent and also hilarious.)

Like the original, there's no shortage of stalking within this script. However, the Shape enters the story on October 29th – the night in which he kills the rock star and then proceeds directly to the Jamison house. (How he knows where Laurie lives isn't explained.) But what's interesting is that he manages to creep inside her house – completely undetected – both nights prior to Halloween. This days-long period of stalk before slash marks *somewhat* of a departure from the original. On both nights, Laurie and her family are easily within his grasp, yet he chooses to postpone his attack. (Guess he really is a stickler for Halloween night). His presence in the neighborhood is noticed by elderly Mrs. Hutchens, who initially suspects the daytime gardener of foul play. On the second night, she calls the cops to no real avail as the Shape is already creeping through Laurie's darkened home once again.

The slasher also takes a ton of abuse in this story's final act. In fact, the damage is so severe that you're left wondering how he could possibly return for a potential *Halloween 5*. This alternate *Halloween 4* charges that Michael's charred corpse simply comes back to life to kill again. Yet its ending sees the slasher's body literally exploded into chunks, which can't make for a very easy resurrection.

## A HASTY RE-WRITE

It was soon after this screenplay's submission that *Halloween 4*'s producers learned that Jamie Lee Curtis – now a major star – would not be reprising her role as Laurie Strode. Given that Laurie is the focal point of this new story, such a development posed a massive narrative challenge that could only be solved through an extensive re-write. Hoping to salvage their script, the screenwriters first tried tinkering with the finale. More specifically, their first draft is marked with notes in pen, crossing out certain passages, and re-assigning Laurie's dialogue and actions to other characters.

The revised finale finds Laurie swapped out with the Aunt Heather role, whom we previously saw killed while Stephie plays outside. Heather somehow learns that the Shape is back and must race home to save her niece. Here it's Loomis – not Heather/Laurie – who reaches the Jamison residence first to save Stephie. It's then Heather - not Loomis - who accidentally slams into the power lines due to failed brakes. Loomis does extensive battle with his former patient, which ends with the Shape being knocked into the pool amid downed power cables. He's again electrocuted, though he doesn't explode this time around. He instead just keels over. When police and first responders go to check the pool a short while later, his body is missing.

If the plot of this revised ending feels mega-similar to the actual *Halloween 4*, that's because it is. Dr. Loomis trying to save an absent Laurie Strode's young daughter from Michael Myers is essentially the same gist as the 1988 sequel.

## WHY IT WASN'T MADE

Had the Kenney/Medina version made it to the screen, Dokken and Alice Cooper may have had competition with their respective Freddy and Jason-themed music videos. Alas, it wasn't meant to be. For over thirty years, this draft has collected dust, never publicly acknowledged by Moustapha Akkad or any others involved. Given this, it's difficult to pinpoint the exact reason of why this draft was passed over. For neither writer having a firm background in screenwriting, their *Halloween 4* reads well enough though it's easy to assume the rock-slasher angle might've been a step too far. The most logical reason – as fans can surely surmise – is that this script is too heavily predicated on the return of Laurie Strode.

Recall that Jamie Lee Curtis had largely put aside the horror genre following her appearance in the second *Halloween*. Since that time, she had branched out to other genres – namely comedies and dramas – and was of this moment filming *A Fish Called Wanda*, which would go on to become another of her staple films. That said, one can easily imagine that another *Halloween* sequel was perhaps furthest from her cards at this point. Ironically, though, the basis of the Kenney/Medina draft sounds strikingly similar to the idea that Curtis had favored for *Halloween*'s first sequel. As she told author David Grove in his book *Jamie Lee*

*Curtis: Scream Queen*, "It would've been interesting if [*Halloween II*] had taken place ten years later and Laurie's living in Chicago. She has kids now and she has an interesting job. Maybe she's a teacher or some kind of businesswoman. Then Michael reappears in her life. I think that would've been interesting."

A draft featuring Laurie Strode no longer works if her well-known portrayer is unwilling to return – and it's safe to say audiences wouldn't have accepted a re-casting. In trying to retain the same story structure, the writers would eliminate the character in later drafts but, in doing so, would've surely impacted Loomis' role as well. As his patient, Laurie's technically the only reason Loomis is present, with him having little purpose outside of his therapy sessions. With such issues to address, one may as well go back to the drawing board, which is what Akkad would ultimately do. The writers may have composed a version sans Laurie but their draft clearly lost favor to others under consideration. Sifting through the submissions, Akkad was particularly impressed with a treatment by another team of writers: Dhani Lipsius, Larry Rattner, and Benjamin Ruffner. This trio was soon hired to expand their treatment into a full-fledged screenplay, thus postponing Laurie Strode's return for another ten years.

# "We had so many scripts for another Halloween sent to us. There were so many stories pitched. Nothing worked."

- Moustapha Akkad, HorrorFan

# MARC ALLYN MEDINA
### Co-writer - Halloween 4 (The Kenney/Medina Draft)

Interviewed by Travis Mullins

**You seem to have an interesting background. Before we dive into *Halloween 4*, could you tell us a bit about that?**

From 1982 to 1990, I had a local LA, medium-fish-in-a-small pond band called Perfect Stranger. We were a top draw at Madame Wong's West. We'd sell out the Roxy or the Whisky in the pre-pay-to-play days. We were very KROQ. We started off B-52s-meets-Quiet Riot, then ended up being more of an INXS-meets-Duran Duran thing. I had some notable players. The founding bass member, Mark Montague, is now known as Tall Man. He's produced albums for Peter Criss and is still an artist out there. We're still friends. The second or third bass player – who was with me for three or four years – was Robert Trujillo, which is just hilarious. He's a fantastic bass player. You just wouldn't have expected him to have come from a new wave band. We were playing at Madame Wong's when we were approached by Rocky George from Suicidal Tendencies. Soon after, Robert left to join Suicidal and then ended up with Ozzy Osbourne and later Metallica. Super great, down-to-earth and wonderful person. The last bass player we had until our record came out to a big *thud* – a little airplay on the coasts but nothing in middle America – was Angelo Barbera. He used to play with The Motels and we're still good friends. He ended up touring with the surviving members of The Doors for two years. They made him a full-time member and he did real well with that. So, I was blessed to have known some great musicians. We were an 'on our way up' local band. We would bring around 200 to 600 people to a gig, as opposed to 20 or 30 people. But we weren't the 2,000 people band.

**Very cool! I've heard your song "Politics of Passion." Definitely has a Duran Duran vibe.**

It was a great time. It's funny; I was watching a documentary on Tom Petty last night. In 1976, I was sixteen and I remember when Tom Petty first came out. He broke on KROQ, and was a part of new wave before he became folksier. He was cutting edge. You had all these new wave acts and then you had The Ramones, The Clash, and Tom Petty, who was punkier. In watching his story, I remember the same thing that happened to him happened to me. When they signed him, they didn't want the band. They just wanted him – but then he kept his two guys that were fantastic. I was lucky enough that my guitar player Randy Szellinky took from Randy Rhoads, who used to sneak us into the Starwood to see Quiet Riot when we were like fifteen or sixteen. We couldn't even get into that place legally. Since my guy played like Randy Rhoads, we had a hard guitar – but then we also had a funky bass. Originally, I couldn't see it all, so we were like, '*B-52s!*' I think we did a song called "The Omega Man" based after that movie from the '60s or '70s. Later, we became more of a Duran Duran kind of thing.

Anyway, there are two or three parallels in this Tom Petty [documentary] I saw last night. There was a point where we had a record deal offered to us, but they only wanted me and Robert [Trujillo]. I couldn't just screw over the other guys and I probably should have. But this guy would've made us do all his own songs, though. We were only allowed one of our songs per album. He had all kinds of gold and platinum-selling records all over the world, but nothing in America. It still would've been a good steppingstone because you could get your foot in the door if you had records selling somewhere on the planet. But he only wanted me and Robert – me, just because I looked good and could swagger. I couldn't really sing. And Robert was an amazing bass player. We would've almost been like a Wham! kind of deal. I didn't do it, though. You know, you think back to sitting in Capitol Records and there's records all over the wall. He says, '*I only want you and the bass player,*' and you're going to stand defiantly? '*No, I can't screw over the other guys!*' What the hell was I thinking? You know, it's hilarious. (laughs) It's not a huge regret. It's just interesting, you know? We all control our destinies and it's all based on our decisions. And if you're always making your decisions for the right reasons, there's not really any wrong decisions.

**Now, your script mentions that you had already composed a version of John Carpenter's iconic theme. Were you hoping to score the film as well?**

I was just hoping to sell a song! I wasn't worried about scoring the whole thing. I've written probably 200 songs and I had hoped to at least play something. If we didn't sell the script, I at least wanted to be in the end credits. (laughs) Actually, I just found a couple of cassettes from that era and will have to search to see if I can find that score.

**Could you tell us a bit about your co-writer Daniel Kenney?**

After Robert left Perfect Stranger and before we got Angelo [Barbera], we had this bass player from The American Lads – and his dear close friend was Daniel Kenney. So, Daniel Kenney started coming to the shows and we became friends. He was a smart, well-to-do kid from over on the Westside, I guess. I was in the Valley. He was pretty well-heeled or came from money. Some of the times when we were writing, if we were going out to dinner, he would pick up my girl and I in a limousine – or he'd offer to get a limo for the band, that kind of thing. And he was only, like, 23 or 24 – and I was a hard-working, starving musician, film technician dude. He could afford the $500 jacket, you know? But he also didn't have an attitude about it. He was just respectful, kind, and nice to everyone.

**Have you kept in touch?**

I've looked for him and I haven't been able to find him anywhere. I've done everything short of hiring a private investigator. We weren't that close of friends, but we were good friends. I seriously haven't talked to the guy since, like, the late '80s. I think he was a couple of years younger than me. He had short *GQ* hair and at the time, I had big, giant Mötley Crüe hair – even though we were new wave. I want to say he had Poindexter glasses. He looked preppy square. You know, a strait-laced kind of guy whereas I was in a leopard shirt and leather pants. Super great guy, though. Really intelligent. Great vocabulary. Brilliant mind. And we had a lot of fun. I mean, we were cracking each other up. Some of these ideas were hilarious.

**How did you guys get involved with *Halloween 4*?**

Daniel was approached by Moustapha Akkad. I guess he was friends with his family or knew him somehow. And he knew that I had a background in film because my dad was a film editor. Growing up, I'm watching *The Omega Man* or *Planet of the Apes* and my dad's going in my ear, '*Did you check out* The Parallax View? *Look how the camera just panned! Did you see that flip focus?*' All of that stuff was kind of instilled in me. So, Daniel and I were hanging out. He dug the band and we got along great. He approached me and said, '*Hey, you've got a clever mind. You want to do this thing together? I've got this opportunity if you want to team up. We can throw this together and there's a chance we might be able to participate and get paid a little bit.*' So, if we were to come up with and write our version of *Halloween 4*, we would possibly have the chance of getting the brass ring and have it filmed. The liaison was Daniel, so I never actually got to meet Mr. Akkad. That was the connection. We wrote it, he submitted it, and then we got paid. But I didn't get to meet him. Daniel knew of him, met with him and said, '*Oh, I presented it and he said we should do this.*' So, I think Daniel may have been in his employ or a friend of the family. That was my impression.

**Were you a fan of the previous films?**

You know, I love all film and I enjoyed the first one. I could see it for what it was. It was amazing what they pulled off. I also knew the kind of money it made. I think it was the highest-grossing horror film of all time. It was certainly scary without really spending a lot of money on special effects. You know, they didn't have to do it like *The Exorcist*. They got you more with suspense. They could've had a better hairstylist for Jamie Lee Curtis, though. (laughs) Horrible hair, man! And she's such a pretty girl! But the basic concept with having Donald Pleasence's voice and demeanor gave it an aura of legitimacy – and they did a lot of original things like looking through the mask. I certainly respected it, but it wasn't like *Planet of the Apes*. I knew it wasn't an MGM musical or *The Wizard of Oz*. It was a cult favorite, but I certainly respected it, and I knew the first and second went together.

Then, the third one went into some sort of Shamrock mask thing, right? I thought that was just sacrilegious. It was cute and funny on its own, but it didn't have anything to do with *Halloween*. So, I was just trying to tie our script back to the first film.

**So, how did the two of you formulate your ideas?**

Daniel would come over to my apartment while my girlfriend would go run errands. We would write for three or fours hours, two to three days a week for three or four months. I'm really great at coming up with ideas and he was more whipping it into shape and making sure it was spelled correctly. But he also had some great ideas and we'd bounce them back and forth. It's great to come up with ideas – but then you'd have to tie them together. I had taken some film classes at Valley College. One of my favorite films was *Battleship Potemkin*, and [Daniel and I] did a lot of the techniques those guys came up with, where you would cut up all of the different lines, scenes, and shots, and then rearrange them. We would take the bottom of the page and put it in the middle – and then take the top of the page and put it at the bottom and see how that played. It was a lot of brainstorming. We would cut up the script, lay it out on a table and try moving a paragraph. I think my girlfriend did the final typing for us, putting it in the proper form.

I know that I was thinking more like a director than a writer. That's why there's so many darn camera angles in the script and Daniel said [Moustapha] didn't appreciate that. But I was thinking of the subjective POV. We'd enter a foggy cemetery, going towards the back of a headstone. Then, I would have the camera flip up and over to face the front of the headstone. You'd almost get dizzy. You're approaching the headstone to music – and then [the camera goes] up, looking down at it – and then upside down, looking forward at it – and it would be Michael Myers' headstone. Basically, it's just a camera trick. But I went to all that trouble. You might have a page or two but it's not really moving the story forward. Another example, I would write a scene where we have the subjective POV – we pan on a large estate, go inside and we hear music playing. We're behind a rock star playing piano. On the reflection of the piano is his music video on MTV – and this is when MTV was still fresh and new. As we go down the hallways, we pan on the gold records on the wall. They've all got horror movie titles on them. While the rock star is playing, you hear him groan and then see blood coming down the piano keys.

Then, we're outside in a six-car garage and Michael Myers gets inside a new Porsche 928. I think the license plate was the name of the rock star's music video – the one we had just seen. The camera pulls back and goes tearing off down the street. Cut to the center of the city and there's a movie theater. From the POV inside the car – *thud, thud, thud*! He runs over these people standing in line for a movie and then races away. The camera pulls back and pans up and we see *Halloween 4* on the marquee. So, we've just seen Michael Myers kill people standing in line to see the movie that we're inside watching!

**It's all very meta. Who would you have cast as the rock star circa 1987?**

Looking back at it now, I actually picture a *Three Lock Box* by Sammy Hagar kind of guy. For ten years, Sammy Hagar was the lead singer of Van Halen after David Lee Roth was fired. But he had a successful career before that. He was already a platinum-selling recording artist. He had a song on the original *Heavy Metal* soundtrack. He had a band called Montrose. They had a big hit called "Rock Candy," and then he had a couple of albums of his own. The song "I Can't Drive 55" will show you exactly the kind of rock star I was thinking of.

**Now, one of the most notable features of your script is that it actually features Laurie Strode.**

That's right. She moved to Chicago and was a photographer for a *Rolling Stone*-type magazine – which would've tied into the rock star getting killed.

**I guess you were injecting a bit of your world into the script?**

Well, I don't know if I was injecting myself, but I was surrounded by music. Music was the culture. Everything was a rock scene – all the way to Pepsi commercials.

**Laurie as a yuppie businesswoman is an admittedly cool take. It almost reads like "the MTV *Halloween*," infused with a bit of *Miami Vice*-style.**

That's exactly what it was like in 1987, too. MTV came out in, what, 1982? By then, pretty much everything was styled like *Miami Vice*. I remember sitting with Daniel and thinking, '*What kind of job do we want to give* [Laurie]?' The first two films were set in the '70s, and we were trying to make her a modern woman that people could relate to in the '80s. I didn't want it to seem antiquated. I wanted it to seem like now. So, we had her being independent, smart, and successful. Not even super successful, but respected and good at what she does. She made it out of that other place and is now having a fulfilling, successful life.

**Yet she's also under the care of Dr. Loomis with deeply repressed memories. Tell us about that.**

Just for intrigue, I thought it was an interesting twist to now have Michael Myers' psychotic doctor as her psychiatrist. What I was excited about was still having Dr. Loomis around because just his voice brought you back into the film. Let's face it, *Halloween* was so bad, it was good. That's why it was so good. I think I was trying to have Laurie think that she was normal and go on with her life – but now, this thing is coming back to get her.

**Something that isn't explained is how Michael survived the fire or the drowning in Lake Michigan. Do you recall how you would've justified that? How would you describe him in your script? Mortal or somewhat inhuman?**

I think we just lost him in the lake, right? I don't think we actually had him drowning in the scene. He's Michael Myers, man! (laughs) He could be standing in the bottom of Lake Michigan and just walk his way out! Even now, thirty years later, how the hell is Michael Myers still around? He was totally burned in the second one, wasn't he? Just having him come back is a stretch. I know that Donald Pleasence would say that he was the essence of all evil. In writing this, I do remember we did research on Samhain and going back to the Druids and the ancient evils. But I don't think we gave it much thought about how we were transcending him across time. Somehow, he's just still alive. It's almost like the Terminator. You can't kill him. It just keeps coming back. You can never really be sure he's gone when he's gone. It's compelling. It's terrifying.

**The script ends with his entire body exploding. Was it your intention to close the storyline? Or could there have been some sort of creative workaround this demise?**

That's a good question. I don't remember. I don't think we thought there were going to be more after this. I think we were doing something that picked it back up and wrapped it. I don't think anybody had an idea there was going to be a hundred of them. It'd be a little tricky for him to come back after that. Unless you did something where the molecules all come back together. But that'd be too magical – like a Terminator thing. But I don't think we were thinking of anything like that. We might've just killed him off. (laughs)

**What's interesting is that throughout the finale all of Laurie's action and dialogue is crossed out in pen and replaced with Loomis. Is there a story behind that?**

Towards the end while we were finishing it, word came back that we weren't going to have Jamie Lee Curtis after all. Originally, I was thinking we still had her. As soon as we realized we didn't, we had to go a different way. If the action or dialogue was viable, useful, or important in moving the story along, we thought, '*How could we still use this to tell that story?*' Part of this would've probably gone along with cutting the script, putting it on the table and moving it around. I believe we did a final clean draft where we made those changes, but it didn't make a difference. I don't remember if she wanted too much money, but she wasn't going to be in it. You know, it's a wonder that anything gets made. There are so many people working on so many different levels. You can build an entire thing around an actor but if the actor doesn't want to do it? Or if the guy at the studio doesn't like the actor? They can even shoot the entire thing, but if the editor or director doesn't like something, then they might take out the character.

**So, did you ever hear as to why the producers weren't going forward with your script?**

Daniel just told me they had chosen something else. I think what killed our script was that we weren't even going to have Laurie anymore. It was my understanding that they had a couple of teams working on scripts together. I figured they had had four or five crews, and then they were supposed to pick the best one. Of course, they didn't pick ours but there are elements of mine that they definitely used. So, I figure they probably just cherrypicked out of all of them and whoever wrote the final professional screenplay would get the credit.

**How did you react?**

I was disappointed but I didn't give it much thought. It was a really fun experience. It was the first thing I had ever written in script form. You know, we threw it together. It's funny because it looks like a real script and it reads pretty good. I mean, you couldn't tell that we hadn't written anything before. My dad was a frustrated screenwriter. When he writes, it's always, '*How can I sell it?*' We kind of did that with *Halloween 4*. But I really looked at this with a creative eye and tried to give it some interesting twists and turns. When I presented this to my dad to proofread, he couldn't have been any prouder of me. He was almost even a little jealous because it was like, '*How is this actually such a script?'* He was blown away. I only went to Valley College for two years, but I did take filmmaking classes. A lot of it is history and learning how other people do things. It's like Tarantino says. *'Everything you do is an homage to something else that you like.'* Although my dad totally loved the band and supported all of that; from a screenwriting standpoint, it was, *'Oh, you're not a screenwriter. You've never written anything.'* Then suddenly it was, *'Wow. Oh, you can write a script! It's a good read. Good job, son.'* So, it was a button on my cap for my dad, for sure.

It was a great learning experience. It was fun to hang out with my friend. It wasn't grueling or really painful. You just had to be disciplined to actually sit down and do it. You couldn't cancel every time. Then, actually getting all the notes together and into script form was a pain in the ass. That took about a month. I would've loved to have seen it made but it was just another fun, creative thing that we were doing. It was certainly disappointing, but it wasn't the end of the world. I still had my band and I was working at the film studios and I was playing the Roxy with Robert Trujillo. When we were writing it, we just believed that they were going to make it. I never had a doubt in my mind. That's probably what helped propel us and actually have it look like a real script. For a first-time effort, it's real. It wasn't a waste of my time. I felt like we created something.

**Did you ever see the final film?**

I did and I thought it was pretty good. Really, I was looking to see what they took from our ideas. Like, having all the Donald Pleasence stuff, talking about the evil Druids. *'He's the embodiment of all that is evil!'* I know we wrote that stuff in there. When we went to see the movie, I was looking to see what they had utilized and the parallels to our script. So, I came to the conclusion – and so did Daniel – that from several groups, they probably gleaned and utilized little pieces here and there. Honestly, I just felt kind of honored by it.

**Were there any specific pieces that you could attribute to your script?**

One of my ideas was the niece. Now, my niece is not exactly like the little kid they used in the movie, but I came up with that idea. They actually made the whole movie about that. Maybe the other guys thought of this, also. The vehicle crashing into the power transformer and the town blacking out? The big explosion? That was mine. I guess they didn't want to destroy an $80,000 car. Instead, they had Michael Myers crash in an old, beat-up, rusty truck.

**Were you involved in the Writer's Guild arbitration?**

No, it didn't even occur to me to pursue that. I felt honored to even have the opportunity. My feeling was that Daniel knew or was associated with Mr. Akkad. I don't remember if he worked for him or was a friend of the family, but that provided us an opportunity, a window to even get a shot. The fact that we got anything was icing on the cake. It was such a fun thing to do, and cool to see the film. I wasn't seeing it to go, '*Aha! What did they take of mine?*' to get an attorney or anything like that. It was kind of like, '*What a trip. We helped put that thing together.*' You know, I had several creative things going on. If I had been just a screenwriter, it would've been devastating. But I had a great relationship with my girlfriend. I had just started doing loans here and there. I had the band playing at the Roxy and the Whisky and I was still working at the film studio. Everything was going great at that time. I was grateful for the opportunity and the experience. Writing with a friend and then seeing it all finished is great. And then, thirty years later, having you guys contact me is great. It was definitely worth my investment, see what I mean? I didn't even get the movie made and then lost the script. Then, you found me, and I get the script back again! My joke is anytime something magical happens, I call upon the power of dead grandmas, and they always come through with a miracle for me.

**They definitely did. That's awesome.**

I think it's amazing that somehow, in some book, I'm going to have some little acknowledgment, so that's just super, super cool as well. It corroborates my story! '*I was telling the truth! I did write a version! They just didn't make it!*' (laughs)

MICHAEL
AUDREY
MYERS

1957 – 1989

*"For in that sleep of death,
what dreams may come..."*
– Edgar Allan Poe

# HALLOWEEN 4

Just when you thought it
was safe to go trick-or-treating.

**Screenplay by**
**Shem Bitterman**

Fall 1987 would see development on *Halloween 4* slowly rev back to life. Upon rejecting the Kenney/Medina script, producer Moustapha Akkad settled on a concept devised by the writing trio of Dhani Lipsius, Larry Rattner, and Benjamin Ruffner. While all three were aspiring screenwriters, none were yet in the Writer's Guild. Nor were they serious horror fans. As per Larry Rattner in his *Taking Shape* interview, their submission came at the suggestion of another friend, who just so happened to work at Akkad's distribution company. To better prepare themselves for the job, the trio rented the first two *Halloween*s and hypothesized Michael Myers' return to Haddonfield.

Like the Kenney/Medina draft, the trio concocted a scenario that would feature Laurie Strode's daughter in a prominent role. With Jamie Lee Curtis opting not to return, their story would instead center on an institutionalized Michael breaking free from his confines in pursuit of his recently orphaned niece. (Something to consider is that while *Halloween II* has been lambasted for its sibling twist, it wasn't technically the film responsible for cementing the Shape as a bloodline killer. That "fault" per se lies with *Halloween 4*, which could have opted to go anywhere yet focused on Laurie's next of kin. But we digress.)

To bridge the gap between films, an early offer was put out to actor Donald Pleasence to reprise his role as boogeyman chaser Dr. Sam Loomis. Pleasence would accept after receiving the casual blessing of John Carpenter. Thus, the good doctor would feature prominently in future submissions. The specifics of the trio's take are unknown, though Larry Rattner asserts that the film's surprise ending – in which Michael's niece violently attacks a relative – had hailed from their material. Akkad requested they expand their rough treatment into a full screenplay, which they did and completed just after Thanksgiving 1987. The trio received feedback that, while the resulting draft was good, it still needed work. Notes were then given on how to improve it. The trio incorporated these changes into a second draft, which they submitted to Trancas sometime in December.

It would seem the trio's submission had still not satisfied producers as Alan B. McElroy would later be hired to revise their story into his own script. But prior to this, another writer was brought to Akkad's attention: Shem Bitterman. If that name sounds vaguely familiar to *Halloween* fans, it should. Bitterman was the first official screenwriter on *Halloween 5* and officially credited for his work on that film. As of this writing, it has been a very little-known fact that his involvement with the series began with *Halloween 4*. Bitterman's hiring came at the suggestion of producer Ramzi "Ramsey" Thomas, another integral figure whose involvement has been regrettably forgotten with time.

An elusive figure (who unfortunately could not be reached for this book), Ramsey Thomas maintained a long-standing partnership with Moustapha Akkad. For over fifteen years, he was the vice president of development at Akkad's Falcon International Pictures, responsible for distributing *Lion of the Desert*, for which Thomas also served as script consultant. He later directed the Akkad-produced *Appointment with Fear*, a low-budget 1985 thriller that served as the producer's first attempt at mimicking *Halloween*'s success. Despite taking an "Alan Smithee" credit on that film, Thomas remained business partners with Akkad. While only credited as producer on *Halloween 5*, it would appear that – like Bitterman – he was also involved in the development of *Halloween 4*, if only loosely.

Bitterman had moved from New York to Los Angeles to pursue a career as a playwright. In November 1987, his play *Tulsa* was running at LA's Callboard Theater. After a performance, Bitterman was approached by Thomas who sought to option one of his plays as a potential film. During this time, Thomas also used his Akkad connection to offer Bitterman the chance to take a stab at *Halloween 4*. (Note: Thomas previously worked with *Halloween 4* actor Michael Pataki on his USC film *Tomorrow May Be Dying* back in 1960. Coincidence?)

Like the trio, Bitterman was neither a serious horror fan nor in the Writer's Guild, but he was up for the challenge. His initial treatment was well-received by the film's producers, who quickly hired him to expand it into a full-length screenplay over Christmas 1987. His two drafts – the second dated January 16, 1988 – mark some of the rarest discoveries in *Halloween* history. As readers will come to find, Bitterman's material bears a *striking resemblance* to the final film, leading one to believe that, much like McElroy, he was brought in to pitch his own revision of the Lipsius/Ruffner/Rattner script.

## THE STORY

The Bitterman treatment opens on October 30, 1988 at the Redding Center for Severe Psychiatric Disorders in Smith's Grove, Illinois. We find the head physician leading several interns on a tour whilst giving short backstories on the more dangerous patients as they go along. ("There are people in this world whose psychic pain is so great that they cannot live among us. Nor can we cure them. They're kept here.") They soon visit an entire unit dedicated to the care of only one patient, the notorious Michael Myers of Haddonfield. Dr. Loomis, visibly burn-scarred from *Halloween II*, joins in on the tour discussion. He mentions that Michael somehow survived his own burn injuries but hasn't physically moved in ten years – nor even eaten. Loomis then gravely errs by mentioning how Michael's only living relatives were killed in a car accident – all except for his adolescent niece who still resides in Haddonfield. Unseen to the group, Michael's hand twitches in the darkness at this mention. Later that night, the Shape kills two romantically involved nurses and escapes using their keys. A traveling preacher mistakes the hitchhiking killer for "an apparition of divinity" and stops to help him on the road. The Shape kills the reverend and his dog before stealing his pickup truck.

We then shift to Haddonfield where six-year-old Amanda Hatch has woken from a nightmare of her uncle. Daughter of the recently deceased Laurie Strode, Amanda is comforted by her seventeen-year-old foster sister, Linda. Though a sweet child, Amanda has a *seriously warped* perception of her uncle, whom she believes is unfairly characterized as "the boogeyman." She thumbs through an old family album the following morning, which includes a photo of her uncle as a boy. While later walking to school, Amanda sprints off in another direction. Running through backyards and alleyways, she is mysteriously drawn to the Myers house. The child enters to find the new owners – a kind yuppie couple – renovating the interior. Amanda then leaves for school where she's teased by her classmates for being the boogeyman's niece. She shouts back, "The boogeyman can be our friend!" Unbeknownst to Amanda, her uncle has already arrived in town and is stalking her from afar.

Hospital staff rightly panic upon discovering the two bodies in Michael's otherwise empty cell. Loomis is especially alarmed at this development. When asked what they should do, he exclaims, "Pray to God it's not too late!" As darkness falls on Halloween night, Linda takes Amanda trick-or-treating, but the little girl notices her uncle off in the distance. He turns to leave, but she chases after him – ultimately arriving back at the now darkened Myers house. Amanda enters once more, exploring Judith and Michael's former childhood bedrooms. In an adjacent room, we notice the yuppie couple murdered, though Amanda does not. Linda catches up to her foster sister and tries to leave, but finds the doors and windows locked tight. The Shape appears and attacks Linda, though she escapes to find Amanda in the basement dressed in young Michael's clown costume. (Amanda is helplessly oblivious to the threat her uncle poses.) The girls move further into the basement to elude the Shape and stumble upon Judith's disinterred corpse, which rests beneath her once again stolen headstone. Horrified, they exit the Myers house through a cellar door and bolt for the police station.

There, a shaken Linda finds Sheriff Brackett and Dr. Loomis, who work together on a plan to keep Amanda safe until morning. Loomis theorizes that Michael believes killing his entire bloodline will free him from his humanity. ("He's not a man. Pure evil, alive in human form. Something no amount of human understanding can touch. Grotesquely brilliant. Almost divine. Only with no compassion. No forgiveness. I believe now that it's after Amanda.") Their plan involves having three deputies – Tom, Jim and Ben – escort the girls to Brackett's isolated hunting cabin outside town using unmarked police cars. Brackett and Loomis will stay behind to search Haddonfield's streets for the escaped slasher. Still sympathizing with her uncle, Amanda views Loomis as "a bad man." Meanwhile, the Shape overhears one of the deputies blabbing to his girlfriend Tammy over CB radio the plan to stash Amanda outside of town.

The deputies accompany Linda and Amanda to Brackett's cabin, which they find without power. Back in town, Brackett and Loomis chase down the Shape, though this turns out to be a mask-wearing drunk they very nearly kill. Having followed Brackett's men as a stowaway in Tammy's car, the Shape descends on the cabin, murdering his ditsy chauffeur and the deputies. Amanda escapes through a window and goes in search of her uncle, prompting Linda to go in search of her. They eventually wind up back at the cabin where Amanda finally comes face to face with her uncle. (Script: "They stare at each other for a long time.") Linda interrupts this eerie encounter and the Shape angrily knocks her unconscious. This upsets Amanda, who screams at him. ("She's dead! You killed her! You're not my uncle! You'll never be my uncle!") She then rushes to Linda's side, apologizing for her behavior. ("Linda, Linda! I'll never run away again. I'll never be a bad girl again. Just please come alive!")

The Shape grabs hold of Amanda and directs her to a make-up mirror. He then instructs her to brush her hair, recreating his final memory of Judith. Amanda refuses, but her uncle shoves the brush back into her hand. Across the room, a bleeding Linda regains consciousness. Playing into the Shape's psychology, she begins brushing her own hair and repeatedly calling the slasher by his human name. Linda then starts to unbutton her blouse, prompting him to approach with his knife raised. With this, she thrusts a pair of scissors into her attacker's throat. The cabin door swings open to reveal Loomis, who fires multiple shots into his patient. Amanda and Linda escape as the Shape crumbles to the floor.

First-responders soon arrive on the scene – including a van from the Redding Center for Psychiatric Disorders. Amanda asks Loomis if her uncle is truly dead. He responds, "Yes, he's dead. He'll never trouble you again." Amanda then asks to see her uncle's face as she never saw him unmasked, but her request is denied. She sneaks into the coroner's van anyway and removes his mask, revealing "the beautiful unlined face of a child." Amanda goes to kiss his cheek and his eyes burst open! She manages a scream as he begins to strangle her – but it's only a dream. She then jolts awake in her bed on a sunny morning. Gazing out her window, Amanda notices the Shape standing off in the distance. After a pause, he steps away, disappearing behind a house. The *Halloween* theme rises.

## SIMILAR YET DIFFERENT

The first act of Bitterman's *Halloween 4* unfolds much like the *Halloween 4* you already know but with several differences. It's not until the second act that the screenplays truly diverge. Yet Bitterman and McElroy are clearly working from the same basic premise. Laurie Strode and her husband have perished in a tragic car accident. Their young daughter has been adopted by a new family. Though still struggling with the loss of her parents, she feels close to her teenaged foster sister. On the tenth anniversary of his 1978 massacre, the Shape wakes from a coma, escapes his confinement, murders several people, and returns to Haddonfield in search of his young niece. Loomis rightly predicts his patient's plans and follows after, teaming with the local sheriff once arriving in town. Familiar enough, right? From that summary, you can easily discern how Amanda and Linda eventually became Jamie and Rachel in the final film.

The Bitterman draft opens with several details that were later incorporated into the McElroy script but ultimately cut from the film. These include a flashback to *Halloween II*'s ending and a narrated tour of the Redding Center (Ridgemont Federal Sanitarium in the film) with brief backstories for the more disturbed patients. Unlike in the final film, there's no mention here of a pending transfer to Smith's Grove. Actor Michael Pataki's Dr. Hoffman is very much present in the Bitterman drafts, though he goes by different names. It's immediately clear that he and Loomis deeply resent one another for a multitude of reasons. Loomis is furious that his colleague exhibits a comatose Michael Myers to visiting interns as though he were "a freak show" and vows to report him for doing so. Just as in the film, the Hoffman character doubts that Michael poses any real threat despite being told otherwise by Loomis. Even after Michael escapes and murders three people, Hoffman refuses to heed his colleague's warning that Michael is headed back to Haddonfield. Judging by this depiction, the degree to which Hoffman is a stubborn asshole was seriously toned down in the final film. He's so unbearable here that you only wish he could encounter the escaped patient he so flippantly insists is no longer a threat to anyone.

Missing from these early drafts are Brady and Kelly Meeker, though early precursors are present in the form of Deputy Ben and Tammy, respectively. In the treatment, Ben is a young rookie cop who is instructed to join fellow deputies Tom and Jim in protecting the girls at Brackett's cabin. Ben remembers Linda from high school and offers his support. (This faint flirtation recalls Jimmy in *Halloween II*.) In subsequent drafts, we meet Ben much earlier as he encounters Linda and Amanda walking to school. Here, he hues more closely to Brady as a relationship with Linda is already established. While there are no love triangles, the relationship is in the early stages of fracturing with Linda's plans to attend college out of state. Ben's fate is the same in every draft. Little Amanda runs into his arms after escaping the Shape's attack in the cabin closet. The poor lad fails to notice the slasher approaching from behind and is stabbed in the back. Tammy, on the other hand, is Deputy Jim's girlfriend, and has a certain reputation for distracting her boyfriend during working hours. She and Jim are fatally impaled to a tree when caught canoodling on the outskirts of the cabin property.

This draft also includes an early version of *Halloween 4*'s Reverend Jackson P. Sayer, though he's named Zachariah here. Like Sayer, Zachariah enjoys picking up hitchhikers while drunkenly crooning gospel tunes in his pickup truck. In the McElroy script, Reverend Sayer gives Loomis a ride to Haddonfield, monologues about damnation, and ultimately lives. In the Bitterman script, however, Zachariah instead gives the Shape a ride to Haddonfield and soon after dies. Why would anyone give the Shape a lift on a dark night? The drunken Zachariah mistakes the white-hospital-gowned slasher for an ethereal being, possibly an angel. Somewhat humorously, the Shape smashes the car radio to stop the reverend's gospel singing before snapping his neck. ("What's the matter? Doncha' like gospel music? (Michael smashes the radio) Hey! They got a knob for that. Hell of a lot easier.")

Dwight Little's *Halloween 4* is notable for being one of the few *Halloween* movies not to feature the iconic house at 45 Lampkin Lane. The Myers house did, however, feature significantly into the Bitterman script. Per his original treatment, a yuppie couple has moved in and are currently renovating. By Bitterman's second draft, the couple had changed to a much less friendly group of drugged-out teenage skinheads. These new occupants wind up murdered in both versions. The scenes of Amanda exploring Judith and Michael's former bedrooms have an eerie quality to them. She sits at her aunt's makeup table and plays with her uncle's antique toys. (Unbeknownst to Amanda, she is already being stalked as she wanders the house.) In a sequence set later that night, Amanda and Linda find themselves locked inside the Myers house with the Shape. This brings to mind the scene in *Halloween 4* where Jamie, Rachel, and Brady are similarly trapped inside the Meeker house. Rather than escaping through the attic, Linda and Amanda find a way out through the cellar – but not before discovering the exhumed corpse of Judith Myers.

It's interesting to note that the bloodshed in this alternate *Halloween 4* owes to the mistakes of two characters – Dr. Loomis and Deputy Jim. In *Halloween* and *Halloween II*, Sheriff

Brackett blames Loomis for his patient's escape, which is a bit unfair as his recommendations had been thoroughly ignored by hospital administrators. Yet in Bitterman's *Halloween 4*, Loomis truly is responsible for everything that transpires. It's he who so carelessly mentions Laurie's orphaned daughter within earshot of his patient, which jolts the dormant slasher awake. With a new reason to kill, the Shape sets about doing exactly that. (Recall that in the actual *Halloween 4*, it's an ambulance attendant who mentions this near the comatose killer.) Had this conversation not taken place at Michael's bedside, he might've continued on in peaceful slumber. Similarly, it's Deputy Jim that mucks up the top-secret plan to keep Amanda safe by divulging it to his girlfriend over CB airwaves. Had the Shape not overheard *this* conversation, he would've had no way of knowing where the authorities had stashed his niece. While the ineptitude of authority figures is a familiar genre trope, it is a major theme within Bitterman's *Halloween 4* and absolutely crucial to the advancement of the plot.

## THE YOUNGEST MYERS

An obvious precursor to Jamie Lloyd, Amanda Hatch is perhaps the most fascinating character in Bitterman's *Halloween 4*. Unlike Jamie, Amanda isn't afraid of her uncle, even though she should be. Rather just the opposite – she desperately wants to form a relationship with him. Having lost both her parents, he's the only blood relative she has left, the last connection to all she's lost. In grieving the death of her parents, Amanda has built up a fantasy that her uncle is, in fact, not all that terrible. She's somewhat aware of his crimes but seems to doubt his true guilt. As she tells the new owners of the Myers house, "He's my friend. And he's coming to get me and take care of me." (If there was ever a candidate for intensive psychiatric therapy...)

Jamie and Amanda also differ in their attitudes on being adopted. In the eventual *Halloween 4*, Jamie adores the Carruthers family and badly wants to become a permanent member. For Amanda, it's again the opposite. While initially close to surrogate sister Linda, she sharply rejects her foster mother's affections. Linda later loses Amanda's trust by cooperating with Loomis and Brackett's efforts to evade the Shape. To Amanda, anyone trying to hurt her uncle or keep them apart must surely be bad. From her perspective, Loomis and Brackett are therefore the villains of the story rather than the Shape. At the police station, Amanda senses everyone plotting against her uncle and tries to warn him. She runs outside and yells into the darkness. ("Run away! They're trying to hurt you! Run away! Please, go! Please. Don't let them hurt you!")

In a sense, Bitterman's *Halloween 4* is the story of a lost little girl caught between the forces of good and evil. In one scene, that tug-of-war becomes quite literal. The Shape grabs onto his niece's hand as she tries to escape the Myers house. Linda grabs hold of Amanda's other hand and pulls with all her might. This image so perfectly encapsulates Bitterman's story. Amanda is being pulled in two separate directions. Yet the ultimate choice of who to side with will be hers to make. It isn't necessarily that Amanda is evil, just that she's spiritually lost. From her confused perspective, her uncle is chasing after her so that they finally can be a family. In reality, he's trying to kill her and everyone around her. It's a painful truth she's eventually forced to accept.

One stand-out role from the Bitterman draft is Amanda's foster sister Linda. As a precursor to Rachel Carruthers, Linda is a wonderfully endearing heroine. Smart, strong, and caring – she never forgets the pain and sadness her foster sister is experiencing. Linda also never abandons Amanda, even when Amanda rejects her for trying to protect her. Unlike Rachel, Linda herself is an adoptee. This gives the character a somewhat stronger resonance as she can – to a larger degree – better understand Amanda's familial yearning. This notion of two orphans banding together amid turmoil nicely mirrors the relationship Kyle and Andy Barclay shared in *Child's Play 2*. In a later draft of the Bitterman script, Linda accompanies a grieving Amanda to her parents' gravesite, believing this will help her process their deaths. (It doesn't.) For a *Halloween* script, it's a surprisingly somber moment. (Their tombstone reads, "Laurie and Kenneth Hatch: 1959 – 1987.") This scene hammers home just how incredibly recent this massive loss is, revealing that Amanda's emotional wounds are still so very new.

Amanda does eventually get a one-on-one encounter with her uncle in the third act. As first written, Amanda and the Shape only stare at each other from opposite sides of the cabin. They're soon interrupted by a rightly alarmed Linda, which causes the slasher to go all stabby. Seeing her uncle so violently attack her foster sister forces Amanda to accept the truth that the Shape truly is evil. This moment is a massively important one for the character. The child's fragile delusion, her only defense against a painful reality, is at once shattered to pieces. She now realizes that Linda, while not a blood relative, is more family to her than her estranged murderous uncle will ever be. Bitterman would modify and expand Amanda's encounter with the Shape in later drafts of the story. A subsequent version of this scene finds the child approaching her uncle with open arms. She hugs him in a warm embrace. The stunned Shape is initially frozen in place, though he eventually places a hand on the top of her head. We might mistake this for a consoling gesture, except that his other hand is raising a knife high in the air. Linda then rushes in and interrupts the scene as previously recapped.

Similar to Jamie in *Halloween 4*, Amanda spends the last half of the story dressed in a red/white clown costume. The difference is in the details, however. In the actual film, Jamie chooses this costume while shopping with Rachel at Vincent Drug Store. It's mere coincidence that it happens to mirror young Michael's costume from the opening of *Halloween*. In the Bitterman draft, however, Amanda is literally wearing the same clown outfit young Michael wore in 1963, which she finds in the basement of the Myers house. (Why this costume would be there and not in an evidence locker somewhere is puzzling.)

Unlike the final film, Amanda's trauma never manifests itself in the form of an attack on a relative. But that doesn't mean she's incapable of igniting terror. It should be noted just how sinister her nonchalant approach to danger can be. As written, the aforementioned chase scene through the Myers house offers one of the most chilling unfilmed spectacles in the franchise. Linda – having already brushed with the Shape – must retrieve her little sister from the house before leaving. Yet Amanda playfully darts from room to room as though a game. She repeatedly spots her uncle in the darkness and even waves to him! This leaves Linda chasing after the sound of Amanda's giggles, knowing full well the Shape is in their midst.

With the Shape closing in, Linda finds Amanda in the cellar creepily donning the infamous clown costume. Unable to escape, Linda proceeds downstairs. Amanda continues to evade her grasp, gleefully spooking her foster sister with a flashlight. Only upon finding Judith Myers' corpse does Amanda finally grasp the reality of the situation. This sequence is made all the more tense by Amanda's childlike carelessness. Her actions pose a great threat for Linda, whose need to protect the girl constantly puts the teenager in proximity of danger.

## RETURNING HEROES

As in the final film, the Bitterman draft brings back Dr. Loomis as a central figure in the story. He remains hyper-obsessed with keeping his patient locked up in the interest of public safety. While we know Loomis' fear and paranoia to be well justified, his superiors feel otherwise. (How quickly they've forgotten the carnage of his last escape ten years prior.) Administrators repeatedly spar with him, first over how to best care for the comatose slasher and later on how much of a threat he poses once escaped. The hospital's head physician expressly forbids Loomis from trying to recapture the Shape, instead demanding that he return to the Redding Center for questioning. Knowing the stakes, Loomis calmly walks away from his superior and *instead steals an unmarked police car.* He speeds so wildly toward Haddonfield that he wrecks the cruiser and catches a ride with a farmer. They stop for gas where Loomis then *steals the farmer's truck* and is nearly shot in the process. (Loomis really needs to chill with the Class A felonies. Recall that he took a state marshal hostage at gunpoint in *Halloween II.* C'mon, Sam.)

Bitterman reunites the slasher-hunting duo of Loomis and Brackett, who previously teamed in both *Halloween* and *Halloween II.* The screenwriter's initial treatment is downright bizarre for glossing over the Shape murdering Annie Brackett in the original film. The sheriff never once mentions or even references the devastating loss he suffered at the hands of Michael Myers. (Brackett casually to Linda: "Dr. Loomis thinks he knows the man who attacked you.") Bitterman corrects this oversight in his next draft, which results in a much different characterization for the sheriff. This Brackett is not at all enthused to see Loomis again and dreads what his return will mean for Haddonfield. ("How come every time you show up here people die?") Their revived partnership is a tense one rooted in a common fear. Brackett still blames Loomis for his patient's escape a decade ago and the deaths that resulted. He only resumes their working relationship due to the fact that no one else will take the situation seriously, not at all unlike that night ten years ago.

LOOMIS: *I'm sorry for your daughter.*

BRACKETT: *I'm sorry for this whole town. Take this. (hands Loomis a gun.) I don't want to see you get killed tonight. It's not that I like you any better, it's just you're my only ally. I called Kansas City for reinforcements and they said I was crazy. Keep feeling like I'm fighting my own private battle.*

LOOMIS: *It does feel like that, doesn't it? Feels almost like it was meant to be this way.*

That Loomis and Brackett reteam with one another doesn't automatically mean they're working toward the same goal. In fact, they're not. Loomis is set on recapturing his patient at any cost to protect the general public while Brackett is most concerned with keeping Amanda safe. It's Brackett who devises the plan to stash Linda and Amanda at his hunting cabin just outside town under police protection. Loomis disagrees with this approach, instead suggesting they keep Amanda in Haddonfield to use as bait for luring the Shape into a trap. (Recall that he does exactly this with Jamie in *Halloween 5*, which very nearly results in her death.) Unwilling to risk the child's safety, Brackett shoots down the idea. Three deputies escort the girls out of town while Loomis and Brackett stay behind to patrol Haddonfield's streets. Little do they know that the Shape is wise to their plan and already trailing the deputies to the cabin.

Each version of the Bitterman story sees Loomis and Brackett nearly killing someone in a white mask and overalls, echoing what happened to poor Ben Tramer in *Halloween II*. In the treatment, this is a town drunk who pisses himself with laughter once unmasked. In the first draft, it's a mischievous teenager. It's the second draft, however, that presents the most interesting version of this scene. While chasing after a prankster in a white mask, Loomis and Brackett notice a similarly dressed figure in the distance. Behind them stands yet another figure in a white mask. And another. Fearing they may lose track of the real Shape in a sea of imposters, Brackett fires his service revolver into the air three times. The masked figures all prove to be teenage punks who scurry off into the night. (This very closely resembles a similar moment between Loomis and Sheriff Meeker in the actual *Halloween 4*.)

For the briefest moment, Brackett truly believed he was chasing after his daughter's killer – that his long-sought revenge was finally within reach. But the shock of this is all too much. Clutching his chest, he collapses beside his police cruiser. Loomis accompanies the sheriff to

Haddonfield Memorial where his condition is found to be most grave. He leans in and whispers to his unconscious ally, "Brackett, can you hear me? I swear to you, this time I'm going to find a way to destroy him. Anything that bleeds can die. Just try to hold on. Please." With this, his heart rate flatlines and medical staff rush into the room. Clutching the revolver Brackett gave him, Loomis leaves in search of their common enemy.

## REVEREND SLASHER

The Shape of Bitterman's *Halloween 4* differs from his theatrical counterpart in several ways. While it was always a superhuman feat to bounce out of a ten-year coma with full-strength ("His muscles would be totally useless!"), this take on the character edges even further into superhuman territory. Loomis tells that his patient hasn't even eaten in the decade since the original *Halloween*, which defies the most basic rules of human biology. The doctor also suggests that his patient's dormant state is entirely voluntary, that he isn't technically in a true coma. This harkens back to the original film when Loomis tells Brackett that Michael is "inhumanly patient."

Visually, this Shape appears much different than in the eventual *Halloween 4*. He notably escapes the Redding Center without the white face-bandage-mask seen in the final film. The character does eventually procure his traditional white mask, though it's never revealed how or from where. Rather than stealing overalls from a garage mechanic, this Shape changes into Reverend Zachariah's outfit instead. (Imagine that for a moment – *Reverend Michael!* Now imagine the pushback from outraged religious groups.) Bitterman never clarifies if the Shape ditches these duds for more familiar killing attire, but he's still wearing them when he stalks Amanda at her school playground in the second act.

If you'll recall, the Etchison draft saw the Shape sporting a black t-shirt and jacket. Similarly, the Kenney/Medina script had him in all black leather. The freedom to which these writers felt in changing the Shape's attire is indicative of how the perceived rules of the franchise were not in place yet. Frankly, this leads us to question why exactly the Shape would don *only* a mechanic's outfit in later films. (Is there room for change or will we throw a fit? A Mr. Zombie wants to know). In another shocking turn, this draft later unmasks the Shape to find he possesses the innocent face of a young child. This strongly evokes the bizarro ending of *Friday the 13th Part VIII: Jason Takes Manhattan*, which wouldn't hit theaters for another year-and-a-half.

Curiously, the Bitterman script hints at a psychic connection between Michael and Amanda long before such an idea would appear in the eventual *Halloween 5*. After murdering the reverend, we get a brief glimpse at the world through the Shape's eyes. Per his POV, the night road is ablaze with giant flames, which are punctuated by the inescapable scream of past victims. (Who knew the Shape was so terribly haunted?) This is later revealed to be Amanda's precise nightmare as she describes it to Linda. ("Why won't they let him come home? He was driving and there were men chasing him, and there was fire everywhere.") Bitterman never references this connection again beyond this early scene, but it remains an interesting precursor to the next film in the series.

We should note that Bitterman's ending serves up a moment that feels... uncharacteristic for the slasher. Having incapacitated Linda, the Shape directs Amanda to brush her hair in a recreation of Judith's final moments. This suggests a warm nostalgia for the past that might've been more appropriate for the Rob Zombie films. That Linda is able to psych out the Shape by pretending to be Judith feels borrwed from the ending of *Friday the 13th Part II* wherein that film's heroine does something similar by pretending to be Jason's dead mother.

## ALTERNATE ENDING

Per the original treatment, Bitterman's *Halloween 4* ended with Loomis bursting into Brackett's cabin to find Linda/Amanda locked in battle with the Shape. Loomis immediately fires upon the slasher until he collapses. Police and EMS soon respond. Amanda later sneaks a look beneath her dead uncle's mask to find the sweet face of a six-year-old child. His eyes burst open and he begins to strangle her – except that this is a dream. Amanda wakes in her bed and looks outside – only to see the Shape standing off in the distance. The *Halloween* theme rises as he disappears behind a house. This original ending is confounding for blurring the line between dream and reality. Michael was pronounced dead at the cabin, so how has he returned? When did the dream begin? And when did it end? Is Amanda *still* dreaming?

The screenwriter would nix the dream angle entirely in his first full draft of the story. Here we see Loomis breaking into a Haddonfield pharmacy earlier in the night – *with police escort* – and stealing a large box of syringes. Flash forward to his arrival at the cabin. After firing upon the Shape, Loomis begins stabbing his patient with empty syringes, each one injecting air into his veins. The slasher flails and spasms in unbearable pain as Loomis yells "Die, die, die!!!" Loomis reaches for the final needle, but the dying Shape grabs his hand and forces Loomis to inject himself. Patient and doctor flail in pain on the cabin floor until both are still – and finally dead. Amanda still sneaks into the coroner's van and peaks beneath her uncle's mask to find a child's face, much like the old photo in her album. (No strangulation here.) She then exits the ambulance and hugs her foster sister. The script ends with a montage – the moon, the cabin, the Myers house, Amanda's photo album, the empty streets of Haddonfield – and the Shape's unmasked face in the ambulance. His eyes pop open. *Cut to black.*

It's difficult to imagine a *Halloween* series where Loomis didn't survive past *Halloween 4*, but that's very nearly what happened with the revised Bitterman script. The plus side, however, is that the character received a noble and heroic death here – unlike his offscreen demises in *Halloween 6* and *Halloween H20*. Bitterman wrote for Loomis to go down fighting, having finally bested his longtime nemesis. Would fans truly want it any other way?

## WHY IT WASN'T MADE

This is where things get a little murky. Bitterman's *Halloween 4* treatment was well-liked enough to warrant not one but two fully fleshed-out drafts. Despite having some leverage with the backing of Ramsey Thomas, the writer's tenure would be cut short with the hiring of director Dwight H. Little in January 1988 – the same month Bitterman submitted his material. Upon his hiring, Little brought on writer friend Alan B. McElroy whom he personally recommended for revision duties. In turn, McElroy would fashion his own take based on the Lipsius/Rattner/Ruffner script, thus creating the Jamie Lloyd and Rachel Carruthers we know today. The finalized billing would see McElroy given the sole "written by" credit while sharing the "story by" credit with the trio.

Lipsius, Ruffner, Rattner, and McElroy. For years, fans had only ever heard of these four screenwriters. While the memories of those involved in *Halloween 4* are awfully hazy given how much time has passed, it would surely *seem* that Bitterman was given the trio's draft to work from in crafting his own script. It would *also* seem that McElroy was given Bitterman's material in creating the final shooting script. So why wasn't Bitterman credited as an official screenwriter? Prior to the film's release, he actually sought an official arbitration in which a neutral third party would determine how the credits should read. Unfortunately for him, the Writer's Guild didn't feel that enough of his material had been utilized to justify awarding him credit. We should note that, as a playwright, Bitterman wasn't all that vested in this horror production. He was paid for his work and simply moved on. Yet looking back at the experience, he notes, "If I had known what the fuck I was doing at that time, I would probably be credited."

Up until this writing, Bitterman's involvement with *Halloween 4* has largely remained a well-kept secret. Furthermore, the story contributions of Lipsius, Rattner, and Ruffner have been similarly downplayed over the years despite being credited screenwriters. It doesn't help that none of these four scribes have ever appeared at a reunion screening or fan convention. Nor were they invited to participate on any of the numerous *Halloween 4* home video supplements. Given their decades-long radio silence on the film, it's incredibly difficult to trace who brought what to the narrative table on *Halloween 4* so many years later. What is certain is that McElroy wasn't alone in sculpting the story.

If Larry Rattner is to be believed, the trio's script featured Michael's niece violently attacking a relative – something that occurs in the final film but is absent from the Bitterman script. Why is this? Did Bitterman take major liberties in adapting the trio's script? If so, what other liberties did he take? Assuming McElroy had read Bitterman's script, did any of these liberties wind up in the final film? Questions to which there are no answers. Something else to consider is that when speaking with the *B-Sides and Badlands* website, director Dwight Little revealed that he had read a draft of the script prior to his hiring:

"My memory of [the script] is that there were so many teenagers being set up as possible victims that it lost the tone of being scary. It just didn't appeal to me. [...] When you get into that teen-romp stuff, I don't think it's scary."

- Dwight Little, B-Sides and Badlands

On the contrary, there is a notable *lack* of teenagers in Bitterman's script. Is Little simply misremembering? Or was there *yet another draft* under serious consideration during this time? To that end, actor Erik Preston – who portrayed young Michael in the film – recalls a script in which Laurie's daughter had *yet another name*. "I wish I still had my audition sides as I know her name wasn't Jamie in the audition," the actor told *B-Sides and Badlands*. "I have been told that there was a script where her name was Britti. However, I am 99 percent sure that my audition had Jamie's character name as Lindsay, at that time." As most fans are aware, Britti was Jamie's name in McElroy's original draft. Perhaps Lindsay hails from the Lipsius/Ruffner/Rattner script? One can't be sure.

If there's anything we can be sure of, it's that Alan McElroy is assuredly the writer credited with the final screenplay. Still, a cursory look at *Halloween 4*'s complicated history reveals that the basic gist of the story had been in place prior to his hiring. This would all culminate in a most winning effort, however. For all of Akkad's struggle in choosing the right script, the final film – *Halloween 4: The Return of Michael Myers* – has been noted as one of the stronger entries in the franchise. (Quite a feat, too, when you consider the lack of John Carpenter, Debra Hill, Dean Cundey, and Jamie Lee Curtis). Throughout the course of development, the character of Laurie Strode's daughter had transformed from a sweet, precocious six-year-old (Kenney/Medina) to a deeply troubled girl longing for a familial connection (Bitterman) to a less psychologically warped girl who later commits the most shocking act of violence (McElroy). It was this ending – in which young Jamie stabs her foster mother – that would shock audiences, reinvigorate the franchise, and lay the foundation for things to come.

# HALLOWEEN 5

## THE KILLER INSIDE ME

Evil is relative.

**Screenplay by**
**Shem Bitterman**

Six long years after *Halloween III: Season of the Witch*, the franchise was finally revived with the release of its fourth installment. The result – *Halloween 4: The Return of Michael Myers* – debuted atop the domestic box office and impressively held that position for two consecutive weeks. To put that success into perspective, one must realize this would be the last *Halloween* to achieve such a feat until the 2018 sequel. With earnings of over $17 million, Moustapha Akkad's efforts to relaunch the series had paid off tremendously. Reviews were never going to be glowing, but the film's climax defined its success, shocking audiences and sending fans into a frenzy wondering just what would happen next. If anything, *Halloween 4* proved the series could hold its own in a market where Freddy and Jason had ruled supreme. To capitalize on the series' newfound interest, another sequel was quickly rushed into development.

Per screenwriter Michael Jacobs, this rush was perhaps hastened by demand from exhibitors. Theater chains had pledged a flat guarantee to Akkad's Trancas International Films should the sequel be available for release by October 1989 – only a scant year after the fourth film. In turn, Akkad would be profiting simply by having the film ready to screen. (In the world of *Halloween*, it's interesting to ponder such a deal. We might remind readers that, unlike their studio brethren, *Halloween 4* and *5* were independent films financed and distributed by Akkad's own company.) To meet the intended release date, production would need to move swiftly. Calls were dispatched to cast members. Alongside Donald Pleasence, it was confirmed that those whose characters had survived the previous outing would return for this follow-up. This meant Danielle Harris, Ellie Cornell, and Beau Starr would be reprising their roles as Jamie Lloyd, Rachel Carruthers, and Ben Meeker, respectively.

With a cast in place, it was now time to settle on a story. Akkad's initial hope was that *Halloween 4*'s creative team – director Dwight H. Little and screenwriter Alan B. McElroy – would return for a fifth installment. After all, their contributions seemed integral to the fourth film's success. The two weren't entirely convinced, however, that their triumph in sequel-making could be replicated. Speaking with *Fear Magazine*, Little remarked, "I think my contribution to the *Halloween* series, frankly, was that I was able to resuscitate Michael in a believable way, bring him back and create a new family for him to terrorize. I think I'll just rest on those laurels." Satisfied with their time in Haddonfield, both Little and McElroy declined further involvement.

Also taking a sabbatical was Paul Freeman, who had previously handled producing duties on *Halloween 4*. (He would return for the sixth, seventh, and eighth films). In Freeman's place was Ramsey Thomas, Akkad's longtime associate who, despite being uncredited, also aided in developing the prior installment. It was through Thomas that *Halloween 5* found its first screenwriter. Unlike on *Halloween 4*, Trancas would not be holding an open call for story pitches. Instead, they would refer back to one of the screenwriting contenders for the fourth film. As producer, Thomas invited back playwright Shem Bitterman to take another stab at the material after his *Halloween 4* script failed to materialize on screen. An elusive figure in the world of *Halloween*, the writer would summarize his efforts in a 1990 interview with *The Los Angeles Times*.

# "I knocked off Halloween 4 in about a week. Then, they asked me to write Halloween 5. I did that one in just three days. It was like writing a comic book, but it paid the bills."

- Shem Bitterman, The Los Angeles Times

History tells us that the creatives behind *Halloween 4* were initially unprepared to manifest the implications of their shock ending. To recap, Darlene Carruthers is preparing a bath for Jamie when she is brutally stabbed by an unseen figure. To Loomis' horror, the assailant is none other than Jamie herself. Having seen this madness before, he raises his gun to shoot but is thwarted by Sheriff Meeker. We close on a heaving Jamie wielding a pair of bloody scissors, seemingly ready to strike again. In addressing this ending, Bitterman had quite a task on his hands. Would Jamie now be the villain of the story? A child version of the Shape, perhaps? Would the *Halloween* franchise break new ground by focusing on Michael Myers' next in line? By most accounts, no.

According to eventual scribe Michael Jacobs, a mandate was imposed by Moustapha Akkad, apparently at the behest of the theater chains pledging a guarantee. Per this, Jamie would return for a sequel – but she could *not* be inherently evil. Or, rather, she should not assume her uncle's role with the intention of replacing him. (It appears Bitterman only discovered this after composing his first draft.) From the project's earliest developments, it was decided the attack on Mrs. Carruthers would be non-fatal. It isn't clear why this imposition was placed upon the story so early on. It'd be easy to assume Akkad did not wish to confuse audiences by creating competition within the franchise. After acquiring the series' rights, he had but one *Halloween* behind his back, its promotion built sheerly on the return of Michael Myers.

As a hired gun, Bitterman would respect Akkad's wishes by reviving the seemingly dead Shape and maintaining Jamie as a sympathetic lead – all the while never shying away from the girl's more violent tendencies. He would formulate his ideas under the guidance of Ramsey Thomas, who is credited with providing the story on Bitterman's script. Dated January 4, 1989, Bitterman's first draft does not feature the subtitle *The Revenge of Michael Myers* – but rather *The Killer Inside Me*, a much more fitting moniker for this version. Bitterman and Thomas fashioned a script that would have deeply explored Jamie's psyche post-attack. The young girl would experience hallucinations of herself committing a series of attacks against her will. For Bitterman, this psychological approach could be attributed to his admiration for the works of Jim Thompson, most notably that author's novel *The Killer Inside Me*, from which this draft derives its name.

Thompson's 1952 novel revolves around a young deputy named Lou Ford. On the surface, Ford conforms to the conservative values of small-town Texas. This is a façade, however, as the character leads a double life. Since childhood, he has been a scheming sociopath, now faced with debilitating mental health and an increased tendency for violence. Although dating a schoolteacher, he engages in a sadomasochistic relationship with a prostitute. A blackmailing scheme and its coverup lead to several murders later culminating in Ford's own death. But for much of the novel, those around the deputy remain oblivious to his crimes. Now, what does that have to do with *Halloween 5*, you ask? The specifics of Thompson's novel were surely *not* incorporated in Bitterman's script. But the writer did take light inspiration, loosely retooling the author's themes. Through this, we can deduce that Ford's languishing mental state, his lack of control and the uncertainty of his guilt would serve as the engine in addressing Jamie's plight.

The writers crafted a clever scenario in which audiences would remain uncertain of Jamie's innocence throughout the film – despite the fact that the Shape would also return to wreak further havoc. Even those who love Jamie most would be unsure of her possible turn to the dark side. Unlike in the final film, she wouldn't be absolved from all blood. In fact, there would be even more of the red stuff on her hands this time around. That said, we now present our commentary on *Halloween 5: The Killer Inside Me*. For years, fans have pondered the long-rumored idea of Jamie emerging as a killer. Had this come to fruition, there's no telling how the series might've changed course. Because of this, Shem Bitterman's script has become the stuff of *Halloween* legend.

## THE STORY

"Halloween night. The sidewalks are wet with blood. Sirens pierce the silence." We rejoin young Jamie Lloyd just after she's stabbed her foster mother in a brutal scissor attack. First-responders arrive on the scene and begin treating Mrs. Carruthers' wounds. She turns to address Jamie but is unable to speak, instead caressing the child's tear-stained cheek before being wheeled to a waiting ambulance. Mr. Carruthers isn't quite as forgiving. ("She's not my daughter anymore! She's a monster! I'm sorry we ever took her in! I'll kill her myself!") He and daughter Rachel depart for the hospital while Jamie is left in the care of a rude Matron, who attempts to wrestle the scissors away from her. Terrified, the child hallucinates knives bursting from the woman's body. Loomis and Meeker hear Jamie's scream and rush upstairs to find her missing. They instead discover the Matron lying face down having been stabbed through the heart. Loomis says to Meeker, "Now, you see it. The girl must be destroyed."

Running off into the night, Jamie finds refuge within an old church several streets over. Inside, she encounters an evil version of herself, who attempts to give her back the bloody scissors. ("You have to kill. You know you want to kill.") Horrified by this, she again flees. Meanwhile, a police manhunt is underway to find her. Meeker gives strict orders that Jamie is to be brought in alive, which Loomis argues against. He even invokes the sheriff's recently murdered daughter in argument, which is still a raw wound. ("Enough!! You're a monster, Loomis! Look at yourself!") Brandishing his gun, the vigilante psychiatrist disappears into the night. Rachel returns home to find Lindsey Wallace scrubbing blood from the bathtub. Jamie quietly enters the room as Lindsey consoles her friend. The distraught child tearfully insists she didn't attack Darlene or the Matron. Unsure what to believe, Rachel hides Jamie from the police. Leaving her in Lindsey's care, Rachel goes out to verify whether Michael Myers is truly dead. If he somehow survived, this could help prove the child's innocence.

Returning to the mineshaft from *Halloween 4*'s ending, Rachel finds two police officers on guard. While inspecting the site, she accidentally tumbles into the darkened pit below. Calling for help, she notices the still-alive Shape from above. He drops a large rock in Rachel's direction which she narrowly dodges. Crashing through the mineshaft wall, she proceeds down a tunnel before reaching a clearing in the woods. Having murdered the nearby officers, the Shape then chases Rachel through the woods until they stumble upon a hungry wolf. The beast turns its attention toward the Shape, who quickly snaps its neck. Exiting the woods, Rachel reaches a farmhouse where a Halloween party is underway. She begs the host, a good-natured jock named Tom, to give her a ride back to town.

Back at the Carruthers' house, Jamie warns Lindsey, "He's coming." Moments later, the Shape forces his way inside, murdering Lindsey and abducting Jamie. Rachel and Tom arrive just in time to see the little girl being carried off. Tracking the slasher to his old home, they enter and locate Jamie in an upstairs bedroom. The trio is soon discovered, however, and a sprawling three-on-one fight breaks out between our heroes and the Shape. Loomis arrives on the scene just as the slasher vanishes. Vowing to keep Jamie safe at an abandoned lodge, Loomis sends Rachel and Tom to track down Sheriff Meeker. Now alone with the child, Loomis padlocks the cabin door before producing a cyanide-filled hypodermic, which he plans to kill her with.

**Loomis to Jamie:** *"What's the matter? I'm a doctor. These are my instruments. You don't even hear me, do you? You were once a little girl, who played in the sunshine out in the yard in front of her house. […] But you're not that little girl anymore. Are you? No. Apparently not. I've had only one regret in my life, but sadly, it's been a major regret. I allowed my instincts to go to seed, you understand, under the pap of institutional purity, funding, scholasticism, legality. There are some things beyond the pale of society. Your uncle, Michael Myers, is one of them. YOU are another. I should have destroyed Michael Myers when I had the chance. I'm not going to make that same mistake twice. Come and get your medicine. Cyanide. Still the most potent poison known to man. No more senseless deaths. One child and the cycle will be complete."*

Loomis goes to inject the child, but a psychic storm hits the cabin. Windows explode, furniture levitates, and the room catches fire. Unbeknownst to Loomis, he's now surrounded by multiple versions of an evil Jamie poised to kill. The actual Jamie screams out for the doppelgängers to leave him alone, which causes them to vanish. Frightened, she runs into her would-be killer's arms begging his forgiveness. Sensing her innocence, Loomis abandons his plan to kill her. He then implores Meeker to release Jamie into his care. ("Listen to me, Meeker! There is a battle going on inside that little girl, a battle between fear and reason. Michael is using fear to get inside her. And once he's in there, he does his evil through her!") Meeker is having none of that, however, calling Loomis' claims "the biggest load of horseshit." He arrests Jamie and has her held at a small highway substation. Meeker also dismisses Rachel and Tom's claim that Michael Myers survived the mineshaft fall. But unable to reach his officers at the mineshaft, he goes to investigate and finds their mutilated bodies. ("No little girl could've done this.")

The Shape tracks Jamie to the substation and murders the attending officers. Jamie, Rachel, and Tom barely escape back to the latter's farm where the Halloween party is winding down. The Shape follows after and quickly dispatches the remaining partygoers. Upon finding the massacred substation, Loomis and Meeker also head for Tom's farm on a hunch. In the interim, Jamie fears she is endangering Rachel's life and runs away. Becoming lost in a dark cornfield amid a rainstorm, Jamie once again hallucinates several visions of her evil self. These doppelgängers slash their knives at her in taunt. ("You're too weak to kill. Now, you have to die.") She soon encounters Loomis, who encourages her to face down her demons in order to beat them. Asserting herself, Jamie confronts her evil doppelgängers and they disappear. ("You've done it now. You've learned how you can defeat him.")

Hearing gunshots in the distance, they rush back to the farm where Tom and Rachel are battling the Shape. Wielding the cyanide-filled hypodermic intended for Jamie, Loomis goes to inject Michael – except the slasher has now projected multiple versions of himself. Surrounded by doppelgängers, Loomis is unsure who to inject and begins unmasking the many Michaels. The imposters vanish upon unmasking whereas the true Shape responds angrily by fatally snapping Loomis' neck. Re-donning his mask, the Shape pursues Jamie and Rachel throughout the farm. Tom comes to the rescue, now behind the wheel of a combine harvesting tractor. He aims the machinery toward their attacker, presumably shredding him. But not so! The Shape yanks Tom and Rachel off. With only Jamie onboard, the tractor crashes into a grain storage bin.

Rachel races towards an injured Jamie and the two girls embrace. In pain, Rachel pulls away to see a knife protruding from her own stomach. ("No. Not you, Jamie. No!") In that moment, the Shape appears from behind, hoisting Rachel into the air by the knife and tossing her aside. Unable to physically best the slasher, Jamie ultimately defeats him using her newfound powers. Standing her ground, she repeatedly shouts "I'm not afraid of you!" as though a chant. Psychically-projected knives begin exploding from the Shape's body and he soon collapses. Jamie unmasks her uncle to find the innocent face of a young boy. ("Now I know you. You can never hurt me again.")

First-responders arrive to discover the Shape has inexplicably fallen back into a coma – much like the one he experienced after *Halloween II*. Rachel is loaded into an ambulance and driven away. The story ends with Tom driving Jamie to the hospital as the sun rises on Haddonfield. The nightmare finally seems to be over – except that Tom suddenly crashes his truck into a tree. Inside the wrecked vehicle, we notice a screwdriver driven into his temple. We close on a lone Jamie walking back toward town.

## THE NIGHTMARE CONTINUES

If nothing else, Bitterman deserves credit for picking up the narrative baton from *Halloween 4* and running with it rather than immediately doubling back as the actual *Halloween 5* did. The last film's twist ending effectively pulled the rug out from under our feet. With this draft, Bitterman ensures we never manage to regain our footing. His story may continue on from the last film, but it carries over none of that entry's grounded sensibility. It is instead an unabashed descent into madness and a huge tonal departure from its predecessor. Bitterman's approach involves frequently and seamlessly alternating between supernatural and psychological terror. This keeps us guessing through to the end as we're never entirely sure how things are playing out. Is Jamie destined for evil? Or is it a case of possession? Or is she just crazy? The screenwriter simultaneously takes Loomis – the great franchise hero – and destabilizes him into an unpredictable madman. It's a new take every bit as bold as Rob Zombie's *Halloween II* – just without the hillbilly grime.

How different is the Bitterman script from the actual *Halloween 5*? Radically different, though there are some similarities. Both stories have Darlene Carruthers surviving Jamie's scissor-attack from the end of *Halloween 4*. Both also feature returns to the Myers house. We can arguably trace the origins of *Halloween 5*'s Tower Farm party to the Bitterman draft, which also sees the Shape murdering young lovers in a barn with a pitchfork. Additionally, both screenplays depict

Jamie as having a psychic connection with her uncle. Theatrically, Jamie convulses uncontrollably whenever the Shape murders someone. Per the Bitterman script, she merely senses when he grows near, usually announcing his approach with the creepy phrase, "He's coming."

The biggest difference between this and the actual *Halloween 5* – time jump aside – involves pacing. The 1989 film begins with everyone going about their normal October business. The Carruthers are off on vacation, Rachel's friends are party-planning, and the children's clinic staff are prepping a costume pageant. Nothing too out of the ordinary. In picking up from *Halloween 4*'s ending, *The Killer Inside Me* never enjoys any such measure of normalcy. We open on Jamie Lloyd having just attacked her foster mother. She then murders a social worker and escapes police custody – all within the first fifteen minutes. Bitterman's story is a chaotic and action-packed one that seldom pauses to catch its breath. Keeping the narrative gas pedal floored is, if nothing else, commendably ambitious.

Unlike most other films in the franchise, *The Killer Inside Me* begins with Halloween already halfway over and continues on from there. (Only two others have tried this approach – *Halloween II* and *Halloween Kills*.) This results in a compressed timeline set almost entirely at night. It also makes this draft feel more connected to *Halloween 4* than the actual *Halloween 5*. It further helps that Bitterman brings back seven characters rather than the actual sequel's four.

## CORRUPTED INNOCENCE

You could easily argue that *Halloween 5*'s screenwriters faced no greater challenge on the sequel than how to handle the next arc of Jamie Lloyd's storyline. How do you now depict a young girl who just savagely attacked her foster mother without provocation? The actual *Halloween 5* would contextualize the attack as an act of temporary madness, swiftly restoring her youthful innocence. As its title suggests, *The Killer Inside Me* takes a much different approach. Bitterman does an exemplary job of showing just how terrified Jamie now is, not only of the monster coming to get her but of the one hiding inside her. Will she kill again? We don't know – and neither does she. This adds a palpable tension to the story.

In spite of the killer within, Jamie remains an incredibly endearing character in this alternate *Halloween 5*. As an audience, we're still genuinely rooting for her to survive the night. Unfortunately, that's not a widely-shared sentiment in Haddonfield. Mr. Carruthers outright disowns her, even threatening to kill her. The officers guarding their home aren't terribly sympathetic either. ("I say, kill her. Kill her before she kills us. Murder runs in her family.") Nor is the Matron assigned to care for her. ("You little monster.") Even Loomis insists she should be put down, which isn't some offhand comment - he firmly believes this. ("The girl must be destroyed.") And yet Jamie continues on being a sweet child in a terrifying situation. She wishes harm on no one, not even those who hate her. Loomis literally tries to kill her, and she tearfully begs for his forgiveness.

Like the actual *Halloween 5*, this draft places Jamie in a number of perilous situations. In one scene, the Shape suspects she is hiding beneath her bed, which she is. Raising a fire poker high in the air, he repeatedly stabs through the mattress – forcing Jamie to contort underneath to avoid injury. The Shape soon tires of this game and flips the bed altogether, revealing his prey. This claustrophobic sequence feels like a precursor to the laundry chute attack in the eventual film.

In continuing her story, Bitterman imbues Jamie with an intriguing set of supernatural abilities. These include telekinesis, precognition, and psychic projection. She also suffers from hallucinations related to these powers, which massively complicate things. These abilities sometimes cause a troubling gap between Jamie's perceptions of the world and her actions in it. Consider the scene where the Matron attempts to retrieve the scissors from her. From the child's horrified perspective, knives are bursting from the woman's arms and face. The script notes the Matron is unaffected, continuing to taunt and pursue Jamie. (How's that for nightmarish imagery?) In reality, Jamie has fatally stabbed the woman through the heart with said scissors. This moment is emblematic of the spiritual battle playing out in Bitterman's story. Who will ultimately win control of Jamie's soul – her or the killer within? It's a fairly high-concept approach for a film series that began with the simplest of slasher stories.

Bitterman never fully spells out Jamie's powers, which may well have frustrated some viewers. The knife-bursting imagery and evil doppelgangers appear to be all within her mind. Yet in the story's finale, she psychically projects knives exploding from the Shape's body. While these soon vanish, the Shape still collapses to the ground without any puncture wounds. The cabin scene with Loomis is also interesting for how the evil Jamie doppelgängers tear apart the room. Loomis can clearly see this fiery destruction unfolding – just as he sees the actual Jamie reversing it after mentally banishing her tormentors. This abstract approach to her abilities feels a little bit Lynch-ian. Whether or not this supernatural twist would've worked within the *Halloween* universe is anyone's guess. (We should note that Jamie's powers in *The Killer Inside Me* appear to have been the inspiration for her telepathic bond with the Shape in the 1989 film.)

One of the story's biggest mysteries revolves around the stabbing of Jamie's foster sister Rachel. Initially, Rachel is aghast, believing Jamie to be the culprit. ("No. Not you, Jamie. No!") But in that moment, the Shape appears from behind, using the knife to lift Rachel in the air before tossing her aside. Was this attack strictly the work of the Shape? Or are Jamie's powers acting up again? Rachel later suggests she never truly believed Jamie to be at fault. But is this true? As written, the details aren't clear. It's possible Bitterman wanted to keep the audience on edge, with the attack serving as a red herring. Frankly, we couldn't possibly know what truly happened; not with the fantastical depiction of Jamie's powers. (The evidence against her is pretty damning.) It's possible the girl is linked to her uncle in such a way that might limit her true culpability. But even so, her actions are unpredictable and, at times, vicious enough to justify second guessing.

And what of this draft's ending? It would seem an effort on the screenwriter's part to match the shock-finish of *Halloween 4* – and it certainly does that. Just when we think Jamie has finally defeated the darkness within, we see the aftermath of her stabbing a screwdriver into Tom's temple. On one hand, such an ending would've adhered nicely to Moustapha Akkad's desire to always leave room for a sequel. On the other, this draft would have largely continued positioning Jamie as the series' future antagonist.

(As an aside, *Halloween 5*'s theatrical poster depicts Jamie Lloyd in her clown costume from *Halloween 4*. While it's arguably an iconic artwork, Jamie never actually wears the outfit in that film. She does, however, wear it for the entirety of the Bitterman script, which would've made *Halloween 5*'s poster a much better fit for this script rather than the eventual one.)

## HALFWAY THROUGH HELL

*Halloween 4* established final girl Rachel Carruthers as a fan-favorite character for her ability to protect Jamie while holding her own against the Shape. Unlike the eventual filmmakers who saw fit to give Rachel an early demise, Bitterman does great things with the role here. At its start, *The Killer Inside Me* finds Rachel exhausted, confused, and scared. She's already spent half the night trying to save Jamie from the Shape only to have Jamie violently attack her mother. Unlike Mr. Carruthers, Rachel doesn't automatically turn on the child following this shocking turn. She hasn't gone halfway through hell just to give up on Jamie now. Rather than rush to judgment, Rachel seeks to understand what has happened. She wants so badly to believe Jamie's tearful claims of innocence, but to do that she'll need some kind of proof. Knowing for certain that the Shape is truly dead would help enormously. If he really is dead, then Jamie has no one to blame but herself for the attack on Mrs. Carruthers. If he's not dead, then they all have a much more pressing problem to solve than the question of Jamie's innocence.

Rachel may be outwardly reserving judgment towards her foster sister, but she secretly fears the worst. Could Jamie be cut from the same cloth as her murderous uncle? Possibly so. This fear bubbles to the forefront in an early nightmare sequence. Returning home from the hospital, Rachel is encouraged by Lindsey to finally sleep off the terrors of the last few hours. As she dozes off, she envisions Jamie stabbing her in a recreation of her mother's attack. She startles awake to find Jamie crying at the foot of her bed. Rachel initially pauses before brushing off the nightmare to comfort the distraught child "like a real sister." In addition to being a pretty incredible surrogate sibling to Jamie, Rachel spends much of this alternate *Halloween 5* being a complete badass. Lindsey warns that returning to the mineshaft from *Halloween 4* will prove a suicide mission if the Shape isn't actually dead. Rachel confidently responds, "I've faced him before. I can face him again." She then charges that the risk is worth it, even if she can't physically best the slasher should she encounter him. ("I can show people he's alive. I can clear Jamie.") Based on her performance in *Halloween 4* alone, Rachel Carruthers ranked high in the pantheon of final girls. Had Bitterman's *Halloween 5* been made, she would've ranked even higher for going toe-to-toe with the Shape again and again. Eat your heart out, Laurie Strode.

Long before she hung out with Tina and Samantha, Rachel's best gal pal was Lindsey Wallace from the original *Halloween*. (Recall that Lindsey made a brief cameo in *Halloween 4* driving Rachel and Jamie to Vincent Drug Store.) Bitterman reintroduces the character early on and gives her a much larger role this time around. Rachel returns home to find Lindsey scrubbing blood from the bathtub as only a true friend would. She later begrudgingly agrees to watch Jamie as Rachel leaves to search the mineshaft. While it's clear Lindsey is a true-blue friend, she makes no secret of her distrust for Jamie following the attack. Curiously, she never mentions having survived her own encounter with the Shape a decade earlier. Her eventual death at the Carruthers home is a painful one. Running to Jamie's room, Lindsey uses her body to physically barricade the door to little effect. The Shape's hands explode through the door, as does a fire poker a moment later, which impales her stomach.

Our new leading man in this story is Tom, a good-natured jock who also serves as a romantic interest for Rachel. The fireworks are kept to a minimum, however. Recall that Rachel had just hours before discovered that her actual boyfriend had been cheating on her with Kelly Meeker. (Oh, and he had his skull crushed by the Shape.) A hysterical Rachel crashes Tom's Halloween party begging for a lift back to town. He drives her home and, being a good guy, stays by her side. This is where Tom deserves some credit. He could've split back to his farm party after their first skirmish with the Shape, but he sticks by Rachel and Jamie through several more encounters. This makes his eventual death at Jamie's hands all the more tragic. The poor guy was killed by the child he fought so hard to protect. Rest in peace, Tom. You were too good for this world. (As a point of reference, if you've seen *A Nightmare on Elm Street 4* or *5*, Tom is equivalent to the Dan Jordan character in those films.)

Rachel may survive this *Halloween 5* but at great cost. Like all involved, her world will have forever changed over the course of this long night. She's battered and bruised. Her ex-boyfriend, crush, and friends are all dead. Her father is seething with grief. And by script's end, it is she – like her mother – who is wheeled off via ambulance, having suffered her own vicious stabbing. As mentioned, it isn't entirely clear just who stabbed her. The Shape is a likely candidate. But now so is Jamie. The knife-happy tyke does appear vindicated in the final moment the girls share together. Before the ambulance drives away, the little girl asks, "Rachel? Did you really think it was me who hurt you?" Although beaten down, the teenager manages a smile. "No. Never. I promise." We know her claim isn't entirely factual as Rachel clearly expressed doubt of Jamie in that one brutal moment. But if anything, this response is to suggest that even after all this turmoil, Rachel still hasn't given up on Jamie just yet. She's all the more endearing for it, too, even if her last shred of faith is potentially misguided.

## BECOMING THE MONSTER

Bitterman's *Halloween 5* begins where *Halloween 4* ended with history having just repeated itself. Another adolescent member of the Myers clan has attacked someone on Halloween night while dressed as a clown. Dr. Loomis has seen this before and knows all too well where things may be headed. But he's not about to stand idly by as more people die. He concludes that Jamie must be destroyed and that he may be the only person willing and able to make that happen. This isn't some impulsive decision. Loomis has clearly thought this through and deemed it the right course of action. It was one thing in the actual *Halloween 5* to see him use Jamie as bait to lure the Shape into a trap, but this is an altogether new level of depravity. In wanting to murder a child, Loomis has now become a villain. It's strange to think about, but both he and the Shape share a common goal in the Bitterman script in that they both want to kill Jamie. (That is one *hell* of a plot point.)

To enact his ghastly plan, Loomis knows he must be alone with the child. He sends Rachel and Tom away to find Sheriff Meeker, padlocking the door behind them as they exit. Jamie is now trapped. Loomis delivers a chilling monologue before producing a cyanide-filled hypodermic. ("Come and get your medicine.") What happens next is most unexpected. Jamie's doppelgängers begin destroying the room before making an attempt on Loomis' life. Jamie intervenes to save him, banishes the duplicates, and undoes their destruction. It's here Loomis recognizes the battle within her. Michael never exhibited any such remorse or empathy in all their years together. That Jamie is now doing so must mean she's not like him, at least not entirely. He reasons that Jamie is not beyond salvation and therefore deserves to live. With this, we have the old Loomis back in the fight. He goes from trying to kill Jamie to trying to save her. Unfortunately, he's unable to convince Meeker of any of this, especially not her supernatural powers.

*The Killer Inside Me* bids farewell to Loomis by giving him a hero's death – just as the actual *Halloween 5* does. The difference is that the 1989 film left enough ambiguity in his demise for him to be easily resurrected in *Halloween 6* if need be. (And, of course, he was.) Bitterman opted for a much more permanent send-off, one that would've made any such comeback difficult. During the barn-set finale, the avenging doctor unmasks his longtime nemesis, who fatally snaps his neck a moment later. In the end, Loomis might not have been able to conquer his own demons, but he made an earnest effort at helping Jamie conquer hers. (You have to wonder if Bitterman didn't have it out for the character. A draft of his unused *Halloween 4* script also saw Loomis trying to inject the Shape with something and being killed for his efforts.)

## THE TOWER FARM PARTY

Fans have long suspected that few, if any, of Bitterman's original ideas made it into the final film. Upon closer inspection, we can see that some actually did. Indeed, it seems quite a bit of this sequel owes to Bitterman's efforts. Some of *Halloween 5*'s most memorable set pieces (the Myers house, the police station) can be traced back to these early drafts, though none feature so prominently as the farmhouse party. In the final film, the Tower Farm is a rural property frequented by Tina Williams and her friends. In the Bitterman draft, it belongs to Tom's family and is introduced much earlier in the story. After battling the Shape, Rachel escapes through the woods and emerges at the farmhouse. It's here that we are introduced to the cowboy-clad Tom and his devil-costumed date Carrie. (Note: The couple's attire is identical to the film's Spitz and Samantha, thus making these two the earliest versions of those characters.)

We later return to the farmhouse as the party is winding down. One couple retreat to an adjacent barn to better engage one another but instead encounter the Shape. He skewers both with a pitchfork, impaling the girl high on a barn wall. (Spitz and Samantha suffered similar deaths in the final film.) Another lingering couple encounter the Shape while making out in a nearby truck, which appears to be an early version of the final film's car chase sequence. In this version, the Shape murders the driver as his date frantically tries to exit the cab, accidentally setting the truck in motion in the process. The corpse-driven vehicle circles around and runs over the girl multiple times as she tries to evade the attacking Shape, which is darkly hilarious.

The farm-set finale of this *Halloween 5* feels ripped from the third and fifth *Friday the 13th* movies, both of which feature extensive chases through a barn. Bitterman's finale utilizes several dangerous pieces of farm equipment including a claustrophobic grain storage bin and a rampaging combine tractor. While the Tower Farm sequence ranks as one of the final film's better moments, Bitterman's version would've been far more chaotic with so much action occurring at this location. You half expect Rachel to turn to Jamie at any moment as if to say, 'Boy… remember the rooftop? That was a cakewalk compared to this!'

## A MORE POWERFUL SHAPE

It's curious that both this unused script and the actual *Halloween 5* pick up from *Halloween 4's* ending – but from different perspectives. The official film follows the Shape as he escapes the mineshaft and shacks up with a hermit. *The Killer Inside Me* instead focuses on Jamie and the Carruthers, withholding the slasher's first appearance until page thirty-two. If we apply the old rule of one-script-page equaling one-minute of film, *The Killer Inside Me* wouldn't have featured the Shape until a half-hour into its story! (For the record, that's considerably longer than any other film in the franchise. Even *Halloween III* gave the Shape a cameo before the half-hour mark!) Not that Bitterman underutilizes the slasher – he definitely does not. The Shape features prominently into a number of sequences including attacks at the mineshaft, the Carruthers home, the Myers house, the highway substation, Tom's farmhouse, and the adjoining barn. Gore fans would've surely delighted in a kill count totaling in the double-digits. At the substation, in particular, the Shape administers some serious brutality, decapitating an officer with the slam of a door while crushing the skull of another.

Looking back on *Halloween 4's* finale, you have to wonder how anyone expected the Shape to return for *Halloween 5*. The guy was knocked around by a truck, blasted by a firing squad, and tossed down a mineshaft. As in the eventual film, Bitterman's script has no explanation for the slasher's death-defying return. Like the Energizer bunny, he simply keeps on going. Unfortunately, the suspension of disbelief required for this means that *Halloween 5* cannot possibly follow in the footsteps of *Halloween 4's* more grounded approach. Bitterman seems to realize this and instead leans into the absurdity, veering his story further into the realm of the supernatural. What does this mean for the character? As with Jamie, it means special psychic powers we previously knew nothing about. This results in radically different characterizations for both.

The Shape may have psychic powers in this story, but he doesn't draw on them until late in the third act. It's here we see him project several disturbing hallucinations into his former doctor's mind. Loomis goes to inject the slasher with cyanide – but discovers he's actually injected a second version of himself! Dying Loomis grabs onto the *real* Loomis, who is absolutely horrified. Brushing off his doppelgänger, he fires several shots into the slasher, which have no effect. Suddenly, Loomis is surrounded by multiple projections of the Shape. ("This is not real. This is not happening. This isn't possible. I'm dreaming you. Only one of you is real. Only one! ONLY ONE!") He begins hurriedly unmasking the fakes. These all disappear until there is only one left. (Script: "Loomis reaches for the mask. It comes free. We do not see the face, but Loomis sees the face. He knows the face.") Loomis is as stunned by seeing Michael's face as Michael is by being unmasked. The pause doesn't last, however, and the Shape snaps his neck.

We see the slasher invoke his powers again in the next scene. Looking for a place to hide, Rachel and Jamie partially submerge their bodies inside a grain storage bin. The darkness frightens Jamie. Rachel tries to calm her by lighting a match, which illuminates the bin to reveal five Shapes surrounding them. Rachel promises they're not real, just her imagination. Michael uses these projections to cause fear. These play out similar to Jamie's nightmare in *Halloween 4* – only if it that weren't a dream. (Perhaps that scene was the basis for Bitterman's tale here?)

Was it a risk on the screenwriter's part to give the Shape supernatural abilities? Yes, very much so. Does it rewrite the rules of the franchise? Absolutely. Would the fanbase have accepted these newfound powers? It's hard to say. Let's be honest with ourselves – are psychic powers any more of a trespass than having the Shape unmask and cry as in the actual *Halloween 5*? It's so difficult to pinpoint where exactly the line is, especially when it changes over time. What we accepted in 1989 is completely different than what we now accept. The visual of Loomis completely encircled by multiple Shapes is a surreal one. It may not make a ton of sense within the *Halloween* universe as we know it, but it is creepy and kind of awesome.

As with his psychic abilities, the Shape now has the power to sustain an unusually high number of grotesque injuries, even by his standards. Never before has the slasher brushed off so many brutal attacks that would've previously rendered him down for the count. Engaged in battle with Tom and Rachel, he is shot several times. He remains unaffected. But then his heart is pierced with a hunting knife. *Nothing*. He simply extracts the knife and plunges it deep into Tom's chest. At this moment, Loomis and Jamie arrive on the scene. Jamie psychically projects two blades emerging from the Shape's eyes. *Still* nothing.

Later, the girls are rescued by a somehow-still-living Tom on a combine harvesting tractor. He plows into the Shape, who is chewed by the teeth of the machinery. Surely, that would be the end of him? As you might've guessed, not quite. He yanks Tom and Rachel off leaving Jamie on an unmanned tractor to crash into the grain storage bin. As usual, there is no rhyme or reason for the Shape's survival. Only this time, things are taken up quite a few notches. And for the most part, that feels okay. With the supernatural clearly playing a part in these proceedings (the ambiguity of it aside), his survival seems but one odd component of an already psychedelic tale.

Like the eventual film, the Bitterman script dares to separate the Shape from his mask. This happens twice in the story, though we only see his face the second time. Just as in Bitterman's unused *Halloween 4* draft, it's Jamie who unmasks the defeated slasher in the final moments where he again has the visage of an innocent young boy. (As with the 1989 film, we must ask – where are the burns from *Halloween II*?) It's also interesting that *The Killer Inside Me* ends with the Shape falling back into a coma as Halloween night draws to a close. ("It's the strangest thing I've ever seen. It's almost as if he had been that way for years.") Is the screenwriter suggesting some kind of seasonal jurisdiction with the character? That he can spring back to life each Halloween but falls dormant as the sun rises on November 1st? If so, that would be a unique take.

## THE SECOND DRAFT

Bitterman later wrote a second draft of *The Killer Inside Me*, which was dated February 8, 1989. This second version contained numerous changes including a new beginning and ending. It's also the draft that fellow scribes Dominique Othenin-Girard and Michael Jacobs cherry-picked from in penning their own script, which was originally titled *Halloween 5… And Things That Go Bump In the Night*. This unused mouthful-of-a-title originated from a poem Jamie reads aloud in the Bitterman draft. "From ghoulies and ghosties and long-legged beasties and things that go bump in the night, the good Lord deliver us."

Whereas the initial draft withheld the Shape's first appearance for thirty-two pages, this updated version gets to him much sooner. Returning to the mineshaft, we find police tossing explosives into the cavernous pit. These fail to kill the Shape as he's already crawled to safety. The wounded slasher then stumbles upon a junkyard shack in the woods. (Sound familiar?) Inside he finds Father Sam, a blind man in his late seventies, and Dora, his teenage daughter. A raving religious fanatic, Father Sam brings the unconscious killer into their home. ("Poor pilgrim of the night. Let us heal you. This man needs our help! As Christians, we must oblige!") Bitterman writes that the walls of their shack are lined with religious artifacts – along with pots of urine and feces. Father Sam performs a strange prayer over his guest, which seems to magically heal the slasher. Restored, the Shape murders his hosts and drives their weathered pick-up truck back to Haddonfield.

This original opening's wounded-monster-meets-blind-man angle feels vaguely reminiscent of *Bride of Frankenstein*. Othenin-Girard and Jacobs would retain the basic structure of this opening in their screenplay, swapping out Father Sam for a voodoo priest named Dr. Death. Moustapha Akkad would later intervene to change this sequence further. He would have producer Ramsey Thomas shoot a new version that traded the bizarre Dr. Death for a more sympathetic parrot-owning hermit.

Bitterman's second draft introduces the Tom character much earlier and in different fashion. Here, Jamie bumps into him and his friends on the street after having murdered the Matron. Tom's friend Rick is dressed as the Shape for Halloween, which causes Jamie to mistake him for the real deal. (*Halloween 5*'s filmmakers would recycle this false scare in the actual film using the Spitz character.) Per the first draft, Rachel encounters the Shape at the mineshaft and escapes up the road to Tom's farmhouse for a ride back to town. Yet Rachel never travels to the mineshaft in this version, instead staying home with Jamie and Lindsey. The actual Shape barges in and attacks the trio whose screams catch the attention of a conveniently nearby Tom. This draws him into the story much earlier where he remains until the end. As an aside, Lindsey also meets her end differently in this version. Here, she is subdued by the Shape after taking a shower in a scene that mirrors Tim Strode's demise in *Halloween 6*.

Since Rachel never returns to the mineshaft in this version, she never discovers the two dead cops who are now presumably never murdered by the Shape. Even so, Bitterman still sends Loomis and Meeker back to the mineshaft in the second act to search for Michael's body. (For some reason, Meeker refuses to believe Rachel, Tom, and Jamie that the Shape made it out alive.)

Instead of finding the murdered cops, Loomis and Meeker stumble upon the junkyard shack from the new opening. Inside they make a horrifying discovery – the bodies of Father Sam and Dora arranged in a macabre Nativity-like scene. Leaving the shack, they encounter Reverend Jack Sayer from *Halloween 4* in what feels like the most random cameo of all time. ("This is HIS doing! The demon! The dark one! The bringer of Armageddon! I've been hunting him. But he cannot be killed! For he is within us all! Run! Run!! But you cannot run away from yourselves!") Unexpected though it may be, it's not that hard to imagine Father Sam and Reverend Sayer bonding over gospel and homemade hooch.

The third act then unfolds as usual until its final moments, which are quite different. Jamie now defeats her uncle without the supernatural knives bursting from his body. She instead screams "I'm not afraid of you" over and over, which drains him of his power. Michael slows in his advance, weakening with each refrain, until he finally collapses at Jamie's feet. Meeker and a swarm of police arrive as the sun begins to rise. Jamie again unmasks her uncle to find a youthful countenance underneath. Here, she repeats a line that actually appeared in the final film: "You're just like me." Police surround and shackle the Shape, defeated but not dead. Just then – Reverend Sayer breaks through the police line for a final cameo: "Don't be fooled. The Devil wears many disguises. He can even pretend to be a man. That's right, a man. Like you and I. Armageddon is coming, I tell you. Armageddon!"

The second draft closes with Rachel holding Jamie in the back of the ambulance as it drives away. Jamie smiles and we cross-fade to the Shape sitting unmasked in a jail cell. "He opens his eyes. Fade to black." Loomis still dies in this draft, though Tom fortunately lives. From this, we can deduce that Akkad's mandate had taken affect, wishing that less focus be placed on setting up Jamie as future antagonist.

## WHY IT WASN'T MADE

As fate would have it, Shem Bitterman's association with *Halloween 5* would come to an end much in the same way as it did on *Halloween 4* – with the hiring of a director. Initially, it appeared *The Killer Inside Me* would reach the screen as there simply wasn't enough time to commission multiple writers. With the backing of Ramsey Thomas, Bitterman's script had satisfied Moustapha Akkad, who had already begun meeting with potential directors including genre mainstay Jeff Burr. At this time, Burr was best known for having helmed the horror anthology *The Offspring* starring Vincent Price and Susan Tyrrell. As of his meeting, he had also completed filming on a sequel to 1987's *The Stepfather*. (His most prominent genre credit – *Leatherface: Texas Chainsaw Massacre III* – wouldn't lens until just after *Halloween 5* already wrapped filming.)

Burr had been given Bitterman's script to work from, offering notes on the material. From his perspective, the meetings went rather well. Not only was he up for the directing duties, but his brother William and friend Darin Scott were being considered as producers. In fact, Burr was so close to securing the gig that he was instructed by Ramsey Thomas to "chill the champagne but don't pop the cork yet." So, how did this all fall apart? It began to unravel with *Halloween* co-creator Debra Hill. It's something of a little-known fact that, unlike John Carpenter, Debra Hill had initially maintained a relationship with Moustapha Akkad even in the aftermath of the series' rights debacle. When speaking with *HorrorFan*, the producer noted that Hill had offered her blessing to Alan B. McElroy's *Halloween 4*, purportedly claiming, "That's the best script out of the hundreds that I've read." Her guidance would also extend to this fifth film.

While attending the 1989 Sundance Film Festival, Hill had met a filmmaker by the name of Dominique Othenin-Girard. As co-director, he had previously been nominated for the prestigious Golden Bear award at the Berlin Film Festival for the 1985 thriller *After Darkness* starring John Hurt. Impressed with his work, Hill phoned Akkad and suggested that he meet with the French-Swiss filmmaker. (Which is all the more interesting when you consider the flack the fifth film receives.) A meeting was arranged and, by Othenin-Girard's account, it was initially unsuccessful. He immediately took issue with Bitterman's script. In a now infamous anecdote, the director shocked Akkad by literally trashing the screenplay in the producer's office. He would later relay his thoughts in an interview with *Fangoria*.

"[Bitterman's script] had too much of an action-oriented, supernatural feel to it. The climax of the movie basically came thirty pages into the script, and there were too many paper-thin characters."

- Dominique Othenin-Girard, Fangoria

Dismissing Bitterman's script, the filmmaker elected to compose a new story alongside a writing partner. This was an audacious request given the project's looming deadline. In his own words, Othenin-Girard desired to "follow the Hitchcock rules of suspense, not mixing the genres like the script they had given me. [The script] had a body count like *Friday the 13th,* and many deaths in nightmarish sequences like the other competing franchise [*A Nightmare on Elm Street*]." (In order to gain knowledge of the horror market, the director admitted to watching all entries of both series prior to taking the meeting.) Initially, Othenin-Girard faced great resistance from Akkad, who took issue with the director's bold demands.

The producer eventually relented, hiring Othenin-Girard under the agreed-upon terms that a new story would be devised. He and his writing partner would be given but six short weeks to compose a new script before cameras were slated to roll. With this development, Shem Bitterman's script – and Jeff Burr's involvement – were suddenly off-the-table. Despite his tenure being cut short, Bitterman remained on the final film's credits. This originally seemed to be a Writer's Guild matter as it had been assumed nothing of his material reached the screen, but we now know this to be untrue. As many already know, the final screenplay for *Halloween 5* was written by Othenin-Girard and Michael Jacobs with certain elements gleaned from Bitterman's earliest drafts. What many don't know, however, is that Othenin-Girard didn't originally pitch his vision for *Halloween 5* alongside Jacobs. Rather, he first brought along another writing partner by the name of Robert Harders. Together, the two men envisioned a *very* different *Halloween 5.*

A scribe of stage and screen, Harders had but one feature credit as one of seven writers on Brian De Palma's 1979 comedy *Home Movies.* Behind the scenes, he was a confidant and script doctor to celebrated filmmaker Robert Altman. Harders was neither a fan of the *Halloween* franchise nor the genre itself, so why bother to pitch *Halloween 5*? Like Othenin-Girard, he relished the opportunity to do something original and unexpected with the slasher sequel. Harders envisioned a story that immediately veered from the direction set by *Halloween 4*'s ending.

"Once I got their attention, I asked Mr. Akkad if I could let in a friend of mine, a writer I had worked with," Othenin-Girard told *HalloweenMovies.com.* "Mr. Akkad was irritated by my boldness, but allowed me to go on. Robert Harders entered and I started to work with Robert in front of them, explaining the story I was going for. He had not read their script and had not seen *Halloween 4.* After twenty minutes, Mr. Akkad interrupted and said that to be a producer is to be able to take important decisions alone. He let us go. "

Harders' pitch told that Michael Myers had truly died after being shot numerous times by police and falling into the abandoned mineshaft. The area would soon experience a violent thunderstorm, which would result in Michael's corpse being struck by lightning. The ensuing jolt would prove strong enough to resurrect the dormant slasher. Upon returing to life, the Shape would have no memory of his former self nor any violent urges whatsoever. He would now instead be a more tragic monster, responding in kind to both friendliness and hostility.

Moustapha Akkad immediately rejected this approach and it's plain to see why. He had just managed, after years of effort, to reinstate the Shape as *Halloween*'s boogeyman. To immediately strip Michael of his boogeyman status would undermine Akkad's efforts to bring him back in the first place. Furthermore, this *Frankenstein*-esque resurrection was much too similar to how filmmakers resurrected Jason Voorhees in 1986's *Friday the 13th Part VI: Jason Lives*. Akkad did offer Harders a chance to re-write the existing Bitterman draft, but he declined. Othenin-Girard would return several days later to pitch a different *Halloween 5* with Michael Jacobs.

In revising Bitterman's script, Othenin-Girard would firmly establish Jamie as an innocent, rationalizing Mrs. Carruthers' attack as an act of momentary madness. To underline Jamie's guilt, she would lose the ability to speak. Furthermore, the film would now take place a year later rather than serve as a direct-continuation of *Halloween 4*'s night of horror. Jamie would be subsequently confined to a clinic under the watchful eye of a distrusting Dr. Loomis.

The decision to eliminate Jamie's culpability in the crime was contested by Donald Pleasence who, in speaking with *Fangoria*, stated, "I think they should have gone with the fact that the little girl is now totally evil. I was disappointed that we now discover that she did not kill her mother." Likewise, actress Danielle Harris was excited at the prospect of becoming a killer, or Michael Myers' "sidekick" as she's referred to it, though her perspective would shift in later years.

In any of its iterations, *Halloween 5* would mark a turning point in the series. Concepts would be introduced that would stray further from John Carpenter's original. With the knowledge the fifth film initiated what some fans might consider a momentary decline, it is difficult to say whether audiences would've been truly receptive to Bitterman's take. Both of his drafts excel in areas the film may falter while also featuring elements that would've proved even more polarizing. What stands is this – the fact *Halloween 5* could never properly capitalize on the prior film's great shocker of an ending is often bemoaned as one of the series' greatest missteps.

**How did you meet Dominique Othenin-Girard?**

Dominique and I met through our mutual agent. Our meeting was set up because he was a director looking for a script and I was a writer with a script. I liked Dominique right away and we have remained friends. Dominique liked my script – a thriller called *Burnt Hills* – and with each of us attached, it was set up in a development deal with Raffaella de Laurentiis' production company, but was never produced. I wouldn't want to speak for Dominique as to why he brought me to the *Halloween 5* pitch meeting exactly. I think it's fair to say we recognized that we worked well together and responded to each other's ideas.

**Were you a fan of the *Halloween* series or of the genre?**

I thought the original *Halloween* movie was impressive story telling and on a par with *Night of the Living Dead* and some of the films I remembered from growing up like *Invaders from Mars* and *Invasion of the Body Snatchers*. What I'm trying to say is that I liked good stories, regardless of the genre. The stories mentioned above are, in my opinion, actually quite sophisticated in that they operated on multiple levels – employing horror and suspense to entertain, but entertaining in order to draw the audience into participating in a deeper, perhaps even unspoken, social, political, or moral conflict – and that it was this sophistication that made the films great. Once the franchise potential was realized for movies like *Halloween* then it became a matter of turning out sausage. In other words, a formulaic and gratuitous chase. Get the girl or group of teenagers isolated and bring on the monsters kind of stuff, which was not at all anything I ever wanted to be involved with. I guess what I'm trying to say is that if it hadn't been for my relationship with Dominique, I don't think I would have even taken the meeting.

**You presumably met with Moustapha Akkad and Ramsey Thomas. How did this initial meeting go for you and Dominique?**

If Moustapha Akkad was the man in the meeting, I remember him as being friendly. He listened to the whole pitch and I remember feeling that I had him for a moment or two during the pitch, but I'll readily admit that what I thought might be a spark of interest could merely have been a businessman trying to understand what the hell I was talking about and how I had gotten in there in the first place. In other words, I had absolutely no illusions that the powers that be would jeopardize the franchise with so drastic a departure from what was expected by audiences around the world. There was a Ramsey connected with another project Dominique got me involved with but I don't know if it was the same Ramsey you mention. To my horror, again, this second project was a horror story called *The Dollhouse*. We got a script written but it was never made. That one was a terrible experience because of the producers involved.

**Do you recall why you were not involved with the film past the meeting? Did you ever discuss the project with Dominique while the film was in-production?**

Turns out they offered me the job of re-writing the original script, but I turned it down, so my involvement with the project ended with that meeting. I was too excited about the ideas I had come up with, and knew myself well enough to know I would hate doing what I felt they wanted. Fortunately, Michael Jacobs was available and he worked on the script. Michael's a good writer and a nice guy. I remember Dominique telling me Michael saved the day because he came up with the house having a laundry chute, which I assume facilitated the chase. I never actually saw the film.

**What was your role during this meeting? What input did you have in the changes that Dominique was suggesting?**

I had a dilemma. I knew what kind of story they wanted, of course, and I knew that kind of story wouldn't interest me. So, I put together a pitch that, as I remember it, started precisely where *Halloween 4* had ended, which, as I am remembering it right now, had the Michael Myers character at the bottom of a collapsed mine shaft or some similar place and dead. And I imagined him there and remembered the classic scene in the original *Frankenstein* movie in which the creature is brought to life in Dr. Frankenstein's lab surrounded by all that equipment. I proposed opening the story with a tremendous storm of thunder and fierce lighting. The shattered timbers, concrete, wires, and rebar entangling and supporting the lifeless body of Michael Myers would channel the storm's life-giving electrical current from the heavens into the body of our creature, bringing him back to life.

From there the *Frankenstein* story took over my imagination. You've probably seen *Frankenstein* the movie, but have you ever read the book? If not, you should. There's a different kind of horror at work in the novel and I became very excited about trying to tell a story that evoked both *Frankenstein* the movie and *Frankenstein* the book. The details of the pitch are long forgotten, except for one key element, which was that the revived Michael Myers would no longer be the embodiment of pure evil. Instead, the harm caused by him – and I should say the significant harm that he would cause throughout the movie – was to be incidental. Unintentional. In response to attacks upon him. The result of his own need to survive in a world that was out to destroy him because it believed him to be the embodiment of evil he once was. In this scenario, Michael Myers was to have only one friend. The person who knows him better than anyone else, who knows to his horror the evil of Michael Myers past. I mean Loomis, the Donald Pleasence character. Think of the scene in *Frankenstein* when the creature meets the child by the pool of water. That's the innocence I would have loved to try to have Loomis discover in Michael – can you imagine Loomis' disbelief at even the possibility – thereby creating a terrible conflict for Loomis: how to save Michael Myers from the mob to see if he can get through to him, communicate to him. Loomis is a scientist, don't forget. And that he is capable – and often the only one capable – of understanding of the depth of the evil that has existed in Michael – testifies, I believe, to the depth of Loomis' own understanding of humanity. The movie then becomes about Loomis trying to save Michael Myers from the mob as he gets closer and closer to reaching Michael as a human being. The movie would have to end with Michael's demise – something closer to the way it was handled in the novel, I thought.

**The film's original opening featured Michael escaping from the mine shaft and stumbling upon a young voodoo priest's shack in the woods. During a rainstorm, this odd figure performs an incantation, which revives the Shape. The scene was later reshot with an older hermit in place of the priest, yet both versions feel somewhat in the league of *Frankenstein* and *Bride of Frankenstein*. Was this particular opening an idea from Dominique's mind that you expanded upon, justifying with your *Frankenstein* connection? Or was this an idea of yours that Dominique took a liking to?**

I honestly don't think I made any contribution at all to the way Michael Myers was revived for *Halloween 5* or was any kind of catalyst for any of the ideas that ultimately made it into the script.

Your description of the young man and his demonic arts ritual strikes me as pure Dominique who had a penchant for the supernatural and had already explored supernatural themes in some of his earlier films. I, on the other hand, really didn't take to the supernatural as an explanation for anything. Instead, what I pitched took place within the mine shaft itself and relied on horror movie science a la Frankenstein, where the mine shaft becomes the laboratory, the entangling cables/wires become the equipment delivering the jolt of life, but with no human being – no Dr. Frankenstein – present. In other words, my idea was that the monster is reanimated purely through the power of nature – nothing supernatural.

It is logical and most likely that Dominique had the supernatural opening already in mind and he may very well have told me about it before the meeting and that I tweaked it to suit my sensibilities for the pitch.

**You've mentioned your memory is fuzzy on the subject, but do you recall what role Jamie Lloyd, Michael Myers' niece, would serve in this version?**

I don't recall anything specific about the young girl. See, my basic idea turned the whole horror movie concept on its head. Michael Myers was not the monster in my version. The monsters in the movie were to be the townspeople, the authorities, who, spurred by pure irrationality – fear, primarily, based on a lot of false assumptions – were out to destroy something they thought was evil, but, as Loomis grew to understand may not be evil at all and who may even have the potential for great good. That theme resonated for me. The trick for me, had I ever written the thing, would have been to include the young girl in the mounting danger Michael faced, as her sympathy and commitment to his safety grew since she, because of her innocence, would conceivably come to see in Michael the goodness that Loomis comes to see in him. That whatever happened in that mine shaft has brought to life a goodness in Michael's nature that he had been denied previously, and that was equivalent in its potential power to the evil that had once existed but which has been killed off. Or perhaps it's the girl who would have seen it first and helped convince Loomis. But none of this was ever taken seriously. I think they offered me the job because they liked my imagination even though the specifics I came up with were summarily rejected.

So, I don't deserve any credit for anything in *Halloween 5*, and please believe I'm not shy about claiming credit whenever I feel I'm entitled to it. But *Halloween 5* was just not such a case. All credit goes to Dominique and Michael Jacobs and probably Shem Bitterman and the production team, including the actors. They were the creative forces behind *Halloween 5*.

# SHEM BITTERMAN

### Writer - Halloween 4 (Uncredited), Halloween 5 (Credited)

Interviewed by Travis Mullins

**Professionally, where were you leading up to *Halloween*?**

Well, I'm from New York and went to the High School of Performing Arts as an actor. For a couple of years, I went to Julliard and then transferred to Bennington, receiving my Bachelor's in literature, which is something people rarely do these days. Then, I studied at the Playwrights Program at the University of Iowa. When I got out, I went back to New York and started teaching English as a second language just to make ends meet. The [Mark] Taper [Forum] brought me out to Los Angeles to work on a play called *Iowa Boys*. It was a big deal, sort of a nice workshop opportunity with a great association. From there, I had an agent at William Morris that became interested in me. He asked me to adapt the play that I was working on into a film, but I couldn't because I had already licensed the rights to it. So, I adapted another play called *One Plus One Equals Three* into a screenplay called *Remains* [later released as 1991's *Out of the Rain* starring Bridget Fonda]. I was doing another play in Los Angeles called *Tulsa* and Ramsey Thomas came to see that a number of times. He became interested in working together. He wanted to option *Remains,* but he didn't really have the money to option it with. Instead, he asked, 'Can I get you a gig?' and he did. That was my first professional writing job, doing a treatment for *Halloween 4,* which I think he wound up producing.

**What were your thoughts on *Halloween*? Were you a fan of the genre?**

I still think the original is a Hitchcockian masterpiece. I think it's a really brilliant movie for a lot of reasons, the main being the invention of the Boogeyman – an indestructible force – and then the final sixty seconds, in the sense of a driving menace. It was a tough act to follow as has been seen. The second movie, I remember I was in college and grad school and I enjoyed going to see those movies. *Season of the Witch* was actually one of my favorites. I always thought it was associated with Roald Dahl. It has nothing to do with *Halloween*, but it's strong and pretty cool. Ramsey seemed pretty tight with Moustapha Akkad. I guess when Moustapha got the rights back, he went back to the origins of it. They were probably looking for some young writer who was not in the union. (laughs) And for me, I just wanted to survive as a writer. I wrote *Halloween 4* over Christmas while visiting my dad in San Francisco. It was fun.

**We were surprised to learn you had written for *Halloween 4*. Truth be told, I was under the impression we were never going to reach you.**

A bunch of people reach out to me, but I just don't bother responding. But you were so persistent because you contacted three people I know. (laughs) So, there you go! You're a good reporter!

**Thank you. You know, you have to go deep in the trenches in order to make things happen.**

I like it! Whatever you do in life, you're going to be very successful, I already know. Part of the reason I've been a little reclusive about this particular thing is because, bear in mind, this is not my bailiwick. I'm not really a horror guy. I'm mainly a literary playwright, indie filmmaker. This is, like, the distant past. Even when I did this, this was a money gig for me. Even though I loved the series and the people, and I definitely didn't try to write crap, it's not like I was deeply emotionally invested in it. And if anything, I wanted to slightly bury it because it's not in the profile. You know, the world of playwriting and 'quality movies,' it's a segregated society. In another world, I guess I'd do it under a pen name. It's not part of my resume but I'm a very accessible person.

**You mentioned not being completely emotionally invested in the material. Does that mean that you felt pressure in writing? Or was it like writing on the fly?**

More like writing on the fly, or riffing. I wrote both scripts and treatments very fast and I was extremely underpaid. I could have joined the Writer's Guild after the first one, but I chose to stay loyal to Ramsey and Moustapha and to my original deal, and not join at that time. To this date, I have never received any significant residuals from *Halloween 5*, so clearly that was a mistake. Having said that, I very much enjoyed playing around in that world that the brilliant John Carpenter created. It was a fun first gig, but it had nothing to do with my aspirations or intentions. Though I did it for the money, I mainly did it for myself. It made me a professional writer, but as a professional, I've always made it a point to stay true to my own sense of what's good.

**What I like about your *Halloween 4* is that initially, Jamie isn't terrified of Michael. She actually desperately wants to form a relationship with him, which was something lost in translation. What do you propose this would've brought to the film?**

It's hard to talk about films that haven't been made versus those that have. From what you've said, there are a lot of similarities between the finished product and the film I initially wrote. Since my background is theatre, I am always putting the emotional logic of my characters first, in terms of understanding the story. There are always so many old drafts of movies floating around, and I've read so many myself, of my own and other people's projects. Plus, I've been brought in to rewrite other people, and people have been brought in to rewrite me. It's something that would never happen in plays or novels, but it is very much par for the course in film. I wonder why that it is, but a film is a product. A screenwriter is more like a designer. Some might finish an entire design. Others might design parts of the whole. As with any successful product, as new versions enter the marketplace, many decisions are fear-based. No one wants to kill the franchise or weaken the product, and that's why often the second, third, fourth, fifth, and sixth versions tend to increasingly diminish in quality and originality, until someone decides a reboot is necessary. But thinking of films as products doesn't necessarily diminish their impact. There are many fascinating series – *Godzilla*, the Japanese version – that keep getting odder as they grow older. Still, it's always a danger to simply repeat a winning formula until it loses all effectiveness.

**Given the similarities, do you happen to know why you weren't credited for *Halloween 4*?**

At the end of the day, the producer assigns the credit and then the writers have the right to ask for an arbitration. The arbitration gets assigned to three random people who read all the scripts and then determine the credit. I actually had gone to arbitration at the time and I was not awarded any credit. Hard to believe since I've participated in and judged many arbitrations before, and I know the standards. But I guess the Guild was a very different animal then, and I had made a conscious choice not to join, which may have influenced the judges' decision. Who knows? Maybe my stuff was just on the side. I can only speak to *Halloween 5* because I know what happened with that. I believe Michael Jacobs was a Writer's Guild member and when they brought him on, the Guild reached out to me and said, '*You know, this is a Guild signatory project. Therefore, you have the right to join the Guild,*' and I opted not to, which was dumb. Again, I didn't know what I was doing, and I missed out on some of those residuals because of that decision.

I was so naïve. I was twenty-seven years old. I didn't know anything about the movie world. This is a good example of how things were back in the day. You just banged out a script, man. '*Here's a script! Oh, you want a script?*' Honestly, I probably got paid a few thousand dollars. But that's cool. I was pretty young, so I was happy just to get paid. And they hired me again. Bear in mind, my indie movie [*Out of the Rain*], which was a few years later, wound up making everybody quite a lot of money. So, this was a time when you really could make an indie movie with complete indie financing. Because video stores were big and people needed content and it wasn't so corporately integrated, you could make a sort of direct-to-video movie and it was cheaper to distribute. And the margins were quite good. This was a very different time in filmmaking. What was great about those movies is that they were very un-corporate and weren't associated with big integrated companies like Netflix with a vast amount of money and big tentacles everywhere. These really were like labors of love by these producers. Moustapha was an interesting pivot point in a strange way. He was a true independent guy financing this horror movie at the beginning of what became a renaissance.

**What was your impression of Moustapha and Ramsey?**

I remember really liking Ramsey. Talk about a nice guy. Both he and Moustapha were characters. Hollywood was full of characters in those days. Ramsey was a cool dude. I think he was Middle Eastern. He came to my play a couple of times and wanted to option the material, which subsequently got made as a movie by Gary Winick, another interesting indie figure at that time. Ramsey was in my court. He pitched me for the first gig and then hired me again. I did meet Moustapha a number of times. I remember his office was on Sunset Boulevard. He seemed like a cool, nice guy. He was a Middle Eastern businessman. The only reason I was working on the project is because he was nickel-and-diming it, and it was cool. I honestly don't know what Moustapha's process was. I don't specifically remember getting notes. Ramsey must've been involved in talking about the material with me. It was probably Ramsey himself who was pushing for this direction. It must've been shortly after that Moustapha hired Dominique and I don't know what Ramsey's feelings about that were.

I do remember Moustapha specifically saying that I would get a shared screenplay credit on *Halloween 5*. That was a deal point for him. He felt it was important. I didn't have an agent negotiating these things. Anything that I got was because of him and in that sense, Moustapha was a really cool guy because that's not something that you have to give to somebody. I was just as happy not to get it because I didn't really want to be associated with it at the start of a playwriting career. But I guess he felt I deserved it. He made a point of it and it was very important to him, I remember.

**Did you ever meet with Dominique Othenin-Girard?**

Dominique was cool. He was very European. I met him probably after I had finished my second draft. I remember eating at his house and things like that, but I don't think I had much of a collaboration. Once he came onboard, he wanted to do the script himself. I think he told me over dinner that Michael Jacobs was working on it with him. It's the prerogative of the director. I've done eleven or twelve films myself, and around twenty to thirty plays, so I've got a pretty big distinction between working for myself and work-for-hire. I can be passionate about work-for-hire. I have to be. But although I can be passionate, I also feel that it is somebody else's project, so they should do what they want with it.

**What do you recall about *Halloween 5: The Killer Inside Me*?**

That's a good title. That's because I was so into Jim Thompson. My version – because this is who I am, and this is the kind of writing I do – was very fucking twisted. It was very much about how people contain the nightmare within themselves. The only thing that we fantasize or project into the horror world is actually just our own projections of our own world. That's why I like Jim Thompson's *The Killer Inside Me* and that's why I was attracted to the material. Clearly, this was an opportunity to re-examine the character of Jamie. Our own impulses are what we're terrified of. Just like we're terrified of our own heroism.

**Following *Halloween 4*, most viewers assumed that Jamie Lloyd was destined to become a killer herself. What are your thoughts on this?**

They should've fucking done it, man. Come on, dude. I could almost guarantee that my script is one-hundred percent better than what they made. Jamie becoming the killer, that was the door that was opening. Even if it was a surprise ending, the story opened an interesting door. Rather than walk through that door, they chose to take it back and make the same movie again. Unfortunately, that's a failure of imagination. Who knew how people would react to *Halloween*? The whole point of these indie movies is that you don't know. You don't know if *Pulp Fiction* is going to work or *She's Gotta Have It* or *The Blair Witch Project*. You don't know. But you take a shot. The greatest horror is the horror that comes from within. I loved the fact I had Jamie fighting herself. When we watch a movie like *Halloween*, we're not just

the victim. We are also the killer. Don't forget how *Halloween* starts. As the viewer, we are looking through a mask, sneaking around a house and peering in on a sexy, naked woman. We're sneaking in and we're stabbing – which is a metaphor for fucking her, basically – and we're going to be punished. And all of those feelings that arouse the viewer, that's what gives it its strength. Carpenter's genius was that he put us into the eyes of the killer. That's what great horror makes you do. It makes you confront uncomfortable parts of yourself in a way that makes you feel safe.

At its core, *Halloween* was an audacious film, and it didn't become a mega hit because it played it safe. It really challenged people on two important levels. First, it put you in the eyes of the killer. Second, it created a completely natural world, and broke the rules in the last thirty seconds.

In the moment where Jamie Lee Curtis is sitting there and Michael rises in that mechanical way, that's when cinema changed. Carpenter was very clever in the way he built a very naturalistic, almost Hitchcockian world out of low-budget and camera angles. Unfortunately, with *Halloween 4* and *5*, they were not great movies. They were just repeats. At this point, the formula became more familiar after Carpenter cracked the door open. I would say that maybe my draft makes even more explicit some of the underpinnings of what Carpenter was doing. Don't forget, if you start a movie where you are put in the eyes of the killer and you end the movie where the killer disappears, essentially, you're at large. You've become the boogeyman. What Carpenter was doing was infecting the public with their own culpability in horror and that's born out in later films of his. *They Live* also deals with this fundamental denial that people are in, which is unwillingness to see what they don't want to see. There's a great scene that anchors that whole movie, which is a ten-minute fistfight. I mean, it's a crazy ass movie but it's brilliant.

**You mentioned your influence on this was Jim Thompson, having lifted the title of his book *The Killer Inside Me*. What is it about Thompson's work that drew you to the text? In what ways do you think his work inspired you?**

Jim Thompson, for those who don't know him, was a terrific writer of pulp thrillers. Similar to the great French crime writer Georges Simenon, Thompson wrote of deeply flawed characters who, due to crimes of society, were consigned to being misfits or outcasts. See *Monsieur Hire* by Simenon. Though *Halloween* is fairly straightforward – there is a boogeyman out there – and perhaps that's part of its strength, I personally felt it could've used a little more psychological underpinning, though clearly the producer and director disagreed. I have to say I feel it's a missed opportunity. *Halloween* in specific and horror in general is as much about the viewer as it is about the victim or criminal. The viewer is vicariously Michael but less so the victim, who is often objectified. It seems natural to turn the table on both the audience and the genre by making the killer more human and humanly embodied. What better way to accomplish that than by making the killer a little girl? *Peeping Tom, The Turn of the Screw,* and Clint Eastwood's *Tightrope* all play around with the idea that innocence is itself an embodiment of guilt, a form of illusion or self-deception.

**You've expressed admiration for John Carpenter's original, yet your *Halloween 5* radically alters the template by more clearly giving the Shape supernatural-like abilities. Do you remember putting much thought into how to develop this character?**

The original Michael was terrifying because he was so human but what permanently altered the genre is that he was also supernatural – a boogeyman. The most recent *Halloween* restored the human element but it could never match the true horror of the first time audiences were confronted with an evil that cannot be killed. The final sequence of the original, with Michael having been killed and mechanically rising up, then being stabbed and pushed off a balcony, then being gone, with shots of houses in the night surrounded in darkness and vulnerable to something that could not be explained was cinematic genius. Difficult to repeat. One has to find a way to up the game.

**Both of your scripts featured Dr. Loomis, the Donald Pleasence character from the original. Were you aware that you were carrying forward such an iconic character and actor? Is there anything about the character that you enjoyed playing around with?**

It's hard for me to think back now. Loomis is always baggage. I think I felt I had to make him crazy to make him interesting. Of course, he was already crazy, but I had to make him even crazier, even if it meant having him try to murder a little girl.

**Did you ever see the final film?**

I went to the opening with a bunch of friends and it was pretty… *funny*. It was terrible. Obviously, I went in as a writer and went, '*Ugh*.' It was fun, I guess. I will say that I thought they turned it into a standard slasher film. I don't think it rose to the level of Carpenter's original. With the exception of the third one, where people took the real risk, I don't think Carpenter's vision was honored in any of the subsequent material – with the possible exception of the last one with Jamie Lee Curtis, which was quite good. You know, it's very difficult to make a good sequel, anyway. A lot of what drives sequels seems to be the fear the fans are going to be disappointed. Fans *don't* reward a more interesting like *Season of the Witch*. They *do* want the same thing over and over again. Unfortunately, there were great opportunities set up in *Halloween 4* that seem to have been missed in *Halloween 5*.

It didn't have to be my script but why didn't they raise the bar? I think the last *Halloween* showed what could happen if you took a horror series in a new direction. In fairness to David Gordon Green, the distance was probably helpful. The #MeToo movement was probably helpful. A lot of things were helpful in terms of recontextualizing the material. But there were opportunities along the way, and they seemed to have been missed for the most part. It became a series of diminishing returns, and it's a feeling of disappointment the show seemed to have been a one-trick pony until this last adaption. At least the newest film dealt with the after-effects of trauma. It went back to a realistic world and tried to take the slasher movie to the 21st century, making it less of a salacious, puritanical punishment for sexuality. It had an elderly woman as the lead. It dealt with trauma and treated her in a respectful way. You know, nothing's going to be perfect at the end of the day.

One positive thing about Moustapha is that he had the balls to try new things like those surprise endings. That spoke to the spirit of the times, in which everything wasn't so focus-tested and more of the sensibilities of the people making the films could emerge. That eccentricity was good. It left a little bit of mystery in the result.

**Were you ever privy to any discussions about *Halloween 6*?**

No, I never had another chat with Moustapha. I wasn't really interested in any of that. I don't know what happened to the series after that. I don't think anyone was running out to find me. (laughs)

**Where does your brush with *Halloween* sit within the grand scheme of your career?**

It sits way outside the grand scheme of my career, the grand arc! (laughs) It sits on the Lower East Side of my career. It's nostalgic for me, I'll say that. It's nostalgic to remember those people, that time and that Hollywood. Different world. I'm a playwright and screenwriter. I've done a lot of stuff and I've been in the business a long time. I haven't had an interview before and it's not something that I think about very much. But hey, it's definitely cool. I still have the [*Halloween 5*] poster. At that age, it was a big deal to get my name on a poster. But it was mostly my plays that opened doors for me. I would say that even with *Halloween*, every door that opened for me was through my playwriting. But I liked those guys and I enjoyed my experience. It's part of my Hollywood experience. It was the first real paid gig I had and for a playwright to survive in this town, you had to make an entrée. Otherwise, you couldn't survive. So, I really owe it a lot in that respect. And it gives me a bit of street cred. (laughs)

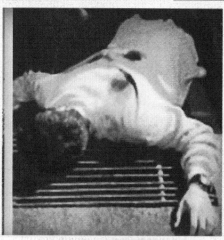

# EVIDENCE

PROPERTY OF THE FEDERAL BUREAU OF INVESTIGATION

| | |
|---|---|
| CASE NO. | 7365219 |
| REF. NO. | 865417784 |
| CAT. NO. | n/a |
| TAG | TOWER FARM CRIME SCENE |

# HALLOWEEN
# 666
## THE ORIGIN

A new dimension.

**Screenplay by**
**Phil Rosenberg**

If ever an award existed for most troubled *Halloween* production, the unlucky recipient would likely be the sixth installment. It's well-known that Miramax/Dimension executives forcibly seized control of the picture from their Trancas partners (including Moustapha Akkad), trimming several key sequences and re-shooting the entire third act for its 1995 release. But the producorial riff that resulted in dueling versions of the film was hardly the start of *Halloween 6*'s troubles. In fact, the project had gone through a handful of filmmakers before Joe Chappelle and Daniel Farrands had even signed on.

Early development on *Halloween 6* first began on the set of 1989's *Halloween 5*. Elated with the positive response to *Halloween 4*, Moustapha Akkad instructed filmmaker Dominique Othenin-Girard to craft a finale that would similarly shock audiences. In turn, this latest *Halloween* sequel would conclude with a mysterious stranger – sharing an equally mysterious tattoo with the Shape – mowing down a police force and escorting the cold-blooded killer out of jail. More so than its predecessor, the ending to *Halloween 5* perhaps elicited one *too* many questions. Who was the mysterious stranger known as the Man in Black? Why did he assist in Michael's escape? Where did the two escape to? What was the significance of the tattoo? What happened to Dr. Loomis? What would happen to Jamie Lloyd? In hopes of attracting returning viewers, Moustapha Akkad seemingly felt these questions were to his favor. In fact, prior to the film's release, Akkad relayed a message to *Fangoria* readers: "The days where each movie was an independent story unto itself are over. It keeps people guessing and interested in the series."

If the reviews from those same readers were any indication, audiences seemed largely ambivalent on the Man in Black and his role in setting up the next installment. While Akkad's exact thoughts on this are largely unknown, history tells us that he was still willing to address this confusing angle in forthcoming films. But in hindsight, the franchise godfather would openly acknowledge several truths about the fifth movie.

First, it had been a rushed production effort, which had negatively affected the quality of the film. Second, with *Halloween 5* arriving only a scant year after *Halloween 4*, the franchise was risking oversaturation with genre audiences. Third, the fifth movie had been the lowest grossing entry in the series, which likely owed to the first two truths. With the slasher subgenre on decline, were audiences still wanting to follow the blood trail of Michael Myers? Akkad still wished to continue the franchise – just with better movies and better box-office results.

## THE ORIGIN OF AN ORIGIN

When creating the Man in Black, Dominique Othenin-Girard had but a faint idea of the character's relation to the Shape. Despite envisioning the two as "soul brothers," the French filmmaker would not be consulted for the follow-up entry. In 1990, Akkad began fielding pitches from prospective screenwriters, including a young Daniel Farrands (the eventual screenwriter) whom he initially turned down. Farrands had, however, gifted Akkad with a *Halloween* "bible" of sorts, detailing the various characters and locales – one which Akkad would frequently refer to when further developing the film.

In the earliest stages of *Halloween 6*, both Danielle Harris and Don Shanks were expected to reprise their roles as Jamie Lloyd and the Shape. In fact, Shanks had been encouraged to drum up interest in the Man in Black's reveal by attending fan events across the country. Also considered worthy for a return at this time was actress Wendy Kaplan; the fate of teenage terror Tina originally left open-ended in the event fans demanded a reprieve. (They didn't – and Tina's neon heart still rests under dirt). The one cast member whose involvement seemed uncertain was series veteran Donald Pleasance. In the context of *Halloween 5*, Loomis' collapse onto Michael was intended to signify the character's death. Only later was this reversed to a non-fatal heart attack. But of this moment, it was entirely possible that Pleasence had donned Loomis' trench coat for the last time – a decision that would have majorly impacted the development of *Halloween 6*.

Said development would progress much more slowly this time. Recognizing that the haste in releasing *Halloween 5* may have resulted in a compromised product, Akkad did not intend to make the same mistake twice. As such, the initial October 1990 release date was missed. Cast members would eventually move on to other projects. In June 1991, Akkad informed *Fangoria* readers the sixth installment was still in development but likely another year from release.

In 1992, Akkad offered Italian filmmaker Michele Soavi the chance to direct. A frequent collaborator of Lamberto Bava and Dario Argento, Soavi had served as assistant director on the giallo kings' *Tenebrae, Phenomena,* and *Demons,* later branching out to helm his own features *Stage Fright* (Italian title: *Deliria*) and *The Sect* (Italian title: *The Devil's Daughter*). He ultimately passed on the project, but one can't help but wonder how his Euro approach might have complimented his predecessor. Concurrent to Soavi's involvement, several screenplays were in development, with at least one given serious consideration.

In October 1993, Don Shanks revealed to *CoverSTORY*, "I was contacted this time last year. The producer of the films, Moustapha Akkad, told me they were working on a script for *Halloween 6* and wanted to know if I was interested in playing the Shape again. He told me they had a script, that they were fine-tuning it, and that this would be the best *Halloween* movie ever. That was the last I heard from him."

## MICHAEL IN SPACE

During this period of development hell, Akkad would encounter a serious setback. In short, he had lost the rights to make new *Halloween* films. Possibly spurred by the delay in producing a new sequel, the lucrative franchise rights went on the auction block. Hoping to regain control of the series, Akkad teamed with Miramax Films to put in a sizable bid. The Disney-owned studio would chip in with the intention of releasing future sequels through their newly formed genre-wing Dimension Films, which was already home to the *Hellraiser* and *Children of the Corn* franchises. Trancas and Dimension would face competition, however. Also seeking to win back control of the series was none other than co-creator John Carpenter. This set up quite the showdown.

Carpenter had initially sworn off his involvement with future *Halloween* installments, yet his interest was piqued with a concept that had been brewing in his mind – one he had revealed to *Fangoria* in 1994: "If you can't kill [Michael Myers], what do you do? You send him up into space, except he gets out up there and ends up on a space station."

Unhappy with the direction of the series under Akkad's guidance, Carpenter teamed with New Line Cinema to outbid his former colleague. Had their collective bid secured the franchise, New Line would have held the rights to not only *Halloween*, but also *Friday the 13th, A Nightmare on Elm Street,* and *The Texas Chainsaw Massacre.* (If there was ever a time for a horror crossover universe, this was it!) Both parties submtited sealed bids with Akkad and Miramax prevailing. Thus, production on the sixth installment could carry forth. At some point, Carpenter would again pitch his "Michael in space" concept, only to be rejected.

# "There was talk of me writing and directing [Halloween 6]. I had an idea for it which would have changed it; correctly and totally changed it forever so that it couldn't go back."

- John Carpenter, Fangoria

As one of the most otherworldly concepts tossed around for a *Halloween* sequel, this long-rumored idea – surely too blasphemous to have come from Carpenter - truly was, in fact, what the director had in mind. Having approved concepts as broad as *Jason Goes to Hell*, *Wes Craven's New Nightmare* and – some years later – *Jason X*, it was not inconceivable to imagine New Line signing off on this idea, thus potentially altering the course of the *Halloween* franchise.

## A DIFFICULT DIMENSION

While Moustapha Akkad had managed to regain control of the series, he now had to share that control with the bosses at Miramax, most notably Bob Weinstein. This would prove a difficult adjustment for the Syrian-born filmmaker, who had previously produced *Halloween*s 4 and 5 with full creative autonomy. The studio originally hoped to fast-track *Halloween 6* into production by October 1993 for release the following year, though they were unable to find a suitable director or screenplay in time.

Director Jeff Burr – who helmed 1990's *Leatherface: Texas Chainsaw Massacre III* – had expressed interest after missing the opportunity to direct the previous *Halloween*. His experiences with the Weinsteins on 1989's *Stepfather II*, however, may have prevented his involvement. Bob Weinstein eventually turned to rising directorial talent Gary Fleder based on the strength of his recent work on *Tales from the Crypt*. His episode, titled "*Forever Ambergris*," was written by another rising talent - Scott Rosenberg – who would become one of Fleder's regular collaborators. (Rosenberg would later pen such Hollywood hits as *Con Air, Gone in 60 Seconds, Venom,* and the newer *Jumanji* films.) But it wasn't Scott who lobbied for the job to write *Halloween 6*. Rather it was his brother – Phil Rosenberg.

An aspiring screenwriter himself, Phil hadn't yet written anything that had been produced. Nor did he have an agent. Nor was he in the Writer's Guild. But he was a genuine horror fan and good friends with Fleder. On the strength of the director's endorsement, Miramax agreed to fly Rosenberg out from Massachusetts to pitch his take on the sequel. Given their penchant for hiring younger (and therefore cheaper) talent, this was not all that unusual. Moustapha Akkad often did the exact same thing.

Phil Rosenberg's *Halloween 6* presentation impressed the Miramax suits enough for them to commission a full screenplay based on his ideas. Returning home to Massachusetts, he would hammer out his sequel script with input from both Fleder and his brother. Rosenberg's first draft was titled *Halloween 666: The Origin* and dated April 6, 1994. The story contained within would leave behind Jamie Lloyd and the Man in Black to explore a previously unknown branch of the Myers family tree. Rosenberg takes us back to Haddonfield by way of an investigative journalist doing a story on the town's bloody history. It's during this trip that she unwittingly stumbles onto the supernatural evil that powers the Shape – along with the slasher himself.

While Miramax responded favorably to Rosenberg's work, Moustapha Akkad was rumored to have thrown the script across the room upon first reading it. Unfortunately, that wasn't the only turbulence happening on the sequel. Citing creative differences with Miramax, Fleder soon stepped down as director of *Halloween 6*. This left Rosenberg, a first-time screenwriter and Hollywood outsider, without an advocate on the project. Fleder would immediately go on to direct *Things To Do In Denver When You're Dead* for Miramax based on a script by Scott Rosenberg. The under-performing crime-drama would be savaged by critics, many of whom drew unfavorable comparisons to the work of Quentin Tarantino. *USA Today's* Mike Clark even called Fleder "a wanna-be Tarantino."

These brutal criticisms are a bit ironic given what happened next with *Halloween 6*. (Spoiler: Miramax tried to replace Fleder with Tarantino.)

## QUENTIN TARANTINO (ALMOST) PRESENTS

March 1994 was an exciting time for Quentin Tarantino. The writer/director was soon to debut his sophomore effort, *Pulp Fiction,* at the prestigious Cannes Film Festival, which it would win. Miramax was also enthused for its release and hoped to continue working with its director for years to come. (Fun fact: The Weinstein's had so much confidence in Tarantino that they funded *Pulp Fiction's* entire budget themselves – a company first.) It was during this time that Executive Vice President Richard Gladstein approached Tarantino with the chance to write and direct the upcoming *Halloween 6.* Tarantino was an admitted fan of the original *Halloween* and even its sequels - despite what he saw as their shortcomings.

"They're like fruit from a poisoned tree," Tarantino told *Consequence of Sound.* "Because Laurie Strode is not the sister of the Shape. I think they just yanked some idea out of their ass and talked themselves into "*Hey, well, this is why…*" and now *Halloween II* has a reason. […] Danielle Harris gives a fantastic performance in those movies. She does what she can to make it legit, but it's just that horrible idea that John and Debra threw in and ruined the entire franchise."

While Tarantino ultimately declined Gladstein's offer to write and direct, he did briefly consider how he might continue the ongoing storyline in his own *Halloween 6.* He was admittedly stumped as to the identity or intentions of the mysterious Man in Black. "I just couldn't figure out who that dude was," Tarantino continued. "The only thing I had in my mind was that the first twenty-minutes would have been the Lee Van Cleef dude and Michael Myers on the highway. They're on the road. And they're stopping at coffee shops and shit. Wherever Michael Myers stops, he kills everybody. So, they're like leaving a trail of bodies on Route 66."

Despite being turned down, Gladstein continued to pursue Tarantino's involvement with the newest *Halloween* sequel. The studio also brought in *Pulp Fiction* co-writer Roger Avary to pitch a new story separate from the Rosenberg script.

"It was too naughts for the nineties," Avary recalls of his *Halloween* sequel pitch. "I remember one person in the room saying, '*I don't know how you shoot that,*' and me responding, '*With a camera, not a gun.*' They validated my parking and I went home and turned my pitch into a spec screenplay titled *Insaniac,* which hasn't been produced. Now, it's too naughts for the twenties!" Next, Gladstein asked Tarantino if and he and business partner Lawrence Bender might consider executive producing the film instead. Both men mulled the possibility.

> ## "When Miramax got Halloween 6 - they asked me and my partner, Lawrence Bender, who we thought would be a good director for it. We both immediately said Scott Spiegel."
>
> — Quentin Tarantino, Fangoria

Scott Spiegel was then best known for having co-written 1987's *Evil Dead II* with Sam Raimi. He had but one directorial credit to his name – 1989's *Intruder,* a thriller about a slasher in an overnight supermarket. Gladstein reached out and found Spiegel open to the idea of directing *Halloween 6.* The Michigan-born filmmaker considered himself a fan of the original *Halloween* and was also complimentary towards *Halloween II* and *Halloween 4.* In considering Spiegel for the director's chair, Bob Weinstein screened an uncut version of *Intruder,* which he liked. Weinstein then met personally with the filmmaker to discuss his vision for *Halloween 6.* Spiegel quickly won over the studio boss, who gave him his full blessing to helm the sequel. There was but one more gatekeeper to meet with – Moustapha Akkad. "He was pretty cool," Spiegel told *Fangoria* of meeting Akkad. "He had some reservations about me, but finally he said, '*Okay, maybe we'll use you to do a polish on the script that we're considering, and then maybe we'll let you direct it.*'"

The prospective director was given a copy of Rosenberg's *Halloween 666* script with instructions to polish where needed. Upon reading it, however, he came to the conclusion that no amount of polishing could salvage the material. This was not a script he wished to direct nor be associated with in any way. He would later share his blunt assessment with journalist Michael Gingold, who would print his comments in *Fangoria 147:* "When I read the screenplay, I said, '*Oh boy.*' It reminded me of a *Friday the 13th* movie and presented Michael Myers as a homeless person. It was really unfocused and corny. I just didn't understand what the homeless element was all about."

Spiegel met with Weinstein again in late April to discuss the project further. The studio boss vented about ongoing disagreements with Akkad, who liked neither Rosenberg's script nor the prospect of Spiegel directing it. With this, Spiegel's short time on the project came to an end. As for the script, Scott Rosenberg next took a crack at polishing his brother's work, but this too failed to satisfy Akkad. "I was really relieved," Spiegel told *Fangoria* of his departure. "The script that we were going to shoot at the time was going to be hard to overcome. And my feeling was that I didn't need to be the one to make a crummy sequel to what had been a decent series of films."

*Pulp Fiction* would debut at Cannes the following month and take home the festival's top prize – the highly coveted Palme d'Or. This massive win catapulted Tarantino to directorial stardom, thus transforming him into a major player within the industry. He would eventually secure a Best Picture nomination for his work. Given this sudden and enormous success, it's difficult to imagine the award-winning director lowering himself to rescue the troubled sixth installment of a struggling horror franchise. (And the franchise *was* struggling. *Halloween 5* remains the lowest grossing film in the series. Even worse, Dimension would briefly downgrade the franchise to direct-to-video following *Halloween 6*.)

With Fleder, Spiegel, and Tarantino off the project, only Rosenberg remained. He was caught between Weinstein and Akkad, who were still unable to agree on the merits of his work. Rosenberg had already incorporated multiple studio notes into his screenplay to no avail, one of which – virtual reality – would prove among the most criticized elements in the entire script.

## THE STORY

*Halloween 666* opens on Dana Childress, our new twenty-something heroine, as she braves a storm in her '73 Cutlass Supreme. The announcer interrupts "Mr. Sandman" on the radio to report the very recent escape of a convicted serial killer in the area. Stopping for gas, Dana is unnerved by the creepy attendant as he stares into her backseat. As it turns out, he was only staring at the real threat in their midst – *the Shape* – who had been hiding in her backseat the whole time. The killer emerges and murders both the attendant and Dana, which jolts her awake from this nightmare. She tells her therapist of the dream, the latest of several involving the Shape, which always seem to occur in the midnight hour. As a Channel 6 reporter, Dana's news team is being sent to Haddonfield to cover the town's first Halloween celebrations since the last murders in 1989. Prior to leaving, she visits her elderly grandmother, whom the script notes having a distinctive cheek mole.

The story then switches to Haddonfield. Here we catch up with Tommy Doyle, whom we last saw as a young boy in Laurie Strode's care back on October 31, 1978. Now a twenty-nine-year-old outcast, Tommy is "tall, lean, and wild haired." His teenaged housemates, Mickey and Bad News, have teasingly dubbed him "Trembling Tommy." They beg him to hide in his attic bedroom during their upcoming Halloween party. Now obsessed with all things Michael Myers, Tommy lives in constant fear of the boogeyman's return. Hoping to gain insight into Michael's past, he visits Dr. Loomis at Smith's Grove Sanitarium but is stunned to learn that Loomis is no longer a psychiatrist there but rather a patient. Having lost his mind in pursuit of evil, Loomis prefers to not think about the horrors of the past. He encourages Tommy to find a different obsession, reasoning that Michael's slaughter should be over if Jamie Lloyd was truly his last living blood relative. ("Unless there's another sealed file out there somewhere – and God knows – the Myers family has more sealed files than the damned Warren Commission.")

As night falls on Haddonfield, we find four obnoxious frat boys harassing a sleeping vagrant à la *A Clockwork Orange* ("Anyone up for a bit of the old ultra-violence?") This vagrant turns out to be the unmasked Shape, who savagely murders all four boys. One bully dies by having a rat forced down his throat, "crushing both vermin and victim." The Shape then visits a homeless shelter and sees a Channel 6 promo advertising Dana's upcoming Haddonfield broadcast.

Upon arrival in Haddonfield, the Channel 6 news team visit a tacky gift shop capitalizing on the town's bloody history. Noticing Dana's arrival, the Shape begins stalking her crew and murders the storeowner after they leave. It's here the Shape steals a souvenir replica of his own trademark white mask, restoring his classic look. Dana and her team next visit the crumbling Myers house to find Sheriff Meeker waiting inside with a loaded shotgun – his now annual tradition in case the boogeyman should ever return home. Dana interviews several townspeople about the holiday's controversial return – including the suspicious Father Carpenter, whom we recognize as the drunken priest from *Halloween 4*. She also speaks with Tommy Doyle, though he declines to be interviewed.

Tommy returns home to learn that his housemates have stolen Judith Myers' headstone as a decoration for their party. He objects to their desecration but is powerless to stop them. Back at Haddonfield Cemetery, rays of light begin to emanate from the earthen hole where Judith's marker previously stood. The Channel 6 crew visit here soon after and discover the missing stone but fail to notice the otherworldly fissure. The caretaker is enraged and accuses them of theft. Dana's team leave at which time the Shape murders the caretaker and his wife. (The caretaker has his face shoved into a food processor set on puree. His wife is killed by having a "Sugar Daddy" candy shoved into her eye socket and brain.)

Dana next interviews Frank and June Wallace – parents to Lindsey from the original film – about their experiences with the Myers family. They screen old home movies of Wallace/ Myers family picnics, which seem idyllic enough. It's here that Dana makes a startling discovery. Michael's grandmother bears a striking resemblance to her own, right down to the distinctive cheek mole. The takeaway from this is that Dana is actually Michael's long-lost sister! She goes to speak with Tommy about her shocking discovery, but he's too pre-occupied with his VR-system to hear her knocking. Tommy does notice their van pulling away – along with the driver's dead body on the roadside. The Shape is actually behind the wheel, unbeknownst to anyone inside. They're driven to a bog where the Shape murders the entire Channel 6 crew as a cackling Father Carpenter watches on. Dana escapes back to Tommy's house where the party is in full-swing.

Stunned by Dana's revelation ("This is fucking insane!"), Tommy soon begins to panic at its implications. ("My God, you've led him back here!") In an effort to learn more about their adversary, Dana straps into Tommy's virtual reality system, which he likens to "a high-tech Ouija board" that "can take you to places you aren't supposed to go." In the VR-world, Dana travels back hundreds of years to the ancient festival of Samhain where Michael's bloodline was first cursed. She next jumps ahead to 1963 to witness this cursed evil taking hold of young Michael. Dana ultimately emerges from the VR-world with the all-important knowledge that – each year on Halloween night – Judith's grave acts as a portal to the otherworld. If they can force the Shape into it between midnight and one, they can vanquish him for good. They'll need to act fast, however, as the midnight hour is nearly over.

Knowing the Shape will follow after them, Dana and Tommy rush to Haddonfield Cemetery amid a rainstorm. (As in the opening, "Mr. Sandman" plays on the radio.) Father Carpenter's disembodied voice echoes throughout the graveyard. After a struggle, Dana manages to trick her brother into entering the portal, seemingly destroying him. ("Go home, Michael! Go the fuck home!") Tommy's housemates arrive a moment later to return Judith's headstone, sealing the portal shut. Feeling confident in their victory, Tommy glances at his watch, which reads 1:14 AM. His face goes slack as he begins to wonder – did they force Michael into the portal before *or after* the 1 AM deadline? Tommy spots Father Carpenter sitting on a nearby tombstone. He laughs menacingly as the *Halloween* theme rises. Cut to credits.

## THE NEW MYTHOLOGY

This original draft of *Halloween 666* has taken a lot of flak over the years and it's easy to see why. The story contains several polarizing elements, notably the otherworldly portal as a means to destroy the Shape, the strange use of virtual reality, and the recycled twist of Dana being Michael's younger sister. But to focus exclusively on these things would be to ignore how much this screenplay actually gets right. The premise of an investigative journalist traveling to Haddonfield for an assignment – and then becoming part of that assignment – is a great one that has yet to be explored. This draft also takes a surprisingly thoughtful approach to the continuing stories of Dr. Loomis, Sheriff Meeker, and Tommy Doyle. Regarding thrills and chills, *Halloween 666* packs several *"Oh shit"* moments that would've surely pleased franchise fans. The scene in which the Shape covertly hijacks the Channel 6 news van is wrought with tension. We know of the danger they're in even if they don't.

But yes, the otherworldly portal does jump the supernatural shark. And the virtual reality element – essentially a "deus ex machina" that doubles as a time machine – veers much too far into science fiction territory. As for the long-lost sister twist, it doesn't play all that well. After all, fans are still debating whether this twist worked the first time in *Halloween II*. To have this happen again just feels redundant. A quick read of *Halloween 666* makes it abundantly clear that there is simply too much going on in the story. Yet there is potential here that might have been seized upon had this draft undergone a proper development phase. A polish focused on emulating the simplicity of the original *Halloween* would've greatly benefited the material. Unfortunately, the Rosenberg draft was jettisoned before such collaboration could take place.

For context, this script is to *Halloween* what *Jason Goes to Hell* was to *Friday the 13th*. Both screenplays offer bold new additions to the respective mythologies by introducing previously unheard-of family members for the killers. They also suggest convoluted new ways to vanquish their monsters. In *Jason Goes to Hell*, that means having a blood-relative stab the hockey-masked slasher with a magical dagger. In *Halloween 666*, that means shoving Michael Myers into an otherworldly portal beneath his older sister's grave between midnight and 1 AM on Halloween night. These stories also depict an unusual physical manifestation of the evil within their killers. For Jason, it's a demon-like snake creature. For Michael, it's a vaporous mass he inhales through his mask. Read on for that to make a little more sense.

While starkly different from the eventual *Halloween 6*, this alternate pitch is oddly similar in several ways. Tommy Doyle is nearly the same character here as in the actual film, socially isolated and obsessed with all things Michael Myers. He teams up with the heroine in both stories, delivering to her (and us) much exposition about the origins of ultimate evil. While Thorn is never mentioned by name, there are references to Michael's bloodline being "cursed." Both stories invoke the ancient festival of Samhain as a possible explanation for the Shape's evil. If not entirely incidental, these similarities were likely grafted onto the actual *Halloween 6* by others as screenwriter Daniel Farrands lacked access to the Rosenberg draft while penning his script. Another similarity between the drafts involves the switch to a more adult cast.

Rosenberg deserves credit for putting forth a compelling new heroine with Dana Childress. After Laurie Strode, Rachel Carruthers, and Tina Williams – you have to wonder how many more high school girls they could possibly pit against the Shape. In this respect, Dana makes for a refreshing change as the first non-teenaged leading lady in the series. As a reporter doing a story on Michael Myers, she brings to mind Joey Summerskill from *Hellraiser III* who similarly investigated Pinhead. Upon learning of her true connection to Michael, Dana comments: "I think subconsciously I always knew." Again, this revelation strains credulity. Its main purpose in the story is to give the Shape a motivation for going after her. Since many feel the slasher seems to work best without such motivation, this detail could've been nixed without harming the story.

As already mentioned, this draft's Tommy Doyle is quite similar to his depiction in the actual *Halloween 6*. His untidy apartment reveals an unhealthy obsession with the past. Tommy has amassed a sick trove of books, papers, computer disks, and religious artifacts – "a virtual shrine to Michael Myers." In a detail exclusive to this depiction, he vocally protests the return

of Halloween this year. We first find him yelling into a megaphone at Haddonfield Center Park: "Brady Johnson! Kelly Meeker! Jamie Lloyd! The victims! They cry out to you from their graves! From a place of darkness! Do not allow Halloween to return to Haddonfield! It is an affront to their memories. They cry out to you. Stop the madness! Stop the horror!" Tommy is also insistent that Michael will one day return to spill blood once more: "You'll see! You won't be able to hide! Not when he returns! Not when he comes home!"

Whereas the actual *Halloween 6* sought to distance itself from *Halloween 4* and *5*, the Rosenberg draft closely aligns itself with the preceding two films. Much of this owes to the return of Sheriff Meeker, but other references to the fourth and fifth installments abound throughout. These include cameos from the families of the Shape's victims, notably the parents of Brady from *Halloween 4*, who give an interview to Channel 6 about Halloween's return to Haddonfield. One major character given only minor mention in *Halloween 666* is Jamie Lloyd, whom everyone assumes was killed in the explosive ending of *Halloween 5*. Speaking of that ending, it's largely glossed over in this story, leaving us to draw our own conclusions.

From this draft alone, you could safely assume that Rosenberg is a fan of the genre as his *Halloween 666* is packed with references to other horror films. Tommy's housemate greets the Channel 6 team dressed as Pinhead while delivering an iconic line. ("Your suffering will be legendary, even in hell – *No way*! Candid Camera? Come in, come in!") Elsewhere in the house, a group is watching the original *Texas Chain Saw Massacre* on television. In a later scene, a partygoer dressed as Jason Voorhees assumes the Shape to be a fellow reveler and asks him for help with a beer keg. The slasher jams the keg tubing through the boy's hockey mask and down his throat. The slasher then pumps the beer at a frenzied pace. Blood and vomit spew from the boy's nose as he drowns. In a fun nod to the original *Halloween*, Rosenberg writes that one partier is wearing a Captain Kirk mask.

Oh – and for those wondering why this *Halloween 6* is titled *Halloween 666*, here's the justification. In a scene set midway through the story, the Shape murders a Channel 6 crewmember and uses their blood to smear two additional 6's on the news van. (It now reads "Channel 666.") Why exactly does the Shape do this? We never find out. Per the New Testament's Book of Revelation, 666 is supposedly the mark of the beast aka Satan aka the Anti-Christ. Rosenberg never suggests – nor even hints – that Michael may be the Anti-Christ or in the service of Satan. The screenwriter instead ties the slasher's origin to the Druids, who didn't even believe in the devil. (Satan, it turns out, is the product of Abrahamic religions, not Druidry.) So Michael finger-painting the mark of the beast in blood doesn't make a ton of sense. But *Halloween 666* sure sounds cool in marketing, right? That's likely why it stuck around well into the film's actual production despite having *even less* relevance once applied to the Daniel Farrands script.

## A TOWN DIVIDED

Like most *Halloween* sequels, this draft ventures back to Haddonfield, Illinois. Driving into town, the Channel 6 team notice a sign that reads "Welcome to Haddonfield – Population 21,000 – Home of the Huskers," except that someone has marked out the sports team and crudely scrawled "Michael Myers" above it. This draft bears further similarity to the actual *Halloween 6* with its approach to Haddonfield as a community. In the Farrands script, the holiday was officially banned following the 1989 massacre. It was only through the effort of Tim Strode's girlfriend Beth that Halloween finally returned to Haddonfield in 1995. This is all much the same in the Rosenberg draft where a similar ban went into effect after *Halloween 5*. Here the town has only narrowly voted to reinstate the holiday in a highly controversial move. Those opposed to Halloween's return won't be opening their doors to trick-or-treaters this night. They'll instead burn memorial candles in their front windows to mourn those lost. The candles will also serve to deter trick-or-treaters from knocking on their doors.

Having lost his own daughter to the Shape in *Halloween 4*, Sheriff Meeker deeply resents the holiday's return. He is especially sickened by those who embrace the town's bloody legacy by donning white masks and roaming the same streets Michael stalked in years past. ("It's like being stabbed in the back for a second time.") As mentioned in the plot summary, his new tradition is to spend October 31 sitting in the darkened Myers house with a loaded shotgun just in case evil ever returns home again. While it's great having Meeker back in this story, it's unfortunate he doesn't have more to do or an opportunity to exact revenge. A showdown between a grieving father and his daughter's killer might've been fantastic.

Among those happy to see the holiday return is Hardy Lomax, owner of a tacky souvenir store that profits from Haddonfield's pain. Rosenberg writes that Hardy's store is filled with t-shirts, keychains, plastic knives, white masks, and back issues of *Fangoria*. (One shirt reads: "*I spent Halloween in Haddonfield and all I got was this shirt. And this slashed carotid!*") In a fun nod to *Halloween III*, Rosenberg writes that Lomax is also selling the three Silver Shamrock masks from that film. After the storeowner suffers a much-deserved death (barbeque fork through the skull), the Shape roams his store in search of a new visage. Browsing the selection, he tosses aside several Freddy and Jason masks to find a more suitable plain white mask. Ripping off the price tag, he puts it on and stares into camera. (Script: "The fit is still good after all these years.")

In a bit of eerie nostalgia, *Halloween 666* travels back to an iconic location from the first film – the Wallace home. (Fans will recall this is where Laurie Strode discovered the bodies of Annie, Bob, and Lynda.) The Wallaces still live here, though Lindsey has moved away to New York City after much therapy. Recall that we only briefly glimpse Lindsey's parents in the original film (though both characters did appear in Dennis Etchison's unused *Halloween 4* screenplay). It's rather Farrands-esque, shall we say, to see the original's rather miniscule characters expanded upon – even going so far as to establish a connection with the Myers family. It's an interesting angle to catch up with Lindsey's parents, who would've surely been *just a bit uneasy* by what happened at their house some years ago. (Hey - that pantry door isn't going to replace itself!)


## THE SHAPE

With respect to the Shape, *Halloween 666* feels like a pre-cursor to Rob Zombie's *Halloween II*. Unlike *Halloween 5*, which largely glossed over how Michael spent his off-time between holidays, this draft offers a feasible explanation. In short, he's a homeless transient. We first find him living on the street as a vagrant without his mask. After killing the four obnoxious frat boys, Michael travels to a large homeless shelter where he's clearly a known presence among the regulars. (Script: "Homeless men nod to him and look away.")

Rosenberg isn't necessarily suggesting that they recognize Michael as the notorious killer at large; just that he's a fearsome stranger not to be trifled with. The Shape effortlessly breaks the hand of a fellow vagrant who tries to change the channel from Dana's news broadcast. If we absolutely must know how the Shape spends his time between killing sprees, this is as good an explanation as any. It's not as if he could go back to the Myers house after the events of *Halloween 5*. Being in a residential area, he would surely be seen coming or going by the neighbors. Never mind the unannounced visits by Sheriff Meeker. (Maybe he could utilize those underground tunnels from *Halloween: Resurrection*?)

This *Halloween 666* doesn't deviate too far from the standard Shape aesthetic apart from the aforementioned homelessness. He soon obtains a fresh white mask and new set of overalls. The kills that follow are chilling – just as we've come to expect. (Fun fact: Had this script been made, it would've been the first *Halloween* where Michael isn't shot by someone. In the eventually-produced *Halloween 6*, he's shot by Tommy with a gas grenade launcher.) Where *Halloween 666* does deviate, however, is in giving the slasher an elaborate backstory, which we'll delve into shortly.

One fascinating aspect of the Rosenberg script involves how Michael Myers has risen to a sort of mythic figure in popular culture – not unlike Charles Manson. With Lomax's tacky souvenir shop selling Michael masks, there are numerous trick-or-treaters roaming the streets dressed as the notorious killer. (Let's all agree on how offensive that is given how many people he's killed in this town.) These imitators allows the *real* Shape to travel undetected in public. He even crashes the party at Tommy's house without freaking anyone out, garnering compliments for his costume instead of the usual screams. One partier does comment: "Hey, buddy. Lose the knife. You'll kill someone with that fuckin' thing." The Shape ignores him.

Among the more interesting Shape moments in *Halloween 666* is one in which the slasher tries to enter the Wallace residence during Dana's visit there. While screening the old Myers home movies, Mr. Wallace hears a knock at the door. Looking through the peep hole, he sees the infamous white mask. Gesturing to the memorial candles in the window, he rebuffs the slasher for knocking. ("Those candles mean anything to you, buster? Please leave us alone, we've got nothing here for you.") Mr. Wallace goes to shut the door, but the Shape sticks his hand inside the doorjamb. He tries to shut the door again, this time successfully, bloodying the Shape's hand in the process. Does the slasher go berserk and force his way inside to kill Dana and the Wallaces in one fail swoop? *Surprisingly, no.* He instead smears blood across the peep hole and storms off. What's behind such an uncharacteristic retreat on the slasher's part? While not outright stated, it's entirely possible the Shape caught a glimpse of his younger self in the Wallace's living room (the home movies) and noped out to avoid that particular trip down memory lane. Just a theory.

## VIRTUAL REALITY

Ascribed as one of Tommy Doyle's hobbies, virtual reality is one of the screenplay's more confounding elements. Rosenberg writes that Tommy is a "virtual reality hacker," though it's unclear what exactly that is. His complex VR-system doesn't meaningfully impact the story until the final act when Dana straps in hoping to learn more about the Shape. As Tommy explains, "It's like a high-tech Ouija board, a conduit. It can take you places, places people aren't supposed to go, to where your brother, to where he came from." Unfortunately, that's not even remotely how virtual reality has *ever* worked. Virtual reality is neither a time machine nor a magical window into the present-day world.

Within the context of *Halloween 666*, Tommy's VR-system is really just a means to communicate a massive amount of story exposition about how Michael became the Shape and how he can be defeated. Some of what Dana sees mirrors actual reality while other images appear too fantastical to be real. She begins her VR-trip soaring over a virtual Haddonfield. Looking down upon the town, she sees disturbing sights including a vision of young Jamie Lloyd imprisoned in a cage of human bones – her *only* appearance in the script. Dana also sees her grandmother, whose cheek mole pulsates until a wet, bat-like creature flies out of it. (*Jesus Christ.*) Some of this imagery calls to mind Laurie's surreal nightmares from Rob Zombie's *Halloween II*.

Dana soon finds herself in a Celtic Village around the year 1,000 BC. Here she will witness the original curse placed upon the Myers family. One of the Shape's ancestors was a Sacral King who was set to be sacrificed at midnight on All Hallow's Eve for the perceived good of the village. The King refuses to go quietly and instead has a Minister killed in his place. This infuriates the High Priest, who places a curse on the King's family. ("I will curse this man's bloodline. His family will feel the wrath of the Gods of harvest. And it will be at the hand of one of their own that they shall fall. No matter how long it takes. The passage of millennia is as nothing to the machinations of heaven. The Gods are hungry. But the Gods are also patient!") A vaporous mass, malevolent and hissing, bellows out of the High Priests' cauldron and into a fissure in the ground. Jumping ahead quite a bit, Dana then sees young Michael Myers outside his home on the night of October 31, 1963. The ground cracks open and the same vaporous mass travels up into the mouth-opening of the young boy's familiar-looking clown mask. In this moment, the Shape is born.

Dana next experiences a "greatest hits" montage of the Shape's kills from throughout the series. Her final vision is of the otherworldly portal beneath Judith's headstone. Pulsing with light rays, the cries of a thousand damned souls can be heard coming from within. Dana emerges from the VR-system having concluded that they need to push Michael into the portal during the midnight hour. This will finally satisfy the sacrifice that should've been made by the Sacral King thousands of years ago on Halloween night. Tommy consults a book to check her theory and finds she may be right. ("There exists sacred, enclosed places designated as holy that become a focus with the supernatural world on the 31st of October – Halloween.") He also cites a unique alignment of the stars as coinciding with the portal opening. This strongly evokes something Paul Rudd's Tommy Doyle said in the actual *Halloween 6* concerning the Thorn constellation appearing in the night sky whenever the Shape does.

Again, if we *must* have a backstory for the Shape, the cursed-bloodline route isn't all that bad. It's certainly no worse than Thorn or the similar origin offered in *Halloween*'s 1978 novelization. But the revelation via computer simulation is all wrong. As it turns out, the push to include virtual reality didn't actually come from Rosenberg. It was added in at the behest of Bob Weinstein. This misguided effort to make *Halloween* current and hip may owe to the popularity of 1992's *The Lawnmower Man*, which had successfully brought virtual reality to the big screen with a horror slant.

## THE LOOMIS CAMEO

Notably absent from most of *Halloween 666* is the franchise's own Van Helsing – Dr. Samuel Loomis. The character instead receives what amounts to an extended cameo in the first act. While the appearance is brief, it is very well-written and offers the good doctor far more closure than in either version of the actual *Halloween 6*. On a tip from Sheriff Meeker, Tommy goes to visit Loomis at Smith's Grove Sanitarium hoping to learn more about Michael Myers. He's shocked to learn that Loomis is no longer a physician there but rather a patient. As it turns out, his many years spent chasing evil have cost him his own sanity.

Loomis is equally shocked to see Tommy again, initially doubting that he's the same boy from that terrible night so many years ago. ("I've suffered two heart attacks, young man. You don't want to assist on a hat trick, do you?") When Tommy inquires how Loomis wound up in this situation, the doctor simply cites having "too many demons." ("Odd, I spent nearly all my life caring for the insane, only to join their ranks in the end.") Tommy first shares his fear that Michael will return to kill again, though the old man dismisses this notion citing the supposed end of his bloodline with Jamie Lloyd. He then explains his theory about Michael's evil being tied to Druidry and the ancient festival of Samhain. Loomis confesses he too once suspected this, though he now dismisses that as well. ("If Michael carried out his insane depredations on Thanksgiving, who would we take to task then? The Pilgrims?") Loomis regrettably tells his visitor that he cannot help him. A fearful Tommy then leaves.

**Loomis:** *"I'm tired, son. Devoting my life to the darkness has placed a shroud on my soul. A shadow. You're on your way there as well. You're a young man. Go out and buy some blue jeans. Meet a girl. Dance on the beach. Put all this behind you."*

While *Halloween* fans might prefer Loomis play a more active role in any given sequel, there is something nice about his appearance here. You could easily argue that Rosenberg gives the character the most satisfying closure of any depiction ever, made or unmade. Though institutionalized with mental decline, Loomis has clearly achieved some measure of peace at Smith's Grove.

## FATHER CARPENTER

One of *Halloween 666's* more surprising developments involves the return of Reverend Jackson P. Sayer from *Halloween 4,* now erroneously named Father Carpenter in tribute to *Halloween's* writer/director. Rosenberg changes not only the priest's name but his characterization as well, shifting from benevolent to malevolent. We last saw the reverend in *Halloween 4* giving Dr. Loomis a ride to Haddonfield whilst drunkenly monologuing about hunting damnation. We find him in *Halloween 666* similarly ranting on the steps of town hall. Noticing the Channel 6 news team, he turns to mug for their cameras. ("Damnation knows no vacation! Think it's safe to babysit in Haddonfield again? Think again!")

Father Carpenter makes sporadic appearances throughout the story right up until the final scene, often appearing just before or after the Shape does. In fact, he consistently shows up in the wrong places at the right time. His comments tend to be brief, cryptic, and unsettling. The suspicious clergyman even cameos in the Wallaces' old home movies they show Dana. In the footage, Father Carpenter approaches a young Michael and quips, "Cute as a devil, isn't he?" Scenes such as this, while certainly creepy, feel less like Carmen Flipi's endearing performance from *Halloween 4* and more like Julian Beck's Father Kane from *Poltergeist II*.

Yet for all his insane cackling, Father Carpenter knows more than he lets on. Later in the story, he teases Dana about her newfound discovery. ("Big brother is watching!") How could he possibly know this long-buried family secret that Dana herself only just learned? Rosenberg never offers an explanation, but he does make one subtle reference to the character's true identity. Late in the story, the Shape chases Dana as Father Carpenter watches on. The scene direction notes that the camera should pan down to the priest's *"black silver-tipped cowboy boots."* Yes – Rosenberg has cast Father Carpenter as the Man in Black! Yet this revelation is curious as Rosenberg never addresses the Man in Black anywhere else, leaving us with far more questions than answers.

The return of Carmen Filpi's Reverend Sayer, coupled with the return of Beau Starr's Sheriff Meeker, might've gone a long way in making this *Halloween 6* feel more connected to *Halloween*s 4 and 5. As is, Joe Chappelle's *Halloween 6* stands apart from its predecessors with only Donald Pleasence returning in a reduced role. It would seem that Rosenberg's goal was to make *Halloween 6* feel like the concluding chapter of a trilogy that began with *Halloween 4*.

## WHY IT WASN'T MADE

This version of *Halloween 666* was a casualty of the franchise's new power split between Miramax and Trancas, the first of many *Halloween* screenplays to die this way. Moustapha Akkad made no secret of his dislike for Phil Rosenberg's take on the property. On the contrary, Miramax did like Rosenberg's work and sought to develop his material further – though they struggled to attach a director with Gary Fleder, Quentin Tarantino, and Scott Spiegel all declining involvement. Rosenberg did receive and apply studio notes to his draft, but these were not enough to change Akkad's mind. Even with production dates looming on the horizon, Bob Weinstein would eventually relent to Akkad's criticisms, assigning two new screenwriters to do a full re-write, effectively canning this draft from ever reaching the screen.

*Fangoria* would later print a slew of disparaging remarks by Spiegel about *Halloween 666* in their October '95 issue. Rosenberg would respond in kind with a letter to editor Tony Timpone, which *Fangoria* would also publish. The screenwriter took aim not only at Spiegel's comments but at the utter chaos that surrounded *Halloween 6* from the very start.

"*I wrote the draft that was deemed "corny and unfocused" by director Scott "Hitchcock" Spiegel of Intruder, (We all remember that instant horror classic, don't we?), who eventually became attached to the project. True, my brother did a brief polish of my script. And he's so "corny and unfocused" that he's under contract to Miramax, has two flicks out this winter, and probably three more over the next few years.*

*Meanwhile, Spiegel himself is the only person apparently more capable of losing a movie gig than me. After all, he (unlike myself) already had a movie under his belt and more importantly, had the backing of Quentin Tarantino. How did he manage to blow it? Now that's scary. I do laud him for co-writing Evil Dead II. Win some, lose some, I guess.*

*Moustapha Akkad hated my script; thought it was "too funny." Silly me. All along, I thought of Michael Myers as the boogeyman incarnate, not some goofy "Shape" from another planet. (What does that mean, anyway – the Shape? I never got that. Myers is just the shape as you or I, just a lot more pissed off.) Clearly, Akkad's (and not Dimension's, mind you) idea of true terror was explaining the mystery of the man in Dingo boots. Apparently, the legion of Fango readers/Halloween fans convinced him of that early on. So in fairness, he did give the people what they wanted. A true showman.*

*I simply want to let the record show – for your readers' sake, of which I include myself – that Akkad is a kind but very old man, who at one time considered the following plot elements/developments for the sixth Halloween: Michael Myers in outer f\*\*king space. Harrowing stuff, indeed. Tonya Harding cast in the movie (incidentally, the best idea Akkad tabled), while Dr. Loomis is discovered to be Michael Myers' father. Michael's mother as a sex slave to the Man in Black. There's a real chilling twist, no? The new movie's cool tagline is "Terror never rests in peace." But whether the late, great Donald Pleasence can do the same is another story altogether. Doubtful.*"

**- Phil Rosenberg, Fangoria 147**

# PHIL ROSENBERG

Writer - Halloween 666: The Origin

Interviewed by Dustin McNeill

**How did you come to be involved with *Halloween 666*?**

This was early 1994, I believe. I was living in Boston at the time. My brother, Scott, who is a big screenwriter now, had just sold a couple things to Miramax/Dimension. Ever see *Things to Do In Denver When You're Dead*? My brother wrote that and his friend, Gary Fleder, directed it. Miramax/Dimension had just recently gotten the rights to do the sixth *Halloween* and Gary was originally attached to direct it. I was such a big horror movie nerd growing up. I loved horror movies, which included the *Halloween* films. With that in mind, of course I wanted to be a part of the new one. I wrote up a treatment, turned it in, and they brought me out to Los Angeles to talk about it. That meeting was fifty-minutes long and absolutely terrifying. It was myself, Bob Weinstein, and about twenty other people. I was mortified, but they liked my pitch enough to order a full script.

So I went back to Boston and wrote the first draft of *Halloween 6*. I didn't even own a computer at the time. I did it on a word processor. It was my first writing job ever. Not only did I get paid for it, but I also got into the Writer's Guild as well. Unfortunately, as you well know, they never actually made my script. It was re-written a few times before Daniel Farrands eventually came on and wrote his own take. This was Miramax's first stab at the *Halloween* franchise and they were wanting it to come out in October 1994. But they had to push the release date back once they started punting it to other writers.

My draft was done by just me. I didn't have anyone helping me write it, not like a co-writer, but my brother and Gary Fleder both gave me notes on it before I handed it in. Gary wanted to be involved because he was attached to direct.

**That explains your involvement. How did Quentin Tarantino come into the picture?**

He was gonna be like a marketing gimmick. He was just becoming popular at the time and a big horror movie fanatic, so they wanted to use him to sell the movie. Miramax thought that maybe *Halloween 6* could be produced by Quentin Tarantino. More like by presented by, really, because he wasn't truly going to be producing it. It would've been cool, but it never happened. At some point, it became clear that he wasn't going to put his name on just anything.

**One filmmaker briefly involved with *Halloween 6* was Scott Spiegel. How di--**

*That guy!* He shit on my script! I read where he did that in an issue of *Fangoria*. I was kind of offended at the time, like '*Who the fuck is this guy?*' I actually wrote a letter about that to Tony Timpone, the editor of *Fangoria*, and he printed it in the next issue. But in hindsight, I kind of wish I hadn't even bothered because what does it really matter? But this was my first real job.

**Wait, how was *Halloween 666* your first job in 1994? I'm looking at IMDb right now and you've got credits going back to the '80s.**

That's not me. Different guy. He's like a hundred-years-old. We get confused a lot. I once got his Writer's Guild residuals by mistake. I had to add an initial to my name to help distinguish myself from him. I'm Phil M. Rosenberg. Not all of my credits are on there. I've written some pretty terrible things under pseudonyms. One of them was a shark attack movie called *Shark Zone*. I took that money and ran. But hey, it was a job.

***Halloween 4* and *5* focused on young Jamie Lloyd, Michael's niece. She's presumed dead in your script, though she does get a very brief cameo in the virtual reality sequence. Why give such a previously integral character such a small role?**

I wanted to try something different with my *Halloween 6*, which meant doing something without her being the focus. The studio might've also asked that I move on from her character – I don't remember if they did or not. I guess they were okay with it because I never heard anyone complain that I wasn't using her enough.

**The big plot twist of your *Halloween 666* is that Dana turns out to be Michael's other long-lost sister. Tell me about why you chose that direction for the new heroine.**

Back then, the *Halloween* series was all about Michael Myers killing his bloodline. Nowadays, he's back to just being the boogeyman and he can kill anybody he wants. But back then, it was all about the relatives. That was one of the rules. He'd also kill you if you got in his way, but he was intent on killing family members. My way of going along with that was to make the reporter character his sister. I made them related. Back then, that familial connection meant something. Today, no one cares about that. My feeling was and still is – who really gives a shit?

I wanted to focus more on the premise of a reporter going to Haddonfield to investigate how the town has moved on from all the killings. I liked that she came to town with a whole news crew, a bunch of dopey guys that Michael could kill in different ways. One scene I especially liked involved when the news team got their van stuck in a bog and the cameraman goes missing. They can't find him, but they find his camera. They go back to the van and watch what was on the tape and it shows him getting killed. Then his head comes crashing through the window or something. I thought that was good!

**How did the studio respond to these story ideas?**

They seemed okay with them at first, but they later quashed them for being too similar to whatever the most recent *Friday the 13th* was. Turns out that one had a similar premise, some kind of tabloid *Inside Edition* program comes to investigate Jason. And then there's some new family members that come into the picture too. They didn't want to seem like they were copying another franchise.

**Oh yeah – that sounds like *Jason Goes to Hell: The Final Friday*, which would've been released less than a year before your script. How did Moustapha Akkad react to your ideas?**

Let me be clear about that – Moustapha wasn't crazy about my script at all. Miramax liked it, though. We had a notes call on it. Moustapha didn't like that I didn't include the Man in Black in my script. I kind of had Father Carpenter as being him, but that's never really directly shown. My script didn't have enough mythology for Moustapha's liking. But look at the end result, the movie they made with Joe Chappelle. You might say that one has a little too much mythology in it.

**Your ending makes it seem as though Dana and Tommy have vanquished the Shape, but then we see the clock and it's just *past* the midnight hour. Did you have a sequel in mind?**

(groans) No, Miramax wanted to leave it open-ended so they could come back and do another one, so that's how I wrote it. They weren't going to let anyone kill off the Shape for good. But that midnight hour thing is something a lot of people believe. It's just a thing you find in folklore, that some believe it's when spirits cross over into the underworld. I thought it was cool to include.

**Do you have a favorite scene from your script?**

It's so hard to remember all these years later, but there was one scene I liked a lot. Michael Myers was homeless in my script, which is different and a bit kooky. I felt like I needed to address what he does between *Halloween* movies. Where does he go? How does he always get a new mask each year? To answer that, I wrote a scene where he visits a joke shop in Haddonfield to get a new mask. This was going to be my pre-Kevin Williamson wink-wink at the fans in the audience. So Michael is browsing and there's all these Freddy and Jason masks. Then he looks over and sees the pumpkin, skull, and jack-o-lantern masks from *Halloween III: Season of the Witch*. Then he finally sees the classic white Shatner mask and grabs it. To me, these were fun nods to other genre films.

**Speaking of nods, I noticed you also referenced Pinhead and Leatherface!**

Of course! Remember that I'm a huge genre fan. Anything I write is going to have references to that stuff in it. The original *Texas Chain Saw Massacre* is like my *Godfather*. (laughs) At this point,

Miramax and Dimension were already doing all their own *Hellraiser* movies, so I thought it'd be an appropriate little wink-wink to throw Pinhead in there. It's just someone dressed up as him for Halloween, right? I had fun writing that.

**What kind of initial direction did you get from Miramax?**

They wanted to have some kind of virtual reality component in *Halloween 6*. That was just starting to be a craze at the time. I didn't know anything about it, so I had to do some research. That was Bob Weinstein trying to keep up with the times. They also had this idea to tell Michael's origin story, which they felt could connect to the Man in Black. That was a big collective discussion that I had to go along with. In hindsight, why would you ever explain the origin of Michael Myers? No one cares about that. Why not go back to the original? Less is more. He's just the boogeyman.

**How about Moustapha Akkad? Did he offer any direction or guidance?**

Yeah, but not much. One day I got a phone call from Moustapha wanting to know if we could put Tonya Harding in the movie somewhere. Remember her? That whole incident with Nancy Kerrigan wasn't that much earlier from this call. He asked me and I said, '*Yeeeaaah..... sure.*' But I never actually followed through with the request because I wasn't sure if anyone other than him wanted me to do it. Fortunately, it was never mentioned again.

**What would you consider the most challenging part of writing *Halloween 6*?**

Are you kidding? The Man in Black! No one knew who he was. The problem I had in writing *Halloween 6* was that *Halloween 5* had been so terrible. They were just trying to rebound from that. As much as they wanted to put the whole thing to sleep, they couldn't. They needed to explain who he was. I think they'd dug themselves into a bit of hole with that character on *Halloween 5*.

At the end of the day, it was really only Moustapha that cared about doing justice to the Man in Black. He wanted to tie the character into the greater mythology of *Halloween*. The guys at Miramax? They didn't give a shit who he was. But Moustapha had some measure of creative control here, so they had to follow his marching orders. Moustapha, by the way, was nice as pie.

He was a good dude. His son, who produces the series now, was in a lot of these meetings too. He was really young back then. Also a good dude.

**When did you start to realize that your script might not pan out?**

Things fell apart after the notes call with the studio. Gary Fleder left over creative differences and Miramax was not happy about him leaving. This was before Joe Chappelle. I was off the project before he came on. My script was given to other writers to re-write until it became unrecognizable.

**Did you ever see the eventual *Halloween 6* that went to theaters?**

Not only did I see it, but I got to read Daniel Farrands' script before it even came out. The Writer's Guild sent me his script to make sure there wasn't anything in it I'd come up with. If so, I might've gotten credit or residuals or something. Daniel's draft was completely unrecognizable to me. Aside from the return of Tommy Doyle, there was nothing in common between his story and mine. It was completely different. As for the movie itself... you saw it, right? It felt like those guys thought they were making *The English Patient* or something. C'mon! It's a *Halloween*. It's a slasher movie!

**How about the newer films? Did you see *Halloween 2018*?**

I did and was quite entertained by it. But c'mon, it's basically *Halloween H20* all over again, isn't it? It's the exact same movie. *H20* also pretended that the other sequels didn't exist just like the new one does. They've now done that twice. How many times can you possibly get away with that? I guess they figured the new one was being made for an all-new audience that might not've even been born when *H20* came out. I was hoping they would bring back Tommy Doyle again.

**Your script leaked online several years ago, which has allowed *Halloween* fans to read what might've been. As a writer, how do you feel about that getting out?**

My script is online? Really? I didn't know that. I should go download a copy. I'm sure I have a physical copy somewhere, but I'd love a PDF.

# SCOTT SPIEGEL

## Prospective Director - Halloween 666: The Origin

Interviewed by Dustin McNeill

**How did you come to be involved with *Halloween 666*?**

This was right at the start of 1994. I was talking with Richard Gladstein of Miramax/Dimension about what he was up to. He told me he was working with Bob Weinstein to develop the sixth *Halloween*. There was a fleeting moment during this time when it was tossed around that my buddy, Quentin Tarantino, might produce *Halloween 6* and that I might direct it. There has been some confusion online with this, though, because I never wrote a script for it and neither did Quentin, not to my knowledge. I did do a treatment, but not a full script. It takes me eons to write a script. I also got to meet with Moustapha Akkad about possibly directing the movie, which was really cool. I admired the guy very much. It was a wild time.

**I understand they also wanted Lawrence Bender to produce *Halloween 6* as well. You, Quentin, and Lawrence go back a few years. How'd you three become friends?**

Lawrence produced the first movie I ever directed, which was *Intruder*. We've done a few more since then. I was also friends with Quentin back then. Sometime after *Intruder*, Quentin was trying to find a producer to help him make *Reservoir Dogs*. He'd written that one very quickly, in about a month. I introduced him to Lawrence and they hit it off. Next thing you know, Lawrence gets *Reservoir Dogs* into Harvey Keitel's hands and the rest is history. It worked out great. So after that, we were all friends.

**What was your experience with *Halloween* at the time? Were you a fan?**

I was and still am a huge *Halloween* fan, though I haven't seen the latest one with Jamie Lee Curtis back in it. Did you like it?

**I did, but I tend to like most of them, so my opinion doesn't count for much.**

I know, right? I just hear the music and I'm in. I'm easy to please that way. I could nitpick each one, but at the end of the day, I'm just a fan. I swear, I took more people to see the original *Halloween*. That and *Jaws*. Everything about the original *Halloween* just worked so well.

**Was Quentin also a fan?**

Yes, I believe so. I might've been a slightly bigger fan than he was. There was also a time where he was looking at producing a *Friday the 13th* reboot. That would've been just before he came out and produced *Hostel,* which Eli Roth directed. So maybe 2004 or 2005. It was a pretty cool time. He eventually just said, '*I don't need to reboot an existing horror franchise. I've got my own franchise now with Hostel.*' Things worked out quite nicely with him coming onboard that.

**And not only did you produce *Hostel* and *Hostel II*, but you also directed *Hostel III*.**

Yes! That was really great. Eli and Quentin, I can't say enough good things about those guys personally and professionally.

**So you're in talks with Miramax about directing *Halloween 6* and they give you the Phil Rosenberg script to look over. What were your thoughts on it?**

Uh... not all that great. They gave me this script for the film that didn't have anyone's name on it. The opening was a vanishing hitchhiker kind of thing. They did this same kind of setup in 1983's *Nightmares* with Emilio Estevez. There's a girl traveling in a car at night when she hears a news alert about an escaped maniac. Naturally, she's scared. She stops for some gas and the guy filling up her tank starts to creep her out. Suddenly, he uses the nozzle to smash in her back window. We start to think he's trying to attack her. Turns out, Michael Myers is in her back seat. The guy was trying to save her. But the whole thing is a dream and she wakes up. It wasn't done badly here, but it had been done before. But overall, I was not a fan of that script.

I ended up doing something really foolish after I read it. Michael Gingold of *Fangoria* called me to ask what I thought of the script. I very plainly told him I didn't care for it and gave all these reasons why. Little did I realize I was being asked that question on-the-record. My comments later appeared in an issue of *Fangoria*. I was so blindsided by that. I thought we were just having a personal conversation between me and him. After I saw the issue, I thought to myself, '*That's the last time I'll ever tell the truth to a journalist.*' I shouldn't say I was tricked into saying those things, because I definitely wasn't. I've always liked Michael Gingold and I still do. I just should've been a little more savvy on my part. It was a heck of a learning experience. Phil Rosenberg ended up seeing my comments and excoriated me in a letter to the editor. I don't blame him. Looking back on it, I did come off unduly harsh with my criticisms. I think both Phil and Scott Rosenberg are excellent writers. That much is obvious now. At the time, I was just trying to get a handle on the script. I was going through it over and over trying to figure out what we could change to strengthen the story.

**I saw the letter to the editor he wrote. I believe he said something like, "How did Scott Spiegel manage to blow it? Even with the backing of his friend Quentin Tarantino! He's apparently the only person more capable of losing a movie than me."**

That's fair! Spot-on, actually! (laughs) I really did not expect to see my comments about his script printed in *Fangoria*. I wish it hadn't happened that way, although I learned something from it. But again, the whole thing wasn't bad. As I recall, there was an idea he had that Quentin and I had also toyed with about Michael Myers being homeless. That wasn't bad at all. I think Rob Zombie later did something with that, didn't he? I only saw the first Rob Zombie *Halloween*. My thought on that one was, '*Gee, Rob. Why even call this* Halloween? *You've got enough cool ideas here that you could do your own thing.*'

**The *Halloween 666* script contained several controversial elements including virtual reality, which Phil Rosenberg included at the studio's request. What did you make of its inclusion?**

I was just going through some treatments and noticed the virtual reality stuff. It seemed like an effort to bring *Halloween* into the present. That's understandable. I didn't think the element itself was a problem. Sometimes you just need to figure out how to reign in an idea and simplify it. That's what's going to make it work within this franchise. That's the greatest thing about the first film – it was so incredibly simple. The *Halloween* series isn't as great when it gets complicated.

**You mentioned meeting with Moustapha Akkad. What was your impression of him?**

Sorry, I don't do impressions. That was such a bad joke. *That was so lame!* (laughs) My meeting with Moustapha was nerve-wracking. That man was partly responsible for one of my favorite films of all time. Sam Raimi and I would constantly do impressions of Donald Pleasence in *Halloween*. And here I am meeting with one of the men behind that film and all the ones that came after. In some very important ways, *Dawn of the Dead* and *Halloween* begat *Evil Dead*.

Moustapha was wonderful, but I could feel at the time that I was only one of several people they were considering to direct. They wanted someone who could expand on the Rosenberg script and get it to where they wanted it. I was trying to do that without much luck. I was trying to reign it in. I eventually came up with a treatment, but it was too late. They informed me they were already going in a much different direction with it. So I lost out on that one. But Miramax did offer me a consolation prize to direct instead. They offered me *Children of the Corn IV*, the one that had Naomi Watts in it – one of her most important roles that launched her into the big time. (laughs) I was like, '*Well, crud.*'

**Wait, I don't remember you directing a *Children of the Corn* sequel?**

That's because I turned it down. I wasn't gonna do that, which is weird because I was flat broke at the time. What a joke I was! I could've been directing Naomi Watts had I taken that job! My feeling at the time was that I didn't really want to be directing a fifth or sixth sequel unless it was going to be *Halloween*. I was okay doing first or second follow-ups like on *From Dusk Till Dawn* and *Hostel*, but not a sixth movie.

## Press Pass

**DANA CHILDRESS**
NAME

Doyle House
1530 N. Orange
Grove Avenue

## COULD IT HAPPEN AGAIN?

Channel Six Investigative Reporter Dana Childress is on location in Haddonfield, Illinois for the anniversaries of the 1978, 1988, and 1989 Halloween slaughters by escaped killer Michael Myers. Join Dana as she speaks with survivors and residents about how the town has moved on and whether or not Michael is still out there.

### SPECIAL REPORT TONIGHT
### ON THE CHANNEL SIX NIGHTLY NEWS
### 6:00 & 11:00 PM

SR-3457-78000 B

# EVIDENCE

Description  Butcher knife          Case No.  SR-78000

Officer  S. Nelson          Item No.  A45-000043

Department  HADDONFIELD POLICE

✂ **TO REMOVE CONTENTS CUT ALONG BOTTOM DOTTED LINE**          SPECIAL FORENSICS

# HALLOWEEN 666

## THE ORIGIN OF MICHAEL MYERS

45 Lampkin Lane has new owners.
But not for long…

**Screenplay by**
**Irving Belateche**
**& Lawrence Guterman**

By late April 1994, Phil Rosenberg's *Halloween 666* was dead in the water – as was the overall project itself. In the wake of Gary Fleder's exit, Miramax had tried unsuccessfully to attach Quentin Tarantino to the sequel. Though the *Pulp Fiction* filmmaker would decline involvement, he did recommend pal Scott Spiegel for the director's chair. But while Spiegel had easily secured Bob Weinstein's vote of confidence, he was unable to win over Moustapha Akkad. Not only that, but Akkad had overwhelmingly hated Rosenberg's screenplay. Spiegel himself disliked the material and would soon depart the project. With no director or mutually agreed-upon script, this sequel might've seemed destined to languish in development hell. But Weinstein wasn't about to let that happen to his newly acquired franchise. Thus, it was time for fresh blood.

The Dimension boss felt that a proper re-write might fix the issues of the Rosenberg draft. Furthermore, a re-write might also satisfy his counterpart at Trancas International. Akkad felt likewise and had even offered Spiegel the opportunity. (He declined.) Like Rosenberg himself, the two writers eventually chosen for the job would be complete industry novices without a feature credit to their name. Irving Belateche and Lawrence Guterman were both film students in the Master's Program at the University of Southern California. The pair had recently landed on Weinstein's radar after having written a spec script for an episode of *Tales from the Crypt*, which executive producer Robert Zemeckis was poised to direct. While the episode never panned out, their proposed script was good enough for Zemeckis to share with Weinstein. (Recall that Weinstein previously hired Gary Fleder based on his own *Tales from the Crypt* episode.) Impressed by the strength of their writing, he offered them the gig. The only catch was that they had a scant ten days to complete their work.

Yet even still, creative disagreements persisted between Weinstein and Akkad. The same feuding producers that could not agree on the merits of the Rosenberg draft could also not agree on what marching orders to give Belateche and Guterman. Prior to starting work, the pair met with Weinstein and Akkad individually and subsequently received different – and even conflicting – instructions on how to improve the existing draft. Weinstein continued to push for the inclusion of virtual reality while Akkad sought to address the Man in Black storyline. Unlike Rosenberg, neither Belateche nor Guterman were particularly big *Halloween* fans though they were familiar with the original. While Weinstein had advocated for a light re-write, the writers instead chose to completely re-imagine Rosenberg's script. Their first and only draft – dated May 1994 – would be titled *Halloween 666: The Origin of Michael Myers.*

## THE STORY

This new *Halloween 666* opens on a decrepit-looking Myers house, which has remained unoccupied for decades; its outer walls graffitied to read "Evil" and "House of Death" in blood-red paint. Suddenly, carpenters and painters descend upon the property. The opening credits play over a montage of the house being restored to its original condition. As the credits end, we meet new owner Jake Ferguson and his seventeen-year-old daughter Dana. Both are newly arrived in-town with Jake having found employment as a janitor at Haddonfield High, which is inherently embarrassing for Dana as she starts her senior year at a new school. With Halloween just days away, they place a festive pumpkin on the front porch.

The story then cuts to the darkened basement of nearby Decatur Sanitarium where four orderlies are engaged in a late-night card game. In an adjacent room, we see "The Stranger" from *Halloween 5* visiting a comatose patient in a makeshift hospital room. On TV, a news report announces that Haddonfield is lifting its longtime ban on Halloween. This news reawakens something within the Shape, who rises from his bed. He goes into the next room and shish kabobs three of the men's heads on his IV poles before stabbing a syringe into the fourth orderly's jugular. The Shape later interrupts a carjacking at a local 7-11, slaughtering the criminal before taking the vintage Chevy Nova for himself. As he pulls onto the highway, he passes a sign - "Haddonfield - 29 Miles Away."

Dana attends her first day at Haddonfield High and finds an insufferably obnoxious student body – save for nice guy Johnny. The most popular girl is the bitchy Sabrina, who manipulates and degrades others for pleasure. Hailing from a rich family, her bad behavior is seemingly beyond reproach. Sabrina is planning a massive party to commemorate Haddonfield unbanning Halloween. (Dana knows not of the ban nor the town's horrific past nor who once lived in her home.) We soon catch up with Tommy Doyle from the original, now a twenty-seven-year-old hermit. Sabrina's parents allow Tommy to rent their spare garage, though she and her friends bully him mercilessly. They've even nicknamed him "Too Slow Tommy" due to a childhood speech impediment. Tommy's garage-apartment is littered with Myers-related research and his main hobby involves a high-tech virtual reality system.

Curious about the town's history, Dana stays after school to research Michael Myers in the library. While leaving school, Dana fears she is being stalked by Tommy Doyle, who has rather creepily warned her against living in the house at 45 Lampkin Lane. (In actuality, this is the Shape.) Dana returns home to find her room torn apart and the words "Get out!" scrawled on her wall in red paint. It's here that Jake confesses he secretly knew he was buying the Myers house. Not surprisingly, she's upset that he withheld this information from her. Elsewhere, Tommy visits an elderly Dr. Loomis, whom he hasn't seen since that fateful night in 1978. Upon hearing Tommy's plea for help, Loomis begrudgingly agrees to warn the new residents of the Myers house.

Loomis first visits the Haddonfield Library to research ancient texts on Samhain. He learns that evil spirits rise out of the earth once a year, creating a multi-dimensional portal. If someone or something were forced into this portal before midnight on Halloween, it would be permanently vanquished to the underworld. He and Tommy theorize that this doorway may exist within the Myers house. Before they can discuss further, Sabrina's friends kidnap Tommy for their party, assaulting Loomis in the process. Tommy is thrown inside a cage and cruelly mocked by drunken attendees. They even plan to stone him, albeit with plastic rocks. Fortunately, he's saved by Dana before he endures any real harm. Having already encountered the Shape with Johnny, a terrified Dana reluctantly teams with Tommy and Loomis to find the portal inside her home. Using Tommy's tricked-out virtual reality system, they deduce that it must be inside Dana's closet.

Meanwhile, the Shape crashes Sabrina's Halloween party, slaughtering guests in a massive kill sequence. He soon finds Dana, Tommy, and Loomis inside the garage. Tossing Loomis and Tommy aside like rag dolls, the Shape chases Dana back to 45 Lampkin Lane. It's here that Haddonfield's law enforcement attempt to stop the slasher, though their bullets have little effect. A brutal fight unfolds inside the Myers house with Dana shoving her attacker through the portal just as the clock strikes midnight - vanquishing him. ("Go to hell, fucker!")

Later in the night, Loomis inspects the renovated Myers house, which is now wrecked from the carnage. It's here he has a chilling realization – the clock in Dana's bedroom is five-minutes slow, meaning the Shape entered the portal *after midnight*. A look of concern falls across his face. Elsewhere, we see a lifeless body being dragged along by an unseen figure. We soon recognize the figure as "The Stranger." He picks up the lifeless body, whom we realize is the Shape, and walks off into the night undetected.

## MOVING INTO THE HOUSE OF DEATH

The first thing to note about this re-written *Halloween 666* is that Phil Rosenberg's name is missing from the title page – and it's easy to see why. This is a complete reinvention of his screenplay. Sure, certain elements transfer over such as virtual reality and the portal – but the characters and circumstances are all so very different. Nary a single original character from the initial draft carries over to this one. At best, Rosenberg might have deserved a "story by" nod. At worst, a "special thanks" in the credits. Even a cursory glance at these two screenplays reveals far more differences than similarities.

Whereas Rosenberg focused on a twenty-something reporter named Dana Childress, the Belateche/Guterman script follows a high school senior named Dana Ferguson. Apart from the first name, these two characters have nothing in common. Unlike her Rosenberg counterpart, this Dana lacks a mole-sporting grandmother or secret familial connection to the Myers clan. Instead, she's a new arrival in town – an automatic social outsider. Strongly evoking Laurie Strode, Dana is shy, quiet, and noticeably repressed – qualities that seem prevalent in *Halloween*'s final girls. There's even the requisite bit where she notices the Shape watching from outside her classroom. Spunky and resourceful, Dana also proves to be a fair match for the slasher. At one point, she rips off a piece of staircase banister in order to beat her attacker with it. (You go, girl!)

As an aside, it appears the final film's Kara Strode owes much to her predecessors. In a departure from the genre standard, Kara is not a teenager but an adult (Rosenberg) while also being the newest resident of the Shape's former home (Belateche/Guterman). Unlike the final film, however, Dana shares a close relationship with her good-natured, if not goofy, father Jake, who always strives to find the silver-lining in their new situation. Though doting, he is away for much of the finale, having found a date in Ms. Mandel, the school librarian.

Belateche and Guterman manage an impressive feat in their *Halloween 666* by making the popular kids at Haddonfield High among the most utterly revolting characters in the entire series. Remember the abusive John Strode from the actual *Halloween 6*? Or Ronnie White from the 2007 remake? The high schoolers in *Halloween 666* are so much worse. It's as if Rob Zombie directed an episode of *Beverly Hills 90210* with zero fucks to give. It's noted the lead popular girl, Sabrina, recently enjoyed a nose-job and drives a BMW to school. Given that, it might not come as a surprise that she's wildly disrespectful, abusive, and woefully entitled. Sabrina is so depraved that she doesn't even run away at first when the Shape begins slaughtering her friends. Rather she

actually pauses to watch the spectacle unfold, mesmerized "like a kid watching a fly have its limbs plucked off." This, of course, makes her eventual death extremely satisfying. But by the time that happens, you've already been rooting – nay – *begging* for the Shape to do something.

We later come to realize the full extent of Sabrina's depravity with a twisted stunt she has planned for her Halloween party. The idea is to trap "Too Slow Tommy" inside a cage and taunt him. One of her gal pals has even rehearsed a sleazy striptease to mock his imprisonment. ("Oh, Tommy, baby. Do you want it? Honey? Tell momma what you want… 'cause you're not gonna get anything from me, you stupid freak!") As if making fun of someone for a speech impediment isn't bad enough, these out-of-control teenagers literally kidnap Tommy. And if *that* isn't bad enough, they kick a frail Loomis in the stomach while doing so. It's way over the line. But, as we'll explore later, Sabrina and her friends all get their well-deserved comeuppance in the end.

Speaking of Tommy Doyle, he's a bit of a cowardly loser in this version – not that he deserves to be locked in a cage for that. Living in a garage-apartment that might as well be a cage, he's only ever heroic inside the world of his virtual reality system. In true reality, his only friend is a pet iguana named Earl and he rides around town on a green motor scooter. (Fret not, Earl survives to the end. If Earl were a dog, it might be a different story.) While Tommy is slow at interpersonal communication, he's pretty quick to yell creepy warnings at people buying

Halloween costumes. ("It's the biggest mistake you'll ever make! You think I'm nuts, but I'm not!") Yes, Tommy has effectively become the "Crazy Ralph" of Haddonfield. He ducks out early in the finale, tossed aside by the Shape, and therefore plays no role in forcing his nemesis into the portal. Given all this, Paul Rudd's Tommy Doyle suddenly seems like a total badass – stopping evil with magical acorns and beating the Shape silly with a lead pipe. Looking back, the character wasn't even this meek in the Rosenberg draft.

A more obvious (and age appropriate) love interest for Dana is Johnny, the lone exception to Sabrina's otherwise terrible social circle. Though he does mingle with Sabrina's ilk, he remains friendly with Dana, even suggesting the two enjoy a coffee date together. Later, he visits Dana at home to invite her to Sabrina's party, though the two are attacked by the Shape. The slasher lifts Johnny in the air and sends him crashing into a far wall before chasing after Dana. Upon her escape – a tense scene mirroring the rooftop chase of *Halloween 4* – Dana manages to track down the local sheriff. But returning to the Myers house, there is no trace of Johnny – his body missing. Thus, we never actually learn what happened to the poor lad. Curiously, he's never referred to afterward though it seems unlikely he made it out unscathed. (Surely, the writers would've expanded upon this in later drafts.)

Not unlike the Rosenberg draft, this re-written *Halloween 666* has quite a bit in common with the eventually made *Halloween 6*. Both this and the Joe Chappelle film feature a new family moving into the renovated Myers house. In both stories, the patriarch knows of its unseemly history but has chosen to withhold that information from their families. Both stories also find Dr. Loomis officially retired and living in solitude. When he does eventually return to Haddonfield, he's warned by the new sheriff not to provoke a public panic. There's even a similar kill with this draft and the theatrical cut of *Halloween 6* where the Shape violently forces someone's body through metal bars. (*Yuck.*)

The Belateche/Guterman draft sees fit to drop the whole Sacral King backstory that originated with Rosenberg. The otherworldly portal as a means to vanquish the Shape still remains, however. In the Rosenberg script, the heroes had to push the Shape into the portal during the midnight hour. Yet in this re-written draft, they must push him in *before* midnight. Belateche and Guterman change not only the rules of the portal but its location as well. Rosenberg placed the portal beneath Judith Myers' headstone while Belateche/Guterman move it into her old bedroom closet. In what seems like an inside joke, the new writers make reference to the Rosenberg draft with a line from Loomis: "Most people believe the portal is in a graveyard, but I've examined Haddonfield's cemeteries. I've spent many a Halloween waiting… for nothing."

This re-written *Halloween 666* scores major points for its blockbuster finale. Not that the original *Halloween 666*'s graveyard ending was lacking. Belateche and Guterman simply kick it up a few notches. Their screenplay winds up back at the Myers house with the Shape chasing Dana, who needs to somehow force her attacker into the portal upstairs. Their scuffle through the house makes for one serious knock-down, drag-out fight. At one point, Dana smashes a sink overtop the slasher's skull. As written here, the actual "into the portal" bit would've required one hell of an effects budget. See below:

> *"An unbelievable array of forces is unleashed – amorphous demons and spirits come shooting through the portal from every direction – crying, screeching, begging. The noise is deafening as Dana shoots to the back of the room, grabbing onto her bed. Lightning explodes from the closet, arcing throughout the room.*
>
> *Now all the spirits seem to have a face – twisted, contorted in unbelievable terror and pain, roaring and bellowing in agony. For an instant, we recognize Michael's older sister from H1 and other victims, hands reaching out from thine gaseous arms, enveloping Myers. Myers' hands grope and grasp frantically, trying desperately to get out of the closet. The demons circle and swirl, hundreds of them now. Enshrouding Michael Myers completely. Grabbing and clawing, pulling him deeper and deeper until, with one concerted effort, they combine to yank the monster into the depths of the portal. An ungodly howl of pain emerges from the flailing monster descending into oblivion.*

Whereas the Rosenberg draft packed in references to *Halloween 4* and *5*, the Belateche/Guterman script makes little effort to connect with the preceding films. Its writers fail to even mention little Jamie Lloyd, whom we last saw crying in the massacred police station of *Halloween 5*. The Man in Black does return for two brief appearances, but we learn nothing new about his identity or intentions. It's almost comical how this draft kicks that narrative chore forward to *Halloween 7* rather than simply handling it here and now. Of course, some of this might owe to the screenwriters' admitted unfamiliarity with the series. This might also explain why a supporting character is named Tina, which would've been odd given that *Halloween 5* already gave us a fairly memorable Tina. (C'mon, screenwriters. "Be sensible.")

Having said that, this draft packs a much-welcome reference to *Halloween III*. After escaping the party cage, Tommy and Dana rush to the former's garage-apartment to find Dr. Loomis tied to a chair with a pumpkin mask over his head. This strongly evokes the image of Tom Atkins' Dr. Challis tied to a chair with a skull mask over his head. (Recall that Rosenberg also planted a *Halloween III* reference in the first draft of his *Halloween 666*.) Oh – and once again, we have a sequel titled *Halloween 666* despite that number having no actual relevance to the plot. In fact, it has even less relevance here than in the Rosenberg version. In the original script, the Shape scrawls the mark of the beast on the side of a news van. In this re-written story, the numbers never come up at all. But *hey* – it would've still looked cool on a poster, are we right?

## A TOWN LESS DIVIDED

It's interesting how the community of Haddonfield changes from the Rosenberg draft to this one. Rosenberg's Haddonfield is a more somber town, still grieving the massacres of years past. The recent decision to lift the ban on Halloween has proven controversial among its citizens. Not so much in the Belateche/Guterman script. In this re-write, Haddonfield welcomes Halloween back with open arms. The residents hang banners in the town square hyping what will surely be the best celebration ever, "a Halloween worth waiting five years for!" It's all a bit distasteful and that seems to be exactly the point. The town may claim the ban was lifted to encourage civic pride, but it's more about economic opportunity. There's good money to be made from selling costumes, candy, and decorations. It's as if Haddonfield had elected the mayor from *Jaws*. At one point, a character tries explaining the town's obsession by likening it to alcohol after the fall of prohibition.

This greed-over-respect approach to lifting the Halloween ban ties into a larger theme within the story about privilege and entitlement. Certainly, the obnoxious cast of high schoolers do as well. They couldn't care less about those who tragically died in years past. This is all very intentional and thematically sound. If Haddonfield hadn't resurrected Halloween, the Shape would still be slumbering in the basement of Decatur Sanitarium. The town has only its own lack of respect to blame for luring the Shape out of retirement to dispense their comeuppance. (And let's be clear about that – he does *not* return to Haddonfield because someone moved into his old home. He returns after hearing a news broadcast about the ban being lifted. There just happens to be someone living in his old home and that *also* pisses him off.)

It all brings to mind the old adage, "Those who forget the past are doomed to repeat it," which was something most endearing about the Rosenberg draft's Haddonfield. Those citizens had not forgotten the past, not entirely. Sure, the younger generation in that script only wanted to resume celebrating Halloween, but the older generations couldn't move on, especially those who lost loved ones. Instead of handing out candy on October 31st, they burned memorial candles in their windows. That kind of reverence is sorely missing in the Belateche/Guterman re-write. The only notable opposition to the ban being lifted comes from Tommy, who expresses himself like a lunatic by yelling into crowds of people buying costumes.

While Tommy and Loomis carry over from the original screenplay, Sheriff Meeker does not. Recall that Meeker was among those who felt stabbed in the back by Haddonfield bringing back Halloween. Instead, he's replaced in the re-write by Sheriff Bill Dogan, who does at least make passing mention of his dislike for the town's decision. Astonishingly, he becomes the third Haddonfield sheriff in the series to not take Loomis seriously. (Did Dr. Loomis terrorize Haddonfield by crying wolf in the years between *Halloween* movies or something? Why will no one ever believe him!?)

**Sheriff Dogan**: *"Listen, Loomis. I didn't want Halloween back in Haddonfield, but I had no choice. The newcomers want their fun like any other town. There's no reason for you to come here and stir up any more of a brouhaha. Listen, Loomis! No brouhaha, got it? You ain't gonna be fightin' any final battles in Haddonfield. And you, Tommy, you don't be botherin' that new family. They've already been on the receiving end of enough Halloween tricks."*

For Brackett and Meeker, the cost of that mistake would be their own daughters' lives. Here, we never learn if Sheriff Dogan has kids, but he does lose his own life by script's end. Driving past Sabrina's house, he notices the Shape charging after Dana on the front lawn. Though stunned, Dogan quickly retrieves his gun and repeatedly fires upon the attacking slasher. The damage, however, does not affect the Shape's mobility and, soon enough, there are no bullets left to shoot. As we follow Dana running towards the Myers house, we can hear Sheriff Dogan's blood-curdling screams in the background.

## THE SHAPE

As with the town of Haddonfield, Belateche and Guterman offer a different take on the Shape than Rosenberg did previously. The original *Halloween 666* found the slasher living as a vagrant, sleeping on the street and, occasionally, in a homeless shelter. (Just picture Rob Zombie's *Halloween II* and you've got it.) This re-written *Halloween 666* finds the seemingly comatose Shape slumbering in the basement of Decatur Sanitarium under the watchful eye of the Man in Black. (This does beg the question – why the previously unknown Decatur Sanitarium and not, say, the more familiar Smith's Grove?) We initially find the Shape unmasked, though he's in full get-up a short while later when he carjacks his way to Haddonfield.

We ascertain from janitorial staff chit-chat that the Shape has been kept in the asylum's basement for the past five years, essentially since the events of *Halloween 5*. He's connected to an IV drip, though its contents are a mystery. This begs a few more questions. How does the menial staff of Decatur Sanitarium know there's a random coma patient kept in the basement? And how have they not blabbed? And how did the Man in Black even secure this peculiar arrangement? One could say this actually isn't all that different from Joe Chappelle's *Halloween 6* where Dr. Wynn kept the Shape in the basement of Smith's Grove, though we doubt the janitors there knew a secret cult had taken root downstairs.

Belateche and Guterman put forth one of the most unstoppable and physically resilient depictions of the slasher we've ever seen. Yes, the Shape has already walked away from multiple bullets, beatings, and fires – but like in Shem Bitterman's *Halloween 5*, the damage in *Halloween 666* seems so much worse. Most notably, he survives an onslaught of bullets fired point-blank in the final act, which cause extensive damage. ("A hole is torn in his abdomen. Pieces of arm and leg come spraying off. But he keeps advancing.")

One eerily great but brief moment worth mentioning is the scene in which the Shape first returns home upon reaching Haddonfield. It's after nightfall and Dana is preparing dinner with her father. Michael stands outside the house and watches through the kitchen window. We not only witness the Shape react to having strangers in his home – we also *hear* it. ("Even through the mask, we can detect a confusion, a mounting anger. His throaty breathing increases in intensity.")

Another question begged by this *Halloween 666* re-write is whether or not the Shape is working alone. We only see the Man in Black in the opening and closing scenes, but it would seem that *someone* was assisting in his carnage. Just prior to Sabrina's party, the Shape shoves a girl through the metal bars of the cage, resulting in a gory pile. Yet her mangled remains are gone that evening when the party kicks off. Did we somehow miss the Shape huddled over with paper towels and trash bags to clean such a mess? We might also wonder how no one discovered the body of Tina – a friend of Sabrina's – left in the driver's ed classroom at Haddonfield High. Or how Johnny inexplicably disappeared after his attack. These events might've provided other interesting opportunities for the Man in Black to step in. Because the writers never spell out his motive nor reveal his identity, we're ultimately left unsure as to the extent of his involvement.

If *Halloween 5* established anything about the character, it was that – for reasons then unknown – the Man in Black worked as a sort of protector for the Shape. This is supported by the jail breakout and, now, his years-long tenure nursing the slasher back to health. What this draft establishes on its own is that, to some degree, the character not only has the power to protect and care for the Shape but the ability to relinquish control and even *encourage* his attacks. In turn, he's even more "the man behind the curtain" than we knew previously. Of course, this take on his role would reach the final film, but it technically originates here – and though it's greatly underexplored, it's interesting to question the implications. How much power does the Man in Black actually hold? What vendetta would he have against Haddonfield and its celebrations to relinquish control after all this time? And what is the connection to Samhain? With these questions unanswered, one can't help but wonder how this role might've played out with future follow-ups.

## VIRTUAL REALITY 2.0

Among the Rosenberg draft's most criticized elements was virtual reality, which he only included at the personal suggestion of Bob Weinstein. In asking Belateche and Guterman to re-write *Halloween 666*, the Miramax boss requested they find a way to keep this odd element. And indeed, they do – all the while changing how it's incorporated into the narrative. Recall that Rosenberg, an admitted layman with VR-technology, had somewhat illogically utilized it as a magical window into the past. Fortunately, Guterman had some experience in this area. Upon graduating from Harvard, he went to work for Pacific Data Images in computer animation. Having relevant knowledge of the technology, Guterman was able to scale back the role of virtual reality within the story to a more grounded depiction. (As an aside, he would later direct several sequences for DreamWorks Animation's *Antz* in 1998.)

In the Rosenberg draft, Tommy likens his VR-system to a "high-tech Ouija board" that allows you to go places you shouldn't be able to. This re-write nixes all of that. Instead, the writers have Tommy utilize his system to search a virtual reality blueprint of the Myers house. (Do such blueprints exist? No, of course not. But it's a more realistic depiction than using VR to spy on the ancient festival of Samhain.) Why search a virtual blueprint? Because Loomis theorizes the netherworld portal may be somewhere in the house and it's far too dangerous to search the actual house given the Shape's return. They do eventually find the portal after Dana notices a strange discrepancy between her actual bedroom and its depiction in the blueprint. (Fun fact: Per Loomis' research, the foundation of the Myers house was laid on October 31, 1926 because why not?)

## CRASHING THE PARTY

If one were to rank the most memorable sequences from the *Halloween 666* re-write, the party massacre at Sabrina's house would likely rate number one. We've become accustomed in this franchise to the Shape lurking in the shadows and only attacking isolated groups of people. The party massacre sequence abandons that modus operandi. Here, the Shape slaughters an entire party full of people with onlookers aplenty. The original Rosenberg draft featured a similar house party, though the Shape never went full-on berserker. Rather he stalked silently throughout the house with everyone assuming him to be one of their costumed peers. He does that same stalking in this draft, but he's triggered into attacking upon encountering "False Myers," a teen dressed up like the Shape. ("Dude! We're two of a kind!") He goes to high-five the actual Shape, who leaves him hanging. (Party foul!) The real slasher instead goes for False Myers' blade, which he plunges into the imposter's stomach before tearing upwards to his neck. And so the massacre begins. The start of this encounter, with a puzzled Shape encountering a Shape imposter, strongly brings to mind Busta Rhymes' bit from *Halloween: Resurrection*. ("Your shit ain't workin' up there?")

The appeal of this wondrous sequence isn't just that the Shape is creatively slaughtering en masse. It's that these victims are the same obnoxious, privileged scumbags that kidnapped Tommy and caged him for fun. Simply put, these kids had it coming. In preparing for the party, Sabrina settles on a '70s theme. Why? To mark "the Halloween to end all Halloweens," of course. Yes, Haddonfield's resident wench aims to "honor" the 1978 murders – a further joke at Tommy's expense. Visual barrage of clogs and bell bottoms aside, this is an opportunity to see Michael Myers at his most creative, violently-speaking. He first skewers several partiers with fondue pokers before impaling a couple, causing them to be "stuck together for eternity in a death embrace." Advancing through the house, the Shape encounters Sabrina's parents, who we find to be just as terrible as she is. The slasher kills them both with a giant disco ball to the skull. He next shoves a football trophy down a teenage male's throat.

This gonzo sequence does recycle one kill from the original Rosenberg draft. The Shape grabs hold of Sabrina's terrified boyfriend and shoves keg tubing down his throat. Pumping the keg forcefully, his stomach fills with beer until it's grotesquely distended, ultimately killing him. Sabrina watches her boyfriend die not in horror, shock, or sadness – but in curious disgust and fascination. This only adds to the lack of empathy we feel a moment later when the Shape finally catches up to her. A brief chase in the house leads outside where Sabrina – wearing clogs – trips on a groove in the driveway. The Shape towers over her. With nowhere to run, and as a last resort, she unhooks her bra and begins coaxing the slasher. ("You want some of this, handsome?") It's here Sabrina dies by having a kitchen knife forced through her mouth and out the back of her head – a moment that would've surely inspired cheers from the audience.

## LOOMIS BACK IN ACTION

Whereas the Rosenberg script only featured Dr. Loomis in a fleeting cameo, the Belateche/Guterman version upgrades him to a major supporting role. In addition to the expanded screentime, the returning franchise hero also fares a little better in this draft, at least where his sanity is concerned. Previously a patient at Smith's Grove in Rosenberg's take, he's now simply retired and living in solitude – much like in the actual *Halloween* 6. One area where the previous draft wins out over the re-write involves the doctor's conscience. In the Rosenberg script, Loomis believed Michael's reign of terror to have ended with the presumed death of Jamie Lloyd. Per this rationale, there was just no more fight left – a noble defeat. Yet in this re-write, Loomis has fled Haddonfield as a means of escaping his demons. He's just plain given up on stopping his former patient from hurting anyone else – a cowardly retreat. As he explains to Tommy, "Take it from an old warrior. You can only fight a battle so long. Then it begins to take its toll. Using man's way to fight evil is a hard battle, indeed." This kind of defeated take on Loomis is a bit harder to root for.

If either of these *Halloween* 666 drafts misses a golden opportunity, it's that they never allow Loomis a reunion with the Shape. (For what it's worth, nor does the actual *Halloween* 6. The two just never cross each other's path onscreen.) Not only was actor Donald Pleasence the longest serving cast member in the franchise by this time, but his character also had the longest history with the Shape among anyone else in the sequel. A one-on-one encounter along the lines of *Halloween 4* ("Don't go back to Haddonfield.") or *Halloween 5* ("Go home, Michael. She'll be there.") would've played very nicely here. Instead, Loomis watches his old nemesis burst into Tommy's garage-apartment. He immediately goes for his revolver, but the Shape is quicker – throwing the old man out into the street like trash. Despite this shortcoming, the character does receive several new lines in his classic style. ("The evil is upon us now...")

Something else to be said about Loomis' depiction here is that both his and Tommy's paranoia appears unfounded. It's no wonder authorities put little stock in their "He's back!" claims. There is nothing in this draft to indicate the Shape's presence in Haddonfield. No bodies. No news reports. No psychic little girl having spasm attacks. The town isn't even aware of the slasher's escape from the asylum as his presence there was generally unknown – mere gossip fodder for the janitors. The audience knows of his return, of course, but neither Tommy nor Loomis should be so adamantly sure. Were it not that she be attacked *late* in the evening, Dana would have every reason to dismiss these two as quacks. All this makes their outbursts – and grand-scheme VR-plan – sound just a bit premature.

## WHY IT WASN'T MADE

Undeterred by production woes, Bob Weinstein hoped to have *Halloween 666* in theaters by October 1994. That the proposed release date was only six months away meant that time was of the essence. Simply put, the project could no longer languish in development hell. A version of this script needed to go before cameras – *and soon*. In a sly effort to deter Moustapha Akkad from scrutinizing the writers' work, the Dimension boss concocted a scheme. Per Weinstein's plan, both he and Akkad would be subject to a personal $10,000 fine each time one spoke to the writers; the idea being that, with such a penalty, only the most crucial of notes would be given to Belateche and Guterman. This would therefore limit the influence of Akkad whose vocal dissatisfaction with the Rosenberg script had already prevented that version from reaching cinemas in the intended timeframe. But Akkad was not one to be provoked into such an agreement. Furthermore, he was still unhappy with the re-written script.

It was during these continued story discussions that Weinstein quickly moved to fill the vacant director's chair. To this end, he settled on filmmaker Matthew Patrick and, somewhat surprisingly, Akkad approved of his choice. Patrick had landed on Miramax's radar based on the strength of his 1989 thriller *Hider in the House* starring Gary Busey, Mimi Rogers and Michael McKean. Prior to this, he had already started turning heads in Hollywood with his critically acclaimed short films, one of which – *Triptych* – had won a Student Academy Award in 1978. He would later score an actual Oscar nomination with his 1985 short *Graffiti*. Had Patrick remained onboard the troubled sequel, he would've notably become the first Oscar-nominated director to helm a *Halloween* film.

Once hired, Patrick immediately flew to Salt Lake City to jump-start production. (This was where the previous two films had lensed due to valuable tax incentives.) Efforts on the new sequel were now roaring at breakneck pace. Patrick began working with a location scout to help recreate the town of Haddonfield. The producers also secured a production warehouse with adjoining offices to work from. Among the first crew hired was cinematographer Billy Dickson whom Patrick had recently worked with on 1993's *Night Owl*. The project was also assigned a casting director who soon began auditioning local actors for the lead roles. For the briefest moment in time, it seemed like this *Halloween 666* was actually shaping up to become a reality – except that Akkad and Weinstein *still* hadn't finalized the Belateche/Guterman script. The project was now greenlit and spending real production dollars – *without an agreed-upon screenplay.*

Not surprisingly, it was Weinstein's desire to forge ahead with this re-written draft in its current form. Akkad, however, still requested further changes before giving his blessing to the project. Yet neither producer actually reached out to the writers to request further modifications. In fact, neither Guterman nor Belateche ever heard back from anyone on the ultimate fate of their screenplay. To further complicate matters, the project's latest director wasn't happy with the script either. In his own words, Patrick claimed that the Belateche/Guterman draft "was not finished."

"[The producers] got the 'go ahead' to do this project in the latter part of 1993, hoping for a 1994 release. They had something like five to six writers working on several drafts of a script, but the ideas were nothing more than Michael Myers wandering around Haddonfield and ending up at a '70s party where he kills kids with fondue sticks. That didn't fly with the producers."

- Daniel Farrands, Shivers Magazine

Looking to appease both producers, Patrick devised an alternate revision. Whereas the Belateche/Guterman script featured a fleeting scene in which Tommy is ridiculed upon being caged in Sabrina's backyard, Patrick's idea – which he seemingly fashioned into his own script – would've seen Tommy literally *living* in a cage of sorts. Equally paranoid as in previous drafts, this Tommy Doyle would've hidden himself away in a custom-built saferoom in constant fear of the Shape's return. Also similar to previous drafts, a female lead would be introduced, teaming up with Tommy to vanquish the boogeyman by story's end.

Patrick's revision of the Belateche/Guterman script seemed to be the winning choice, yet tensions on the project began to rise sharply. This was triggered by a sudden breakdown in communciation between Weinstein and Akkad. Seeking allies on the project, Weinstein pressed Patrick to declare where his true loyalty resided - at Dimension or at Trancas. Meanwhile, production was careening toward the start of filming without having been fully cast. Then – with only two weeks left until cameras rolled – the project was abruptly canceled and thrown back into development. (Oddly enough, this wouldn't be the last time a *Halloween* was canceled so perilously close to filming.) Frustrated and disheartened, Matthew Patrick quit the project, though cinematographer Billy Dickson remained on to eventually work with new director Joe Chappelle.

As for why the project was canceled, it's not entirely clear. It seems likely that Akkad – still dissatisfied with the script – may have stood his ground, demanding that Dimension execs more closely follow his orders as owner of the franchise. Thus, production was now back at square one. The next month – June 1994 – Daniel Farrands would be brought onboard to offer a new take, having already pitched to Akkad four years prior. While his draft would include many elements from his predecessors' work, he would go to much greater lengths to align his story with the previous films. (This meant addressing the fate of Jamie Lloyd while also providing an explanation for the Man in Black and Thorn symbol.)

As for this unmade entry's writers, Irving Belateche would go onto a career in screenwriting before joining the University of Southern California as a Professor of Cinematic Arts. Lawrence Guterman would also enjoy a varied career directing for screens both big and small. His feature credits include family-comedies such as 2001's *Cats & Dogs* and 2005's *Son of the Mask*.

# interview:
# IRVING BELATECHE
## Co-writer - Halloween 666: The Origin of Michael Myers

Interviewed by Travis Mullins

**First things first, how'd you land *Halloween 666*? Were you a fan of the series?**

I landed the job of writing *Halloween* off a *Tales from the Crypt* script, which I'd written with a writing partner [Larry Guterman]. Bob Weinstein read the *Tales* script and called us in to pitch a take on *Halloween 6*. I was a huge fan of *Halloween*, so I couldn't believe that I was going to be a part of the franchise. A good friend of mine – who loved horror films – convinced me to see the first *Halloween* with him and from then on, I was a fan of the horror genre. I saw every horror film that came out over the next ten years. And, of course, I also went back and watched the classics from the '70s that I missed. *The Exorcist, The Omen, Carrie, The Texas Chain Saw Massacre, The Last House on the Left*, etc.

**Can you speak of your meeting with Moustapha Akkad or any other producers?**

[Larry and I] met separately with Moustapha and Bob Weinstein, who ran Dimension. And the meetings couldn't have been any more different. The meeting with Moustapha was like we were proposing to his daughter. He wanted us to know how precious his daughter – the *Halloween* franchise – was and what she meant to him. He had *Halloween* memorabilia decorating his office, and he spoke reverently about the franchise. *Halloween* was his family. My partner and I didn't have to go too much into our specific take on the story. The meeting was about getting his blessing to marry his daughter – meaning we were there to get his blessing to join the *Halloween* family. By the end of the meeting, it was clear to me that Moustapha had the same respect for the franchise as the fans of the franchise did.

196

The meeting with Bob Weinstein was completely different. We pitched him the story, which he liked, but he spent most of the time talking about our *Tales from the Crypt* script. It was clear that he had enjoyed it! Bob quickly approved our take on the story. Then, we met with him a second time after turning in the first draft. I'll never forget that second meeting. It was at the Peninsula Hotel in Beverly Hills, and it lasted one minute. He said, '*Put more sprinkles on the cake*' – which he explained meant add more horror. And that was the extent of our notes.

**Had you watched the previous films for inspiration? What were your goals for the project?**

I think I re-watched the sequels before writing, but I don't remember for sure. What I do remember is that Dimension wasn't into *Halloween 4* and *5*, while Moustapha was more forgiving of the shortfalls of those sequels. Though Moustapha had no specific marching orders, he wanted us to revive the franchise to the best of our abilities. That was the number one goal. My partner and I collaborated on the story and the script. Because I'd been a fan of *Halloween* – and longtime fan of horror films – I brought that knowledge to the table. But both of us were focused on creating a riveting story.

**There happens to be an earlier draft which features a number of the same elements as yours – the return of Tommy Doyle, a lead female named Dana, the virtual reality element, etc. Could you tell us more about that?**

This is how I think it unfolded. After we got the gig, Bob asked us to read one of the previous scripts, and it could have been the script you're referring to. Then he asked us to keep certain elements that he thought worked in the script. So, those elements had to be a part of the story we would write. I don't remember what we chose to alter, but as I said, there were elements that Bob did not want us to change. So, we had to incorporate those elements into our story. This made coming up with a fresh take harder in terms of making some of these elements organic to the overall story. For example, I remember that I didn't like the virtual reality element. As a fan of *Halloween*, that element didn't seem organic to the franchise's core story and theme. But this was one of those elements that Dimension took a liking to from the previous script, so we had to try and make it work. I'm not trying to blame the studio for this decision. Ultimately, we as the writers were not able to make it work organically in any of our drafts.

**Could you speak of the decision to transform Dana from a twenty-something journalist and relative of the Shape to a teenager struggling to fit in?**

It's hard to remember my thought process from so long ago, but looking at it now, I probably thought two things. One, that the set-up with the journalist lacked emotion. And two, that a teenager struggling to adjust to a new town was more in line with the spirit of the *Halloween* franchise.

**Your script brings back Dr. Loomis but not Jamie Lloyd. Was that ever a consideration?**

I don't remember much, but I do remember that *Halloween 4* and *5* were persona non grata! We were to stay away from those films. Dr. Loomis was part of the franchise and its success. I couldn't see writing a sequel where he wasn't a major character.

**The mysterious Man in Black from *Halloween 5* also makes a brief appearance. Did you have any idea in mind as to the character's identity?**

No, but I do remember that we had many discussions on who the Man in Black could be.

**Did you ever see the final film?**

I was too disappointed that the studio didn't use our script to go see the movie when it finally came out.

**Were there any elements of your script that you are proud of? Anything you would've changed?**

Hindsight is twenty-twenty but in hindsight, I would have tied the concept for the story to a real problem or issue like the recent film *Hereditary* did, and also like *Split* did a couple of years ago. At its core, *Halloween* is a reality-based horror film so grounding it in a psychological disorder – which could be used as a twist or not – could have made for a stronger draft.

# LAWRENCE GUTERMAN

Co-writer - Halloween 666: The Origin of Michael Myers

Interviewed by Travis Mullins

**Going into *Halloween 6*, what was your relationship to the franchise? Were you a genre fan?**

I had seen the original *Halloween* a little while after it came out. I've always been a lover of cinema and horror is the quintessential cinematic genre – the one that goes straight for the most primitive part of the brain, straight to your subconscious despite your best efforts! I remember as a kid being absolutely terrified at the shot of the attic door in *The Exorcist* with those guttural sounds emanating from it. I still can't watch it to this day without being terrified. If it pops up on TV, I have to turn it off at that scene. Of course, I loved Carpenter's style in the original [*Halloween*], the POV Steadicam work, all of that.

**How'd the two of you land the job?**

Irving and I were editors in a film class at USC in the Master's program in production. One semester, the legendary Bob Zemeckis taught the 480 workshop, a class where five twenty-minute films were made by the advanced students. You had to edit or DP one of those to get a shot later at writing or directing one, so we had to go through the gauntlet of editing one first. So, we'd see Bob once a week when he'd come in to comment on dailies and then he would teach the directors and writers exclusively a couple of other times during week. Anyway, at the end of the semester, I had heard from the director of the short I was editing – Raoul Rosenberg – that Bob had told the writers and directors that if they were interested, they could pitch ideas for a *Tales from the Crypt* episode. The last day of the semester – while Bob was pulling out of the film school loading dock area for the last time, in his giant black boat of a Mercedes – I ran over to his car impulsively. He lowered a blackened window slightly and I asked him if Irving and I could pitch him a *Tales from the Crypt* episode. Amazingly, he said yes, but to keep it on the down-low, and to call his office.

After three months of incessant calls to Bob's office, with his assistant politely blowing us off, we finally asked Irving's wife Lori, who was a marketing manager at an engineering firm, how to get the meeting. She basically told us that when the assistant says, '*Oh, can you please call back the next week?*' just say, '*No, I'm sorry. I won't be able to; I'm busy,*' no matter how many ways and times she tries to stonewall. It was one of the hardest things I've done but, on that call, I basically kept saying, '*I'm sorry, I won't be able to,*' repeatedly, until she finally said, '*Okay, you guys are persistent. Let me call you back in thirty minutes.*' Thirty minutes later, we got a call, and, while still in film school, we were invited to pitch ideas to the legendary director. We had six fully fleshed-out pitches and when we were in the middle of pitching the second one, Bob started chiming in. I suddenly realized I should pull out my pencil and legal pad as he waxed on about the story, throwing in new elements. I remember having the exhilarating out-of-body experience that Bob Zemeckis was about to buy a *Tales from the Crypt* episode from us while were still film students. To top that, he then said he was going to direct our episode as part of a three-part anthology with Walter Hill and Richard Donner. We were in heaven.

Unfortunately, Bob got busy with another project and our *Tales from the Crypt* never got made. The other project was a little movie called *Forrest Gump*. One thing that we did get to do, though, was come to the set of *Death Becomes Her* a few times to work with Bob on the *Tales* script. Long story short, the *Tales* episode we wrote got seen by Bob Weinstein and he apparently loved it. When we met him, he couldn't stop talking about the scene between the rapacious freak show owner and the beautiful three-armed lady. We had actually met with Dimension just prior to this on a rewrite of *Scary Movie*, which was the original title of Kevin Williamson's *Scream* – but we didn't get that gig. But on *Halloween 666*, Bob offered us the job.

**Can you speak of your meetings with Bob Weinstein or Moustapha Akkad?**

Bob had us come to the Peninsula Hotel in Beverly Hills where he and Harvey would stay in Los Angeles in a couple of suites – their main offices being out of New York City. Bob's lieutenant Paul Freeman came out into the hallway and, in hushed tones, promised us that if we deliver on this script, the world would be our oyster – Bob would give us movie after movie. Simply witness

Quentin and Robert Rodriguez, etc. This was their standard M.O., from what I had heard, I guess to pull artists in and motivate them to deliver. In retrospect, the fact that they were hanging out in hotel suites should've struck us as being a bit odd, but at the time, we were so new to the game, we just went where we were told to meet company heads. So anyway, we go up to the suite where Bob and Moustapha Akkad are waiting. Moustapha was the original rights holder of *Halloween*. An elegant Syrian film producer who wore tweed and carried himself with great dignity, smoked a pipe, and spoke beautifully. He was seated opposite Bob in an ornate chair. Bob had sweatstains under his shirt and was scarfing down chocolate-covered strawberries.

We pitched the basic story and they liked it. Bob said he was ready to hire us to do the re-write but Moustapha was concerned there wasn't that much time to execute it. Right there in the room, Bob challenged Moustapha. *'I'll bet you $10,000 right now that these guys can write the script in ten days. Right now.'* Moustapha demurred but Bob kept pushing it. Anyway, we got hired. We had ten days and we dug right in. We were so thrilled to be doing this while still in school. As we were given notes to develop the script, we, of course, had meetings with Paul, and at one point, he brought us to see Moustapha. We sit down in Moustapha's well-appointed office. Paul starts talking about the things that Dimension wants in the script. Moustapha politely rebuffs some of the things. Paul digs in, politely, but with a bit more vigor. Moustapha rebuffs those ideas, again with class and poise.

Finally, Paul just won't back off. He's been sent on a mission by Bob. Now, Paul is a very nice guy, but he was forced to do his boss' bidding, so he brings up something or other that really gets under Moustapha's skin. All of a sudden, Moustapha lifts his fists and pounds on his old, heavy, mahogany desk, and in a deep, booming voice, proclaims, *'I am the father of the* Halloween *series! Look! Look!'* and he pulls out letters – handwritten letters – from kids and fans he got from all over the world, about how much they loved the *Halloween* movies. When I think about it now, can you imagine having hundreds of handwritten letters in your drawer? Of course, it would all just be internet ephemera now. But it was great he had the original copies. And I think he probably scared the daylights out of Paul at the time.

**Had the two of you watched the previous films?**

We did watch what we could. Remember, at the time, the only way to see a film was via Blockbuster Video, and we only had like 10 days to do the re-write. So, I don't actually recall which ones we had the ability to watch and which we didn't. I don't think Dimension sent us videos. We really had to deliver this script at a breakneck speed. I'd say Irving and I were pretty much 50/50 contributors on the script. I focused a bit more on action and scares while he focused a bit more on character and dialogue but there was a lot of crossover. We just wrote round the clock at his place on Park LaBrea with our Mac SE-30s grinding away on Microsoft Word.

**Do you recall in which ways you had altered from Phil Rosenberg's draft?**

I remember specifically there was a much larger component of a TV reporting crew in a van following events in Rosenberg's draft. That was removed. By the way, when we had met Bob, originally he said, '*I don't want to change much of the script. Just put, like, sprinkles on the ice cream.*' In the end, although we kept elements, it ended up being a lot more work than 'sprinkles on the ice cream.' The story veered away from the journalism angle towards where we ended up. I think reprising the innocence of a teen struggling to fit in seemed to have an emotional resonance.

**What were your thoughts on carrying over the virtual reality angle?**

After re-reading the script, I can certainly see why fans don't particularly love that angle. While I buy that in lieu of being able to get close to the house because of danger possibly lurking there, they might resort to VR to search it instead and discover the closet portal that way, I did think it was a stretch that supernatural sparking elements would manifest themselves in the VR. That seemed to jump the shark a bit. Certainly, visually cleverer and cooler than scouring blueprints, and you could even make the case that in VR, you might be able to view the closet whereas it might not be visible in a standard overhead blueprint.

When we wrote that, I'm pretty sure it was in the *Lawnmower Man* era – so pretty old school VR. I worked in computer animation in 1987, out of college, and then again in 1989. Back then, I remember working with a guy who knew Jaron Lanier, the VR guru. I had also met Jeff Kleiser at Kleiser/Walczak, who was working on his Synthespian idea, which we were going to incorporate into some commercial work. This, of course, morphed through various iterations in the industry to become the water creatures in *The Abyss* to the metal man in *Terminator 2* all the way to the CGI creatures in *Avatar*. And now, of course, in every Marvel movie. But back then, it was right at the beginning.

Out of college, I worked at Pacific Data Images for a summer as an assistant animator and during the day, I digitalized flying logos for network animation. But at night, I worked on my own computer animations – character-animated shorts using their system which required scripting in an animation programming language rather than having a user interface with a mouse to do a lot of animating. Pretty old school. It was like the second wave of CGI after the pioneers from the late '70s / early '80s – but pre-dating the third wave when *Toy Story* came out. Of course, then, I went to direct sequences in *Antz*, which became the second biggest studio computer animated film of all time to be released.

In fact, back in 1984, I saw a talk given at MIT by Ed Catmull and possibly John Lasseter. He showed not only the *Star Trek* genesis terraforming effect from one of those movies – *Wrath of Khan*, not sure – but also *Andre and Wally B.*, which was Lasseter's first computer animated short. So, VR was sort of running in parallel, I guess, with CGI, and appearing in pop culture and entertainment in fits and starts at the time, but never quite grabbing hold. Then came *The Matrix*, of course, which was sort of an abstraction of VR. And now, there's real VR, which is pretty cool.

**The Man in Black from *Halloween 5* makes a brief appearance in your script. Did you have any idea as to the character's identity? Likewise, could you speak of writing for Dr. Loomis?**

As far as I can recall, we did not [address the Man in Black]. That mystery was left for whoever might pick it up in the next film. I know Irving and I enjoyed the character of Dr. Loomis. Including him allowed us a dramatic vehicle to help uncover the mystery of Myers, Samhain, and provide the necessary exposition.

**What was the reaction to your script?**

I remember after we finished our draft, we were told to bring it back to Bob at the Peninsula and he would read it. We waited in the lobby while he read it. Then he came down and said some nice things at the time. But beyond that, we never really heard anything and ended up moving onto other projects.

**Did you ever see the final film?**

I think we were deep into each making our Master's thesis films by that point, so we weren't following that closely at that point. It becomes an all-consuming endeavor as you can imagine, and they weren't using our script anyway. So, I never actually saw the final product. Maybe I should watch now and give my feedback!

**Having recently re-read your draft, were there any elements that you enjoyed? Anything that makes you shake your head?**

Having "Too Slow" Tommy locked in a cage and pet rocks being thrown at him by drunken, entitled students seemed like a particularly twisted and callous moment. Also, it has weird cross-resonance twenty-plus years later in the wake of some of the real-life depravity that took place in the Middle East in the past few years. Cages, torture, etc. Having the real and fake Mike Myers coming across each other was sort of fun. The way he kills Laura with a fondue poker – with no anticipation whatsoever – was intended to evoke the kind of sudden and unexpected violence that actually is presented in a near-identical way towards the end of *Ex-Machina*, when the female robot kills the tech entrepreneur. Zero anticipation, zero emotion – just efficient and then each killer moves on.

The sudden mirror ball killing of the parents is effective, though a bit arch. Myers jamming a trophy into Eric's mouth and down his throat has a weird metaphorical resonance about privilege. Also, I imagine that at the time, the effects would have been done through some combination of practical effects – *American Werewolf in London*-style – with maybe some CGI enhancement to sell the trophy shape distorting the silhouette of Eric's neck. Myers lifting Derek by the ankle and raising him effectively evokes Darth Vader doing the same to one of the Empire officers at the beginning of *A New Hope*. I sort of shake my head at what comes next – jamming the keg into his mouth and filling him up until he explodes – but maybe that would've been a crowd-pleaser.

On pages 89 through 93, Michael Myers is relentlessly pursuing Dana, getting shot at by Sheriff Dogan – body parts flying off, but he keeps advancing. This sequence was meant to have a kind of *Terminator* intensity thus setting up effectively that no physical confrontation would be able to stop the monster. The only way to do so would be to somehow trick him, then send him straight to hell.

# interview:
# MATTHEW PATRICK

Original Director - Halloween 666: The Origin of Michael Myers

Interviewed by Travis Mullins

**Now, you were hired as the original director of *Halloween 6*. What led you to this?**

Well, I had won a Student Academy Award when I was in college. Later, I was nominated for an Academy Award for a short film called *Graffiti*. I had directed a feature called *Hider in the House* with Gary Busey, Mimi Rogers, and Michael McKean that did really well in Europe. It got great reviews by *Variety* and *Time Out*. Then, the company – Vestron – went broke in America. 1,200-screen release. That was it for that. My agent submitted me to Miramax and a development exec saw *Hider in the House*, liked it and I was hired. What's interesting is that *Hider in the House* is more of a suspense film, not a gore film. There was really no blood in it. So, I wanted to make *Halloween* like a classier, suspenseful picture. It was quite a process. We were originally going to call it *Halloween 666*. There were two people involved, Bob Weinstein and Moustapha Akkad, who theoretically owned the rights, which I later found out may not have been the case. I inherited a script and a couple writers. I had a direction I wanted to go in. But Bob and Moustapha kept having conflicts because they were 50/50 partners so they both had to agree to things.

**Getting into that conflict, what was it like working with Bob Weinstein?**

Wild. Those guys are really tough. Sort of like the old studio heads where they get really emotional. It was quite a ride. In the beginning, I had a hard time getting my first payment, but my agent finally got it. You know, the project went forward until a week or two before shooting. We in production just didn't know what to think because those guys – Bob and Moustapha – kept fighting over the script. Bob wanted the writers to have ten days on their own. We were meeting at the Peninsula Hotel and there was this bet where Bob said, '*Listen, Moustapha, we're rich men. If one of us speaks to the writers, we'll pay each other $10,000.*' Then Bob said, '*Nah, nah, we're rich men. Let's make it $100,000!*' It was just wild. The style between the two men was so different. I liked Bob because he went by his gut a lot. But Miramax was a really tough company to work for. They're very tough with money. They were trying to hold it back because they didn't know if the movie was going to go through or not. Finally, we got a script which, as far as I'm concerned, was not finished. I ended up re-writing it to take it where I saw it. To make it where you could actually shoot it. I wasn't interested in getting credit. I was just the director.

**So, what exactly did your version of the script entail?**

My concept was to follow a young man connected to Jamie Lee Curtis' character. This character had been terrorized by this whole experience, so he created what is now known as a safe room. He had set up a metal shipping container in an abandoned factory, setting up cameras all around. He would lock himself in there all the time because he was afraid of Michael Myers coming back. He lived this defensive life because he was totally terrified. I took another angle which was the safe room. That is what my script was about – him living in this safe room, but he's not really living. He's not able to really live life. He becomes interested in a young woman. He falls in love with her from a distance. She somehow becomes a target of Michael Myers and he comes to her rescue and must bring her to the safe house. And that's when Michael Myers comes, and the excitement ensues. There was also some big party featuring school kids on Halloween night. I remember the location we were going to rent.

It's funny because I didn't do the research on the previous films and here I am taking on *Halloween 6*. I just wanted to make it like my own film, which may not have been as successful depending on the audience we were going for. I wasn't planning on making it ultra-bloody or gory. I really liked the first film because it didn't really rely on that. It was much more about the characters and creating situations about near escape. I saw one of the more recent ones – the one where Rob Zombie directed. They definitely took it in another direction. The script was a real mess, as far as I'm concerned. It was more about episodes of pretty explicit violence. I think it did really well, which shows the power of the franchise. But it was very different from what I wanted to do. Who knows? Maybe I would've disappointed a bunch of fans.

**Earlier scripts for this sequel featured virtual reality. Do you recall this?**

I can remember a little bit about it. Bob would come up with an idea on how to sell a film and it might've even been under my administration that he brought up virtual reality. I don't think I ran with it, but I might've had to. The writers that I was working with were good guys and sort of caught in the crossfire. I mean, we had to do what Bob said. I'm trying to remember if I could work in the VR thing somehow, but not make it a major thread. I do remember some mention of it. It would've come from Bob because his interest is in marketing. He's a genius for marketing. He knows how to sell a picture. It would not surprise me at all if that appeared when Bob was around. But like I said, it wasn't at the forefront of my mind. I might've somehow worked it into the story to accommodate Bob. There's a lot of creative things you can do in support of the main story using those kinds of elements. I would've tried to weave it in without it taking over.


**How was it working with Moustapha Akkad?**

I really liked Moustapha. Bob was wild but Moustapha was a really calming influence. He had a certain gravity to him, a certain kind of presence. He seemed like a true gentleman. I liked him a lot. It was really a shame. I was fond of him. And Malek, his son, was a young guy who was sort of like my right hand. I liked him a lot and he was very supportive. We would get coffee for each other because we were friends. We had a good relationship. I was pitching some projects to him once. This was way after *Halloween 6*. He said, 'Oh, I'm finally free of Dimension. Thank God, it was a nightmare.' Not a lot of producers are necessarily nice guys. He's pretty down to earth. He's kept the franchise alive. He's been able to survive working with Bob Weinstein which is a feat in itself. I admire him for being able to turn it into this big money machine. It's really remarkable to make that much money. From a $300,000 film that revolutionized the entire horror realm. I was young, but [*Halloween*] was a breakthrough. Everyone went to see that film.

Moustapha wasn't really involved in the day-to-day matters, quite honestly. Even though there was this power struggle between he and Bob, it wasn't *really* about the content of the script. That's what was so weird. I don't know what the conflict really was. Bob loves conflict to begin with, so I'm sure it all came from him. I see Moustapha as being able to work things out. He was a calm guy. Bob would get really excited and start screaming. One time, he asked, '*Are you with me or Moustapha? We're gonna make a lot more films.*' I made the mistake, maybe, of saying, '*Well, you know, each of you own 50 percent of the movie. I gotta be good to both of you.*' Caught in the crossfire – and I don't think Bob liked that. I think he wanted me to be his boy or his spy, whatever. I already knew that he wasn't always being honest with me. And he kept deferring my payments, so I was working for free for a long time. So, this was not an honorable guy. It's tough. They try to take advantage of you as much as they can. He didn't earn my respect as an individual but being able to make any movie is very difficult. I mean, I had to put up with a lot of shit.

**Billy Dickson [*Halloween 6*'s director of photography] revealed that he had actually been hired under your tenure. How involved were you in production? What had you already completed?**

*Halloween* was just its own horror show in terms of production because we didn't know if it was going forward or if it was being scrapped. We didn't know how serious we should take the preparation. We didn't have enough time. I hadn't even cast the leads in the two weeks before we were shooting. I did location scouting and found certain areas, but I honestly didn't see *Halloween 6*, so I don't know how much was left over from my administration. Obviously, they liked Billy enough to hire him. They were impressed enough with him. I had shot two movies with him and he's a really good DP. I don't know who else carried over. I hoped they changed because we weren't getting the support we needed. The casting director was not effective. We could've hired someone a lot better. They were not bringing me people that were really that good. Hopefully, they fixed that when I left. But I didn't have a lot to choose from and that was a real problem.

I worked with Paul Freeman. He was a nice enough guy but man, he wasn't up to the caliber of producers I was used to, in terms of organizing, being effective, and hiring the right people. That was the problem. I'm glad I was hired, and I appreciate the trust they had with me. But I didn't get a good casting director. I didn't get a good costumer. I wished I had been involved

in that process. I was able to pick Billy, which was good. I should've pressed for a better casting director. But at the same time, it's possible that as a *Halloween* movie, more 'name' people may not have been interested. But even in regard to hiring a non-name person, like the male and female lead, they weren't going to be name people. They didn't need to be. But the people he brought in were just not up to caliber.

**You've secured the job and things are moving forward. What led to your exit?**

It was two weeks before shooting and we were still working stuff out. We were looking at locations, but I still had not cast the two leads. I was going to do this whole thing with UV black lighting, and I was there in the production warehouse when the company guys announced over the intercom, '*Matthew, Billy, come to the front. Your project has been canceled.*' Like, '*Yeah, nice, two weeks before.*' I thought it was really unprofessional in the way it was handled. Very frustrating. Never before had I been through anything like that. I didn't know who to believe about what was going on. From the very beginning, they were not being straight with us. It may have been a rights issue.

We would've been shooting in the spring. That's when the show was shut down. It had nothing to do with me. It had everything to do with Bob and Miramax – and possibly this rights issue that they never talked about which I think may have been an underlining trigger. That's my feeling. It wasn't personal. I wasn't the one getting beaten up all the time. They didn't blame me. I was just a cog.

**So, it wasn't a production issue?**

Well, I don't know if it's because we weren't ready – because we weren't – but they never seemed concerned about that before. It was always a bit of a mystery, honestly. Once I was out, I never followed up with what was going on. It was a really difficult situation. Unless I was going to get hired again, there wasn't any reason to put any work into it.

**In retrospect, are you satisfied with not having helmed that particular installment?**

Am I satisfied? It's always fun to make a new movie but at the same time, I knew that there were going to be issues. I have to say I have mixed feelings about it. When I saw Billy, I asked, '*How'd the shoot go?*' and he kind of just gave me this look. So, all I know is that it was a horrible experience. And Billy's a real pro. I don't know. Maybe I dodged a bullet? When I was involved in the show, it felt horrible. I was thinking, '*Honestly, I don't even know if I want to do it.*' One day, we're on. The next, it feels like we're off. It was very hard to get motivated.

**If you had creative control over a *Halloween* film, how would you approach it?**

I would make it more of a suspense picture, more in line with the first movie where we got really attached to Jamie Lee Curtis. They had taken the right approach by building a sympathetic character and following that person who behaved in a rational and courageous way. We could get behind that person. And I would've kept Michael Myers the same size as he was before and have him behave in the same way. I wouldn't have celebrated gore. I would've made the story compelling in the central force so that it would have the stalking and murder element, but there would be a reason for it. Personally, I like suspense thrillers, so I would've pushed it in that direction. In the *Terminator* films, you're dealing with the ultimate killing machine and that's what Michael Myers is. They were able to do it with a lot of class and without gore and creating the Linda Hamilton role, whom you really cared for. Just like they did with Jamie Lee Curtis. I would want to bring it back to that realm again.

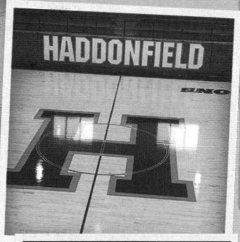

**LAMPKIN LANE AREA**   Fixer-upper with good bones. 3BR + 2B. Close proximity to Haddonfield High. Fenced-in backyard. Price seriously *slashed.* Make an offer.

Interested? Contact **Sean Clark** @ Hallowed Grounds Realty at (856) 555-3435

# HALLOWEEN 7
## TWO FACES OF EVIL

All trick. No treat.

**Screenplay by**
**Robert Zappia**

Production lore tells that the fifth *Halloween* was detrimentally rushed through every phase of its development and production. Lessons were learned, however, and producers took a different approach on *Halloween 6*. That film underwent a much lengthier development spanning no less than five years. Unfortunately, this didn't necessarily result in a stronger film. By most accounts, *Halloween 6* was a critical and commercial disappointment. Numerous battles permeated its production, resulting in a product even more compromised than its predecessor. Even *Fangoria*'s Fred Raskin remarked, "There is nothing in *Halloween: The Curse of Michael Myers* half as frightening as the possibility of a *Halloween 7*." (It's a bad day when a *Halloween* can't even charm a *Fango* reviewer.) Sure, the fifth film received equally bruising reviews, but the future of the franchise had now been condemned by its own fanbase. This was a blow to all involved.

The loose ends posed by *Halloween 5* had tasked a heavy burden on *Halloween 6* scribe Daniel Farrands. To his credit, Farrands went to great lengths to connect his entry to the previous films. His script not only concluded the Jamie Lloyd storyline but also re-introduced Tommy Doyle and set the stage for a final showdown between Dr. Loomis and the Shape. In making sense of the fifth film's ending, Farrands also brought back the original's Dr. Wynn, now unmasked as the mysterious Man in Black. The screenwriter rationalized that Wynn had overseen a cult that either encouraged or controlled the Shape's violence. Unfortunately, Farrands' work had been badly marred by studio meddling. "I feel so bad for the fans," he informed *Fangoria* readers months after the film's release. "That wasn't my version of the film. Only thirty percent of what I wrote made it to the screen."

Heading out of 1995, the future of the franchise seemed most uncertain. The working relationship between Miramax and Trancas had badly deteriorated across numerous story battles. No longer the sole driver, Moustapha Akkad faced great resistance from the Weinsteins, who elected to rewrite and reshoot the film's finale without his involvement. These battles would mirror Akkad's own frustrations with John Carpenter years earlier – only on a significantly worse scale. Having lost control of his own production, Akkad immediately sued the Weinsteins, but dropped the lawsuit to avoid negatively affecting the film's release. Alas, the damage was done. As per *Fangoria*, Akkad elected to have "complete control" of future *Halloween*s going forward. This must've been easier said than done as the two companies soon put aside their differences and began co-planning the next sequel. By this point, it was unclear what the story might be.

Upon first being hired to write the sixth film, Daniel Farrands had pitched such a vast story to Akkad that the producer deemed it enough material for two films. (Note: Farrands' original treatment was titled *Halloween 666: The Hunt for Michael Myers.* "The Night *She* Came Home!") His original *Halloween 7* treatment – tentatively titled *Michael Myers: Lord of the Dead* – would've picked up after one of the sixth film's rejected endings. After a showdown at Smith's Grove, Tommy, Kara and Danny would've escaped the carnage with Jamie's baby. Arriving at the same bus depot seen earlier in the film, Kara takes the children to the restroom while Tommy searches for help. Hearing a blood-curdling scream, he rushes downstairs to find Kara's throat slit and a giant Thorn symbol painted above her in fresh blood; the implication being that *whatever* happened at Smith's Grove had propelled Danny to finally kill his mother.

Farrands' *Halloween 7* began with authorities arriving at the bus depot to find Kara dead, the children missing, and Tommy at the scene of the crime. With the Shape having disappeared from Smith's Grove (in some unknown fashion), authorities would accuse the Myers-obsessed Tommy of having committed these most recent murders. Speaking with the *Halloween Daily News* website, Farrands described this idea as a "road movie" in which Tommy must elude police while racing back to Haddonfield to clear his name, find the children, and defeat the Shape once and for all. In the process, Tommy makes the startling discovery that the *entire town* is involved in the cult conspiracy. This idea – which Farrands attributed to Shirley Jackson's *The Lottery* – actually represented the writer's original vision for the sixth film before Akkad requested the cult's reach be scaled back from the town's denizens to just the staff at Smith's Grove.

In his *Taking Shape* interview, Farrands revealed that one of the earliest iterations of this sequel idea would've seen Jamie Lloyd survive her appearance in *Halloween 6*. In turn, the follow-up would culminate with the presumed dead Laurie Strode returning to save her daughter's life just in the nick of time. Ultimately, the main gist of this treatment would rely heavily on the sixth film's outcome which, as we know, had diverted considerably from Farrands' original script. Per the final film, Jamie Lloyd was now dead and Kara Strode still alive. As for Loomis and Wynn?

Well, their fates had always been left for debate. Should Farrands' ideas for the seventh film ever come to fruition, an extensive rewrite would've been necessary to retain the main plot. Such a revision would prove moot, however.

The Weinsteins and Akkads had many clashes on the sixth film. But if there was anything these men could agree on, it was that *Halloween 7* needn't be a direct continuation of the previous film's storyline. If reviews were any indication, the series' continuity had become too convoluted and difficult for the casual moviegoer to follow. Both Trancas and Dimension were looking for a fresh start – but with no more existing protagonists to follow, this would present a challenge for the next film's writer. Tommy Doyle and Kara Strode were being left behind. Jamie Lloyd and Laurie Strode were both considered dead. Dr. Loomis may as well have been dead with the unfortunate passing of actor Donald Pleasence. (A re-casting would've surely proven disastrous.) Going forward, the franchise had only its monster left.

Perhaps most interesting to consider about early attempts to get *Halloween 7* off the ground isn't what the story would've been, but *how* and *where* that story would've been seen by audiences. The failure of the sixth installment had led Dimension execs to question the viability of the *Halloween* franchise. As such, the studio chose to downgrade the series to direct-to-video. Mind you, this was not a decision made by Moustapha Akkad. This had become standard practice for Dimension, who had done much the same with once theatrical franchises like *Hellraiser* and *Children of the Corn*. The studio initially released theatrical sequels to these properties before transitioning them to home video after box office underperformance. This downgrade is typically associated with a steep decline in budget, quality, and critical regard. As of this writing, the two franchises have yet to make the leap back onto theater screens. There's a strong case to be made that the decades they've spent going to direct-to-video have badly tarnished their mainstream appeal. Circa 1996, this is exactly where *Halloween* was headed.

Sometime after settling on this release strategy, Dimension exec Richard Potter met with aspiring screenwriter Robert Zappia. While Zappia had written for several sitcoms including *Home Improvement*, he had yet to earn his first feature credit. The two had initially met to discuss *Population Zero*, a sci-fi spec script the writer had penned. Although Potter passed on the script, he took a chance on Zappia by asking if he would be interested in taking a crack at the seventh *Halloween*. As a fan of the original, Zappia jumped at the opportunity to pen the sequel – even if it was headed direct-to-video. Rather than continue the storyline of the previous three films,

Zappia's instructions were to take the series in a new direction. For him, this meant having a mostly blank narrative slate. He would work closely with Trancas and Dimension to develop his screenplay – titled *Halloween 7: Two Faces of Evil* – across the next several months.

## THE STORY

*Two Faces of Evil* opens in Nauvoo, Illinois, on the night of October 28, 1998. Teenage Debra Wiley is begrudgingly tasked with babysitting her younger brother and his friends while their parents are out for the night. As the boys are busy playing hide-and-seek, Debra engages in a phone conversation before being murdered upstairs by an unseen killer. Police respond and Detective Richard Kinkade is assigned to the case. He immediately suspects Michael Myers as the culprit given that a babysitter has just been stabbed to death in the days before Halloween not far from Haddonfield. His younger partner Janet Blake scoffs at this suggestion, noting that Myers has been incarcerated at Middle Rock Penitentiary for the past three years. They decide to personally verify his incarceration for good measure.

Sure enough, Blake and Kinkade find the Shape securely locked away deep within Middle Rock. Not long after their visit, the slasher collapses. Backed by a team of guards, the prison physician cautiously approaches the airtight cell. After failing to detect pulse or respiration, the Shape is pronounced dead. His body is then transferred to an off-site morgue where it returns to life and murders two attendants. Stealing a hearse, the Shape drives to a nearby drugstore with a garish Halloween display that includes a mannequin dressed as Michael Myers. Donning the mannequin's mask and overalls, the real Shape takes its place before murdering unsuspecting employee Eddie Catero and his girlfriend Sherry Hackney, a student of the all-girls Hillcrest Academy. Sherry's body is left for police to discover though Eddie's is removed from the scene.

The next morning, the slasher begins stalking the nearby academy where he targets two students – Joanne Wittington and Linda Kang – as they prepare for the school's annual Halloween dance. Meanwhile, police uncover a possible suspect in the Debra Wiley murder – criminal-turned-magician Cain Gabriel. Obsessed with all things Michael Myers, Gabriel has a poor history with law enforcement. He also recently performed his magic act at a birthday party for the babysitter's little brother, directly linking him to the victim. Blake and Kinkade soon deduce that Gabriel was already in police custody when the morgue and drugstore murders occurred, meaning they now have a second killer on the loose. Without hard evidence, Kinkade is forced to release their suspect on bond. He convinces Gabriel to stick around, however, under the guise of helping solve the subsequent murders and potentially meeting his idol face-to-face.

While strolling off-campus that night, Joanne is asked to the Halloween dance by Frank Roth, a student at the neighboring boys academy. All throughout this, the two remain unaware they are being trailed by the Shape. Before he can strike, however, the teens are caught by the headmaster, who bars Joanne from attending tomorrow night's dance for leaving campus. Elsewhere, Blake and Kinkade are following the coordinates of the Shape's prison-issued tracking device. With Gabriel in tow, the trio is led to the woods outside Hillcrest where they discover the device strapped to the mutilated body of the missing drugstore clerk.

With Halloween now upon us, the Shape continues stalking Hillcrest, murdering one of Joanne's friends in the gymnasium pool before zeroing in on his main target. That night, Kinkade and Gabriel are led to a marshland just outside town where the Shape's getaway hearse is found submerged in a lagoon. They also discover the bodies of the missing morgue attendants in its trunk. On a tip from Gabriel, Kinkade tracks the resurrected slasher to Hillcrest. With the dance in full swing, the Shape murders Linda and her boyfriend in the school kitchen. He then sneaks into Joanne's dorm, slashing her thigh before she escapes to the gymnasium where the dance is taking place. Unfortunately, the gym has been padlocked shut as part of a student prank, preventing anyone from entering or exiting.

The Shape chases Joanne to the school bell tower. Climbing to the top, she finds a janitor's corpse stuffed inside, which she removes in order to ring the massive bell. This alerts Kinkade and Gabriel, who are just arriving with police backup. Before they can reach her, an unseen figure approaches Joanne. It's Frank, her prospective date. He collapses, revealing a knife in his back and the Shape behind him. Joanne extracts the knife and stabs her attacker in the shoulder. The slasher then grabs hold of Joanne's neck before dangling her over the bell tower's ledge. She's narrowly saved by Kinkade who shoots the killer off the tower, plunging him four stories down. After consoling her, the detective goes to look upon the dead Shape only to find his body missing.

Down below, Gabriel vanishes concurrent with Blake revealing that forensic evidence has confirmed him as the babysitter's killer. Police search the woods outside Hillcrest and eventually encounter the Shape. They open fire and strike him numerous times, dropping him to the ground. Kinkade peels off the white mask to discover a fatally wounded Gabriel. ("Impressed yet, Kinkade? I made Michael Myers disappear.") As he dies, the real Shape escapes under the cover of darkness.

## THE TRICK IS THE TREAT

With a first draft dated July 11, 1997, *Two Faces of Evil* clearly represents an attempt to do something different with the franchise. Yet it's also careful not to betray the original film's mythology. Nor does it contradict the events of the sequels that followed after. This is an important distinction to note between this draft and the eventual *Halloween H20*. Neither story continues on from *Halloween 6*, but only *H20* acts as though that film didn't happen. Given its noble intentions, *Two Faces of Evil* is a strong effort for what would've sadly been *Halloween*'s first direct-to-video installment. Zappia brings several new elements to the table including detectives and flashy magic tricks, which integrate surprisingly well into the franchise.

Had this draft been produced, it would've stood apart from the rest of the series for several reasons. Like the eventually-produced *Halloween H20*, it would've been the only Shape story to sidestep Haddonfield completely. It was also poised to become the only *Halloween* to show Michael Myers in custody at its start. (Ignoring *Halloween 4*. Here the slasher is awake and alert.) Furthermore, this was going to be the first sequel without any returning characters, Michael aside. To date, we have never actually seen a *Halloween* sequel without at least one returning protagonist somewhere in it. That alone would constitute a daunting challenge for any screenwriter.

There's yet another reason why the Zappia script would've marked a huge departure from earlier films. *Two Faces of Evil* was set to become the first *Halloween* where the Shape wasn't actively trying to murder a blood relative, something that's even referenced in-story. In one scene, Kinkade and Gabriel theorize on where Michael will go next. Kinkade mentions that he has someone working to locate Jamie Lloyd's baby, who had been adopted by an out-of-state family following her death in *Halloween 6*. Gabriel laughs off his suggestion, dismissing the old Loomis-fueled theory that Michael's only goal was to end his bloodline. And within this story, he seems to be correct. Zappia effectively does for the Shape what *Halloween 2018*'s filmmakers did twenty years before it was fashionable. He restores the slasher to his original characterization as the ultimate boogeyman. Of course, Zappia would reverse course on this direction entirely with the return of Jamie Lee Curtis for *Halloween H20*.

Giving credit where credit is due, *Two Faces of Evil* is cleverly written. Take the opening sequence with the babysitter. As horror fans, we've grown accustomed to the trope of the first kill. Being that this is a *Halloween* film, we automatically assume the killer to be Michael Myers because we don't yet have reason to think otherwise. The heavy use of POV-camerawork feels less like a trick to conceal the slasher's identity and more like a natural homage to cinematographer Dean Cundey. But it is a trick. The scene is written so that we never actually see the killer's white mask or full figure. It's not until much later in the story that authorities confirm this was not the work of Michael Myers but Cain Gabriel. Additionally, Zappia stages the babysitter's murder in chilling fashion with much of her death unfolding offscreen. The scene soon cuts to her little brother and his friends downstairs. Hearing the guttural screams of her murder, they slowly climb the staircase to her bedroom, terrified out of their minds. The boy eventually finds his sister in a closet. (Script: "She falls right on top of him...her throat slit, gushing blood.")

It's almost remarkable just how inconsequential *Two Faces of Evil* is. That's not an aspersion on the material, either. By this point, the *Halloween* franchise had become so serialized that a strong familiarity with previous entries was required to understand new ones. Not so on this script, which operates more like the direct-to-video *Hellraiser* sequels Dimension was known for during this time. You don't need a bachelor's degree in *Halloween* studies to enjoy *Two Faces of Evil*. It's a one-off story that doesn't continue on from the previous movies. Nor does it change the series in any lasting way going forward. Zappia's tale is standalone in the best sense of the word.

Given that Zappia would later pen *Halloween H20*, it comes as no surprise that his script has several similarities to the later produced anniversary sequel. The "secondhand smoke kills" joke occurs at almost exactly the same part of the story. Both drafts also feature medical professionals who erroneously declare the Shape dead. This draft's Joanne sees the Shape standing outside her classroom at Hillcrest whereas in *H20* this happens to Molly.


## TO CATCH A KILLER

By this point in the series, there existed a reliable formula to writing a *Halloween* movie: Vigilante psychiatrist and small-town lawman team up to catch a returned killer as he targets young people. That's essentially the plot of *Halloween, Halloween II, Halloween 4,* and *Halloween 5.* (The sixth installment applied some variation.) With *Two Faces of Evil*, Zappia charts a different narrative course that more closely resembles a police procedural. It's a far cry from Loomis shouting at skeptics that death has returned to their little town. We instead find detectives leading a sprawling investigation to catch a killer-at-large. (Think *Law & Order* meets *Halloween*.) Blake and Kinkade are utilizing every tool at their disposal to find and capture the Shape. That means forensic testing, crime scene analysis, and a county-wide manhunt.

Our lead protagonist, Richard Kinkade, is a hard-nosed gumshoe who takes his job seriously. His role feels like an attempt on the screenwriter's part to fill the void left by Dr. Loomis in the wake of Donald Pleasence's passing. Like Loomis, Kinkade has some history with the slasher, though we're unsure what that is exactly. ("You haven't seen what I've seen, the carnage this thing has inflicted. He's defied death before and maybe now he's finally conquered it. And if he has, God help us all.") He also maintains a healthy level of fear for the killer they're chasing after, spouting familiar lines like "We're not talking about a man." Zappia even recreates *Halloween*'s ending using Kinkade and Joanne in place of Loomis and Laurie.

*Two Faces of Evil* further cements a connection between the characters when Kinkade finds several boxes of Loomis' personal files in an evidence locker. He takes them home to study, hoping they might reveal something that could help in catching the slasher. One box contains Myers family photo albums, which allow us a rare glimpse into Michael's childhood. Another box houses several film canisters marked "Myers Home Movies." Kinkade projects these onto a blank wall of his apartment but finds nothing unusual. Exhausted, he falls asleep as they continue to play. With this, the Shape steps out of the dark and into the path of the projector beam. The light falls onto his mask and jumpsuit, juxtaposing the image of young Michael onto the adult Shape's form. He slashes Kinkade's throat ear-to-ear, jolting the detective awake from his nightmare.

Kinkade's partner on the investigation is Janet Blake, a new recruit to the force. Though smart and savvy, Blake lacks the gut-intuition that comes from years of experience. As a result, she never fully accepts that Michael Myers may have come back to life to kill again. ("With all due respect, Kinkade, I think it's more likely these kids went to show Myers' body off to their friends, than it is to believe he actually rose from the dead.") Blake is also alarmed by the lengths to which her partner will go to catch their killer, which occasionally means breaking the law. In one scene, Kinkade bashes in a suspect's mouth for a blood sample to avoid having to wait on an order from a judge. (He's similarly impatient when it comes to search warrants.) Blake winds up dying in several early drafts of *Halloween H20*, though she survives in this version of the story.

The detective plot remained a large part of *Halloween 7* right up until cameras rolled on *H20* in February 1998. It was ultimately deemed unnecessary to the overall story and cut from the script at the last minute. That is not at all the case in *Two Faces of Evil* where it's the detective plot that drives the story forward. The scenes at Hillcrest Academy with the teenage protagonists aren't at all bad, but they lack the engaging drama of the Blake/Kinkade scenes, especially once Cain Gabriel comes into the picture.

## NOW YOU SEE HIM

With criminal-magician Cain Gabriel, Zappia gives us what is arguably the most interesting new character in *Two Faces of Evil*. An unsavory chap with a criminal history, Gabriel makes for an intriguing secondary villain. You never know what he'll do next, but trust that he has at least one proverbial card up his sleeve. He's also eerily obsessed with all things Michael Myers. A glimpse into his apartment reveals the extent of his slasher worship – crime scene photos, newspaper clippings, and disturbing artwork. (Per Zappia's description, it rather resembles Tommy's room from *Halloween 6*.) Kinkade not only suspects Gabriel of committing at least one murder, but feels the case could also benefit from his Myers expertise in catching the Shape. According to Zappia, this "using-a-killer-to-catch-a-killer" angle was originally suggested by producer Paul Freeman. It's an interesting riff on *The Silence of the Lambs* with Gabriel playing the Hannibal Lecter role.

As far as villains go, Cain Gabriel is wonderfully conniving. His schemes are never apparent to those around him until they're already in motion. Upon first being arrested for Debra Wiley's murder, a restrained Gabriel sits opposite Kinkade in interrogation. The trickster intones, "If I really wanted to escape, I could." Kinkade laughs off his comment. A moment later, Gabriel hands him the cuffs that only seconds before secured his wrists. Feigning indifference, the detective pulls out a cigarette but is unable to find his matchbook. Gabriel reaches behind Kinkade's ear, pulls out a match, and lights his smoke. These would be simple parlor gags in any other situation, but here they have a threatening undertone. ("Your little tricks might impress the kids, but they don't impress me.") In this fashion, Gabriel will remain two steps ahead of Kinkade throughout the story.

In a surprising twist, Blake and Kinkade eventually invite Gabriel to join their investigation of the other murders. While they could genuinely use his Myers expertise in tracking the Shape, they also want to keep him as close as possible. Without any hard evidence, they cannot legally detain him any longer despite the fact that a pending forensic test might yet incriminate him in the babysitter's murder. Releasing Gabriel now would allow him to escape justice by fleeing the country. Having him nearby as part of the investigation will also make for an easier arrest in the event forensics returns a DNA match. Of course, Gabriel isn't stupid. He knows he's being played, but it's well worth it for the opportunity to meet his longtime idol. If *Two Faces of Evil* has a fault, it's that Gabriel never gets his wish – at least onscreen. An encounter between Gabriel and the Shape would've been one hell of a confrontation. How would Michael regard his most devoted fan? Unfortunately, this is left to the imagination as we never see how Gabriel managed to switch clothes with the killer.

> **Cain:** "*Evil never dies. It just finds a new host. I can help you. I know how Michael thinks. I can help you track him down. Halloween is tomorrow and time is not your friend. [I want a] chance to feed my obsession... to meet Michael Myers. Face to face, eye to eye...*"

## SLASHER FODDER

What would a *Halloween* movie be without misbehaving teens? Possibly not a *Halloween* movie, but not to worry – *Two Faces of Evil* has a plotline to satisfy that requirement. This part of the story focuses on two charming students at Hillcrest Girls Academy – Joanne Wittington and Linda Kang, both seventeen. We meet Joanne and Linda early on, even before the Shape escapes Middle Rock Penitentiary, which at first makes you wonder about their relevance to the plot. It all comes into focus when the Shape arrives on campus, however. The scenes at Hillcrest may well constitute this draft's "B-plot," but Zappia still makes the most of the setting and characters. He sets up several novel scares throughout campus, the likes of which we've not seen before or since in this franchise.

Joanne fills in as this story's final girl, a surrogate Laurie Strode who senses the approaching threat before anyone else does. This includes catching peripheral glances of the Shape just as Laurie did. (Linda makes fun of her for repeatedly seeing an "invisible man.") Joanne's first actual brush with the slasher is an especially creepy one. Skipping the school dance, Joanne lazes around in her dorm. Reaching over the side of her bed, she goes to pet what she thinks is Lurch, the school dog. A moment later, the actual Lurch enters the room and starts growling in her direction. (Script: "She instantly stops petting whatever is under her bed. Terrified, she slowly leans over the edge and comes eye-to-eye with... THE SHAPE!") A cross-campus chase ensues in which the slasher kills one of her schoolmates.

Pursued by the Shape, Joanne heads for the school gymnasium where the Halloween dance is well underway. Unfortunately, she won't be able to gain entry. Several freshmen have devised a prank in which they open the gym's retractable floor during the dance to reveal the pool underneath. This will cause much of the student body to fall into the water. To ensure maximum effectiveness, these same freshmen have also padlocked the exit doors. This not only prevents students from leaving – it prevents Joanne taking refuge inside. *But wait* – there's more. Earlier in the day, the Shape drowned Sharon here, a friend of Joanne's, and hid her corpse beneath the gym floor. As it retracts, helpless students are forced into the pool with the waterlogged corpse of their peer. Pure pandemonium ensues inside the gym, drowning out Joanne's screams for help outside. Zappia would later write both the dog and pool scenes into *Halloween H20,* though neither concept would survive to the final shooting script.

Joanne's best friend, Linda, is written as being a bit spunkier and more comedic. Unlike Joanne, Linda plans on attending the dance and dresses as the Bride of Frankenstein. (Recall that Tim Strode's girlfriend Beth previously cosplayed as the Bride in *Halloween 6.*) Her boyfriend, Jeff Delacruz, plans on attending as Count Dracula. Neither will actually make it to the dance,

however. The Shape first murders Jeff in the dormitory kitchen before cramming his body into a refrigerator. With Linda approaching, the Shape puts on Jeff's Dracula costume and turns his back to her. Tragically unaware of the deception, Linda walks right up to the slasher, who spins around to reveal *Michael Myers in a Dracula cape*, flared collar and all. (Picture that for a moment.) He grabs her and she fights back, accidentally kicking open the fridge to reveal her dead boyfriend. The Shape eventually kills Linda by impaling her on a pot rack, in a manner similar to Pam on Leatherface's meat hook in *Texas Chain Saw Massacre*.

You may wonder why Hillcrest Academy chose to forge ahead with their Halloween dance given the nearby murders of at least four people. There's a reason for that and it involves a boneheaded decision by town officials. They ultimately decide to keep things quiet so as not to alarm the citizenry just before Halloween. (It would seem the mayor from *Jaws* moved to Illinois after losing his re-election bid in Amity.) Rather than acknowledging the murders committed inside Freeman's Drugstore, police instead tell locals it was a simple burglary. Not everyone buys this, however, given the alarming amount of crime scene tape on the building. Had there been competent law enforcement in this town, Hillcrest would've been locked up tight on October 31st. (Also, the naming of Freeman's Drugstore is nice nod to series producer Paul Freeman.)

## THE REAL SHAPE

As already mentioned, *Two Faces of Evil* uniquely opens with the Shape already in federal custody. While he's been here before, the difference now is that he's awake and fully alert – none of that *Halloween 4* coma business. The details of his capture are scarce, but we do learn that he was apprehended by a SWAT team at Smith's Grove Sanitarium three years ago. This would appear to line up with the theatrical ending of *Halloween 6*, which saw the slasher confronting Dr. Loomis deep within Smith's Grove. Zappia allows the specifics of that offscreen confrontation to remain a mystery. We do glean from character dialogue that the retired doctor has been missing for some time now. He might've fallen victim to his former patient in that final encounter, but again, Zappia leaves that to the viewer's imagination.

The Shape's accommodations at Middle Rock bring to mind Hannibal Lecter's ultra-secure cell in *The Silence of the Lambs* – only with more protective measures in place. The slasher is housed in a windowless cell with walls, floor, and ceiling made of three-foot-thick concrete. He's kept in a straitjacket and leather muzzle around the clock, the latter added after he bit a guard's fingers clean off. His now takes meals through a straw to prevent the further finger loss. Michael's cell door is electromagnetically sealed and requires two pass keys to open. Furthermore, he's under 24-hour camera surveillance. *As if that weren't enough*, the Shape also wears a satellite tracking device strapped to his ankle, which can locate him anywhere in the world. As the warden tells it, "I can assure you that Michael Myers is a permanent guest of Middle Rock."

With the original *Halloween*, John Carpenter and Debra Hill were careful not to depict the Shape as some unstoppable monster. If you stabbed him in the neck with a knitting needle, he went down. That film's ending does strain credulity a bit as he walks off six bullets, but it's a grounded story otherwise. The sequels that followed would sully this approach with the slasher being shot, stabbed, hanged, blinded, thrown from towering heights, hit with multiple vehicles, and set ablaze. With *Two Faces of Evil*, Zappia returns the Shape to his original, more grounded characterization. He doesn't incur any wounds here that would otherwise kill him, beyond being shot again in the finale. The screenwriter does tease that Michael might've figured out a way to cheat death as a means of escaping Middle Rock. Even Kinkade begins to consider the possibility. How else could he have been pronounced dead by a prison doctor only to rise later that day? Cain Gabriel has a theory on that.

> **Cain:** *"Michael must have learned to do what many Hindus can do. Through deep meditation he was able to take control of his bodily functions to the point that involuntary functions like his heartbeat and breathing were shifted into the domain of his conscious mind. He learned to slow down these bodily functions to the point where he was perceived dead, when actually he was still quite alive."*

The Shape spends the first act of *Two Faces of Evil* without his trademark white mask, though Zappia never indicates whether audiences would've seen his naked face. Within Middle Rock, the character wears a constrictive leather muzzle that guards remove once he's found unresponsive. The Shape later dons a mass-produced Michael Myers mask he swipes from a drugstore mannequin, which would have offered filmmakers an in-story chance to tweak the iconic design. Zappia did write one moment into his story that would've allowed us a brief look at Michael's unmasked face – albeit as a young child. This comes as Detective Kinkade screens old home movies of the Myers family. The footage reveals the innocent face of a young boy with "no signs of the evil lurking inside." Compare that to young Michael's depiction in the deleted opening to *Halloween: Resurrection*. In *those* Myers home movies, the boy appears quite sinister with what are most certainly "the devil's eyes."

Historically, the Shape has never been averse to grand theft auto. It's then unsurprising that he steals a vehicle in *Two Faces of Evil* to better navigate suburban Illinois. That vehicle just happens to be a hearse in what might be his most appropriate ride ever. (Given that he comes back to life at the county morgue, it's reasonable to assume there'd be a hearse nearby.) He's not dumb, though, and quickly remembers the satellite tracking device strapped to his ankle. The Shape soon affixes the tracker to one of the corpses from the drugstore murders before dumping the body in a remote area. By the time Blake and Kinkade locate the device, wolves have already half-devoured the body. As for the slasher's methods, they're as nasty as ever. At the morgue, the Shape drains one attendant of blood with a trocar to the jugular before using a skull saw on the other.

*Two Faces of Evil* muses on what exactly motivates the Shape to kill in a chat between Kinkade and Gabriel. The former believes in Dr. Loomis' theory about Michael wanting to end his own bloodline. Gabriel disagrees and offers his own take, which is that Michael is sexually obsessive-compulsive. He fixates on a victim and, unable to act on his feelings, stalks and murders them in a macabre courtship. Kinkade briefly considers this theory before dismissing it himself. That's when Gabriel chimes in: "Of course, there's always the most popular theory... that he *is* the boogeyman." It's a fascinating scene between the man currently hunting the Shape and the slasher's biggest fan. Zappia is most wise to only peak into the dark abyss of the character's motivations without drawing any firm conclusions.

## WHY IT WASN'T MADE

Screenwriter Robert Zappia spent six weeks writing his *Two Faces of Evil* screenplay, which he submitted on July 11, 1997. He soon received word from his agent that Dimension execs had responded favorably to his script and that head honcho Bob Weinstein wanted to meet personally with him. (While Weinstein was known for his hands-on approach to developing new *Halloween* movies, he didn't always meet one-on-one with the screenwriters involved.) In their meeting, Weinstein told Zappia that he had good news and bad news. The good news was that he liked Zappia's work on *Two Faces of Evil* very much. The bad news was that Dimension would not be moving forward with his script.

Unbeknownst to Zappia, original *Halloween* star Jamie Lee Curtis had been quietly plotting her return to the franchise for much of 1997. She envisioned a twentieth-anniversary sequel for the following year as a way to thank fans of the genre that helped launch her career in Hollywood. Prior to meeting with Dimension about the idea, Curtis reached out to filmmakers John Carpenter and Debra Hill to gauge their interest. Both were agreeable to signing onto *Halloween 7* as co-writers and producers with Carpenter again filling the director's chair. Now a unified front, this trio met with Bob Weinstein to formulate a path forward. Unfortunately, this is where things began to fall apart. Feeling he was owed many years of unpaid *Halloween* profits, Carpenter was rumored to have demanded both a lofty directing fee and a multi-picture deal. Weinstein reportedly scoffed at both demands, which prompted Carpenter's exit. Hill would follow soon after.

Even amid this setback, Curtis did not abandon the push to make an anniversary sequel starring herself. Weinstein too felt the idea was still worth pursuing and reached out to screenwriter Kevin Williamson to secure his involvement. Williamson's star had recently risen meteorically with the blockbuster release of Wes Craven's *Scream*. Dimension moved quickly to capitalize on this success by jumpstarting development on *Scream 2*. Yet that sequel would have to wait as Williamson was busy writing and producing the pilot for *Dawon's Creek* in his hometown of Wilmington, North Carolina. He was also in-development on an original screenplay entitled *Teaching Ms. Tingle*. Recognizing *Scream* as a love letter to *Halloween*, Weinstein felt strongly that Williamson was the right person to champion *Halloween 7*. The scribe declined the opportunity, however, citing an overload of prior commitments.

While Weinstein continued to pursue Williamson's involvement, time was running out. The studio could not afford to let the project languish in development hell if it were going to reach theater screens the following year. To this end, Weinstein invited Robert Zappia in for the aforementioned meeting about his *Two Faces of Evil* script. Moments after quashing his screenplay, Weinstein invited Zappia to submit a new *Halloween 7* draft centered around Laurie Strode. The screenwriter enthusiastically accepted this new assignment. He would complete his first draft of this new sequel – titled *Halloween: Blood Ties* – in late fall 1997. Further unbeknownst to Zappia, efforts were still ongoing to recruit another screenwriter to the project.

Despite the re-hiring of Zappia, Weinstein persisted in his efforts to bring Kevin Williamson on board *Halloween 7*. Likewise, Williamson remained resolute in his refusal, citing his busy schedule. One of Weinstein's tactics involved sending in *Dawson's Creek* helmer (and future *Halloween H20* director) Steve Miner to convince Williamson, but he again declined their invite to write the sequel. In a last ditch effort, Weinstein sent in his biggest gun with actress Jamie Lee Curtis, who managed to seal the deal on Williamson's involvement.

"When Jamie Lee calls and asks you to do something, you *always* say yes," Williamson said in his *Taking Shape* interview. "It was impossible to turn down at that point." (While Curtis was surely persuasive, it also likely helped that Weinstein had sweetened the deal by offering to produce Williamson's *Teaching Ms. Tingle* at Dimension and allow Williamson to direct it.)

Given his other commitments, Williamson was only initially available to pen a six-page treatment for *Halloween 7*. His take incorporated several elements from Zappia's *Blood Ties* script such as the private school setting. The *Scream* scribe's treatment found Laurie Strode very much alive and now living far away from Haddonfield. Having faked her death in an auto-accident, she's since forged a new life as Keri Tate, headmistress of the posh Hillcrest Academy where her teenaged son attends school. This reincorporation of the Laurie Strode character owes much to *Halloween 4*, which first suggested that Laurie had perished in an auto-accident a decade earlier. Producers would next give Williamson's treatment to Zappia, who would in turn expand it into a full-length screenplay titled *Halloween 7: The Revenge of Laurie Strode*.

"I didn't necessarily feel the need to change Kevin's treatment," Zappia told the official *Halloween* website. "After all, he doesn't need help from me. There were certain elements that I had a difference of opinion on and discussed those things with the producers and director. Some things I was able to change. Others remained the same." One of these elements included inserting the detective subplot back in.

"This was a unique situation because I had already written a draft pre-Jamie Lee. So, I used elements from my previous work in the later drafts. [...] Kevin's treatment was very brief, which allowed me to embellish quite a bit during the process. That gave me a lot of creative freedom."

- Robert Zappia, HalloweenMovies.com

*Halloween 7*'s screenplay would remain in-flux right up until (and even after) cameras were set to roll on the project. Zappia would ultimately depart the sequel just before the start of principal photography. "You can imagine that after seven drafts and over a year on one project, you begin to see double," the writer had informed the official *Halloween* website. "I was beginning to lose sight of the whole picture and was too busy trying to fit all the various pieces of the puzzle together. Everyone agreed – including myself – that it was time to get a fresh pair of eyes in to look at the script in a way that I wasn't able to anymore." To this end, *Scream* scribe Kevin Williamson was brought back to orchestrate a page-one rewrite in just a week's time. His focus was on polishing the teenage dialogue and creating an additional scene between Laurie and the school's secretary. This expanded on an already-planned cameo appearance by Curtis' mother Janet Leigh, another notable scream queen given her iconic role in Alfred Hitchcock's *Psycho*.

One of Williamson's biggest additions – or subtractions, as it were – was to ixnay the detective subplot that ran parallel to the Hillcrest material. The screenwriter would argue that this deletion would help streamline the plot and allow for more action at the school. Such a last-minute revision resulted in the unfortunate dismissal of actor Charles S. Dutton who had already been cast as Detective Richard Carter, a revision of the Richard Kinkade character from *Two Faces of Evil*. Williamson would now limit the detective's role in the story to just the opening sequence after the murder of Marion Whittington. Now named Detective Fitzsimons, the role would be played by the lesser-known Beau Billingslea.

As filming commenced, however, it was determined that further revisions were still needed. In particular, the deletion of the detective subplot had left quite a gap in the story's narrative runtime. To amend this, Matt Greenberg was brought in as the film's third and final writer after

Zappia and Williamson had already completed their duties. Greenberg was a frequent Dimension collaborator, having co-penned the direct-to-video sequels *Prophecy II* and *Children of the Corn III: Urban Harvest*. On the theatrical side of things, he had also supplied uncredited revisions for Guillermo del Toro's *Mimic*. For *Halloween 7* – now titled *Halloween H20: Twenty Years Later* – Greenberg composed the scene in which a mother and her young daughter encounter the Shape at a rest stop. The slasher leaves the two unharmed, instead electing to steal the mother's vehicle – his previous having suffered a flat – before proceeding to the school. With this sequence, both Zappia and Williamson commended Greenberg for propelling the story forward.

Bob Weinstein had originally hoped that Kevin Williamson would be credited with providing the final film's story in an effort to capitalize on the writer's burgeoning popularity. The Writer's Guild felt differently, however, and assigned story credit exclusively to Zappia, citing how much *Halloween H20* owed to his original *Two Faces of Evil* draft. In another snub to Williamson, the WGA then assigned the final "screenplay by" credits to Zappia and Greenberg. While Weinstein disagreed with this distribution of credit, he was ultimately powerless to change it. In response, he would name Williamson an executive producer on the film as a consolation prize for his otherwise uncredited efforts. That – in a nutshell – is how the well-received *Halloween H20* came to be. Zappia's *Two Faces of Evil* may not have reached home video shelves, but his work on *Halloween H20* would eventually land somewhere even better – theater screens around the world. All's well that ends well.

# ROBERT ZAPPIA
## Writer - Halloween 7: Two Faces of Evil

Interviewed by Dustin McNeill

**How'd you first land the opportunity to write *Halloween 7*?**

I was working in television at the time writing for sitcoms. I had written for *Home Improvement* and had finished work on a short-lived sitcom starring David Chapelle called *Buddies*. During that hiatus, I wrote a spec sci-fi feature called *Population Zero*. Writing feature films was always my ultimate goal, so every hiatus I would write a new spec with hopes of selling it. And while *Population Zero* didn't sell, it did catch the attention of an executive at Dimension Films named Richard Potter. My agent arranged for a general interview with Richard. I remember sitting in the Miramax/Dimension lobby waiting for the meeting to start. I was sitting there for nearly forty-five minutes and seriously thought about leaving. I had been on so many of these general meetings that never amounted to much more than a handful of compliments about my writing. Boy, am I glad I didn't just get up and walk out!

So Richard eventually came out and apologized for being behind and we talked about the spec script and such. I clicked with Richard from the minute we started chatting. Just a really good, down-to earth executive. Richard said they'd really like to work with me but the only writing assignment they had open was a direct-to-home video release of *Halloween 7*, would I be interested? *Would I be interested*?! Uh, *yes*....yes, I would. I was a huge fan of the original *Halloween* and any chance to be a part of that franchise was such an exciting thought, whether it was being released theatrically or not!

**And this results in your *Two Faces of Evil* draft. Were you given any direction before starting?**

I was told by Richard Potter that I would have to meet with Moustapha Akkad along with a few other writers. We would pitch our ideas to Moustapha and producer Paul Freeman. They would then decide who to hire based on those initial pitches. So, I set about coming up with a pitch in June of 1996. Having seen Moustapha's name on screen for so many years, it was a thrill (and quite surreal) to be sitting across from him pitching an idea for *Halloween 7*. Moustapha looked like he stepped out of a time machine. He was impeccably dressed in a sport coat with patched elbows, pipe in hand, sitting in a high back leather chair. Salt and pepper hair neatly combed. And he had this great smile – a very subtle wry smile. It sounds cliché, but he even had a twinkle in his eye when he smiled.

I made my pitch to Moustapha, Paul Freeman, and Moustapha's son, Malek, who was a student at USC Cinema School at the time. I was incredibly nervous, but I had prepared a brief document to help me through the nerves! I think it was within a week that I heard I got the writing assignment. As far as rules or parameters, Moustapha was *very* protective of Michael Myers. And they wanted him to be consistent in his motivation and actions. As much as I loved the franchise, I had no issues with that.


**Your *Two Faces of Evil* draft seems mindful of previous storylines, though not overly preoccupied with any of them. Was it at all difficult picking up the story after the conclusion of *Halloween 6*, especially given the passing of Donald Pleasence?**

I have never seen the "producer's cut" of *Halloween 6* that everybody says is *so much better* than the theatrical release. Having said that – I was not a big fan of this one. It was way too campy. The story bordered on the absurd with the Man in Black and genetic experiments. Michael also looked like he could use a personal trainer. I considered *Two Faces of Evil* to be my opportunity to help right the ship after that one.

My original pitch for *Halloween 7* was to set the movie at an all-girls boarding school. The movie starts when Michael is found dead in a maximum-security penitentiary. He's transported to the local morgue. As you can imagine, things don't go well for the mortician and soon Michael Myers is out and about wreaking havoc on the students at the boarding school. I believe it was producer Paul Freeman who had the idea of adding a copycat killer to the fray who was captured and served the same purpose as Hannibal Lecter in *The Silence of the Lambs*. My *Two Faces of Evil* draft, the two faces being Michael Myers and the copycat killer, evolved from there.

Before it became *Halloween H20* with Jamie Lee Curtis reprising her role, I really just wanted to make a film that I would enjoy as a fan of the original. I wanted to try and recapture as best I could what John Carpenter had in the first *Halloween*. It had the lowest budget of any of them and yet, in my mind, it was the scariest of them all. Carpenter couldn't rely on big budget effects, he didn't have unlimited set-ups and unlimited shoot days. He had to boil down the story and characters to their most primal level.

Ultimately, the boarding school afforded me a "micro-Haddonfield" where I could let Michael Myers loose and focus on the inventiveness rather than the goriness of the murders. And the copycat element added a distinct story device that added a layer of complexity to the script. It also afforded me the opportunity to bring in a character to "fill the shoes" of Dr. Loomis, as impossibly large shoes to fill as they were!

**If you could've cast anyone in *Two Faces of Evil*, who would you have chosen for the lead roles of Detective Kinkade and Cain Gabriel?**

Remember you said "anyone" in your question. Taking myself twenty years ago to 1998, the first names that come to mind are Bruce Willis or Denzel Washington as Detective Kinkade and Kevin Spacey as Cain Gabriel.

**Tell me about the next step in *Halloween 7*'s evolution as Kevin Williamson came on. What was your impression of his initial treatment?**

Let me back up to the beginning drafts before Jamie Lee was involved… I completed the first draft of *Two Faces of Evil* and turned it in. It might have been the second revision, I'm not sure. The next thing I knew my agent called and said Bob Weinstein was thrilled with the script and wanted to meet with me. It was in that meeting that he told me he had personally spoke to Jamie Lee Curtis and she agreed to the do the film for its twentieth anniversary. He said they loved the boarding school idea and asked my thoughts regarding working her into the current story. I suggested she be a teacher or head mistress at the school. The first draft I turned in with Jamie Lee was called

*Halloween: Blood Ties*. The proceeding drafts were called *Halloween: The Revenge of Laurie Strode*. I am a big *Star Wars* fan and I remember when *Return of the Jedi* was originally called *Revenge of the Jedi*. I always preferred that title, so I had fun with the idea of *Halloween 7* being called *The Revenge of Laurie Strode*.

The strange thing is I had no idea Kevin had even written a treatment until months after turning in my revised draft. I don't even know what Dimension might've told Kevin – in regards to my involvement – or the existence of the drafts I wrote. They could have suggested the prep school idea to him.

There was some dispute regarding credit. I know Dimension wanted Kevin to be credited with story by. The credits went to WGA arbitration where an independent panel reviewed all the outlines and drafts. All material is labeled anonymously (e.g. Writer A, Writer B, Writer C). After the panel reviews, they determine final credit. Everyone who has a stake in the game has their own opinion of who deserves what credit, which is why it's so important to have a non-biased independent panel review and determine credit. The original pitch and subsequent versions were crafted by myself along with input from Moustapha, Paul Freeman, and Malek Akkad. Later, Kevin Williamson was brought aboard as a producer. I had one notes call with him on a first or second draft of the film. Moustapha was *heavily* involved with the concept. He really had an affinity for the franchise and Michael. He was incredibly protective, in the best possible way, of the characters and the franchise as a whole.

**How did you initially view Jamie Lee Curtis' big return to the franchise? And did this at all complicate your work on the screenplay? Did she have any input or notes?**

*I was thrilled!!* Did I just yell that?! *Yes, I did!* The project literally went from a small direct-to-video seventh installment to a major theatrical event. Did it mean more laborious hours at the keyboard for me? *Absolutely*. Did I care? *Absolutely not*. I honestly don't know if I was more excited as a fan or as the writer.

I believe it was Jamie Lee herself who had strong ideas about where the character would be emotionally after twenty years of dealing with her tormented past. The functioning alcoholic angle, while not wholly original, certainly was believable. Before it was determined that there would be no reference to *Halloween 4* through *Halloween 6*, I attributed much of her pain to the

234

fact she thought by staging her death she was protecting her daughter, Jamie. Of course, Michael found his niece and the rest was history. But even without this backstory, having gone through the terror of Halloween night twenty years prior was certainly enough to drive her to drink.

Jamie Lee was also so gracious. When I visited the set one day she asked if I'd seen any of the dailies. When I said I hadn't, she invited me to watch some of them in her bungalow. Another surreal and very memorable moment! I first saw the complete film at the premiere in Westwood. My wife and I sat behind Jamie Lee, Tony Curtis, and Janet Leigh! Watching the film was (and still is) one of the highlights of my career. I was extremely proud of the end result. And all that everyone in that theater contributed to the final product!

**Your *Two Faces of Evil* detective carried over to *Halloween H20* but was cut before filming began. The theatrical version of *H20* is quite fast-paced. Would you have rather kept the detective sub-plot in *H20* or does his absence improve the film by making it more lean?**

The detective character worked well when the film was more of an ensemble. He nicely filled the unfillable-shoes of Donald Pleasence. But once Jamie Lee signed on, I just found myself wanting to get back to her story. My father, Marco Zappia, was an Emmy award-winning editor. I grew up in an edit bay watching him craft story in the edit room. In many ways I credit those experiences to my seemingly innate ability to keep writing screenplays that are tightly woven and are always driving the story forward. In this case, the detective scenes seemed to get in the way of what I wanted to see as fan…LAURIE "FREAKIN'" STRODE! So onto the chopping block they went!

**In both *Two Faces of Evil* and your original *H20* script, there are scenes involving a retractable gym-floor pool, which is a pretty unique idea for a horror film. Creatively, where does this come from? Did you have a traumatic incident earlier in life involving such a pool?**

No traumatic incident that I can recall, at least not one that involved a retractable gym-floor pool. It actually comes from one of my favorite holiday films, *It's A Wonderful Life*. I remember seeing that film on television as a kid and thinking, '*Whoa! There is such a thing as a pool under a gym-floor? Cool!*' So yes, in one draft the floor of the gymnasium opens up to reveal a pool, Michael crashes the dance, and Laurie impales him with a javelin. He falls into the pool as the floor closes above him. Sounds crazy, right? But in the context of the draft it was a lot of fun!

Another ending involved Laurie driving a bus from the school full of students trying to escape Michael Myers. He makes his way onto the bus, it crashes and teeters on the edge of a cliff. Laurie manages to get all the students off the bus and leaps to safety as the bus falls hundreds of feet with Michael dangling from the bumper to his death. Another fun one!

And I know we had one ending that involved a helicopter decapitating Michael Myers, which was a version of the teetering bus scene. That was our *Mission: Impossible*-style ending. Way too pricey for the for the folks at Dimension Films!

**One of the crazier internet rumors I've read regarding your abandoned copycat killer plotline was that you considered using Stephen Lloyd, the baby from *Halloween 6* who would now be an adult. Any truth to that?**

Nope. No truth to that, whatsoever. Dimension Films had wanted to distance *Halloween 7* from *Halloween 6* right from the very beginning, even before it became *Halloween H20*. So I never considered the killer to be Stephen Lloyd.

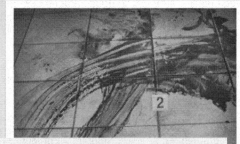

# Hillcrest Academy

# Student Handbook

**Find yourself here.**

## Hillcrest Academy

### Keri Tate
*Headmistress*

Phone: (818) 555-2104
Fax: (818) 555-2109
keritate@hillcrest.edu

2280 Durand Avenue,
Summer Glenn, CA 91750

# THE HELLRAISER CROSSOVER

Hell comes to Haddonfield.

**Treatments by
Dave Parker &
Josh Stolberg / Bobby Florsheim**

Frankenstein and the Wolf Man. Godzilla and King Kong. Alien and Predator. In the annals of legendary horror match-ups, these are the most touted showdowns. But Michael Myers and Pinhead? While not usually among the first names mentioned, these two icons have also been tossed around for decades as a possible pairing – and not just on fan forums. But why? *Halloween* and *Hellraiser* are starkly different franchises. The two have virtually nothing in common. Technically, Pinhead isn't even a slasher. The reason these two cinema monsters almost crossed paths most obviously lies in the fact that, for around twenty years, both franchises were controlled by Dimension Films. This made a potential hybrid-sequel that much more of an actual possibility. And for the briefest moment in time, it was a very real possibility.

For the uninitiated, the general premise of the *Hellraiser* series is roughly this. There is a black and gold puzzle box known as the Lament Configuration, often kept by a homeless-looking transient known as the "Puzzle Guardian," who gifts it to unsuspecting victims. When opened, the puzzle box summons extra-dimensional beings known as the Cenobites, who self-describe as "explorers in the further regions of experience. Demons to some, angels to others." (Demon would seem most apt.) These denizens of the underworld are led by the nefarious Pinhead, who functions as "the High Priest of Hell." The Cenobites can only reach Earth when summoned by the box and prefer to take with them fresh souls for the return trip home. Pinhead and his Cenobite cronies have a recurring nemesis in final girl Kirsty Cotton, who has tricked them into sparing her life more than once.

Before discussing the ill-fated *Halloween/Hellraiser* crossover, one must first acknowledge the influence of what is undeniably the biggest monster mash of all time – *Freddy vs Jason*. The 2003 horror showdown debuted atop the domestic box office and remained there for two consecutive weeks before ultimately grossing $82 million. New Line's success with the project led many of its rivals to develop their own potential crossovers. Though few of these projects were ever greenlit, the following year did see 20th Century Fox finally crank out the long-awaited *Alien vs Predator* to mixed results. Elsewhere on the small screen, the Sci-Fi Channel premiered *Puppet Master vs Demonic Toys* and *Boa vs Python*. This was also the year Dimension had planned to release their own crossover between *Halloween* and *Hellraiser*. But we're getting ahead of ourselves. Though *Michael vs Pinhead* only became a strong possibility after *Freddy vs Jason* murdered its box-office competition, the earliest rumblings of such a project pre-dated the New Line film by several years.

It's unclear to what degree Dimension execs seriously considered pairing the franchises, but it was an idea tossed around as far back as the mid-1990s. *Halloween* and *Hellraiser* were already connected in a roundabout way through their shared studio parent. Not long after helming *Halloween 6*, director Joe Chappelle was brought onboard *Hellraiser*'s troubled fourth installment as a replacement director in post-production. (*Hellraiser: Bloodline*'s original director would refuse to return for studio-mandated reshoots and ultimately remove his name from the project altogether.) Bizarrely, clips from *Hellraiser: Bloodline* would feature in various TV spots promoting *Halloween 6*'s September 1995 release.

The crossover idea must've been percolating in the minds of those at the far ends of the company, as the creators behind *Hellraiser* seemed aware that such a mash-up might happen. Two of its most notable alumni would even mention the possibility to press – not always favorably, mind you. Screenwriter Peter Atkins, who had penned the second, third, and fourth Pinhead ventures, confessed to the magazine *Lost Souls*, "Frighteningly, [Dimension does] own Michael Myers, so *Pinhead vs Michael Myers* might become a distinct possibility somewhere down the road, but I'll have nothing to do with it." Calling the idea "creatively bankrupt," the writer would, however, express that he was "tickled" by the idea his Pope of Hell could join the ranks of those featured in the Universal crossovers. "It kind of amuses me that, hey, maybe our monster will get to be part of this big monster mash. Tag teams from hell!"

Even more damning than his statement was the one by Pinhead actor Doug Bradley. During publicity for *Bloodline*, he remarked to *Fangoria*, "With New Line producing this Freddy/Jason crossover, my biggest fear is that, since Dimension has bought the rights to both the *Halloween* and *Hellraiser* films, some bright spark is going to come up with a *Pinhead vs Michael* script." His instincts weren't wrong. In anticipation of *Freddy vs Jason* reaching the screen, a crossover between these two baddies had already gained momentum outside the company with aspiring horror filmmakers, many of whom grew up with these characters.

## HELLRAISER: HELLOWEEN (1998)

The first known attempt to crossover *Halloween* with *Hellraiser* was by genre fan and filmmaker Dave Parker in the late '90s. A man of many hats, Parker is variously a writer, director, editor, actor, and producer. Most notably, he's the writer/director of such films as *The Dead Hate the Living!, The Hills Run Red,* and *Tales of Halloween* (segment: "*Sweet Tooth*"). He's also one of three credited screenwriters on Uwe Boll's 2003 film *House of the Dead,* though he takes that film's critical reception in stride. Oddly enough, Michael and Pinhead weren't the first horror icons he had tried to bring together. Parker had previously pitched *Freddy vs Jason* to Sean Cunningham's Crystal Lake Entertainment in 1995 without success.

Anticipating that the in-development *Freddy vs Jason* would trigger a wave of horror crossovers, Parker considered other characters he could square off against one another. That's when he realized the rights to both *Halloween* and *Hellraiser* were held by the same company – Dimension Films. This detail was important as a *Halloween/Hellraiser* crossover wouldn't require any messy licensing deals with other studios. Parker not only wrote a treatment for his story; he also created a faux-trailer as a visual aide using clips from the existing films. The project's working title was *Hellraiser: Helloween* or more simply *Helloween.*

"I was a big fan of *Frankenstein Meets the Wolf-Man, House of Frankenstein,* and the other monster rallies," Parker told *Fangoria* in 2003. "I was like, '*Oh God, Freddy vs Jason would be so much fun in a geeky sort of way.*' Then I started thinking about what other ones you could feasibly do, and obviously Dimension had both Pinhead and Michael Myers. So, I started thinking about how it might work and came up with a take that wasn't one-hundred-percent true to both mythologies, but there was something there that definitely worked."

Parker's *Helloween* immediately veers into sacred territory with a new spin on the Shape's origin – a risky move by any measure. The story takes us back to that fateful night in October 1963, just moments before young Michael murders his older sister. While trick-or-treating, the boy comes across the shady-looking "Puzzle Guardian." Instead of candy, the vagrant hands Michael the infamous puzzle box. On the walk home, he unwittingly opens it. This would ordinarily summon Pinhead and the Cenobites, but not this time. Instead, a demonic entity named Sam Hain (aka the "Lord of the Dead") escapes hell through the box and possesses young Michael, transforming him into the Shape as we now know him. Michael/Sam Hain then return home to kill Judith per the original *Halloween*'s opening scene – and the rest is history. (Interestingly enough, this wasn't the first time a screenwriter has gone back to the original's prologue to explain Michael's reason for killing. Recall that Phil Rosenberg's *Halloween 666* suggested an evil vaporous mass had possessed Michael that night. The actual *Halloween 6* alternately told how Michael heard evil voices telling him to kill.)

Parker's story then jumps ahead to present day where we find several characters breaking into the old Myers house. This crew of trespassers consists of new and returning characters from both franchises – including Kirsty Cotton. They're on a mission to find something, though we're not sure what. Breaking through a wall in Michael's room, they stumble upon the puzzle box. Naturally, someone accidentally opens it, which calls out to Sam Hain aka the Shape, who returns home. This also summons Pinhead and the Cenobites to the Myers house, who immediately recognize the Shape as the escaped demon. A knock-down, drag-out fight ensues with the trespassers caught in the middle. The action eventually spills out of the Myers house and down into the bowels of Hell for the final act.

## "I'm not saying this is the greatest idea ever or anything like that; I was just trying to come up with a plausible way to get these two guys together to fight."

- Dave Parker, Fangoria.com

It's a tall order to bring together two such disparate franchises, but Dave Parker manages it with his *Helloween* pitch. He also makes an earnest effort at intertwining the two mythologies as a pretext for the central conflict. The notion of a dark soul escaping Hell is not unprecedented in *Hellraiser* mythology. As "the High Priest of Hell," Pinhead would surely want to recapture the Shape, whom Parker charges is actually Sam Hain. Per this pitch, these two would be natural enemies from the start. Each horror icon gets a shot at home field advantage by fighting on their own turf – be it the Myers house or Hell itself – not unlike how the title characters did in *Freddy vs Jason*. Parker also plants several satisfying callbacks to each series. The Sam Hain character is itself a reference to the Celtic holiday Samhain, which the Shape scrawled in blood on a school chalkboard in *Halloween II*.

(Recall that *Halloween III* scribe Nigel Kneale had used "Sam Hain" as a character name in his original script for that film, which we detailed in the first *Taking Shape*. Both he and Parker are actually using a popular misreading of the word, however. Even Dr. Loomis says it wrong in *Halloween II*. For a correct pronunciation of Samhain, see how Dan O'Herlihy's Conal Cochran says it in *Halloween III*. It's pronounced "sow-in." Okay, grammar lesson over.)

Parker managed to score a meeting with a Dimension executive in late 1998. Armed with his story and proof-of-concept trailer, he pitched *Helloween* to a studio suit who immediately responded that they weren't interested in merging the two properties. In the studio's defense, there hadn't been a successful horror crossover in decades as *Freddy vs Jason* was still several years away. Factor in *Hellraiser*'s diminishing box office returns and the studio's reluctance is perfectly understandable. Little did Parker know that the *Hellraiser* films were about to nosedive in quality as Dimension embarked on a string of unfortunate direct-to-video sequels. Some of these weren't even originally written as *Hellraiser* scripts, but rather purchased on the cheap and retrofitted with cameos from Pinhead and the Cenobites. The first of the direct-to-video entries, *Hellraiser: Inferno*, would arrive in November 2000. The *Halloween* franchise would suffer its own dip in quality with the 2002 release of *Halloween: Resurrection*.

## HALLOWEEN IN HELL: MICHAEL VS PINHEAD (2002)

The next significant crossover pitch came several years later from the writing team of Josh Stolberg and Bobby Florsheim. A screenwriting veteran of twenty years, Stolberg has since written such genre hits as *Piranha 3D, Sorority Row, Jigsaw,* and most recently *Spiral: From the Book of Saw*. Along with writing partner Florsheim, Stolberg also wrote *The Passion of the Ark*, a spec script that became the basis for 2007's *Evan Almighty*. Yet at the time of their crossover pitch, Stolberg was known primarily for his work in television writing for shows like *So Weird* and *Honey, I Shrunk the Kids: The TV Show*.

Stolberg and Florsheim made their pitch in late 2002 not to some random Dimension exec, but direct to Moustapha Akkad at Trancas International Films. Titled *Halloween in Hell: Michael vs Pinhead*, the two envisioned a crossover between the horror icons as a major event film that could reinvigorate both franchises. Their pitch to Akkad was comprehensive and even included details of how the film could be marketed to audiences. Florsheim visualized a boxing-style poster that pit Michael against Pinhead complete with fight statistics, kill counts, and their preferred weapons of choice. (The tagline: "This Halloween, they're gonna raise a little Hell!") This approach was very similar to how New Line would later market *Freddy vs Jason* with a Las Vegas boxing match weigh-in.

*Halloween in Hell* opens outside Chicago with a support group for horror film survivors. Most notably in attendance are Kirsty Cotton and Jamie Lloyd, but other attendees include characters from films such as *Critters*, *The Prophecy*, *Leprechaun*, and *Phantasm*. Jamie explains the Thorn curse to her peers and shares how it's been a terrible hardship for her. ("I can't date. I can't hold down a job without everyone getting massacred. I have to keep a blood supply in the hospital for the next attack. He just keeps coming.") She also mentions that it's been seven months since the Shape last tried to kill her, which he tries again as the meeting ends. The other survivors rush to her defense, resulting in a giant melee. Holding the puzzle box, Kirsty dives in front of Jamie to deflect one of Michael's stabs. His blade pierces the box, the force of which fatally embeds it into Kirsty's chest. Having been summoned by the stabbed box, Pinhead and the Cenobites arrive to find Kirsty dying. She uses her last breath to taunt her old adversary. ("You never got me.") Pinhead is furious that Kirsty has died by someone else's hand and vows revenge against her killer. He instructs his Cenobite followers, "Find out who did this. Her soul belonged to me. I will collect from someone."

Having escaped the Shape's attack, Jamie heads for the nearby hospital where she has a personal blood supply on tap. After giving Jamie an infusion, her nurse gravely errs by returning her blood to general storage rather than her private stock. This gaffe results in seven unfortunate people being given Jamie's cursed blood this evening, which makes them all automatic targets of the Shape. (He can instinctively sense other members of his bloodline.) Not only that, but Pinhead and the Cenobites have declared war on both Michael Myers and those in his bloodline. Jamie and the seven transfusion-recipients are now caught in a hellacious battle between a relentless slasher and literal demons. This motley crew of seven are soon whittled down to just one – a hyper-intelligent ten-year-old named Betsy – who teams up with Jamie to stay alive.

Jamie and Betsy wind up inside the spooky mansion of the monster-obsessed Horace Merryweather, who earlier stole the puzzle box from the hospital morgue. Horace reveals there are one-hundred-and-sixty Lament Configurations on earth – and that he now possesses all of them. While they can't be used to kill Pinhead or the Shape, they can be used to trap both monsters in Hell. To do this, the puzzle boxes must be combined in just the right manner – as though a Rubik's cube made by Satan. They manage this uneasy task just as their monstrous pursuers close in, which opens a portal to Hell. The final act unfolds with a showdown between the entire surviving cast in Hell.

The finale would kick an already exhilarant crossover into overdrive. As Stolberg and Florsheim pitched it, "The unstoppable force is meeting the immovable object and all Hell is coming down around them." The Shape decapitates several Cenobites before moving in on Pinhead, even using his own chains against him. The slasher pulls out half of Pinhead's pins while shoving the other half further into his skull. The two titans battle it out until one emerges victorious. (We'll address this later.) The victor then sees Jamie and Betsy attempting to close the Hell portal using the giant Lament Configuration. The girls manage this at the last second, sealing the portal closed and their tormentors within it. An injured but still alive Jamie and Betsy limp away into the sunset.

Stolberg and Florsheim's vision for *Halloween in Hell* would've arguably made it the most bloody, action-packed, and big spectacle entry in either franchise. It would've also required a budget millions above what was usually spent on these films. Their pitch has a strange relationship with the existing continuity, particularly on the *Halloween* side. No explanation is given for how the Shape continued on from the ending of *Halloween: Resurrection*. (Recall that he was looking extra-crispy in that film's final moments.) The decision to return to *Halloween 6*'s Thorn storyline is a surprising one given that *Halloween H20* essentially erased it from the timeline. Not only that, but the screenwriters inexplicably resurrect final girl Jamie Lloyd, whom we most assuredly saw die in *Halloween 6*. Even so, fans would've surely cheered on the return of not only Jamie, but of actress Danielle Harris, whom the writers mention by name in their pitch.

While this treatment wastes no time in killing off *Hellraiser* heroine Kirsty Cotton, it does find a way for her to still win even in death. Kirsty goes down fighting on her own terms, depriving Pinhead the pleasure of claiming her soul. Her death then clears the way for Jamie to take center stage as the lead protagonist of our story. The later pairing of young adult Jamie with adolescent Betsy would seem a winning move, warmly evoking the sister dynamic Rachel and

Jamie shared in *Halloween 4*. To this story's credit, the blood transfusion plot device could've allowed for some much-needed diversity in the cast. Whereas the Shape typically stalks white high schoolers from Haddonfield, he would now have seven new targets of varying age, race, background, and characterization.

The writers inject much humor throughout their story, but never at the expense of the battling monsters, which is an important distinction to make. Some of that humor is incredibly prescient. Take one of the transfusion recipients – a goth known as "Fangula, Dark Lord of the Underworld." In actuality, this is Ed, a vampire-wannabe who still lives with his mother. Upon first encountering Pinhead, Ed believes he's found a kindred spirit and asks where the Cenobite leader got his piercings. He's also convinced they've met somewhere before, possibly at a Rob Zombie concert. (Ha! For the record, this pitch pre-dates Zombie's involvement with the series by several years.) Pinhead ultimately dispatches poor Ed by giving him several thousand new piercings all at once.

Stolberg's deep-rooted horror fandom manifests itself frequently throughout his *Halloween in Hell* pitch. He not only envisions a shared universe between the two titular franchises, but with other franchises as well. Consider the various horror heroes in attendance at the opening support meeting. Stolberg and Florsheim reference survivors from *Critters, The Prophecy, Leprechaun,* and *Phantasm* – "an assortment of characters that any horror fan would recognize." (It's worth noting that Dimension only held rights to characters from *The Prophecy* and that others would require licensing from rival studios.) The screenwriters pack in additional horror references through the Horace Merryweather character, whose mansion is a veritable museum of horror oddities. Horace's collection includes such prizes as Freddy Krueger's glove, Hannibal Lecter's mask, and Jeffrey Dahmer's cutlery. (Creepily enough, it also includes a locket of Laurie Strode's hair.)

One crucial detail missing from the plot synopsis several paragraphs back was who exactly won the title fight – the Shape or Pinhead? As Stolberg and Florsheim wanted it, both monsters would've won in their own way. The screenwriters originally wanted two endings created for the film – each with a different winner. These would then be randomly distributed to theaters so that audiences would have no way of knowing which ending they would receive. They might then pay to see the film again and again hoping to catch the alternate finale. While the winner would've varied depending on the print, the film would've still concluded with Jamie and Betsy closing the portal to Hell and limping into the sunset together. This randomized ending gimmick had been previously considered for *Freddy vs Jason* but ultimately abandoned. Director Rick Rosenthal suggested a similar approach on *Halloween: Resurrection*, though producers rejected the idea there as well.

Should the duo's meeting with Akkad turn south, a last-ditch effort had already been devised to impress the producer – an alternate prelude to the finale. Like Parker's pitch, this set piece would have altered the course of past *Halloween* history. Following the same basic premise, the duo would divert their story in the third act. Angered that the Shape has racked up a higher body count, Pinhead would attempt to settle the score by traveling back in time to October 31, 1978 – the night of the first two *Halloween* films. Scenes from these films would be recreated with the High Priest notably knocking off several of the Shape's past victims. As pitched, "We know Michael kills the one girl (Annie) by waiting for her in the backseat of the car and strangling her from behind. So, we see Michael waiting in the car – but Pinhead kills the woman outside the garage before she even gets into the car." When considering this pitch, Stolberg admits that he prefers this alternate finale, likening it to the sequence in *Jason X* where the hockey-masked slasher ventures through a virtual Camp Crystal Lake

So, how exactly did Stolberg and Florsheim's pitch go over with Moustapha Akkad? Well, we know it wasn't fruitful. It's no secret that, by this time, Akkad had established a series of rules to guide future *Halloween* films – literally. He kept in his desk a photocopied set of narrative guidelines intended for prospective writers looking to pitch new sequel stories. The *Halloween in Hell* treatment went against several of the producer's firmly-held views. Akkad took issue with the story's artificial expansion of the Shape's bloodline via transfusion. He was also reluctant to return to the Thorn storyline from *Halloween* 6, an installment he described to *Fangoria* as being "a major disappointment." Furthermore, Akkad has long felt that the *Halloween* series should be as grounded in realism as possible, an approach at odds with Cenobites from Hell.

"I always try to keep to realistic stories. Somebody with ten ears and ten eyes isn't scary. But if you're locked inside a house with somebody who wants to kill you, that could happen to anybody."

- Moustapha Akkad, The Producers: Profiles in Frustration

## THE CREATORS STEP IN (2003)

By 2003, both Dimension and Trancas had independently received and rejected multiple pitches for a *Halloween/Hellraiser* crossover. Oddly enough, it was only after these rejections that the project began to pick up major steam. So, what changed? The industry itself did after the August 13, 2003 release of *Freddy vs Jason*. The New Line monster brawl brought in an impressive $116 million worldwide gross and its home video releases debuted in the number one spot as well. Consider also the wave of merchandising that followed. *Freddy vs Jason* enjoyed a novelization, action figures, costume accessories, comic books, various apparel, and two soundtracks, one of which actually made it onto the *Billboard* charts.

Eagerly hoping to replicate New Line's success, Dimension immediately set about fast-tracking a *Michael vs Pinhead* project through development and into production for release the following year. Surprisingly, they had somewhat noble intentions with the film as evidenced by who they reached out to – series creators John Carpenter and Clive Barker. Dimension's plan was to secure Carpenter to direct the film from a screenplay by Barker. The only problem was that both men had long ago walked away from their respective franchises, each frustrated by the direction taken with the sequels. Barker had told *USA Today* that sequels were generally "a wretched business" and that most were "imaginatively impoverished."

Of his first exit from the *Halloween* franchise in 1987, Carpenter told *Fangoria*: "It was like a great weight had been lifted from my shoulders. I could finally stop feeling guilty about being responsible for the outcome. I told the producers, '*Don't put my name on [Halloween 4.] Don't even credit it as based on characters created by John Carpenter and Debra Hill.*' But they're trying to attach my name to it anyway. I suppose they will, at least in terms of the music." On the subject of his exit from *Hellraiser* in 1998, Barker told *SFX Magazine*: "I have a limited time on the planet to make things, so I can't watch over the sequel to the sequel of *Hellraiser*. I just can't do that. […] At the end of the day, film is a director's medium. So, as executive producer, I might say, '*We really shouldn't do this, guys; or this makes Pinhead look ridiculous; or this is inconsistent with the mythology.*' But, when I walk away, the director is going to be doing what he should be doing, which is directing the movie. Also, I have no contractual control over any of this material."

An initial meeting with Barker and Carpenter was scheduled only days after *Freddy vs Jason* racked $36.4 million across its opening weekend. Astonishingly, both men agreed to participate in a *Halloween/Hellraiser* crossover dependent upon the other creator's involvement.

While neither had worked together before, they were old friends who had long held each other in high regard. "I was kind of stoked by the idea," Barker said in the *Halloween: 25 Years of Terror* documentary. "I called up John and said, '*What do you think about this? Because if you don't want to do it, I won't do it.*' And he said, '*No, I'll do it.*'"

## "I thought it would have been a pretty cool idea."

### - Clive Barker, Penny Blood Magazine

On August 20th, *Creature-Corner* became the first website to break the news on a potential crossover. The site's Ryan Rotten reported that as of then, Dimension execs were "scrambling" to assign a story to the project. (Fun fact: Ryan Rotten is actually Ryan Turek, one of the Blumhouse producers responsible for *Halloween 2018* and its sequels. Bravo, Ryan. A fan that could and did!) Around this time, the site also published a rumor claiming that Carpenter was circling a remake of the original film. His wife and producing partner Sandy King Carpenter denied this but did reveal that discussions with Dimension regarding a *Hellraiser* crossover had occurred, publicizing that the horror maestro would be interested in directing if Barker was also involved.

Despite earlier hesitation, Doug Bradley was also game to reprise his character for a match-up against Michael Myers. The actor recounted learning of the project to *Your Movie Magazine* in 2016: "I was told that Dimension Films had rejected two pitches for a *Hellraiser/Halloween* crossover the year before *Freddy vs Jason* was released. I was told the reason they turned it down was because they didn't think it would work. They predicted that *Freddy vs Jason* would bomb, but it opened at the top of the box office and stayed there for a second weekend. I think I'm right in saying that it was the first movie that year to do so. After its success, Dimension wanted a *Hellraiser/Halloween* movie made immediately, so it was certainly going ahead. I had a couple of phone conversations with Clive Barker about it and I was getting quietly excited. Clive said he would write it and I heard reports John Carpenter would direct."

## WHY IT WASN'T MADE

With Carpenter and Barker on board, what could have possibly stopped such a blockbuster project with so much momentum from going forward? Moustapha Akkad himself. While Dimension had changed their tune on a *Halloween/Hellraiser* crossover following *Freddy vs Jason*, Akkad had not. It was his gut instinct to block the project from moving forward. And being that he still retained ownership of the *Halloween* brand, he was a gatekeeper the studio could not bypass. There was no such issue on the *Hellraiser* side of things as Dimension outright owned that property.

While Akkad had long been keen to work with John Carpenter again, despite their previous disagreements, this was not how he wished to do it. Concerned with maintaining the integrity of the *Halloween* brand, the producer may have felt that *Hellraiser* wasn't a good match. Not simply in story, but also the disparity in viability between the two series. Sure, *Halloween: Resurrection* hadn't been a huge success, but the overall franchise was faring far better than *Hellraiser*. By the time Dimension began seriously looking at a crossover, Pinhead had already become stuck in another kind of hell – the world of direct-to-video. At this moment in time, the series' seventh and eighth installments were already shot (back-to-back) and due for release soon.

It's interesting that *Hellraiser* would befall such a fate as the series held a unique position in the company's history. 1992's *Hellraiser III: Hell on Earth* marked the first title Miramax released under the newly-created Dimension label. Reviews were largely positive but after a disastrous fourth installment, the company demoted the series and had been cranking out home video sequels ever since. (In a twist of fate, *Hellraiser* is now earmarked for a theatrical reboot from Spyglass Media *and* a series on HBO – with *Halloween 2018* director David Gordon Green earmarked to helm the pilot.)

## "[Moustapha Akkad] didn't want the crossover to be made. I guess he didn't want Michael Myers hanging around with the likes of Pinhead."

- Doug Bradley, Yahoo Movie Magazine

"Michael is so viable that you don't need to combine him with anyone. You don't need to use that trick to introduce him to a larger audience."

- Nick Phillips, Halloween: 25 Years of Terror

Despite Akkad's hesitations, discussions persisted for about a month. Dimension pursued further development with Barker and Carpenter though Akkad remained steadfast in his disapproval. To gauge fan interest, the Trancas producer requested a poll be featured on *HalloweenMovies.com* inquiring whether fans would be interested in a *Halloween/Hellraiser* crossover. In less than two weeks, over eighty-thousand fans voiced their opinion with fifty-four percent voting a resounding 'NO' to the idea. Presenting these results to Dimension was enough proof that *Michael vs Pinhead* wasn't the right direction to head in. The brakes were applied and efforts to conjoin the franchises quickly ceased. Trancas and Dimension would return to the drawing board in developing the ninth *Halloween* entry.

A month later, Akkad would personally poll the audience at the *Halloween Returns to Haddonfield* 25th Anniversary convention. Fans applauded at his dismissal of the concept. Curiously, they cheered at the prospect of a crossover with fellow slasher Jason Voorhees. The producer would further explain his reasoning for ixnaying the project, stating, "I was against [the idea to match Michael against Pinhead]. Michael Myers, we always have a real person. He's not going through walls and killing at random. He's not someone who fell from the sky. He's a real person, so we have to match him with somebody real. I've had lots of pressure, but I've resisted."

"In the wake of Freddy vs Jason, any other team up is just going to look derivative. [...] When it comes to Michael, we don't feel we have to jump on any matchup bandwagon."

- Malek Akkad, Fangoria.com

In March 2004, John Carpenter was questioned by the Australian version of *Empire* on how the Shape would fare in a match-up: "He'd kick [Freddy and Jason's] asses. Well, the original Michael – my Michael – would. The modern Michael wouldn't stand a chance. These days, all the *Halloween* movies have xeroxed the formula to the point it isn't scary anymore. It's depressing." On whether he would ever direct another entry in the series, he said, "Well, my motto is: never say never. I have some ideas up my sleeve that would blow people away. Watch this space." Now, that phrasing is interesting. Was he referring to *Michael vs Pinhead*? Or perhaps his long-rumored idea of sending the Shape to space?

Rumors of a *Halloween* crossover persisted in the following years. In November 2005, Freddy Krueger actor Robert Englund informed *Bloody-Disgusting.com* that alongside a *Nightmare on Elm Street* prequel, New Line Cinema had been developing a potential crossover that might've involved the Shape. "New Line has commissioned two scripts," the actor said. "One is *Freddy vs Jason and Michael Myers*, or *Freddy vs Michael Myers*. I'm not quite sure how that works." If true, it's curious how New Line prepared for such a crossover. Had Dimension been involved in these discussions? Or would New Line reach out to the company only after having a complete concept to present? Nothing would come of this, however.

In retrospect, the idea of the crossover was but a brief craze of the 2000s that fizzled quickly, never truly latching onto the creative sphere in a way that remakes and reboots eventually would. One of the most notable examples – 2004's *Alien vs Predator* – made respectable bank yet it's a small miracle that film merited a sequel three years later. Not even *Freddy vs Jason* managed that feat despite several attempts. (One potential sequel – *Freddy vs Jason vs Ash* – was relegated to comic book form). As audacious as it might have been, it's easy to lament the inability for *Michael vs Pinhead* to grace theater screens. There was a brief time for it – but it appears that time has long since passed.

**Before we get into *Helloween*, you also pitched *Freddy vs Jason* around 1994, didn't you?**

Yes! I was one of around eight thousand people who did. There was a point in time where they would meet anyone who had an idea for *Freddy vs Jason*. Honestly, I can't even remember my pitch. It was probably not all that good, most likely a harebrained fan-ish kind of thing. It couldn't have been very good because I never made it beyond that first pitch meeting.

**What did you think of the *Freddy vs Jason* we eventually received in 2003?**

I think it was a lot of fun. I don't know that anyone could've done it much better than that. Sure, it's silly, but these things are already kind of silly by their very nature. You also have to consider the time in which that *Freddy vs Jason* was made in. It's not like they could suddenly go back and make Freddy super serious and scary. That's not where the character was at that time.

As a horror filmmaker, one thing I've learned is that there's a difference between what the hardcore fans want to see and what the general public wants to see. The general public are your more casual fans. They're also the ones that have the biggest impact on the box office, which is the studio's first consideration. Sure, they want to make a good movie, too, but they're out to make a hit. And *Freddy vs Jason* certainly served that purpose in that it was a huge money-maker. When you're a hardcore fan, you tend to believe the bullshit minutia you care about is important, when most people don't actually care about that stuff. People generally just want to be entertained and have an escape for ninety minutes. Every movie doesn't need to be this huge emotional catharsis, especially when you're talking about a slasher movie.

253

**How many years later was your *Halloween/Hellraiser* pitch?**

My *Freddy vs Jason* pitch was years and years before it was actually made. Anticipating that, I was like, '*This is gonna be so big.*' Just by the sheer nature of it. I was predicting that other studios would also want to make their own big horror crossover movies. And why not? Most of the big horror franchises were starting to wane in popularity and box office. I started looking at which companies owned which properties. At the time, Miramax owned both the *Halloween* and *Hellraiser* franchises. It seemed like a no-brainer to combine those two.

Because I'm also an editor, the first thing I did was make a proof of concept promo. I took footage from both franchises, recorded narration, and came up with a fake trailer for it. For the title, I combined *Halloween* and *Hellraiser* to come up with *Helloween*. I had this idea to bring back that iconic skull pumpkin from *Halloween II*'s poster, except that I wanted Pinhead's pins coming out of it. I was friends with an artist named Michael Hoover, who came up with that for me. And that's how my trailer ended with the title and that art. I showed it to some friends and it was a fun little video. I remember the narration went like, '*For years, Haddonfield has been haunted by this one thing. And this year, you'll find out the evil behind the mask*' or some bullshit. (laughs) And then I went, '*And it will tear your soul apart.*' That's when the trailer went into *Hellraiser* territory and I blended the footage to look like Michael and the Cenobites were facing off.

Around this time, I was brought in to do a trailer for *From Dusk Till Dawn 2* at Dimension Films. While I was there, I showed my *Helloween* trailer to guys like Scott Spiegel and Bob Murawski. I even sent it to Clive Barker just for fun. That's when Dimension heard about it and called me in to hear my pitch. I guess they were like, '*Alright, we'll take a meeting with this kid and see what he has to say.*'

**I've read that your pitch involved introducing a new character named Sam Hain, is that right? And that this character possessed young Michael in 1963, thus turning him into the Shape?**

That was the idea, yes. Sam Hain was my way of connecting these two very different properties. My story would've gone back to that night in 1963 where young Michael is out trick-or-treating. And someone, I don't know who, instead of giving him candy gives him the puzzle box from *Hellraiser*. Not knowing what it is, Michael opens the box, but it doesn't bring out the Cenobites like it usually does. It instead frees this demonic entity from Hell named Sam Hain. I thought I was being so clever tying it back to *Halloween II* because that's what Michael had written on the school chalkboard. So, Michael is now possessed, and that's what makes him kill his sister and become this unstoppable killer. He's been possessed by a demon this whole time. For the record, I realize that I was completely bastardizing what John Carpenter had done with the original film. Had this been made, it would've probably really pissed him off.

**That's the origin part. What about the present story of *Helloween*?**

It's difficult to remember exactly, but I think my story involved a group of people breaking into the old Myers house. I don't know why that place is even still standing. It's dilapidated and old. The town should've torn it down, but they haven't. So, these people are there searching for something. They break through a wall in Michael's room and come upon the *Hellraiser* puzzle box. There might've been a relative of Dr. Loomis in the group, I don't know. Kirsty Cotton from the first two *Hellraiser*s was definitely there. They find the box and someone accidentally opens it. This not only calls out to the Cenobites, but it alerts the Shape to return to his childhood home and he does. So, this group of characters is facing off with Michael Myers, but then Pinhead and the Cenobites show up. That's when Pinhead sees Michael for the first time and immediately recognizes him as Sam Hain. He even calls him that. The main goal of Pinhead and the Cenobites is to bring Sam Hain back to Hell since he'd escaped all those years before. Sort of like Frank Cotton did in the first *Hellraiser*. The Cenobites are like the enforcers of hell, you know? So, then it becomes a face-off between Michael and Pinhead.

**For a match-up that's inherently hokey, that's a pretty fun idea. I'm really intrigued that the Shape might be its own character apart from Michael. That's a novel concept.**

Thanks. There were just so many questions around the Shape. Why is this thing like it is? Why can't he be killed? Why won't he stop killing? Why is he mute? And why is he pure evil? Combining *Halloween* with *Hellraiser* allowed me to answer those questions. How cool would it have been to see the Shape stalking the labyrinthian halls of Hell that we saw in *Hellbound: Hellraiser II*? I also had an idea that the Shape might get Cenobitized. That could've been interesting. I envisioned them permanently affixing his mask to his face. Then they'd graft these two huge knives onto his arms. I was asking myself, *'If this match-up were to go down, what would I want to see as a fan?'* Cenobite Michael is what I came up with. Dragging Michael down into hell just seemed like the logical thing to do.

**It makes sense for that crossover. It's just like what happened to Dr. Channard in *Hellraiser II*. He ventured into hell and became a Cenobite himself. Do you recall how your story ended?**

I honestly don't remember, but it was all resolved in the end. I found a way to reset everything so that both franchises could go back to normal and have their own independent sequels again. I don't think anyone would want a permanent Cenobite Michael in the *Halloween* franchise. It was all kind of like what DC Comics does with their *Elseworlds* stuff where it's not entirely canon, but it is a fun way for two awesome characters to fight one another.

**How'd your pitch go over with Dimension?**

Not well. (laughs) I met with a guy at Dimension who was your typical studio executive. I showed him my proof of concept trailer and made my pitch. He was the most sullen-faced person I'd ever met. No emotion on his face whatsoever. At one point, I wondered if he even had a heartbeat. It seemed like he couldn't have been less interested if he tried. And then I left. That was it.

Years later, I read a story on *Dread Central* about Clive Barker and John Carpenter possibly teaming up to do *Helloween*. I was like, *'What!?!'* They just took the title and idea and approached them with it, I guess. And they did hold talks, both of them. I have a feeling Moustapha Akkad probably killed it. I can imagine him going, *'No. Absolutely not. I'm not doing that to my franchise.'*

**Moustapha did hold a poll asking fans what they thought of a potential *Hellraiser* crossover on the official *Halloween* website. The fans voted it down, but only narrowly so.**

I don't remember that, but it doesn't surprise me. That must've been around the time that they were seriously considering it. I wasn't expecting that they'd ever come back to me for it, though. I was just the bastard that jump-started the idea. I never got to meet Moustapha or show him my trailer. I don't know if Dimension ever shared it with him. The only thing my *Helloween* pitch ever led to was that this same executive also mentioned that Dimension was taking pitches for the next *Hellraiser* sequel. So I ended up pitching them on one of those as well, which also led nowhere.

**If you don't mind me asking, what was your *Hellraiser* pitch like?**

I don't remember much of that, either. It was a long time ago. But I did have an idea for a character I came up with for *Helloween* that I carried over to my standalone *Hellraiser* pitch. It's the one thing you never see in any of the *Hellraiser* movies. Who makes all of their blades and weapons in Hell? I came up with a character who was essentially "the Blacksmith of Hell." He created all of the weapons that the Cenobites use.

I had some conceptual art made for my *Hellraiser* pitch as well. By that point, I felt like the series had gotten too far away from the classic Cenobites of the earlier films. I wanted to bring them back to the forefront, but also update them. My designs weren't complete re-imaginings, but I did spruce them up a bit.

**What was your approach towards depicting Sam Hain? How would you have visually represented him? Another actor? Special effects? CGI?**

He was just Michael Myers. That's how I was going to represent him in my mind. We look at Michael and see only the Shape. But Pinhead looks at him and immediately calls him Sam Hain. He recognizes him. So in that sense, he would be unseen. We would only see him through his possession of Michael first as a young boy and later as an adult.

**What were your thoughts on *Halloween 2018*?**

I did like it, but it's complicated. Being an uber fan of this stuff, I would've obviously done it differently. I felt a little like we'd already seen this movie twenty years ago with *Halloween H20*, but it's still exciting to see Jamie Lee Curtis back as Laurie Strode. And also seeing Michael back to his old self from the original movie. I thought the Dr. Sartain character was a little wonky. For me, his motivation was explained a little too quickly and simply. It felt out of place, almost like they just did it just to facilitate something in the story. That part didn't work for me, but it was cool seeing Michael and Laurie face off again.

I didn't love *Halloween 2018*, but if I'm being honest, do I really love any of them besides the first? I really don't know. The original *Halloween* is such a juggernaut and trend-setter. The expectations on a *Halloween* sequel are going to be far higher than on, say, a *Friday the 13th* sequel. It's a daunting thing to try and make a great *Halloween* follow-up, especially when almost none of these movies have had a singular vision behind them. They're all saddled with a bunch of outside influencers that try to change things. The *Halloween* series is now controlled by all these producers who don't want to do anything that might risk the future of their golden goose. Unless you're someone like David Gordon Green, who comes in with a lot of respect from the company making the film, you're going to get a lot of input forced on you from other people. That's how things get muddled.

**How do you look back on this all? Is it weird having this unmade crossover attached to your legacy? You're mentioned online and in a great *Hellraiser* book as having pitched it. Most fans just sit at home writing fan fics, but you took a real shot at it. Do people ever ask you about it?**

No, never. I had no idea that people even knew about it. I've mentioned it publicly maybe once or twice before, but only fleetingly. This is the most detail I've ever discussed it in. I feel like people will hear about this and go, '*Aw, fuck! That writer from* House of the Dead *came up with a* Halloween/Hellraiser *crossover? I bet that would've sucked!*' (laughs) But honestly, I'd rather my name be known for having pitched *Helloween* than for having written *House of the Dead*. That's just the honest truth.

In the end, it's probably for the best that they never made it. I can't even imagine the potential damage a crossover like this could've done to both series, regardless of where either franchise is right now. In terms of mucking up the works, it could've been really bad. At best, a *Halloween/Hellraiser* crossover might make for an interesting comic book. Like a "What if?" kind of thing. But not a movie. The whole thing is just a small footnote in the histories of *Halloween* and *Hellraiser*. It's just something the studio considered for about ten seconds around the time of *Freddy vs Jason*. Then they came to their senses.

# JOSH STOLBERG

## Co-writer - Halloween in Hell: Michael vs Pinhead

Interviewed by Travis Mullins

**First things first, could you speak of your background as a fan of the genre?**

I've loved horror ever since I was a kid. Most little boys my age were into action figures and Legos but I spent every Saturday afternoon glued to the screen watching old horror movies. In my hometown of Sarasota, Florida, they had a double feature every week. It was called *Creature Feature* and the host was Dr. Paul Bearer. I fell in love with Boris Karloff and Vincent Price. But one of the first R-rated horror movies I ever saw was on HBO at my parents' friend's house on Halloween night. It was – as luck would have it – the original *Halloween*. I snuck out the bedroom that they tucked me into, and I watched from behind their living room couch. I was hooked. Fascinated. Disturbed. When my parents eventually got HBO, I'd sneak out some nights and watch movies at 2AM while they slept. One of the next horror films I remember seeing was *Humanoids of the Deep*. I still remember the main character's name was Peggy because I remember telling my mom how "Poppy popped" at the end! It was a blatant rip-off of *Alien*, which I wouldn't realize for a few years, but the pregnant woman's belly burst open and this bloody, fanged creature popped out, smiling. My exposure to these films changed my life. At that young age, I wasn't able to put a finger on what I loved about *Halloween*, only that I knew that I liked what it did to my "insides" – sort of like riding a roller coaster or swinging too high on the swing set. But even today, I can't stop watching it when it comes on TV.

**What were your thoughts on the *Halloween* sequels?**

I really enjoyed the first sequel. Picking up the story the same night was kind of perfect if you loved the original the way I did. It felt like the movie continued and would never stop – just like

Michael. It was like a homecoming for me. And following the legend that was John Carpenter, I thought Rick Rosenthal did a really nice job setting the film up for a franchise. Those second films are so important in helping to launch a franchise. If they don't work, your goose is cooked. Look no further than my own *Piranha 3D* and that subpar sequel. Anyway, years later, I hired Rick's son, Noah, as the DP for one of my first films – a romantic comedy called *Conception* – and we spent hours chatting about *Halloween*. While I know some people love *Halloween III*, I didn't really see what the filmmakers were trying to do when it first came out. I just really missed seeing Michael, so it landed with a thud for me. In recent years, I've learned to appreciate it more. The middle years of *Halloween* had some upsides to them. I really love Danielle Harris and was excited by the promise that her Jamie character was going to go to really dark places, but then they went in a different direction for *Halloween 5*, although I do love that film, too. Her performance is great and there were some stellar moments in both of those movies.

In later years, I thought Rob's films were really intriguing. To be honest, I look at them as Rob Zombie films instead of *Halloween* films. He really brought so much of what makes his movies so cool to them. Brutally violent, no holds barred, almost nihilistic in its delivery. It's hard to compare them to the rest of the catalog. They are almost as different as *Halloween III*. I might lose a lot of cred with *Halloween* fans by saying this, but my guilty pleasure favorite – besides the original – is *Halloween H20*. Everyone talks about how the new film made the brave choice of ignoring all the sequels but that's exactly what *H20* did! And sue me, I love Kevin Williamson's dialogue. With *Scream*, the guy single-handedly reinvigorated a dying genre and I love him for it. *H20* just hit me at a time in my life when I was really, really excited to see Curtis back in action. While certainly the new film takes Laurie's emotional journey to new heights, seeing her face down Michael in *H20* was, for me, one of the highlights of the franchise.

**So, how did the idea of a *Halloween* / *Hellraiser* crossover come about for you?**

As I mentioned earlier, I fell in love with horror watching *Creature Feature* as a kid. During that Golden Age of horror, when the audiences began getting bored of *The Mummy* and *Frankenstein* and *The Wolf Man*, the studio started putting the monsters together in films. *Frankenstein Meets The Wolf Man*, etc. So, I was already obsessed with the idea of these kinds of pairings. Right after high school, I made a little video that I edited on two VHS decks. It was a trailer for *Michael vs Pinhead: MVP. Halloween in Hell*. It's the dorkiest thing you've *ever* seen! I mean, *really* embarrassing! But I was barely out of high school. I still have the video; I'll send it to you if you want to see it. Anyway, I was a kid and had no way of getting my idea to Moustapha Akkad or Clive Barker or anyone else. It was just a kid's idea. So, the VHS tape went into the bookshelf and I forgot about it for years. Then, much later, when I was actually writing films, I saw that they were making *Freddy vs Jason,* so I dusted the VHS tape – it was so ridiculously cheesy I didn't show it at my pitch – but I talked my writing partner at the time, Bobby Florsheim, into working up a pitch with me. And my agent got us into a room with Moustapha Akkad.

**Speaking of Bobby, do you recall his input? How did the two of you formulate your ideas?**

Bobby is much more of a summer blockbuster kind of writer. Our films together would attach actors like Jim Carrey, Zach Galifianakis, and Todd Phillips. I've always been the horror guy. I will say that I do remember, specifically, that it was Bobby's idea for the posters, to design them to look like boxing matchups. And I remember that the victim support group was something that I was excited about. We wrote up two different versions of this same pitch. One was *Halloween in Hell,* and the other was called *Halloween: Bad Blood,* which was basically the same story with blood contamination, but it was all in the *Halloween* world and didn't bring *Hellraiser* into it. It was very similar in plot but without the Pinhead element. We pitched *Michael vs Pinhead* instead because we felt that after *Halloween: Resurrection,* the franchise was in need of a reboot. A clean start. And with *Freddy vs Jason* about to come out, we gambled, and it just didn't pay off.

**The idea of a blood transfusion is an interesting one and introduces a slew of new victims with distinct character traits. In a way, it seems very *Dream Warriors*.**

Yes, there are definitely similarities to [*A Nightmare on Elm Street 3: Dream Warriors*]. And when we came up with the blood transfusion idea, I thought it was a home run – a way to get Michael off the treadmill of the Strode storyline. At the time, the idea of Jamie Lee Curtis coming back wasn't even a consideration. I was excited to find a way to have both Jamie Lloyd and Kirsty Cotton in the same film. Being a horror nerd, that was really what I was pushing for.

**Your story immediately kills Kirsty albeit heroically as she dies to save Jamie. Did you have any apprehension in offing the *Hellraiser* franchise's leading lady?**

Yes! 100%. We thought there was a good chance that this would turn into a Jamie/Kirsty movie. And that would've been fine. But how much more fun is it to *think* you know how the film is going to go, and then it goes off in a completely different way? Like, how we killed Richard Dreyfuss off in the first scene of *Piranha 3D* or the way that *Scream* killed off Drew Barrymore. Part of the fun of a horror film is to kill the ones you love. It means *so* much more to an audience when they experience that loss with someone that they love. But yes, we were prepared to pivot if need be.

**Was there ever a concern about maintaining a balance between the two franchises?**

Yes, that was definitely a concern. Generally, Michael Myers is of this Earth, while Pinhead and his crew are very much not. So, there was a leap of faith you needed to make. But no more than *Freddy vs Jason*. They had a similar problem, and maybe even more of an issue, because *A Nightmare on Elm Street* has a fantasy element to it that the other three do not.

**Going off on that, which franchise would you consider yourself a bigger fan of?**

I am definitely a bigger fan of *Halloween*. Not that I don't love *Hellraiser*. It's a great film. And Clive Barker is a *monster* in the horror world. Getting a chance to work with him on *Weaveworld* and *Nightbreed* has been a dream, but you can't forget that *Halloween* was my first horror film. It was the first time I fell in love with the genre. And it was more "palatable" as far as the violence. *Hellraiser* is fucking dark! And I didn't find a taste for that kind of darkness until later in my horror development. Also, to me, *Halloween* was real. It felt like my neighborhood. It felt like people in my world. Jamie Lee Curtis felt like she could be my babysitter. There was a strong connection to the material at a young age – and it imprinted on me.

**Speaking of Jamie Lloyd, I love that you brought her back as the lead for this. Her relationship with Betsy hues similar to the relationship she shared with Rachel in *Halloween 4*, which is a nice touch. That said, it appeared that Jamie died in *Halloween 6*. Did you formulate an idea to get around that? What led you to pursue her as lead as opposed to say Laurie or Tommy?**

When we were coming up with storylines for *Michael vs Pinhead*, having Laurie in it felt too crazy because she was also dead. And Tommy Doyle had too much Thorn backstory that we didn't want to deal with. We just knew that there's always a way around a death in these kinds of movies. The question you need to ask is: "Will the audience forgive you for this far-fetched rescue because they are *excited* to have the character back?" We were also trying to set up many different bloodlines to follow after that. Which would allow us to step away from the bogged-down mythology.

**The horror collector Horace Merryweather certainly stands out among the newly introduced characters. If you could've cast that role with any actor, who would it be?**

At the time, we had Steve Buscemi in our heads. Quirky. Weird. Possibly dangerous. The kind of guy that collects horrific artifacts. My old writing partner Monica Johnson had bought a painting by John Wayne Gacy and I was both repulsed by it and fascinated. But the idea of someone collecting *all* the greatest serial killer weapons was interesting to me. And we thought of him with a bit of a rat-tat-tat-tat dialogue. A fun character. We even wrote out some of his dialogue in the pitch document to show that he's not stuffy and self-important.

**Tell us about your meeting with Moustapha Akkad.**

At the time, Moustapha was a *giant* of cinema to me. I mean, *Halloween* made me fall in love with slasher movies, so I was kind of blinded by his presence. We pitched our idea and while they seemed intrigued by the general concept – probably because *Freddy vs Jason* was about to open – Moustapha couldn't get past the "rules of *Halloween*." God, I wish I still had it, but Moustapha handed me a photocopied list that I'm sure he gave to everyone. The "rules of *Halloween* and Michael Myers." By this time in the franchise, there were a *lot* of fucking rules – because the direction the franchise went with followed the curse of Thorn, druids, cults and sacrifices. After

the meeting, Moustapha basically said that he couldn't make the movie we were pitching because it broke the "rules of *Halloween*." The rule that we had broken had to do with the bloodline. He felt that our story went against the rules of the franchise, so he didn't want any part of it.

I think there might have been an element of not wanting to kill the golden goose. It's hard to put the genie back in the bottle once you go big like that. That might've been a concern. Maybe they just hated the pitch, I really don't know. *Freddy vs Jason* came out in 2003 and we definitely pitched ours before that was released, because we mention it in our verbal pitch. I thought about trying to get a meeting with Clive Barker to talk to him about the idea, thinking that if he got excited, perhaps we could back into it that way. But I couldn't find a way to meet him. The crazy thing is that I'm currently working with Clive on a TV adaptation of *Nightbreed* and worked with him on a draft to expand out *Weaveworld* as well. He's one of the nicest guys in the world. I haven't mentioned to him my *Michael vs Pinhead* pitch yet, but I don't think he would've gone for it, either. His approach to horror is completely different from anyone else I've worked with in the business. The way he looks at the genre is totally unique and very Barker. He would *not* have liked what we cooked up. I'm actually very lucky it never happened because I treasure our working relationship now.

**Were you under the impression that you and your partner were the first to suggest such an idea or had there been prior rumblings about a *Halloween* / *Hellraiser* crossover?**

I honestly don't know. It certainly wasn't the most original idea, with *Freddy vs Jason* already in pre-production. I'm sure someone had thought of the idea. But I can promise you this. No one was thinking about it when I cooked up my VHS tape based on *Creature Feature*.

**Looking back at your pitch, what are your thoughts now?**

It's a relic of the writer I was over a decade ago and if I were to pitch a similar movie now, it would be *completely* different. This one is way too silly. It's very dated now. It leans way too much into humor. It's funny. We have a little notation at the end of the document, sort of a "in case of emergency, break glass" idea, which I always have at-the-ready in case a pitch goes sideways, and I actually like that idea more than what we pitched so many years ago.

# the Lament Configuration

*Avoid directly handling if at all possible.*

The Lament Configuration is a lock puzzle or puzzle box. The best known of these boxes is Lemarchand's Box. This was designed and made by Simon Sayer, one of the original creative team. A Lemarchand's box is a mystical/mechanical device that acts as a door — or a key to a door — to another dimension or plane of existence. The solution of the puzzle creates a bridge through which beings may travel in either direction across this schism.

The demonic being intoned, "The box. You opened it. We came." And then came the chains.

The interior surfaces were brilliantly polished. Frank's reflection — distorted, fragmented — skated across the lacquer. Lemarchand, who had been in his time a maker of singing birds, had constructed the box so that opening it tripped a musical mechanism, which began to tinkle a short rondo of sublime banality. The puzzle draws the player onward until suddenly [...] opened.

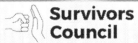

# HALLOWEEN
# H25

The Shape vs the Showman.
Round Two.

**Treatment by**
**Tim Day**

In the wake of *Halloween H20*'s runaway success, an eighth installment was a sure bet. There was but one problem. *The Shape was dead!* For most involved, the seventh film was truly meant to conclude the original storyline with Laurie Strode beheading the Shape in the sequel's final moments. This was the preferred ending of the screenwriters, Dimension execs, and even Jamie Lee Curtis herself. The singular holdout to this plan was Moustapha Akkad, who was banking on his ability to produce future sequels. To amend this, a compromise was proposed. As part of the eighth *Halloween*'s opening, it would be revealed that the slasher had switched places with an EMS worker. This meant Laurie had decapitated an innocent man, not her brother, thus sending her sanity into tailspin. While *Halloween 8* lacked even a rudimentary premise at this embryonic stage, it at least had a way to continue on from *H20*'s showstopping finale.

In August 2000, screenwriter Larry Brand was hired to formulate what would eventually become *Halloween: Resurrection*. His premise was undeniably unique, centering on the Shape attacking a group of college students shooting a live webcast from inside the abandoned Myers house. While chockful of nuances – Brand's concept being an inversion of the legendary *War of the Worlds* broadcast – studio meddling would see the final product devolve across all areas of development. While the genesis of any sequel is arguably related to business motives, *Halloween: Resurrection* would too obviously hue as a commercial product rather than a sincere artistic endeavor. (The most obvious example of this being the blatant stunt casting of rapper Busta Rhymes and supermodel Tyra Banks.)

Shot in the spring of 2001, *Resurrection* was initially due for release that fall. However, a series of poor test screenings necessitated re-shoots that would see the film opening in July 2002, instead. Hopelessly out of season amid giant summer blockbusters, the film debuted fourth at the box office with $12.2 million. While fan response was tepid (and that's being generous), culture critics declared open season on the eighth installment. As of this writing, the film holds a bruising 11% on Rotten Tomatoes. At the end of its worldwide theatrical run, *Resurrection* had grossed a modest $37 million against a $13 million budget, which is substantially less than *Halloween H20*'s $55 million. Given the film's negative response and fair box office, there didn't seem to be any obvious reason to rush a ninth *Halloween* into production for release the following year. And yet, that's very nearly what happened.

Before we discuss this proposed sequel, let's first look at where Dimension Films was in 2002. The genre-wing of Miramax had theatrically released three horror films this year – *Below*, *They*, and *Halloween: Resurrection*. The first two were outright bombs, each losing the studio many millions of dollars. Dimension did release a fourth horror picture this year, *Hellraiser: Hellseeker*, but it was a direct-to-video effort. Two bombs, a mediocre sequel, and a direct-to-video *Hellraiser* didn't exactly constitute a great year in horror. These disappointments were nothing at all like Dimension's previous year, which saw the release of horror blockbusters like *Scary Movie 2* and *The Others*. These two titles alone collectively grossed several hundred million dollars for the studio. Yet 2002 was an entirely different story.

One could even argue that Dimension's grip on the horror genre was starting to slip around the time of *Halloween: Resurrection*'s roll-out. With a disappointing year of genre releases and no new *Scream* in active development, Dimension was in need of a horror hit for 2003. Unfortunately for them, they had already downgraded most of their recognizable horror franchises to direct-to-video. (Which ones, you ask? *Hellraiser*, *Children of the Corn*, *From Dusk Till Dawn*, *Mimic*, *Dracula 2000*, *The Prophecy*, and *The Crow* – just to name a few.) Dimension had but two ongoing theatrical horror franchises left with *Scary Movie* and *Halloween*, the former of which already had a sequel scheduled for 2003.

Given all this, it's easy to see why Dimension might have some interest in getting another *Halloween* into theaters by the following year. That's where screenwriter Tim Day comes in. Having just co-written *Hellraiser: Hellseeker* – his first screenwriting credit – Day was approached by the studio to gauge his interest in writing a new *Halloween* sequel. He responded positively, and discussions began on where a possible ninth film might go. One of the studio's earliest requests was that Day utilize Busta Rhymes' Freddie Harris from *Resurrection*. As Bob Weinstein explained it, Rhymes was still under contract for two films at Dimension at a relatively low rate given his rising stardom in Hollywood. Day would submit his initial treatment for *Halloween H25* on December 5, 2002 – just five days before *Resurrection* arrived on home video.

The inherent challenge in making a sequel titled *Halloween H25* – as it was so dubbed by the studio – is that its title necessitates a very specific release window. The *H25* in *Halloween H25* obviously references *Halloween*'s twenty-fifth anniversary – a milestone it would reach only once in 2003. You couldn't roll that same movie out in 2004 or else it'd be *Halloween H26*, which somehow isn't quite as catchy. Being that Day had only just written a treatment in early December, he would've needed to scramble to complete a full screenplay. And Dimension, in turn, would've needed to rush to get it before cameras and completed before an October release date. That's all assuming that Trancas didn't have any major issues with the material. Best case scenario, this production was going to be a challenging race against time.

As we'll cover in future chapters, there were a handful of proposed *Halloween 9* scripts that attempted to wrap up the Dangertainment storyline. Not continue it, mind you, but conclude it. They tended to do this by having the Shape finally murder Busta Rhymes' character in their opening moments. *Halloween H25* is therefore a rarity among lost *Halloween* sequels for daring to continue on from *Resurrection*'s ending. Continuing this storyline may well be one of the most unenviable tasks for any screenwriter because – let's be honest – *Resurrection* wasn't exactly a bright spot among sequels. Despite this, screenwriter Tim Day tackles the assignment with gusto.

It's important to keep in mind that *Halloween H25* was never developed beyond an initial treatment, so this story doesn't represent the finalized version of a complete cinematic vision. Any kinks, oddities, or plot holes should be attributed to this fact. It's a little unfair to judge such an unfinished work, but we're here to dissect lost sequels in any form, so let's get to it.

## THE STORY

*Halloween H25* picks up where *Resurrection* left off inside a darkened Haddonfield morgue. A badly burned Shape rises from the slab to attack an attending worker. Her screams attract a nearby police officer, who fires on the slasher multiple times. Suddenly, a director yells, '*Cut, cut, cut!*' In actuality, this is not a continuation of *Resurrection*'s ending, but a staged recreation of it for an upcoming documentary on Michael Myers. It's now October 29, 2003 – one year after the Dangertainment fiasco at the Myers house. Survivor Freddie Harris has spent the past year self-financing and producing the documentary in hopes of bringing closure to Michael's victims and their families. Its gala premiere is set for Halloween night in Haddonfield with an audience comprised of victims, their families, nurses, doctors, and police. All proceeds are being directed toward the Haddonfield Victims Fund.

As part of his documentary, Freddie interviews Tracy Woods, a forensic psychologist with the FBI's serial killer unit. Agent Woods assures Freddie that Michael truly died last year, having actually risen from the morgue slab and been fired upon by multiple police. She then produces an urn containing his supposed ashes. ("I was there when they put him in the oven. He's gone, Freddie. End of story.") In actuality, Michael is still very much alive and being kept in a secret underground research facility outside of Chicago. Woods is well aware of this, having spent the past year studying him in great detail. Her goal has been to find what triggers Michael to kill. He's shown photos of his family, his victims, and even childhood toys, though the slasher's heart rate never changes. It does spike, however, upon being shown a Myers family heirloom, a music box that plays a cheerier version of the familiar *Halloween* theme. (Does such an upbeat composition even exist?)

The following day, the Shape manages a bloody escape from the FBI's underground facility. Upon exiting his cell, he notices a television playing a news story about Freddie's documentary premiere. He stops by Agent Woods' office on his way out, stealing an invite list for the premiere tomorrow night. This guest list contains names and addresses for countless faces from throughout *Halloween* history – everyone from Tommy Doyle and Sheriff Brackett to John Tate and Sara Moyer. The Shape travels to Haddonfield and begins visiting the addresses on the list. He first murders several now elderly ex-staff members from his time at Smith's Grove Sanitarium. Agent Woods follows after and uncovers a trail of bodies, which local authorities suspect her of committing. Once arrested, she tries unsuccessfully to convince them of her role at the FBI. Unfortunately, her boss has disavowed knowledge of her employment as payback for Michael's escape. (FBI chief: "Michael Myers is dead. And I never heard of Tracy Woods.") Having acquired a new mask, the Shape visits Agent Woods at Haddonfield PD. He doesn't kill her, though. He instead decapitates the on-duty officer and tosses the poor man's head into her cell as a threatening gesture.

As night falls on Haddonfield, the premiere event begins inside the town's tiny one-screen movie theater. Unbeknownst to the audience of survivors within, their worst fear is now lurking just backstage. The Shape first encounters Tommy Doyle in the men's room, whom he swiftly murders. As the documentary plays, Freddie notices the Shape hiding at stage left. Believing him to be a stagehand with a poor sense of humor, he goes to confront him. He instead finds Sara Moyer, who thanks him for the sense of closure his documentary has brought her. Meanwhile, a Halloween conspiracy theorist springs Agent Woods from jail and they rush to the premiere to alert Freddie. They search the packed theater for the escaped slasher but instead find Sara murdered. Freddie rushes onstage to warn attendees that Michael has returned, but the Shape slashes through the screen and attacks him. The panicked crowd try to leave but find the exit doors locked. Freddie engages his nemesis in a fight to the death. He finally gains the upper hand when Agent Woods distracts the Shape using the music box. The Dangertainment founder uses this opportunity to fatally impale the Shape with a piece of an old set. ("How's that for closure?")

## BREAKING THE MOLD

As a sequel to John Carpenter's 1978 original, *Halloween H25* is a strange beast. Comparing it to that first entry will surely make you wonder how exactly we got here. Truthfully, this 2002 treatment doesn't feel anything at all like Carpenter's original masterpiece. (And if we're being totally honest, neither did any of the sequels that directly preceded this proposed installment.) But maybe emulating the original was never this treatment's intent. Whereas *Halloween 2018* was nostalgic comfort food, *Halloween H25* picks up the story from where we left off and runs with it. As a sequel to *Halloween*, again – it's strange. Yet as a follow-up to *Halloween: Resurrection*, it's all in good fun. Had it actually been produced, *H25* might even have retroactively boosted *Resurrection*'s standing with fans by giving its story a better sense of purpose and direction.

Why does *Halloween H25* feel so different? It could be the documentary angle or the high-tech underground prison. It could also be that it ventures from Haddonfield to Chicago in the first and second acts. Most notably, *H25* lacks a final girl character. Every *Halloween* thus far has had a final girl, be it Laurie Strode, Rachel Carruthers, Jamie Lloyd, Kara Strode, Molly Cartwell, or Sara Moyer – but not here. Our lead female protagonist is instead Agent Tracy Woods, an ass-kicking femme fatale from the FBI's serial killer division. There has never been another character like her in the *Halloween* universe. Similarly, Freddie Harris doesn't fit anywhere within the standard formula, either. As a young, strong, black man, he could not be more opposite from the franchise's

HALLOWEEN

former leading man (Dr. Loomis). It's hard to say whether or not this unique approach would've won over audiences, but it is an admirably bold attempt at something new – a clean break from the traditional *Halloween* formula. In its defense, *H25* isn't even trying to be the original film.

*Halloween: Resurrection* had a clever hook in that it often cut to the headset cameras worn by the Dangertainment contestants. This was a novel idea that sadly never lived up to its potential. *Halloween H25* was set to have its own hook in that we could glimpse snippets of Freddie's documentary throughout the film. This could've proven *very* interesting. Imagine juxtaposing recreations of famous moments from throughout the series against sit-down interviews with the characters. What would an interview with Sheriff Brackett look like in 2003? Tommy Doyle? Jimmy the EMT? The documentary plot device is a great excuse to bring back veteran characters from throughout *Halloween* history, fan favorite roles that haven't been heard from in decades. (You can almost hear the impassioned cries of fans lobbying for a Danielle Harris cameo!)

Speaking of *Halloween* history, this franchise has earned a certain reputation for re-writing its own timeline whenever it's convenient to do so. While this does simplify the narrative for mainstream audiences, it's an arguably lazy approach to take with the material. Surprisingly, *Halloween H25* modifies the continuity even further by re-incorporating the sequels that *H20* tried to erase from existence! That's right – this treatment directly incorporates the *Return/Revenge/ Curse* trilogy into its story. In doing so, *H25* positions itself as a sequel to every *Halloween* movie thus far excepting *Season of the Witch*. The push to make *H25* a more timeline-inclusive sequel might've gone unappreciated (or even unnoticed) by most critics, but a large sect of the fanbase would've likely embraced it at the time.

The *H25* treatment envisions a highly meta-sequel, which hasn't really been done before in this franchise – at least not to this degree. In one scene, Agent Woods produces an antique music box that plays a rendition of the *Halloween* theme, meaning Carpenter's music now exists in-story. Oh – and so does Carpenter himself! The filmmaker is said to be in attendance at the documentary premiere in Haddonfield, "rumored to be developing a movie based on Michael Myers." (Now *that* is hilarious. Whether Carpenter would've agreed to such a cameo is uncertain. His comments on *Resurrection* contained multiple variations of "Oh lord, god.") With Freddie's docudrama on the Shape, *Halloween H25* begins to evoke story developments in the later *Scream* films. Recall that *Scream 2* introduced *Stab*, a franchise-within-a-franchise that dramatized the events of earlier *Scream* movies.

## FREDDIE'S REDEMPTION

Had it been made, *Halloween H25*'s greatest accomplishment would've likely been transforming showman Freddie Harris from comedic caricature to actual character. If you read *Taking Shape*, you may recall one of our biggest problems with Freddie was that he never took responsibility for what happened that night, at least not in the theatrical cut. Larry Brand's original screenplay (and the first cut of the movie) alternately had him apologizing to Sara Moyer in the end for everything that had happened. It was a moment of much-needed humility that studio execs swapped out for yet more levity. Calling Michael Myers a "killer shark in baggy ass overalls" on live television right after eight people were murdered as a direct result of your actions... makes you a remorseless clown. Fortunately, *H25* does better things with the character. Here, he becomes a more fleshed-out character, someone the audience can really root for.

We catch up with Freddie one year after the Dangertainment fiasco. No longer a joker, he now lives with the guilt of having caused eight deaths with his webcast stunt. Like so many survivors, he's begun to experience symptoms of post-traumatic stress disorder. Freddie even starts to imagine that the Shape has tracked him to Chicago and is seeking revenge for last Halloween. As the treatment puts it, "Everyone thinks Freddie is losing it. Even Freddie starts to think so. Maybe he's snapped and this is the onset of a breakdown." As an audience, we too might wonder – is Freddie really seeing the Shape about town? Or are these visions all in his mind? There's an air of mystery to his paranoia as we don't yet know what has become of the slasher.

And what of Freddie's documentary project about Michael Myers? You'd be forgiven for thinking this was just another get-rich scheme to exploit tragedy à la Dangertainment, but that's not the case. For once, Freddie's heart appears to be in the right place. He's self-financed the entire production with all proceeds going to the Haddonfield Victims Fund. His documentary has a dual aim in that it seeks to figure out *why* Michael kills while also providing closure to victims and their families. (It's unclear how it might achieve either of those lofty goals, but there you have it.) With survivor interviews, expert analysis, and dramatized recreations of his crimes, it sounds like the kind of thing Netflix would be all over if it came out today.

## A HIGH-TECH CAGE

*Halloween H25* isn't the first unmade *Halloween* to open with an incarcerated Shape, but it is the first to find him in the custody of the FBI. We eventually learn that federal agents faked his death and cremation and have since been holding him at a secret underground facility. The subterranean compound's entrance is located inside the Xamarin Pharmaceuticals building, which is situated inside an unassuming industrial park on the outskirts of Chicago. Authorities hold the Shape prisoner inside a maximum-security wing six floors underground. The treatment describes the location as part high-tech prison and part hospital laboratory. For the briefest moment, it feels as though we've stumbled into another movie altogether.

This covert facility is run by Agent Woods, who gives Freddie an interview for his documentary. Of course, she withholds the bombshell fact that Michael is still alive. Why involve herself in Freddie's project then? It could be that she wants to continue pushing the false narrative that Michael Myers is truly dead. She even brings along an urn containing his supposed ashes to prove her point. As written, Woods' deception leads readers to believe she may very well be an antagonist of sorts. Who could possibly want to protect the Shape – and joyously so? In actuality, Woods has spent quite a lot time with the slasher in attempt to understand him, though she's gotten nowhere. That, it turns out, is the FBI's entire goal in keeping him alive. If they can understand what triggers Michael to kill, they might be able to prevent future killers before they're triggered into violence.

As for the Shape's accommodations, they make Hannibal Lecter's cell in *The Silence of the Lambs* look like the Hilton. His cell is encased in two-foot-thick bulletproof plexiglass. He wears an electronic shock collar around his neck and a GPS-tracking bracelet around his ankle, neither of which are ever removed. The Shape is constantly wired to medical equipment, which monitor his vital signs – not that they ever change. To enter his cell, one must pass through two separate passcode-locked doorways – each manned by a guard – and moving around the facility requires a biometric handprint scan.

Agent Woods regularly enters Michael's cell in a brazen display of power, questioning him and even taunting him in hopes of provoking a response. She could easily have him restrained to either his chair or his bed, but she opts not to. While in the ultra-secure cell, she reads aloud the names of Michael's many victims and even projects crime scene photos onto the wall. The silent slasher remains so completely unaffected that not even his heart rate changes. Why doesn't he simply reach out and snap her neck? It's not that he doesn't want to, just that he likely knows that 5,000 volts of electricity will pulse through his body before he can finish the job.

It's fascinating to witness such a proud character fall from grace. Upon being blamed for Michael's escape, Woods is essentially fired from the FBI and thrown to the wolves. She does the right thing by trying to recapture her former prisoner however she's doing so entirely on her own. Her superior supports her efforts though demands that the operation be kept secret. ("I want a complete lockdown of this facility. Nobody outside this room finds out about this. Last thing we need is a panic.") But when arrested on suspicion of murdering the ex-staff of Smith's Grove, Woods has no alibi whatsoever. She comes off as crazy for trying to pin the murders on Michael Myers, whom authorities pronounced dead a year prior. Agent Woods' situation worsens considerably when her FBI boss denies knowledge of her employment with the bureau, which makes her seem even more delusional.

## GHOSTS OF HALLOWEEN PAST

In what might've proven one of *Halloween H25*'s most winning touches, it brings back a slew of survivors from throughout the series to attend the premiere of Freddie's documentary. In fact, it was this story beat that served as the genesis for Day's concept. Upon learning that Busta Rhymes was still under contract at Dimension, the writer considered that the same might be true for other franchise vets, perhaps Paul Rudd or Josh Hartnett. And while the idea of the Shape's past victims returning once more certainly floated around the internet around the time *Halloween 9* was being developed, never before have we been treated to such a concept that actually made it before studio execs. A *Halloween* reunion sequel - what an idea!

Of these survivors, the treatment specifically mentions Sheriffs Brackett and Meeker, Tommy Doyle, John Tate, Myles Barton, and Sara Moyer, though there are plenty more in attendance. These six names alone mean that every Myers-centric film in the franchise is represented in *H25*, which ties into the aforementioned goal of uniting the timelines. This sequel was poised to become the first *Halloween* without an appearance by either Dr. Loomis or Laurie Strode. Given that, the return of so many familiar faces would've likely helped in forging a nostalgic connection to earlier entries. Is it fan service? You bet! But honestly, who doesn't want to see these characters all in the same room together with the Shape?

Interestingly, *H25* resurrects Sheriff Meeker, who was widely assumed dead following the shoot-out that ended *Halloween 5*. While we never saw him die on-screen in that sequel, his demise was written and even filmed, albeit left on the cutting room floor. The assumption of his passing was further reinforced by his absence in *Halloween 6* as well as the appearance of a new sheriff (in the Producer's Cut, at least.) Nevertheless, *H25* finds Meeker back in action as Haddonfield's top lawman. Meeker is depicted as being somewhat chummy with the still-retired Brackett. These two might've had a strong onscreen chemistry together given their similar losses.

Screenwriter Tim Day gives brief but important mention to another familiar survivor – EMT Jimmy from *Halloween II*. From everything we've seen, *Halloween II*'s filmmakers never gave the character a last name, but this treatment does. Here, he's known as Jimmy Lloyd! Yes, the same last name as Jamie Lloyd from the *Return/Revenge/Curse* trilogy! Had this treatment been made, it would've confirmed what many have speculated on over the years – that Laurie and Jimmy's budding romance in *Halloween II* resulted in the birth of Jamie. This small detail opens up a huge can of worms, however. Where's he been all these years? How much does Jimmy know about Jamie and Laurie's deaths? Does this mean he's also John's father? (Per canon, John is slightly younger than Jamie.) *H25*'s screenwriter might not've been prepared to answer all these questions, but fans would've surely been asking them regardless.

While *H25* brings back numerous survivors, not all of them live to see its ending. Curiously, there are two returned characters whom the Shape finally kills – Tommy Doyle and Sara Moyer. Why these two? It's not entirely clear. The Shape finds Tommy mid-piss in the restroom just before the premiere and fatally slams his head into a toilet. Tommy's sudden death is a little disappointing in that he never sees it coming or even realizes what's happening. (The treatment mentions Tommy as being from *Halloween 6*, so maybe the Shape still holds a grudge over the events of that film.) Sara is choked to death backstage shortly after the documentary's conclusion. Her final words are to thank Freddie for the sense of closure his project has given her. ("It finally feels real. It's finally over.") In a bit of tragic irony, the only closure Sara will know tonight is that of her windpipe.

If there's one missed opportunity with these cameos, it's the ending. Recall that Freddie and the Shape duke it out onstage as frightened attendees flee the theater. Freddie is pretty much alone in this fight, though Agent Woods steps in to distract the slasher with the music box. But let's not kid ourselves – that's *not* how this would've gone down. Had the Shape actually appeared onstage, Brackett and Meeker would've been tripping over themselves for a shot at the monster who killed their daughters. And they would've likely lagged behind a younger and spryer John Tate looking to avenge his mother's death. (We don't know what Jimmy would be doing, but Myles Barton would probably be among those trying to escape.) In defense of the screenwriter, he might've addressed this had he been given the chance to expand his treatment into a full screenplay. But could you imagine it? The Shape versus a posse of angry survivors!

## THE SHAPE

When it comes to the Shape, *Halloween H25* contains a unique depiction in that the slasher is no longer out to end his bloodline. (By re-incorporating *Halloween 4-6*, we're presuming that bloodline still flows with Stephen, the orphan son of Jamie Lloyd.) Instead, this Shape is out for revenge against pretty much everyone he's ever come across. After finding Agent Woods' copy of the premiere guest list, he sets about visiting each name on it. For the Shape, this is less of a guest list and more of a to-do list. He first visits several of the now elderly staff from his time at Smith's Grove Sanitarium, whom he easily dispatches. (Low-hanging fruit, if you ask us.) He doesn't get far down the list, however, before the night of the premiere is upon us.

Visually, this Shape doesn't much resemble the white-masked slasher we're accustomed to until the end of Act II. That's due to him being incarcerated at the FBI black site at the start of this new story. His prison duds are... eerily fitting. The Shape sports an orange jumpsuit along with a special white medical mask intended to help with the healing of his burns. (Might this medical mask have resembled the Shape's white-bandaged look back in *Halloween 4*? A winning move, if so.) How does the character eventually come by his more classic look? Upon arrival at the premiere venue in Haddonfield, the Shape encounters a stage grip who'd pranked Freddie by dressing up as Michael Myers. The slasher immediately murders the grip and dons his mask and overalls. (It should be said that writer Day was a grip early on in his career thus making this one of *H25*'s more meta moments.)

The Shape's escape from the subterranean FBI facility is clever and nicely staged. Scientific researchers have spent the past year studying Michael in this high-tech cage. They've subjected him to a barrage of tests and experiments, none of which have yielded anything useful. Unbeknownst to staff, *he's studied them, too.* The Shape has obsessively watched and memorized even the most subtle nuances of the guards' routines. He waits with inhuman patience for the right moment to strike – and manages a full escape upon doing so.

In a swift move, the slasher removes his security collar and places it around the neck of one of the guards. He then uses the remote to crank up the voltage causing the guard's head to incinerate and explode, splattering across the cell. One grisly detail suggested but not shown is how exactly he made his way up to the surface level of the facility. As already mentioned, movement around the complex requires a biometric handprint scan. It's likely he severed one of the dead guards' hands to use as a key in escaping this prison.

## WHY IT WASN'T MADE

Why did Dimension Films suddenly pump the brakes on *Halloween H25*? Truth be told, they didn't – not entirely. Upon submitting his treatment, Day received positive marks from Bob Weinstein, who took to the writer's idea of the franchise survivors returning once more. While the Dimension boss favored this treatment, he maintained that it needed more development before proceeding to the script phase. To this end, Weinstein suggested that Day reconfigure the documentary angle, fearing this highly meta sequel would draw too many comparisons to the studio's own *Scream 3*, released two years prior. As an alternative, the producer suggested that the release of a book penned by Freddie might be better suited as the catalyst for rallying up the franchise's survivors.

Day was receptive to this idea yet his involvement in the project would be cut short before he could enact such changes. Not only would he exit his work on *Halloween* but his work at Dimension entirely; his three-picture deal absolved, and a proposed *Children of the Corn* sequel unmade. This hadn't stopped his ideas from remaining in development, however. In fact, the studio had offered his ideas to other writers to revise which, in turn, means that Day's material serves as a loose blueprint for the next unmade *Halloween*s to come.

That aside, perhaps it's best the franchise's silver anniversary would not be celebrated on film. Frantically rushing a new sequel to theaters – and so soon after a disappointing prior entry – isn't the most thoughtful way to guarantee a return on investment. Recall that *Halloween: Resurrection* brought in $18 million less than *Halloween H20* had just four years prior. A similar fall-off in ticket sales would make this proposed sequel an unprofitable venture, and for Dimension, that would've easily doomed the franchise to the direct-to-video shelf.

Then again, studio execs might've looked ahead to the following year and noticed a crowded playing field at the box office. Both Freddy and Jason were headed back to the big screen in August 2003. Historically, that didn't bode well for the Shape. Both 1988 and 1989 had seen Freddy, Jason, and Michael all vying for box office dollars with *Halloween* coming in third both years. Not to mention, a revamped Leatherface had already staked a claim on mid-October 2003. Did Dimension Films really want the Shape going up against New Line's House of Horror? Likely not. But this is all just speculative. At any rate, *Halloween H25* never advanced beyond an initial treatment.

# HALLOWEEN
# RETRIBUTION

The most CHILLING Halloween yet!

**Screenplay by**
**Dudi Appleton & Jim Keeble**

Tim Day left the ninth *Halloween* after only a few short weeks – yet the ideas contained within his treatment carried forth for quite some time. Dimension continued developing the notion of the surviving victims returning once more with Bob Weinstein, in particular, liking the idea enough to instruct future writers to incorporate this element. One such writer was Joe Harris, whose first feature – *Darkness Falls* – had just been released by Sony in January 2003. Not long after, he signed a deal that saw him pitching sequels to Dimension's various franchise properties. (He very nearly made his feature directorial debut on a *Children of the Corn* sequel that never materialized.) Among these properties was, of course, *Halloween*, though the writer's work here would be relatively minimal.

While Harris submitted neither a script nor a treatment for *Halloween 9*, he had engaged in discussions about the project. Per his account, Dimension had strongly considered bringing back not only Busta Rhymes' Freddie but also LL Cool J's Ronny from *H20*, thus uniting the two rappers in a showdown against the Shape. "Figuratively speaking, Ronny had an axe to grind with Michael Myers," the writer exclusively tells us. "And Freddie – who I think I suggested being destitute following lawsuits – would also have a score to settle. I also have this hazy memory of an opening scene involving a book launch in which an investigative journalist was publishing some sort of Michael Myers tell-all book. Michael would appear and kill someone, which is frightening enough to discover, but things are complicated by the fact that everyone in attendance is wearing the iconic mask as part of the festivities."

With the arrival of 2003, it seemed less and less likely that the ninth *Halloween* would be a celebration of the franchise's silver anniversary, meaning the *Halloween H25* title was effectively out. Dimension would soon settle on a new title – *Halloween: Retribution*, which would stick for much of the foreseeable development future. (This title would also embed itself in the project's rumor mill, even long after it had been discarded.) On April 25th, 2003, the *Dark Universe* website leaked news of the new *Retribution* title for *Halloween 9*, further telling their readership, "The legendary Michael Myers will be brought back to his true roots [...] in what Dimension hopes will be the definitive chapter." Trancas International was slow to address this new rumor, though would eventually do so two months later through the official *Halloween* website, stating "Moustapha Akkad reported today that a storyline has been chosen and the screenplay is being written right now. With discussions taking place with actors and the film set for a summer 2004 release, shooting isn't too far off. We will, of course, keep everyone updated as things progress."

Development would be temporarily sidelined in August 2003 due to the high-profile release of New Line's *Freddy vs Jason*. The success of this monster mash-up immediately led Dimension to consider doing the same with Michael Myers and Pinhead. The idea was swiftly rejected by the Akkads. Speaking with *Fangoria*, Malek Akkad confirmed, "That idea did come from Dimension, and I can honestly say that I was against it from day one. As soon as it was proposed, my father said no. But then it kept going back and forth for a couple of months and we lost a lot of time. There was also some casual talk at one point about a possible *Michael vs Leatherface* or a *Michael vs Jason*. But in the wake of *Freddy vs Jason*, any other team up is just going to look derivative. And besides, when it comes to Michael, we don't feel we have to jump on any matchup bandwagon."

The ninth *Halloween* was further impacted by another momentous event – the *Halloween Returns to Haddonfield* convention in Pasadena, California. Set across Halloween weekend 2003, the three-day event celebrated the franchise's twenty-fifth anniversary with discussion panels, autograph signings, film screenings, a costume contest, and an extensive locations tour. Over three-thousand fans attended from across the globe, many of whom expressed their opinions and desires for *Halloween 9*. Both Malek and Moustapha Akkad were on hand to directly respond to these comments. In one discussion panel, fans lobbied the Akkads for cameo appearances by series veterans such as Dick Warlock and Danielle Harris. While these names drew applause, the biggest audience response came when someone suggested Charles Cyphers, who had portrayed Sheriff Leigh Brackett across the first two *Halloween* movies. With this, Akkad turned to son Malek during the panel and humorously quipped, "Are you taking notes?" Given this exchange, it would seem that Cyphers' involvement with *Halloween 9* was all but confirmed.

Horror sites such as *Bloody-Disgusting* quickly picked up on the idea, reporting that the next sequel would revolve around the former sheriff as he finally avenged the death of his daughter Annie. For Dimension execs, this idea gelled nicely with the "returning survivors" concept that had already been percolating within the studio.

The following month, Malek Akkad mentioned to *Fangoria* that Trancas International was in ongoing discussions with both writers and directors to tackle *Halloween 9*. Of potential directors, the younger Akkad commented that there weren't yet any clear frontrunners for the sequel, but that there were "some real interesting names in the mix." He also mentioned a personal desire to have a first draft by mid-December, a deadline that would not be reached. While it remains a mystery who exactly the Akkads were in discussions with, we do know that they reached out to *Halloween 4* screenwriter Alan B. McElroy at some point. Rumors of McElroy's involvement soon reached the internet.

"I was contacted by the producers and asked if I had any interest in working on it, but I had to politely refuse," McElroy told the *Creature-Corner* website. "I want to thank Moustapha and Paul Freeman for thinking about me. They are always extremely complimentary of *Halloween 4* and I must say that working on that film was one of the highlights of my career."

Trancas' November discussions resulted in the hiring of British writing team Jim Keeble and Dudi Appleton. In retrospect, these two might've seemed an unorthodox pick. Even now, they are relatively unproven talents in the horror genre. Having met as students at the University of Oxford, the two began a working relationship that first culminated in a short drama for the British Film Institute. They would next co-write *The Most Fertile Man in Ireland*, an indie-comedy for which Appleton received the "Best Director" award at the 2000 U.S. Comedy Arts Festival. Keeble, on the other hand, garnered positive reviews for his travelogue novel *Independence Day*, which chronicled his misadventures looking for love in America.

These successes among others eventually led Keeble and Appleton to gain representation by the Gersh Agency, subsequently leading to multiple writing opportunities. Prior to working on *Halloween 9*, the two had sold the romantic comedy *What a Man's Gotta Do* to New Line and were adapting Ayn Rand's *The Fountainhead* with Oliver Stone. We know little of the duo's introduction to *Halloween*, but it would seem their diverse work caught the eyes of the powers that be at Trancas. Aligning with rumors of the time, their script – dated February 20, 2004 – would operate under the aforementioned *Halloween: Retribution* title. Per the studio's request, their script would also incorporate several elements cherrypicked from Tim Day's *Halloween H25* treatment. These included the return of survivors from earlier films and the release of a book by Freddie Harris chronicling his Halloween experience. (Recall that Bob Weinstein felt a documentary was too much like the plot of *Scream 3* and preferred a book instead.)

## THE STORY

*Halloween: Retribution* opens on October 31, 1964 – exactly one year after young Michael Myers brutally murdered his older sister on Halloween night. Now catatonic, seven-year-old Michael is an extended-stay resident of Smith's Grove Sanitarium. His caregivers are unable to agree on how to best help him or whether he can even be helped. The optimistic Dr. Hill provides Michael with art supplies and encourages him to draw whatever comes to mind. He raises the writing utensil high in the air before *stabbing it into his own hand* with tremendous force. As orderlies rush to subdue the child, we see that he has covertly stolen something – Dr. Hill's glasses. We then jump ahead fifteen years to the evening of October 30, 1978. A retiring and less optimistic Dr. Hill bids Michael farewell while also taunting him. ("You're never going to leave here. This is your home. This is where you will die.") Having fashioned a shiv from the glasses years before, Michael fatally stabs Dr. Hill. Maneuvering out of his straitjacket with alarming ease, he lifts a grate in the floor and slips inside. Now free from his confines, the Shape moves toward freedom. This opening ends with a familiar station wagon pulling up to the hospital gates to find numerous escaped patients wandering the grounds.

The story then shifts twenty-five years later, one year after the events of *Halloween: Resurrection*. Dangertainment founder Freddie Harris is now on tour in promotion of his new book, *Unmasking the Monster*, an exaggerated chronicle of how he managed to "kill" Michael Myers. At one book signing, he encounters a young man who questions whether he really slayed the slasher. This man turns out to be John Tate, son of the deceased Laurie Strode and nephew of the boogeyman himself. After the signing, the Shape murders Freddie with John arriving just a moment too late to intervene. Hoping to avenge his mother's death and also learn about his newly discovered past, John travels to where it all began – Haddonfield, Illinois. The town has once again banned Halloween and enacted a 6 PM curfew for all residents. Strangely, this October 31st finds central Illinois forecast to receive a blanketing of snow. Between the inclement weather and the ban, Halloween is assuredly canceled this year.

But several Haddonfield High students have found a way around that by sneaking off to a party cabin in the woods over in Warren County. This group includes your typical high school stereotypes – along with Lea, a shy senior markedly more mature than her peers. The teenagers' van breaks down en route to the cabin, stranding them amid heavy snowfall. They seek shelter at a nearby structure – the long abandoned ruins of Smith's Grove Sanitarium. Little do Lea and her friends know that they're already being stalked by the Shape, who's returned to his former institutional home. Having murdered the sanitarium's caretaker, he follows close behind as the teens explore the shuttered facility.

John arrives in Haddonfield and immediately visits the burned-out lot where the Myers house once stood. It's here he encounters the new central lawman – Sheriff Shaw. John then visits the local library to research his infamous uncle but is unable to turn up a single public record. It's here a voice calls out to him from behind. ("You won't find anything here. They've deleted all that stuff.") He turns to see the town's former sheriff, Leigh Brackett, who charges that Michael is still alive and killing. Research reveals that an alarming number of Smith's Grove ex-employees have been turning up dead. Concluding that the Shape must've returned to the abandoned hospital, John begs police to investigate. They refuse, however, on account of the treacherously icy roads. Police also mention the stranded teenagers at Smith's Grove, whom they plan to rescue in the morning once conditions improve. Unwilling to wait, John alerts Brackett of his plan to rescue the teens and heads for Smith's Grove alone. Hoping to join the fight, Brackett steals Sheriff Shaw's police cruiser before speeding off toward the abandoned hospital.

The Shape picks off the teenagers at shuttered Smith's Grove one-by-one until only Lea and Noah remain. Having barely escaped their encounter with the slasher, they take refuge in the old medical records vault. It's here the teens learn about their attacker's history through old therapy notes and video recordings. The Shape forces his way inside, though he's momentarily stalled when Lea impersonates his older sister Judith. With John and Brackett's arrival, a bloody battle unfolds through the hospital. This spills out into the snow and onto a frozen lake. John buries an axe into Michael's chest, who collapses onto the thin ice, which soon breaks. The Shape pulls John down into the frigid water with him, but Lea, Noah, and Brackett manage to pull him out. The seemingly dead slasher sinks into the dark abyss. As the heroes drag John to safety, they notice he's holding onto something tightly – the pale white mask of Michael Myers, into which he stares intensely.

The script's final words are spoken over darkness. These are, in fact, the same words that began the story, a snippet of conversation between the optimistic Dr. Hill and the cynical Nurse Spence in October 1964. The young Dr. Hill rosily insists, "Everyone can be reached. No one is beyond redemption." The older Nurse Spence flatly retorts, "You obviously haven't met Michael."

## IT'S SNOWING IN HADDONFIELD

When it comes to *Halloween* sequels, the filmmakers seem to fall into one of two camps. They either seek to closely emulate the tone and style of John Carpenter's original or instead try for something completely different. With *Halloween: Retribution*, it's immediately clear that Dudi Appleton and Jim Keeble are trying for something different. Their screenplay ditches many of the most basic tropes we've come to expect. Gone are the trick-or-treaters, the jack-o-lanterns, and the rustling of autumn leaves. Halloween has been officially banned by town officials with seemingly little pushback. Even if it hadn't been, there's an approaching snowstorm. While sure to be a memorable one, this All Hallows' Eve isn't going to be like anything we're used to.

Before we dive into the story, let's first address the title – *Halloween: Retribution*. If you're hazy on that word, retribution means to inflict punishment on someone as vengeance for a wrong or criminal act. Who in the story does this word apply to? *Virtually the entire main cast.* John Tate is obviously seeking retribution for his murdered mother. Brackett still wants retribution for his murdered daughter. Lea wants retribution for her murdered friends. On the flip side, Michael is seeking retribution against multiple people. He first seeks his revenge on Freddie Harris for burning down his family home. (This is an interesting and widely-held fallacy. Technically, only the garage burned down in *Resurrection*, though you'd be forgiven for thinking it was the entire house.) We later learn that Michael has been murdering the ex-staff of Smith's Grove Sanitarium where he was held for more than fifteen years. Why exact retribution on these old souls now? As we glimpse in the opening, these caregivers tortured him with cattle prods and leather straps. Given that, it's no surprise he still has a bone to pick with them. Why not just call this *The Revenge of Michael Myers*? Because that title is already taken, silly.

The most immediately obvious element that would've set *Retribution* apart from other films in the series is the unseasonably early blizzard that blankets Haddonfield in snow. (For those curious, it's rare but not unprecedented to have snowy Halloweens in Illinois. 2019 marked the second whitest October on record in Chicago.) Snow isn't something most mainstream slashers have had to deal with, though it does work to the Shape's advantage here. Not only can his teenage victims *not* escape out into the frozen wilderness beyond Smith's Grove, but authorities refuse to brave the icy terrain to provide them help. The Shape may as well be shooting fish in a barrel. Aesthetically, this would've also made for a more visually interesting *Halloween* movie. Forget the orange, yellow, and brownish-red color palettes we're used to. *Retribution* was poised to be wintry white.

Tonally, this script marks a huge departure from *Resurrection* and feels much more in line with *H20*, minus the overt *Scream* vibes. There is some humor, but it's kept to a respectable minimum. (No one gets to kung-fu kick the Shape, thankfully.) As in Robert Zappia's *Two Faces of Evil*, the teen drama unfolds as a secondary plotline. While their exploration of a shuttered Smith's Grove is certainly interesting, it just can't compete with John Tate and Leigh Brackett's quest for vengeance. Had this script actually been made, there's no doubt that actors Josh Hartnett and Charles Cyphers would've absolutely carried this sequel on their shoulders. The roles of both John and Brackett are well-written continuations of the characters as we last saw them.

Unsurprisingly, this story's lead teenager is a good girl in the Laurie Strode tradition. Described as "thoughtful but withdrawn," Lea is a socially reserved bookworm, maybe even a little more so than Laurie was. Personality-wise, she's slightly more endearing than *Resurrection*'s Sara Moyer, but not quite as charming as *Halloween 4*'s Rachel Carruthers. Preferring her own company to that of others, she's encouraged by her school psychiatrist to seek out more social interaction for her own well-being. This sets the stage for her to join the popular kids on their trip to a remote party cabin over in Warren County.

Lea's friends run the gamut of usual slasher movie stereotypes. There's Tim the wealthy jock, Tonya the vacant but pretty blonde, and Phil the uptight nice guy. There's also Jenny, the sassy daughter of Sheriff Shaw. Given what happened to Annie Brackett and Kelly Meeker in previous films, you can easily guess Jenny's ultimate fate here. One interesting addition to the potential victim lineup is Noah, Lea's fourteen-year-old mute brother. Charged with watching her little bro on Halloween night, Lea has no choice but to bring him along to the party cabin if she's going to attend, which she's peer-pressured into doing by Tonya. The idea of incorporating a non-verbal character into a slasher movie is a novel one. Unable to communicate with anyone but Lea, Noah can't scream for help or alert the others to what he sees. This raises the stakes considerably.

## FREDDIE'S FINAL BOW

Like *H25*, *Retribution* revisits Freddie Harris, one of the most polarizing characters from the previous film. In place of a documentary, though, Keeble and Appleton's story tells that Freddie has alternately published an embellished account of his brush with the Shape, not at all unlike Dr. Loomis in Rob Zombie's *Halloween II*. Titled *Unmasking the Monster*, Freddie's book charges that he single-handedly killed Michael Myers. (Never mind that his body went missing from the morgue that same night. Probably just a coincidence.) We first find Freddie performing a dramatic reading from his book at Antrim College in Newry, Illinois:

> **Freddie:** *"There is a contract in fear. It requires someone to be afraid of, and someone to be afraid, perpetrator and victim... Back in the day when you knew everyone on your street we used to call these 'Stranger Murders'... Today, in our sprawling suburbs, lawless inner cities, and failing institutions we are all strangers. It's harder to spot the outsider, the sociopath, the killer. We're all anonymous, we all wear a mask."*

From that alone, it's clear to see Freddie is still the same showman he was while running Dangertainment. Unfortunately, the scene that follows after reveals just how much more crass he's become. The Freddie of *H25* sought to bring closure to himself and others. This Freddie instead revels in his newfound exposure. Whatever humbling effect losing Nora and six college students to a murderous psychopath had on him has clearly worn off. He's since succumbed to the sleazier side of celebrity. Freddie grows angry when asked if Michael Myers is truly dead until he realizes he's being asked this by John Tate. ("Ladies and gentleman, we are honored. [...] It's truly a pleasure to meet Michael Myers' nephew.") Throwing an arm around John's shoulder, Freddie immediately mugs for an impromptu photo shoot. We further cringe as Freddie voices concern that John might write a competing book about Michael Myers that would outsell his. No fan of the limelight, John heads for the exit. He leaves Freddie with a warning, which goes unheeded. ("I'd watch your back, Mr. Harris. My uncle never liked publicity.")

Given Freddie's irreverent attitude towards the webcast tragedy, it's no surprise that he soon finds himself targeted by the Shape. Leaving the book signing that evening, Freddie discovers his SUV's tires have all been slashed. A campus police vehicle idles nearby. Assuming this to be a jerk cop, Freddie shouts obscenities at the driver for not offering to help. Shock and disbelief wash over him when the Shape steps out of the car a moment later. ("Who are you? You're not him. I killed him. I'm not afraid of you! Take off the fucking mask!") Raising his blade high, the Shape goes in for the kill. Freddie blocks the stab using his book, though the Shape forces his blade through the book and into Freddie's heart, killing him. Retribution achieved.

With *Halloween: Resurrection* having two survivors, you might wonder why the Shape chose to go after Freddie Harris and not Sara Moyer. Consider that, as the proprietor of Dangertainment, Freddie was chiefly responsible for the webcast invading the sanctity of Michael's childhood home that night. He also kung-fu kicked him in front of a live-stream audience and electrocuted him in the nuts. Given all that, Freddie definitely appears to have landed on the Shape's bad side in a way that Sara did not.

## A FATHER'S REVENGE

In a winning move, *Retribution*'s screenwriters reintroduce Leigh Brackett to the storyline after a long absence. They're not the first scribes to bring back the character nor would they be the last. Similar to his other characterizations, we find Haddonfield's former sheriff a broken man. He's clearly never recovered from the murder of his only daughter by the Shape so many years ago. The writers describe him as "a disheveled figure" and "not in great shape, his eyes sunken in his face." John Tate first encounters Brackett forty-five pages into the script while trying to research Michael Myers at the Haddonfield Public Library. We immediately realize that Brackett has been down this road before, having obsessed over his arch-nemesis for many years now.

Like John, Brackett refuses to buy into the popular theory that Michael died in the Myers house fire. ("He's alive. The Evil that killed your mother, the Evil that killed my daughter… is alive. Alive and killing.) More importantly, both men believe that Michael can be caught. It's through these shared beliefs that Brackett recognizes a kindred spirit in the young man. He presents John with a massive dossier of unsolved murders in Illinois dating back to 2001. ("I left out Chicago or we'd be here all night.") He believes that some of these, possibly many, are attributable to the Shape. If they can figure out his killing pattern, they might be able to predict his next victim and thwart his attempt on their life. John is skeptical and charges that there is "no pattern in insanity." In a very Loomis-esque moment, Brackett slams his fist down onto the table. ("He's not insane. Others have made that mistake. It's much worse than insanity.")

Halloween night finds Brackett at home in the dark. Clutching a photo of his daughter, he flashes back to a conversation from the original *Halloween*. In it, he assures Dr. Loomis that the only things happening in Haddonfield this night are kids playing pranks, trick-or-treating, or parking. Loomis replies with his famous "Death has come to your little town" speech. Snapping back to the present, Brackett is forced into action upon learning that Michael may be at Smith's Grove *and* that a group of kids are trapped there. He steps up not only to save the teenagers, but also to exact his long-sought revenge. Brackett visits Sheriff Shaw under the ruse of needing a friend to talk to on this difficult anniversary. In actuality, he's there to steal his successor's car, which he does rather stealthily. With Shaw's cruiser, he catches up to John on the snow-covered highway. John notices Brackett wearing Shaw's badge and asks if he thinks that will somehow frighten the Shape. "No," Brackett replies, "but it makes me a little less afraid." Armed with his old service-weapon, the former sheriff approaches Smith's Grove on foot alongside his new ally.

Venturing inside the shuttered hospital will force Brackett to relive the painful memory of his deepest trauma. Searching its empty halls with John, he encounters the dead body of Sheriff Shaw's daughter and is immediately taken back to the night of October 31, 1978. Kneeling by her corpse, he's mentally and emotionally gutted. ("Oh, Lord. Oh, Annie.") Remembering the situation at hand, Brackett shakes off these feelings. He soon finds himself alone with the Shape deep within the bowels of Smith's Grove. Aiming his gun squarely at his enemy's head, he yells out, "This is for Annie!" *Click* – and nothing. His weapon jams right when he needs it most, the result of years of disuse. In this moment, Brackett is truly defeated. Retribution will not be his this night. Yet amazingly, he survives to the end of the night and beyond. Of all the scripts that sought to bring this character back, only *Retribution* allows him to live.

## LIKE MOTHER, LIKE SON

Truth be told, John Tate wasn't quite the most interesting character in *Halloween H20*. He was pretty much your average seventeen-year-old, interested in girls and not in the rules. Like most teens, he was also eager to have his own space apart from his overbearing parent. You could argue that John only became interesting after having survived the events of *H20*. You could further argue that he became even *more* interesting after the events of *Halloween: Resurrection,* which he wasn't even a part of. Why wasn't John around for that sequel? There's both an in-story and out-of-story answer. In-story, Laurie was supposed to have hidden her son where Michael couldn't find him. (Dialogue shot but later cut: "I knew you'd come for me sooner or later, but you would never find my son. I made sure of that.") Out-of-story, producers doubted that Josh Hartnett would ever return to the franchise. In the final film, we only briefly glimpse his photo on Laurie's nightstand.

Keeble and Appleton's story finds John older and wiser than when we last saw him. (He's no longer the same messy-haired Creed-loving youth from Hillcrest.) There is brief reference made to him having spent time off the radar in Europe, which would align nicely with his mother's omitted *Resurrection* dialogue. (It's difficult to imagine the Shape crossing the pond, so Europe was probably a safe bet.) It's never explicitly stated, but John's visit to Haddonfield in *Retribution* seems like his first trip there. Given that it's now a few years after Laurie's death, this begs the question – how deep in hiding was he? And when did he find out about his mother's murder? Upon arriving in town, he visits her grave in Haddonfield Cemetery. Another question – who buried her here, if not John? The tombstone reads: "Laurie Strode. July 14, 1961 to October 31, 2002. Beloved mother of John. At peace at last." An unprincipled caretaker approaches John as he's deep in thought at his mother's final resting place. The dirtbag tells him, "I'm not supposed to do this, but for twenty bucks I'll let you take a picture." John doesn't respond.

(Some food for thought: Laurie Strode didn't simply vanish from Haddonfield and later reinvent herself as Keri Tate. In *H20,* she specifically mentions having faked her own death. Did Laurie then have another gravesite before this one? If so, where? And was it removed upon her cover being blown following *H20*? Or was it simply amended? Does she now have two graves? Why would she be buried in Haddonfield and not Summer Glen, California? On that note, just where was Grace Andersen Sanitarium? Surely not in Illinois, right?)

After visiting Haddonfield Cemetery, John travels to the burned-out house at 45 Lampkin Lane. He immediately notices that police have fenced off the property and erected strict "No admittance" signs. Being October 31st, Sheriff Shaw is parked out front to discourage anyone hoping to trespass on the site of Michael Myers' childhood home. He approaches John with hostility. ("I had a feeling this was going to be a long day. Do you want to move on or should I just throw your ass in jail?") Not easily provoked, John remains calm and hands over his California license when asked to. Oblivious to the familial connection, Shaw comments that he's a long way from home. Staring into the charred Myers house, John replies, "Not really."

In avenging her death, John is channeling his mother's incorrigible fighting spirit. The image of an axe-wielding John stalking Smith's Grove in search of the Shape warmly recalls the image of an axe-wielding Laurie heading into Hillcrest for the same reason. If it wasn't already clear, we can tell from this that Laurie's badassery was genetically passed down to John. He will eventually bury this axe in the Shape's chest – just as his mother did years before. Yet *how* he does it is completely different. Battling the Shape out on the hospital's front lawn, John throws the axe toward his enemy. It spins through the air before landing perfectly in the slasher's chest. Michael stumbles backwards and collapses into the snowbank.

While John Tate proves himself a formidable foe in *Retribution*, his heroics ultimately fail to land him a happy ending. This sequel story ends not with him riding off into the sunset but staring into the dark abyss of his uncle's mask. Having been dragged into icy waters by a badly injured Shape, John appears to have drowned. Lea, Noah, and Brackett retrieve his unconscious body from the water a moment later. As they revive him, they notice a strange object held tightly in his grasp.

> As Lea wraps the coat around him, hugging him tight, she sees something in JOHN'S HAND. It's MICHAEL'S WHITE MASK. Lea: "Leave it. It's evil." But John can't leave it. He clasps the WHITE MASK tighter, drawn to it by an irresistible force. A moment as John holds the mask. He stares at it. The DARK EYES of the MASK and JOHN TATE'S DARK EYES.

## HOSPITAL ON HAUNTED HILL

While nowhere near as location-locked as the unproduced sequels that would follow it, most of *Retribution* does unfold in a singular space – Smith's Grove Sanitarium. The story's extensive focus here makes for a refreshing change of scenery from *Halloween*'s usual suburban setting. We first see Smith's Grove as a functioning hospital in 1964 and later on as an abandoned facility in present day. The backdrop of a rundown psychiatric hospital ties neatly into the franchise's trope of isolated locations. (Haddonfield Memorial in *Halloween II*, the grade school in *Halloween 4*, Hillcrest Academy in *Halloween H20*, the Myers house in *Resurrection* – just to name a few.) In returning to Smith's Grove, the writers infuse much intrigue and mystery into their story. The modern-day scenes here feel reminiscent of *Session 9* in the best possible sense.

In retrospect, it's strange to think how little we've actually seen of Smith's Grove over the years. The hospital is only briefly glimpsed in the first two *Halloween* films. (Yes, we saw more of it in *Halloween 6*, but remember – that film doesn't exist in this continuation of the *H20* timeline.) Despite being a hugely important part of *Halloween* mythology, Smith's Grove has largely remained a gray area. We know virtually nothing of Michael's fifteen-year incarceration there – except that someone might've taught him to drive. *Retribution* aims to shine some light on this part of the story. Not surprisingly – it ain't pretty. The orderlies mercilessly beat, kick, whip, and electro-shock him. Given that Michael is only seven at this point, it's incredibly difficult not to feel some sympathy for him – even though we also recognize that he's pure evil. This material seriously calls into question the entire spectrum of right and wrong. Who exactly is the good guy here? Is Michael later justified to seek revenge on these people as an adult? Are they just doing their job? Were they justified in torturing a child because they view him as evil? It's not as though these doctors, nurses, and orderlies are malicious in their intent. Not at all – they're a far cry from Noel Kluggs in *Halloween 2007*. They instead seem to be acting on pure conviction. If nothing else, it's a thought-provoking story development.

These opening scenes include a character named Dr. Hill, an idealistic young man who hopes to help Michael if at all possible. This character is surely named in tribute to *Halloween* co-writer and producer Debra Hill. Such a tribute is undercut, however, by the fact that Dr. Hill is male. Debra Hill is well remembered for being a trailblazer for women in Hollywood at a time when most filmmaking jobs were held by men. Gender-flipping the male Dr. Hill would've made a more fitting tribute and a potentially more interesting narrative choice given that Michael killed his sister in the midst of the Women's Rights Movement of the 1960s. Not that *Halloween* has to get all socio-political, but a gender-flip would've made this nod more emblematic of the person being honored. (To those who might argue that women doctors weren't as common back then, the same could be said of women filmmakers, no?) Still, we'll take our nods where we can get them.

At one point, having already been attacked by the Shape, Lea and her friends hide out in the hospital's medical archives room. Her mute brother finds a large box labeled "Myers, Michael. Patient #413075." Contained within are documents, photos, audio cassettes, and old film reels. Hoping to learn something about their attacker, Lea screens one of the reels using a nearby projector. This is where we're given a unique glimpse into the past – a filmed therapy session between seven-year-old Michael and Dr. Loomis. The conversation is predictably one-sided with Loomis asking many questions and Michael appearing unaffected and stoic. (Recall that we previously saw such a session in Etchison's unused *Halloween 4* where Loomis was depicted as a raving madman.)

> **Loomis:** *"How are you feeling, Michael? Are you hungry? Do you want to play? (Loomis hands the boy his old clown mask.) Do you want to put it on? Does the mask scare you? Or does it protect you? Why won't you speak? I know you can hear me. Tell me about Judith, Michael. Did you love your sister? Were you angry that she was kissing that boy? Do you think she loved that boy? She was meant to love you... That must have made you angry. It would make me angry. Are you angry now, Michael? [...] Why won't you talk to me Michael? Miss Blakemore tells me you used to be a very talkative first grader... [...] You like hurting people, don't you Michael? You're very conscientious. You're determined, when you start something you always finish it, don't you? So how does this end, Michael?"*

The very notion of depicting Dr. Loomis in the wake of Donald Pleasence's passing is a sensitive one. Fans would surely reject any other actor stepping into the role within this continuity. *Halloween H20* and *Halloween 2018* were able to get around this by having voice-over cameos performed by Tom Kane and Colin Mahan, respectively. *Halloween: Retribution* was scripted to proceed accordingly with most of Loomis' appearance being an off-camera voiceover. He was written to step forward into camera-view once, though we would only see him from the back.

That so many sequels – both made and unmade – keep trying to bring back Donald Pleasence's iconic protagonist speaks volumes about how integral he is to *Halloween*. Fans came back for Dr. Loomis as much as we did Michael Myers – to an extent, of course. The masks and stuntmen changed with each film, but Pleasence did not. Ever reliable, he was in some questionable sequels, but he was never questionable in them.

One lingering question with this screenplay is – why does the Shape return to Smith's Grove? What significance does this place hold for him? Is it at all special to him? Or did he simply have nowhere else to go after the Dangertainment crew burned down his childhood home? And if it's not special to him, why not destroy or burn it to the ground? Is this his first time returning here in three decades? We're left to draw our own conclusions. As a stalking ground for picking off the trespassing teenagers, Smith's Grove is *perfect*. Not only does the Shape have home field advantage here, but we also learn of an underground tunnel system running beneath the facility. (Oddly enough, the Myers house also had such a convenience in *Resurrection*.) This tunnel system allows the Shape to stalk and travel undetected by his prey.

## A SOUL BEYOND REDEMPTION

Unlike its predecessor, which at least offered an explanation as to how the Shape cheated death in *Halloween H20*, *Retribution* makes no attempt to explain the slasher's continued survival. When we last saw him in *Halloween: Resurrection*'s final moments, the Shape had miraculously come back to life on a morgue slab after having burned to death. *Retribution* acknowledges this, but never attempts to explain it. We later glean from John Tate's research that the morgue burned down that same night, leaving the bodies inside burned beyond all recognition. By this, the proposed ninth entry in the *Halloween* franchise seems content to simply gloss over the details of Michael's survival. Any and all attempts at realism have been fully abandoned. If you haven't yet suspended disbelief, now's the time.

With regard to ability and appearance, *Retribution*'s Shape is largely the same slasher from *H20* and *Resurrection*. This story does, however, call into question the character's lifelong obsession with ending his own bloodline. Recall the moments after Freddie's murder in the parking lot of Antrim College. The Shape climbs into his nearby truck – and waits. John Tate soon happens upon Freddie's corpse and, noticing the idling truck, immediately suspects this to be the work of his estranged uncle. Approaching the Shape's truck, he bangs on its tinted windows as the vehicle pulls away. ("Is it you? Let me see you! I need to know!") In this moment, John appears to be alone and unarmed in an empty parking lot – a ripe kill opportunity if there ever was one. And yet, the Shape leaves him here. Why? Is Michael no longer interested in killing blood relations? Or does he understand John's personal hell of wanting to avenge his mother's death, that such anguish is worse than any physical pain he could inflict? If so, that would make him even more depraved and evil than we previously realized.

*Retribution* later gives credence to this second theory near story's end when Brackett catches up to the Shape. Aiming his weapon, the former sheriff intones, "This is for Annie!" He pulls the trigger, but the gun jams. Alone and defenseless with nowhere to run, Brackett is now at the mercy of his enemy. Turning to face him, the Shape performs his signature head-tilt. This silent pause between the two lasts a tense moment, after which the Shape turns and continues on his way. In sparing Brackett's life, he's leaving him to a fate worse than death – reality. Not just the reality of having lost his only daughter, but one where he had the chance to slay her killer yet was unable to do so. (God, that is savage.)

> *"Sheriff Brackett is standing there, waiting for Michael to finish him off. But Michael's not interested in him. He destroyed him long ago. Michael turns away, to go after Lea and John. He walks away and disappears around the corner. Sheriff Brackett collapses on the floor."*

With this ending, we're again left to wonder if this isn't truly the end for Michael Audrey Myers. The Shape takes an extraordinary amount of abuse here, far more than in *H20* and *Resurrection*. At one point, John buries his axe so deep into the slasher's face that we hear the sound of metal-hitting-skull. (*Yikes.*) Sure, Michael's been down-and-out before, but being fatally wounded and left for dead at the bottom of a frozen lake... sounds like a career-ending finish.

## WHY IT WASN'T MADE

In truth, we don't know why Keeble and Appleton's *Halloween: Retribution* stalled in development hell. Their involvement was kept secret until years after they had already departed the project, so the specifics of their dealings with studio execs remained largely unknown. What we do know is that their pitch was well-liked enough by both Trancas and Dimension to move forward into the script phase. Trancas, in particular, seemed especially enthused by it. They would update fans on March 2, 2004 – just weeks after the submission of Keeble and Appleton's first draft – on the official *Halloween* website.

"The producers cannot make any official announcements until the screenplay is finalized," Webmaster Anthony Masi wrote. "Although there is a story in place, Miramax is finalizing the draft that was submitted. Once that's finalized, [our website] can make an official announcement. You can be sure to expect a great storyline and for the film to be one of the best in the franchise."

At some point, Keeble and Appleton were replaced with writer Jake Wade Wall, who was hired to pitch his own version of Tim Day's concept. Little is known of Wall's *Retribution* – aside from it dating May 2004 – although from his interview, we can deduce that not only did his version feature John Tate, Leigh Brackett, and Freddie Harris, but also a plethora of other *Halloween* notables including the original's Lindsey Wallace and the second film's Jimmy. Wall completed his duties that summer before being tasked with writing the remake to 1979's *When a Stranger Calls,* which did move forward into production.

Somewhere in the development process, the idea of a sequel featuring numerous franchise veterans must have lost its luster. While Busta Rhymes was still under contract for a cameo, it seemed increasingly unlikely that Josh Hartnett would reprise his role as John Tate, having risen in the Hollywood ranks with roles in *Pearl Harbor, Black Hawk Down,* and *40 Days and 40 Nights.* This would require a significant revision to the material, something that Wall's re-imagining didn't provide as his script also featured John Tate. Uncertain of how to proceed, Trancas and Dimension began fielding entirely new pitches. With that, *Halloween: Retribution* began to gather dust, never having the chance to enact vengeance upon audiences.

**You and Jim Keeble don't appear to have a background in writing horror films. How'd you both manage to land *Halloween: Retribution*?**

I was working with a guy in Los Angeles named Louis Nader, who had been helping Malek and Moustapha Akkad try to figure out what to do next with *Halloween*. Louis really liked our work, even though we were mostly doing comedy. We weren't doing much in the way of thrillers at that point. He introduced us to Malek and I got along very well with him. We became friends. One day, Louis said, '*Listen, this is a really out-there suggestion, but why don't you guys try writing a* Halloween *movie?*' I think Malek and Moustapha felt there had been some missteps with the franchise and they wanted to fix it. So, they asked us to do a treatment, which we agreed to do. We knew the original movies, of course, but we hadn't caught the last couple of ones. So, we went off and re-watched all the movies up to then.

The bit I was fascinated by was – what terrible things happened to Michael inside Smith's Grove? We were interested in the double evils that might have existed inside there. Without trying to pretend that Michael was some poor innocent kid, we wanted to show that his evil was fueled and abetted by the awful treatment they gave him. Our idea was that Smith's Grove got a monster and then made him a much worse monster. That's my memory of our concept, anyway. We were also really interested in the different doctors and their obsessions with Michael. We thought Michael was scariest as a kid and wanted to mix in some of *The Omen* with it. That was only part of it. We also wanted it to be a great ride and feel authentic to young lives with the teenage characters in the present. Coming off *Halloween: Resurrection*, we didn't feel a lot of pressure. Maybe if that one had been really successful, we would've felt that pressure, but we didn't.

**That's a rich concept – the double evil of the Shape and of the staff at Smith's Grove.**

I obsessed over that, the idea of them carting little Michael off to this strange place. If you think about it, he came out of Smith's Grove so much scarier than when he went in. That sometimes happens in real life, believe it or not. People will go to prison for something petty and often come out proper criminals. The institution makes them a certain way. So, what would that be like in a place for the criminally insane? Do the people there get better or worse? We also had references to things like *One Flew Over the Cuckoo's Nest*. So, just the idea that, on some level, Michael might be the product of American institutions seemed really interesting to us.

**What kind of direction, if any, did you get from Malek or Moustapha in figuring out the story?**

Honestly, I'm finding it hard to recall. I do remember them being very open in asking where we would take the story. They were very supportive and friendly in that way. At one point, they gave us a sheet that listed all the rules for the character of Michael Myers. '*This is what he does. This is what he doesn't do.*' I think they had to write those out because Dimension kept coming to them with ideas that were terrible. Like, at one point, Dimension or someone wanted Michael to talk, which broke one of the rules. Michael doesn't talk, right? For us, Malek and Moustapha basically said, '*So long as you don't break the rules, you can do whatever you want.*' And we liked that about them. They were really just into the creation of advancing the story.

**What was your experience like working with Dimension Films?**

*Awful.* It became quite clear very quickly that we were but pawns in a war between the Akkads and Dimension. That was the disappointing part of it, I suppose. I don't blame the Akkads for it. It seemed like a great big dick-swinging battle on Dimension's part. We eventually got into a dispute with Dimension and were asked to create a timeline of everything we'd done on the project. I'm looking over that timeline now. Right here, we wrote that a Dimension exec told us, '*Look, I need to get some changes made to the treatment.*' And we'd already started writing the script by this point, so why would we go back to the treatment? He explained that they weren't really creative changes and that he didn't even really agree with them. Oh, look – right here – we quoted him. He told us, '*If I go back to my boss at Dimension without these changes, he'll call me an asshole, so that's why I need these changes made.*' It was really depressing to have to work with someone like that.

The guy was just spineless. It's tough when you're making changes without any decent creative reasoning behind them. All you've got is, '*My boss told me to tell you.*'

I remember an early conference call we had with Dimension, Malek, and Moustapha about the treatment. The Dimension execs started to talk about the creative direction of the project. And Moustapha cut right across them and said, '*That's none of your business! You don't have those rights. You have no right!*' I think Moustapha had been expecting that moment. He knew they were going to step over the line and he intended to pull them back. After that, we were probably seen as the Akkads' writers and I imagine that made Dimension pretty suspicious of us. Moustapha became angry at them and so were we. They were wanting to make unreasonable changes and he told them, '*No, we've already approved this. You've had sight of it. You agreed to it. And now you're going back and wanting changes. No.*' And Moustapha didn't go back to the treatment. He and Malek encouraged us to continue working on the script draft we were on and to just submit that, which we did.

**You're not the first writer we've spoken to that had issues with Dimension.**

I don't know what their problem was. Did they already know they wanted to remake *Halloween* and were biding their time until they found the right person? In the end, they really screwed us. We delivered the *Halloween: Retribution* script as agreed and Dimension goes, '*Yeah, we're not paying for that.*' And we said, '*But we have a contract.*' We had a Writer's Guild contract with them. So we went to our agent, and agents are always really bullish until you need them to do something. And he goes, '*There's nothing really we can do. Try the Writer's Guild.*' I couldn't believe that response, but we did talk to the Writer's Guild and they told us the same thing. They said that, unless we had the money to sue Dimension, there was nothing that could be done because no one was going to sue on our behalf. They told us, '*If you do sue them, you'd have a pretty good case.*' We told Dimension that this was a breach of contract and they came back saying, '*Oh, no. This falls under artistic differences,*' which was pure nonsense.

In the end, I think we got paid fifty-cents on the dollar for our script. I vowed that I would never do another day of work for them. I would never take another Miramax/Dimension gig. And that really showed them! (laughs) That obviously destroyed their business terribly! (laughs) But it was a horrible experience. It was a wake-up call to that side of the business. But actually writing *Halloween: Retribution* was a great time and we enjoyed working with Malek and Moustapha.

**That's a shame because it's a good script. Surely, you know that.**

Malek and Moustapha felt that it was, but I've learned something in this business, Dustin. It's that good scripts don't mean much. Films rarely get made or not made because the script is good or not good. We really liked it, but what do we know? We weren't even particularly horror-heads. We just wanted to be respectful of the franchise and what it meant to the fans.

**_Halloween: Retribution_ opens with Michael Myers as a child, but then catches up to the present with Freddie Harris, Busta Rhymes' character from _Resurrection_. Was he a lingering plot thread you felt you needed to address or was that requested by someone?**

I think that was something Dimension had asked for. They had a lot of research about what had worked and hadn't worked on the previous films. I never really knew why we were bringing him back. Did the audience love him and want more of him? Or did they hate him and want to see him killed? (laughs) I can't remember which it was. Bringing back John Tate might also have been one of Dimension's suggestions.

**How about Sheriff Brackett? You and Jim bring that character back after a five-film absence.**

I can't remember who first thought of bringing him back, but he was a great character. Looking back at the early _Halloween_ movies, yes – you had the Dr. Loomis character, but he always felt a little bit malevolent to us. Sheriff Brackett, however, seemed like a genuine good guy, kind of like the police chief from _Jaws_. We had this idea of Brackett being your classic American western hero.

There was also an added benefit to bringing him back. Often in these kinds of movies, there's no lasting traumatic impact from the murders that occur. You've got these unspeakable things that happen year after year, but no one talks about them. No one seems bothered by them. We wanted to show that these murders, even decades later, still affected people. They still had an impact. The people who lost loved ones will always have lost them and that doesn't just go away. They'll never, ever get over it. So yes, we wanted to have the fun of the craziness of _Halloween_, but we also wanted to show that these losses were serious. They leave a lasting residue of the evil that caused them. Trauma is itself a residue of evil. It seemed stupid to us to think that life would ever go back to normal in Haddonfield. It would never be normal again.

**Did you ever have any conversations about which cast members might be open to reprising their roles from previous films?**

No, we weren't a part of those discussions. The guy who played John Tate in *Halloween H20* – Josh Hartnett – we liked him quite a bit. He was just becoming a big star back then. We just felt that he was becoming a proper actor and could do something great with the role in *Retribution*. We thought we could give him interesting material to work with and that he'd be able to eat it up.

**Your script very uniquely takes place amid an October snowstorm, which is an uncommon backdrop for a slasher film. Tell me about that decision.**

I think we just loved the idea of blood in the snow. I'm not sure if that was entirely ours or if we took it from something else at the time, but we loved it. That was something we had many long conversations about, whether it might ever snow in late October. Story-wise, it really helped in getting the characters isolated. Isolation is so key to horror films, you know. Isolation of place and time and situation. Those are the things that fuel your nightmares. We'd never seen it snow in a *Halloween* before, so it felt like we were doing something new with it.

**Late in your story, the main characters come across Michael's patient files. Contained within is an old film reel of a therapy session with Dr. Loomis. This affords us a quick cameo for the franchise hero. Why bring back Loomis for this story?**

Why did we do that? Because we wanted to see Donald Pleasence in a *Halloween* movie again! Who doesn't want to see that? It's not much more complicated than that. At one point, we had an idea to only use things Loomis had said in earlier movies so that it could actually be Donald Pleasence doing it, but I'm not sure we stuck with that approach. He was just another person who had really helped drive the franchise forward, so we wanted to get him in there somehow.

***Halloween: Resurrection*** **ends with part of the Myers house burning down. Rather than have Michael go back there, you instead have him go to Smith's Grove, even though you say horrible things happened to him there. Why go back to the sanitarium at all?**

I remember having a conversation with Jim that began with, '*Well, they've burned down the Myers house in the last film. What are we gonna do now?*' But then we realized that he only lived there for six years. He lived at Smith's Grove for an awful lot longer. That may not be where the evil was born, but it was certainly where the evil expanded and took hold. So, really, Michael would probably feel that Smith's Grove was actually his home. I loved the idea of being able to explore his time there a little. The doctors think they're studying him, but really he's studying them. Twisting that around was fun. I also loved the idea of Michael traveling around Smith's Grove in these underground tunnels because this was his home. He knew this place. That was to his advantage upon going back there.

We do have a little bit of the Myers house in it, don't we? We have the wreckage of it, I think. John Tate visits it at one point, right? I mean, c'mon... by then they'd pretty much done as much with that house as they were gonna do. It was time to go somewhere else.

**Your script ends with Michael drowning in a frozen lake. John Tate has his mask, however, and stares into it, "drawn to it by an irresistible force." Is the implication here that John may follow in his uncle's footsteps?**

That's where we were going with it, but we wanted to leave it open to be explored later on. There could've been a possible handover there because, to be honest, Michael was getting a little old, wasn't he? And even if John wasn't going to become a killer, there still might be something evil inside of him that he has to deal with. I think we were interested in John's fascination with evil and whether it's something in the bloodline. To some extent, there's a little evil inside all of us. And given John's proximity to Michael being his uncle, maybe it's a little more so inside of him. What if his fascination with evil draws it out of him?

**I mentioned earlier that your *Retribution* script has leaked online in recent years. As a writer, how do you feel about people being able to read your unproduced work?**

I'm delighted! I'm delighted it's doing more than just sitting on my hard drive. That's the thing. As a writer, you put a lot of work into these projects. Most of the time, no one ever gets to see an unproduced script. I have no idea how it's out there, but it's great! I thought maybe only ever ten people got to read it, but I'm amazed and delighted that people can read it

# HALLOWEEN
## HADDONFIELD

# HALLOWEEN
## ASYLUM

To embrace the past,
you must first relive it.

**Treatments by**
**John Sullivan**

When it comes to movie franchises with waning popularity, there are several ways to continue churning out profitable sequels – all of which involve dramatically cutting costs. One way is to release future installments direct-to-video rather than theatrical, which saves enormously on prints and advertising. Another way is to shoot in a foreign country with generous tax incentives and low working wages. Yet another way is to shoot not one but two sequels back-to-back to save on overhead investment. (This is something even major franchises do, such as on *Superman, The Matrix,* and *Back to the Future.*)

Being the shrewd genre arm of an indie studio, Dimension Films had been utilizing these cost-saving tactics for years, all the way back to its initial formation in 1992. In fact, the studio's very first production – *Hellraiser III: Hell on Earth* – was shot back-to-back with its second – *Children of the Corn II: The Final Sacrifice.* Dimension would repeat these tactics on films throughout the '90s but never all three at once. At least, not until the early 2000s. That's when the studio produced back-to-back, direct-to-video sequels to *Hellraiser, The Prophecy,* and *Dracula 2000,* all of which were filmed on location in Bucharest, Romania. This strategy paid off exactly as intended, yielding six sequels to three well-established franchises for well below industry costs.

Believe it or not, for the briefest moment, Dimension reportedly mulled taking the back-to-back sequel approach with the ninth and tenth installments of the *Halloween* franchise. Granted, this was but one of several directions under consideration at the time. Never was it a front-burner priority for the studio. But such an assignment was given to screenwriter John Sullivan, who was then a rising young talent within the industry. Circa 2003, Dimension had brought Sullivan into their offices to hear pitches on several in-development properties. (These included sequels to *Mimic* and *Rambo,* and also a prequel to *Total Recall.*) While the studio passed on his pitches to these three franchises, they did offer him the opportunity to write back-to-back sequels to *The Prophecy.* Yet upon viewing the original trilogy, Sullivan realized he already had a pair of unproduced screenplays that could be easily retrofitted to align within that franchise's universe. He sent them to Dimension, who agreed with his assessment and bought them outright. Sullivan was then hired to customize his own stories into what would become *The Prophecy: Uprising* and *The Prophecy: Forsaken.*

Pleased with his work, Dimension then offered Sullivan a chance to pitch back-to-back *Halloween* sequels – an opportunity the writer jumped at. Sullivan had long been a fan of not only horror films but of the entire *Halloween* franchise as well. While the distribution fate of these potential follow-ups was never explicitly stated, Sullivan maintains that from his impression, they were to be lower-budget efforts intended for the direct-to-video market. (Recall the franchise had almost been here once before with *Halloween 7*.) This in mind, Sullivan began to envision sequel stories that could be shot economically. This would mean limiting special effects, focusing on smaller locations, and avoiding elaborate set pieces.

## "[We were being] asked to create these sort of lower-budgeted takes that they could shoot for maybe $5 million with $2.5 being allotted for both movies."
- John Sullivan

One of Dimension's clear goals with their direct-to-video sequels was that they not be dependent upon the storylines of previous installments. In other words, you wouldn't have needed to see any other *Hellraiser* movie in order to understand *Hellraiser: Deader*. The same was true of Sullivan's *Prophecy* screenplays, which told entirely new stories. Dimension outright requested this approach with the writer's prospective *Halloween* sequels. Per their instructions, Sullivan's sequels were to exist within the *Halloween H20* timeline but not reference or even acknowledge the events of *Halloween: Resurrection*. And while his story would be a spiritual successor to *H20*, he was not to use any characters from that or any other installment. (The logic here was fiscally sound. *H20*'s surviving cast members, Josh Hartnett, Michelle Williams, and LL Cool J, were now likely out of Dimension's price range.)

While Sullivan's *Halloween* sequels were never developed beyond the treatment phase, they were formulated at Dimension's request. Like all lost *Halloween* sequels, they represent a fascinating "What if?" Even more interesting to consider is what would've become of the franchise had these two sequels been made. What might they have led to? Dimension had earned a solid reputation for churning out these direct-to-video horror sequels at a rapid pace. Had Sullivan's sequels come to fruition, we would've likely received even more *Halloween* movies with far less time between productions – but at what cost?

Sullivan's first treatment operated under a few different titles. It was originally conceived as *Halloween: Haddonfield* though was soon re-titled *Halloween: The Legend of Michael Myers* on the suggestion of a Dimension executive. This was changed yet again to *Halloween: Retribution*, which was still a likely title for whatever storyline the ninth *Halloween* composed. The writer's second treatment was titled *Halloween: Asylum*, though it bears little resemblance to other takes sharing that same name, one of which was being developed separately around this time.

## HALLOWEEN: HADDONFIELD

John Sullivan's first treatment introduces a new protagonist in Dr. Jason Loomis, the now adult son of the late Sam Loomis. A psychiatrist like his father, Jason has recently authored a best-selling book on his father's exploits with his most famous patient. In the days leading up to Halloween, Jason learns that Haddonfield has chosen to embrace its bloody past in a most macabre way. This year, the town has planned an entire Halloween festival celebrating the legend of Michael Myers. In a bold move, such revelry will even include a re-enactment of the murders. The younger Loomis feels this is not only distasteful, but also extremely dangerous as some believe the Shape to still be at-large. He decides to personally visit Haddonfield to argue against holding this event.

Jason arrives in town just before Halloween and begins tracking down the mayor, the police chief, and city councilmembers. He charges that such an event is a slap in the face to the countless families who've lost loved ones over the years. However, the town officials prove unsympathetic, citing the massive economic downturn Haddonfield has suffered as of late. Investment in the area has ground to a halt, which has sent unemployment soaring. Meanwhile, curious tourists have continued to pass through in pilgrimage to the birthplace of ultimate evil. Rather than scoff at these visitors, Haddonfield has finally chosen to embrace them and its own past. The event itself has already created numerous jobs and the mass of tourists expected will have plenty of opportunities to spend cash within city limits.

Unbeknownst to anyone, the Shape is still alive, having spent the last several years living off the grid on the outskirts of town. Waiting for an opportunity to strike again, which the festival more than provides, he returns to Haddonfield on Halloween morning just as preparations are underway. With multiple people brandishing knives in white masks, the Shape blends in more easily than ever before. He first stalks and murders several of the town elders who are responsible for planning the event.

As the night kicks off, local actors recreate the murder of Judith Myers before an audience. The Shape observes this bizarre re-staging and fixates on the young girl performing the role of his sister. Meanwhile, Jason Loomis has begun to notice the suspicious disappearance of several local leaders and worries that Michael may have returned to take revenge. He takes his concerns to the sheriff, a younger lawman new to Haddonfield, who agrees that Michael may indeed be back. Unfortunately, the celebratory chaos of the festival makes it impossible to tell if the real Michael is present – or even if actual murders are being committed. (With so many re-enactments, the night would be filled with screams and the streets littered with fake blood.)

The festival eventually builds towards the night's main attraction – a big dance at Haddonfield High School with multiple live music acts. Jason and the sheriff, both in attendance, somehow confirm that the Shape is back and that he's now targeting the actress portraying his sister. Police interrupt the dance and lock down the high school in an effort to protect the teens, but the slasher is already inside. A fire soon breaks out, forcing everyone out in the open. This final act culminates in a three-way fight between Jason, fake Judith, and the Shape inside the burning school gymnasium. Their struggle unfolds before a gigantic papier-mâché pumpkin, which is also on fire. (This pumpkin was to resemble the one from *Halloween*'s opening credits.) The Judith actress eventually gains the upper hand and stabs the Shape multiple times, presumably to death.

The lost sequels detailed in this book have alternately depicted the town of Haddonfield as either trying to ban or unban the Halloween holiday. None yet, however, have found it embracing its dark past with such extravagance. Had it been produced, *Halloween: Haddonfield* was poised to become the most meta and self-reflective *Halloween* ever. Sullivan envisioned his first sequel as a social commentary on the culture of serial killer worship. Just as real-life killers John Wayne Gacy and Ed Gein have developed cult-followings over the years, Sullivan reasoned that Michael, too, would've gained an unsavory fanbase. With its macabre re-enactments, the *Haddonfield* treatment blurs the line between performance art and reality. Viewers would've been left constantly guessing whether the violence on-screen was actually being perpetrated or just part of a harmless re-enactment. This uncertainty would've proven a major obstacle for Jason Loomis and local law enforcement as they try to bring the true slasher to justice.

This actually ties nicely into one of the original themes behind *Halloween: Resurrection*. Screenwriter Larry Brand had initially envisioned the eighth installment as a clever commentary on life imitating art and vice versa. While that noble intention was ultimately lost en route to the big screen, the seeds of his premise are still there. *Resurrection* drew inspiration from Orson Welles' famous 1938 *War of the Worlds* broadcast in which listening audiences believed a dramatized news story about aliens attacking was real. With *Resurrection*, Brand sought to flip Welles' premise. Within that story's reality, Dangertainment contestants were actually being killed, but viewers at home believed they were watching staged murders. (If you didn't walk away from that sequel pondering its social commentaries, you're not to blame. Studio execs muddied those waters.) Unlike *Resurrection*, Sullivan's self-aware treatment seemed much better poised to communicate its themes to the audience.

Sullivan scripted several thrilling sequences that would've drawn on familiar traditions of the Halloween holiday. One of these involved the Shape attacking riders one-by-one on a haunted hayride through a large cornfield. (Think back to the nighttime raptor attack from *The Lost World: Jurassic Park*.) The beauty of this sequence is that the tall rows of corn would've given the Shape ample coverage to stalk and slash as he pleased without being seen. The unsuspecting riders would've been blind to his approach and to the mutilated corpses of their fellow riders strewn amongst the cornfield.

With Dr. Jason Loomis, Sullivan gives the franchise something it has been sorely lacking since *Halloween 6* – a hero in the tradition of the elder Sam Loomis. As this story's lead, Jason comes off as an upright guy like his father, a man looking to do whatever he can to protect others. The subject of Sam's offspring is a strange one that's never been fully addressed in the theatrical canon. The original's novelization saw Loomis make brief mention of his teenage son when passing by a liquor store. Early drafts of *Halloween H20* also tried giving Loomis an adult daughter named Rachel. (The screenwriters originally envisioned that in place of Marion Whittington, it would be Rachel's home that the Shape ransacks in the film's opening sequence.) Furthermore, writer Stef Hutchinson envisioned the late doctor as having a son named Dr. David Loomis in his 2003 comic, *Halloween: One Good Scare*.

In what may be its strongest attribute, *Halloween: Haddonfield* envisioned a different kind of sequel for the franchise. It abandons the Shape hunting down members of his family. And, thankfully, it avoids introducing any new family we didn't know about. It also never tries to explain what may be driving the Shape to kill, leaving the secret of his evil unexplained. Though in providing a target victim, who better for the slasher to pursue than a young woman bearing a passing resemblance to his older sister? Sullivan's treatment features just that with the Shape zeroing in on the actress playing Judith in the town's murder re-enactment. It's a rather thoughtful idea, with the finale – in which fake Judith stabs Michael – also serving as a nice twist on the original film's prologue. All in all, we say the writer deserves kudos for creating a tale so simple yet strong enough to have warranted a potential last-minute conversion from direct-to-video to theatrical.

## HALLOWEEN: ASYLUM '04

While Sullivan mapped out the story for his second *Halloween* sequel, he never fully developed it into a proper treatment. His follow-up would've found Jason Loomis continuing in his father's footsteps by enlisting as the new head administrator of Smith's Grove Sanitarium. Per the screenwriter, Jason would've been compelled to join the staff of Smith's Grove following the incident in Haddonfield. While the still-missing Michael Myers was presumed dead in that sequel's ending, the younger Loomis is concerned that another young slasher might pass through Smith's Grove and emerge (or escape) unrehabilitated. But this isn't exactly his father's sanitarium.

Following the 1978 breakout, authorities have continuously upgraded Smith's Grove so that it functions like a high-tech prison. Patient rooms have been converted into cells with electronic locking mechanisms. In fact, the security of the entire facility is now managed by computer software. This new system has drastically scaled back the need for guards and orderlies, resulting in a minimal skeleton crew overseeing things. Unfolding mostly on Halloween night, this *Asylum* finds Jason Loomis, a young female reporter, two orderlies, and a security guard as the only non-patients in the hospital. A raging thunderstorm causes a short-circuit in the power grid, which results in a dangerous situation. The resulting blackout throws the facility into lockdown mode while simultaneously releasing patients from their cells. This traps the aforementioned staff and reporter within the facility with a roaming hoard of incredibly dangerous patients.

How does the Shape factor into this? Well, he doesn't, *not really*. Yet there is a delusional patient named Richard Raines, however, who actually believes himself to be the real Michael

Myers. As the evening begins, Richard seems like any other raving patient. But as the night rages on, he slowly disappears into his fabricated identity as the Shape. Richard grows increasingly withdrawn until becoming entirely non-verbal. He also fashions a crude white mask that he stitches together from old bed sheets. Upon either obtaining or making a weapon, he begins stalking the locked-down Smith's Grove and picking off our heroes one-by-one. To make matters worse, Richard isn't the only homicidal maniac running loose this evening. He just so happens to be the only one impersonating the Shape.

Trying to survive the night, Jason and the others attempt to reach the only traversable exit in the entire building. This path takes them through the hospital's long abandoned basement, which was once the site of ghastly medical experimentation. They move quickly through this hall of horrors as their most dangerous clientele trails close behind. Richard eventually picks off the remaining staff until only Jason and the female reporter remain. Having cornered his prey in the basement, the faux-Shape now moves in for the kill. It's here that Jason plays into Richard's delusion by making a desperate plea as though this were a conversation between Sam Loomis and the actual Shape. ("I always tried to help you, Michael.") With this, Richard steps back silently as if he's going to spare them. *But he doesn't.* After a pause, he raises his knife to strike, but is instead fatally stabbed from behind by the *actual* Shape. Having heard the speech, the real Michael allows Jason and the reporter to escape through the basement exit before disappearing into the night himself.

Without a doubt, Sullivan's *Asylum* represents one of the boldest visions for a *Halloween* since *Season of the Witch*. A sequel where the killer is a Michael Myers impersonator? Where the true Shape doesn't appear until film's end? And he only kills one person? *What a gamble!* This approach would've surely drawn comparisons to 1985's *Friday the 13th Part V: A New Beginning*, but any such comparisons would be inaccurately made. *A New Beginning* doesn't reveal its fakery until the final act, thus tricking the audience into thinking they've been watching Jason Voorhees the entire time. When we do finally see Jason at film's end, he's but a hallucination inside Tommy Jarvis' mind. *Halloween: Asylum* would've alternately been upfront about its primary killer being an imposter. Whether or not Dimension would've been capable of keeping the real Michael's limited appearance a secret remained to be seen. (They may well have included the reveal in the film's trailer – you never know these days.)

The shock ending of this proposed sequel would've undoubtedly inspired tremendous debate amongst fans, if not some uproar. The Richard Raines character receives his well-deserved comeuppance from the true Michael Myers, who then allows Jason and the reporter to go free. The Shape isn't exactly known for his mercy, so why spare them? It's possible he'd try to kill them in any other scenario, but not this one. His legacy has been muddied by an impersonator. Perhaps the Shape isn't here to kill, but to clean up that mess. Or maybe Jason's speech somehow reached whatever human part of the slasher still remains. (It did seem that in *Halloween 5* both Loomis and Jamie nearly reached him in much the same way.)

Whether or not this treatment would've succeeded as a film would've largely depended on the scare appeal of the Richard Raines character. Sullivan would've needed to create a horrifying characterization – one that would be worthy of stepping into the Shape's role as a Halloween killer. The filmmakers would've also needed to ensure that his crudely fashioned bed sheet mask was capable of striking fear into those who gaze upon it – much like the modified Shatner mask. Lastly, it would've been important to cast the role with a powerhouse performer – someone with a unique physicality to their acting that could also deliver insane dialogue. Bill Moseley? Doug Jones? Crispin Glover? You could skew young or old with it, lanky or heavy build. This isn't the true Shape, so it would've been a unique opportunity to try a different physical look.

Taken as a double-feature, Sullivan's proposed sequels really are standalone in the best sense of the word. At their start, the Shape is at-large. At their conclusion, he's still at-large. Sullivan doesn't inflict any permanent damage to the universe, ensuring that it remains intact for the next filmmaker. (He doesn't burn down Smith's Grove or lop off any of the Shape's fingers.) He also doesn't try to explain or reinvent the Shape's origin.

Would such a radically different sequel have been able to win over fans, critics, and audiences? It's hard to say. Bad movies have been made from good scripts, so it would be dependent upon execution and advertising. If nothing else, it would've been an interesting experiment to once again test the boundaries of the franchise. There's certainly intrigue in focusing on a copycat killer, as well as the Shape's reaction to this and his sparing of lives. (Were a *Halloween* TV series created, experimental tales such as this would be fascinating to explore.)

Sullivan's *Asylum* didn't envision an entirely new story à la *Halloween III*, but it did tell an alternate story within the *Halloween* world we already know. Does that technically make it a spinoff? *Possibly*. And what other spinoffs might this franchise have within it? A Loomis prequel set before he meets the Shape? A Brackett prequel? What about old Charlie Bowles who one night excused himself from dinner and went to retrieve a hacksaw from the garage? Had it been successful, *Halloween: Asylum* might've even revived John Carpenter and Debra Hill's anthology approach. Or it could've crashed and burned like a police cruiser into Ben Tramer.

## WHY THEY WEREN'T MADE

Unlike other concepts featured in this book, John Sullivan's back-to-back treatments weren't quite as close to reaching the screen. To start with, his second treatment hadn't been entirely fleshed out and only comprised a few pages. But as already mentioned, plans to produce future *Halloween*s as back-to-back and direct-to-video hadn't been a high priority for Dimension. Rather, these ideas were developed as a sort of back-up plan if nothing better were to materialize. It's also unlikely Moustapha Akkad would've ever approved the direct-to-video route. Recall that Trancas had already nixed a potential *Hellraiser* crossover in fear that that franchise – which had gone direct-to-video – might impose on *Halloween*'s own theatrical viability. The dual-sequel approach also didn't fit with what was then a hot new movement within the genre – remaking the classics for modern audiences. Beyond that, there was a storm brewing with Miramax/Dimension, but we'll get to that in the next few chapters.

That said, both Dimension and Trancas liked the idea of featuring the Smith's Grove sanitarium as a primary location and, as with Jim Keeble and Dudi Appleton's *Retribution*, would continue to develop this element for later iterations. Likewise, the location of Sullivan's first treatment – a Halloween carnival of sorts – would also gain some traction. (A non-descript idea titled *Halloween: Abusement Park* would be jotted down in a list of potential scenarios considered by Dimension. More on that later.) As for John Sullivan, he may not have written a *Halloween*, but he did go on to script the action films *Recoil* (starring Steve Austin and Danny Trejo) and *Security* (starring Antonio Banderas and Ben Kingsley).

# JOHN SULLIVAN

## Writer - Halloween: Haddonfield & Halloween: Asylum

Interviewed by Travis Mullins

**Prior to *Halloween*, you worked on *The Prophecy* sequels for Dimension. Could you tell us a bit of your backstory leading up to that?**

I had written a horror film called *Fear of the Dark* back in 2001 that wound up being made by a Canadian production company. It was a low-budget movie – probably $2 million – and [the company] didn't have distribution. They sent it to Dimension to look at. Now, Dimension passed on the movie, but they liked it. That kind of put me on their radar as a writer. But I was still pretty young – only 21 or 22 – so they didn't bring me in for what they'd call a general meeting yet. A couple of months after that, I sold a major spec script to Sony – an action movie called *Rapid*, which unfortunately didn't get made. By then, I was very much on Dimension's radar. Shortly after, they brought me in for *The Prophecy* movies. They hadn't really looked at any other writers. It was almost like they offered me the job in the room, and I was happy to take it. I loved the Christopher Walken original, familiarized myself with the other sequels, and wrote *Prophecy 4* and 5 back-to-back. That went well. I had a really good experience with everyone involved. Then, I had one or two options on my contract, which meant Dimension had the option to look at anything else I did. They also had the option to bring me in with a pre-negotiated rate.

**How did you come to be involved with *Halloween*?**

After *Halloween: Resurrection* was released, Dimension had what they call a bake-off where they ask different managers and agencies, '*Do you have any writers who would be good for this?*' My manager remembered that I had the relationship with Dimension, so I got in the room. I had one general meeting. They didn't want a direct sequel to *Halloween: Resurrection*. They wanted a standalone sequel – a new storyline with Michael Myers that didn't have any other returning characters. That's when I heard from my manager that they were thinking of going direct-to-video. Obviously, that didn't happen, but I was working with the idea that this would be a lower-budgeted *Halloween* sequel and that they were looking to do *Halloween 9* and *10* back-to-back. I was a little confused because I had talked to other writer friends of mine who had talked to different execs at Dimension. They were saying they had never heard of the back-to-back sequel idea and they thought they were pitching on a theatrical sequel. But it made sense because I had done *The Prophecy* movies back-to-back and those were direct-to-video sequels. So, I'm thinking, '*Okay, they're looking at me for THAT version.*' That's sort of what I was given as far as any sort of mandate. It probably had to be done on a significantly lower budget than *Resurrection*. They didn't lose money on *Resurrection*, but it wasn't a significant hit and it wasn't well-regarded by fans.

Talking to the executives, I was under the impression they were giving different mandates about what it should be about. '*Okay, we're looking for this!*' or '*We're looking for that!*' Depending on which executive you talked to, it would be *different* every time. I had friends who pitched on this and they were telling me, '*Oh, yeah, they want me to do this version in New York.*' I'm like, '*What? They never said that to me!*' There were just a lot of writers coming up with *multiple* takes and neither one was necessarily the one that Dimension was totally targeting for. I had a suspicion they were going to be direct-to-video. I was never told that, but it was my suspicion. I think they wanted to have their lower-budgeted *Halloween* movies ready in case the mandate came down, '*Okay, we're not going to spend $20 million on another* Halloween *sequel after we only made, like, $5 million on* Resurrection.' Ultimately, they decided to do that. But I think they wanted to have ammunition – bullets in the gun in case they did decide to go that route. I think that's why I – and maybe a couple of other writers – were being asked to create these lower-budgeted takes that they could shoot for maybe $5 million with $2.5 million being allotted for both movies.


**It's so interesting that may have been an option at some point. Or at least was an idea percolating in the back of their minds.**

It happens more times than you think. On *Fast & Furious* – after *Tokyo Drift*, there was an idea to do two back-to-back direct-to-video sequels. That almost happened but cooler heads prevailed. (laughs) They kind of left me to my own devices. At the time, I was living in New York and that was convenient because Dimension was one of the few production companies that had offices in the city. It was very easy to get on the phone with them or if they needed me to come in for a face-to-face and pitch Bob [Weinstein] or any of the higher-level executives. I never did that, though. I never got to Bob. I think my treatments did, but I never met Bob Weinstein or Moustapha Akkad. I never met any of the real heavy hitters. Obviously, if my treatment had gone to script, that would've eventually happened. So, my role in the franchise was slim. I mean, I worked on it from roughly 2004 to 2005. I don't know the exact year. But I was really flattered that you reached out to me. It's one of the things in my past that I always bring up because everyone knows the *Halloween* franchise. A lot of the other stuff I've worked on is great, but it doesn't have the name recognition of *Halloween*.

**Going back a bit, were you a fan of the series?**

I saw the first *Halloween* at a very young age. I still put it on loop in the background whenever my wife and I have a Halloween party. Just the way it catches the autumnal vibe of October, it's an iconic Halloween movie. It's the *Jaws* of slasher movies. For me, there's no better slasher than *Halloween* just as there's no better monster movie than *Jaws*. I also loved *Halloween II*. I became a fan of *Halloween III* after the fact – as did everybody. *Halloween 4* was a movie I had to sneak on VHS when it came out. My parents wouldn't let me watch R-rated movies, so that was a tough one. The only *Halloween* I've seen in the theater, actually, was *Halloween 6*. I'm not sure why I didn't see *H20* in the theater. For whatever reason, I just didn't make it out. I would've loved to have seen that on the big screen. That was a good one. One of my favorite sequels.

My first movie [*Fear of the Dark*] was a very kid-oriented horror film but it was built around suspense. There was no real gore. It was mainly about mood and that's what *Halloween* always meant to me. The best sequels are the ones that favor mood over gore. Like *Jaws*, *Halloween* was also a movie where the killer *was* the soundtrack. I think that's why both of those movies just work so well. So, I was always a fan. When my manager called and said, '*They're looking for* Halloween,' I mean, I flipped out. It was one of those things where I may have been overeager because I *really* did want to write *my* ideal sequel. But I always suspected that Dimension already had what they wanted to do in mind. I was hearing different ideas from different executives on what to do. Ultimately, those movies didn't go forward. They scrapped everything and went with Rob Zombie's version.

**Tell us about the first of your proposed sequels.**

The first was the Haddonfield one which, depending on whatever version it was, was either called *Halloween: Haddonfield, Retribution,* or *The Legend of Michael Myers.* That one largely took place in the town. Every Halloween, Haddonfield gets transformed into what amounts to an amusement park. There are cornfields, a haunted hayride, Shape masks everywhere, and the Judith Myers murder is reenacted by local actors. Basically, this town embraces the legend of Michael Myers. I got the impression they liked the idea of multiple people looking like Michael Myers. I just remember the pushback we had was finding an engine for why Michael was killing people again. Jason Loomis is in town – actually being against the celebration – and we thought he might be a good target. But it didn't really work out, so we wound up having Michael go after the actress playing Judith Myers after he interprets her as his sister. She would've been the female lead. It was a cool twist – a nice fix because we didn't want to invent any more family members.

Michael was alive after *Resurrection,* so we didn't have to address that. But in the opening, I had him in the same hermit hole from *Halloween 5.* I remember not having to explain that it was a reference to *Halloween 5.* No one picked up on that right away. (laughs) It was his retreat. Initially, I couldn't figure out where Michael would go. He needed to be laying low somewhere. The timeframe was always up for whatever I needed it to be. But a year or two years later, where was he the entire time? He wasn't killing anybody. He hadn't shown up. I needed him to be somewhere. It harkens back to *Halloween 5,* but it was more of a wink than an intentional callback because *Halloween 5* doesn't exist in this universe.

I remember one of the junior executives or someone I was talking to at the time said, '*This is kind of like* The Wicker Man.' Like, it's not. It's nothing like *The Wicker Man.* I'm not going to use that for a reference. (laughs) But I guess a town holding a festival honoring what amounts to an evil deity is sort of like *The Wicker Man*, I suppose? It was a lot of fun. Ultimately, I think it was bigger than what they wanted. It wasn't quite there. I think we had second act problems. Also, I think it was like, '*Would Haddonfield actually do this?*' Would they actually turn their town into a money-making venture honoring a really brutal murder? Even Amityville, they

*hate* being associated with *The Amityville Horror*. I'm from Long Island, I know. But I thought it was really interesting. We've seen a couple movies since then that have utilized that premise. I think *Hell Fest* did it. I think even *Scream 4* touched on it a little bit.

**It does remind me of *Scream* a bit – the reenactments and the idea of not being certain if the murders are staged or not.**

This was something developed post-*Scream*. We were living in a post-*Scream* world at that point, so I was trying to do something that recognized *Halloween* and recognized that if there were a Michael Myers and these murders did take place, there would be this sort of culture around him. Like people who idolize Jeffrey Dahmer and Charles Manson; these horrible serial killers yet there's this cult following. I think I had set it up in such a way almost like how Amity was having budget problems in *Jaws 2* because the shark had ruined their commerce. (laughs) Haddonfield needed to recoup. No one wanted to live in the town, so why not make a negative a positive? It happened with Salem, too. Salem embraces the fact the witch trials happened there. I think what we bumped up against was the timeframe. Like, yeah, that might make sense ten years after *H20* or *Resurrection*, but we were pretty much setting this in present day. Essentially, it would seem to the audience like this was taking place immediately after *Resurrection* – and nobody wanted to set *Halloween 9* ten years in the future. Ultimately, I think those were the roadblocks. In going back and forth and revising it, I kind of knew, like, this is cool, but it's not working. I would've loved to have written that script, but I don't think that's what they were looking for.

**You said an alternate title for this was *The Legend of Michael Myers?***

*Halloween: Haddonfield* was my original title. Then, I heard, 'Oh! The Legend of Michael Myers! We can keep that in line with Return, Revenge, Curse.' The only reason I didn't like that title is because it felt like a King Kong movie. It sounded like *The Legend of King Kong* – like it needed to take place in an older era, like a 1930s swashbuckling adventure rather than a slasher movie. I didn't like that title, but it was sort of a placeholder. Eventually, I learned that it was going to be *Retribution*, which still worked. Whenever you have a *Halloween* movie, you can always call it *Retribution*. It's retribution for something. In this case, I guess Michael – if he had emotions – would take offense to him turning into a pop culture thing.

**When I spoke with Nick Phillips, he mentioned that while working for Dimension, he kept a document of loglines from over a dozen concepts. One of the titles he mentioned was _Halloween: Abusement Park_. Do you think there's a connection there?**

That could be it. That could've been a title that they were thinking of that wasn't expressed to me. (laughs) Thing is, with these sort-of [writing] bake-offs, you're really taking a risk at shot-gunning these takes to the studio. They might like your title, one or two elements and then they may talk to another writer and say, '_What about something like this?_' It's not always intentional. These producers – they hear multiple pitches and takes. They hear it all the time. After a while, it seems like they thought of it. Something like _Halloween: Abusement Park_? That's almost like you have a logline in your title. '_Yeah,_ Abusement Park! _I get that right away!_' That might've been it. But I'm sure there were other writers who might've come up with that, too. It's a good idea and a different venue for Michael Myers, so it definitely seems like something they were looking at.

**From this concept, do you remember any notable set pieces?**

There was a set piece that I had sketched out where Michael would be picking off people in a cornfield which I hadn't seen before, so I thought it would've been creepy. This is largely why I wanted to do something that took place within the town.  It was a cat and mouse chase. I think it was Michael chasing the Judith Myers character and she was hiding in the cornstalks. But there were also other people in the corn. Remember the scene in _The Lost World: Jurassic Park_ where you can see the raptors chasing the characters from above? You would've seen the path of the corn from an aerial view. That was something that I wanted to expand upon if it had gone to script.

The other aspect was a haunted hayride. It was an automated hayride. There wasn't a horse; it was an automated horse. As the hayride moves through the woods, people just start disappearing from the back and getting killed off. Again, this goes back to my love of _Jaws_. I always saw Michael as the shark, and I wanted him to be evocative of _Jaws_. You have four characters on a hayride, and they start getting pulled into the darkness one-by-one.

Those are two that stick out in my head – and then the ending which took place at the dance. The dance would've been lit up by a massive, glowing jack-o-lantern. I'm guessing it was papier-mâché. But in the ending, it's on fire. It's sort of like the opening of _Halloween_ with the flaming jack-o-lantern.  You actually see the jack-o-lantern slowly dissolve. This is during the fight with Michael, Jason Loomis, and the fake Judith – and the backdrop is this jack-o-lantern which is slowly turning into the jack-o-lantern that we know from the credit sequence. That was just a visual that I really wanted to do. (laughs)

**What I like is that this is so holiday centric.**

I really wanted to embrace the holiday. That's what I love about the first one. It's just such a quintessential October film. I wanted to up that. I wanted the entire movie to take place within the Halloween universe – the physical and spiritual Halloween universe. The ending set piece taking place with a backdrop of a gigantic, flaming jack-o-lantern? I mean, I wanted to write that. I wanted to see that in a *Halloween* movie. Even if I didn't do it, I wanted to see that, at some point, in a *Halloween* movie.

**Tell us about your second treatment.**

Since we were thinking of doing this back-to-back, Jason Loomis would've carried over to *Halloween: Asylum*. This never developed further than probably a couple of pages. The idea was that he would be the new doctor at Smith's Grove, which had been completely redone and modernized with secure cells. We would've gone into more of the inmates at Smith's Grove. That movie pretty much took place inside the asylum during a blackout. It became this gritty, horrific thriller – still very much a *Halloween* movie because we still have the Michael Myers character even though it's not Michael Myers. You know, I was worried that it was going to be like *Friday the 13th Part V* where it's not Michael Myers – but we also know that it's not him. It's never a question.

**So, the audience isn't being tricked.**

No, we save that for the end. It comes down to Jason Loomis and the young reporter. They've managed to kill or block off the inmates who are trying to kill them. Now, it's just them and Richard Raines. Because Richard thinks he's Michael Myers, he wants to kill a Loomis. But Jason tries to reason with him. He speaks to this fake Michael as if he really was Michael. '*I always tried to help you, Michael. I don't know why you're doing this. I don't know why you want to kill me. I was always there for you. I was the only one who tried to help you.*' There's a moment where you think you see the humanity in this fake Michael Myers. But he takes out the huge knife, steps forward and is about to kill the young reporter. But then, the fake Michael just rises in the air because he's suspended on this gigantic machete – and behind him is Michael Myers. So, the real Michael Myers kills the fake Michael Myers and lets Jason Loomis and the reporter go. That's how the movie would've ended. Jason Loomis and the reporter go free – and Michael Myers is still alive.

**What's the psychology behind that?**

Uh, I didn't want to get hired? I don't know! (laughs) I was playing around with the idea of where, in the *Haddonfield* treatment, the Judith Myers is not the real Judith Myers, and I wanted to do one where Michael is not the real Michael. Towards the end, Dr. Loomis wants nothing more than for Michael to be dead. But in the beginning, Loomis was trying to help and find the humanity in him. That's what Jason Loomis was trying to get across to this maniac who thinks he's Michael. But this maniac is not Michael, so that isn't going to do anything for him. But the real Michael sneaks into the sanitarium. I don't think I worked out why he was there. It was really one of those shock endings that hopefully no one would question. But that speech would appeal to him. He lets Jason go because he was right. His dad was always trying to help him in the beginning. Loomis only became this vigilante, Van Helsing-type after Michael started killing everyone.

I remember having this chase sequence that took place in the bowels of Smith's Grove. I've always been fascinated with the old sanitariums and what they used to do to inmates. I thought these places would have these subbasements that they never cleaned up and I wanted to do a set piece in one that was filled with this old equipment and horrific blood stains. I thought that would've been interesting. It got to the point where I have this idea with this really suspenseful sequence – but I don't have Michael Myers. This is a guy who just *thinks* he's Michael Myers – and then we're going to be faced with the *Friday the 13th Part V* problem where the audience just watched a *Friday the 13th* movie without Jason. So, I wanted the real Michael to show up.

I felt like this was an opportunity to show just a *bit* of humanity with Michael. He kills the fake Michael trying to kill Loomis and lets Loomis go because he realizes that Loomis was right. His father had tried his best. There was no Judith Myers character in this. There wasn't a new relative or anything, so there wasn't any reason for Michael to kill Loomis' son. I thought he would let him go and it was going to be the shock ending. You know, it worked in the pitch – like the reaction you had, '*Holy shit!*' But I don't know if it would've worked on-screen.

**Honestly, I like both of these ideas. I doubt they'll ever stop making *Halloween* films, but I feel like Michael letting someone go could be a concluding chapter. If you were going to conclude the franchise, then that's one way to do it without Michael 'dying.'**

I'm flattered! (laughs) You know, in the treatment, you don't really write a lot of dialogue. You might have one or two lines that you definitely want to hit for whoever is reading it. But I remember thinking, 'Yeah, that Loomis speech. That would be cool.' I remember having the line, '*I was the only one ever trying to help you. My dad was the only one ever trying to help you*,' and Jason hoping against hope that it would work on this maniac Michael Myers and it doesn't – but it works on the real Michael Myers. I don't know where it would've gone after. He lets them go – and then Michael is also alive and free. At least, it's an open ending that the next writer can tackle.

**What's interesting is that this would've had multiple killers running around. Not just the fake Michael Myers, but the other inmates as well.**

I can't remember what exactly, but they all had different traits. That was one of the things that was mentioned to me. Like, '*Oh, they should all be unique. They should all be different types of serial killers.*' That might've meant different masks. I didn't want to do that, but they were all different types of serial killers. Richard – the fake Michael Myers – was their leader. They were taking their various forms of revenge against the orderlies and the security guards. Literally, the inmates were running the asylum. So, the leads didn't have to just worry about the fake Michael Myers. If this were a video game, he'd be the big boss at the end – but there were other lesser serial killers to contend with. It became very much like a run and chase – almost like *Aliens* – in terms of going through darkened corridors, having to lock doors behind them.

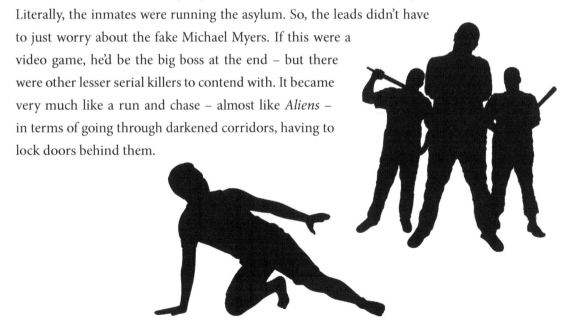

**Tell us more about this female reporter and her role in the story.**

She was a reporter, but she was also writing a book about Loomis. So, Jason Loomis was sort of getting his just deserts getting a book written about him. Jason doesn't want to do the interview, but he knows that if he doesn't agree, she's just going to find some other way. It's sort of a push-pull relationship. In the beginning, he doesn't want her there, but he knows that if he doesn't allow her access to him, his history, and his dad's experiences with Michael Myers, then she's just going to dig up some other stuff. So, they have a very tumultuous relationship in the beginning. Then, they bond a little more as they have to fight for their lives. I guess she was sort of a Gale Weathers-type.

**Did you ever refer back to the Judith actress from that first treatment?**

I think her name was Annie. That might've been a throwback. But no, she wasn't in this one. I wanted to have a new sort of romantic interest. And the girl playing Judith was way too young for Jason Loomis. I wanted someone more his age, so that's why I had a slightly older reporter in this one. So, no, she's never referenced. But we never really get out of the asylum, so the rest of the town isn't really referenced. The only character ported over was Jason, so it was going to be a Jason Loomis twofer – and I'm surprised the other scripts didn't have him as a character because I always thought that was the caveat. Like, '*Oh, we are going to have this.*' If it wasn't going to be Jason Loomis, I thought maybe a Nancy Loomis or something. (laughs) This was like a set piece treatment I had. Like, the three major action or suspense set pieces would be a page, so there wasn't a lot of character development [with this female reporter] – whereas with the *Haddonfield* treatment, I remember the Annie character was an aspiring actress. She had every intention of moving out of Haddonfield to Los Angeles. She wanted to be an actress, so this was just a steppingstone for her. I really had that character mapped out.

**Did you develop any of the orderlies or security guards?**

I know that I killed somebody with a shock paddle. One of the orderlies was the asshole orderly. He was an orderly who was abusive to some of the patients. He gets cornered in the basement towards the top of the third act. It's almost a torture porn sequence – because he gets cornered by these three main inmates who he had been abusing and they literally tear him to pieces. It was of its time. Keep in mind, this is like 2004 or 2005. There was a little bit of that *Saw / Hostel* vibe with some of the sequences. But as far as blood goes, the security guard gets killed by the maniac Michael Myers. I think he gets impaled over one of the railings of a hospital cot. He was a good character. I guess that was the death that might've affected the audience. I would say there were only two or three major kills in that treatment because the cast would've been so small. It was more of a survival movie than a body count movie.

**Between these two treatments, you spent a lot of time with this Jason Loomis character. Did you ever envision a specific actor for the role?**

He wasn't super famous yet but at the time, Timothy Olyphant. He never would've done it. (laughs) But that's who I had in my head while writing it. I guess I needed someone who was a little more mature. I didn't want anybody who was super young. Not middle age but at least mid-30s. It was between him and maybe Colin Farrell, I guess. But again, it was one of those scenarios where he never would've done it.

**I was curious if you'd go for an accent.**

Yeah, Colin would've worked for that. This is all fantasy casting but, in my head, Jason Loomis was raised in the United States, so you could go either way. In fact, I thought that might've been an interesting character beat. Timothy Olyphant – in something like *Go* or *Scream 2*, he's very much not Donald Pleasence. He's more of a Southern California guy. I thought that might be interesting in that he's the opposite of Donald Pleasence. That's sort of how I pictured it.

**Another take that later made it to script was also titled *Halloween: Asylum*. In your memory of it, did you come up with that title or was it suggested to you? Is there a connection?**

No. I mean, I'd love to say, '*Oh, that's my title!*' But that was something that was floating around – to make a contained *Halloween* in an asylum. That was not unique to me. That was something that I utilized. But that was all you got, like, '*What about* Halloween: Asylum? *And maybe it takes place in the asylum?*' and then the writer would just run with that. Then, it's however you want that story to play out. But that's something that was just floating around. I'm not surprised there's an existing script called *Halloween: Asylum*. I wouldn't be surprised if there's more than one. (laughs)

**What kind of feedback did you receive?**

It was always good. You never really get bad feedback. You'd get notes, like, '*We feel that this is not necessarily what we want to move forward with.*' It was always good. I was under the impression I was close. It was definitely communicated to me, like, '*Oh, yeah, we're getting there!*' I'd check in with my manager. '*They really like you! They really like what you're doing!*' But what winds up happening is that it just sort of fades away and then you hear that someone else got hired. And that's how it works in this business. You don't usually hear '*No,*' but you will hear that someone else got hired for the job. (laughs)

**So, how did you feel about where the series ultimately went?**

I was glad. There were so many cooks on *Halloween 9*. There really wasn't a choice but to wipe the board. Rob Zombie's take? It wasn't for everybody, but I think the franchise needed that sort of scorcher to rise again. I understand why they went that route. They commissioned a couple of scripts and heard a lot of takes. Ultimately, though, when you have that much development for those many years, it doesn't always turn into a great sequel. And I think once you start getting into the part eights and part nines of a franchise, you really need to reboot at that point. So, depending on how you feel about it, I thought the Rob Zombie version was a necessary evil in a way. It led to Danny McBride and David Gordon Green coming onboard and I really liked what they did. I'm excited to see what they do with *Halloween Kills*.

**Of your two concepts, which would you say was your favorite?**

I think I would've had the most fun with *Halloween: Haddonfield,* or whatever it would've been called. *Asylum* was more of a straightforward, contained horror film. That's fine, but for me as a writer, I'm more known for action films. My last movie [*Security*] was actually an homage to *Assault on Precinct 13*. I also have a family movie at Disney. I mean, I love all types of movies, but I think *Haddonfield* would've provided me with – for the lack of a better term – more of an amusement park to play with. I think I would've enjoyed working on that more than, say, *Asylum*, which would've been a horror film – which is fine. But I think that's all it would've been. *Halloween: Haddonfield* would've been more colorful.

# HALLOWEEN
# ASYLUM

Death comes to Death Row.

**Screenplay by**
**Matt Venne**

By the end of 2004, *Halloween: Retribution* was thoroughly dead. In search of a new storyline, Dimension exec Nick Phillips, an ardent fan of the genre, continued reaching out to agents to see if any of their clientele had an original idea for the franchise. This led him to screenwriter Matt Venne, another genre fan, who most certainly did. Like Jim Keeble and Dudi Appleton before him, Venne was a relatively new but promising talent with no significant horror credits yet to his name. A graduate of USC's film program, he had already sold a horror spec script entitled *Second Sight*, which would later be repurposed as a sequel to 2005's *White Noise*. (Venne's revised script – *White Noise 2: The Light* – would be directed by *Halloween H20* editor Patrick Lussier, another important figure in the saga of unmade *Halloween*s.)

In moving on from Jim Keeble and Dudi Appleton's script – as well as other concepts such as by John Sullivan – Dimension continued favoring a return to the Smith's Grove Sanitarium. This would remain a popular setting for the ninth *Halloween*, with scribes like Todd Farmer and David Bergantino also pitching similar ideas for the project sometime in the mid-2000s. Venne's pitch would follow suit; the location particularly exciting him as he drew parallels between Smith's Grove and the hospital from *Halloween II*, one of his personal favorite sequels. His pitch had been well-liked by both Dimension and Trancas, thus leading to a full draft commissioned – the second of three *Halloween 9* concepts to achieve this feat.

Whereas *Halloween: Retribution* found Smith's Grove shuttered and abandoned, Venne's script would alternately find it still in operation and having been expanded into a maximum-security penitentiary. His version would mark the last gasp of Dimension's efforts to bring back survivors from earlier *Halloween* films. It would stand far apart from previous *Halloween 9* efforts in that it focused neither on Freddie Harris nor a group of unsuspecting teenagers who venture where they shouldn't. Like one of John Sullivan's treatments, the first draft of Venne's sequel – dated January 28, 2005 – was also titled *Halloween: Asylum*. It wouldn't be the last script to bear this name, either. To help avoid confusion, especially during comparisons, we'll refer to Venne's script as *Asylum 2005* going forward.

Buzz began to build online for *Asylum 2005* before the project was even written. On January 7, 2005 – several weeks before the submission of Venne's first draft – series producer Malek Akkad gave an update to the *Creature-Corner* website: "There's nothing to report on *Halloween 9* right now but keep in touch because there will be next month. We're going to make a major announcement about the direction the film's going to take." Unfortunately, *Fangoria* would beat Akkad to the punch a week later with a juicy scoop on the still formulating script:

> "The new movie is called *Halloween: Asylum* and it's being written by Matt Venne [...] [The film] is set in Smith's Grove, which became a maximum-security penitentiary/asylum after the breakout of '78. It's filled with deranged killers and Michael is awaiting execution, harking back to the horror-hospital setting of *Halloween II*. This is not going to be some neutered 'vs.' movie, not filled with campy one-liners, etc. Rather, it takes the iconic Michael Myers back to his roots in a very cool setting. It's really serious/scary/suspenseful in tone, like all the best *Halloween* films have been."

Unlike most *Halloween 9* rumors floating around online at the time, *Fangoria*'s scoop was 100% accurate in its description of the still in-progress screenplay. Like *Retribution*, Venne's script would feature the return of Freddie Harris and former sheriff Leigh Brackett, though it should be noted that John Tate is noticeably absent. (Perhaps the filmmakers learned that Josh Hartnett would not be returning after all, thus leaving no reason to reintroduce his character.) For reasons unknown, possibly due to *Fangoria*'s highly informative leak, Trancas never made their February announcement on the direction of *Halloween 9*.

## THE STORY

*Asylum 2005* finds the charred Shape right where we left him – undeniably dead on a morgue slab. Yet it's soon revealed that this is *not* the infamous slasher, but Haddonfield University student Jim Morgan. A flashback to *Resurrection*'s ending depicts the Shape escaping the burning garage, but not before putting Freddie's discarded white mask on Jim's corpse. The alarmed coroner gravely proclaims, "Michael Myers is still out there!" Elsewhere, the Shape has tracked Freddie to his motel room and fatally stabs him. Defiant to the end, Freddie spits a glob of blood onto Michael's white mask. ("Fuck.... *you*.") The Shape spins around to see a "cavalry of officers armed with taser guns." They fire, lighting him up like "the fourth of July during an electrical storm." The Shape crumples to the ground as the officers celebrate. ("I can't believe it! I can't believe we've caught Michael Myers!") The title sequence plays over a montage of Michael's trial.

The story then jumps ahead two years to the evening of October 30, 2004. We meet a young twenty-something nurse named Lucy Garrety as she heads into her night shift at Smith's Grove State Penitentiary. Formerly a sanitarium, Smith's Grove now houses the state's most criminally insane citizens, whom Lucy rightly fears. This night will mark a momentous occasion – famed killer Michael Myers is scheduled to be executed for his crimes just after midnight. For the past two years, the Shape has been confined to a maximum-security cell and forced to wear a white leather restraint mask, which is eerily similar to his killing mask. The head administrator, Dr. Phineas Craine, has invited a salacious documentary crew to capture Michael's execution for posterity. Just before midnight, the facility receives a surprise visit from Leigh Brackett, the former sheriff of Haddonfield. He begs for an opportunity to face his daughter's killer, which Craine reluctantly allows. Brackett grows hysterical and attempts to kill Michael himself with a firearm he snuck inside. He's quickly taken down by armed guards in a huge scuffle, however, and placed in solitary confinement until after the execution.

Michael's eventual death by electric chair is a grisly spectacle carried out at full power, "moderation be damned." It's so intense that his head bursts into flames as his body spasms. Unbeknownst to anyone, this was not actually Michael Myers – but a helpless guard. In the chaos of Brackett's assassination attempt, the restrained Shape managed to palm a small piece of metal, which he used to escape his handcuffs. He was then left alone with a single guard as his colleagues escorted Brackett to solitary. It was here the Shape attacked the lone watchman, swapped outfits, and ripped out his tongue to prevent him from speaking. As Dr. Craine celebrates Michael's apparent demise, the actual Michael roams the facility dressed as a guard, face-shield and all. He immediately sets free a ward of inmates. Noticing their escape, Craine activates a high-tech lockdown, which mechanically seals all doors and windows shut. Suspicious over this turn of events, he goes to inspect Michael's corpse in the morgue. Peering beneath the leather restraint mask, he finds the poor de-tongued guard from earlier. Dr. Craine now realizes he's locked down the entire prison with an escaped Michael Myers stalking its halls.

The Shape works quickly to unleash a reign of terror upon Smith's Grove. He first murders Brackett in solitary confinement before freeing the remaining inmates. The slasher then sets a clever trap for the guards, locking them inside the hospital's giant industrial freezer. With no one to stop him, he begins indiscriminately slicing through patients, staff, and documentary crewmembers alike. Teaming with a patient and one of the crew, Lucy tries hiding out in the old medical records archive. She's followed by the Shape, however, who kills both men. A fierce battle unfolds, the end of which finds Lucy cornered and unarmed. In a desperate move, she presses play on an old audio cassette deck. This blasts audio of a decades-old therapy session between Dr. Loomis and a six-year-old Michael. Hearing his own adolescent voice stuns the Shape long enough for Lucy to escape, though he soon catches up to her. Lucy is ultimately saved by Dr. Craine, who fires upon a badly wounded Michael with his pistol, seemingly killing him.

Having nulled the threat, Dr. Craine removes Smith's Grove from lockdown. Lucy emerges from the facility and heads home. (It's now mid-afternoon on October 31st.) There is a problem, however, in that authorities are unable to locate the Shape's body within the hospital. They instead find a trail of blood leading from medical archives to employee records – with Lucy's folder missing. Concurrent with this, Lucy discovers her roommate and boyfriend murdered in her upstairs bedroom. The Shape attacks and another fight ensues. Lucy is again saved at the last moment by Dr. Craine, who crashes his car into her living room in order to thwart the attack. He exits his vehicle unharmed but is unable to find the slasher in the wreckage. Lucy and Craine look out as trick-or-treaters take to the streets. Halloween night has begun with Michael Myers once again loose in Haddonfield. "God help them," Craine says. "God help us all," Lucy retorts.


## THE ORANGE MILE

With *Asylum 2005*, Matt Venne takes the series in a stark new direction by veering *Halloween* into the prison movie sub-genre. That might not seem like the most obvious place to take the story, but it works well there. The penitentiary backdrop allows for a plethora of new tropes and scares, which this franchise desperately needed heading into its ninth installment. This storyline also feels somewhat inevitable. Surely Michael was going to be caught sooner or later and tried for his crimes? He's certainly an easy candidate for the death penalty. (Ironically, Illinois would outlaw capital punishment six years after this script was written.) Had it been committed to film, the Shape's supposed death by electrocution would've likely ranked among the most intense sequences in the franchise. If the electric chair strikes you as a rather archaic way to kill someone, you might be surprised to learn that it's still a legal method of execution in some states. (And unlike John Strode in *Halloween 6*, the faux-Shape's head does not explode – it merely catches fire.)

The degree to which *Asylum 2005* follows the structure of both *Halloween H20* and *Halloween: Resurrection* is... kind of strange. It's probably coincidence, but all three stories begin with a prologue involving a known character's demise (Marion Whittington, Laurie Strode,

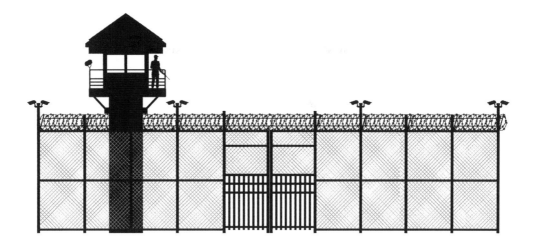

Freddie Harris). The main stories then play out primarily at one location (Hillcrest Academy, the Myers house, Smith's Grove) with the exception of the final scene, which unfolds elsewhere (a country road, a morgue, and a neighborhood.) Structurally, all three films seem to operate from the same narrative blueprint. But that's not to suggest *Asylum 2005* is derivative – not at all. In fact, had it been made, it would've stood apart as one of the most original entries in the franchise.

In a notable departure from most *Halloween* sequels – made and unmade – there's no lineup of expendable slasher movie stereotypes here. (You know the usual suspects - the jock, the prankster, the slut, etc.) Nor does this story center on high school or college students. This cast is alternately comprised of medical staff, security guards, documentary filmmakers, and inmates. From this alone, it's evident that Matt Venne was thinking far outside the box with his sequel pitch. Another *huge* difference is that *Asylum 2005* ends just as Halloween night is beginning – a definite first in the franchise. This is the moment where most *Halloween* movies are just starting to kick things into high gear. It's a bold choice that leaves the door wide open for an immediate sequel continuation this same night.

Whereas *H20* and *Resurrection* ignored the existence of earlier films, *Asylum 2005* seems perfectly comfortable referencing their events. These nods, which appear throughout the script, would've surely pleased longtime fans. Take the opening title sequence, which was to play overtop images from Michael's trial. These visuals were to include numerous crime scene photographs "culled from iconic moments throughout the *Halloween* franchise." Then flash forward to Michael's execution ceremony, which was to have a viewing audience comprised of survivors from previous movies. (This could've proven a wonderful excuse to bring back some fan-favorite cast members.) The final act contains even more references as Lucy scours Michael's files in the old hall of records. Here, we would notice file folders marked "Thorn," "Jamie," "Samhain," and "Druids."

In the end, *Asylum 2005* answers a question that absolutely no one asked – can you have a movie about Michael Myers that isn't also a *Halloween*? Yes, Halloween is technically in this script's title and, yes, half the movie is set after midnight on the morning of October 31st but this doesn't much read like a *Halloween* movie. It reads like a Michael Myers movie. Where are the costumes? The decorations? The jack-o-lanterns? The parties? The suburban trick-or-treating? The foggy nighttime landscapes? Venne's *Halloween: Asylum* has only the Shape, some Dean Cundey-esque POV shots, and the familiar theme music. So... can you have a non-*Halloween* movie with Michael Myers? If Venne's winning script is any evidence, *you definitely can*. You could alternately set this story in April and it wouldn't change much beyond the final scene. *Asylum 2005* demonstrates the surprising versatility of the character regardless of whether that was ever its intention.

## UNFINISHED BUSINESS

Before *Asylum 2005* can begin its own story, it must first wrap that of its predecessor – *Halloween: Resurrection*. Accordingly, this sequel was written to open late into the night of October 31, 2002 at Haddonfield Memorial Hospital. Venne's description of the clinic warmly evokes its appearance two decades earlier in *Halloween II*. A reporter outside the hospital catches viewers up to speed:

> *"Earlier tonight, a publicity stunt ended in multiple tragedies when serial killer Michael Myers returned to his childhood home. The publicity stunt was Dangertainment, a live webcast featuring eight youths who were to spend Halloween night in the Myers house for a monetary reward. Dangertainment was the brainchild of one of the night's only two survivors, Freddie Harris, a modern-day P.T. Barnum-type, who even went so far as to have several dozen Michael Myers costumes created in an attempt to illicit cheap scares on his captive contestants. We have also been told that Michael Myers is dead, having burned to death in a fire that broke out in the house shortly after midnight..."*

When last we saw him, the slasher was in rough... *shape*. Burned to a crisp and pronounced dead, his eyes inexplicably burst open on the morgue table just before *Resurrection* cut to black. Sure, that made for a shocking ending, but it didn't make much sense. Even so, Venne continues down this path for a moment. Upon inspection, the morgue tech finds that the Shape's white mask has fused with his skin in "a macabre melding of flesh and latex." We're briefly left to wonder – is this the character's new look? Is Michael Myers now an overcooked zombie slasher? Actually, no. *Asylum 2005* soon reveals that this wasn't the Shape at all, but instead Dangertainment contestant Jim Morgan. (It would seem the Shape accidentally left Jim's wallet in his back pocket. D'oh!) Okay, but why did Jim's eyes suddenly pop open? There's an explanation for that, too. The startled morgue attendant mumbles to herself, "Postmortem nerve palpitations are common in burn fatalities." Well played, *Asylum 2005*. In a bit of fan-service, this opening morgue sequence plays out as The Chordettes' "Mr. Sandman" blares on a nearby radio.

Having established that the Shape is still at large, we cut across town to a cheap motel where the webcast crew had been staying. We follow Freddie into his room, which is alarmingly filled with a dozen Michael Myers! Not to worry – these are all mannequins originally intended for use in the broadcast. (Why Freddie would let such elaborate props go unutilized is a mystery.) He takes a shower and emerges to find the power out. Surrounded by Shapes, Freddie begins to worry that one of the dummies might not be a dummy. Now scared, Freddie runs from his room, but not before striking several of the mannequins just to be sure. This unique sequence had the potential to be quite memorable. As written into the script, it somewhat echoes the moment in *Halloween 4* where Loomis and Meeker are surrounded by fake Shapes, which turn out to be teenage pranksters. It's also a precursor to the moment in *Halloween 2018* where the Shape hides in a darkened room of creepy mannequins inside Laurie's fortified home. The difference, of course, is that the Shape was actually there in *Halloween 4* and *Halloween 2018*, but seemingly not in *Asylum 2005*. He is instead waiting outside.

Freddie runs to the motel office and encounters its elderly proprietor, who is apparently quite racist. ("You tryin' to rob me, boy? […] Whenever I let one of your kind stay here, I watch my back real careful. Eyes in the back of my head, boy.") In a darkly hilarious turn, the manager's eyes are indeed soon in the back of his head as the Shape exacts some grisly social justice. The slasher then impales Freddie to the wall using a foot pedal ripped from the manager's wheelchair. Freddie spits a glob of blood onto his killer's white mask before intoning a final "Fuck.... *you*."

On one hand, Freddie Harris was among the most divisive characters not only in *Halloween: Resurrection*, but in the entire franchise. He turned the Shape's childhood home into a livestream circus before burning it to the ground. And let's not forget his unfortunate displays of martial arts. His death here feels almost like an apology to the audience for the last movie. On the other hand, Freddie is one of very few characters to ever stand up to the Shape – and that takes some real chutzpah. Even in his dying moments – with his final breath – he stands up to the Shape. He doesn't cower or beg for his life. He instead tells evil incarnate to go fuck itself. Good night, sweet Freddie. May the kung fu masters of yesteryear sing thee to thy rest.

## A SCARIER SMITH'S GROVE

One of *Asylum 2005*'s most interesting innovations is the conversion of Smith's Grove from a sanitarium to a hybrid sanitarium/penitentiary for the criminally insane. (It's now officially titled "Smith's Grove State Hospital-Penitentiary.") The co-housing of psychiatric patients with convicted criminals is, of course, a horribly insensitive move by state officials, but it opens up all sorts of in-story possibilities. And yet it gets even worse – Smith's Grove now has a death row complete with an electric chair! This facility has always been a place of mystery within *Halloween* and inherently a little spooky, but this is so far beyond a little spooky. With *Asylum 2005*, Matt Venne has effectively turned Smith's Grove into a depraved nightmare factory. Why set this new story at Smith's Grove and not some generic prison somewhere else? Because this is a place of ghosts for Michael. He has a long history here. And some of that history will return when Lucy searches the old hall of records.

Like John Sullivan's *Asylum*, the conversion of Smith's Grove into a hybrid sanitarium/penitentiary allows for the introduction of secondary villains, which the franchise has historically been light on. These unsavory characters hail from "Killer's Row," a ward so dangerous that it's located underground. Lucy's chronic tardiness results in her being given this most dreaded assignment. ("You're a good nurse, Karen. I'd hate to lose you, but you've got to learn to be on time." *Halloween II* déjà vu, anyone?) Killer's Row is currently home to exactly three patients – serial slasher Michael Myers, murderous cult leader Jake Gracie, and necrophile self-mutilator Wade Ludlowe. (The naming of these last two appear to reference *Halloween: The Missing Years* screenwriter Jake Wade Wall.) When the Shape eventually frees his fellow inmates, it's Gracie and Ludlowe the heroes will be running from as much as the Shape himself.

Another intriguing innovation to Smith's Grove in *Asylum 2005* is its total lockdown feature, which was devised following the last mass escape in 1978. Recall that we actually glimpsed that particular escape in the original *Halloween*. ("Since when do they let them just wander around?") Dr. Craine swiftly initiates lockdown in the story upon seeing the first round of inmates released by the Shape. In an impressive display of prison tech, massive barricades and bolts slam shut overtop windows and doors throughout the facility. The screenplay doesn't mince words here – "There is absolutely no way in or out." Once more, this feels cut from the same cloth as John Sullivan's second treatment. *Asylum 2005*'s lockdown feature is also wonderfully reminiscent of a similar trope in 1999's *House on Haunted Hill* remake. (If you've seen that film's lockdown sequence, this one unfolds in similar fashion.) Within the story, the lockdown mechanism functions much like the snow did in *Halloween: Retribution* – trapping Michael's victims inside Smith's Grove while also preventing outside authorities from entering to assist. Basically, a perfect storm for *Halloween* horror.

## NEW TAKES ON OLD CHARACTERS

In the wake of *Halloween: Resurrection*, the series' most beloved and iconic protagonists are all now either dead or written out of the continuity. This arguably posed a huge challenge to screenwriters looking to write the next sequel. In doing so, they would be tasked with creating new and engaging characters for audiences to care about. While *Asylum 2005* envisions itself as an aggressively original sequel, there are certain familiar elements at work. Take the new characters of Nurse Lucy Garrety and head administrator Dr. Phineas Craine. As final girl and monster hunter, these two are clearly patterned after Laurie Strode and Dr. Loomis. They help fill the tremendous void left by *Halloween*'s original leads while also being distinct enough to not come off as carbon copies. In that respect, these characters work well for their intended purposes. They're even interesting enough to have warranted a return in potential *Asylum 2005* follow-ups had the franchise gone down that path.

Not unlike the *Halloween* heroines that came before her, Lucy Garrety is the kind of girl you'd consider the quiet type. She may be shy, but a virginal bookworm she's not. Now out of school, Lucy works the graveyard shift at Smith's Grove as a nurse. In a huge departure from other final girls in the series, Lucy is no stranger to sinister characters, whom she routinely works with. That doesn't make her any less afraid of them. It does make her more aware and prepared when things go bad, however. Late in the story, she finds herself trapped by the Shape in the hall of records. With nowhere to run, Lucy quickly engineers a clever fake-out. Strategically placing her shoes behind a desk, she tricks her attacker into thinking he's discovered her hiding spot. As the Shape goes to investigate, Lucy leaps onto his back and stabs a transorbital ice pick so deep into his eye socket *that it rams the back of his skull*. (What is a transorbital ice pick? A nightmare instrument used in lobotomies from 1946 to 1967. Those with a strong stomach should Google it. We dare you.) In short, Lucy is a low-key badass.

As head administrator of Smith's Grove, this story's Dr. Craine is another likable hero. Unlike most authority figures in the series, he gets it. Truly. Michael Myers is "purely and simply evil" and not one to be underestimated. Craine comes with all the high-powered perception of Dr. Loomis with none of the doom and gloom. (Unlike Loomis, Craine doesn't have any blood on his hands at the start of this story.) Craine works so hard to not be outsmarted by his most notorious inmate and yet somehow still is. It's not long after the Shape's supposed execution that Craine feels something is gravely amiss. The sudden escape of an entire ward is too well-timed to be mere coincidence. He rushes to the morgue to verify Michael's demise, which is where he learns the shocking truth.

In further contrast to Loomis, there's an element of showboating to Dr. Craine. He's not quite the celebrity douchebag Loomis was in Rob Zombie's *Halloween II*, but he also doesn't mind the cameras, either. He allows a film crew to capture this momentous evening – including the Shape's actual execution – for a documentary titled *The Life and Death of Michael Myers*. (We might remind that such an element obviously harkens back to Bob Weinstein's reaction to Tim Day's *Halloween H25*.) Craine's on-camera interview comes off a tad theatrical: "Death has been residing in my asylum for the past three years and tonight...? Tonight, I exterminate it." Craine's post-execution mood is initially one of self-congratulation. He wastes no time in lighting a celebratory cigar while phoning the governor to report the good news. In defense of Craine's character, however, he more than rises to the occasion when all hell breaks loose. As a pencil-pushing administrator, he could've easily hidden in his office until police arrived, but he instead grabs his pistol and runs out into the penitentiary to find the Shape.

**Dr. Craine in his on-camera interview**:

*"I've been running Smith's Grove for over two decades. In that time, I've encountered the most severely deranged men in the country. A collection of human specimens so depraved – so deeply disturbed – it literally staggers the mind. Under most circumstances, our two current violent offenders, Wade Ludlowe and Jake Gracie, would make anyone's stomach churn. But over three years ago, I admitted Michael Myers into Smith's Grove – and it was only then that I realized how little I knew about true malevolence. How little I knew about the desire to inflict harm and pain and suffering on another human being. How little I knew about true evil. […] Shortly after the stroke of midnight, we're scheduled to bring the good people of Haddonfield closure. I refuse to let them down."*

## BRACKETT'S DARK FATE

As already established, *Halloween Kills* wasn't the first attempt to bring back the retired sheriff Leigh Brackett. The character was originally poised to return in Dennis Etchison's *Halloween 4,* Shem Bitterman's *Halloween 4,* Tim Day's *Halloween H25,* and Dudi Appleton/Jim Keeble's *Halloween: Retribution.* None of these efforts saw the tortured lawman killed by the Shape, but that's exactly what happens to him in *Asylum 2005.* We reunite with Brackett early in the story and immediately find that time has not been kind. Venne writes that Brackett's "weight and cholesterol are now roughly in the same dead two-hundred-something ballpark." His evidence-littered apartment reveals an unhealthy obsession with Michael Myers. Staring intensely at a photo of the Shape, he mutters to himself: "Took my little girl's life twenty-seven years ago. Tonight, it's your turn."

Brackett's eventual face-to-face meeting with the Shape is a tense one. Choking back tears, he demands an apology for Annie's murder. When the slasher remains silent, Brackett grows hysterical and then violent. It's positively wrenching to envision this poor man, so desperate for revenge, botching his attempt on the Shape's life. He's immediately restrained by guards in a violent scuffle. An irked Craine demands he be thrown in solitary confinement until after the execution, which utterly destroys Brackett. He pleads with Craine to allow him to watch the execution to no avail. ("Don't take this moment away from me - please! Don't take it away from my little girl - we deserve to watch him die!") We later revisit Brackett in solitary during the execution itself, which is a huge drain on the facility's power supply. Rocking back and forth, he smiles a "hateful smile" as lights strobe with the hum of electricity. It's a sad portrait of a once strong man, but not as sad as the end that approaches.

The Shape later visits his old foe in solitary. An irate Brackett presses his face against the tiny cell window in an effort to see who has come to free him. The Shape steps into view before repeatedly stabbing the former sheriff's eyes, blinding him in gruesome fashion. Brackett falls screaming to the ground where he bleeds to death. The last image he saw in life? The Shape's haunting white visage. A tragic end to an already tragic life. Those hoping for Brackett to enjoy a happy ending will need to look elsewhere. Then again, those looking for any kind of a happy ending will need to look elsewhere. *Asylum 2005* is an unrelentingly brutal tale. Dozens of lives are lost and those that survive will likely never be the same.


## TRUE MALEVOLENCE

Fans who prefer the Shape as he was depicted in the original *Halloween* would've found much to like in Matt Venne's *Halloween: Asylum* as it marks a return to form. Per the 1978 film, the Shape is not some mindless slasher but a conniving prankster and a skillful deceiver. The same is true in *Asylum 2005*. Michael doesn't simply bumble around Smith's Grove Penitentiary looking for people to kill. No, he's a schemer with an agenda and, as in the original, that agenda has nothing to do with tracking down long-lost relatives. Once free, he orchestrates a carefully devised plan that turns Smith's Grove into a hellish nightmare. (Contrast that with his role in *Halloween: Resurrection*, which was more reactionary in nature. The slasher returned from Grace Andersen Sanitarium to find numerous unwelcome house guests.)

Recall that in *Halloween* – and many of its sequels – the Shape remains two steps ahead of everyone else in the story. When Bob came downstairs for a beer, he was already hiding in the closet. When Annie left to drive over to Paul's, he was already inside her car. And when Laurie

Strode went to investigate the darkened Wallace house, he was there too, lurking in the shadows. This trope is very much still at play in *Asylum 2005*. The Shape maintains his advantage by laying traps and staging distractions throughout the facility. Even when almost beaten, he still thinks ahead to the long game. Take the moment in Act III when Lucy and Dr. Craine leave the Shape for dead. The badly-injured slasher knows he can't take on an armed Dr. Craine, not in this moment. He instead waits for them to leave before limping over to employee records to find Lucy's address. This way, he can be there waiting when she arrives home. Who's to say he didn't also look up Craine's home address? For these two, the nightmare is only beginning.

*Asylum 2005* takes one of *Resurrection*'s most groan-worthy twists and attempts to legitimize it. In the previous sequel's opening moments, we learned that Michael Myers swapped places with a first responder at the end of *Halloween H20*. Venne has the character employ this identity-swap trick twice more in his story. We first see him trade places with *Resurrection*'s Jim Morgan, whom authorities initially believe to be the dead slasher. Michael does this again just before his execution by switching places with an unconscious security guard. As in *H20*, the right people mistakenly kill the wrong man. But is this really an altogether new facet to the character? The Shape pretended to be Bob in *Halloween* and a goon-masked Mikey in *Halloween 5*. He even traded duds with Dr. Wynn to escape Smith's Grove as the Man in Black in the producer's cut of *Halloween 6*. In retrospect, Michael has been an opportunistic master of deception from the start. Given his history, these identity-swaps now feel a little more organic to the story.

It's always interesting whenever a character is able to stun the Shape, whether it's Tommy Doyle with some magical rocks or Freddie Harris telling him to take his ass out back with Nora. Lucy Garrety manages this in *Asylum 2005* in an unusual way. While hiding in the old hall of records, she stumbles upon a box of Michael's files. Contained within are audiotapes of his earliest therapy sessions with Dr. Loomis, which she listens to. Lucy will later find herself trapped in this very room, cornered by an angry Shape. In a last-ditch effort to distract him, she grabs the portable tape deck and presses PLAY. The familiar voice of Dr. Loomis fills the room – as does that of a six-year-old Michael. Venne writes that the Shape halts and stands completely motionless as the tape plays. Loomis repeatedly asks

the boy why he killed his sister. Young Michael is initially silent before finally intoning, "I don't want to talk anymore." With her attacker transfixed by the sound of his own voice, Lucy smashes the tape player across his skull and the fight resumes.

This taped therapy session represents one hell of a window to the distant past. We're finally able to witness a tremendous moment in series history – the final spoken words of Michael Myers. It's worth noting that this part of *Asylum 2005* plays out remarkably similar to a scene from *Halloween: Retribution*. In that script, a teenaged Lea and her friends hide from the Shape in the medical archives department of an abandoned Smith's Grove. It's here they too uncover records of Michael's earliest sessions with Dr. Loomis. (It's entirely possible that Dimension execs asked multiple writers to give Loomis a voiceover cameo.) While generally similar, these two scenes differ considerably in the details. In *Retribution*, the heroes find and view an old film reel of Michael's therapy session in which the boy never speaks. In *Asylum 2005*, Lucy finds an audio cassette of the session and Michael does speak, albeit minimally.

Aesthetically, Venne depicts the Shape in standard form as he appeared in the last several films. Continuity-wise, he should technically still have the same mask from *Resurrection* as it wasn't Michael who burned to death in the Myers house fire. Venne does resurrect the iconic "blood tears" visual from *Halloween II* for one scene near story's end. Fighting to escape, Lucy jams a transorbital ice pick deep into the Shape's eye. He soon pulls this out, causing a "rivulet of blood to trickle down from his gouged eyeball." The effect would've been chilling, no doubt, as Michael once again "appears to be crying tears of blood."

## WHY IT WASN'T MADE

At the time of the project's informal announcement, the involvement of Matt Venne had not yet been confirmed by either Trancas or Dimension Films. The writer submitted his first draft in early 2005, initially receiving positive feedback from execs. The lines of communication soon went to cold, however. Unbeknownst to Venne, his script had fallen into the much-dreaded development hell alongside several other stabs at *Halloween 9*. He was never given any notes to incorporate into a second draft, which meant his work on the project was technically complete. Looking back, it might have fared better at Dimension had it not been written during a time of great turmoil between its studio parent and grandparent.

For years, rumors had swirled that the Weinsteins had grown unhappy with The Walt Disney Company's heavy-handed management of Miramax Films. Recall that the "House of Mouse" had purchased Miramax in 1993 for $80 million. This same year saw Miramax launch Dimension Films as an outlet for less prestigious genre fare such as horror, action, and science-fiction. *The New York Times* reported that, under Disney's watch, Miramax had distributed over three-hundred movies and generated a collective $4.5 billion at the box office. Furthermore, Miramax had garnered over two-hundred Academy Award nominations with an impressive fifty-three wins. While the Harvey-managed Miramax brought in the Oscars, it was the Bob-managed Dimension that delivered the most profitable productions. In Dimension's founding year of 1993, the off-shoot distributor delivered a mere 9% of Miramax's total box office earnings. By 1997, Dimension was responsible for an astounding 45%. (These numbers per Alisa Perren's marvelous *Indie, Inc: Miramax and the Transformation of Hollywood in the 1990s.*)

Despite their successes, the Weinsteins were constantly feuding with Disney Chairman and CEO Michael Eisner. The relationship between the two parties had soured considerably, spurred by conflicting egos and what many viewed as the Weinsteins' reckless spending. Eisner, nearing the end of his Disney reign and concurrently engaged in his own turmoil, repeatedly pressured Miramax execs to make cutbacks to their operational spending. These warnings were not heeded as Miramax continued to produce a series of well-reviewed commercial flops. In turn, Eisner placed a cap limiting Miramax's per-movie investment to $35 million with special permission needed on any productions that would exceed this amount.

The Disney CEO also rejected the Weinsteins' efforts to produce the *Lord of the Rings* trilogy through Miramax, which resulted in the blockbuster franchise landing at New Line Cinema instead. Their professional relationship deteriorated even further when Eisner refused to allow Miramax to distribute Michael Moore's *Fahrenheit 9/11,* which the Weinsteins had a considerable stake in, production-wise. These are but a few of the many spats Disney and Miramax had throughout the years. In June 2004, *The New York Times* reported that Eisner was open to selling Miramax back to the Weinsteins for a sizable fee, though a Disney spokesperson quickly refuted this rumor.

In his essay "*Dimension Films and the Exploitation Tradition in Contemporary Hollywood,*" Bradley Schauer notes that during 2004 contract renewals, an offer was proposed by the Weinsteins that would have seen the Dimension label reside at Disney under the guidance of Bob

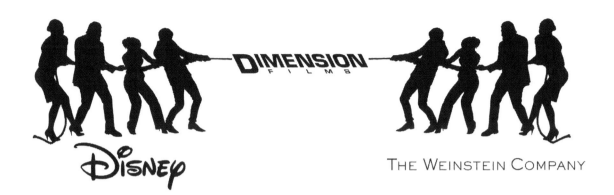

while his brother would be free to strike out on his own. One may assume this would've been an agreeable option. After all, it was technically Harvey's Miramax that had seen the continued losses amid skyrocketing budgets. Anchored by the *Spy Kids* and *Scary Movie* franchises, Dimension's investments were relatively sound, holding steady in their budget-to-box office ratio. (The immense fumbling of Wes Craven's *Cursed* notwithstanding.) But Disney counter offered that if such a deal were to pass and Bob remained with Dimension at Disney, his profit share would be reduced dramatically.

Insulted by Disney's offer, Bob elected to stand by his brother. The two agreed to renew their contract, which was now due to expire in September 2005. There would be an option for Disney to extend their management, but this seemed unlikely given the ongoing struggles. The quiet formation of the Weinsteins' own company was beginning to take shape. On March 30, 2005 – two months after Matt Venne submitted his draft of *Halloween: Asylum* – it was officially announced that the Weinsteins would be splitting from The Walt Disney Company. The brothers would soon announce a new filmmaking venture in their namesake, leaving the Miramax brand and its extensive library of films behind at Disney.

It wasn't immediately clear what this shake-up would mean for the future of the *Halloween* franchise. Certainly *Halloween 6, Halloween H20,* and *Halloween: Resurrection* would be staying behind at Miramax/Disney, but what about new sequels? Were the Weinsteins relinquishing their stake in one of the genre's most valuable properties? Or was Disney going to allow one of Dimension's biggest franchises to escape to a newly formed competitor? Rumors circulated online for months about *Halloween*'s future before the record was finally set straight.

To contextualize it more simply, Matt Venne's *Halloween: Asylum* was caught in the crossfire of the Weinsteins' initial split from Disney. Therefore, work on *Halloween 9* would come to a screeching halt. Yet even in development hell, Venne's story wasn't entirely dead. Despite failing to reach the screen, the idea of the Shape being held on death row at Smith's Grove remained a favored idea of Bob Weinstein who, as we'll come to learn, attempted to resurrect the concept as a potential sequel in the post-Rob Zombie era. But for the time being, Venne's script was dead. It wasn't until several months later in November 2005 that the writer would even confirm his involvement via an interview with *Bloody-Disgusting*.

As for Matt Venne, don't feel too bad for him. His screenwriting career soon took off in the wake of his aborted *Halloween* effort. As already mentioned, his *Second Sight* spec script was produced in 2007 as *White Noise 2: The Light*. Prior to that, he adapted an F. Paul Wilson short story for Showtime's *Masters of Horror* anthology series, which Dario Argento directed. He would go on to write screenplays for *Mirrors 2* and *Fright Night 2* in 2008 and 2013, respectively, as well as adapt the Stephen King novel *Bag of Bones* into an A&E miniseries to be directed by Mick Garris. More recently, he penned an episode of Shudder's *Creepshow* anthology series. (*Halloween 5* fans take note – this show was produced by effects maker Greg Nicotero and features cinematography by Rob Draper!)

"[Halloween: Asylum] was a very strong premise but the Dimension split from Disney really threw a lot of projects into a type of limbo and I'm not sure exactly what the status of that project is."

- Matt Venne, Bloody-Disgusting

# MATT VENNE

## Writer - Halloween: Asylum

Interviewed by Dustin McNeill

**Were you a *Halloween* fan prior to writing *Asylum*?**

I was a huge fan of the franchise. Isn't everyone that's involved with these movies? The original was truly one of the most formative films of my life. I just remember watching the hell out of it growing up with my little sister. I loved it so much, not only the first *Halloween* but the second one as well. I later grew to love *Halloween III*, but not initially. I grew up pre-internet, you know. I remember roaming the aisles of my video store and first spotting that now iconic cover with the silhouetted trick-or-treaters. I went, '*Holy crap, there's a* Halloween III?' My sister and I were only allowed to rent one movie each visit and that was going to be mine. Then I remember going home and, about twenty minutes into it, I began wondering where the hell Michael Myers was in all of this. I was completely baffled. I now deeply love *Halloween III*, but back then I was so confused. So yes, the *Halloween* franchise has been ridiculously important to me throughout my life.

**How did you wind up scoring the assignment to write *Halloween 9*?**

You always hear how they're trying to get a new *Halloween* made and they're looking for scripts. And you always hope your name gets tossed into that ring. There was a gentleman working at Dimension Films named Nick Phillips, a great supporter of genre films. Our paths had crossed somehow over the years. He reached out to my agent and said, '*We're trying to do another* Halloween. *Does Matt have any ideas for it?*' And I was so thrilled because that's the greatest news ever. But then you sit back and start to wonder, '*Wait a minute, do I have any ideas for it?*' Yes, I loved the franchise and it's meant so much to me over the years, but can I bring something new to it? There's now a blank page in front of me waiting to be filled. This was right after the release of *Halloween: Resurrection*, the much-reviled sequel with Busta Rhymes. I still think there are things you can enjoy in that one, even though a lot of people hate it. So, whatever I came up with for *Halloween 9* had to work from that chronology, but that was all the direction I had. They basically offered me a blank slate.

I began to think about what I would want to see in a *Halloween* sequel. In my opinion, the first film worked so well because of its simplicity and also that sense of isolation. That's what I wanted to go back to. But simplicity can be difficult when you're writing the ninth film in a franchise. So the question became, '*Can I still do this even though we're so far down the river in terms of mythology, story, and quality?*' We're a long way from Carpenter's original by this point.

But then I started thinking more about *Halloween II*, which I know they've ignored now with *Halloween 2018*, which I thought was phenomenal. I see why they took away the sibling thing, but that first sequel is still a special film for a lot of people. I know John Carpenter derides it a lot, but I didn't care. I didn't know he felt that way when I first watched it as a young man. I thought *Halloween II* had a great twist and a wonderful setting with that hospital. Then I had my '*Eureka!*' moment. I said, '*What if we copied that approach with the isolated hospital setting?*' The franchise already had the perfect location to do it in with Smith's Grove Sanitarium. That premise started to pop for me and then caught fire. The idea was to do an updated riff on *Halloween II*, very simple but also cool. That kind of isolated horror goes back to classic films like *Alien* and *Night of the Living Dead*.

**That is a great approach! By this point in the franchise, there were so many things unavailable to you. Laurie Strode and Dr. Loomis were both dead. The Myers house was played out. Even the Shape was burnt to a crisp when last we saw him. Where else would you have gone if not to Smith's Grove? What was left?**

I know, right? It did feel like the franchise had painted me into a corner. This was still 2005, so the idea of going '*Screw it all, let's just reboot*' wasn't really in vogue yet. That's certainly what I would've pitched if I could've. But this was 2005 and we still felt tethered to the original continuity. Even so, I didn't really want to go back to Uncle Michael and the Thorn cult. I was only really giddy about writing my own *Halloween* until I realized how much was already off the table, story-wise. But I still had Smith's Grove, so I wanted to tap into that part of the mythos.

As for Laurie, she's one of the great heroines not only of horror but of cinema in general. We live near South Pasadena and I've taken my daughters to the iconic Strode house. We've taken pictures out front sitting just like Laurie did holding her pumpkin. She's an inspiration for many people, particularly young women. With *Asylum*, I was trying to create a Laurie-esque character, which is how I came up with the Lucy Garrety role. She's young, maybe in her twenties, and struggling with her relationships while working at Smith's Grove. I wanted to let past elements of the franchise continue to shine light into the creative darkness. So Lucy is very much my Laurie Strode. And, of course, Dr. Crane is my Loomis. That's how I planned on staying true to the franchise.

**With respect to Lucy and Dr. Crane, who would you've cast in those roles? Who did you see in your mind's eye while writing the script?**

It's a funny thing, but I never see anyone in my head when I'm writing. I know that sounds weird, but I'd tell you if I had someone in mind. It's probably different for every writer. I know generally what the characters look like in my head, but I didn't pattern them after anyone in particular.

**The Shape goes unmasked for a portion of your *Asylum* script. Would we have seen his unmasked face or would it have been obscured somehow?**

I wanted to show his unmasked face. I think it would've been that much more chilling for the audience to see that he's a real person. That's what I've always found fascinating about this franchise, especially in the earlier films. I don't think it would've lessened his mystique any to see his unmasked face. Just look at Jason Voorhees from *Friday the 13th*. Jason's mystique has never suffered despite the many times we've seen underneath his hockey mask. They kind of showed us Michael's face in *Halloween 2018* and there was nothing oogly-boogly about that depiction. He was just an old dude, a real human being who is seriously fucked up. It would've been interesting on *Asylum* to cast someone beaten and weathered that looked the part. But it's just a man behind Michael's mask. In some ways, that makes him the scariest monster of all.

**One really interesting part of your script involved you essentially giving Michael an alternate look with the restraint mask. Tell me about that idea.**

Wouldn't that have been friggin' cool? That's what I love about being a screenwriter. I get to imagine these things on the page before handing it off to someone else to make it happen. Then it's the director that has to fight with the studio and producers and costume designer about bringing those concepts to life. In my head, the restraint mask would've been a really cool and contemporary way to re-introduce the character to audiences. We find him on death row awaiting execution for his horrible crimes. Of course, he would've eventually stumbled upon the evidence locker and retrieved his more iconic white mask. I never envisioned him *not* getting that back at some point. But the restraint mask would've been something cool and different. This was supposed to be *Halloween 9*, after all. You can't be too artsy or precious with it. I kind of viewed the restraint mask like a cross between his more classic mask and a Hannibal Lecter mask.

**You'd have to trust the director and mask makers to execute your idea to its fullest potential, right? Because it's an idea that, if done right, could've been quite visually striking.**

Well, that's the leap of faith you have to take as a screenwriter. In my experience, it's usually a fifty-fifty proposition. Fifty percent of the time you're blown away with how the filmmakers realize what you've put on the page. Sometimes, they even make it stronger or better than what you came up with. And fifty percent of the time you turn into that typical screenwriter going, '*That's... not what I wrote at all.*' It's just the gamble you take as a writer.

**Had it been made, *Halloween: Asylum* would've been the first sequel in the franchise *NOT* to have Michael Myers chasing down a blood relative. He's now back to being a force of ultimate evil. It's a great creative choice, but did you feel any compulsion to go back to the old formula?**

This was a conscious choice on my part to reset the franchise and make Michael Myers scary again. I didn't want to write off the old films, but I also didn't want to continue those storylines. I was basically saying, '*Look, all of that stuff that happened before still happened. It's just not relevant to the story we're telling right now.'* I know the official canon is important to a lot of fans, so I didn't want to contradict the previous films. I just wanted to go back to the simplicity of the very first film where there's no rhyme or reason for what he does. As I said, it's never bothered me that John Carpenter and Debra Hill came up with the sibling connection in *Halloween II*. It bothered them, but not me. I do see both sides of it, though. The original *Halloween* is so scary because it's all so damn random, these two paths crossing for no reason. Sometimes in life, you cross paths with the wrong person. What if that person turned out to be Michael Myers? The thought is terrifying. Getting back to the first film's simplicity was my goal. And to do that, I needed to strip away a lot of the narrative baggage.

**I caught several subtle nods within your script toward other films in the series. I remember one moment where Lucy is thumbing through file folders at Smith's Grove, some of which are labeled "*Jamie*," "*Thorn*," and "*The Druids*."**

That was my way of acknowledging the continuity of the franchise up until that point. It was an easter egg to the hardcore fans who've followed the previous films so diligently. I personally love these kinds of things in movies. I just wanted to give some kind of shout-out to the previous eight installments, all of which I enjoy. I even maintain that there was some merit in *Halloween: Resurrection*. When you're working with an established franchise, you're really standing on the shoulders of other writers whether you like it or not. It's a good thing to throw some love to those who've come before you. And you can even have a little fun while doing that. I just didn't want to throw the previous sequels under the bus and pretend they didn't happen.

**Your script brings back Sheriff Brackett from the first two films. Coincidentally, it was just announced that Charles Cyphers would be reprising his role for the upcoming *Halloween Kills*. Tell me about your take on the tortured lawman.**

Sheriff Leigh Brackett is a character that I've always loved. He just pops whenever he's on screen in those first two movies. He's captivating to watch. Watching his scenes is a little different for me now that I'm a father with two daughters. It breaks my heart to see this man desperately trying to save his town, unaware that his own daughter has already been brutally murdered. How was he supposed to save the town when he can't even save her? That's a fascinating construct and really hard to watch as a parent. What would he be like after that? He would be so ripped apart by it. I think he would become one of the most interesting characters in the entire franchise right behind Michael, Loomis, and Laurie. So, I definitely wanted to revisit him and continue his story in *Asylum*. It seemed logical that he would be chomping at the bit to watch Michael Myers die.

**I totally get that. As an adolescent watching *Halloween*, those scenes played one way. But now as a father with a little girl, those scenes hit on a different level.**

Exactly. It's the same for me. Brackett is such an incredibly tragic character and Charles Cyphers just fucking nailed it. I love that they cast him in the new one. It's going to be so awesome to see him back. I just love what they're doing with the franchise right now.

**I would honestly love for your script to be realized on screen. I could even see it working within the present continuity following *Halloween 2018*. Couldn't you? Just nix the opening with Busta Rhymes and it fits.**

Thank you. I would love that. Here's something funny about *Halloween 2018*. Whenever you've written on a project with multiple writers, the Writer's Guild rounds up every previous writer hired to determine who should get credit. They actually reached out to me prior to the release of *Halloween 2018* over that. Someone felt I might have a credit claim on it and wanted to send me a finalized shooting script to look over. I immediately responded that I didn't have any claim to what they'd done. None whatsoever.

**One of *Asylum*'s more surprising touches involved how you managed to resurrect Dr. Loomis for a cameo appearance in your story. Tell me about that.**

That was one of my favorite things to write in the script. We get to hear these old recordings of the first therapy sessions between young Michael and Dr. Loomis. I absolutely loved those. I thought it would be chilling to hear them, kind of like *Session 9*. It would be so unnerving to hear that little boy's voice in the hours and days after he first murdered his sister. I was very careful with that material, though. The goal was to harken back to the earlier mythology, not explain it. I hate when films do that. They did that with the *Star Wars* prequel trilogy. Darth Vader worked so well for me as a character. I didn't need to see how he came to be Darth Vader. That kills it. I was careful not to use the therapy tapes as a way to explain why Michael killed his older sister. Like, '*The reason he killed her was because she forgot to feed his favorite cat and the cat died!*' Any explanation you come up with will immediately diminish the character. The scary thing about Michael is that, no matter how much you delve into his mind and situation – you'll never know anything more than you already know. It will always be confounding. And you will *never* understand him.

The inspiration for those tapes goes back to my enormous love for *Friday the 13th*. Maybe to a fault, maybe not. Think back to the ending of *Friday the 13th Part II* where the child psychologist gets into Jason's head by dressing up as his mother and pretending to be her. I wanted a version of that moment in my story where Lucy Garrety manages to get inside Michael's head. She gets her hands on these therapy tapes and figures that they may have some effect on him if played out loud. So, she plays them as he's trying to attack her near the end. Suddenly, Michael hears the voices of his younger self and of his father figure, neither of which he's heard in a long, long time. She figures this might pause him in his tracks for a moment and it does. I thought it was a great moment for that character.

**I noticed you had two characters within Smith's Grove named Jake and Wade. Your immediate screenwriting predecessor on *Halloween 9* was Jake Wade Wall. Were these a nod to him?**

No, but that is one hell of a coincidence. That's a trip! I'm aware of Jake Wade Wall and a big fan of his remake of *When a Stranger Calls*. I knew he had been the writer before me, but that wasn't a conscious shout-out. Maybe I did that subconsciously? I didn't realize the connection until this very moment as you were asking the question.

**Who did you collaborate with in developing *Halloween: Asylum?***

That may be the coolest thing about this whole experience. Like I said, Nick Phillips had reached out to me from Dimension Films. I developed my idea into a treatment, which I then submitted. Nick liked it and gave it to Bob Weinstein, who also liked it. Nick then sent my treatment to Malek and Moustapha Akkad. Malek really dug the pages, so Nick and I went over to the offices of Trancas International to discuss it. This is where I got to finally meet Moustapha Akkad, which was one of the greatest experiences of my professional life. I'd been seeing his name written in that beautiful orange credit font ever since I was a little boy. He had such an influence on me from a very early age. And now I was going to meet him.

Our meeting only lasted maybe thirty minutes. He mainly wanted to talk about the character of Michael Myers. He was very protective of the property and adamant about Michael not being written in certain ways. That may sound silly to some, but it wasn't. Moustapha had very concrete opinions and rules such as Michael never speaking or running. I just remember leaving that meeting going, '*Wow. I can't believe I just met that man.*' It was an honor.

**Tell me about your approach to the subject of Michael's mortality. Is he immortal?**

I wanted to go as realistic as possible with it. It's interesting to me that, even at his most real, Michael still has borderline-supernatural qualities and abilities. There's just no other explanation for the ending of the first *Halloween*. He's been shot multiple times, falls fifteen feet over a balcony, and is just gone. I'm not saying that's entirely supernatural, but it makes you think. Your mind just boggles the first time you see that.

Then in *Halloween II*, he's shot in the eyes and cries tears of blood. That's a beautiful image, but come on! *He was just shot in each eye!* How did that not blow out the back of his head? The blood tears thing is such a good visual, but it's not realistic. Even so, I think Michael is overall more realistic than characters like Freddy, Jason, or Chucky. There's nothing that happens to Michael in my script that couldn't happen to a real person and have the same consequences. I didn't want him to be smashing through walls, WWE-style. They did that to Jason, which is okay if you're writing a *Friday the 13th*. That's not okay if you're writing a *Halloween*.

**We caught brief glimpses of it in the first two movies, but your *Asylum* script was poised to give us our first real look inside Smith's Grove Sanitarium. Rob Zombie's *Halloween* eventually took us there in 2007. How did his depiction of the hospital compare to your own?**

Rob's depiction was very different from my own. That's not at all how I saw it. But give the man credit, that's how he saw it and he stuck to his creative guns on it. It's so easy to rag on Rob Zombie's *Halloween*s, but I was into them. You had to know what you were getting into with his films. The disclaimers were there in full-force before you got on his ride. You couldn't get off complaining that you thought it was going to be Haunted Mansion but it turned out to be Matterhorn. You knew what it was beforehand. I was baffled by the people who were so shocked by it.

I personally envisioned Smith's Grove being more austere, more clean, and more real. Mine would've had a much less grungy production design. I imagined a real state-run facility for the criminally insane.

**You've written three horror sequels that were made into films. Is there anything appealing about coming into a project and being able to work with existing rules and mythology from previous movies? Or is that more of a challenge?**

It's a funny story. My first sequel script was for *White Noise 2*, which began life as an original screenplay I'd written called *Second Sight*. In that screenplay, this man has a near-death experience and goes into the white light but is brought back from it. Once he's resuscitated, he begins having these ocular distortions of a blinding white light. He comes to discover that he can now see when someone is going to die. Gold Circle Films liked that script, bought it, and decided to turn it into *White Noise 2*. Not to completely undermine my role in that process, I said, '*Absolutely, yes. Let's do that!*' There are times I desperately wish it hadn't been reconfigured into part of *White Noise*.

As for *Mirrors* and *Fright Night*, I like to joke with my wife that I have written two sequels to horror films I hadn't seen until I was hired to write the sequels. I'm a fan of Alexandre Aja but I didn't see *Mirrors* until they reached out to me. And then with *Fright Night*, I was friends with the producers but hadn't seen the remake until they reached out to me for ideas on a follow-up. Writing sequels is kind of a fun puzzle-making experience, although my sequels don't really have anything to do with the original films. They're standalone tales that use the original film's conceit to tell their own stories.

**How do you look back on your script for *Halloween: Asylum* all these years later?**

I am very proud of it. I haven't looked at it in years, but I took another look at it before this conversation and yeah, I'm pleased with it. When you reached out wanting to talk about it, I was more than happy to. It's something I look forward to sharing with my daughters one day.

**At what point did you realize your script wasn't going forward?**

In my experience, screenplays die a slow death. In fact, you're never even really sure if they're fully dead. You send off your draft and it's incredibly well-received. I was much younger when I wrote this, so I was less emboldened to be checking in with my executives to ask how it's going. I just assumed they would update me as needed. But you eventually start to get the feeling that it's never going to get made, but no one ever calls to say that. There's just no reason to ever make that call to a writer. But you get the feeling it's dead. And then maybe it comes back to life only to die again.

I got a call several years later from a writer named Josh Stolberg who said, '*Hey, we've never met, but I've been hired to rewrite your* Halloween: Asylum *script and I think it's incredible. I don't even think it needs rewriting. But Bob wants to try to get this script made.*' This was back when Dimension still controlled the franchise. I had always heard that Bob Weinstein liked my script. But my thing is, if he liked it so much, why didn't he just make it? For whatever reason, they felt it needed a polish. That was one of Bob's things. Josh told me that Bob wanted Michael to actually be electrocuted for his crimes, but that he wouldn't die. He would become like Super-Michael with bolts of electricity surging through him. I was like, '*Oh God. That sounds like an abomination.*'

I truly knew my script was dead when the Rob Zombie remake was officially announced. Clearly they weren't going to do my *Halloween 9* script after that. But until the remake was actually shot, you never knew which of the scripts they'd been developing was going to be chosen or not.

**We also interviewed Patrick Lussier about his unmade sequel scripts and he mentioned that your exit from *Halloween* was spectacular, but wouldn't elaborate. What did he mean by that?**

I know exactly what he's talking about. (laughs) It doesn't have anything to do with *Halloween: Asylum*. I was just e-mailing with Patrick this morning. About six years ago, Dimension still had the rights to *Halloween* and was looking to get a new film going again. Bob still liked my

*Asylum* script and wanted to hear some new ideas. At this time, Platinum Dunes was going to be producing the film for Dimension. I had a good relationship with the guys over there. So a small handful of writers went in to pitch some ideas. They really responded to mine and we worked for several weeks to flesh it out. At that point, my idea was to essentially reboot the franchise. If we weren't going to do *Asylum*, I felt we should go back to the original. This was just after they had just rebooted the *Spider-Man* franchise with Andrew Garfield. I know that film has its detractors, but I liked it a lot. So, I said, '*Why keep building onto the mythology when you can just do a total reset?*' And that was my pitch. I worked very hard with the guys at Platinum developing how we'd go about doing that.

So, I go into the meeting with executives from both Dimension and Platinum Dunes. Bob Weinstein is running late in classical Bob fashion. He finally arrives and sits down and then, about three minutes into a fifteen-minute pitch, he basically says, '*Eh, hurry it along. What else do you got here?*' And I told him that was it and that he was being extraordinarily rude. I then told him that I was through presenting to him if that's how he was going to act. Bob gets up to leave the meeting and I proceed to tell all his executives how their boss needed to get back on his meds and that I did not envy them working for him. I also explained how I would never be pitching to them or Bob ever again. And that was my spectacular '*Fuck you and fuck off*' ending to that meeting. He was such a dick.

**Sections**
A. News/Editorials
B. Memos/Obituaries
C. Style/Television
D. Sports/Business/Comics
Inside: The Weekend
Review Today's Contents: Page A2

# Haddonfield News

**Weather**
**Today:** Partly Sunny, low humidity
High 94 Low 64, Wind 6-12 mph
**Tomorrow:** Partly sunny, breezy
High 82, Low 66, Wind 8-16 mph
**Yesterday:** temp. Range 68-82
AQI 33 Details on Page B2

**CIRCULATION**
1,635,210 DAILY 5,250,320 SUNDAY

November 1, 2009
No. 215

**DAILY $.35**
DESIGNATED AREAS HIGHER

# HALLOWEEN KILLER CAPTURED!

By Andrew M. Miller
*Staff Writer*

Michael Myers, the so-called "Babysitter Killer," has been so ...

When reached for comments, Dr. Terence Wynn, chief of staff at Smith's Grove Sanitarium, declared: "Every effort is being made ...

Smith's Grove, and then insisted on his continued incarceration instead of treatment.

Doctor Loomis even made pressure on his superiors to have his former patient transferred to a higher security facility. At press time, no officials from Smith's Grove had commented on the situation.

It is report... staff that... room at Smi... the word... before break... leased the o... rooms, crea... helped his e...

At the sa... and Nurse N... arriving at t... Myers for hi... ing the pat... outside the... out the car t... attacked Ma... the sanitariu... order... the... whelm... mough... have... wandered... ng rain... is...

ding to this orderly, who asked to remain nameless, "every precaution was taken with Myers, as well as every other patient. What happened was impossible to predict and unfortunate, but should by no means reflect the security measures of Smith's Grove Sanitarium."

Smith's Grove Sanitarium, declared: "Every effort is being made to secure the return of Myers to the hospital and ensure the well-being of the residents of Warren County."

After learning of Myers' escape, the hospital collaborated with the

police and established two road-blocks at 30 miles intervals as well as send out an all-points bulletin on the stolen vehicle.

The beige station wagon bears the official seal of the state of Illinois and the words "For official use only" on the sides. Any infor-

## Halloween Killer Sentenced To Death

By Mary-Austin Klein
STAFF WRITER

Infamous serial killer Michael Myers was found guilty and sentenced to the death penalty last Tuesday after a lenghty trial.

Myers, dubbed "the Halloween Killer" after his modus operandi of attacking his victims on or around October 31st, was seen in the courtroom with a vacant expression, seemingly unaware of his situation or surroundings. The officers in the courtroom confirmed that the suspect was heavily sedated, after his many attempts of escaping and subduing police officers.

The violent nature of Myers' crimes and his apparent lack of remorse were a key factor in determining his sentence. The defense attempted to rationalize Myers' behavior by recalling his mental health history and his period of treatment in Smith's Grove Sanitarium in Warren County but the evidence against him was too overwhelming.

...or Myers' execution.

FREDDIE
HARRIS
CEO / FOUNDER

(232) 555-0429
freddie@dangertainment.com
dangertainment.com

# HALLOWEEN
## THE MISSING YEARS

No one heard their screams… until now.

**Screenplay by
Jake Wade Wall**

In the formation of The Weinstein Company, it was decided that Miramax and its vast library of titles – including the *Halloween* sequels – would remain under Disney's ownership. Though the Mouse House refused to relinquish control of Miramax, agreements were already in place for the more genre-focused Dimension Films to be ported over to the Weinsteins. Essentially, this would allow the new company to continue producing sequels to that label's most lucrative franchises. To proceed, all that was necessary were fees to be paid to Disney, along with the continued development of these properties. Were there to be a lapse in development, the sequel rights would revert back to the now Disney-owned Miramax. Thus, in the world of *Halloween*, it seemed the Weinsteins' split from Disney would not affect the ninth film, after all.

Though with no release date in sight, fans continued to remain skeptical about the series' future. For the most part, official news on the project had evaporated. The rumors of Matt Venne's involvement was but a flash-in-the-pan that had been neither confirmed nor denied. In April 2005, only a month after the Weinsteins' announcement, the website *Creature-Corner* brought further worrisome news from an insider formerly associated with the project: "I did a draft about two years ago on this thing – and rudely, found myself removed from it about a month later. […] It's dead, according to my agent. Dimension have abandoned all plans for it, apparently. The Weinsteins are going to start out at their new company doing lucrative projects and anything with a 'risk factor' is off-the-cards at this point. It didn't help that they couldn't come up with a reasonable storyline either. The most recent version had Jamie Lee Curtis' Laurie Strode returning as sort of a vision to Myers."

Taking an increasingly active role in the series' affairs, Malek Akkad was quick to offer a rebuttal to this rumor. A day after the article was posted, the Trancas producer also sent a message to *Creature-Corner* himself, reading, "[*Halloween 9*] is happening. We have been seriously delayed due to the recent split of Miramax/Disney. Hopefully, we will be able to make an announcement on our website, *HalloweenMovies.com*, shortly. With regards to your 'inside source,' I, of course, do not know who he is, but his supposed script has no resemblance to any of the story treatments we have developed." (What's curious is this *Creature-Corner* rumor sounds very Rob Zombie's *Halloween II*, no? Possibly fake but prescient nonetheless!)

Whether this rumor was true or false, fans did not need this inside scoop to wonder whether the ninth *Halloween* would ever come to fruition. (In retrospect, for as much debate as there was, these fears seemed premature considering the *nine* years it took for the 2018 film to reach the screen). At this moment, though, it had been nearly three years since *Halloween: Resurrection*. There hadn't been a shred of news that seemed to progress further than the rumor stage. The film would not be arriving in 2005 and already a fall 2006 release seemed unlikely. But even as The Weinstein Company was in its infancy stage, Trancas continually fielded new pitches.

In search of a new angle, attention turned to Jake Wade Wall. This wouldn't be the writer's first involvement with the project. He had previously submitted two fully fleshed out drafts to the studio, one titled *Halloween: Abduction* and the other – what else? – *Halloween: Retribution*. Both were Wall's take on different concepts the studio had been considering, the latter being a revision of Tim Day's original "returning survivors" concept. For all his efforts to bring Michael Myers back on the big screen, Wall would relay to *MovieHole.net*, "I've been hired three times for [*Halloween 9*]. At times, it was really exciting and at other times, it really wasn't." This time, Wall may have been considered a hotter commodity than previously. He was originally known for scripting the well-regarded spec thriller *Next Door*, which had been in development at Lionsgate but has thus far not yet made it to the screen. But as of his latest *Halloween* meeting, his first foray into big studio fare – a remake of 1979's *When a Stranger Calls* – had been shot, was in-the-can and being prepped for a February 2006 release through Screen Gems.

For this third attempt, the writer would follow the studio's suggestion to focus on the Smith's Grove asylum – but in doing so, he would be pitching an alternate concept altogether. By the time his involvement became known that summer, Wall's take – *Halloween: The Missing Years* – had already been pitched and was well-liked enough to have a first draft commissioned. As the title might suggest, the writer proposed a prequel in which audiences would've been treated to a view of young Michael's fifteen-year stay at Smith's Grove, which had been only scantly addressed in the original film. (Loomis: "I spent eight years trying to reach him and another seven trying to keep him locked up.") The idea seemed to excite those fans who had often wondered about this little slice of *Halloween* history which had yet to be realized on screen.

Given the previous film's reception (and the hardships in producing a follow-up), a prequel might've seemed the most logical choice at the time. With no draft in hand, however, we can only speculate of Wall's vision – which we will now explore to the best of our ability.

"We agreed it was time to get back to the early Halloween films in terms of style and story. [...] In the original movie, you go from seeing Michael Myers as this 10-year old who has just butchered his sister to a 25-year old escapee from a mental institution. I wondered what happened to him in those missing years."

- Jake Wade Wall, Bloody-Disgusting

## THE STORY

Dated April 18, 2005, *Halloween: The Missing Years* was to open with a flashback to the original film's prologue. In Wall's own words, the camera was to "turn on right where it turned off the in the original." In line with this thought, we presumably would have caught up with what happened on the night of October 31, 1963, in the aftermath of six-year-old Michael Myers' murder of his older sister Judith. The story would've then briefly touched upon his apprehension and sentencing to the Smith's Grove Sanitarium. With a segment of the script covering his years of incarceration under the care of Dr. Loomis, the audience would've followed Michael's time at the asylum right up until his escape on Halloween 1978.

Prior to the second act, the story would then shift to pick up after the events of the second film. Burnt to a crisp after the fiasco at Haddonfield Memorial Hospital, we would've learned that the Shape had survived his night of terror, having managed to avoid detection while escaping the building's fiery ruins. With Laurie Strode and Dr. Loomis transferred to other medical facilities, the Shape would've had nowhere to go and no one to hunt. In turn, he would venture back to his true home – the town of Smith's Grove. The story would again shift to presumably a year later – considered present day in Wall's script – as that small town prepares their Halloween celebrations.

During this, we learn that the Shape's former residence – the local asylum – had shut down its doors in the wake of 1978's mass breakout. In the interim, the facility has been abandoned and left to rot. The derelict building now plays host to a number of parties held by the town's rebellious youth, many of whom are familiar with the Michael Myers legend, his antics in Haddonfield, and the relation to their town. With no reason to fear, however, another batch of soon-to-be unlucky teenagers pop into the old asylum for a Halloween night party, only to come face-to-face with their former neighbor. And that's all we have.

## THE PREQUEL-SEQUEL

It should be noted that contrary to popular belief, *Halloween: The Missing Years* was not intended to act solely as a prequel – but as a "prequel-sequel," as Dimension exec Nick Phillips would call it. If following Michael's early years wasn't enough, Wall's take would've been groundbreaking in that it would've marked the series' first period piece, taking place a year or so after the first two films. (In essence, this was to be *Halloween III* if that film had featured Michael Myers.) Had this come to fruition, genre fans would've surely been pleased with the displays of late '70s / early '80s culture. (Might we have suggested Ti West as director?)

As of now, the franchise hasn't often provided a look-back at past events in the form of serious time jumps. Given this, we must first acknowledge the implications of a prequel. Wall's script was to have taken place within the timeline set forth by *Halloween H20* and as such, his idea would've filled in one piece of that timeline's puzzle by establishing what exactly happened to the Shape between narrowly avoiding a fiery death in 1978 to tracking down his sister Laurie in 1998. With this, one wonders what sort of effect Wall's script might've had on that simplified timeline. Keep in mind, as per the 1998 film, the Shape had not been seen or heard from in twenty years. (Detective Fitz: "They never found his body.") This leads to several questions. How exactly did *The Missing Years* end? More importantly, what happened to the Shape?

In *Halloween: Resurrection*, it is established that for some period of time, the Shape has taken refuge in the tunnels beneath his former home in Haddonfield. Ignoring the "What?" factor of that, had he always been there? Perhaps not. If you'll recall, the prior film featured a memorable opening credit sequence in which the audience is treated to a full view of Dr. Loomis' office in Nurse Marion's home. We can easily deduce that the doctor's obsession with the Shape had not ceased in the years before his death. The office is plastered with Myers-related news reports and crime scene photos. While many of these artifacts were in relation to the first two films, others were not. (The bloody scissors? That polaroid of a deceased man in a bathtub?) Could Wall's script have provided insight in these unsolved crimes? Crimes that Loomis presumably believed were caused at the hands of the Shape?

One must ask what exactly happened during these Smith's Grove murders that allowed the Shape to remain undetected in those twenty years he was supposedly M.I.A.? Perhaps Wall's script would've skirted continuity errors by having the Shape walk away from the scene with no survivors – like *Texas Chainsaw Massacre: The Beginning*? Or – assuming there were survivors – maybe the crimes simply couldn't have been pinpointed to him given a quick escape and a delusional final girl? Any other scenario just might've posed a problem with the timeline.

## ESCAPING HADDONFIELD

One of the most interesting ideas Wall proposed for *The Missing Years* – aside from the prequel aspect – was its change in locale. Having survived the inferno at Haddonfield Memorial, the Shape disappears without a trace; his body never recovered. This presented the writer with a fresh start. With Loomis and Laurie out of the picture, there would be no reason for the Shape to linger in Haddonfield. Instead of wandering around town aimlessly, Wall proposed that the killer return to his second home. His real home. In pursuing this angle, *The Missing Years* would have diverted from well-worn territory by moving its prime location to Smith's Grove. Not simply the asylum, mind you, but the town itself.

(Note: In the comic *Halloween: Nightdance*, writer Stef Hutchison also used a different locale to nice effect – the town of Russellville, mentioned as being nearby to Haddonfield in the first two films.)

Now, many *Halloween* sequels have emphasized the Shape's connection to Haddonfield and his childhood home. Likewise, the town has become haunted by his crimes. Wall's reasoning for his change in geography would be that the residents of Smith's Grove were to have their own relationship with the boogeyman. To the writer's credit, this was a rather thoughtful idea. After all, the troubled youth had spent much of his life in custody at their local asylum. Wall may not have been the first writer to conjure a return to Smith's Grove, but his intent for doing so thoroughly stands to reason. Knowing the boogeyman resided within their immediate vicinity must've surely left some residents on edge. One can assume his former presence spooked the town much in the same way his memory stained Haddonfield. Let's not forget the asylum breakout. Surely, that would've been front page news. The Shape may have hitched a ride back to corn town, but in his rearview mirror, he left a madcap group of lunatics running amok around Smith's Grove. Who knows how long it was before the patients were rounded up? If at all?

In setting up the story, Wall would introduce several new Smith's Grove denizens who would have relayed their knowledge and history with the Shape – only for these poor souls to eventually become new blood as the killer returns home. In particular, Wall envisioned one of the asylum's nurses as being the sole employee who treated young Michael with kindness during his incarceration. In that sense, she might've recalled Ismael Cruz from Rob Zombie's eventual remake. ("I was good to you, Mikey.") The writer enjoyed the idea that, while strictly positioning the slasher as evil, the Shape might recall such acts of kindness prior to his killing spree, thus opening the door to a dynamic yet brief character beat. In print, the idea of a *Halloween* prequel may have perhaps sounded tonally different from the previous films. But the basis of Wall's take leads us to believe it would've fit in with the *Halloween* pantheon just fine. Free from any prior baggage, it may have even made for a strong addition. By focusing on the boogeyman hunting a new batch of teenagers in sleepy suburbia, fans who had yearned for a scenario mirroring the original might've been pleased.

"What I wanted to do was to say, 'Forget about all of those old characters. This is about Michael.' There will be new characters – new kids. And it will be set around Michael's real home – Smith's Grove – which is where the asylum was, some 150 miles away from Haddonfield."

- Jake Wade Wall, MovieHole.net

## THE SHAPE

When *Halloween: The Missing Years* was first announced to the public, fans initially expected the film would strictly revolve around young Michael's tenure at Smith's Grove. Although we've come to learn this is untrue, we would've indeed been treated to a series of scenes set throughout the killer's years at the asylum. As such, we first meet the Shape as a six-year-old boy. Presumably, he has already ceased communication by this point. (Loomis: "He hasn't spoken a word in fifteen years.") Might we have gained further insight into the boy's mind post-attack? If so, how? Or would we have simply been treated to Loomis' interpretation?

Speaking of Loomis, it isn't clear how much of a role he would've played in these proceedings. As you'll recall, previous concepts for the ninth film also flirted with showing brief glimpses into Michael's incarceration. Yet in place of Loomis, the boy's interactions were often with other figures. It's entirely possible there may have been some hesitation to recast the role after Donald Pleasence's passing – particularly for what would've amounted to integral flashback scenes. Would Wall's script have similarly avoided addressing Loomis? Or might we have caught a glimpse of the good doctor in his younger years? In passing, the writer has basically confirmed as much. But most of the script's action occurs post-*Halloween II*. By that point, Loomis is already out of the picture therefore limiting major screen time.

One issue that Wall's take would've skirted was the killer's advancing age. Come *Halloween: Resurrection*, he was approaching middle age, begging the question: how long can this possibly go on for? By traveling back in time, we would've been presented with a Shape fresh from the oven yet still in his prime. It isn't clear how his survival from the hospital would've been addressed. Or how he tended to his injuries, for that matter. Or whether he ever receives another copy of his trademark mask. (Of course, we'd have every reason to believe he does manage to get ahold of the ol' Captain Kirk. It's the anniversary of his escape and the town's celebrations are in full swing. There is no way Wall missed an opportunity to showcase a few teenage clowns donning the mask.)

What we can be sure of is that Wall's script would have inadvertently shifted the motive typically associated with the killer. By focusing on a different set of teenagers in a different locale, *Halloween: The Missing Years* would have seemingly underlined that while the Shape may have an eye for targeting family members, he is, above all, an equal opportunity slasher.

His attacks on Laurie (in 1978, 1998, and 2001, respectively) could be re-contextualized as circumstantial events of an isolated nature – the effects of tending to the one that got away. Along with *Halloween: Resurrection*, this unmade installment – chronologically third – would have reinforced the Shape's motive as being more geared to the intrusion of his perceived homes, whether that be the Myers house or the Smith's Grove asylum. (Recall that the masked maniac only discovered Laurie as she was dropping a key off at 45 Lampkin Lane.) This in mind, Wall's take may have gone a long way towards negating the bloodline motive introduced in the second film, which had been heavily contested by fans come the fourth, fifth, and sixth installments.

## WHY IT WASN'T MADE

What seems to have prevented *Halloween: The Missing Years* from reaching the screen – at least initially – could be chalked up to being developed at a rather precarious time. Jake Wade Wall's script was written in the aftermath of the Weinsteins' split from Disney. Although founded on March 15, 2005, The Weinstein Company didn't officially launch until October 1st, a day after the brothers' contract with Disney had expired. To boot, the acquisition of Dimension Films and its properties hadn't been finalized until late that summer. Production on the ninth *Halloween* would simply have to wait. During the transition, many Dimension employees would exit the company including executive Nick Phillips, who had overseen previous developments of *Halloween 9* and had championed Wall's involvement.

The most interesting bit of news about the project occurred just a week after the launch of The Weinstein Company. On October 7th, *The New York Times* reported that – as per the licensing agreement with Disney – a *Halloween* remake was listed among the fifteen projects now in the works at the newly-formed Dimension Films. Entertainment websites were quick to pounce on this report and the response from franchise fans was largely negative. Malek Akkad sought to clarify, telling *Dread Central*, "We have had talks with [Dimension] about [a remake] and it is something we would consider but we are focused on getting *Halloween 9* made right now. It is a touchy subject because *Halloween* is such a classic and it still holds up today. It's a case of why fix what isn't broken – but we never say never." He followed by mentioning that a remake could perhaps be in store for the franchise's tenth installment.

One could argue the seventh and eighth *Halloween* films were indirectly influenced by the horror genre's recent revitalization, spearheaded by the success of Dimension's *Scream*. From a business perspective, it seemed only natural the ninth installment might be similarly influenced by the changing market trends of the time. In 2003, Platinum Dunes' *The Texas Chainsaw Massacre* brought home an impressive $107 million worldwide. The following year, Universal's *Dawn of the Dead* remake followed suit, grossing over $102 million. (For comparison, *Halloween: Resurrection* grossed $37 million.) These early efforts were just the start of what would become Hollywood's latest fad: transforming the classic horrors of yesteryear into slick, updated revamps that might help reintroduce these properties to modern audiences. In hopes of replicating this success, Dimension quickly snatched up rights to '70s genre classics *The Amityville Horror* and *Black Christmas*.

As of this remake rumor, Dimension's update of *The Amityville Horror* had already been unleashed, besting its ilk with a gross of over $108 million. This same October, in fact, a remake of another John Carpenter classic – *The Fog* – was being geared up for release through Sony Pictures. Alas, it seemed that no matter how revered the original *Halloween* might be, a start-from-scratch remake remained entirely plausible. Truth be told, this wasn't even the first time such an idea was mentioned in the press. Two years earlier, *Creature-Corner* reported that Dimension might've been circling an update with none other than John Carpenter behind the helm again. (This could've easily been misinterpreted with the director's faint involvement in a *Hellraiser* crossover.) Furthermore, according to writer Carl Dupré, Rick Bota – best known for directing the sixth, seventh, and eighth *Hellraiser* sequels – had apparently pitched a *Halloween* remake whilst working for the studio.

With the Weinsteins' affairs remaining in flux, it was too soon to tell what might happen with the *Halloween* franchise just yet. The following month would see the project's development cease in light of tragic news.

On November 11, 2005, it was reported that Moustapha Akkad had tragically passed away alongside his daughter as the result of injuries sustained in a terrorist attack in Jordan. For the last eighteen years, Akkad had overseen development of the *Halloween* franchise. Frankly, it is to his credit – along with Irwin Yablans – that *Halloween* became a franchise as this was not the original intention of either John Carpenter or Debra Hill. Picking up the reigns from his father, Malek Akkad would now serve as president of Trancas International, assuming his father's supervisory role over the franchise. Having co-produced the last three films, this was not a new role for him. But it would mark his first time charting alone. In turn, the unexpected death of the series' longtime producer would momentarily halt all developments on the ninth film.

The news of Akkad's passing had sent shock waves throughout the horror community – many of whom would've remembered meeting the producer during the *Halloween Returns to Haddonfield* convention. The news even brought confirmation from Matt Venne that he had previously scripted his own version of the ninth installment. Speaking with *Fangoria.com*, the writer said, "Mr. Akkad is the man whose name I have known for as long as I can remember – written in huge orange letters accompanied by John Carpenter's *Halloween* theme. I only met him three times, but he was ultimately the man who gave me the go-ahead to write the script."

"I'll never forget how larger-than-life [Moustapha Akkad] was," Venne continued. "So regal and wise behind his gigantic desk. He had such an endless well of experience gained from a lifetime of making movies and so much more. Yet amidst all of that knowledge and power and wisdom, there was constantly a mischievous little twinkle in his eyes – a spark of life and playfulness that will live on in the minds of anyone who had the privilege to meet him."

The following months would see Dimension and Trancas slowly begin to field directors for the ninth *Halloween*. One such director who reached out for the job was Dante Tomaselli, best known for helming the abstract low-budget flicks *Desecration* and *Satan's Playground*. An avid *Halloween* fan, Tomaselli proposed a sequel that would "bring back the spirit of the original" – one that might feature a John Carpenter cameo and the return of Jamie Lee Curtis. In March 2006, Tomaselli revealed that in his call to Trancas, the younger Akkad informed him that the studio had already been courting a certain director.

Throughout this, it appeared that Jake Wade Wall's idea for a prequel remained in development at Dimension. In an interview with the website *MovieHole* dated May 3, 2006, the writer indicated that his take – *Halloween: The Missing Years* – was indeed the appointed script. There would be one little snag, however. Despite believing the project was "finally set to go," the writer revealed that he had been privy to internal studio discussions that, lo and behold, might limit the extent of his involvement. Unbeknownst to Wall, these discussions would actually cease development of his script altogether.

> "I know they're in the process of nailing down a really big director, but I haven't been able to figure out who it is yet. The problem is [...] whoever this big director is apparently fancies himself a bit of a writer-director. I do know that it's my script that they're going off, but that's about it."
>
> - Jake Wade Wall, MovieHole.net

On June 4, 2006, *Variety* reported that rocker-turned-filmmaker Rob Zombie would be helming the next entry in the *Halloween* franchise. While not the most obvious choice to direct a *Halloween*, it had been almost four years since the last film and this project had languished in development hell. Behind the scenes, Dimension set sights on hiring a well-known director whose personal vision might account in overcoming the story issues plaguing the project since its inception. An accomplished musician, Zombie turned to film in the early 2000s, helming the ludicrously bonkers *House of 1,000 Corpses*. His 2005 follow-up *The Devil's Rejects* cemented his reputation as an auteur filmmaker. The blood-soaked scenery of his work generally conflicted with what most fans had come to associate with *Halloween* and in that sense, he was considered the perfect choice to revive the franchise.

After giving an "impressive" pitch that explored the Shape's childhood incarceration, Zombie was hired, and the ninth *Halloween* was finally given the greenlight for a fall 2007 release. And true to Wall's belief, Zombie did not intend on working from another's screenplay. (To date, he has only helmed one project that could not be solely attributed to himself – a 2010 episode of *CSI: Miami*.) If the hiring of Rob Zombie wasn't earth-shattering enough, what also surprised fans was the announcement that his film would not carry forward from the previous installment. As announced, this new film would be a re-imagining of the original told through Zombie's cinematic lens. To many fans' dismay, a remake – not a sequel – was indeed on the horizon.

"I am not making *Halloween 9*," Zombie wrote on his official MySpace account. "That series is done, complete, over. But what I am doing is starting totally from scratch. This is the new *Halloween*. Call it a remake, an update, a re-imagining or whatever, but one thing that's for sure is this is a whole new start."

Alas, after numerous pitches, meetings, treatments, and drafts, *Halloween 9* – at least in that exact form – was simply no more. Still, one can't help but wonder if Jake Wade Wall's script may have provided some sort of template for the Rob Zombie remake – specifically in its exploration of the life of young Michael Myers. Perhaps the similarities are merely coincidental; the result of an angle the studio favored. It should be said that Zombie initially elected to shoot two *Halloween* films, the first exclusively focusing on Michael in Smith's Grove with the second being a more straightforward remake of the original film. These two ideas were eventually combined to create the 2007 film we know today.

Jake Wade Wall would later script Platinum Dunes' 2007 remake of *The Hitcher* as well as *Amusement*, *Devil's Backbone, Texas*, and *Cabin Fever 3: Patient Zero*. More recently, he was credited with providing the story for 2019's *Jacob's Ladder*.

"We actually commissioned three different scripts for a sequel. [...] All of them touched on Smith's Grove in some way. But when you get to part nine in this series, the storylines get convoluted and you need answers for all of these characters. There were so many ways we could have gone, but it just didn't feel right."

- Malek Akkad, Fangoria

**Tell us about your relationship to *Halloween* prior to getting the gig.**

It's the horror cliché but the original is one of my all-time favorite films. I was just a crazy fan. It's so funny. For me, it sets off an entire genre of horror – the slasher film – but that very first *Halloween* is so far from a slasher film. It's surprisingly not gory and more suspenseful, which I always really admired. I was really young when I first saw it. I'm the youngest of a bunch of brothers and sisters so they always forced me to watch scary movies when I was young. (laughs) It had already been released theatrically and I think they aired it on television when I was young, so I saw kind of an edited for TV version.

**What were your thoughts on the sequels?**

I have to be honest, I really loved *Halloween II*. I wanted more of that night and we got more that night. I thought it was so exciting and ambitious that a sequel would be more of the same film. That's what it felt like as a kid. So, I was a big fan of the first two and from there, I just loved the franchise. Even if there were installments that I wasn't exceptionally crazy about, I always enjoyed being able to see Michael Myers onscreen and to hear the John Carpenter score. That always satisfied my horror itch. But I was particularly intrigued by *Halloween III*, which is what my *Halloween* was going to go back and explain.

**Really? Were you going to tie the universes together or would it've been more symbolically?**

What I wanted to do was play with the concept of, okay, the first two films are the night he comes home. We don't hear anything about Michael Myers in *Halloween III*, and then he comes back in *Halloween H20*. What happened in those years? For me, I wanted to play with the notion of, '*Well, we had to tell* Halloween III *because we didn't know where Michael Myers was during these years.*' Where did he go? What was he doing in those missing years of the franchise? That's what I thought would be a fun addition. Because it was technically going to be *Halloween 9* when I came on board.

**And yet it would be *Halloween 3.5*-ish?**

(laughs) Exactly. I wanted it to be *Halloween III*. There was something fun about that for me. The producers were on board for it. This was in, like, 2004 or 2005, so my memory is not super sharp on the particulars of it all. But it was going to be that fun hook of, '*Hey, let's go see what* Halloween III *was supposed to be.*' Not to do any discredit to *Halloween III* as its own standalone film, but for the Michael Myers fans.

**Most have assumed *The Missing Years* was going to be a prequel with young Michael in the sanitarium. Is this true?**

There's truth to that, yes. In essence, what I wanted to do was pick it up right where that iconic first scene [in the original] ends with the parents coming home and Michael has just killed Judith. I wanted the camera to turn on right where it turned off in the original. We were going to pick it up and see what happened to Michael right after his parents came home. That was the beginning of the engine to the film. The concept was, the first two films were the night he came home. If you think about the span of Michael's life, Smith's Grove is actually his real home. That is where he actually grew up before he broke out. So, I thought, '*Why not make* The Missing Years *the film where Michael went back to his second home?*' (laughs) He went back to the other place that was home for him in actuality. In *The Missing Years*, we pick it up and meet him as a young boy with Loomis. We kind of go through his years growing up in the asylum, filling in the missing pieces all the way up until he breaks out.

Then, the main action would pick up in Smith's Grove. So, it was going to be, here's what happens in Smith's Grove. Here's what their youth culture is like. Here's what their Halloween traditions are. Here's their relationship to the myth and legend of Michael Myers. Because even though he would come to Haddonfield and butcher some teenagers, [the residents of Smith's Grove] were aware of the fact their asylum was the place where he grew up. They had their own personal mythology with him. So, that's kind of what *The Missing Years* was. I wanted to fill in and expand on some of the franchise mythology without interfering with what Carpenter had laid in the first two films – and with a different set with characters. Michael has his Haddonfield mythology and we were simply filling in what his Smith's Grove mythology would've been like, independent of Laurie and everyone in Haddonfield.

**How much of the film would've comprised of young Michael?**

You know, that's always arguable. In script form, we probably spent fifteen pages on him. It was lengthy and more than just a cold open. We spent some time laying down some of the important facts, but it wasn't an entire first act. It was enough to fill in the parts that you had always wondered about – what happened from him being six years old to breaking out while introducing a couple of Smith's Grove characters that were going to become significant in our current day story. So, when *Halloween III* technically took place, he went back to Smith's Grove. He had unfinished business.

**So, the second half of your script took place after *Halloween II*?**

Yes. It would've been the next Halloween. It was going to be a period piece. It was kind of a fun way to go in and tell a little more of the story without unraveling the whole sweater of the franchise.

**What would the majority of the film have entailed?**

In my mythology, after the Halloween night that Michael Myers escaped, the Smith's Grove institution was shut down. It was out-of-commission. It was this rundown structure outside of this kind of violent, young town – and the majority of the film did take place in that institution. I played with the notion that the Smith's Grove youth had their own tradition of going into that building on Halloween night. And these kids have always been safe because Michael Myers has been killing in Haddonfield. He does what needs to be done in the first two films and then he goes back to Smith's Grove that next Halloween. He starts a new bloodbath, if you will. But the youth in Smith's Grove have no reason to believe that he has anything personal to do with their town, other than he was in an institution there and broke out and left.

**I take it you worked with Moustapha Akkad. What was that experience like?**

He was such a lovely man – and that sounds like such a cliché, but he was. And so vibrant. I do not have enough praise to say about Moustapha. He was an incredible gentleman and just loved the franchise. I was really honored to be able to work on a *Halloween* with him while he was still alive. And the same with his son. Malek was very much involved in these scripts. In fact, he was in the room more than Moustapha was. They're a fantastic pair. They just love the franchise and it's very special to them.

**What were their thoughts on *The Missing Years*?**

They were excited by it. At this point, when you're coming in for *Halloween 9*, you clearly want to be careful because in any franchise, there can sometimes be a bit of a fatigue. Moustapha was really excited about it because he was a part of making *Halloween III*, and that was a decision they made that was later changed. They decided to go back to the core characters. So, I think he was excited by the notion of being able to tell an origin story without negating or disrupting any of the sequels' universes. He was fantastic. I don't have enough great things to say about him. He was very enthusiastic and liked this direction. It was after this one, though, that the studio decided to just flat out do a remake. I think Moustapha was excited about keeping the mythology going. I can't speak for him and I don't want to but there was definitely a lot of excitement about taking a moment in franchise – *Halloween III*; fans have an opinion, positive or negative – and say, '*Hey, guys, this is what Michael did that year.*' So, I think he was excited for it.

**Did you ever meet with Bob Weinstein?**

Never in person, no. Whether it be fortunate or not, I didn't have to go through much of that. There were some phone calls to them. I'm LA-based and they were in New York. I do know they were very involved with the franchise but there wasn't much of that in front of my face. There's no telling what was being said between parties. They had zero input on this concept. I'm sure they might've had notes. To be honest, at this moment, they felt a little hands-off when I was involved.

**Going back, how did you first become attached?**

I had recently sold my first spec called *Next Door*. It was kind of a throwback to the old *Halloween* films. I believe it was 2003 or 2004 and, in that moment, the horror genre was not quite there yet in terms of doing retro horror and this script was. So, *Next Door* was sold at New Line and it kind of put me on the horror radars. When they were looking for writers to come in with a take on *Halloween 9*, I was on the list.

**Was *The Missing Years* your first idea or had you any drive to follow-up *Resurrection*?**

Technically, I was hired and did three versions. I know that I wrote three *Halloween* scripts. The first one was *Halloween: Abduction*. That one was, the studio had a concept and it came with a pretext. '*Here's what we're looking to do next.*' I can't find that script. I've tried to dig it up. So, it was *Halloween: Abduction*, then it became *Halloween: Retribution* and finally *Halloween: The Missing Years*. The latter two, I remember better. The concept for *Halloween: Retribution* was that in every *Halloween* film, there's the person that survives and gets away. So, *Retribution* was taking one survivor from every film – whether that be Lindsey from the first or Jimmy from the second – and basically bonding them as survivors of Michael Myers. They were all kind of wounded and had their own support group. They spoke their own private language as far as survivors' guilt went. The premise was that someone writes a book about the Michael Myers survivors and now he comes back and kills the people that got away. It was a lot of fun. I think I delivered a couple of drafts to the studio for that one.

**We actually know of another script by a team of writers also titled *Halloween: Retribution.***

Yeah, I mean, it's not a shock or a surprise that a studio will get a script or an idea, have elements of it that they like and then hire another writer to add additional elements that they like. And I know they had plenty of money on working on developing *Halloween* scripts.

**With your *Retribution*, it's awesome you had Jimmy from *Halloween II*. I love that character.**

I do, too. (laughs) And yeah, Lindsey's in it. A lot of them were brought in for fun cameo kills but Jimmy was kind of a meatier role in this one. Brackett was in mine. John Tate was also in mine.

**Do you recall what the reaction to *Resurrection* was at the time?**

I think they were pleased with it. I know that in my *Retribution* script, they did want Freddie – the Busta Rhymes character – to have a cameo. I do want to say that at least the executives I was dealing with wanted to go in a different direction than *Resurrection*.

**Were you aware other pitches were being considered, like Matt Venne's *Halloween: Asylum*?**

Vaguely. Again, it was so long ago. I do know that back then – and I'm sure it still is today – it was such a sought-after job for horror writers to be included on that franchise on any level. I knew that it was a very competitive field trying to get these jobs. Even though I wrote three scripts, I didn't necessarily write three consecutively. In my memory of it, I would fulfill the contract and then get rehired. If you're hired for a script, sometimes you'll be guaranteed two drafts and a polish. I would fulfill those steps and then get rehired. So, I fulfilled the contract twice and then got offered two more jobs to keep working on it. But there was also a lot of concern about what direction to take that franchise next. I think by the time it came around to *Halloween 9*, they had already tried so many different elements. (laughs) The producers wanted to be very protective and make a very smart decision about where to go next with the franchise. And because there were so many people involved, I think it just naturally slowed the process.

**Back then, I know it seemed like it took forever for any film to come out.**

Yeah, it did. You had so many people that had significant opinions on it, from the studio to the producers to the Akkads to the studio execs. I think people just got really protective about what direction to take next. They maybe had one more shot to keep it going, I think, which is why – maybe my own opinion – they decided to then say, '*Oh, let's not actually strike out in a different direction. Let's just do a remake with a hot filmmaker in the moment.*'

**At what point did you realize your script wasn't going forward?**

I realized it when Bob Weinstein made the announcement that Rob Zombie would be doing the next *Halloween*. That's pretty much when I knew.

**Not much of a heads up. Was it a major blow for you?**

I wasn't thrilled. (laughs) You know, I had spent so many years working on different variations of where to take the franchise next. What was disappointing for me was the decision had been made to no longer fulfill any future story developments. The decision was, '*Okay, now let's go back and start remaking them.*' I was disappointed as a fan, even, that they weren't going to take the opportunity to further explore the franchise and the characters. A lot of times, writers sometimes get leery when a writer-director gets hired to come on board with the script that you had gotten greenlit. For a multitude of reasons. I was aware that was [Rob] was there in the talks. But I didn't know that in those exchanges, it would be, '*Let's toss out the script and do a remake.*'

**Hypothetically, do you think your script would've benefited under Rob's direction?**

I mean, I always admire the directors that can come in with their own unique vision. The writer puts it on the page, and you lose it in your head. Then, executives and producers get their hands on it. When a director that has his or her own vision can take that script and then show a different depth to it, I've always thought that's a fun part of the process.

**Do you find it curious that Rob's film also focused on Michael's years in Smith's Grove? Is there a connection there?**

Yes. Well, absolutely. I know that I was the last writer before Rob came in. That was the last *Halloween* script that the studio had before hiring him, so I think it's quite obvious. I can't pretend to know how it unfolded. I do know one of the things the studio was most excited about in the drafts I turned in was seeing some of young Michael. You know, they owned it. So, it's completely within their right if they hired someone next and said, '*By the way, we really like the idea of seeing Michael as a boy in the institution.*' It would make total sense that they would do that.

**Did you ever watch the remakes?**

Oh, God. I hate to admit this. I have not. For no particular reason – and nothing against Rob, personally. *Halloween* is such a special film for me. I worked for so many years on it that I would have gladly gone to see another installment in the franchise. But personally, I wasn't really ready to have somebody else redo or re-show me the original film that had such an impact on me. So, it was just as a fan. I didn't want to see somebody else's version of what I think is such an iconic film. That's how it started. It was for no reason other than that. And then after time, it's just… and then I *meant* to see it… so no, unfortunately, I can't… I didn't see those.

**Oh, okay. Do you have any urge to now?**

(laughs) Yeah, I do! Every Halloween that comes around, I'm like, '*Oh, I need to finally watch those.*' Now, it's just time has passed.

# NICK PHILLIPS

## Development Executive - Dimension Films

Interviewed by Travis Mullins

**First things first, how did you land the job at Dimension?**

Well, I started as a receptionist at Miramax. At the time, Miramax and Dimension were different divisions of the same company. I did a year in business affairs working as the assistant to two attorneys. Then, I moved over to Dimension in 1998. I was the assistant to the co-heads of production. It was a pretty straightforward, entry-level job and then just rising through the ranks. By the time I left Dimension, I was the vice president of production and development. What was cool about working there was Miramax was known for the prestige, Oscar-bait films and Dimension was pure genre. In moving over, they really ask, '*Are you a fan of genre movies?*' and fortuitously, I was. I loved the Universal classics and Hammer movies; all the amazing films of the '70s and slashers of the '80s. I loved John Carpenter movies; just everything. So, in terms of my formative years and my tastes, Dimension just felt like a really good fit for me. I mean, I love all types of movies, but I do have a special affinity for horror films, most certainly.

**What was your relationship to the *Halloween* franchise?**

Growing up in the age of VHS, I discovered *Halloween* at the video store. I was just blown away. From the atmosphere to the way it was shot to the score, of course, and all the performances. I was just really taken by every aspect of that movie. I think Dean Cundey's cinematography is incredible. As a director, Carpenter's work is phenomenal, of course. The cast was all great, too. They seemed like real, relatable teenagers. And even though it was shot in Pasadena, it felt like small-town America. From there, I discovered the sequels. I've always had this fantasy of editing the first two films into one, big three-hour epic. Even though Jamie Lee Curtis' wig is *terrible* in the second one. The continuity would be a little screwed up.

**I must be honest. I love the wig. I don't know why. It does not look natural.**

(laughs) It's a terrible wig! And she spends most of the time lying down! She doesn't get to do anything until the end when she finally gets to be that kickass final girl that she does so well. With *Halloween III*, I remember being angry – like a lot of fans were – at the fact it didn't feature Michael Myers. Conceptually, I respect the idea of doing an anthology and I knew that's what they were going for. But when you're ready for another Michael Myers movie, you're a little pissed. In hindsight, though, that movie has obviously aged well. In and of itself, I think it's a cool little movie. It's a lot of fun and has all the trademarks of a great Carpenter film. I saw *Halloween 4* and *5* on opening weekend as a teenager. Liked, didn't love. And *Halloween 6* came out right before I started working at Dimension.

So, my introduction to the franchise was *Halloween H20* and I remember being really excited about that. At the time, I was only an assistant, but I was privy to a lot of the conversations about its development in bringing Jamie Lee Curtis back and having Kevin Williamson write the story. Growing up with the franchise, it was cool to be a part – a minor, minor part – of reintroducing it to a modern, post-*Scream* audience. Bringing Kevin Williamson in to do the initial story treatment was very of its time, both at Dimension and within the genre itself. He was obviously one of the biggest writers at the time and that was the sensibility that was working. I liked that it wasn't super heavy on kills. Like the original, it's fairly subdued in that sense. So, *H20* was the first time that I was tangentially involved with the films. I didn't have anything to do with *Resurrection*. That was another Dimension exec that did that movie. So, my first official hands-on participation came afterward when I was basically tasked with developing *Halloween 9*.

**Ah! The long-fabled *Halloween 9*.**

Yes! There was a process during which I heard *dozens* of pitches. Honestly, maybe forty to fifty. At one point, Bob Weinstein asked me to put loglines for all of these pitches into a single document and send it to him. I wish I still had that document today. It would be a treasure trove for anybody who is curious about the process in developing a sequel. I can remember some of the loglines.

There were some classics in there. Some usual places you'd think it would go. There was definitely one in space. There was one where Michael Myers was put on a secret government research boat because they were trying to harness his powers – his pure evil – to create super soldiers. There was another where Michael Myers was at an amusement park which is basically what that movie *Hell Fest* was. Just dozens and dozens of variations on extending the timeline. Some were good. Some were not. But nothing ever really caught the eye of the powers that be at Dimension. There was one take, however, that made it all the way to the script phase which I developed with a writer named Jake Wade Wall. Jake ended up directing a movie I produced called *Devil's Backbone, Texas*, but he and I go way back to my time at Dimension. He also wrote the remake to *When a Stranger Calls* for Screen Gems, which I later worked at as well.

But Jake was a writer I really liked. I enjoyed his writing and trusted his instincts. We developed a sequel called *Halloween: The Missing Years*. For me, the jumping off point was to make a prequel-sequel. Conceptually, it was supposed to be like *The Godfather Part II*. Now, just to be clear, I'm not comparing this script to inarguably one of the greatest movies ever made. (laughs) I'm merely saying that conceptually, we wanted to explore a prequel *and* sequel in the same film – which is to say that Jake and I were always interested in those fifteen years that Michael was at Smith's Grove. You know, he kills his sister at age six, goes to the asylum and escapes at age twenty-one. That's fifteen years of his life that were never explored in any sequels. Basically, the idea was to see what Michael's life was like in the asylum while concurrently, you would've had your classic group of teenagers going to Smith's Grove – which is now abandoned – and spending the night there. Michael comes, obviously, and they all meet gruesome ends. So, that was the sequel idea that made it the furthest in development. We had a script written and I felt really good about it. I thought Jake did a great job but ultimately it was never made.

After I left Dimension – even *before* I left Dimension – it seemed like the development [on *Halloween 9*] had gone so far and yielded so little, there was nowhere to go except remake the first one. Subsequent to my leaving, they obviously decided to do that. Once you realize the initial timeline of any franchise has gone far enough, it was the logical decision to go back and start at the beginning. I thought Rob Zombie made sense because you're not going to get that same atmosphere and the same bloodless, low-kill count as Carpenter's original. That's what's really interesting about the original. It really is a bloodless film. I know this sounds depraved but there's only, what, five kills? That's a pretty low body count on a relative scale of modern slasher movies. I thought there was a certain logic to bringing Rob on because he would bring his own aesthetic and his own world to these movies. It was an interesting way to go because he'd take it in a completely different direction. Obviously, Rob has a hyperviolent style and this edgy, hillbilly aesthetic, which I thought was an interesting choice. You couldn't just remake Carpenter's original. No one can touch that movie. But if you're going to remake it, you might as well go with somebody whose style and aesthetic is completely different. So, after having exhausted every possibility for *Halloween 9*, there was a certain logic to handing the reigns over to Rob.

**Now, before Rob and before Jake Wade Wall, there were actually two other scripts developed: *Halloween: Retribution* by Jim Keeble and Dudi Appleton and *Halloween: Asylum* by Matt Venne. These scripts featured the return of John Tate, Freddie Harris, and Sheriff Brackett. Do you recall this?**

(laughs) Yes! Oh my god! I should be interviewing you! This is so funny. I mean, I worked on these, but this was fifteen years ago.

**I hope you love the book!**

Exactly! I mean, I feel like I'm contributing nothing right now because I don't remember half of what we did back then! I liked Matt [Venne]. I haven't talked to him in years, but he was another writer that I worked with. We always tried to find something to do together. There was definitely an idea to bring back Sheriff Brackett and have him become the new Loomis. Everybody liked that. As far as I knew, Charles Cyphers was really game to do it. Obviously, he was a fan favorite. He goes back to the original and essentially, he was to become the new Loomis; to the point where he almost started to look like Donald Pleasence, I believe. You know, his head was shaved, and he had a goatee. I was excited by that. Amongst the lower level execs at Dimension, that was a really well-received idea. All of us fans wanted to do something that referenced the first couple movies and make [*Halloween 9*] feel like it lived within that world. I thought it was a fantastic idea because Brackett had lost a child to Michael Myers. He was a law enforcement official, so he had that gravitas and that edge. I thought it was a great idea and I'm just bummed it never happened.

With John Tate, we actually had a seven-picture deal with Josh Hartnett. We had a bunch of options on him. But I don't think there was any talk of bringing Josh back. I think he may have gone on to do bigger things by that point. I can't speak to Josh specifically, but we definitely wanted to bring back Sheriff Brackett. Wait, is *Halloween: Retribution* the one where Michael goes back and kills anybody that survived the previous films? There was definitely an idea to bring back any surviving character from the previous movies. We basically made them the kill list for that movie. This would include Jimmy from *Halloween II*, Sara from *Resurrection* or even LL Cool J from *H20*. I specifically remember that idea and I guess it only got so far as having Brackett, John Tate, and Freddie, in the context you're referring to. But we really liked exploring that idea. We thought it was really fun. It would've brought back this cool, eclectic cast that spanned multiple movies. Having them all on-screen at the same time was exciting. But it obviously didn't get far enough. Man, this is amazing. I really haven't thought about this stuff in fifteen years.

**Could you speak about the decision to bring Busta Rhymes back?**

The idea was to provide some sort of continuity. In these sequels, there's always the notion of trying to bring something back from the previous film. It's why Jamie Lee Curtis appears in the prologue of *Resurrection*. The idea was to do that again, basically, and to have him being the opening kill as Dimension had done with Drew Barrymore in the first *Scream*. Conceptually, it was A) to bring him back for continuity's sake, and B) to provide a surprise kill at the beginning. That device actually goes back as far as Adrienne King being killed off in the first few minutes of *Friday the 13th Part II*. Also, I think Busta was just really popular with test audiences when we screened the movie.

**It just seems an interesting choice given how *Resurrection* was received by fans.**

The fact there was a script written with him in it, I think, just speaks to trying to bring back a character that at least tested well when we screened the movie. To be honest, I can't really speak to that. I knew it wasn't a good movie. I knew at the time it wasn't a good movie. But I didn't have anything to do with it, so I can't really speak to that. I think we all wished we had done better. I know we had wished the movie had done better. But it sort of was what it was.

**Do you remember working with Jim Keeble and Dudi Appleton?**

I do but to be honest, my recollections are hazy. I would imagine it was mostly done over email. What would've happened is, I would've read a sample or two of their writing. If I liked it, I would've gotten approval to bring them on to develop a take. Basically, [the bosses] say to you, '*Go develop* Halloween 9.' So, you call agents and managers around town, or you go to writers you already know and like, and say, '*Hey, can you come up with an idea for* Halloween 9?' They'll send you an idea, come in and pitch that idea. You put forth a few of these ideas that you like to the bosses. They pick one they like and then you commission treatments. The writer will send you anywhere from a five to fifteen-page treatment. You mark it up, revise, and send it back. They make changes. And then you just keep developing it until everybody is happy with the results.

**It's curious that *Retribution* also had John Tate, especially if Hartnett wouldn't return.**

It just provided some continuity with the previous films, and he was a direct descendent of Laurie Strode. Most of the time, in these franchises, they don't mind recasting people when necessary, which I don't like. I always like the same actor playing the role.

***Halloween H20* was still so current at the time. I feel like recasting him would've been more noticeable than say a lesser character. I was curious whether *Retribution* didn't go forward because it became known he wouldn't be coming back?**

Maybe if Josh wasn't coming back, yeah. At the end of the day, I just think the idea of bringing back people from the old movies didn't feel current or exciting to them. For fans, it feels great, right?

But maybe those people weren't current marquee names that could draw people to the theater. It would draw the hardcore fans. But I think they were probably like, '*Oh, young audiences don't know Jimmy from the second one or Brackett from the first one. They don't know these characters.*'

**It is a bit fan service-y.**

It's *very* fan service-y. And it didn't feel of the moment at all, right? I'm not saying anything to disparage anyone, but I just don't think those actors, at that time, would've felt like major enough star power to greenlight a movie. If you wanted to do a fan fic movie, it would've been awesome, right? But I think they were looking at it from a marketing perspective and what names they could attract to the movie. I don't think Josh was coming back, so that was definitely a drawback in not having him reprise the role. He was becoming too much of a name at that point. It was just a variety of factors. Like I said, after putting yourself in circles trying to develop another sequel, sometimes it's easier to just stop the carousel and say, '*Alright, let's go back to the beginning.*' Because there were so many ideas floating around and so many iterations of those individual ideas. It just got to the point where I think people sort of threw their hands up and said, '*Let's remake this.*'

**Was there ever an idea to follow through with the *Halloween 4-6* timeline?**

In those forty to fifty pitches I heard, there may have been a Jamie Lloyd storyline but nothing that I can remember. To my knowledge, there was never any inkling of continuing that storyline. It was really always about trying to continue the continuity of the first two and *Halloween H20*. I'm sure it was considered but I can also imagine that maybe they felt like *Halloween 6* wasn't the best movie. Maybe they felt like they had explored that timeline enough and didn't do the best job of it. It never felt like that was part of the franchise worth exploring.

**Was there ever an idea to feature one of Loomis' relatives?**

What's so funny is that you probably know better than I. (laughs) I don't think so. Again, maybe in one of those takes. I would love to get my hands on that document I wrote to Bob Weinstein. It had the title of the pitch and the logline. I remember one in the amusement park was called *Halloween: Abusement Park*, which is just hilarious. The document would say, 'Halloween: Abusement Park.

*Michael Myers kills people in a Halloween-themed amusement park.*' But no, I don't think we ever had a relative of Loomis because in the films, it was never hinted at whether he was married or had kids. Not that that would've stopped anyone from retconning things.

**What do you remember about a *Halloween / Hellraiser* crossover?**

(laughs) So, *Freddy vs Jason* comes out and it's a big success. It opens huge. I went and saw it opening weekend. It was a very big deal. That next Monday, Bob Weinstein says, '*We are going to do* Halloween / Hellraiser.' Clearly, any studio that had more than one franchise in their library was looking to do something akin to this. Immediately, the idea was to combine the two biggest icons we had at Dimension, which were Michael Myers and Pinhead, into a *Halloween / Hellraiser* mashup, which I personally think would've been fuckin' awesome.

Clive Barker comes into the office. So, it's myself, my boss at the time, Clive Barker, Bob was on the phone from New York, and John Carpenter was on the phone. And we talked for an hour about potential ideas. Clive had some really good ideas, if I remember correctly. And you know, John was agreeable to all of this. He seemed really up for it. He would chime in here and there and give his approval on a certain idea. Overall, I think everyone in that room seemed really receptive to the idea and I have no idea why it didn't come to fruition. Maybe it just lost steam in people's minds, internally at the company. Also, I think when you try to make a movie that imitates something that just came out – the gestation period for a movie is so long that by the time this movie would've come out, maybe that wouldn't have been what's working in the marketplace anymore. Because if you're starting from scratch the Monday after *Freddy vs Jason* comes out, our movie wouldn't have come out for a year or a year and a half. Who knows what the market would've been wearing at that point?

But I do remember sitting in a meeting with Clive in the room and Bob and Carpenter on the phone and having a really interesting conversation about how to potentially merge these two franchises. One is obviously an earthbound, grounded horror series while the other one involves this otherworldliness and other dimensions; cenobites, demons and that kind of stuff.

**It's definitely more of a stretch than *Freddy vs Jason*. In retrospect, I would've loved it.**

*Definitely* more of a stretch than *Freddy vs Jason*. But I was so excited when Bob brought up this idea. I was just jumping at the chance to do it. And yes, the big main challenge that we faced was trying to mix this grounded slasher franchise with this mythology-laden, other-dimensional, cenobite-based body horror franchise. Those were two different flavors that may or may not have gone together. We'll just never know. But I do remember trying to figure it out. In all of these mashups, it's always who is pulling whose strings? Who wins? You could have almost approached it like they did with *Freddy vs Jason*. Because Freddy is the more ethereal, otherworldly being and I think we were looking into doing something where Pinhead was sort of pulling Michael's strings in order to get Michael to kill, torture, and maim for him. That was definitely something that we had touched upon, trying to figure out the mechanics of how and why they interact and who's controlling whom. But I will tell you, that meeting was one of the best meetings I've ever been involved with. Everybody in that room seemed really excited and agreeable to it and for the life of me, I don't know why it didn't go forward.

**What did the Akkads think of this idea?**

I'm assuming Moustapha or Malek must've been on the phone. Now that I remember it, they were not total fans of the idea. They were not fans of mixing the franchises and I'll tell you why. In their mind, I think *Hellraiser* needed *Halloween* more than *Halloween* needed *Hellraiser*. *Halloween* was still a viable, theatrical franchise whereas the *Hellraiser* sequels – a few of which I worked on – were mostly in the direct-to-video world at that point. I think they saw *Hellraiser* as being a bit of a drag on their franchise. With all due respect to Clive and the franchise, I don't think *Halloween* needed to do that. They weren't super enthusiastic on the idea. *Halloween* was still a very viable franchise; one that always gets big theatrical releases and still had a few sequels – at least a remake – on the horizon, whereas *Hellraiser* felt like it was a bit more long in the tooth and needed an injection of life – like one of these mashups – in order to bring it back to the theatrical scale.

**In general, what was it like working with the Akkads?**

I loved going to see Moustapha in his office. I always thought that was like going to see the wise man, you know? It was really neat to sit across his desk from him. You'd hear him talk about his career and this franchise and how much his family were the guardians of the franchise. I just really savored every moment I was able to sit there and listen to Moustapha. You didn't really meet with him; you listened to him – and I mean that in a good way. I think Malek has done a fantastic job with keeping the franchise alive and introducing it to new generations. He's a smart guy and I became friendly with him over the years. So, I think the Akkad family deserves a lot of credit for being the champions of this franchise for, what, forty years? You know, they had input on the writers we selected and the story ideas. They were given every treatment or draft and gave their notes and input. Personally speaking, I trusted them to know what was best for the franchise. These were the keepers of the gate, so I put a lot of faith and trust in them. They were an integral part of the process. They really helped steer whatever direction was going forward at the time.

**What was it like working with Bob Weinstein?**

To be honest, I never got a ton of face time with Bob. Never. You know, he was very direct in his opinions. He was always thinking about things from a commercial point of view – what would work for the audience and what would attract the biggest box office numbers. I believe he really liked movies. But it's so interesting to work with someone who what they say goes. It's just an interesting hierarchy to work within. At the end of the day, we could all come up with our ideas, pitches and takes and all that, but whatever he wanted to do was what we were going to do. You basically got your orders handed down through the other top execs and you just went and did it. So, I don't have a ton of insight into Bob. I just didn't have a lot of direct contact with him. But I knew that he knew a lot about marketing. He knew how to sell movies. I believe he was passionate about movies. And for a time there, I think he was really innovating. With things like *Scream*, I think he was leading the market. But after a while, sometimes you end up trying to follow the market and I think that's where you start to lose what made you great in the first place, perhaps.

I left Dimension in 2005 just as they were leaving Disney to start their own company. A lot of us left around that time and used that as an opportunity to pursue other things. But as an aside, I can tell you that Bob became *obsessed* with remakes after we – I should say he, not I, but he – passed on the *Texas Chainsaw Massacre* remake. We went into a screening room in New York with him and his brother and we watched a teaser [Platinum Dunes] made for *Texas Chainsaw*. It was those two and a bunch of the Dimension people and we were all a bunch of film geeks. And the teaser was nothing, really. It was just a soundscape of a woman running and screaming down a hall. Suddenly, this chainsaw comes right through a piece of wood or a door in the screen. You'd see this light and a little bit of Leatherface or something like that. And they asked, '*What did you guys think?*' And we were all pushing them to do it. I remember they had a phone call with Michael Bay and maybe some of the writers and producers and they pitched what would become the *Texas Chainsaw* remake. They passed on it, and it ended up working. It kicked off the entire modern remake boom. I would've loved it. We were all into doing that but for whatever reason, they just didn't see it.

After that, we just snatched up every remake property we could. I brought in *The Hills Have Eyes* which Bob later put into turnaround and eventually Fox made it. But they did *Piranha*. They did *Black Christmas*. People were just coming out of the woodwork with remake rights. I got approached with the rights to *C.H.U.D.* I was trying to do *Hell Night*. Every property was remake-based. It was just so funny. That became Bob's thing after missing out on the *Texas Chainsaw* remake. I was bummed because we were really close to making *The Hills Have Eyes*. We had conceptual drawings and we were scouting locations. We had a budget. But for some reason, he just put it into turnaround and gave it to Fox who then made two movies out of it. But for a while there, it was all remakes.

**I know you left prior to Rob Zombie but was there talk of a remake while you were still there?**

Only early chatter but yes. It was right when I left when that idea came up. Like I said, I thought it was a good move. Sometimes, the only place to go is back to the beginning. I went to the premiere when [Rob Zombie's *Halloween*] came out. The movie has a completely unique feel. It has the title *Halloween,* but it doesn't feel like Carpenter's original – and I mean that in a completely good way. If you're going to remake the original, you might as well do a different version. You might as well try to add some of your own idiosyncrasies and that's what Rob did. I was pretty pleased when I saw it. I don't think you need to overexplain why Michael Myers is Michael Myers. To say that he has an abusive stepdad and his mom is a stripper was maybe a little too straightforward, I don't know. I love the way Loomis talks about him in the first two movies. '*The blackest eyes. The devil's eyes. Staring through the walls.*' He's just abstract, you know. He's a myth. To boil that down to him just being an unhappy kid, it took away some of that mystery and lore for me. But again, Rob made the movie his own. In and of itself, I think it was a really cool movie.

**What are your thoughts on the 2018 film?**

I thought the movie was really good. I thought they did a good job of updating and making it feel relevant. It wasn't this big bombastic thing with crazy kills. It felt grounded, real, and believable. I loved the opening sequence where [Aaron] holds up the mask. There was some really cool stuff in there. I did think it was interesting that everybody's always in such a hurry to erase all the other movies. (laughs) They went even farther! Now, *Halloween II* didn't happen – which is fine but in a weird way, it is conceptually very similar to *H20*. But I thought it was really good in terms of fan service in addition to introducing it to mainstream audiences. I thought it succeeded on several levels. I know a lot of those guys at Blumhouse and I know they care about these movies in ways that you and I do as well. I always feel like we are in good hands when they reboot a franchise.

**Out of the three pitches that made it to script, which would you say was your favorite?**

I'd say *The Missing Years*. That would be my favorite because, again, it just felt like it could serve the current marketplace while also servicing the fans. I just thought it was a nice conceit to do a prequel and a sequel. If I'm not mistaken, I think *Retribution* made it the farthest. That was the most seriously considered idea and came fairly close to moving forward, or it's just the one that seemed to stick around the longest. But my favorite would be *The Missing Years*. I loved that one.

**Had you yourself ever pitched any ideas?**

(laughs) No. Other franchises, yes. But not *Halloween*.

**Why not? *Halloween* was the big one.**

I don't know. Maybe at that point, I just – yeah, I don't know. It depends. Maybe it wasn't my place. Sometimes, they'll tell you to come up with something for, like, *Mimic 3*, right? Which is neither here nor there. But they said, '*Oh, you come up with an idea!*' So, I said, 'Rear Window *with cockroaches*'. Sometimes, you're the one who is tasked with coming up with an idea but there's other times where it's like, '*Go find an idea*'. And you just don't know whether it's your place to self-generate or commission other people to do it. But no. God, geez… now, I have another regret to add in life! Amongst a long line of other regrets, I never had the initiative to pitch my own *Halloween* movie! (laughs) But I do think the prequel-sequel idea was something that Jake and I brewed up together. That conceit – that *Godfather Part II* template – was something that I felt like I helped generate. I never singularly went in and said, '*Okay, here's my take*,' but I definitely helped plant the seed for *The Missing Years* and the prequel-sequel idea.

**Here's a broad question. Do you think the franchise is perhaps hindered by fan expectations?**

I think any franchise – especially horror franchises – are hindered by fan expectations. They always will be. And I'm part of that, right? As a fan, I have certain expectations for what I want to see, whether it's *Star Wars* or James Bond or any other franchise I grew up with. You always want it to feel a certain way. When you develop one of these movies, you just have to thread that needle. You have to address the fans' wants and needs for what they feel the story is or what the timeline extension should be. But you also have to introduce it to new audiences. You know, I'm forty-six years old. When I make a horror movie, I have to keep in mind that I'm not making it for forty-six-year-old middle-aged men who grew up on these movies. You have to introduce these movies to a new generation of young audiences, moviegoers who might not know anything about the original. Whenever you go into a remake or sequel, you just gotta thread that needle. You have to service the fans while also introducing these characters or concepts to a whole new audience.

**It's interesting because the fans are such purists. You can take risks with Freddy and Jason that you can't with Michael. It's difficult to project where the series will be in twenty years.**

Yeah, Jason became more of a lumbering, unbeatable zombie in the later movies. I'm a fan of Jason in *Friday the 13th Part II* when he's wearing the burlap sack. He feels like a real feral person out there in the woods. That's terrifying. By the eighth, ninth and tenth movies, you rooted for Jason. He became the protagonist. You wanted him to do his best inflicting damage on these filthy kids. He became sort of cartoonish whereas Michael hasn't gotten there yet. But where do I see the franchise in twenty years? I think it'll always go back to the basics. With any good horror movie, you can reduce it down to a single element that is universally felt or feared by people. So, in twenty years, the franchise will probably be right back where it was, teenagers in jeopardy at the hands of a maniacal serial killer.

**I think that's what fans were expecting before the 2018 film. Now, with Jamie Lee Curtis back, these next few sequels have a hook. I'd still like to see a standalone with Michael stalking babysitters. But after that itch is scratched, what is the hook going to be next?**

I mean, I love the fact Blumhouse is committed to doing two more. I think that's really cool. I'd assume this new trilogy will be the final struggle between Laurie and Michael. Isn't that how it always is? But I would love to see it go back to the basics. Jake Wade Wall actually wrote a great script called *Next Door* which was sort of a new franchise. It sucks that it never got made because that's really what it was, a back-to-basics approach of a serial killer stalking teens in suburbia. I know that *Scream* was basically that, in that it brought back the slasher movie, but it was also meta. *Scream* existed in a world with horror movies. In the Dimension era, I read plenty of good scripts that weren't as self-referential or tongue-in-cheek that never got made because it wasn't what was working in the market at that time.

**So, if you were brought in to helm your own *Halloween*, how would you approach it?**

I'd still go back to the basics with a new set of characters. The simple concept of an escaped killer on the loose is as timeless and universal as a fireside tale. So, I'd try to make it a simple and clean story that relied more on atmosphere, suspense, camera work and performance as opposed to just blood and guts. I will say the good thing about *Halloween* is that it never veered too far into highly cartoonish, super gory territory. Now, I love *Friday the 13th*, I really do, but by the end, he's bashing people in sleeping bags. It became more of a funny sport to see just how ridiculously Jason was going to do away with people. I don't think *Halloween* ever veered too far into absurdism. That's what I always liked about the films. I'd love to make a simple, suburban slasher movie; small, intimate, straightforward and scary.

**Well, you've gotta go pitch it, okay? Don't let it be another regret!**

Exactly! (laughs) I mean, the rights situation was messy there for a while, but they obviously fixed that. But yeah, that would be my pitch. Thank you for asking.

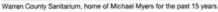
Warren County Sanitarium, home of Michael Myers for the past 15 years.

# Child Murderer Escapes Mental Hospital

**Michael Myers, criminally insane killer, now 21, is reported missing from Warren County Sanitarium.**

By Jonathan Stack
STAFF WRITER

**Michael Myers**, the so-called "Halloween Killer," has been reported missing from Warren County Sanitarium. Myers, now 21, killed his sister by stabbing her repeatedly with a kitchen knife. He was six years old at the time.

Myers escaped by climbing out a second story window. He had fashioned a homemade rope out of stolen bed sheets. He then overpowered a security guard and scaled the East wing wall.

To create a diversion for his escape, Myers also managed to free every other patient of his wing. The resulting commotion allowed him to sneak off the hospital grounds undetected.

Once outside the gate, Myers attacked his own psychiatrist Dr. Samuel Loomis and Ms. Marion Chambers, the nurse accompanying him. The patient then stole their vehicle, despite claims that Myers' never learned how to drive.

Dr. Loomis and Ms. Chambers were scheduled to assist Myers' transfer to the courtroom where he was to be tried as an adult. The patient was to be highly sedated with Thorazine and then transferred to the courtroom's prison cell awaiting his trial.

When reached for comments, Dr. Terence Wynn, chief of staff at Warren County Sanitarium, declared: "Every effort is being made to secure the return of Myers to the hospital and ensure the well-being of the residents of Smith's Grove."

After learning of Myers' escape, the hospital collaborated with the police and established two roadblocks at 40 miles intervals as well as send out an all-points bulleti

The beige stat state of Illinois a the sides. Any in this vehicle or N investigation.

# Laurie Strode Sole Survivor of October Mass Murders

By Sharon Walsh
Staff Writer

Tragedy struck last night when escaped mental patient and former Haddonfield resident Michael Myers murdered more than ten people in cold blood.

After escaping from Smith's Grove Warren County Sanitarium on October 30th, Myers made his way to Haddonfield. He is suspected in the killing of a mechanic working at Phelps Garage, who was beaten do death and stripped of his clothes found outside of Russelville.

Early last night, Myers then attacked Laurie Strode, 17, who was babysitting on Orange Grove Avenue at the time. Three friends of Miss Strode were also babysitting in the house across the street, where it's presumed that Myers attacked and killed them.

The identities of these first victims are not confirmed at the moment, but local residents are saying one of them is Annie Brackett, 17-year-old daughter of Sherrif Leigh Brackett, who was unavailable for comment.

Laurie Strode was then rescued by Myers' former

psychiatrist Dr. Samuel Loomis, who claims to have shot the man six times at point blank in an attempt to stop him. Miss Strode was then taken to Haddonfield Memorial Hospital to be treated for cuts and bruises, as well as nervous shock.

Myers, who was apparently unharmed by the shots, followed Miss Strode to the hospital, where he murdered most of the small staff on duty that night, including five nurses, an orderly, a doctor and the security guard.

An orderly was also found unconscious in the parking lot, having suffered a severe concussion. He was then sent to a hospital in Pontiac County. His condition is unknown at this point.

Strode was once again rescued by Loomis, who according to her testimony, caused an explosion in a successful attempt to kill Myers.

Myers is also suspected in the killing of Alice Samantha Martin, 17, who was found stabbed in her home on Brubacher Rd. A marshall on the scene also had his throat slit by Myers in front of Nurse Marion Chambers, who was accompanying Dr. Loomis into custody on orders from the state governor. The nurse was

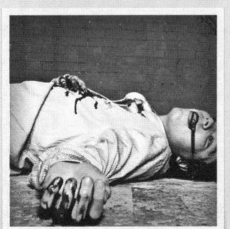

# HALLOWEEN 3D

This time, the terror won't stop at the screen.

**Screenplay by**
**Todd Farmer & Patrick Lussier**

**N**ow for one of the strangest chapters in the unmade *Halloween* saga – a sequel effort that materialized almost overnight and fell apart just as quickly. At first glance, Rob Zombie's *Halloween II* doesn't come off as the kind of film that needs a follow-up, but that's exactly what the Weinsteins had in mind for the franchise. They sought to continue the stories of Zombie's Laurie Strode and Michael Myers – just without Zombie at the helm. Recall that Mr. Zombie had been hired to reinvigorate the franchise with his 2007 remake, which received polarizing reviews and continues to be a hotly debated entry among fans. That said, it certainly left its imprint on audiences, making enough bank to warrant a sequel. (The film grossed over $80 million worldwide, also scoring the highest domestic opening for a Labor Day weekend release.)

After initially considering a sequel concept by *Inside* filmmakers Julien Maury and Alexandre Bustillo, Dimension fast-tracked *Halloween II* with Zombie back at the helm for an August 2009 release. Zombie was initially reluctant to return but sought to further elaborate on the emotional damage bestowed upon his characters. Aside from receiving even more polarizing reviews, *Halloween II*'s shoot was fraught with difficulties. In terms of *another* follow-up, the desire from Zombie to part ways with the Weinsteins seemed more than mutual. He widely asserted that he wouldn't return for a *Halloween III*, even telling reporters such on the red carpet of *Halloween II*'s Hollywood premiere. And while the filmmaker had claimed much the same after the 2007 film, he seemed to really mean it this time.

"*Halloween II* was a big problem," Zombie said in his *Fangoria Legends* issue. "There was a lot of shit going on behind the scenes where I'm pretty sure certain people were stealing lots of money and doing various fucked up things. No matter what we asked for, it was '*We don't have the money*.' [..] And then the day before filming began, '*Oh, you have to lose fourteen days of shooting*.' Now, for people who don't know, a movie's schedule is so exact, what scenes you're going to shoot and what day. To lose fourteen days, it's like – *how*? Losing one day is a nightmare, but fourteen?!"

Unbeknownst to Zombie, the Weinsteins had been planning a third *Halloween* without him for quite some time. In fact, the studio reached out to filmmakers Todd Farmer and Patrick Lussier even as Zombie was still shooting *Halloween II* in the spring of 2009. Bob Weinstein would formally announce *Halloween III* to the *Los Angeles Times* on August 31, three days after its predecessor opened in theaters. His announcement revealed that The Weinstein Company did not expect Zombie to return and that they were actively talking with other filmmakers to take over the series. Farmer and Lussier would pitch Weinstein their vision for *Halloween III* in early September even as *Halloween II* was still playing on theater screens throughout the country. Both screenwriters were coming to the franchise with solid backgrounds in the genre. Farmer had previously written screenplays for *Jason X* and *The Messengers*. Lussier had directed half-a-dozen films including the *Dracula 2000* trilogy, *The Prophecy 3: The Ascent,* and *White Noise 2: The Light.* His resume as an editor was even more impressive with credits like *Halloween H20, Wes Craven's New Nightmare*, and the *Scream* trilogy.

One of the Weinsteins' earliest ideas for *Halloween III* involved shooting it in 3D. In one respect, Michael Myers was a little late to the game. Both Freddy and Jason had already dabbled in the 3D format decades earlier, but it wasn't always going to be that way. Michael Myers very nearly became the first slasher to kill in three dimensions back in 1981. Producers on the original *Halloween II* briefly considered shooting *Halloween's* first sequel in 3D but nixed the idea over cost and the restrictive limitations of the format at that time. In retrospect, the decision to shoot this new *Halloween III* in 3D seemed a knee-jerk reaction given the timing. Bob Weinstein announced the project on Monday, August 31st. This immediately followed the new *Halloween II's* opening weekend in which it was bested by *The Final Destination*, a 3D entry into the ongoing New Line Cinema franchise. Surely it wasn't a coincidence that Bob Weinstein announced *Halloween 3D* the day after a 3D horror sequel beat his newest *Halloween* at the box office.

Farmer and Lussier were certainly well-qualified to work on a potential *Halloween 3D* given their success with *My Bloody Valentine 3D* earlier that year. Lussier had directed the 3D remake for Lionsgate from a script co-written by Farmer. The project went on to gross $100 million at the worldwide box office, more than recouping the studio's investment.

On September 12, the screenwriters had a conference call with Malek Akkad, Dimension exec Matthew Stein, and head honcho Bob Weinstein. Both Farmer and Lussier found Akkad congenial and supportive of their concept. On his official blog, Farmer wrote, "Malek was on his game. His questions were smart. We had smart answers. Once we won him over, there was zero hesitation. He was a powerhouse. '*We do this. We get this guy. We move now. I can make this call. I can make that call.*' We left that meeting and suddenly it was all very real."

Dimension aimed to get *Halloween 3D* made as quickly as possible so that it could be released into theaters by October 2010. Writing, planning, shooting, and editing a feature film in under a year would prove an enormous challenge, not to mention a possible detriment to the overall quality. There was a snag, however. Both writers were set to begin work on *Drive Angry* in January with Lussier directing from a script he'd co-written with Farmer. Writing and shooting *Halloween 3D* after *Drive Angry* would make the October 2010 release date an almost impossibility. If the new sequel were going to happen, it would need to be written and filmed before year's end – *which was three months away*. All parties agreed this was do-able. For the record, no *Halloween* movie in history had ever come together so quickly.

We should note that, at the time *Halloween 3D* was taking shape, there was only one official cut of *Halloween II* – the theatrical version. Rob Zombie hadn't yet assembled his director's cut, which would debut on home video in January 2010. Theatrically, *Halloween II* ended with Laurie stabbing Michael to death after he's hit by a sniper bullet. She then stumbles out of the rundown shack wearing his mask. The final shot finds an institutionalized Laurie seeing visions of her mother and the white horse. The eventual director's cut would end quite differently. In this version, which Zombie dubs his true ending, Michael dies outside the shack in a hail of gunfire. Taking his knife, Laurie goes to stab an already dying Loomis, but is instead fatally shot through the chest by police. The final shot remains the same, though the context is now different, alluding to what may be the final thoughts of a dying Laurie. In writing *Halloween 3D*, Farmer and Lussier would work from the only ending they then knew of – the theatrical ending. Their eventual script would not connect to the Zombie-preferred director's cut ending in which almost everyone dies.

## THE STORY

*Halloween 3D* picks up where the theatrical cut of Rob Zombie's *Halloween II* ended. (Or rather just before that since it technically ends with Laurie institutionalized.) Having just fired upon Michael in the rundown shack, Sheriff Brackett and his officers rush in to find Laurie alive, Loomis dead, and Michael missing. (We learn it was actually Laurie who killed Loomis after hallucinating he was her brother.) Laurie immediately confesses to Loomis' murder, but Brackett insists she be placed in his car uncuffed. Psychiatrist Josey Blair arrives on the scene to help. Michael soon reappears and attacks Brackett. To the sheriff's horror, Laurie willingly leaves with her brother for Haddonfield Cemetery to exhume their mother's corpse. An unfortunate group of trespassing teens stumble upon this macabre family reunion. All are killed except one – Amy – whom they trap in Deborah Myers' empty coffin along with her boyfriend's severed head. Police soon catch up to the Myers siblings and a violent clash ensues. Laurie fatally shoots Brackett as he rushes to her aide. Dr. Blair is slashed across the back but escapes. Officer Cooper Goodman engages Michael in brutal hand-to-hand combat, which ends with the slasher trapped inside a burning ambulance as it hurdles into a dam. He is presumed dead, though his body is never recovered. Goodman is severely injured but lives.

The story then jumps forward a year to the J. Burton Psychiatric Hospital. Amy has been receiving intensive treatment here for the trauma she experienced the previous Halloween. In an unfortunate move, Dr. Blair admits Laurie Strode to the girl's wing on the same day Amy is scheduled to leave. They cross paths in the hallway, which leads Amy to attack Laurie, thus scuttling her planned discharge. This results in Laurie and Amy being housed on the same behavioral unit with Halloween rapidly approaching. Elsewhere, we catch up with Cooper Goodman, who strongly believes Michael somehow survived the burning ambulance, even if no one else does. Hellbent on revenge, Goodman harbors a secret plan to catch the slasher – part of which involves having Deborah Myers' corpse cremated. As we already know, his instincts are correct. Haddonfield's most infamous son has returned. He immediately steals a new copy of his white mask from a local costume shop, killing an employee in the process.

Back at the hospital, Doctors Blair and Kibner struggle to help Laurie using conventional therapies. Kibner opts to directly confront Laurie over Brackett's murder, which she has previously been in complete denial of. It's here the cracks in her identity begin to show – is she Laurie Strode or Angel Myers? Good girl or psycho-killer? Laurie will waver between these identities throughout the story, which leads to much conflict with her peers. Having tracked Laurie to the hospital, Michael infiltrates its psych wing. He murders much of the patients and staff in gory fashion including Dr. Kibner. Laurie and Amy's delinquent hallmates team up against the slasher, though they're unable to stop him. Having anticipated that Michael would return for Laurie, Goodman catches up to them both at the hospital. He plans to destroy Michael – and possibly Laurie as well – with a bomb hidden inside an urn containing their mother's ashes. They don't take the bait, however, and flee the facility while also setting free its patients.

Michael and Laurie head for a giant Halloween festival at nearby Plissken Park with Cooper, Dr. Blair, and Amy in tow. The heroes beg Laurie to reject her family's madness while still trying to destroy her brother. Keen to Goodman's plan, Michael takes the bomb from his mother's urn and gorily implants it into his stomach. It soon explodes, obliterating the former cop. Amy cuffs herself to Laurie to prevent her from rejoining her brother, but Laurie cleaves off her own hand to escape and goes to him anyway. Bleeding to death, Laurie pleads, "I'm sorry. I just want it all to stop. Michael, I'm not you." Appearing to understand, the hulking slasher takes Laurie into his arms while fatally stabbing her. He gently cradles her until her final breath. A further traumatized Amy watches on in horror as Michael escapes into the night.

## BACK TO THE ZOMBIE-VERSE

As a continuation of the Rob Zombie saga, *Halloween 3D* is appropriately insane, much like how its nightmarish predecessor was. Screenwriters Todd Farmer and Patrick Lussier manage a flawless transition from Zombie's creative vision to their own while impeccably matching his spirit and tone. Fans of the remake continuity would've surely delighted in this proposed threequel, which carries over many of the remake's best attributes. Conversely, *Halloween 3D* might also have lured back some fans previously turned off by the remake and its first sequel. In a wise move, the screenwriters completely drop the white trash shtick that permeated the previous two installments. They also reduce fan-divisive roles such as douchebag Loomis and Deborah Myers to quick postmortem cameos. Aesthetically, Farmer and Lussier move on from Michael's controversial homeless look with its reverse-*Phantom of the Opera* mask. The combined effect of all this makes for a much more palatable moviegoing experience.

Tonally, Farmer and Lussier's threequel would've taken the franchise in two completely new directions. This story is partly about Cooper Goodman plotting his revenge on Michael Myers, which is a fresh new angle. Sure, we've seen characters obsess over Michael before and even try to stop him, but not like Goodman. This guy's plan involves bringing C4-grade explosives to a knife fight. Tyler Mane's Michael has never had reason to fear anyone before now, but he might consider fearing Goodman. *Halloween 3D* is also partly a women's prison flick. (Think *Sucker Punch* crossed with *Orange is the New Black*.) No, the J. Burton Psychiatric Hospital isn't technically a prison, but it might as well be with its locked doors, barred windows, and padded seclusion rooms. Laurie and Amy's peers on the female ward further contribute to the prison vibe. They're whom you'd consider "bad girls," oversexed, foul-mouthed, and easily provoked to violence. On second thought, Michael might also want to fear this deranged lot.

It's interesting just how differently this remake continuity was set to evolve compared to that of the original franchise. Earlier *Halloween*s desperately clung to Dr. Loomis as the main protagonist, making him a reliable constant for five installments. Producers only moved on from the character when absolutely forced to by the sudden passing of actor Donald Pleasence in 1995. Even then, he was resurrected for voice cameos in *Halloween H20* and *Halloween 2018*. But the Zombie films have a different relationship with Malcolm McDowell's Loomis. His Loomis was left for dead in *Halloween 2007* before returning as a total sleazebag in the sequel. Having died in the last film's finale, he is entirely absent from *Halloween 3D*, though not to the detriment of the story. In a shocking twist, we learn that it was actually Laurie who stabbed him to death, not Michael. How strange that, in the original franchise, Laurie and Loomis were the clear-cut heroes. Yet here, one murders the other, who had become an antagonist in their own right. This speaks to what seems to be a core theme running throughout the entire Zombie-verse, which is not to put your faith in heroes. They don't really exist here.

Not unlike the opening of its predecessor, *Halloween 3D* warmly evokes 1981's *Halloween II* throughout its story. This is first apparent when Michael cuts power to the hospital, forcing the emergency generators to kick on. Subsequent scenes of the slasher stalking darkened hospital corridors would've surely brought to mind the original *Halloween*'s first sequel. In a later scene, Michael tries to stab a hypodermic needle through Dr. Blair's eye in a clear callback to Dr. Mixter in *Halloween II*. (Script: "The needle pushes on Dr. Blair's contact lens, pressing until its beveled sides pop.") She's saved at the last moment by an orderly with a mean baton swing, however. Amy rushes in to grab the needle, which she jams into the killer's eye in a reversal of the infamous *Halloween II* kill. (Script: "Michael rockets back, the syringe protruding from his mask.")

Being horror fans, Farmer and Lussier pack their script with fun genre references. This includes prominent nods to three different Kurt Russell characters from John Carpenter films. First up, there's the MacReady Dam (R.J. MacReady from *The Thing*), then the J. Burton Psychiatric Hospital (Jack Burton from *Big Trouble in Little China*) and finally Plissken Park (Snake Plissken from *Escape from New York*). The writers also tip their hats to *Halloween III: Season of the Witch* with the Silver Shamrock commercial appearing twice in the story. Noticing the familiar jingle on a nearby television, Dr. Kibner – played by *Season of the Witch* star Tom Atkins – was to impatiently and hilariously change the channel. (Kibner: "Enough of that crap.") There is also a reference to comedian Mike Myers when one patient describes Laurie Strode as "Austin Powers' fucking sister."

*Halloween 3D*'s finale takes place during something called the Great Pumpkin Dance at Plissken Park. (Imagine the town festival from *Halloween 6* mixed with the Phantom Jam from Rob Zombie's *Halloween II* and you've got it.) In another fun nod to the original *Halloween III*, the event is mentioned as being sponsored by the Silver Shamrock company. This sequence would've contained most of the film's holiday-related imagery including a giant pumpkin as the festival's centerpiece. This oversized decoration later catches fire after Goodman's bomb detonates on-stage. Striking would've been the 3D image of Michael standing before the great pumpkin as flames plume out from its eyes and mouth. Speaking of Michael, this ending would've marked a rare event – Michael slashing out in the open at a crowded public event.

## THE THIRD DIMENSION IS TERROR

*Halloween 3D* was slated to open with a recap of *Halloween II*'s ending in standard 2D format, just as it was originally filmed. Recall that the Rob Zombie sequel ended with Loomis dead, Michael seemingly dead, and Laurie further traumatized but still alive. She emerges from the rundown shack wearing her brother's mask in a shocking visual. This is where *Halloween 3D* begins. As Laurie stumbles from the shack, we cut to a newly filmed in-mask point-of-view shot. Laurie removes the mask, revealing her full point-of-view in glorious 3-D. (Script: "The world floods with 3-Dimensions.") Police and medics rush in and quickly realize that the blood covering Laurie isn't her own, but that of Dr. Loomis. Even worse, they're unable to find Michael inside the shack. They do find a suspicious crawlspace in the floor, however.

Having already teamed on *My Bloody Valentine 3D*, Farmer and Lussier make frequent and creative use of the 3D format. Their screenplay is brimming with objects that fly toward or near the camera: fire, pumpkins, steam, blood, etc. The opening sequence envisioned an ambitious shot of Michael trapped in a flaming ambulance, which careens over a guardrail into the MacReady Dam. (Script: "The ambulance rushes at us – ass first. We fly up through the back doors – to Michael trapped and on fire within, his mask melting around his face.")

Many of the kills are written to take advantage of the 3D format. One of the more visually striking gags would've involved the death of Tom Atkins' Dr. Kibner. While giving an interview on Michael via phone, the slasher himself would've appeared from behind, grabbing hold of Kibner's head and shoving it through a nearby aquarium, sawing his head off on the broken glass shards. Another grisly spectacle would've occurred early on with Michael visiting a pop-up Halloween store. After stealing a new mask, the slasher would've used a broken side-view car mirror to bash in the face of Clark, a store worker. This kill would've been executed from Clark's POV, treating the audience to a 3D gag of the broken mirror propelling towards the camera along with a close-up view of the destruction of the man's face via that mirror. In a cheeky touch, no doubt we would've been able to read the text, "Objects In Mirror Are Closer Than They Appear." (Script: "WHAM! Clark goes down! The mirror keeps slamming into his face... DRIVING AT US - with each hit we see Clark getting bloodier and bloodier... in the cracking reflection...")

Somehow, neither of these scenes feel quite as disturbing as Laurie's self-mutilation in the finale. Unwillingly handcuffed to Amy, she lops off her own hand with a meat cleaver, spraying the camera with blood as she wails in pain. It's so shocking that even Michael stops what he's doing and takes notice.

## THE NIGHTMARE CONTINUES

Rob Zombie's *Halloween II* plunged a knife into Sheriff Brackett's heart with the murder of his daughter Annie. *Halloween 3D* was poised to excruciatingly twist that knife around before pouring salt on the still-fresh wound. In short, things get much, much worse for the sheriff in this story. No doubt actor Brad Dourif was sure to give another heart-wrenching performance as the tragic character. With Annie dead, Brackett focuses on saving Laurie at any and all cost. He rushes her to his car as she tearfully confesses to Loomis' murder. Headed for the nearest hospital, they initially ride along in silence as Brackett fails to find the right words to say.

Consider the raw emotional charge of this scene. You have Brackett, who just hours before lost his only daughter to a monster that had already tried to kill her once before. He failed to protect her just as he failed to protect Laurie, whom he took into his own home as a surrogate daughter. Then you have a shell-shocked Laurie in the backseat. She's still alive, of course, but clearly spiraling into madness. Laurie is also still furious with Brackett for not telling her about her true heritage. Recall that she spent yesterday morning reading Loomis' new tell-all book, *The*

*Devil Walks Among Us,* which publicly divulged that she was actually born Angel Myers. After speaking with Annie, Brackett deduced that Laurie had read Loomis' book, but she spent the day avoiding him, so they hadn't spoken about it yet. That is some hugely important context to this scene.

> **Sheriff Brackett:** *"Laurie, darlin, I want you to know, we're gonna get through this. I should'a...I should'a told you who your real parents were. I'm sorry. I am so fucking sorry. You're all I got left now and whatever happened back there, well, it don't matter now. Not to me. I won't let them take you away."*

A grief-stricken Brackett desperately *needs* to save Laurie in this moment. He needs it for his own sanity. He's scraping rock bottom, but Laurie isn't having any of this. ("Jesus Christ. Would you just shut the fuck up?") Before Brackett can even respond to that, Michael's massive hand bursts through the windshield, causing their vehicle to crash. Approaching the wreckage, he rips off Laurie's door and extends a hand to her. As directly noted in the script, he's offering her a chance to join him. After a pause, she reaches into the front seat to retrieve evidence bags containing her brother's belongings. Laurie then places the mask over Michael's head and they leave together. Trapped in the car, Brackett yells out in protest but is unable to stop them. Despite the sheriff's best efforts, Laurie has finally embraced her family's darkness. It's difficult to fully grasp the magnitude of this betrayal. Brackett hasn't just been fighting to save Laurie's life this past year, but her soul as well. He's now defeated in every possible sense of the word. ("Halloween is over. He won.")

You have to admire Brackett for not giving up at any point during this night of unrelenting hell. He could've easily called it quits upon finding his daughter murdered in their home. And again after the failed takedown of her killer at the shack. And yet again after Laurie betrays him to join her brother. But Brackett is still determined to find them both so that he can kill Michael and save Laurie. Why? Why would he *still* be trying to save Laurie? The script contextualizes her as his "last thread to sanity." As a precautionary measure, Brackett has stationed officers at the Myers house and Smith's Grove in case Michael decides to return home, but Dr. Blair has another theory. ("He's got no reason to go to either. He's looking for something else. No. He's looking for *someone* else.") She rightly guesses that Michael and Laurie are headed to exhume their mother's corpse for a macabre family reunion.

Brackett and his deputies catch up to the slasher siblings and a nasty fight ensues. The officers prove no match for Michael, who tears through them with ease. In an effort to save his men, Brackett retrieves a shotgun from his car. He fires it repeatedly not at Michael or Laurie – but at their mother's exhumed corpse! (This would easily qualify as the biggest "Fuck you" gesture anyone has ever made to Michael in this series.) Brackett's shotgun blasts utterly decimate Deborah's rotted corpse, infuriating Michael. The slasher is so angered by this that he attacks the sheriff *using one of his own men*. Slinging the dead officer's body like a weapon, Michael knocks Brackett to the ground before stabbing him. An out-of-control ambulance soon speeds through the scene, accidentally crashing into Laurie. A badly injured Brackett approaches her twisted, bloodied body. Believing her dead, he mourns her fate, even after all that's happened this night. ("No... no.... no...") Unbeknownst to him, Laurie still clings to life.... and also to one of the deputies' guns. She raises the gun and shoots Brackett pointblank in the face. He collapses next to her.

## THE NEW SURVIVORS

With only Laurie and Michael returning from *Halloween II*, the franchise was again in need of new characters for the audience to care about. Farmer and Lussier cleverly tackle this unenviable task. Our new leads are Officer Cooper Goodman, psychiatrist Dr. Blair, and traumatized teen Amy. The writers introduce all three early on during the extended ending to *Halloween II*. Each has their own harrowing brush with Laurie and Michael this night, which leaves them scarred physically and emotionally. By the time the story jumps ahead a year, we feel like we've known them for at least a film or more. They're already survivors. It's an effective tactic that embeds them into the ongoing story.

Our first new lead is Cooper Goodman, who charges the old shack from *Halloween II* in search of Michael Myers – only to find it empty. He's also among the officers who respond to the cemetery slaughter a short while later. While there doesn't initially appear to be any survivors, Goodman discovers Amy trapped in Deborah Myers' coffin with her boyfriend's headless corpse. Rescuing her from this nightmare, he accompanies her in the ambulance, which is soon attacked by Michael. It's here that he and Goodman engage in a brutal fight. Michael eventually stabs his opponent in the thigh before slashing him shoulder to hip. One of Goodman's stray bullets strikes an oxygen tank, which lights the vehicle ablaze. Authorities believe Michael to have perished in this fire, but Goodman knows better. He'll spend the next year tracking Michael across nine unsolved murders. His colleagues will think him crazy for having such an obsession.

The next new lead is Dr. Josey Blair, the Smith's Grove psychiatrist Brackett calls for help during the extended ending to *Halloween II*. She arrives on the scene just after officers storm the rundown shack. Second only to Loomis, Blair is considered the leading authority on Michael Myers. She's not terribly phased by news of her colleague's death. ("Loomis was a prick.") Blair smartly guesses that Michael and Laurie would try to exhume their mother's corpse. Catching up to Laurie, Dr. Blair tries to reach her through empathy. Laurie responds angrily, however, and tries to escape. Blair tackles her by the roadside, ultimately pinning her to the ground. Unbeknownst to both, Michael is rapidly approaching from behind and slashes the psychiatrist across the back. Physically, Dr. Blair will survive this Halloween night and heal. She'll take on both Amy and Laurie as patients at the J. Burton Psychiatric Hospital, the latter of whom will prove a challenge. She'll also bond with Goodman over their shared trauma, resulting in a hushed affair. Unfortunately, Dr. Blair is among those who believe Michael to be dead, which will prove a dangerous fallacy.

Our third and final new lead is Amy, who arguably fares the worst of anyone in the opening sequence – Brackett excluded. She and several friends are out partying this Halloween night when they make the fatal mistake of cutting through Haddonfield Cemetery. They cross paths with the fugitive Myers siblings, which results in immense bloodshed. In a shocking turn, it's actually Laurie who traps Amy in the coffin with her dead boyfriend. (Farmer and Lussier spare no hellacious detail here. The freshly decapitated corpse of Amy's boyfriend is still gushing red when the coffin lid closes. His warm blood drenches Amy, even landing in her mouth, choking her. (*Good Lord, fellas.*) Naturally, she is already beyond traumatized when Goodman hears her screams for help and rescues her. He and Amy will form a lasting bond as well, platonic of course, as she idolizes him for being her savior.

## WE EAT CRAZY

The bulk of *Halloween 3D* plays out on the female ward of the J. Burton Psychiatric Hospital, which houses a handful of wayward teenage girls aged sixteen to nineteen. This is where the threequel explores wondrous new territory in the exploitation sub-genre of women's prison cinema. The ward's roster includes Margo, Rabbit, Kat, and Gina. Foul-mouthed, sex-starved, and easily provoked, these are not women to be trifled with. Having lived alongside Amy for the past year, they have allegiance to her as one of their own. You can easily imagine then how they respond when Laurie Strode – the bane of Amy's traumatic experience – arrives as the newest patient on their floor. As Gina tells Laurie, "You think you do crazy, bitch? We eat crazy."

The hospital is run by Dr. Kibner, who – as already mentioned – was to be portrayed by *Halloween III*'s Tom Atkins. Old school cool, Kibner is a bit of a hard-ass. He'll let the patients watch *The Three Stooges* in the common room but not *SpongeBob SquarePants* ("SpongeBob is clearly OCD.") Kibner has an extremely confrontational approach to behavioral therapy, which is something Dr. Blair isn't quite on board with. This includes forcing Laurie to break through her denial about what happened last Halloween in her very first session. Kibner is fascinated by everyone's seeming obsession with Michael Myers but refuses to believe any of it until he personally encounters the slasher.

**Dr. Kibner:** *Michael Myers embodies that reptilian part of us all. Whatever humanity he was born with was either beaten or bled out of him. Over time, that primal instinct for blood lust was all that remained. The importance of Halloween and its rituals to his fantasy possibly stem from his fascination with masks, that need to become 'another,' to deny his human identity and let this 'Shape' of evil, for lack of a better term, dominate. Halloween is all about hiding who we really are. Allows us to embolden our darker impulses by assuming whatever persona our subconscious aspires to. In the case of Myers...the face he chose was a blank. An emotionless, empty, white void. Who knows what Myers was truly like under the mask? I think he wore it so long that he may have fully assumed it as his true self. That Michael Myers, in the end, was ONLY the mask. There was, frankly, no one and nothing left beneath it.*

[Michael snatches the phone HURLS it against the wall. Kibner turns... As Michael pushes the door to the office closed.] *Oh...fuck. You really are here.*

The J. Burton Psychiatric Hospital features nicely as a backdrop to Michael's carnage in Act Two. The screenwriters mark his arrival inside the facility with a wonderfully tense sequence that crescendos into explosive violence. Laurie creepily whispers to Amy that her brother has returned and is going to kill her, which provokes Amy to lash out in rage. Orderlies swoop in to break up the fight and Amy winds up restrained in the padded room. Believing Laurie's claim, Amy begins to panic as she's unable to escape her confinement. Back on the main hallway, the other patients surround Laurie, eager to avenge her trespass against Amy. (Script: "There's a tidal wave of madness rising. And no way the orderlies can get it under control.") Chaos erupts throughout the hospital as the lights go out. Michael now begins his attack. Having glimpsed the slasher, Dr. Blair works frantically to loosen Amy's restraints, but she's not quick enough. This very quickly becomes a two-on-one fight.

Elsewhere in the hospital, Margo, Rabbit, Kat, and Gina corner Laurie in the facility's industrial kitchen. Having confirmed Michael's return, they duct-tape Laurie to a chair and arm themselves with various cutlery. This includes affixing knives to mop handles to form makeshift spears. Michael eventually comes in search of his sister and encounters the fearsome four. A melee quickly unfolds. (Script: "Suddenly the girls charge Michael. They ram him with their makeshift spears – like insane sexy cave-girls trying to slaughter a grizzly.") Margo, Rabbit, Kat, and Gina eventually take down Michael – or so they think – and turn their attention to Laurie. ("Now the only Myers left is her.") Unbeknownst to them, Michael does his trademark sit-up from the original *Halloween* behind them and murders all four. He then frees Laurie and they escape together to Plissken Park, but not before releasing the entire patient population.

## ANGEL FROM HELL

The cinematic journey of Rob Zombie's Laurie Strode leading up to *Halloween 3D* has been... strange. Laurie was arguably one of the least interesting characters in *Halloween 2007,* but that all changed in its 2009 sequel. In that entry, we found Laurie struggling with the after effects of her encounter with Michael the previous year. She's an emotional wreck for most of the film, especially after learning she was originally born Angel Myers. It was only in *Halloween II*'s final moments that Laurie began to embrace that identity by donning her brother's mask. We see much more of that play out in Farmer and Lussier's *Halloween 3D.* Their Laurie is trapped in a deep crisis of identity, trying desperately to figure out who she's meant to be. Is she Laurie Strode? Or

Angel Myers? She wavers between victim and villain in this story, which is a horrifyingly brilliant turn for the role. It proves to be one of the most complex characterizations ever suggested for this franchise. Screenwriters with lesser visions might've reneged on Laurie's descent into madness, but not these two.

Making Laurie a wild card in this way adds tremendous unpredictability to *Halloween 3D*. We're never sure when or if we can trust her. Take the opening in Haddonfield Cemetery, for example. Laurie warns Amy and her friends to "get the fuck out of here if you want to live." They ignore her warning and suffer Michael's wrath because of it. She does nothing to stop the slaughter and is actually the one who seals Amy in the coffin with her headless beau. Later, at the hospital, Laurie makes what seems to be a heartfelt apology to Amy over the incident. ("For what it's worth and I know it's not worth shit, I am sorry.") Yet several scenes later, Laurie whispers one hell of a threat to her. ("My brother's here. And he's gonna cut you from your throat to your cunt.") As already mentioned, a catfight ensues.

There's a little bit of what seems like split-personality disorder going on here. Laurie is remorseful of her actions and mentally blocks her most painful memories. Angel, on the other hand, doesn't mind the violence and seeks to rejoin alongside her brother. In their first therapy session, Dr. Kibner forces Laurie to confront the painful truth that she – not her brother – personally killed Dr. Loomis and Sheriff Brackett. She howls in remorse as the memories flood back. ("Oh god...what have I done?! Oh god! Lee! Nooo! Make it stop! Take it back! No! I don't want these memories! Pleeeease!") It's a wrenching scene that Scout Taylor-Compton would've no doubt knocked out of the park. Like its predecessor, the success of *Halloween 3D* would've rested on the shoulders of her performance.

*Halloween 3D* would've allowed audiences a brief but fascinating glimpse into Laurie's living quarters at the J. Burton facility. Embittered during her stay, she questionably engages in a... *physical relationship* (read: fuck fest) with a highly tactless orderly named Desmond. (When in Zombieland, right?) Furthermore, her digs appear eerily similar to Michael's old room at Smith's Grove Sanitarium. Laurie's walls are covered in homemade masks, though we never see her hiding behind them as her brother did. The script also mentions Laurie having drawn pictures of a woman in white standing beside a horse. This is a clear nod to her mother's postmortem appearances in the previous film. Yet after completing the drawing, Laurie promptly rips it to shreds, another example of the internal conflict she faces with her true lineage. And while we never see Deborah Myers' ghostly form in *Halloween 3D*, it's safe to assume that both Laurie and Michael still do on a regular basis. Why wouldn't they? And why not include these visions in the story? It's possible that the screenwriters took into account that Sheri Moon Zombie seldom appears in films not directed by her rocker husband. As such, she was very unlikely to reprise her role as the dead Myers matriarch for *Halloween 3D*. (There's also the fact that the white horse scenes weren't universally loved by fans.)

In a tragic end to an immensely tragic life, Laurie dies at the end of *Halloween 3D*, ultimately by her own choice. Speaking from her broken heart, she tells Michael that she cannot go on like this. No longer fit to battle her own emotions, she simply wants to die. Grabbing his hand, she aims the knife at her stomach and nods. After a beat, Michael embraces her, forcing the knife into her stomach. He then holds her until she's gone. This would've marked an emotionally devastating moment in a trilogy that is otherwise completely batshit insane. By this point, we'd have come to realize that Laurie just wanted the same thing her brother did – a place to belong in this crazy world, even if that place is standing alongside a psycho slasher. As Laurie follows Michael into the festival at Plissken Park, Goodman yells out that she doesn't have to go with him. Laurie turns back and tellingly replies, "I have nowhere else to go."

## MICHAEL LIVES!

With *Halloween 3D*, Farmer and Lussier try their best to re-mystify the character of Michael Myers after his controversial depiction in Rob Zombie's *Halloween II*. Recall that many fans took issue with the slasher going mask-less, his hobo-inspired fashion sense, and the fact that he finally spoke before killing Dr. Loomis. ("DIE!") *Halloween 3D* abandons all of that early on for a more traditional depiction. If there's a cop-out here, it's that we never learn how Michael escaped the flaming ambulance from the opening as it crashed into the MacReady Dam. We're simply expected to accept that he's back and move on. In *Halloween 3D*'s defense, its predecessor did the same thing by glossing over the bullet Laurie shot into her brother's face at point-blank range in *Halloween '07*.

By the end of *Halloween II*, Michael's mask was covered in grime and quite literally falling apart. What remained of the formerly white mask only covered half his face in a bizarro *Phantom of the Opera* kind of way. Farmer and Lussier quickly dispose of Michael's old mask in the first act by *melting it onto his face* in the aforementioned ambulance fire. The story then jumps ahead a year to find the slasher acquiring a fresh mask and jumpsuit from a Halloween costume shop in a welcome return to the original *Halloween*'s visual style. Michael is later unmasked while attacking Dr. Blair, which reveals a sight far ghastlier than the mask itself. We would've seen that portions of his old mask were now permanently and horrifically fused to his face. The script notes that it would be impossible to tell where Michael's face ends and the mask begins.

In a shocking turn of events, this story sees Michael and Laurie working together as forces of evil. It's fascinating to see the slasher with a sidekick, especially one that can speak. Unfortunately for him, their partnership is short-lived as Laurie ultimately turns away from the darkness that united them. The story's ending contains a surprisingly vulnerable take on the slasher as he realizes Laurie cannot go on living this way. Michael seems to understand that the only peace his sister will ever know will be in death. With that realization, he performs an act of mercy by killing her. Laurie's death is strikingly different from every other kill in the remake continuity in that it's neither violent nor angry. In fact, Michael takes Laurie into his arms and holds her until she's gone. It's a stunningly well-conceived ending on the screenwriter's part. Would this same moment have worked with John Carpenter's version of the Shape? No, not at all. But with Rob Zombie's take on the character, it truly works.

Most interestingly, *Halloween 3D* was set to end with Michael escaping into the night. With the Laurie Strode storyline so neatly wrapped up, you have to wonder what might've come next? The story could've gone absolutely anywhere.

*CLOSE ON MICHAEL. Cold. Malignant. Eternal. The Halloween theme rising like an anthem of infinite madness. An Ambulance WIPES the frame... and Michael is gone. AMY -- her face haunted as we crane back, the giant pumpkin roaring fire into the night sky.*

## WHY IT WASN'T MADE

Something to keep in mind about this *Halloween*'s inability to grace the screen is that, unlike previous unmade entries, it was practically already greenlit before falling by the wayside. If you've been following along, then you've surely noticed by now that the Weinsteins have historically had no problem whatsoever letting *Halloween* scripts languish in development hell. Why then would they suddenly be so gung-ho to rush *Halloween 3D* into production? As it turns out, the studio was in serious financial trouble. It's not as if Rob Zombie's *Halloween II* had been some massive hit for them. *It hadn't been.* The grunge-horror sequel earned less than its predecessor had on the same budget, returning $39 million worldwide against a $15 million investment. To be clear, that doesn't mean the Weinsteins made off with $24 million in profit. They had to share that box office gross with theater owners while also taking into account the cost of prints and promotion. So, *Halloween II* was not a hit. It likely didn't lose money, but a hit it wasn't.

Even the most cursory look at 2009 will reveal a bruising year for The Weinstein Company. They released twelve films in 2009, seven of which were outright bombs. (These include *Outlander, Killshot, Crossing Over, Janky Promoters, The Road, Nine,* and *Fanboys.*) Yes, Rob Zombie's *Halloween II* did okay for them, but *Outlander* lost the company $40 million alone, which more than eclipsed *Halloween II*'s modest profits. You might point to Quentin Tarantino's *Inglorious Basterds* as a box office triumph, but the Weinsteins co-financed with Universal Pictures and were therefore only entitled to half its profits. Unfortunately, the project's earnings were not enough to offset losses incurred by the company's seven bombs. (Their many non-film investments fared even worse, but that's a story for another book.) By June 2009, barely four years after the company's inception, there were already credible rumors of a possible bankruptcy as the Weinsteins hired a financial advisor to restructure their debts. There were also waves of layoffs within the company.

But just how broke were they? So broke that they couldn't afford to release one of their own movies. Box office records show that 2009's *Janky Promoters*, a comedy starring Ice Cube and Mike Epps, only returned $9,069 theatrically against a $10 million budget. If you don't recall hearing about *Janky Promoters* hitting theaters, that's because it never did – not as intended, anyway. The Weinstein Company couldn't afford to give it a proper theatrical release. According to Ice Cube, the Weinsteins canceled planned re-shoots, cut the movie in secret, and dumped it onto DVD in November 2009. (They did eke out a 22-screen release in October, which is where its pitiful $9,069 gross comes from. Janky promoters, indeed!)

The bungling of *Janky Promoters'* post-production and theatrical release happened concurrent with the Weinsteins' efforts to ram *Halloween 3D* through pre-production. If the threequel was going to go from rough pitch to in-the-can in just three months' time, the filmmakers would need to work at a frantic pace. Regarding the script, there would be no time for overdevelopment, nitpicking, or feet dragging. Farmer and Lussier churned out their forty-page treatment across two days, which was immediately used for prepping the shoot.

The production started coming together very quickly. Tyler Mane and Scout Taylor-Compton were approached to reprise their roles as Michael Myers and Laurie Strode. No deals were signed but the interest was there. (Taylor-Compton would later express conflicting views on her prospective return – an interest in reprising the role but frustration over the initially rushed production.) Original *Halloween III* star Tom Atkins – last seen in *My Bloody Valentine 3D* – agreed to appear in *Halloween 3D* in a role written specifically for him. Edi Gathegi had also been in discussions to play Deputy Goodman. Makeup effects designer Gary Tunnicliffe (returning from the sixth and eighth *Halloweens*) began prepping a master list of effects needed based on the initial treatment. Producers agreed to shoot *Halloween 3D* in Shreveport, Louisiana out of convenience for Farmer and Lussier as they would begin prepping *Drive Angry* there immediately after filming wrapped. Location manager Stanley Pearse quickly sourced a locale to serve as the sequel's main setting and photographed it for the writers.

Upon submitting the first and only draft – two days earlier than expected – Farmer and Lussier's *Halloween 3D* was reviewed favorably by both Malek Akkad and Dimension's Matthew Stein. Bob Weinstein, however, was mysteriously silent. Two days later, the movie mogul dispatched a call to Lussier, informing the prospective writer/director that he had not yet read the script. Why? Because more time was needed to develop the project. The primary source of this shutdown would be related to their crippling money matters. Despite urge from all parties to see *Halloween 3D* come to fruition, the studio was simply too broke to finance the project. Thus, as quickly as the project unfolded, it was now on hold – indefinitely.

One might assume the technology needed to shoot in 3D might've proven costlier than the budgets of previous *Halloweens*, but this was not the case. Lussier had consulted with the same 3D company responsible for *My Bloody Valentine*, upon which it was deduced that the ultimate cost of *Halloween 3D* would've nearly equaled the same budgets for the previous two Rob Zombie films, as well as *My Bloody Valentine*, which astonishingly only cost $14 million. (Chump change in those days!) Regardless, such issues and delays would mean that Farmer and Lussier could no longer waste any more time on the project. Disappointed, both men turned their attention to *Drive Angry*, which would begin shooting in January 2010. As we'll come to find, while their *Halloween 3D* would languish and die in development hell, this wouldn't be the last to be heard of them in regard to *Halloween*.

"We took Rob Zombie's story and continued it, but we did it in a way that sort of pulled it back to the John Carpenter tone and intention. We didn't break any of the rules. We used the rules Zombie had established. It felt like a complete story."

- Todd Farmer, Fangoria.com

"The day after [Halloween II] came out, we were back in production for Halloween 3D. We were about two weeks from going down to Louisiana to shoot it and for whatever reason, the studio thought we were maybe moving a little bit too quickly. I disagree. I think we had a great script and a great team, and it would have been a massive hit."

- Malek Akkad, Collider.com

# TODD FARMER

### Co-writer - Halloween 3D

Interviewed by Travis Mullins

**Genre fans obviously know you for your connection to *Friday the 13th*, but what is your relationship with *Halloween*?**

Without any doubt, it was my favorite slasher growing up. It didn't even strike me as a slasher. You were just terrified. To me, the *Friday the 13th* films were more fun. They were goofy. You know, you'd order pizza with the guys and just watch. With Jason, it's not just this unstoppable guy. It's this unstoppable guy who also fights telekinesis. (laughs) It just goes all over the place. And when Freddy came out, it was horrifying but also completely different. People have asked, '*What's your favorite of the scary movies?*' I don't have favorites but certainly *Halloween* was one of those movies that influenced what I do today. It influenced my even being in Los Angeles. It's a big part of who I am. I'd say you could throw *Jaws* into that. You could throw *Alien* and *Star Wars* into that. There's a handful of films that sort of make me who I am, and *Halloween* is definitely one of them.

**What were your thoughts on the sequels?**

Other than *Halloween III*, which I *adore* every frame, I felt the sequels were a little more cookie-cutter than, say, *Friday the 13th*. I didn't enjoy them as well. The first three, yes. The others, I followed but they weren't movies that I would stop and watch again. *Halloween H20* was fun. I also really did enjoy the most recent one [*Halloween 2018*]. I thought it was fantastic. There were a couple of places where I physically jumped. I really dug it. I thought Jamie Lee Curtis played it perfectly. I'm curious what they're going to do next. Overall, though, if I had to choose, I think I would choose the *Nightmare on Elm Street* or *Friday the 13th* sequels over the *Halloween* sequels. You know, everybody's different.

**How did you and Patrick Lussier come to be involved with *Halloween 3D?***

Patrick had edited most of Bob [Weinstein]'s movies so that was the main 'in.' From what I remember, they would have a movie with issues, and Patrick would come and fix it. Towards the end, that was a big part of their relationship. We reached out with our take on *Halloween.* This would've been either 2008 or 2009. We pitched *Halloween, Hellraiser,* and I think *Scanners,* almost back-to-back. Nothing came of it. Rob Zombie was probably a week or two into filming *Halloween II,* and Bob reached out and said, '*We want you guys to come in and do the third one.*' So, Patrick and I took our original pitch and made it fit with Rob's take. The first act was mostly new because we would be following Rob's film, starting before the night was even over. But the asylum setting and everything else was from the original pitch.

**It seems the project was developed in the blink of an eye. Could you speak of your process collaborating with Patrick?**

It's an interesting thing because we wrote it, quite literally, in eight days, and then never worked on it again. (laughs) I don't think I've ever gone back and read it. My process is, every day, I start on page one and read until I catch up to where I was. The first half of my scripts tend to be a lot tighter than the second half because I spend a lot more time on them. Patrick and I don't have a set way of how we do things. He tends to come up with a story idea. He'll either flesh it out on his own or we'll banter back and forth, and I'll write the first draft. Then, he'd come in and follow me. I think that's how it worked on *Halloween 3D.* I'm pretty sure he came up with the original idea of that initial pitch. When we went into this, it was pretty much all on paper. The outline was very detailed. A lot of people were like, '*Wait, you wrote the script in eight days?*' Well, it's hard to write a script in eight days unless you know exactly what you're doing, and we knew everything. *Drive Angry* wasn't like that. That went down the road of things changing while we were on set. But with *Halloween,* we knew exactly what everything was going to be. We had just set up *Drive Angry,* so we didn't have a ton of time. Bob wanted to go into production before the end of the year so that he would have it for the following October.

It was tight. We had that outline which I'm pretty sure Patrick did most of the heavy lifting on. Then, I went through that outline in about seven or eight days and wrote the draft. It was never rewritten. We never had time. That was the first and only draft because realistically we had to be in pre production before I was even done with the script. So, Patrick was hiring crew. I mean, it was all moving forward while I was still writing the script. I was, quite literally, eating and sleeping at the office because it was just non-stop. I finished on a Saturday and we handed it in that day. We didn't want to wait until the Monday when we were supposed to hand it in because that'd just cost us time. One of the biggest worries was that if we didn't get finished before Christmas, it would screw up *Drive Angry* because that was supposed to start shooting in January. So, we got it done, turned it in on a Saturday, and on Monday, Bob pulled the plug. He also tried not to pay us but that was sort of a notorious Weinstein thing, anyway.

**Both of Rob Zombie's films were noted as being darker and grittier than your usual *Halloween*. What are thoughts on his style? How'd you feel about being tasked in following his work?**

For me, *Halloween* was the unexplained. It was the idea that it could be your brother. That was the scariest thing to me. I love the fact there are remakes. I have no problem with that. There are some people who freak out, like, '*Oh my god, it's destroying my childhood*.' If you feel that way, you need your childhood destroyed. The more, the merrier, to me. I'd want Rob Zombie to do a remake and I'd want a dozen other directors to do a remake. Why not? Doesn't hurt. I never had a problem with it but it's not what I would've done, personally, because I like the idea of Michael being unexplained. You know, John Carpenter described the Shape as this force of evil that rolls into town without any rhyme or reason. I like that. Tyler Mane is one of my best friends, and as far as Rob's style and the movie itself, I think it's amazing. It's just a dark and unendingly brutal movie. It's not what I would've done, but that doesn't mean his version is wrong. I think his work is great and it reaches a fanbase that loves it. But I didn't like knowing all of Michael's secrets, and neither did Patrick.

So, our take was to reintroduce the Shape. By the end of our first act, Rob Zombie's Michael Myers was dead. Psychologically, he dies. When the ambulance goes over that cliff, the mask melts to his face, and by the end of our second act, it's John Carpenter's Michael Myers that returns. He goes to one of those fly-by-night Halloween stores, and there's a single mask left over from last season. It's the old Captain Kirk mask. Michael kills the kid, puts the mask on and psychologically, he becomes the Shape. It's still the same character, the same hulking beast that is Tyler Mane. But in that world, he becomes the Shape for the first time. It's the Shape that stands at the end of the street and just stares at you. Or covers himself with a sheet with the glasses on. Michael Myers is a dick. If he wants to scare you, he can do it any old way. But to pretend to be the

boyfriend? That was a dick move. That's what we liked about it. And Bob liked the idea of going back to the Shape, going back to the silent force that once it sees you and marks you, it's not going to stop until you're dead.

**Out of curiosity, did you ever hear as to why Rob wasn't coming back with the third film?**

I heard lots of things that were all different. I don't know who was telling the truth. One entity was saying he had no interest in ever coming back. Another said that he wanted to come back and they took it away from him. I don't know what the true story is. It came across as though Rob didn't want to do another one. In fact, it came across as though he didn't even want to do the one he was doing. In retrospect, I don't think that's the case, but we didn't have anything else to go on, so we didn't feel like we were stepping on Rob's toes. We proceeded to make the best movie we could make. Or at least the best script. The best story.

**I honestly thought your script fit with his films rather well. It's an interesting mix. You were obligated to follow in his footsteps, yet I could see a lot of your stuff in there. It's toned down but not to a drastic degree.**

I mean, if you look at his *Halloween II*, it is a brutal, non-stop snuff film. It just doesn't stop. Betsy Rue – who I knew from *My Bloody Valentine* – was in it. Had I been writing the scene that she was in, Michael wouldn't have killed her, in the same way that when he sees the kid with candy, he doesn't kill the kid. It's almost like there's a cowboy code and in that situation, Michael did have a code. But for him to kill Betsy's character when she's actually the one trying to help him? To me, that's fine. That's one way to do it, and it certainly makes the character darker and, in some ways, more evil. But to me, it almost made the character more unintelligent. I don't know. Tyler will probably bust me in the balls when he hears this.

**You spoke of wanting to harken back to the original Shape. What were your thoughts on Rob's Laurie and writing for that character?**

We always tried to stay true to the characters. What we wanted to do was offer Laurie the journey to make the decision on whether she wanted to join Michael or not. She's faced with the fact that she has this brother who's done all these things. Was he just an abnormality or is this something in the blood? Over the course of her journey, she has to come to that conclusion. We liked the idea that she watches Michael killing Loomis – or so she thinks. Then, you pull back and reveal that she's actually the one stabbing Loomis. He puts the mask on her face, which was him introducing her to the insanity. She stumbles outside, takes the mask off and then we go into 3D. So, up to that point, the whole opening was supposed to be in 2D. I do remember really liking the point where Laurie makes the choice, '*I can't do this with you.*' I remember feeling emotions at that very last scene with them, and even, to a degree, feeling sad for him because now he's alone. His sister can't make the journey with him. I remember really liking that.

**And then he kills her and the Laurie Strode chapter concludes.**

And I liked that. I thought it was a ballsy way to go. I'm not sure we ever talked about a sequel to this. I don't think we did. This was standalone. I mean, Michael could go on to do whatever. But this wasn't one of those sequels where it's like, '*Did he make it or did he not?*' At the end, the fucker just walks away.

**Did you ever consider bringing back Deborah Myers or was that a no-go from the start?**

I don't remember discussing it. For us, it was always the brother and sister story. It was about coaxing Laurie into her first murder. Then, having the Shape come back to finish the job. Not to kill her but as if to say, '*So, are you with me or not?*' We never talked about the mother. I think there was a moment when Laurie draws a white horse when she's in the asylum and then she rips it up. I had thought about taking that out because I thought it would be interpreted as making some sort of statement about Rob's movie, which was not the case.

**In developing the plot, had you or Patrick ever considered the issue of the director's cut of *Halloween II*, which had a vastly different ending?**

We talked about that. We saw *Halloween II* early on. Bob kept sending us DVDs of the movie, early cuts before it had even come out, so we were watching it on our computers. I know I saw a version where everybody died. We followed the theatrical ending. The reason Bob came to us was because of that ending. I'm pretty sure we knew reshoots were going to happen. The storyteller in me preferred Rob's ending because it's the ballsy ending. But the businessman in me knows there's no way you can kill all of your main characters. It's not viable. It's a ballsy thing to do and I appreciate that. (laughs) But why on earth would you end someone's franchise? It would've forced us to reboot or '*It's all a dream!*' which, to a degree, our script does with revamping who kills Loomis. But if they had all died? That would've made it an impossibility. My suggestion would be, '*Do* Halloween III*! Do* Season of the Witch!' I still want to do *Season of the Witch*. (laughs)

**Do you remember any characters, set pieces or 3D gags that you enjoyed writing for?**

I still think the opening would've been fun, where you pull back to reveal Laurie as the one stabbing Loomis and having her take off the mask. Whether you're a fan of Rob Zombie's films or not, I'd like to think following the rest of that night would've been interesting. You don't often get the opportunity to do that. To go back and say, '*Okay, you saw what happened. But this is what really happened,*' and do it in a way that hopefully wasn't breaking any rules. Some of this would be playing out in Laurie's head, so she's losing her mind as well. I thought it was fun going to the asylum the next year and not knowing just where her head is at. That ambiguity was fun to write.

With all of our movies, we wanted to give Tom Atkins an opportunity to shine. We brought him in as the doctor. He even gets to have a wink at *Halloween III* when the Shamrock commercial is playing on the TV in the common room. And the asylum girls were red shirts, but they were never supposed to feel like red shirts. The idea was that any one of them could rise and become the new Laurie, the new hero. It was all about making them fun and goofy. My own death,

I thought would've been fun. You would've had my severed head flying at you in 3D. Also, Tom Atkins dying in the aquarium.

**I think my personal favorite is when Michael steals the mask at the store. He's shoving a broken sideview mirror in the guy's face. You'd be able to read, '*Objects in Mirror Are Closer Than They Appear.*'**

And in 3D, that would've looked stunning. I mean, we didn't know. When we went in to do *My Bloody Valentine*, we didn't know 3D could look like that. There's a sequence where the miner pickaxes the door and looks inside. Just the depth and suddenly, the audience is inside the movie. It was just wild. We grew up with *Friday the 13th Part III* and *Jaws 3D*. We expected the eyeball coming at your face. We didn't expect an immersive feeling. So, this would've been a really fun movie. We had the same 3D effects crew and they would've come in, done this and then we'd all go into *Drive Angry* right after. It would've been fun; even though, even now, when I go see a movie, I rarely go see the 3D version. For us, I think the straining part was when *Valentine* came out, suddenly everyone started doing 3D movies. Yet they were saying things to us, like, '*Well, you know, yours was just a fluke because of the 3D.*' Like, we did it okay and it wasn't bad. We did a pretty good version of it.

**What was it like working with Malek Akkad?**

Malek was great. I didn't know what to expect at first. I grew up in construction and my dad was the boss. You know, I was always 'the boss' kid.' I wondered if that's what it would be like [with him]. '*Is he the boss' kid?*' And it wasn't. From day one, he completely won me over. His passion for the project, the actors, the story; it was wonderful. I really liked him. And I don't like anybody. I don't often go into a situation where I feel like the producer has my back, but I knew he had our back. And what we were trying to do was ballsy. I mean, Rob hadn't even finished his movie and we were already talking about doing a third one.

**What was the reaction to your script? Were there any notes offered?**

No, everyone agreed on the outline. Malek really dug the script. I mean, even the lawyer read the script and was like, '*This is great.*' So, Malek was completely on board. And he knew we were in a tricky situation because we didn't have an automatic 'out.' It's not like if we hit December and weren't done, the Weinsteins couldn't screw us. They could. Malek was well aware of that and he was going to do everything in his power to make sure we wrapped when we needed to. Because had we not done that and had we run into some sort of problem and couldn't get finished, we'd lose *Drive Angry*. So, Malek was bending over backwards. While I was writing, in my own sweat for eight days, Patrick and Malek were non-stop. They were both in prep because we *had* to be in production. All of the stuff that had to happen fast – costumes, set design – they were talking about. I know we had brought in Gary Tunnicliffe [for special effects]. I believe he may have done some sketches, but he was mostly just planning. I was talking to Patrick every single day while he's doing all this stuff. He's calling me up going, '*Oh my god, Gary just found the original mold for the very first* Halloween. *We got that mask!*' I mean, we were so frickin' happy. We were stoked. It was so frazzled during that time that I don't remember everything Patrick was doing. But we were moving. It was going to happen. So, Malek was a force of nature. Very supportive.

**In terms of casting, were Tyler Mane, Scout Taylor-Compton, and Brad Dourif all expected to return? Had any of them read the script?**

I knew Tyler's wife [Renae Geerlings] from the comic book industry. I gave them a call and said, '*Hey, I'm swinging by. You guys want to grab a drink or something?*' I ended up for staying for 24 hours and that was the night we toilet papered Derek Mears' house. The three of us have been fast friends ever since. The reason I went there is because Patrick and I wanted Tyler to be in *Halloween 3D*, and Scout as well. I don't know if she read the script. As far as being an actress, we both adored her. Brad was expected to return but I don't think we had reached out to him yet. If you're following Rob's film, you're using Rob's actors. It wasn't like there was anyone we wanted to replace. I don't know all the details, but I know in some areas, there was no desire for Loomis to come back, so we introduced a female doctor to fill that structural role. For Goodman, I'm pretty sure we had talked to Edi Gathegi, who played the deputy in *My Bloody Valentine*. At least verbally, they were all in. No deals were made. We really didn't have a lot of time because Patrick's prep was eight days, and then the plug was pulled. So, it's not like we were in production for a month or two. We were in pre-production for a week. That was it. And then it all just went away.

**So, what exactly lead to the film's cancellation?**

Patrick would know better. It's just speculation but I believe it was money. They didn't have the money to do it and the fear was they wouldn't be able to finish the movie and it would derail us on *Drive Angry*. We turned in the script on Saturday, and Bob called Patrick on Monday and said, '*I'm so sorry but we can't do this. If we do this, we won't finish, and we'll derail* Drive Angry.' I still to this day believe that Bob genuinely didn't want to hurt Patrick. He didn't give a shit about me. But if you go and look at Patrick's credits, most of the movies he edited were theirs. He saved Wes Craven's job on *Scream*. They were going to fire Wes, and Patrick stayed up all night editing that Drew Barrymore sequence. Sent it back to the Weinsteins and that saved Wes' career. Then, Patrick became their go-to on all their big movies.

They pulled the plug and to this day, as much as I hate that they pulled the plug, I feel like Bob was trying to protect us. The next part is probably Harvey. I don't know for certain, but I know that they didn't want to pay us. We had to go to war to get the money. It had come down to this. Bob called our agent and she sent us an email saying, '*Look, I just got off the phone with Bob. He said you gotta trust him. He'll pay you everything he owes except the $10,000.*' Within ten seconds, without talking to each other, we both responded via email, '*Fuck him.*' (laughs) We were so pissed off at that point, we didn't care. Plus, we had *Drive Angry* money coming in, so we were feeling a little more cocky. We had all our money by that afternoon. We were told, '*You guys will never work with him again. They're never gonna work with you again.*' Sure as shit, we worked on *Hellraiser* and made twice the money that we made on *Halloween*. At the same time, I think they did respect Patrick because he made a fortune with them. And I think they also respected us for fighting. They wanted an opportunity to screw us. They can't screw us if they don't work with us.

**How did Malek feel about the shutdown?**

I remember him being upset this wasn't happening. I remember for a long time, he wanted to make this movie but couldn't because of their unending shenanigans. Even after we were done, they would bring in more people. It reached a point where – I don't know if Malek ever said this – but you certainly got the sense that he knew they had no intention of making the movie. This was all just to keep the rights until they were ready to make the movie, and Malek was always jumping through these hoops. I may be wrong, but that was the impression I got. Blumhouse now owns everything. I'm okay with that because they'll continue to make the movies.

This will sound weird, but *Halloween 3D* is the, '*Show me on the doll where it touched you,*' that I block out. Because this was the one that hurt the most. *Halloween* was one of those movies that made me who I am. I have now sat down with Carpenter on many occasions. To be able to work with him and have him do the music and all of those things would've been just fantastic. Then, on a completely financial level, it would've changed our lives in that suddenly, we would be doing what I consider to be one of the horror royalty movies. You know, '*We're a part of the* Halloween *franchise*.' And I guess we'll always be a part of the history. But we never got to make our movie. So, that always feels like a sucker punch when I think about it. It's the one project that I really don't think about much. I don't like thinking about it.

But I'm glad Patrick and I were the first to send Malek a congrats when they announced they were moving forward. I wish them the best. I'm glad that Ryan Turek was able to be a part of it. Back from the first time Ryan was running his website, he was always passionate about the movies. I can remember busting his balls, '*Why don't you stop writing about other people making movies and why don't you do it yourself?*' And he's doing that and that's great. At least you know *Halloween* is in good hands when there are guys that are passionate about it. I know Malek is. I know Ryan is. I know Jason [Blum] will make sure they're protected.

**You attempted to come back to *Halloween*, though, right?**

When we got home from *Drive Angry*, we reached out to them, saying, '*Hey, let's see what's going on with* Halloween,' and then fairly immediately, Bob responded, '*Eh, let's do* Hellraiser.' I would guess it's because they were being threatened with losing their rights, so they probably had some arbitrary, '*Go to this step, go to that step.*' For a while, I held out hope for this *Halloween 3D* because I really did like the script. We worked on it and then I know we played around with some other ideas. The next version would've completely ignored Rob's films because too much time had passed. Then, Bob wanted to do found footage and we were like, '*No, we ain't doing found footage.*' And then there was a whole thing about doing a PG-13 version, and we were like, '*No, we won't do PG-13.*'

That was his thing. Whatever is hot at the moment, he wants to mimic. And then he was always stuck on this idea of Michael being in an asylum for the bulk of the movie. That didn't come to anything, but I kept hearing stories. We would reach out to Malek every now and then, and they were working with somebody else. Other stories were coming in, but nothing ever happened. And I'm like, '*What is happening? They've got this script that everyone liked. We did it for a budget.*' I think we were between $10 to $15 million. I mean, it was the Weinsteins. Two things, they can never make up their minds, and they want to make the movie that is hot at the time. We certainly saw that with *Hellraiser*. I know Malek had to put up with that stuff all the time, so I'm glad it landed with Blumhouse.

**Would you ever come back to take a crack at another script?**

I would gladly work with Malek again, but I don't think they're going to bring us back. We sort of had our shot, didn't do it and we're tarnished now. We're not the shiny new coin when it comes to the franchise. By the way, Malek came back to us four years after. Right before the most recent film, Malek called Patrick and I, and he wanted to do a soft reboot and start from scratch. He was like, '*I want this to be the sort of thing where if you watched it, it could be cut right out of the newspapers as a real serial killer, that no part of this feels like a slasher movie.*' We came up with a pitch that was Michael Myers right out of high school, and we loved it.

**As the man who put Jason in space, how do you feel about the vocal distaste for change in the *Halloween* franchise? Do you think the franchise is perhaps hindered because of this?**

I mean, if you look at the last film's box office, I think that's not true at all. I think there's a very loud, vocal minority who don't like change. If you look at *Friday the 13th*, every single film is change. The first film is completely different from the second because it's a different killer. The third film is in 3D. You keep going on and then you have zombie Jason, and then Jason fighting the supernatural. Everything about it is change. What I didn't like about the *Halloween* sequels is that it felt like there wasn't enough change. So, I like how [the Blumhouse version] is going. I probably wouldn't have gone that route, but I love that that story is now out there to tell. I feel the same way with my comic books. How many versions of Spider-Man are there? How many versions of Captain America? Or Batman? They don't have to all fit together in the same world. I feel the same way about my slashers and my scary monsters.

My reasoning for putting Jason in space was that *Freddy vs Jason* was in development and we didn't know what they were going to do. So, if we set our movie in the future, then that'd be our way to avoid any issues. I wanted to set it in the *Blade Runner* world, and they said, '*We can't afford that.*' So, I said, '*Great, let's do* Aliens. *Stick him on a spaceship.*' I wasn't trying to reinvent anything. I was just trying to get the movie made. And I loved *Aliens* and thought, '*Well, that would be fun. Take aliens out and put Jason in.*' I can see why hardcore fans would just lose it over that, but I never understood it. I mean, I'm fifty. I'm a hardcore fan. I grew up with all of these franchises. Why on earth would I just want more of the same? As long as the movie is good, as long as the telling is good, then you've won me over already. I get that fans – when they want something, they want it. (laughs)

**Let's say Malek does bring you back into the fold. If you could do anything with Michael, if you could go off the path and break any rules, what is the *Halloween* film you'd personally want to see?**

Good question. Part of me would do all the versions that I've written. (laughs) If I could go crazy with it, then I'd probably do what I did with Jason. I like the idea of the military using him like a virus, capturing and dropping him somewhere to cause havoc. We always talked about different places we could put Jason before we landed on space. We talked about Jason in the hood and Jason in the Middle East, all these different places. I like a fish-out-of-water story. Michael and Jason are always in their one little spot. But what if you took either of them out and put them elsewhere? I liked *Freddy vs Jason* because it crosses the boundaries. So, I think my best would be to figure out a place to put Michael where he is either captured and escapes to somewhere he shouldn't be, or someone physically puts him somewhere. That's probably what I would do. That's a big question, something I hadn't thought about, but I like that question.

# PATRICK LUSSIER
### Co-writer, Prospective Director - Halloween 3D

Interviewed by Travis Mullins

**Years after editing *Halloween H20*, you were brought onboard to write *Halloween 3D* along with Todd Farmer. How did this come about for you?**

We literally got a call from Bob [Weinstein] after Rob Zombie's [*Halloween II*] opened. We had just done *My Bloody Valentine 3D*. It had released in January of that same year, had been very successful both domestic and foreign, even though it only had, like, three weekends because of the 3D at the time. There weren't enough theaters to have more than that. Anyways, Bob wanted to shoot the new film in 3D. He wanted someone with 3D experience, and experience with the franchise. I guess we got the call right around the time of when *Inglourious Basterds* came out. They wanted to do a sequel to Rob's movie and asked if we would be interested. It's like, '*Okay, well, you've sort of made it tricky to do a sequel to Rob's movie, but we can figure it out.*' We sent them a forty-page treatment that they approved. Now, we already had the deal to make *Drive Angry* but because of Nic Cage's schedule, we weren't going to be shooting until the spring. So, they were like, '*Can you shoot [Halloween 3D] in the fall?*' and I was like, '*Um, yeah, we can make that work.*' I think it was going to be a six-week shoot. We were prepping off the treatment. Todd did the first draft of the script and then I went through behind him.

**What I like about your draft is that even as a new team coming in, you really honor Rob Zombie's approach. After a certain point, the style is altered but it still fits with his work.**

What we wanted to do was transition from what Rob had done back to something that was more of an echo to the simplicity of what Carpenter had created in the beginning. That was very much our approach in tackling it. Part of what we were thinking is the moment where the mask melts into Michael Myers' face, Michael Myers no longer exists. All that is left is the Shape. It's the idea of Bruce Wayne just being swallowed by Batman. As a visual motif, there was something about that we found intriguing. I don't know if people would've got it or thought that much about it, but it was something we had fun messing with. Then, the girls in the asylum and how they became our heroes – sort of like the stalker version of *Girl, Interrupted.* The other film we talked about a lot in the scene where they all try to kill Michael in the cafeteria was *Lord of the Flies.* The idea of them all gathering around with the spear and trying to stab it to death. (laughs) Becoming primal. That was very much something I had learned from Wes [Craven], the idea of becoming savage. He talked about that a lot – the primal stories told around a campfire. You know, at the end of the day, we're all just cavemen. And the reason so many of those stories resonate has to do with that.

And then, Rob's Laurie was so damaged. We felt that we should leave her to that as opposed to try and redeem. To redeem her based on how Rob had ended her at the end of *Halloween II* would not be true to what he did. I've never met him. We never talked to him about this but that was our take on it. He might say, '*You guys are full of shit,*' and not be wrong! (laughs) But we tried to be respectful to the tone that he had set out. It was interesting, I remember having a brief conversation with Kevin Williamson about Rob's version of the movie. He said the thing he loved about the Carpenter version is that you never justify why Michael went crazy. You never gave him a reason to do it, so you didn't have hidden sympathy for why he did it. Whereas with Rob's movie, you really go out of your way to say, '*His childhood was fucked.*' These people around him, it's like, '*Jesus, no wonder he turned out the way he did.*' I think Carpenter's version is actually scarier – the idea that there isn't an explanation. The idea that you don't need a reason to be evil. You can just be it because you can be. That's more terrifying.

**Laurie suffers a pretty dark journey throughout all this. Even if one isn't a fan of the Rob Zombie storyline, the way you conclude her character does it justice. Tell us about that.**

Initially, she begins to think, '*I'll just surrender to this dark side of who I am. I will become this thing because this is my destiny to become,*' and then the idea of her realizing what that actually entails and what that costs. It's like, '*I can't fucking do it.*' He lets her go. And I always saw that ending as very compassionate on Michael's part. He kills her but it's a compassionate thing that he does. He does it because no matter how much she is willing to surrender to become like him, she can't be like him. We tried to give that sense of conclusion and wrap-up. If somebody else wanted to take that story and go on, we'd give them enough of a leap-off point that you could take the mythology whatever direction you wanted to take.

**Going back to Laurie, we also discover that she's actually having a fling with the hospital orderly Des, which isn't really an action we would typically associate with her, especially under those circumstances.**

Oh, yeah! (laughs) I liked that aspect in that it was an unpredictable thing. She wasn't the final girl virgin anymore. She was no longer the final girl! That, to me, was the thing that told you she was no longer the final girl. She had surrendered that right. She was so damaged; she could no longer carry that mantle. Her need to have control over her environment is why she slept with Des. It wasn't just about the sex. Being in that position of power over somebody who is supposed to be her jailer, essentially, is significant because it gives her a strength in that environment she doesn't otherwise have.

Also, it felt like it gave you all sorts of different family dynamics that made Michael and Laurie as a family more relatable. It's the simple idea of, '*Oh, you fucked my sister, I'm going to break your face.*' That's an old, old human archetype of how family dynamics work. To me, there was something about that that just rang true and, in its own way, sort of normal – to normalize that relationship in a relatable way when there are so many things about it that aren't. With Des' realization – '*Oh my god, I've been banging Michael Myers' sister!*' – there's something about that that I also felt had merit. So, those are the two different components, with the primary being the idea of giving Laurie control over a part of her life and over people she's beholden to. Again, it wasn't something we would do with the Jamie Lee Curtis version of Laurie, but with Rob's version, it felt like a natural extension.

**Speaking of family dynamics, you make only passing reference to Deborah Myers. Were there any talks of having her appear as a ghostly visage once more?**

We talked about it but discounted it. We talked about that being a component of *Halloween II* that neither of us bought into. That felt very outside, and this was deliberately counter to that. We had an echo of that but never any kind of angelic thing. We also felt that we would never get the same actress to play the part for obvious reasons and as such, didn't want to back ourselves to where we felt that was even a direction we needed to go. We echo it and then let it go. It was a part of the mythology but at the same time, it didn't need more acknowledgment than that.

**Loomis isn't here but you do have a surrogate in the form of Dr. Josey Blair. What led to this character and the decision to leave Loomis behind?**

We were told that Loomis was dead. Unequivocally, Loomis was dead, and they literally just didn't want to pay Malcolm McDowell to come back. So, it was like, '*Okay, that's fine*.' In this version, it actually works better without him. He wasn't the character that was introduced. He wasn't the Donald Pleasence version. So, not being that, he was quite different. I remember hearing, '*Don't write him in!*' very succinctly. Josey was actually a character that we wrote for the sequel to *My Bloody Valentine*. We wrote about forty pages of a scriptment – half script, half treatment – for a sequel before the film had come out, thinking that if the movie was successful, we would do a sequel. Of course, the movie was successful, but we didn't do a sequel. So, we thought, '*Okay, let's take that character and put her in here*,' sort of a reinvented counter to Loomis.

In the *Valentine* sequel, Josey was a villain. She had an affair with Tom Hanniger when he was in the hospital and had been encouraging his disassociation. She was not a sterling character. But you thought she was. To me, Tom is always the hero of that movie. I mean, everybody he kills sort of deserves it. (laughs) You know, they leave him! They're all cowards who leave him to Harry Warden in the beginning. His vengeance is what they had coming to them. In my mind, it was always sort of a twisted, '70s revenge movie. Covertly, that's the movie that I was having fun making in my head. So, the *Valentine* sequel is where Josey first appeared in a negative way. And when it looked like that wasn't going to happen, we added that character to *Halloween 3D*. You don't need any extra villains beyond the Shape, so we thought she would be a good, true blue character along with Amy and Goodman.

**Which characters did you most enjoy writing for?**

I really enjoyed Amy, Josey, and Goodman – the three of them. With Tom Atkins' character, it was so much fun to write the Silver Shamrock references and all of that. I think Todd really latched onto all of the asylum girls and their dynamics, but I was very much into the troika of heroes. I thought it was really fun to put them into those circumstances. I loved the sort of obsessive nature of Goodman and the fact that just his name told you everything you needed to know about him. He was a good man! He was trying to do the right thing! You know, it's as subtle as a train wreck. (laughs) And I liked the idea of Amy being sort of complicated. She ends up in a place she shouldn't be, dealing with something she shouldn't have to deal with. And you know, this version of Laurie was interesting. To make somebody so damaged that they were beyond redemption. I felt that was an interesting way to take that character. That's certainly not a way you would go with Jamie Lee Curtis' version of the character but with Scout's version and what Rob had done, it felt like that was a very short trip. We weren't going outside of the box.

**How did you find working with Malek Akkad and Bob Weinstein? Did either offer input?**

Malek was great to work with. Obviously, I met him on *H20* with Moustapha when he was still alive. And Moustapha, I thought was pretty brilliant. He was such a great champion of Michael Myers. He understood what made that character work, why the character was important, why the franchise was important, and what you could and couldn't do. You know, he was a real keeper of that. He was a great caretaker and steward of Michael Myers, and Malek has carried that on. Not only the character but also his father's legacy and I think there's a lot to admire about that. For Bob, it was just about, *'How many killings do you have?'* and *'We don't want this movie to hinge on Laurie Strode,'* so we took care of that.

**Todd mentioned that as he was writing, you and Malek were already in prep on the movie. Which production tasks had you already completed? How close were you to shooting?**

Prior to the shutdown, we had found the primary locations – the hospital, the outside concert area and I believe where we were going to do the opening sequence with the ambulance. We were going to shoot in Shreveport because the whole idea was to shoot in the same place where *Drive Angry* would be shot, so that we could piggyback the prep. A friend of mine, Tom Elkins, was going to cut and edit the film, so he could basically take over the post-production and be cutting in Shreveport while I was in prep on *Drive Angry*. We had a production designer. I want to say Clark Hunter, but I could be wrong about that. We had the first assistant director, and the director of photography Bryan Pearson. Mary McLeod was going to do the wardrobe and design the costumes. Gary Tunnicliffe had already started designing some of the gags and how the kills were going to work. Gary's my special effects make-up person. We've worked together on pretty much everything but one project since *Dracula 2000*.

We had talked to Tom Atkins about playing the doctor. We had talked to Edi Gathegi about playing Goodman. I believe Todd talked to Tyler Mane. I don't think a conversation had been had with Scout yet, but Malek was very confident about talking to her. We hadn't talked to Brad Dourif yet, but I had worked with Brad briefly on the very first thing I ever directed [*The Prophecy 3: The Ascent*] so I didn't feel that was going to be an issue. We talked to the 3D company. I had talked to Michael Wandmacher about doing a score that obviously used the *Halloween* theme but that would later do its own version. Michael and Tyler Bates are friends, so we talked about doing something that encompassed both of what John Carpenter had done and what Tyler had done – especially for the opening sequence, but then creating its own identity later. You know, budgets were done. Accounts were on. We had a shooting schedule. Everybody who read the script was very complimentary. *'Great! Good! We'll do some tweaks as we go. We can make this work.'* So, lots of shit happened!

**You mentioned Edi Gathegi as Goodman. Did you have anybody in mind for Amy or Josey?**

For Amy, we had some great actresses audition for the role of Megan for *My Bloody Valentine* that we considered. We talked to Nancy Nayor about doing the casting as well. Somebody who we wanted for *Valentine* that we didn't get was Sarah Shahi. She auditioned for the part that Jaime King played. We thought she would've been great in this and we wanted her for Josey. We didn't offer it, so this'll come as news to her but that's who we wanted for that part.

**With things moving forward, how did this all come to an end?**

Five weeks out, the script is ready and everybody's like, '*Okay, we're ready to go!*' Then, the heads of the studio go dark. Suddenly, they're not talking to us. It's like, '*What's going on?*' Finally, I get a call on a Tuesday after a long weekend. '*Um, I hate to tell you this, but we don't have the money. We just don't have the money to make it. We don't have the money to shoot it in 3D.*' It would've been an extra $2.5 million to shoot it in 3D. You know, we had already talked to the 3D company. We had it all lined up and it was suddenly, '*We can't put it together.*' I think at the time it would've been $12.5 million. Now, that feels like a gazillion dollars when people are spending either less than $5 million or more than $200 million. (laughs) But they just didn't have it. You know, *Inglorious Basterds* had made money for them, but they had to sell some of the other rights in order to get the movie released. So, they weren't actually pocketing money from that. They had a string of failures and huge overhead that was crippling them. It was a really weird call. '*Yeah, we just can't.*' So, it was like, '*Huh, okay. Well, then.*' Then, we just put all of our energy into *Drive Angry* and went off and did that. But it was disappointing because there's some suspense sequences in there that I'm tremendously proud of and think would've been great. I know Tom Atkins was excited to be getting his head cut off in a fish tank. (laughs)

**Of the set pieces and 3D gags you concocted, did you have any favorites?**

Certainly, Tom Atkins' death. I thought that would've been great fun. And he was so bummed that we didn't get to do that. I loved the sideview mirror gag. I absolutely loved that one because I could just see how that worked and how it was sort of cheeky and sly. '*Objects in mirror are closer than they appear,*' and then getting smashed over and over in the face. Seeing both the killer and the killee (sic) in the same frame. I thought that would've been a really, really fun gag. That – and

I very much liked all of the girls trying to kill the Shape in the cafeteria. I thought that was just a great sort of set piece. And then the ending. The whole cutting off of Laurie's hand and the pumpkin, I liked all of that stuff. And then just the suspense sequences in the hospital. And, of course, Todd's head being thrown at you in 3D would've been cool as well.

**Having worked with Bob Weinstein for over fifteen years, did the events of *Halloween 3D* sour anything between you two?**

Bob and I had a short disagreement about getting paid for the work we had done, but then it all worked out. He called me one day when we were in the middle of shooting *Drive Angry*. I think it was the scene out on the freeway with Nic Cage driving the wrong way through traffic. We were leading Nic in this camera car with a crane on it and my phone is vibrating and it's Bob Weinstein calling. (laughs) And he called up to say, '*Look, I shouldn't have done that. I wanted to thank you. If you get a chance to come back to* [Halloween], *maybe we can come back to it.*' My working relationship with Bob was always reasonably good before, reasonably good after. I think I only worked for Harvey a couple of times and it was never a great experience. I worked for Bob many times and he always treated me... *well*, in terms of his trust in my ability to get the job done. You know, he's a complicated guy. When I first directed for them, I believe Bob's comment was, '*Yeah, we'll kick the shit out of ya,*' and true to their word!

In terms of things that have led to the demise of their company, you always sort of heard rumors about Harvey, but I was never directly involved with him except for via Wes on *Music of the Heart*, which we were cutting in Los Angeles. They tried to send us versions of the film that Harvey had cut with his own editor. I remember Wes taking it, watching the first three minutes, tossing the tape into the garbage, calling him and saying, '*Yeah, we're not even watching it. Fuck off.*' That was a great experience – and then briefly [working with Harvey] on *54*, which I recut for three weeks after *Halloween H20*. The rest of my dealings were with Bob. You know, I got along with Bob. He's a guy who had a lot of creative thoughts, a lot of business thoughts, and they would occasionally be in conflict so one didn't always support the other. Not easy people to work for but at the same time, as a dear friend of mine said, '*They didn't pay you for what you did. They paid you for what they did to you.*'

# HALLOWEEN 3D

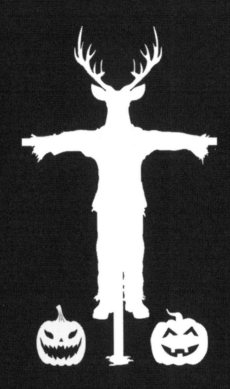

This Halloween, who's hunting who?

**Treatment by
Stef Hutchinson**

While Todd Farmer and Patrick Lussier's *Halloween 3D* died a sudden death in late 2009, there was another iteration of the project that cropped up immediately after. Briefly developed on the Trancas side of things, it would take a different approach to the continuing storyline of the Rob Zombie era. This second take on *Halloween 3D* didn't get nearly as far as the first, but it remains a fascinating "What if?" in the annals of *Halloween*'s lost sequel history. This second draft was championed by writer Stef Hutchinson, a name that many *Halloween* fans will instantly recognize.

Growing up in the United Kingdom, Stef Hutchinson had two passions – horror movies and comic books. His childhood enthusiasm for these mediums would endure through to adulthood where, as a writer, he would combine them to great success. In 2002, he caught wind of the *Halloween Returns to Haddonfield* convention, which was being planned for the following year. He connected with organizer Anthony Masi, who asked if he would be interested in filming the event for posterity. Hutchinson and his crew would capture a gaggle of footage across the weekend, enough to comprise a documentary. This concept soon took flight with Hutchinson pitching Malek Akkad the idea in London later that year. Won over by the pitch, the younger Akkad agreed to help bring the documentary project to life with Hutchinson in the director's chair. Ultimately titled *Halloween: 25 Years of Terror*, the film would land distribution through Anchor Bay Entertainment in July 2006. Reviews from fans and critics alike were overwhelmingly positive. Even still, as co-writer, director, and producer, Hutchinson was disappointed with the documentary's final cut, which he had hoped would be longer and more in-depth. Oddly enough, *25 Years of Terror* would pave the way for much longer horror docs such as *Crystal Lake Memories: The Complete History of Friday the 13th* and *Never Sleep Again: The Elm Street Legacy.*

Hutchinson's involvement with *Halloween Returns to Haddonfield* wasn't solely limited to filmmaking. As a writer, he had long sought to tell stories within the *Halloween* universe through the medium of comics. With the twenty-fifth anniversary celebration, he was finally afforded this opportunity, which resulted in a special one-shot titled *Halloween: One Good Scare*. Released as a convention exclusive, this comic introduced fans to David Loomis, son of the late Sam Loomis, as he explores his father's tragic legacy. The issue was well-received enough to warrant the commissioning of a second one-shot titled *Halloween: Autopsis,* which Anchor Bay packaged with the *25 Years of Terror* DVD release. Set within the *Halloween H20* timeline, *Autopsis* told a self-contained story about a photographer hired to follow Dr. Loomis in hopes of getting a rare photo of the elusive Michael Myers.

Given the success of *One Good Scare* and *Autopsis*, Hutchinson teamed with Devil's Due Publishing to write additional official *Halloween* comics. These included the four-part *Nightdance* series, the *30 Years of Terror* anthology collection, and *The First Death of Laurie Strode* trilogy. He would also publish a pair of official short stories titled *Sam* and *Charlie*. The consensus among critics was clear: Hutchinson might not've been the first person to write *Halloween* comics, but he was certainly among the best to do so. *Dread Central*'s Steve Barton called Hutchinson's work "better than some of the sequels it was leading into." *Bloody-Disgusting*'s Jason Jenkins argued that the first two issues of *The First Death of Laurie Strode* "cemented Hutchinson as one of the better writers the *Halloween* saga has ever had."

## "Stef is responsible for what are arguably the best Halloween and Michael Myers stories told since the original two films."

- Jason Sheppard, TrueHorror.net

Unfortunately, Hutchinson's acclaimed run with Devil's Due Publishing did not end well. The company fell into financial turmoil, which it first blamed on the 2008 economic downturn and later on its distributor. The resulting cashflow problems brought their *Halloween* publications to an abrupt halt. This left the concluding issue of *The First Death of Laurie Strode* trilogy in limbo. Though written and even partially illustrated, this final issue has yet to see release even today, which is a terrible shame given what a powerful conclusion it is to the mini-series. (Fans would be wise to lobby for this comic's release. It's the sequel we deserved but never got.) While Devil's Due is unlikely to ever publish a *Halloween* comic again, Hutchinson continued to collaborate with Malek Akkad at Trancas International Films on various projects. Having heard about the sudden collapse of Farmer and Lussier's *Halloween 3D*, Hutchinson inquired about pitching his own *Halloween III* concept. Akkad responded that he could do so given that his story was compatible with the 3D format. This was the only stipulation placed upon his pitch. The narrative canvas was otherwise blank. Spanning eighteen pages, the resultant treatment was titled *Halloween 3D* and dated November 18, 2009.

## THE STORY

This *Halloween 3D* opens at the Nichols home in Langdon, Illinois on October 27th. Little Bobby has begun to suffer nightmares lately of a terrifying boogeyman. Shortly after being tucked in, he's attacked by an unseen figure in his bedroom. Hearing his scream, Mrs. Nichols wakes to find her husband in bed beside her – his throat slit. Panicked, she runs into the hall and directly into Michael Myers, who kills her. At once, the house is again quiet, the outside world blissfully unaware of the carnage within. The opening credits play overtop footage of a jack-o-lantern in darkness. The background slowly illuminates to reveal an entire field of glowing jack-o-lanterns.

Jumping ahead to October 31st, we find a retired Lee Brackett laying flowers at his daughter's grave. (It's been three years since *Halloween II*, which ended with Loomis and Laurie dying. Michael's body was never recovered.) Brackett now lives in Langdon, a good distance from Haddonfield. We learn he was fired from his job as sheriff when his own officers caught him burning down the Myers house. Being the anniversary of his daughter's death, Haddonfield authorities ask that Langdon's Sheriff Hall check on Brackett. Hall finds the former lawman's home littered with case files related to Michael Myers. Most think Brackett crazy for still hunting his daughter's killer, but not Hall. He somberly asks whether Brackett wants to kill Michael to save lives or to exact revenge, but never gets a response. (Brackett is unaware that Hall has two officers shadowing him today.) Just then, the retired sheriff's teenaged niece, Alice Brackett, arrives with a gift of homemade cookies on this most difficult of days.

A perpetually single bookworm, Alice is the least popular of her social circle. Her best friends include Cassie, a happy-go-lucky seventeen-year-old, and Phoebe, a cheerleader whose boyfriend is a star player on the football team. Tonight is Langdon's first-ever homecoming, which is being commemorated with a parade, fireworks, a football game, and a school dance. As part of a bitter love triangle, Cassie becomes the target of a mean-spirited prank in which her crush plans to seduce her, but only to get nude photos to distribute amongst their peers. Elsewhere, a local hunter finds Brackett using pumpkins for target practice. The two men set off for a local diner, but their truck slams into a large horned whitetail buck. Uneasy over the animal's death,

Brackett leaves the hunter to dispose of the roadkill. Michael Myers appears a moment later and impales the hunter on the buck's antlers. The returned slasher then ventures into town to begin stalking Cassie, even coming face to face with her during the homecoming parade. Hearing news of Cassie's stalker, an unsettled Alice alerts her uncle.

As night falls on Haddonfield, we see Michael in the Nichols home from the opening. Standing over Mrs. Nichols' corpse, he dons his classic white mask in preparation for a night of terror. Brackett, too, is preparing, arming himself with heavily artillery and a photo of Annie. Cassie falls victim to the aforementioned prank during the homecoming game, though Michael kills the prankster soon after. He chases a horrified Cassie back to school where teachers phone Sheriff Hall. Tipped off by Alice, Brackett rushes to the school and begs Cassie to remain in an open space as bait to draw Michael out of the shadows. Hall strongly objects to this, but Cassie agrees and goes to the dance. Michael enters the school soon after, slaughtering Phoebe and the entire cheerleading squad in the girl's locker room. He then crashes the dance by lighting Phoebe's boyfriend on fire and sending him into the crowded gymnasium. This causes a panic while also setting the school ablaze. The final chase boils down to Cassie, Brackett, and Michael. Brackett is forced to choose between saving Cassie's life or ending Michael's. He ultimately chooses to save Cassie, redeeming himself from his self-destructive quest for vengeance. Michael vanishes into the night once more.

Sheriff Hall wonders aloud why Michael didn't kill Brackett when given the chance. The retired sheriff replies that, having already murdered his daughter, "There's nothing else he could do to hurt me." Hall then makes a startling confession. Some time ago, Annie's grave had been dug up in Haddonfield Cemetery. Authorities later found her body and casket on display at Bracket's former home, presumably as revenge for burning down the Myers house. Believing Brackett to be Michael's true target, Hall withheld this information and used him as bait to catch the slasher – similar to how Brackett used Cassie as bait. Arriving home, Brackett notices something unsettling across the street – a scarecrow decoration with the severed head of the whitetail buck from earlier. Brackett rushes into his neighbor's house, which we recognize as the Nichols family home, to find the slaughtered family of three. Written in blood on the wall is a name – "*Alice.*"

With this, Michael's true plan comes into focus. To further hurt Brackett, he would go after someone else he loved – his teenage niece. By slaughtering the Nichols family, he was able to use their home to spy on his nemesis from across the street. (This is where he took notice of Alice.) Michael therefore only pretended to focus on Cassie as a diversion, manipulating the situation to his advantage. With so much focus on Cassie, he was able to isolate his true target. A panicked Brackett phones Alice's home. We see the bodies of her parents in their living room as the phone rings unanswered. Elsewhere in a vacant field, a large bonfire rages amid a sea of glowing jack-o-lanterns. Having been tied to a wood pyre, Alice screams as the flames envelop her. Tilting his head, the Shape watches as she burns to death. He has won.

## WELCOME TO LANGDON

As with Farmer and Lussier's take on *Halloween 3D*, Hutchinson is clearly trying to reign in some of Rob Zombie's more polarizing stylistic choices. For starters, he immediately ditches the remake's portrayal of Illinois as a depraved hillbilly haven. Hutchinson also moves the action from Haddonfield to Langdon, which he sets up as a quaint Anytown, USA. (Langdon is basically what Haddonfield was before Zombie had his way with it. Recall that we last saw Langdon in 1998 with *Halloween H20*'s opening moments.) By switching the focus from Laurie to Brackett, Hutchinson also ditches the psychotic madness that permeated the previous installment. The screenwriter instead grounds his sequel in reality without so much as a nightmare sequence. (Given its continued focus on Laurie, the Farmer/Lussier draft retained some of the madness angle.) We're no longer privy to Michael's hallucinations of his ghostly mother and the white horse, though there's no reason to think he's not still having them. While these choices would mark a huge departure from Zombie's artistic vision, they would've also helped to make the franchise more accessible to mainstream audiences again.

The inherent difficulty in creating a sequel to *Halloween II* is that the film *technically* has two official endings, though they are distinctly different. As theatrically released, Laurie Strode exits the rundown shack, dons her brother's tattered mask, and winds up institutionalized but alive. Per the director's cut ending, which Zombie strongly prefers, Laurie exits the rundown shack, attempts to stab a dying Loomis, and is shot dead by one of Brackett's men. Since it charges that Laurie died, you would naturally assume that Hutchinson's *Halloween 3D* was a sequel to the director's cut, but it is not. This draft was submitted some two months before the director's cut was first released onto home video. It's by sheer coincidence that Hutchinson writes off Laurie Strode as having died. Recall that the previous Farmer/Lussier draft was alternately a sequel to the theatrical cut in which Laurie survived. Despite this discrepancy, both drafts were technically written while Rob Zombie toiled away in the editing room on his preferred version.

With regard to continuity, this *Halloween 3D* is surprisingly versatile in its storytelling, which may well be intentional. There's almost nothing in it that would prevent the filmmakers from casting Charles Cyphers and declaring it a sequel to the original *Halloween*. (It would even fit after *Halloween: Resurrection* without any messy retconnning.) Given its tonal departures and vague continuity, would this *Halloween 3D* have even felt like part of the Zombie timeline? Contingent upon the return of Brad Dourif, Tyler Mane, and the 2007 Myers house, possibly still yes. As a dark character study, this fits in marvelously with the previous two installments. Together, they would've made a fine trilogy. Focusing on Michael, *Halloween 2007* is the horrific tragedy of a boy trying to regain his family. Focusing on Laurie, *Halloween II* is about our inability to escape who we really are. Focusing on Brackett, this *Halloween 3D* is a study in grief and a cautionary tale of revenge. It's all too perfect and a shame the story couldn't have ended this way.

This treatment's opening sequence is interesting for the simple fact that we don't yet know its relevance or if it even has relevance. Why would Michael murder this young boy and his parents? And in Langdon, no less? Is this just a random triple murder to open the story? We're initially unsure. *Season of the Witch* aside, no other *Halloween* has ever opened with such narrative ambiguity. As viewers, we've become accustomed in this series to knowing what's happening most of the time. But our uncertainty here is by design. As a storyteller, Hutchinson withholds certain details that he'll only reveal when the time is right. In the case of the opening murders, we won't know their true relevance until the story's final moments. On a similar note, we're initially unaware the opening titles depict the location of the movie's closing scene. The title sequence's field of glowing jack-o-lanterns is the same one in which Michael later roasts Alice in the bonfire. So, the end is actually the beginning – we just don't realize it the first time around.

Speaking of Hutchinson's writing style, he's every bit as conniving as the characters he writes. In his *Halloween 3D*, we're really only privy to Brackett's plan, which involves using Cassie as bait to lure Michael out into the open. Unbeknownst to Brackett and the audience, Sheriff Hall also has a plan, which involves using Brackett as bait. Further unbeknownst to anyone, Michael has his own plan, which involves targeting Alice as a way to hurt Brackett. None of this is evident until the finale, however. Hutchinson likes to play his cards close to his chest, which is an effective way to keep the viewer engaged with the story. We're constantly left wondering what everyone's true agenda might be.

With *Halloween 3D*, Hutchinson makes welcome reference to the ancient festival of Samhain, which is something the franchise has not done since 1995's *Halloween: The Curse of Michael Myers*. This reference comes during a montage sequence as the sun sets on Halloween night. We overhear Cassie's father telling her little brother a story about the holiday's origins. His words play overtop images of Michael and Brackett preparing for a night of mayhem, each in their own way. These words faintly echo those of Conal Cochran in *Halloween III*. (Recall that Dr. Loomis made similar comments in the Kenney/Medina draft of *Halloween 4*.)

**Cassie's Dad in *Halloween 3D*:**

*"During the witching hour, the walls break down. The gap between the spirit world and what we see as real becomes as thin as a veil. And some people... some monsters... see right through to the other side."*

***Conal Cochran in Halloween III:***

*"The barriers would be down, you see, between the real and the unreal, and the dead might be looking in...to sit by our fires of turf. Halloween...the festival of Samhain!"*

Given that *Halloween 3D* was poised to become the franchise's first three-dimensional installment, it should come as no surprise that Hutchinson packs plenty of spectacle into his story. The kills are as numerous as they are inventive. In one scene guaranteed to secure a hard R-rating, Michael slashes through an entire locker room full of cheerleaders. This is but a tease of an even bigger set piece when he later crashes the dance by sending a flaming victim into a crowd of people. The ensuing panic is so great that no one seems to notice (or care) that Michael himself strides into the crowd after Cassie. With an entrance framed by the mouth of a giant pumpkin, Langdon's homecoming dance would no doubt make for a terrific 3D visual – especially as it burns down around the heroes during the finale.

When it comes to *Halloween* films, you never know how they're going to end. Sometimes the endings are happy, sometimes they're not. Sometimes the heroes prevail and it's still an unhappy ending. And there's always the strong chance that the next sequel is going to undo whatever has just been done. Even so, *Halloween 3D*'s ending is a dark one. Anyone familiar with Hutchinson's work in the franchise knows he likes an ending where evil triumphs and this is exactly what happens in *Halloween 3D*. Not only does Michael escape relatively unscathed, but he successfully enacts his murderous plan. By story's end, he's left a long trail of bodies leading up to Alice Brackett, whose death is slow and agonizing. If there remained any part of Brackett left to break, it's surely now broken. Evil has solidly defeated good. An ending this bleak feels right at home in the Rob Zombie timeline.

## A BROKEN HERO

The final moments of *Halloween 2007* found Sheriff Brackett in a rough spot having just discovered his only daughter in a pool of her own blood. She'd been attacked by a killer whose recent escape he hadn't taken seriously enough, at least not at first. The character would fare even worse in the final moments of *Halloween II*. It's here Brackett not only loses his daughter to the same killer, but also the surrogate daughter he took in after the first film. (Having orchestrated Laurie's secret adoption as an infant, he'd come to feel responsible for her well-being.) With these devastating losses, Brackett is now a thoroughly broken man. His pain is made worse by the fact that Michael's body was never recovered after *Halloween II*, which strongly suggests that he escaped. This is where we find the character in *Halloween 3D*.

At the outset of this new story, we learn that Brackett is no longer sheriff or even residing in Haddonfield and for good reason. Sometime after the events of *Halloween II*, he brazenly set fire to the old Myers house and stood out front in full uniform to watch it burn. Having committed third-degree arson in a residential neighborhood, he's soon fired from his job as sheriff. Now looked upon as a threat to the community he once served, Brackett relocates to Langdon. His only hope for any measure of closure is to find and destroy his daughter's killer. His new Halloween tradition involves walking the streets of Haddonfield with a loaded gun, which cannot possibly help his public image.

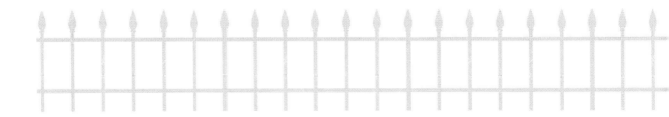

**Brackett:** *It's not... It's not like today is worse than the others. I don't miss her any more because it's this day. I miss her every single day and each one hurts the same. He stole her from me, ripped the only sunshine I had right out of the sky and... there's no making peace with that. I want her back, Alice. I want her back. A father shouldn't bury his daughter – that's not how it's supposed to be and it can't ever be made right. This day - Halloween – is different, but not because I remember what happened any less. It's the day I get to be selfish – the day it's about my pain as much as her loss. The day I want to get out there and find him and destroy him and kill him and – yep. The day I get to be selfish. Anything to make it hurt less. Just for myself – just for a moment. I don't know what sort of person that makes me.*

Make no mistake, this *Halloween 3D* would've absolutely rested upon the shoulders of Brad Dourif's performance as Lee Brackett. The actor's wrenching portrayal of the character in *Halloween II* was among the strongest of his long and varied career. Hutchinson demonstrates a strong grasp of the role and does great things with it. One early scene would've found an emotional Brackett standing over his daughter's grave in Haddonfield Cemetery. He speaks to her as though she were still alive in a haunting portrait of a still grieving father. Again, this film would've been Dourif's to dominate. Without him, it just could not have gone forward as written.

Langdon's Sheriff Hall makes for a solid counterweight to Brackett in this story. Professionally, the two men are kindred spirits. Hall is deeply concerned at the appearance of his friend's home, which is littered with Myers-related articles and case files. He's

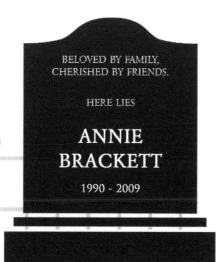

BELOVED BY FAMILY,
CHERISHED BY FRIENDS.

HERE LIES

**ANNIE
BRACKETT**

1990 - 2009

quite worried – not that Brackett is wrong and wasting his time, but that he may be right and Michael is still out there. Hall challenges Brackett to look inside and question what's driving him to hunt Michael Myers – is it concern for others or revenge? The answer is initially revenge, which is why he burnt down the slasher's childhood home. Tragically, it's this grave misstep that lures Michael out of retirement, meaning Brackett now has a lot of blood on his hands. This seems to be *Halloween 3D*'s central message, that revenge is but a terrible stop on the road to self-destruction. Brackett does eventually redeem himself, but it's far too late.

Hutchinson would later change Sheriff Hall to Sheriff Harry Brackett, Lee's older brother. This would lead to a dynamic shift in how the two characters interacted. Lee would have left Haddonfield to stay with his brother in Langdon, though it's a tense living situation. In one re-written scene, Harry would come home to find Lee firing off illegal weapons in the backyard. ("People are scared of you, they think you're dangerous. I spend half my days telling people otherwise and here you are firing a nuke in my backyard!")

## THE NEXT GENERATION

The Rob Zombie *Halloween* films were, if nothing else, extremely unconventional entries in the series. His 2007 remake was largely a prequel set inside a depraved sanitarium. Its 2009 follow-up revisited the surviving cast for a close-up look at the horrors of post-traumatic stress. The main story of Hutchinson's *Halloween 3D* – a grieving father hellbent on revenge – is equally unconventional for a *Halloween*. It's the treatment's secondary story about a group of high-schoolers preparing for a Halloween dance that feels like a throwback to earlier films. Given all the bold new directions, this old school-style plotline is a welcome inclusion.

The story's younger lead is Cassie Morgan, a perfectly likable and seemingly well-adjusted seventeen-year-old at Langdon High. Michael begins stalking Cassie early on Halloween day, which she takes notice of. They eventually come face-to-face at the homecoming parade, though Michael is wearing an alternate mask presumably so as not to alarm. As if these sightings weren't unsettling enough, Cassie and Alice return home from school to find a ladder propped outside the former's bedroom window. While initially scared, she's soon distracted by a visit from her crush. Alice remains spooked, however, and phones her uncle. He urges her to remain calm to keep from needlessly upsetting her friend.

As already mentioned, Cassie will become the victim of a cruel prank this night. While carried out by her crush, this prank was fiendishly conceived by head cheerleader Suzie. A truly awful type, Hutchinson gives the teenaged bully her comeuppance twice in his story. The first occurs when Michael chases Cassie back to Langdon High after her crush's murder. Encountering Suzie outside the dance, Cassie delivers an incredibly satisfying and well-deserved right hook, which bloodies the girl's nose. Suzie will later be among those slaughtered in the girl's locker room as the dance starts. As Hutchinson writes it, "she receives a fate far more graphic than the rest!"

Cassie's best friends include the socially awkward Alice and peppy cheerleader Phoebe. If that trio reminds you of Annie/Laurie/Lynda from the original *Halloween*, it's because they're quite similar. (In all likelihood, they're a direct homage.) The teens' interactions are fairly ordinary, a far cry from the foul-mouthed Annie/Laurie/Lynda of *Halloween 2007*. Further like *Halloween*'s original gal trio, only one of these ladies will survive the coming night. Surprisingly, it's not the virginal Alice in a twist that would likely confound final girl scholars. As this story's Laurie Strode archetype, we assume her to be safe. But Hutchinson isn't about to let us feel confident in our preconceived notions.

## THE GHOST OF HALLOWEEN PAST

Set three years after the events of *Halloween II*, Hutchinson's story never directly addresses how Michael survived the sniper bullet he took in that film's ending, nor how he escaped past the police that surrounded his location. This is really no different than how *Halloween II* dealt with *Halloween 2007*'s ending. We're never told how Michael cheats death, only that he does time and time again. The Farmer/Lussier draft of *Halloween 3D* pulled this same move, so fair enough. Suspension of disbelief has always been part of the cost of enjoying these movies. Simply put, Michael is back in action at this story's beginning, explanation be damned.

Like the previous draft of *Halloween 3D*, Hutchinson immediately seeks to reset the slasher's aesthetic back to something more familiar. Recall that Rob Zombie had controversially devolved Michael's look into a hobo-esque *Phantom of the Opera* in the previous film. In this story, Michael sports a fresh set of overalls and a brand-new white mask. Oddly enough, it's the unsolved murders behind these new duds that first lead Brackett to believe his nemesis has returned. (A murdered gas station attendant without his uniform and a costume shop owner killed during a break-in/robbery.) In a unique touch, we also see Michael briefly wearing a clown mask that he steals from Cassie's home. Aside from being just plain creepy, this alternate mask allows him to attend the homecoming parade without completely freaking everyone out.

The character's return in *Halloween 3D* brings to mind a recurrent question – what draws Michael out of retirement on certain years and not others? Is it learning a relative's whereabouts (*Halloween 4* & *H20*), the alignment of the stars (*Halloween 6*), or is it – in the case of *H3D* – revenge for the destruction of his family home? This last motivation is interesting since, up until this proposed installment, Zombie's Michael hadn't demonstrated the same level of fondness for the homestead as Carpenter's Shape had. Sure, the slasher went home in *Halloween 2007*, but not in its 2009 sequel. In actuality, this was due to last-minute budget cuts and not Zombie's preferred vision. As first written, Michael was to return home in *Halloween II* to find two police officers waiting, whom he'd quickly dispatch. In Hutchinson's story, Michael seems fond enough of the old fort to bitterly avenge its fiery destruction. This begs the question – had Brackett not set fire to the Myers house, would this have been just another uneventful Halloween?

Hutchinson's take on the slasher closely aligns with what we already know of the character. This Michael is ruthless, relentless, and incredibly violent. He's also a schemer who enjoys leaving macabre displays to strike fear into those who would find them. (In *Halloween 3D*, Michael poses the bodies of three dead cheerleaders on the homecoming throne, which is unveiled at the dance to everyone's horror.) He's seemingly also without fear as evidenced by a scene near story's end. As the dance erupts into chaos, Brackett points his gun directly at the slasher. Michael immediately grabs the nearby homecoming queen as though she were a human shield – but that's not his intention. He instead slits her throat right in front of Brackett, as if to taunt him. As if to say, "You can't possibly stop me." Knowing the girl will succumb to her injury, Brackett fires his gun through her body in order to strike Michael, who charges at him. Slamming Brackett to the floor, Michael has a perfect opportunity to kill him in this moment – but that's also not his intention.

With his *Halloween 3D* treatment, Hutchinson breaks one of Rob Zombie's most steadfast rules with the character by allowing him to drive. Zombie had been a vocal critic of the Shape's driving abilities in the original *Halloween*, one of several changes he made in his 2007 remake. The rocker-turned-filmmaker argued that his Michael – having been incarcerated since the age of ten – would be unable to operate any motor vehicle. He upheld this rule in the remake's 2009 sequel. Hutchinson, however, restores the character's driving privileges by having him chase Cassie through darkened woods in a stolen vehicle. (This sequence has strong *Halloween 5* vibes.)

Michael toys with his prey by never actually running her over, just repeatedly slamming into her and knocking her to the ground. For a guy who's never been to driving school, Michael is apparently a decent stunt driver.

In a scene set before the car chase, Cassie's crush wanders further into the woods to review the pictures he just snapped of their lovemaking. Flipping through the images, he begins to notice a strange shape behind Cassie in the darkness. By the time he realizes they're not alone, Michael is already beating him to death with a large tree branch. Deafening fireworks from the nearby homecoming game drown out his screams. Picking up the dropped cell phone, Michael snaps a picture of the boy's bloodied face and sends it to Suzie, the one who put him up to the cruel prank. (Forget how Michael learned to drive, who in the hell taught him to use a smart phone!?)

## WHY IT WASN'T MADE

There were essentially two reasons why this *Halloween 3D* died in development. First, Hutchinson was never all that enamored with his pitch. While he received positive feedback from Malek Akkad, he declined to pursue the gig further due to his own reservations. Part of that owed to the incongruity of writing a bleak tale of revenge that was also supposed to be in 3D. Having to create dark character moments for Brad Dourif's Sheriff Brackett while also figuring out things to throw at the camera never felt quite right for the screenwriter. As such, he moved onto other projects.

(Hutchinson has a valid point here. This darkly serious material just was not a good tonal fit for the 3D format. Contrast it with 2009's *My Bloody Valentine 3D*, which billed itself as a "date movie" in advertising materials. A "date movie," Hutchinson's *Halloween 3D* was definitely not.)

The second reason this draft never moved forward was that The Weinstein Company was still flat broke. This was, after all, mere weeks after Todd Farmer and Patrick Lussier's version had fallen apart. The Weinsteins were still in no place to fund a new *Halloween*, much less a 3D one.

## "The treatment itself never felt quite right – there was the sense that something was missing, or that some elements didn't line up with each other."

- Stef Hutchinson

# STEF HUTCHINSON
## Writer - Halloween 3D

Interviewed by Dustin McNeill

**What were your impressions of Rob Zombie's *Halloween* and *Halloween II*?**

I was not a fan of his *Halloween*. We'd interviewed Rob a few years prior for *25 Years of Terror*, and he clearly understood what made *Halloween* tick, so I couldn't get my head around the approach he took. But that's the problem with any franchise like this – we all have our own ideas of what it should be and what works the best. I thought the whole notion of delving into Michael's past missed the point completely although, admittedly, that material was the best part of the film. The problem is, you can't reconcile that with the traditional *Halloween* of the second half as, by contrast, it didn't deviate *enough* from the source. And do we really need a graphic rape in the middle of a *Halloween* movie?

That being said, I *loved* his *Halloween II*. Rob's *Halloween II* was exactly the sort of film I'd hoped we were going to get the first time around. It was visually exciting, visceral, surreal, and ambitious in a way we hadn't seen in the series. It was unashamedly artistic and beautiful. And it was character-driven, too. It dealt heavily with the ugly repercussions of trauma, which is something that is a thread through all the *Halloween* comics I've written – the question of where these characters are 'the morning after'. The performances, too, are bold and fearless – stripped away from the remake structure of the first film. Tyler Mane's Michael is genuinely terrifying.

I didn't like everything about it – the 'mother' angle is already a core element of *Psycho* and *Friday the 13th* and adding it here felt distracting, although it did fit with Rob's more human take on Michael. I think what hurt this film more than anything was the reception to Rob's first film. That was a huge hit, but I don't think all of the *Halloween* audience wanted a world as ugly as the one presented within that, so they didn't come back for the sequel.

Both of his films take a lot of flak, but I believe *Halloween II* is going to be like 1982's *Halloween III*. As we know, that film wasn't respected at the time at all, but has grown in stature as people have learned to take it on its own terms. I hope and expect the same will be true of Rob's *Halloween II*, as it's a genuine high point of the franchise as a whole.

**Was the decision to drop Laurie and Loomis your own or did you have instruction to do so?**

Completely my own. I asked about pitching, and the only criteria to adhere to was the then omnipresent 3D hook. I don't think it's a good idea to bring a character back purely for the sake of it. At the ending of *Halloween II*, I think it's pretty fair to say that the storylines for both Laurie and Loomis are done. To bring either back would undermine the tragedy and boldness of that ending (I'm going with the Director's Cut as the definitive take here). I'd be forcing a narrative onto them for no good reason – either distorting the characterization or repeating what we've already seen, while diluting another creator's work.

You could easily say that about bringing back Michael Myers, but that's something you have to accept as part of any *Halloween*, for the most part. In the remake and its sequel, however, Myers has clearer motivations than in the original films, so I had to consider that in the writing.

Sheriff Brackett, to me, was the character left at the ending with a bunch of potential. Where does he go after losing his daughter – how does he process that pain? And how does that align – or collide – with the story of Michael Myers? What became clear was that this was a story of grief – and how being unable to deal with that shadow of loss would lead to a consuming desire for revenge.

**You drop some of the remake's more controversial choices, notably Michael's hallucinations, his homelessness, and the white trash vibe. How intentional were these changes?**

All of this was fully intentional. In regards to the 'white trash' element being sidelined, I didn't think I could write it convincingly without it coming off as parody. There was also a commercial consideration, too. Mainly though, it was a creative call. In the original 1978 film, the Shape is, in every way, a violation. He isn't simply a product of his environment – he goes *against* it. This isn't just a narrative concern but a stylistic one. We see this from a cinematic perspective when he intrudes into the frame with a sudden jolt, or hovers in the periphery of the audience's vision, creating that constant unease.

The Haddonfield we are presented with in 1978 feels mythical and antiquated even by the standards of its day (the use of "Mr. Sandman" in the sequel only accentuates this pseudo-1950s feel of suburban 'innocence'). As far as we know, the Myers family background is as wholesome as it could be. A little boy simply slaughtered his sister on a Halloween night, and it's something that horrified and scarred a whole town. This is important – and it needs that contrast between event and environment to work. It's something evil in an idyllic place.

With the remake, Michael Myers (who definitely is NOT The Shape here – he's too defined a character to be that) is the product of a horrifically mean-spirited landscape. It's no real surprise that he becomes a murderer – it's the logical outcome in many ways. He's very much a part of his world, so there's no real sense of either intrusion or anything uncanny. Shifting the location from Haddonfield to another small town allowed me to try and recreate that sense of small-town naiveté, and of something abhorrent walking behind its homes and gardens.

In regards to the hallucinations, they're unique to Rob's take and thus intrinsically related to Myers' motivations in his films. When you step away from the family side of the narrative, they lose a lot of their relevance. Again, a lot of this comes down to what your individual take on the character is or isn't. I've always been vehemently opposed to giving the character too much relatable back-story. I like the information to remain minimal, and when not that, abstract and evocative rather than literal. For example, in the 1978 original, we see that Loomis – a psychiatrist – has rejected all of his medical training and knowledge to denounce Myers as '*purely and simply evil*'. It's a simple and brilliant statement.

What has he done that we know of? He's stared at a wall for fifteen years. He's given away *nothing*. And this is perfect – true evil should remain unknowable, other than through its actions.

I know there's takes on the 1978 mythology out there (in the Chaos! comics and the original novelization) that have Myers killing other people in Smith's Grove, but to me, this is reductive.

Bringing it back to my treatment, I ultimately felt it best to remain outside Myers again, particularly if I was going to bring elements of the Shape into the story. I wanted to remove any sympathy we may have remaining from Rob's portrayal, but not without acknowledging where we're coming from. It's a transitional story in many ways. This Myers has motivations that we may initially relate to – the burning down of his home and sacred memories – but the story ends in a place where he is utterly monstrous and irredeemable.

**Did you want this to be in 3D or was that something mandated by Trancas/Miramax?**

It wasn't my intention to pitch a 3D film at all. At the time, I was working with Malek Akkad on a separate project entirely, not *Halloween* – or horror – related. The planned *Halloween 3D* (by Todd Farmer and Patrick Lussier) had hit some walls within Dimension, so after a while, I asked if I could pitch something. I had the core concepts and tone of the story in mind.

The 3D aspect was still locked in place even though the studio had pulled back from the previous script. It was not something I was ever a fan of or had any interest in myself. I've always found the *Halloween* series to be the darkest and most esoteric of the slasher franchises, and felt the 3D gimmick would be a distraction (especially when watched back later on a 2D screen!). In this case, it felt even more jarring to go this route following the darkness of *Halloween II*.

I tried to emphasize a few moments organically, but they were considered in terms of the depth of the image – looking inwards, rather than shit flying out at you at every opportunity. The stalking sequence at the parade is an obvious example, particularly as we move through the costumed crowd. There's a scene where Michael Myers stood on a tree-lined slope, silhouetted against a backdrop of exploding fireworks, that I think could have looked fantastic. There's another moment when one character, set alight by Myers, runs screaming out of the mouth of a giant jack o'lantern and into a crowd of trapped onlookers. I swiped that one from my first ever attempt at a *Halloween* pitch (*Halloween Legacy*, way back in 2003), because it might have had a strong visual punch to it in 3D. However, despite those moments, I couldn't get to that synthesis of what I wanted to write, and what this would have needed to be for those making it. That's the biggest failure of this treatment.

My treatment was quite dark, and focused heavily on character, whereas I feel that 3D films, in general, are more crowd-pleasing, popcorn affairs. The only people who should have been doing a 3D *Halloween* film were Farmer and Lussier. That was key to the foundations of their pitch (whereas it was something arbitrary and 'stuck on' to subsequent ones), and something they'd been trailblazing in the films that led them to this.

**Your story is a direct sequel to Rob Zombie's *Halloween II*, but it could also pretty easily be a sequel to the original *Halloween II* as well. You wouldn't even have to change that much, really. Was that by design or just coincidence?**

This was a deliberate attempt to make it more accessible, but it was more related to the character at the core of my treatment. The only really specific difference is that Laurie and Loomis are explicitly dead where my *Halloween 3D* begins, which you could still take as an outcome from the original *Halloween II* (made easier with the idea that Laurie faked her death). The starting point of my treatment is a character thread from both versions of the film, and that's the aftermath of Halloween night for Sheriff Brackett. He's shamefully dumped from the original *Halloween II* storyline at the point he's about to get *really* interesting. I went back to that portrayal several times in the comics with the intention of following the fall-out all the way through. This would have culminated in a story set on a very cold and snowy day.

Here in *Halloween 3D*, the imagery was the opposite of that. Brad Dourif portrayed a very different Sheriff Brackett than Charles Cyphers, so their paths and fates would inevitably differ. Despite being different characters, however, they each leave their own *Halloween II* in the same place – dealing with the loss of their daughter, Annie.

**Brad Dourif would've had some incredible moments to shine in your *Halloween 3D*. What were your thoughts on his role and performances in *Halloween* and *Halloween II*?**

He was great in the first film but didn't really get too much to do. However, in *Halloween II*, he's phenomenal throughout. He's the heart of that film for me, and his scenes towards the end are the most memorable. The moments in which we fade from his silent grief to the dreamlike shots of Laurie running through the woods are transcendent.

Brad Dourif is a wonderful, captivating actor who can do anything, but we don't always get to see him in roles that allow this. He can convey so much with a single expression, and throughout the film, we see many facets to his character. His warmth as an aging father, out of his depth with the emotional situation he's found himself in, adds so much impact to how it feels when he loses his daughter.

When I'm writing a treatment, I usually write a few 'test scenes' to get a feel for the character, and to find the tone I want. Doing that here was a joy – visualizing Dourif in the role would push me to write the quality of material that he deserved, and I could do that by either giving him the best dialogue I'd be capable of, or leaving everything to be told just by his gestures. It made me very confident that this story could work.

**Your treatment is very cleverly composed. You strategically withhold certain details until the end and there's a twist – that Michael was actually after Alice Brackett. Tell me about your approach to storytelling here.**

You're essentially stuck with a specific formula for these stories, at least in terms of how they unfold. If you deviate too far from that, the audience generally freaks out (and if you put a white horse in there, they shit their pants in confused rage). It's a bit of a trap, really. In this case, a lot of the construction is based on how I could – hopefully – still surprise people while working within those constraints. So, a lot of the approach there comes from providing those elements that are expected, but also attempting to recontextualize them so they pay off in different ways. We follow Myers as he stalks Cassie, but she's ultimately a distraction as he knows he is being hunted by Brackett. Similarly, the opening stands on its own as a traditional *Halloween* set-piece, but takes on a new importance when we find out the actual location it took place in.

Additionally, there's a problem with ending ANY *Halloween* story – and that's the 1978 original. *That* ending is perfect in every way and I can't throw enough praise upon it. Unfortunately, it means you're always working in the shadow of perfection (you can say that about the whole film.) There's unison of narrative and cinematic technique throughout, and the ending encapsulates this perfectly. Throughout the film, we're aware of the Shape by his absence as much as his presence – there are empty voids throughout the Haddonfield backdrops. When Loomis looks over the balcony to where the Shape's body should be, it's again this sense of absence that is terrifying. The simple act of him not being *there* means he could be *anywhere*.

We then see the locations where the Shape has been. Again, he's not there, but his stain remains. The breathing dominates the soundtrack, and the Shape thus becomes the dominant force of the film. He may not have killed Laurie, but it doesn't matter – the damage is done, and the Shape is in control of the narrative. He's not just a person anymore, but an abstract force. So, that's what I was going for here in a lot of ways. I wouldn't try and repeat the original in a literal sense, but I wanted to capture at least the subtext and implication.

Sheriff Brackett's story in this is about pain and grief being purged through revenge. We've all been wronged by someone at some point (hopefully not to the extent Brackett has) and we have a choice in how we deal with that. Brackett burns down the Myers house, and this seems like *his* story. He's hunting Myers right from the start, and he's even a few steps ahead of the local authorities – he's seemingly driving the narrative.

Brackett finds himself in a place where he can have his vengeance, or he can save a life. And he makes the right choice. Normally, this would be the happy moral resolution we see in revenge tales – the character chooses to save somebody, and possibly saves himself by doing so. Not here. Myers' actions at the end completely undermine all of Brackett's growth. It's very nihilistic in this way. While it seems we've been following Brackett's hunt, we've actually been following a different storyline, one in which Myers is completely in control – right from the opening scenes. It's just

that Brackett doesn't realize this until it's far too late (and I hope that would be the same for the audience). It also plays into the 'trick or treat' game playing of the Myers character that we really don't see enough of. We end, as in the original, with Myers asserting dominance.

Alice is, for all intents and purposes, a surrogate Annie. She's a warmer character, too, more open and articulate with emotion. In some ways, Brackett has a chance to be a father again, and the test scenes I wrote mostly surrounded the closeness of their growing relationship. It was his desire for revenge that started this story, however, and it's that spark that leads to the fire at the end. Brackett could have pursued a new life instead, but he didn't. His actions have led to the death of his 'daughter' all over again.

**Farmer and Lussier's *Halloween 3D* fell apart because The Weinstein Company was out of funds. Being written so soon after theirs fell apart, it would seem that yours fell victim to the same problem. Did you ever get a reason for your script not moving forward?**

I knew there had been a back and forth regarding the budget of the film, with Dimension being reluctant to spend what was needed. Beyond that, I was completely in the dark. I've never really been privy to such things. It was surprising that it did get canceled, given that it was just about to go into production. The reason for my pitch not moving forward, ultimately, is me. That's not to say that if I'd pushed it further it would have actually happened, though. Unlike the other writers featured in this book, I don't have the film credits behind me for there to be any weight behind what I submit.

The treatment itself never felt quite right to me – there was the sense that something was missing, or that some elements didn't line up with each other. It was on an instinctual level, I guess, because initially I couldn't put my finger on it. I'd sent the outline over to Malek and he really liked it, which encouraged me to continue. I took my test pages, and started writing the script itself. Everything *seemed* to be working – the opening scene was strong and scary, Brackett and Alice were a joy to write, as was Cassie…

One of the notes I received was to highlight the 3D moments throughout the script. Literally make them **bold** – so some studio exec somewhere could simply look at the pages without reading and count the gimmicks. That sounds like parody, but it's not. And it was doing that which made me realize what was wrong. My story was darker in feel, and it just wasn't meshing with what a 3D crowd-pleaser needed to be. I'd be writing an introspective character moment, and all that would be going through my head would be the popcorn and yo-yo from *Friday the 13th Part III* and it was making me fucking nauseous. So, at that point, I just left it alone. I just knew inside that I couldn't write something specifically driven by the tonal needs of the 3D format. At least not a *Halloween* film.

**Unlike nearly every other writer featured in this book, you actually did get to drive the *Halloween* story forward via the comics. I know those came with their own challenges and frustrations, but how do you overall look back on your work there?**

I look back on my work there with happiness for the comics themselves, and deep sadness at their lack of completion. The books that came out comprised about the first third of the storyline I had mapped out. We had a long way to go, with some really interesting – and *scary* – tales that would lead to a big emotional climax that would take in the history of all the characters from 1963 to the present day. The working title for the whole storyline, and the very final issue of the final series, was *Black Rose*. The unreleased (yet completed) final issue of *The First Death of Laurie Strode* solidified all the key themes and started to draw together the ideas that had been in the background right from *One Good Scare.*

There are a few minor things I'm not happy with – a couple of lines of beginner's dialogue in *One Good Scare,* and the first issue of *Nightdance,* which got tweaked by the publisher and was also overwritten on my part. Other than that, I unashamedly love those stories. Writing them was a great experience. Prior to these, I'd directed *25 Years of Terror,* and I wasn't completely happy with how that turned out. It was compromised. It's uneven, and it became more superficial as we went on - the frustration of that likely colored my view of it for a long time. It's good, don't get me wrong, and I think it's somewhat important, particularly as a gateway to the horror documentaries that followed in its wake. But it's better on a conceptual level than an actualized one, I guess.

With the comics, I had full control of the stories. I know they are not for all tastes – for everyone who praises them, there's a bearded YouTube man telling the world how shitty they are – but at least the mistakes and stumbles are all my own and I can defend or apologize for them accordingly! Even with a decade of hindsight, there's very little I'd change.

Malek was exceptionally supportive and a pleasure to work with on these, backing me up when it came to dealing with the publisher, too. I had great editors and a wonderful group of artists to collaborate with. Everyone along the way had the same goal – making these stories the best they could be, and it's rare you get that.

Those stories could never have been told on film. They're driven by damaged and lonely characters, but are more fatalistic there than the films are. Can you imagine pitching *Nightdance* to a studio? '*So, there's a girl afraid of the dark, and she imagines herself as a ballerina…*' They would have been demolished along the way. Here, I got to tell the stories I wanted to exactly *how* I wanted to.  I got to approach it differently, too – I could think several stories ahead, and think beyond the commercial pressures. There was time and space to explore the psychological impact of the characters beyond the immediate scares and suspense, which is how the whole *Black Rose* storyline originated. I would think about where the themes and characters would go and where they would intersect (or wouldn't) with others and how this would coagulate into one singular saga. If you look at the books, you can start to see the ideas develop throughout. The black rose image itself appears in a very literal fashion in several of the released episodes. There are hints as to the character it represents scattered throughout, and it's the character who would become the comic's own 'final girl'. It's frustrating that I never got to share the conclusion.

I saw *Halloween* when I was very young, and it's impossible to overstate the impact it had on me. In creating the comics, using characters that I couldn't put on the screen, such as Donald Pleasence's Loomis, or Jamie Lee Curtis' teenage Laurie Strode, I got to tap into a lifetime of ideas. And in writing the Shape, I would recall how utterly terrified I was when I first saw *Halloween*. I wrote him as he appeared to me in John Carpenter's masterpiece: merciless, sadistic, cruel and relentless – a shadowy abstraction of pure evil, and a terrifying embodiment of abject horror. I didn't want him to be someone an audience would cheer for, like in the later sequels.

So, I'll be forever grateful I got to do that. And even though the subsequent stories were never released (those being *The Mark of Thorn, Fate Never Changes, The Babysitter Murders, Valley of Shadows, The Frozen Ghost* and *The Last Harvest*), they do sit on my hard drive and live on in my head, happily ever after.

# HALLOWEEN 3.0

Forget what you THINK you know.

**Treatment by**
**Todd Farmer & Patrick Lussier**

When we last spoke of Todd Farmer and Patrick Lussier, their *Halloween 3D* had fallen apart just weeks before cameras were set to roll in October 2009. The sequel production had been canned over serious issues related to its budget. In short, The Weinstein Company had recently suffered a string of box office bombs and was now too broke to fund a new *Halloween*. While extremely frustrated, Farmer and Lussier didn't have long to dwell on the project's sudden collapse. Lussier was set to begin directing *Drive Angry* in January 2010 on location in Shreveport, Louisiana from a script he'd co-written with Farmer. This Lionsgate-backed action film was set to star Nicolas Cage and had a rumored budget of $50 million, which was more than the last three *Halloween* movies combined. Like *My Bloody Valentine* and their abandoned *Halloween* before it, *Drive Angry* was slated to shoot in 3D and would feature Tom Atkins in a supporting role.

An unabashed grindhouse-action flick, *Drive Angry* roared into theaters on February 25, 2011 but sadly failed to find its audience. Despite being in 3D, the project opened ninth at the box office and garnered a worldwide gross that fell short of its production budget. (It would fare slightly better on home video.) Yet reviews were surprisingly strong for a film of this type with Elizabeth Weitzman of *New York Daily News* claiming "[*Drive Angry*] is so committed to its own junkiness that it is, in its way, a pleasure to behold." Even the grindhouse-averse Roger Ebert found something nice to say about it. While he didn't entirely like it, he did "appreciate it" as "well made," noting that *Drive Angry* was "so jaw-droppingly excessive that even Quentin Tarantino might send flowers." *Bloody-Disgusting*'s John Squires would later hail it a "bona fide cult classic."

Following their work on *Drive Angry*, Farmer and Lussier continued developing genre projects for The Weinstein Company. Together, they formulated several pitches for a potential *Hellraiser* reboot aimed at elevating Pinhead and his cronies out of the direct-to-video market and back onto theater screens. True to their reputation, the Weinsteins were unable to settle on a direction for the failing franchise. Such chronic indecision would nearly cost them the property. Having failed to commit to a theatrical reboot, the company now faced a contractual ultimatum – immediately produce a new *Hellraiser* film or risk losing the rights altogether. In response to this, the Weinsteins rushed a slapdash effort into production titled *Hellraiser: Revelations*. Filmed on a microbudget across two weeks in September of 2011, the project would draw sharp rebukes from series creator Clive Barker and original Pinhead actor Doug Bradley, who declined to reprise his iconic role for the first time in series history. The resultant film was, by all accounts, an unparalleled disaster even by *Hellraiser* standards.

(We should note that *Hellraiser: Revelations* ought to serve as a cautionary tale for how badly studios can plunder and ruin once great horror franchises. Were it not for Trancas International running quality control, the *Halloween* series could've very easily suffered a similar fate at the hands of the Weinsteins.)

Having successfully preserved their stake in the *Hellraiser* franchise, The Weinstein Company now turned its attention back to *Halloween*. On June 17, 2011, it was officially announced that the series' eleventh film had been slated for an October 2012 release. While this may have seemed premature given the project's already long-gestating yet fruitless development, it was still achievable. The studio would've simply needed to act fast. By this point, two years had passed since the controversial release of Rob Zombie's *Halloween II*. In January of the previous year, the studio released an unrated director's cut of the sequel that featured a radically different ending in which Laurie, Loomis, and Michael all unequivocally die. While not released theatrically, this director's cut quickly became the most widely circulated version of the sequel on home video. In fact, the studio withheld the theatrical version of *Halloween II* from Blu-ray for several years in an effort to push the director's preferred version. The highly coveted "Complete Collection" boxset from 2014 includes theatrical cuts for every *Halloween* – except the Rob Zombie entries. As of this writing, you can only obtain theatrical cuts of these two films in a bare-bones Canadian double-feature release. Simply put, *Halloween II*'s theatrical presentation is arguably the lesser-seen version and something of a rarity. With his new director's cut, Zombie effectively closed out the stories of Laurie, Loomis, and Michael – all the while completely negating Farmer and Lussier's unmade *Halloween 3D*. Beyond that technicality, the Weinsteins were just no longer interested in continuing the Zombie saga. After passing on their *Hellraiser* pitches, Bob Weinstein invited Farmer and Lussier to take another stab at Michael Myers.

With a release date locked in, Weinstein began mulling various scenarios for the latest film, ideas that would include not only a PG-13 version but also a found footage film, neither of which impressed this team of writers. While they'd held out hope for the revival of their *Halloween 3D* draft, Farmer and Lussier were also enthused at the possibility of starting over with a new take on the *Halloween* franchise. After receiving some basic guidance from Weinstein, the pair formulated a spec treatment only tentatively referred to as *Halloween 3.0*. This was not to be a sequel to the original nor a straight remake of it. Similarly, it was not to be a period piece set in the past. Farmer and Lussier instead envisioned a new story based on a modernized version of the classic *Halloween* mythos. The tragically intertwined stories of Laurie, Loomis, and Michael would already be unfolding at the start of this new treatment. As such, *Halloween 3.0* operates as though it were a sequel to a remake that was never produced.

> **Opening notes from the treatment:** *"Think Batman Begins and The Dark Knight then apply it to the legend of Michael Myers, Laurie Strode, and Dr. Loomis and you'll be stalking down the same dark streets we intend to travel in HALLOWEEN. This isn't a gimmick-filled sequel or an unnecessary rehash of the original film. This is a WHAT IF. What if John Carpenter's story, with today's money and technology, turned left rather than right and revealed a whole new world to the audience?"*

## THE STORY

*Halloween 3.0* kicks off with a recap of the original *Halloween*'s ending – all newly re-filmed to feature an updated cast. We find teenaged babysitter Laurie Strode under attack by Michael Myers in a darkened house. This is all very familiar – right up until the moment we expect Loomis to rush in and save Laurie from strangulation. That doesn't happen here. Instead, windows shatter as police in tactical gear come crashing into the room. Michael is shot numerous times and apprehended in a violent confrontation. Dr. Loomis then enters, revealing that this was a trap intended to catch his escaped patient. ("Michael would never have let his guard down for anyone but Laurie.") Even while shackled, Michael still manages to kill two officers before being unmasked and loaded into a police van. Some time later, we find Loomis begging a state review board to allow his patient to be tried for his crimes and ultimately put to death.

> **Loomis:** *"We can never allow him to escape again. But he will. No matter what we do. No matter what precautions we take. Michael is smarter than any of you realize. And he counts on us to underestimate him. His silence is nothing more than a weapon to lull us into making a mistake. And any mistake with him will result in another murder spree. That is why I BEG you to find Michael Myers "sane." He must stand trial. He must be convicted. And he must be executed. We must seek and get the death penalty. There is no rehabilitation. There is no redemption. To stop Michael Myers from ever killing again, there is only one solution: death."*

This dramatic speech is intercut with clips of Michael's murders set during and before the first *Halloween*. It's here we glimpse a slightly different origin story for the character. Instead of only murdering his sister on Halloween night fifteen years ago, we find that he also murdered her boyfriend and his own parents. Back in the present, it seems that Loomis' warnings fall on deaf ears as Michael remains institutionalized rather than imprisoned. Two years later, Loomis arrives to work one October night to find the hospital engulfed in flames. Worried that Michael might escape in the chaos, he rushes inside with a shotgun intent on finally ending the slasher's life. (Script: "He must be sure Michael dies, but it's like hunting a raptor in a maze of fire filled with shrieking lunatics.") The vigilante-psychiatrist manages to corner his escaped patient just as the building explodes. Loomis barely escapes with his life. First responders scour the burned-out hospital and discover a charred corpse with a mask melted onto its face. Authorities assert that this is clearly Michael Myers, but Loomis isn't so sure. He insists on DNA identification, which will take days to complete.

Loomis grows increasingly paranoid about the hospital fire and fears that Michael is somehow still alive, which, of course, *he is*. The escaped slasher steals a new white mask from a nearby Halloween store before murdering its two teenaged employees and burning it to the ground. Loomis immediately suspects his former patient, but police maintain that Michael Myers is dead. Concerned over this turn of events, Loomis tries phoning Laurie to warn of her brother's likely approach, but the number has been disconnected. In actuality, Laurie has secretly moved west to Seattle to live with the Tate family. Loomis visits her former boyfriend, Desmond, who divulges Laurie's secret whereabouts. Unbeknownst to either, Michael is hovering nearby and kills Desmond and his new girlfriend following this meeting. Loomis returns a moment later to find their bodies and immediately phones Haddonfield's Sheriff Tyler. Police arrive and discover fabricated evidence that it was Loomis – not Michael – who murdered Desmond and his girlfriend. ("Jesus Christ. He wanted us to believe Myers was back bad enough to kill these two innocent kids.") Having fallen into a trap, Loomis is arrested on Halloween morning on suspicion of murder.

Using his one call, Loomis phones the Tate family from jail to warn them of the approaching danger. Unfortunately, Michael is already there. Mr. and Mrs. Tate then phone Laurie, who's babysitting their young daughter at a friend's house. Both are murdered just as the call connects, which Laurie overhears. Alarmed, she calls Loomis for help and learns he's been arrested for murder. Michael immediately travels to the house where Laurie is babysitting with sixteen-year-old Kit Tate and friends. A stalk-and-slash sequence unfolds, resulting in several deaths. Only Laurie, Kit, and the children make it out alive. Discovering yet another grisly scene at the Tate residence, Laurie offloads the kids and heads for Haddonfield's Police Department. Her brother is but a few steps behind, arriving at police headquarters just after she does. Michael slaughters much of the night shift en route to his old doctor. Thinking quick, Laurie grabs a dead officer's keys and – rather than freeing Loomis – locks herself inside the cell with him. Michael tries reaching them through the bars but is unable to. In a shocking gesture, he instead offers Laurie his knife. (Loomis: "He's offering you an out. He wants you to kill me.") Rejecting this invite to kill, Laurie insists she's not like him. Michael retrieves his own set of keys and tries entering the cell, prompting a violent struggle that ends with Sheriff Tyler shooting him several times. Though wounded, the slasher puts up a fight and ultimately bests his opponent in gory fashion.

As Laurie and Loomis flee the station, they notice Michael disappearing into a nearby house with a hostage – *Kit Tate*! Inside they find the word "home" scrawled in blood on a wall. Realizing the old Myers house is nearby, Loomis and Laurie follow after for a final showdown. Michael quickly murders Kit and stabs Loomis in the stomach before again offering Laurie his knife. Sensing her refusal to kill Loomis, he removes his mask and places it on her head. After a tense pause, Laurie stabs her brother in the heart, and they collapse to the floor. She cradles him as he appears to draw his last breath. Police and EMS soon arrive on the scene. A wounded Loomis tries explaining the situation to Laurie. ("He needed you to be like him. That was the only thing that kept him going.") As the ambulance pulls away with both inside, Laurie notices the driver dead on the roadside, meaning *Michael is behind the wheel*. He slams on the brakes and attacks the vehicle's occupants. Their scuffle eventually ignites an oxygen tank, which blows Laurie out of the vehicle. She watches on in horror as the ambulance burns, a giant fireball rising into the night sky, her brother's ultimate fate unknown.

## THIRD TIME'S A CHARM

By 2011, the *Halloween* franchise had once again fallen into a narrative bind. The various continuities of the original series had long been deemed too convoluted to continue after *Halloween: Resurrection* – and yet the new Rob Zombie continuity had already concluded after only two films. A second remake was certainly an option, but did audiences really want to see an adolescent Michael Myers murder his sister *again* just four years after the last time? (A similar issue has long plagued the Batman franchise. How many times must we see Bruce Wayne's parents murdered?) Farmer and Lussier seem to understand that it was much too soon for another retelling of Michael Myers' origin story. Instead, they alternately envision a reboot that picks up an already-in-progress story within an all-new timeline.

While the *3.0* of *Halloween 3.0* refers to the third iteration of the franchise, this treatment's story functions much more like a *Halloween II* despite there not being a *Halloween* to precede it. Farmer and Lussier's treatment has virtually no setup, instead hitting the ground running with the action already underway. It begins where the 1978 and 2007 films ended with Laurie Strode being attacked by her slasher brother on Halloween night. These aren't the exact same versions of the characters we've come to know, but they're familiar enough that we should recognize them instantly. Considering we've been here twice before, we'd feel confident that we already know what happens next. Dr. Loomis is going to rush in to save Laurie by firing six shots into his patient, who will then tumble off a balcony and vanish into the night. But that's not what happens. We'll instead see SWAT officers storm the room and do battle with the Shape, whom they'll eventually arrest. This is but the first of several tricks the screenwriters play on the viewer. Farmer and Lussier realize that much of their audience will already know the basic *Halloween* story and use this to their advantage. As the treatment itself reads, "*Forget what you know or think you know...*"

If you were to take the *Halloween H20* trilogy and blend it with the Rob Zombie films, you might get something similar to *Halloween 3.0*. It's from these five installments that the screenwriters primarily derive inspiration. (That's not an assumption, either. The treatment outright dubs the *H20* trilogy as "the best films in the franchise," which some fans would certainly agree with.) These five entries may seem like an odd bunch to mix, but Farmer and Lussier make it work. And while their treatment clearly pulls elements from *Halloween H20* and the Rob Zombie films, it never tries to replicate their distinct styles.

From *Halloween,* we have the opening sequence that follows along a familiar path – until it doesn't. From *Halloween II,* we have the sibling connection between Laurie and Michael, and its fiery finale. From *Halloween H20,* we have mention of the Tate family, Laurie moving out of state, and her briefly wielding a fire axe. (There's also a great visual of Michael swiping his blade at Laurie/Loomis through the bars of a jail cell that recalls a similar moment from *H20* with John and Molly.) From the Rob Zombie films, we again have a version of Michael that wants to team-up with his sister as sibling slashers. Vehicle-wise, we would first see Michael driving the station wagon he stole from Smith's Grove in *Halloween.* He will later acquire a Buick Skylark and Harvester Travelall as seen in *H20.* Why does he need three rides? As we'll get to shortly, there's quite a bit of driving in this story.

Farmer and Lussier's unproduced *Halloween 3D* script also serves as major influence on their *Halloween 3.0.* Not content to let those ideas die in development hell, the screenwriters port over several characters and set pieces for use here. Oddly enough, *Halloween 3D*'s beginning became *Halloween 3.0*'s ending with Michael presumed dead in a fiery ambulance crash. In *H3D,* Desmond Lee was an orderly on the J. Burton Rehabilitation Wing with whom Laurie was having an affair. In *3.0,* he is now the teenaged boyfriend Laurie leaves behind in Haddonfield. (Despite being different characters, these Desmonds die similar deaths.) In *H3D,* Kit was one of Amy's ill-fated friends in the opening massacre whereas now she's the teenaged daughter of the Tates. The two endings are also eerily similar. In *Halloween 3D,* we find Michael cradling Laurie, whom he's just stabbed. In *Halloween 3.0,* it's the reverse – Laurie cradles Michael, whom she's just stabbed. In both drafts, Laurie ultimately rejects her brother's invite to kill alongside him.

There is one potentially major goof in the treatment, however. It's established early on that Laurie moves to Seattle for a fresh start. Perfectly understandable, but Haddonfield is roughly two thousand miles from Seattle. How does the Shape manage this thirty-hour journey so quickly after framing Loomis for Desmond's murder? Upon the slaughter of her new friends and family, Laurie then makes the exact same journey back to Haddonfield *with her brother in tow!* That puts the Shape driving over sixty hours almost consecutively. Timeline issues aside, how could he possibly stalk anyone after that? Wouldn't his legs and glutes have turned to jelly? (Fun fact for *H20* fans: Seattle is about the same distance from Haddonfield as Summer Glen.) Of course, Farmer and Lussier are pretty savvy, so we should consider possible explanations. One, maybe this new Haddonfield isn't in Illinois but instead Washington. The treatment doesn't mention a change in state, but it also doesn't mention the Land of Lincoln. (This isn't entirely unprecedented. The

2013 *Bates Motel* series moved the iconic lodging from California to Oregon.) Two, it's possible that Seattle was left over from an earlier concept and that they intended to change it to somewhere closer – like Chicago. Then again, the screenwriters mention that the Shape has three different rides in this story, all obviously stolen, which lends support to the long-haul theory. Ultimately, *Halloween 3.0* is but an unrefined spec treatment that shouldn't be judged too harshly. Even so, analysis is what we're here to do.

It's also a credit to the screenwriters that they leave the door open for future sequels with their story's ending. Sure, it seems as though Michael burns to death in the flaming ambulance, but the scene direction notes that Laurie has no way of knowing whether he truly perished or managed to cheat death once again. This would've been a very easy ending to follow-up had *Halloween 3.0* been made and a subsequent sequel ordered.

## FRAMING LOOMIS

In re-envisioning Dr. Loomis, Farmer and Lussier push the envelope. This is no longer the soft-voiced monologuing Brit played by Donald Pleasence, but a shotgun-toting badass ready to do what's necessary. Pleasence's Loomis was constantly on defense whereas this Loomis goes on the offense. This version is also a little younger and spryer than his predecessors. "Forget the versions we've seen before," the treatment reads. "Think Sean Bean and you'll see what we're going for."

Interestingly, this new Loomis doesn't argue to his colleagues that Michael Myers is insane and must be kept locked up to protect society. He instead posits that Michael is *perfectly sane* and well aware of what he's doing. Loomis' goal is *not* for Michael to enjoy a lifetime of incarceration. Rather, he wants to see the slasher put to death. In order for that to happen, he'll need to be declared sane by the courts. But aiming for the death penalty takes so much time and legal wrangling. As the treatment notes, Loomis has already lost faith in the system and the cops. ("Loomis knows what he must do. [...] *Holmes must kill Moriarty.*") Knowing his mindset, the asylum fire sequence becomes so much more interesting. We suddenly realize that Loomis isn't there to make sure Michael doesn't escape. He's there to make sure Michael doesn't survive. Arming himself with a shotgun, he runs into the inferno, which Farmer and Lussier describe as "a nightmare in full scream." Hippocratic oath be damned, Michael has pushed Loomis so far beyond his breaking point. His evil has defied everything Loomis was ever taught or believed. He's turned Loomis into an attempted murderer.

That last point becomes incredibly ironic given what happens next. Loomis goes to visit Desmond, Laurie's ex-boyfriend, for information on her secret whereabouts. Little do they know that the Shape is lurking nearby and overhears this sensitive info. Loomis departs at which time the Shape murders Desmond and his new girlfriend. Having forgotten his cell phone, Loomis returns a moment later to find their fresh corpses. He doesn't hesitate to call police though he probably should've. Sheriff Tyler arrives and finds evidence suggesting Loomis was their killer, not Michael. It's here Loomis realizes he's been ensnared in a trap, one he might should've seen coming. (His previous words to the state review board: "He counts on us to underestimate him!")

Believing the evidence at face value, Sheriff Tyler promptly arrests Loomis and charges him with murders he didn't commit. (Recall that authorities similarly accused FBI Agent Woods of committing Michael's murders in the unproduced *Halloween H25* draft.) The doctor's final fate in this treatment is a little hazy. He's in a precarious spot when Michael attacks within the ambulance – restrained to a stretcher. The slasher buries his knife into Loomis' stomach before accidentally igniting an oxygen tank within the vehicle. It would seem at first that Loomis perished, but this was also our assumption at the end of 1981's *Halloween II*. Without a body, we can't be too sure. For all we know, Loomis escaped out a side door with minimal burns.

## LAURIE'S FRESH START

Per this story's opening, Laurie Strode is said to be eighteen-years old, one year older than her 1978 and 2007 counterparts. With the first act time jump, we find her two years older and having been taken in by the Tate family in Seattle. At twenty, Laurie may seem a bit old to have been adopted by a new family but then she'd likely need a change of scenery and a supportive home to regain her sanity. And what of the Strodes back in Haddonfield? The treatment never indicates whether they survived per *Halloween 1978* or perished per *Halloween 2007*. That Laurie left them behind and Loomis doesn't seek their help in finding her may suggest they fell victim to the Shape.

*Halloween 3.0*'s Laurie stands as one of the least developed characters in the treatment, which could've been an intentional move by the screenwriters. With the story still coming together, she remained a blank canvas to utilize down the road. As of this writing, we've seen three starkly different takes on what happens to Laurie after that tragic October night. In *Halloween H20*, she became an emotionally wrecked but still functioning alcoholic. In Rob Zombie's *Halloween II*, she became a drugged-out psychotic spiraling into madness. In *Halloween 2018*, she became a paranoid recluse and a much-less functioning alcoholic. We're unsure to what degree Laurie may be struggling in *Halloween 3.0*, but she doesn't seem to be crashing anywhere near as badly as Rob Zombie's *Halloween*. Had Dimension execs ordered Farmer and Lussier to expand *Halloween 3.0* into a full screenplay, they would've likely formulated their own unique spin on the character. Still, this treatment raises questions. Michael and Laurie are siblings in this universe, but when exactly did Laurie discover that information? Prior to the opening or subsequently? Given that Loomis set a trap using Laurie as bait, he must've already known this information, which is in contrast to 1981's *Halloween II* where he didn't know until the governor unsealed certain records. So, when did he find out?

This treatment's third act would've given us two marvelous things that we've never, ever had before in the series. First, we would've gotten to see Laurie and Loomis working together as a team. In both the Carpenter and Zombie timelines, the two main characters only cross paths in the final moments and hardly speak to one another. There's just no connection there, much less a friendship. In *Halloween 3.0*, Laurie and Loomis work together to escape and eventually challenge the Shape, which would've been fantastic to see onscreen. Secondly, the finale would've had Laurie returning to the Myers house with the full knowledge that it was once her home, that her biological parents and sister were murdered here. Laurie never once entered the Myers house in the Carpenter timeline. She did venture inside in *Halloween 2007*, but she knew not its full significance yet. That she would be forced to return here in order to save Kit – knowing her brother was waiting inside – could've been an incredibly powerful moment for the final girl.

There is one moment of hilarity amid tension worth mentioning here. Having slaughtered the entire night shift of Haddonfield's police force, the Shape chases Laurie and Loomis into a cell, which they slam shut. Unable to stab Loomis through the bars, the Shape hands Laurie his knife and motions for her to stab him. She staunchly refuses and, in doing so, hands her brother back his knife, which stuns an indignant Loomis. ("*Laurie!*" he yells. "*You could have just refused! You didn't have to give him the knife back!*") This humorous moment recalls a similar laugh in Farmer's *Jason X* where Professor Lowe gives the reawakened Jason Voorhees his signature weapon. ("Shit, it's yours! Take it! Just remember who got it back for ya. Guys, it's okay! He just wanted his machete back!") *Halloween* fans might also consider this some form of tribute to the original in which Laurie, against all logic, drops a knife not once but *twice* (!!!), rendering her defenseless each time.

## A SMARTER SHAPE

As with Laurie Strode, Farmer and Lussier blend the original and remake versions of Michael Myers for their *Halloween 3.0*. They're very particular, however, in the qualities they pull from the *Halloween 2007* iteration of the character. "This isn't the 'Michael' from the Zombie version," their treatment reads, "the one where we understood why he became the monster." The screenwriters stress that this Michael, much like Carpenter's original, hailed from a seemingly normal family. His sudden turn to evil at age six was therefore shocking and unforeseen to those around him. There were no warning signs or red flags for anyone to pick up on. That, they would argue, is what makes Michael terrifying – the lack of reason or justification for killing.

Further unlike the Zombie version, this take on the slasher de-emphasizes his size and strength to instead focus on his intelligence. Whereas Zombie's Michael was pretty much a blunt instrument of death, this Michael is alternately conniving and incredibly smart. He spends two years of his re-incarceration putting together a plot to not only escape custody but frame his psychiatrist for murder while doing so. These differences are most obvious during his attack on Haddonfield PD in the final act. Farmer and Lussier specifically note that their Shape doesn't bluster in and fight off multiple cops at once. ("He's not the Terminator," they write.) Instead, their Michael enters the station quietly and murders the dispatch officer "with malignant stealth." He then moves silently from room to room, slaughtering the night staff as he goes along. Admittedly, this level of cunning was sorely missing from the remake installments.

Surprisingly, the one story element the screenwriters do borrow from Rob Zombie (or at least the aborted *Halloween 3D*) involves the Shape wanting Laurie to join him in killing. This makes for a fascinating cross-section of characterizations. On one hand, Farmer and Lussier want their Michael to be the unexplainable and unknowable evil. On the other hand, they assign him a motivation in wanting to recruit Laurie as his partner in crime. From the treatment, we're not sure if she's ever truly tempted by his invitation, but it's enough to make Loomis concerned that he might soon become the target of two Myers rather than just one. Their climactic meeting in the Myers house would've undoubtedly proven tense. As Loomis lay wounded, Michael urges Laurie to finish him off. He hands her his bloodied knife and places his mask upon her head, which recalls a chilling visual from Zombie's *Halloween II*. Laurie refuses, of course, and instead stabs her brother in the heart in a wrenching rejection.

In a rare turn, we find the Shape communicating to Laurie and Loomis. Not verbally, of course, but with the written word. Before anyone cries foul, this isn't unprecedented for the character. Recall that he foreshadowed his own plans back in *Halloween*'s TV Cut by writing "SISTER" in blood on his cell wall. He later inscribed the word "SAMHAIN" on a blackboard in *Halloween II*. Here, he writes another message in blood – "HOME" – which indicates where he wants Laurie and Loomis to meet him for their final confrontation. This isn't him just trying to be creepy. As the treatment notes, Michael *wants* Laurie to remember their home where he murdered their parents and sister. He wants her to remember and feel that – *and then join alongside him!*

## THE ALTERNATE THIRD ACT

Farmer and Lussier's *Halloween 3.0* treatment concludes with a fascinating oddity – an alternate third act tacked onto its final pages. Just how different is this alternate conclusion? *Wildly different.* In fact, it's a complete inversion of the first ending described several pages back. As already mentioned, the treatment itself is a unique blend of the *H20* and Zombie-verse timelines. This alternate third act abandons that even blend for a bit of the old Rob Zombie madness – the kind last seen in the final moments of his *Halloween II*.

(For a quick refresher, the first ending saw Michael lure Laurie and Loomis to the Myers house where he nudges her to stab Loomis. She refuses and instead stabs her brother, seemingly fatally. Despite that, the slasher returns for a final scare in an ambulance, which Laurie sees explode into a fireball as a result of their struggle. The fates of Loomis and Michael are left unresolved.)

This alternate finale picks up as Laurie and Loomis exit the police station. They steal a cop car but are rammed by the Shape in another vehicle before they can escape. The Shape abducts Laurie and disappears into the night. Dazed from the crash, Loomis runs to a nearby neighborhood where a giant Halloween party is underway – complete with a massive decorative pumpkin. Recognizing the area, he realizes where Michael has taken Laurie – to their old family home. Inside the Myers house, the Shape places his mask on her head before handing her his knife and gesturing to his chest. Sobbing and confused, Laurie refuses to stab her brother. Before he can respond, police in tactical gear storm the house. Michael immediately kills several officers, but he's taken down with a bullet to the back. Another cop aims his gun for Michael's head, but is stabbed by Laurie before he can pull the trigger. As the officer recoils, he shoots Laurie.

A wounded Shape escapes the carnage carrying his also-wounded sister. They stop down the road near the giant pumpkin. Laurie places her brother's mask back onto his head and apologizes, "I'm sorry. I'm not like you." With this, she takes his knife, gripped tightly in his hand, and places it over her chest. After a pause, Michael buries it into her heart. An injured Loomis arrives a moment later to find Laurie dead and her brother gone. A short time later, Loomis is being tended to in an ambulance when he thinks he sees the Shape off in the distance. A moment later, the figure is gone.

Examining this revised ending, the implications of Michael's "assisted suicide" are interesting to ponder. This marks the first time in franchise history in which the writers envisioned the Shape actually *wanting* an opponent to end his life. That the opponent in question here also happens to be his own sister offers much in dramatic weight. By giving Laurie the mask in the first ending, encouraging her to kill Loomis, it would seem to be Michael's way of initiating Laurie as his equal. But by giving her the mask in this context, it might appear to be some form of communication – something that might make Laurie feel more equipped to perform the act of killing him, thus, in his mind, making her his successor still. Yet in either scenario, Laurie's not prepared to kill – not Loomis, not even Michael. Instead, she opts for her own death. With this shocking reversal, it's strange and even a little eerie to see the

469

Shape regard another human with such affection and consideration. Farmer and Lussier write that upon reaching the giant pumpkin, the Shape checks Laurie's injuries and notices her gunshot wound. He stares at a nearby ambulance, but Laurie refuses treatment and instead steadies his knife above her chest. That alone is a stunning development – that Michael Myers is considering *saving* a life rather than taking one. Is it out of character? For previous iterations of the slasher, yes – very much so. But that doesn't make it any less powerful here. If any of this reminds you of the duo's *Halloween 3D*, you're on the right track. Remember how that proposed sequel saw a similar mercy-killing set against the backdrop of a giant pumpkin decoration.

These endings differ not only in their content, but also in how they leave the franchise. Per the first ending, the stories of Laurie, Loomis, and Michael will seemingly continue on across more films. Per the second ending, Laurie is dead, and the focus will now shift to Loomis. Both endings answer a very specific question – does one want this new *Halloween* universe to center on Laurie Strode again? In writing separate endings, Farmer and Lussier were prepared to let the studio make that important call.

## WHY IT WASN'T MADE

Simply put, The Weinstein Company never followed up on the story submission. This is less a reflection on the quality of Farmer and Lussier's work and more an indication of the company's now notorious reputation for being wishy-washy. The *Halloween* franchise sorely lacked direction just as Dimension Films sorely lacked the creative leadership to choose that direction. It wasn't as if they didn't have a broad range of viable options at their disposal – they most certainly did with *Halloween 3.0* being one of them. The *Halloween* franchise also had something that the studio's other horror properties did not – the guiding voice of Malek Akkad, whom they just were not utilizing properly. If you can't seem to figure out what to do with a *Halloween*, why not turn to the family whose name has graced the credits of every installment thus far for input?

Knowing the studio's nature and recognizing the project as a longshot, Farmer and Lussier didn't get their hopes too high for *Halloween 3.0*. Their spec treatment recycled a number of concepts and characters from their also unproduced *Halloween 3D* script. While that earlier effort very nearly went before cameras, their *Halloween 3.0* treatment would die in development without being ordered to full script. Given their inability to commit, it felt to some as though Dimension would never actually produce another *Halloween* again. Such feelings were incredibly... prophetic.

# PATRICK LUSSIER

Co-writer - Halloween 3.0

Interviewed by Travis Mullins

**In getting back to the franchise, were you still holding out hope for *Halloween 3D*?**

Sure, we thought it was possible. Like, '*Hey! That's just sitting there! Let's make that movie!*' But because there's such a short attention span in Hollywood, that eventually went away. We had a pitch for *Hellraiser*, and they were still figuring out what they were going to do with *Halloween*. They were like, '*Oh, we want to do a whole new version!*' Originally, we were making a sequel to Rob's version and the further you get away from Rob's version, the less anybody gives a shit about doing a sequel. '*We still like the franchise, but we no longer want to tie it to that.*'

**Also, the more widely available director's cut of *Halloween II* killed everyone, even Laurie.**

I didn't see that one. If we'd made *Halloween 3D*, all they would've had to have done was not allow that [director's cut] to have happened. I wouldn't have seen that as an obstacle. It's something we were ready to shoot. I think at one point we talked about doing a version without Laurie, but then a year later, we pitched a totally different version of *Halloween*.

**What do you recall about that version – *Halloween 3.0*?**

I just read it this morning. We came up with the idea of, '*What if you were to cast Sean Bean as Dr. Loomis?*' What would that character do? How would he play it? How smart would he be? Because that's a very different guy from Donald Pleasence or Malcolm McDowell, so how would that work? And then the idea of being ahead of Michael Myers and making it a real chess game. So, that was the jumping off point

471

**The way it's described in the treatment, '*Instead of going right, you go left.*' You're picking up right after the end of the original film – or a completely different version of that film.**

That was very much it. When we did *My Bloody Valentine*, we wanted the opening to be the whole end of the original film. We didn't want to address it as a remake. We wanted it to be something that had a fondness for the source material. One of my favorite films is the 1978 *Invasion of the Body Snatchers*, the Philip Kaufman film with Donald Sutherland and Leonard Nimoy. There's a film that's not only a remake but also a spiritual sequel to the original because they have Kevin McCarthy in the opening who was the star of the original 1956 film. It's a fantastic, brilliant film.

**The concept sort of homages not only the original but also *Halloween II* and *H20*.**

That was the idea, that we would fall into those sorts of echoes. That was something that we were excited to do. We didn't spend a ton of time on it. You'd have to be careful with how much sweat equity you put into anything with the Weinsteins because it was always a moving target. You never knew whether you'd be able to hit or not. It's like, '*Ugh, I don't know what you want! I don't know if you know what you want! But here's something. Let's see if you want to talk about it more or not.*'

**On that note, you also used a few elements from your *Halloween 3D*.**

Dimension owned it so we felt it was fair game. It wasn't like the set-pieces no longer worked. It also made it easier in terms of doing a spec pitch. Nobody's paying for it. You could spend every second of your life doing spec pitches and end up nowhere. It's like, '*Okay, let's put effort into it but at the same time, nobody's paying us, so let's be cautious of how much time we're spending.*'

**Re-reading the treatment, were there any new aspects to it that you liked?**

I always liked the set-up trap at the beginning and Michael's vengeance for that trap. I actually thought all of that stuff was really cool and very effective. I liked the time jump and, all these years later, the idea of, '*Hey, this isn't about rehabilitation. This is about locking him up and having him declared sane so that we can execute him.*' That's actually pretty fun.

**One of the most interesting bits is that you have actually have Michael framing Loomis for his crimes. Tell us about that.**

This is the thing about the original *Halloween* that's so much fun. Michael's kind of a dick. He's so clever. He's a prankster and he's mischievous. He's not like Jason, who always sort of felt like the Terminator. I never felt that Jason had a sense of humor. Michael Myers actually has a sense of humor. Like, when he shows up in that ghost sheet and he's standing there? It's like, what the fuck? That is just so *weird*. He's like, '*Oh, I'm going to dress up as a ghost and stand here with the glasses on.*' Not just the sheet, but also putting the glasses on. Jason would never do that. Michael is hyper aware. He's smart and patient. I never felt that with Jason. He was always just a tank that was going to run you over. If you came in proximity, you were dead, period. Whereas Michael felt like he was going to go out of his way to fuck you up for his own amusement. That's one of the reasons where in *Halloween 3D*, we were writing for Des and the [effects of] banging the sister. Michael would take offense and fuck you up for that. That felt like a legitimate thing, something that Michael would do. He's calculated and that's a calculated thing. So, the idea of framing Loomis came out of, '*Okay, this is a really smart character. Let's lean into how smart he is. Let's not shy away from it and really enjoy the fact that he's that smart.*'

**Aside from his positioning of corpses, it feels like this calculated humor isn't something that's greatly touched upon in later films. You wouldn't be breaking any rules by framing Loomis.**

It's there! It's just sitting there in the source material! (laughs) For whatever reason, John Carpenter and Debra Hill created that moment [with Ghost Bob]. The moment exists and it perseveres. It's part of the M.O., and it's fair game. You can attribute meaning to it. With framing Loomis, it's the idea of, '*You fucked me, and I will not be fucked.*' You know, vengeance is best served cold. It's the, '*Oh, I'm going to get you, motherfucker.*' It's personal. To me, the whole thing about Michael always felt like hyperintelligence that so many of the other slashers do not have. That's what I think sets him apart and why he persists and has had so many other films and such. Because it's not just about how you kill somebody. There's more to it than that.

PLATINUM DUNES'

# HALLOWEEN

The Night THEY Came Home...

**Treatment by**
**Scott Milam**

As originally planned, the eleventh *Halloween* – in the form of Todd Farmer and Patrick Lussier's *Halloween 3D* – was slated to hit theaters sometime in October 2010. Those plans quickly fell apart, however, even before 2009 came to a close. Some two years later, in June 2011, The Weinstein Company rescheduled the next sequel for October 26, 2012. With a year-and-a-half to go, such a date may have seemed achievable, yet it was still unknown who would be helming the picture or if Farmer and Lussier's screenplay would still be utilized. Even Farmer himself was unsure, casting doubt on a direct continuation from the last installment. "So much time has gone by that I don't think a sequel to Rob's *Halloween II* would still play. I'm not sure that our original script would work," he told *Bloody-Disgusting* in September 2011. To this end, he and Lussier devised several alternate concepts though none garnered further development.

Months went by without further news. Only recently have we come to learn that during this quiet period, scribes Ben Collins and Luke Piotrowski were brought in to pitch on the project. Relative unknowns at the time, Collins and Piotrowski would later cement their mark in the horror genre with the *V/H/S* spin-off *Siren*, followed by the thrillers *Stephanie* and *The Glass House*. (The two are currently attached to script Spyglass Entertainment's *Hellraiser* relaunch. Should this come to pass, it'll mark the first theatrical Pinhead venture in over 25 years. Can you even believe that?) For *Halloween*, the writers devised their own treatment which they then pitched to a Dimension exec in the spring of 2012. Nothing further was heard, however. With October quickly approaching and no clear direction on how to proceed, The Weinstein Company once again removed *Halloween* from their release schedule. While disappointing, huge news was just around the corner.

On April 1, 2012, *Bloody-Disgusting* broke a few major scoops on the franchise, which they assured readers was *not* part of an April Fools prank. First, they reported that not only was Farmer and Lussier's *Halloween 3D* now off the table, but the entire 3D approach as well. The site also refuted rumors that the new *Halloween* would be PG-13 or part of the found footage sub-genre. By far, the biggest bombshell from this report was that The Weinstein Company had brought on Michael Bay's Platinum Dunes production company to produce the next installment in the series. Under the guidance of filmmakers Brad Fuller and Andrew Form, Platinum Dunes had already produced very successful remakes of *The Texas Chainsaw Massacre, The Amityville Horror, Friday the 13th,* and *A Nightmare on Elm Street*. Each of these four projects opened atop the domestic box office and grossed near or above $100 million worldwide. Apart from the original, no *Halloween* had even come close to those kinds of numbers.

As far as internet rumors go, the Platinum Dunes scoop was a believable one, especially since they had already partnered with Dimension on a 2005 remake of *The Amityville Horror*. Founded by Bay, Fuller, and Form in 2001, Platinum Dunes had single-handedly kickstarted the remake craze of the 2000s with *The Texas Chainsaw Massacre* in 2003. It was a project they initially brought to Bob Weinstein, who turned them down. The film eventually found a home at New Line Cinema and went on to become one of the year's biggest horror hits. Weinstein bitterly regretted having let *Texas Chainsaw* slip through his fingers and immediately sought to replicate its success with other horror properties. This is in part what led Dimension to abandon plans for a follow-up to *Halloween: Resurrection* in lieu of a remake. Having overseen reinventions of Leatherface, Freddy Krueger, and Jason Voorhees, Fuller and Form were vocal in having long wanted to re-imagine Michael Myers as well. It was a desire they held onto even in the aftermath of the Rob Zombie remake and its sequel.

Unfortunately, *Bloody-Disgusting*'s reporting of a partnership between Dimension and Platinum Dunes lacked the proper context. *Shock Till You Drop*'s Ryan Turek would pump the brakes on their scoop later this same day. After making some phone calls, Turek discovered that Platinum Dunes was but one of several companies Dimension was taking pitches from. No agreements had been signed between the two companies, making news of their producing a new *Halloween* nothing more than wishful thinking.

Based on their spirited approach to the project, it's evident that Platinum Dunes badly wanted to add *Halloween* to their already impressive horror lineup. It's also evident that, throughout this period of development, Dimension Films was as fickle and non-committal as ever. Not surprisingly, the studio failed to give Platinum execs a clear idea of what they wanted to see in a new *Halloween*. Consequently, Platinum Dunes never settled on a singular pitch to fully rally behind. Rather, they brought multiple pitches before Dimension from various writers. Some of these were straight remakes while others were direct sequels to earlier films in both timelines,

Carpenter and Zombie alike. Some pitches – like the one made by *Halloween: Asylum '05* scribe Matt Venne – Platinum Dunes developed and refined before sharing with Dimension. Others, such as the one described in this chapter, were accepted and subsequently lost in development hell. (If you somehow missed Venne's colorful anecdote about pitching Bob Weinstein his Platinum Dunes remake, turn back to the last page of his interview now. We'll wait.)

One of the pitches fielded by Platinum Dunes belonged to screenwriter Scott Milam. Though Milam had only one feature credit to his name at the time, it was a recently-produced slasher remake. He had long worked in film and video production but first landed on horror radars with his spec script *Wichita*, one of the selections of the 2006 Black List. Milam's script was quickly purchased by Dimension with *Saw* franchise veteran Darren Lynn Bousman set to direct. Though Dimension never made *Wichita*, the script did form the basis of *Mother's Day*, the 2010 loose remake of the 1980 cult-slasher favorite. (Directed by Bousman, the film's release was unfortunately botched, finally reaching video stores in 2012.) Milam would first learn of Platinum Dunes' involvement with *Halloween* from Dimension Films executive Matthew Stein. Intrigued by the prospect, he reached out to Brad Fuller, whom he knew personally, for more details. Fuller invited him to submit a pitch, the result of which was a seven-page treatment simply titled *Halloween*.

Before we dive into Milam's unique vision, we should stress that his treatment was never officially championed by Platinum Dunes, just as Platinum Dunes had not yet been officially hired to produce a new *Halloween*. Milam's pitch was but one of several that Platinum execs were bringing to Dimension for consideration. Nonetheless, very little has ever emerged publicly about Platinum's work on their prospective *Halloween* project. Milam's treatment is therefore a fascinating insight into an otherwise secretive period in lost sequel history.

## "I'd heard through the grapevine that I was a contender out of probably a thousand pitches."

- Scott Milam

## THE STORY

Scott Milam's tale opens with a prologue set in the unspecified past. On Halloween night, young Michael Myers and pal Sean Carver are abducted by a mysterious stranger while out trick-or-treating. Their little sisters, Laurie and Rachel, are witness to this shocking kidnapping, all the while Michael and Laurie's older sister Judith, tasked with watching the children, is distracted by her boyfriend. Despite an intense search, the two boys are never found, leading the oldest Myers son, Daniel, to forever resent Judith for her irresponsibility this tragic night.

Ten years later, we find Rachel Carver and Laurie Myers now in high school. Rachel has grown to hate Halloween as a result of her childhood trauma. Her boyfriend suggests they spend this holiday taking the ferry to Port Townsend, a nearby community that doesn't celebrate All Hallows' Eve. With her parents having died six years ago, Laurie has moved in with brother Daniel. (Judith left home at eighteen though she and Laurie keep in touch.) Daniel is now a homicide detective – a career path we can attribute to his enduring obsession with what happened to Michael and Sean a decade ago. He's soon called to the abandoned grounds of what used to be the Smith's Grove Sanitarium, where a teenage paintballer claims his friends were murdered. Daniel searches the property and locates the mutilated youths along with some very strange graffiti. In launching an investigation, he calls upon Dr. Sam Loomis to assist.

No longer a practicing psychiatrist, Loomis now works as an advisor for the FBI's homicide division. After some initial discussion, Loomis and Daniel hear gunshots in the distance. They rush outside to find two mutilated agents and an old truck fleeing the scene. A chase ensues which leads them to an old farmhouse where several people had been living. Contained within is the decayed body of a young blonde-haired boy, whom police suspect may possibly be Sean Carver. A DNA sample is sent out for identification. Meanwhile, Laurie's best friend Annie offers to handle her babysitting assignment so that Laurie can join Rachel and friends in Port Townsend.

As night falls, we see a shadowy figure – the Shape – stalking Laurie's home in Haddonfield with Annie and the children inside. Glued to a horror movie marathon downstairs, little Tommy Doyle and Lindsey Wallace never hear Annie's screams upstairs. Upon finding their babysitter murdered, the children call for help. Loomis and Daniel rush to the house while, across town, Rachel and friends board the ferry to Port Townsend where spirited Halloween celebrations are underway. Having been lied to, Rachel is immediately upset and wants to go home. After struggling to regroup, most of the friends get back onto the ferry. Unbeknownst to them, the Shape has already murdered two of their ilk and is now on the ferry as well. (Milam in the treatment: "I know what you're thinking. If the Shape was in Haddonfield, how could he also be on the ferry? Keep reading folks.")

Isolated from her friends, the Shape attacks Rachel, resulting in a violent chase across multiple levels of the ferry. Rachel's boyfriend tries valiantly to defend her but is soon killed. On a different level, Laurie receives a call from Daniel, who is en route to the ferry with Loomis via helicopter. Daniel reveals he's learned that Michael might've returned, murdered Annie, and could be coming to kill her next. Baffled and horrified, Laurie and her boyfriend rush to find Rachel, who is still under attack. The Shape slaughters the boyfriend before throwing Laurie to the ground so forcefully that her bones crack. Just then, Daniel and Loomis reach the ferry. Daniel calls out his brother's name. In an effort to de-escalate this nightmare, he tells Michael that he never stopped loving him nor did he ever stop searching for him. ("Put the knife down, Michael. It's over. Please. Let her go.")

For a brief moment, this seems to work. But the Shape soon raises his knife to kill Rachel and is shot by Dr. Loomis before he can do so. Even this fails to stop him, however. Rachel crawls to a nearby car on the ferry and rams it into the Shape, sending them both overboard into the frigid waters below. Rachel swims to the surface though the slasher remains pinned underwater by the car. (Loomis to Daniel: "That… wasn't your brother… not anymore. That… that was evil. Pure evil.") In the aftermath of the ferry attack, Daniel receives a disturbing call from the crime lab. The DNA sample from the farmhouse corpse does *not* match Sean Carver. Concurrent with this, we notice the dead Shape's corpse floating in the sound – blonde-hair protruding from the tears in his mask. In actually, this killer was not Michael Myers, but a now adult Sean Carver. The treatment ends with Judith Myers returning home from work to find her boyfriend slain. In the shadows of her apartment, a dark figure emerges and unmasks. She recognizes the face. ("Michael?") A knife hovers into frame and she gasps. Cut to black as the *Halloween* theme plays.

## NEW WORLD, NEW RULES

In the world of lost *Halloween* sequels, there are those that use the 1978 original as a template for success. Scott Milam's *Halloween* is definitely not among them – at least not obviously. If anything, Milam uses John Carpenter's film as a guide on what *not* to do. He would rather break free of the norms and tropes that have defined the franchise for decades rather than conform to them. If it's not already evident from the plot summary, Milam is playing by his own rules, which audiences wouldn't yet be privy to. This adds a very intentional and effective level of unpredictability to the narrative. Milam may be playing with story and visual elements from the original *Halloween,* but he never once tries to ape what Carpenter did. When following in the footsteps of a horror master, that takes testicular fortitude.

This *Halloween* is so different that, even as a fan, you can't make any assumptions heading into it. The Shape is no longer an escaped psych patient. Therefore, there's no doctor to chase after him. (This shatters the traditional Loomis/Shape dynamic.) If there's no psychiatrist, then there's also no local sheriff for him to nag. (Annie Brackett is here, but not her father.) Similarly, the Shape has a target this time around, but it's not some virginal teenage babysitter. (Laurie's here, but repressed she's not.) The final act includes the traditional stalk-and-slash chase, but it's not set in a darkened house as we might expect. Milam knows well that audiences would be bringing these and other expectations to his story and uses this to his advantage. The biggest trick he pulls involves the revelation near story's end that there are actually *two* Shapes. How would fans have reacted to such a bold re-imagining of the classic formula? It's very difficult to say.

Among the script's many uniquities is the character of Judith Myers, who benefits from a serious boost in screen time. In the 1978 original, Judith died six minutes into the movie. In the 2007 remake, she survived to the twenty-three-minute mark. Here, she's been expanded into a more fleshed-out character who survives until the final scene – and *possibly* even beyond it. If Michael does murder Judith in this story's concluding moments, then Milam will have cleverly flipped the original *Halloween*'s opening kill to his story's final kill. The treatment hints at, but does not fully explore, what would surely be an interesting tension between Judith and her siblings. Having been responsible for young Michael on the night of his abduction, how would she cope with that unbearable guilt? Milam writes that Daniel deeply resents her for it, but that Laurie has maintained a relationship with her big sister. Interestingly, we also learn that Judith has since become a nurse. Might this career choice be an attempt at redemption on her part? How many lives would she need to save before she could forgive herself for the one she didn't? In the unlikely scenario Judith lived beyond this treatment's ending, she could've become one of this universe's most interesting characters.

Further breaking from tradition, Milam sets much of his third act not in suburban Haddonfield but on a large ferry headed back from Port Townsend. This gives us something quite new – the Shape on a boat! (While we've never seen our landlubbing slasher on the water before, we have seen Jason Voorhees get his mask wet in *Friday the 13th Part VIII: Jason Takes Manhattan.* Given that, it would be impossible not to draw comparisons between the two.)

The Port Townsend ferry makes for a surprisingly strong backdrop to the final chase. Being loaded up with cars, it's full of dark places to hide and creep around. And given that this is Halloween night, the costumed partiers onboard wouldn't think anything of the Shape stalking its decks. In one scene, an ill-fated reveler unwittingly blocks the Shape's path as he's chasing after Rachel. The plus-size reveler, dressed as a clown-ish John Wayne Gacy, soon meets with the business end of the slasher's blade in a highly meta spectacle. Just picture it – a fictionalized slasher murdering a real-life one. (You may recall that the Shape last met a John Wayne Gacy impersonator in *Halloween: Resurrection.* Instead of killing him that time, Michael gifted him his knife.)

Speaking of Port Townsend, there's no such port in Illinois. There is, however, a Port Townsend in Washington state, from where Milam hails. Was the screenwriter suggesting his Haddonfield existed in Washington as *Halloween 3.0* seemed to? Possibly, but maybe not. This might've simply been a tribute to his home state similar to how Debra Hill named the fictional Haddonfield, Illinois for her hometown of Haddonfield, New Jersey.

The original *Halloween* was, by design, a straightforward story. The film's only mystery surrounded the Shape's motivations, which were unknowable. (Why did he start killing? Why escape now? Why target Laurie Strode?) That aside, we always had a clear understanding of what was happening onscreen. That's not at all the case in Milam's *Halloween*, which unfolds much differently. This is a story that, also by design, is rife with lingering mystery. The screenwriter teases plotlines and backstories that likely wouldn't be explored until later films. His intent isn't only to scare you, but to also draw you in with intrigue. This is a big part of Milam's long-term plan. With this first treatment, he's simply world-building.

A story with this many unresolved plot threads would absolutely require a sequel, if not two or more. By the end, we're maddeningly left with so many more questions than answers. Who abducted Sean and Michael as children? What happened to them during that time? Why come back now? What's with the strange graffiti at Smith's Grove? Whose body did they find at the farmhouse, if not Sean? What does Loomis know that he's not telling? All this, and so much more. Of course, introducing story elements that have yet to be hammered out hasn't always worked out well for this franchise. Recall that *Halloween 5* infamously hinged its ending on a plot point that had yet to be finalized, which proved disastrous. How is Milam's approach any different from that of *Halloween 5*? The difference may be that his treatment's mysteries involve the past whereas *Halloween 5*'s involved the present and future.

Visually, this *Halloween* wasn't going to be anywhere near as clean or bloodless as the original film. Milam envisioned multiple messy kills that would've surely kept the effects team busy the entire shoot. There are two memorable visuals on the ferry involving blood worth mentioning here, the first of which reveals the screenwriter's dark sense of humor. Using his knife, the Shape uppercuts a janitor tethered to an automatic floor-waxing machine. The machine continues waxing while dragging along the bleeding corpse of its operator. This leaves behind a smeared sanguinary trail wherever it goes. (The image of a floor-waxer dragging a corpse throughout a ferry is both sick and kind of hilarious.) A short while later, an injured Rachel tries to hide from the Shape in a public restroom on the ship. Hiding in a stall, she stands on the toilet to avoid revealing her location. Unfortunately, Rachel is unable to stanch the flow of blood from her wound, which functions like breadcrumbs for the approaching slasher.

Curiously, things in Milam's treatment seem to come in pairs. We have two Shapes (Sean and Michael), two final girls (Rachel and Laurie), and two evil-chasers (Daniel and Loomis). This doubling-up would seem to result in twice the danger, twice the peril, and twice the action. In the original *Halloween*, less was more. Here, more is more.

## FINAL GIRLS

As mentioned, this *Halloween* runs with two final girls, though neither fits the Laurie archetype from the original film. Our lead final girl would seem to be Rachel Carver, described in the treatment as "smart, attractive and strong with a giving nature." We first see a teenaged Rachel doing laps at swim team practice, which low-key sets up how she'll later escape the sinking car during the finale. Rachel is not only still traumatized from seeing her brother kidnapped as a child, but bitter about it as well. She hates Halloween and avoids celebrating it at all cost. Milam also writes that Rachel resents the Myers family, whom she blames for Sean's abduction. (After all, it was Judith Myers who was babysitting.) Given that resentment, Rachel and Laurie aren't exactly besties despite sharing a social circle.

Our other final girl is Laurie Myers, not to be mistaken for Laurie Strode. (The Strodes don't exist here.) This Laurie is nothing like her predecessors and more akin to a "normal" teenage girl. She's quite social, has a boyfriend, and uses a fake ID to go out drinking on Halloween night. Given the death of her parents six years ago, she's now being raised by her workaholic older brother Daniel, which has apparently allowed her a greater measure of freedom. Laurie doesn't seem to be affected by her brother's disappearance in the same way that Rachel is. Rachel very much blames herself for not intervening in their kidnapping. ("I saw what happened. But I did nothing. I didn't even scream.") In a bonding moment, Laurie reasons that they were only children – what could they have possibly done differently? ("You might've been taken, too.")

Rachel and Laurie both have boyfriends here, neither of whom survive the ferry slaughter. Laurie is currently dating Ben Tramer, a responsible type with plans to attend medical school. Fans will surely remember that Laurie had a crush on Ben Tramer in the original *Halloween* and that we later saw him perish in a fiery auto-accident in *Halloween II*. The poor guy doesn't fare much better in Milam's story. (Script: "The Shape breaks Ben's body in half on the railing and drops him into the cold, frigid water.") Rachel's boyfriend is the well-meaning Graham, who lies about Port Townsend not celebrating Halloween in an effort to get Rachel to socialize on All Hallows' Eve. That deception proves to be a fatal mistake on his part. It's on the Port Townsend ferry that Graham meets a grisly end. The Shape stabs a knife into his throat and slices upward, "parting his face like the red sea."

Laurie is initially unable to go out partying due to a prior babysitting commitment, which Annie Brackett takes over for her. When the Shape later slaughters Annie at the Myers house, we can only assume that he intended to kill Laurie there instead. In a hyper-meta moment, Tommy Doyle and Lindsey Wallace fail to hear Annie's cries upstairs because they're watching *Scream* downstairs. Interestingly enough, the characters in *Scream* watch the original *Halloween* near that film's end, meaning the tributes would've come full circle with this proposed remake. (We're still trying to figure out how Molly and Sarah watching *Scream 2* in *Halloween H20* could fit into this.)

## THE SHAPE VS THE FEDS

One recurrent theme in *Halloween* is that of the local lawman reluctantly chasing down the Boogeyman. With little-to-no backup, you already know this will surely prove a dark night for Haddonfield's chief law enforcement officer, especially if he has a daughter. Though tried and true, it's a theme we've seen play out multiple times by now. Sensing this, Scott Milam takes a much different approach with his treatment. In place of Sheriff Brackett, this *Halloween* finds the FBI's homicide division on the case, which shakes things up considerably. They're not cruising around town in a '73 Dodge Polara but swooping down in a tactical helicopter. They're not hiding in bushes outside darkened houses but doing DNA testing and establishing psychological profiles.

Given that Milam's treatment works in pairs, we have two evil-chasers in this story. The first is homicide detective Daniel Myers, who obviously has a very personal connection to the unfolding situation. The treatment tells that it was young Michael's abduction, now a cold case, that led Daniel to pursue this career path and that he still hopes to one day solve it. Prior to the return of Sean and Michael, Daniel had been charged with tracking down "The Black River Killer," a mysterious case we're told very little about. In investigating the slaughter at Smith's Grove, Daniel wonders if this all might be connected to the Black River Killer given the ritualistic nature of the killings and the strange graffiti. By story's end, we're still not sure if there's a connection here, thus leaving the door wide open for future developments.

Possibly the most interesting moment with Daniel Myers comes during the finale. Believing the Shape to be his long-lost brother, Daniel makes a heartfelt and desperate plea for him to stop the killing. As Milam writes, "he plays the brother card." He stresses to Michael that he never stopped loving him or trying to find him. It's touching and might've had some effect if only this *were* Michael Myers. As we later find out, it's not – it's Sean Carver, who doesn't seem to give a damn about such sentimentality. More interestingly, this leaves the possibility of an actual reunion between Daniel and Michael open for a sequel.

Upon being summoned to Smith's Grove to investigate the murdered paintballers, Daniel calls in Dr. Sam Loomis. Once again, Milam tries something different with the role. This Loomis doesn't practice medicine at Smith's Grove as the hospital is already shuttered. As we find him, he's not even a practicing psychiatrist at all. Nor has he ever met Michael Myers. *This* Loomis works as an advisor to the FBI in hunting down serial killers. As Milam writes, "He's the guy you call when Hannibal Lecter is ready to talk." Further adding to the mystery, Loomis behaves strangely when investigating the graffiti at Smith's Grove, "as if he knows more than he's willing to tell." In all, this Loomis plays a surprisingly small role in the story, though he would've likely returned in follow-up installments. Even with his reduced screen time, it's still Loomis who shoots the Shape on the ferry. (Milam doesn't specify but we're assuming six shots.)

## TWICE THE SHAPE

In a creatively risky move, Milam's *Halloween* has two Shapes. Only two other lost sequels in this book have doubled-up on the white-masked slasher – Robert Zappia's *Halloween 7: Two Faces of Evil* and John Sullivan's *Halloween: Asylum '04*. Unlike those efforts, we don't realize we're seeing double in this story until the ending in which only the true Michael Myers remains. Of course, we'd have already realized something strange was afoot watching the Shape simultaneously attack Annie in Haddonfield and Rachel's friends over in Port Townsend. Teleportation is not, as of this writing, one of the character's many abilities.

Milam's new take on the part of Michael Myers may be among the most radically different in this book. He doesn't kill anyone in the opening scenes and he's never committed to a psychiatric institution. If anything, we may have reason to feel sorry for him given that he was abducted as a boy. What could've possibly happened to him in the years that followed to transform him into a silent killer? We don't yet know. In a sense, Michael is himself a victim to a larger evil we're not yet privy to. Why go to such great lengths to alter the character's backstory? Milam explains his creative thought process in the treatment itself.

**Milam's notes:** *"The reasoning behind the abduction instead of Michael killing his sister and being sent away to a Mental Hospital is because I feel that version of his back-story is dated and not scary anymore. It was done to death in Zombie's version and I would suggest staying away from it. All the clinical mumbo jumbo is boring for today's audience. By making this an abduction we don't know what horrors Michael experienced and what turned him into a killer. It's a clean way to create an air of suspense and mystery of why Michael was taken. We'll never know who took him in this film because I think it can be one of those mysteries that are milked for a few more films. I think it's a way to get back to the less we know the scarier it is."*

As the Shape, both Sean Carver and Michael Myers seem identical in appearance and intention. They're both white-mask-wearing slashers intent on murdering their siblings – virtually indistinguishable. This would surely make Milam's *Halloween* even more interesting on re-watch as we wonder from scene to scene – are we seeing Sean or Michael? In retrospect, it's clearly Michael in Haddonfield and Sean on the ferry, but who murdered the paintballers at Smith's Grove? Sean, Michael, or both? And why were they even at the abandoned Smith's Grove if they were never admitted as patients there? Mysteries for future entries, perhaps. It seems apparent that most of the Shape-activity in this story is carried out by Sean, leaving Michael with little screen time and a kill count of one, possibly two if we're counting Judith.

The eventual reveal of Sean as the ferry slasher in the final moments is an effective one. As an audience, we've grown accustomed to view any white-masked slasher in this series as the Shape aka Michael Myers. But why then does Daniel make the same assumption that the killer is his long-lost brother? Milam writes that there was evidence at the farmhouse that Michael had been living there for some time. Prior to the DNA results, Daniel had assumed that the farmhouse corpse was young Sean. Given the subsequent victims, it's a short walk to pin this all on Michael.

## WHY IT WASN'T MADE

To state the obvious, Dimension execs were never quite able to settle on an initial direction for the eleventh *Halloween*. This same indecisiveness remained in effect in the months that Platinum Dunes began bringing pitches to the studio. On July 23, 2012, *Bloody-Disgusting* announced that "after nearly four months, [Platinum] Dunes is no longer working on [*Halloween*]." Upon hearing this, Scott Milam reached out to Brad Fuller, who confirmed the news. The studio was no longer developing *Halloween*. Just as earlier, Dimension was unable to choose from any of the suggested pitches, much to the frustration of Platinum's development execs. *Bloody-Disgusting*'s announcement also seemed to irritate the website's founder, who, in his announcement, noted, "There are plenty of brilliant writers out there dying to tackle these franchises, and it's mind-boggling that [Dimension] can't settle on a single pitch to get excited about."

Ultimately, Platinum Dunes would never again re-team with Dimension Films, making their *Amityville Horror* co-venture a one-off project. Platinum would, however, begin partnering with Blumhouse Productions in 2013 on franchises like *Ouija* and *The Purge*. Jumping forward, it would eventually be Blumhouse, not Platinum Dunes, that would secure the producing deal to make a new *Halloween*. Thus, despite his passion, Brad Fuller has yet to make his mark in Haddonfield. "The property I wanted […] was *Halloween*," the Platinum co-founder told *SyFy Wire*. "We really wanted *Halloween*. But it looks like what [Jason] Blum has done is awesome. Everything I hear about [*Halloween 2018*] is so positive. As a horror fan, I'm super excited to see that movie. As a producer, it's the one that got way."

Internally, Platinum Dunes would soon shift their focus from remaking classic horror films to producing entirely new ones. This would lead to the creation of several lucrative franchises including *A Quiet Place* and the aforementioned *Purge* series. Though not planned as such, their final horror remake would be 2010's *A Nightmare on Elm Street*. Fuller would later publicly acknowledge his company's retirement from the remake craze it itself had launched.

## "[Platinum Dunes has] rebooted enough. We're not going to be doing that anymore."

- Brad Fuller, CinePOP

As for Scott Milam, his next project would still involve a classic movie slasher first introduced back in the 1970s – it just wouldn't be Michael Myers. He would instead be hired to write the sequel to 2013's *Texas Chainsaw 3D*. This later morphed into the 2017 prequel *Leatherface*, which dramatically re-envisioned the character's backstory for modern audiences. (Milam would be credited as co-producer.) Beyond that, he also provided the screenplay for the 2016 thriller *Submerged* and the upcoming *Tension*, collaborating with Darren Lynn Bousman once more.

# interview:
# SCOTT MILAM
## Writer - Platinum Dunes' Halloween

Interviewed by Travis Mullins

**It's a little-known fact that Platinum Dunes briefly worked on *Halloween* alongside Dimension. What can you tell us about their association, as well as your own involvement?**

How I got involved was actually through Brad Fuller. I had heard about the opportunity through Matt Stein, who worked at Dimension. Nothing was announced but I had heard that Platinum Dunes had come in, and I didn't even know if it was true, either. I thought, '*Is this even worth me reaching out to Brad?*' But I did and said, '*Hey, Brad, I hear you guys are hearing pitches for* Halloween.' He said, '*Yeah, it's true. We're in talks. If you've got anything, send it to me.*' So, I took a shot. I'd heard through the grapevine it was a contender out of a thousand pitches. (laughs)

If they could find something that they liked and could get behind, then that would seam out their relationship with Dimension. It wasn't like they had a deal to go out and look for it. It was more like, '*If we find it, great. If we don't, then good luck.*' (laughs) I think because Platinum Dunes had success with *Friday the 13th*, Dimension was probably like, '*Hey, we've got* Halloween. *You guys should come onboard and we'll produce.*' I think Platinum was a little weary because first of all, it's Dimension. (laughs) I mean, they hadn't really worked with Dimension before. I think it was a handshake agreement. '*Look, if we can find a treatment that we all like and can get behind, then of course we'd love to try to do this.*' That was the deal as far as I know.

**Everyone regards *Halloween* as a classic but which of the sequels did you like best?**

I like the first two films; the original, of course. Some people dislike the second film, but I like it. I didn't really buy into the third one because it didn't have Michael Myers, but it is creepy on its own

488

and I do like it. Taking that one out of the equation, I like *Halloween 4*, but I'll be honest, I never really got into the sequels and that's because the mask took me out of them. (laughs) I hated the mask in the sequels, so it's always hard for me to dig in. I've seen them all, though. I was always bummed that we never got to see whatever they had in mind for the Man in Black. I was always curious like, what was that all about? *Halloween H20* was interesting. I thought it was a pretty decent sequel with Jamie Lee Curtis coming back, and then bringing her and Michael together again. But I was a lazy viewer when it came to that stuff. I didn't watch the sequels as many times as I watched the original.

I think I own the original in four different formats. It's a tradition to watch it every *Halloween*. As a kid, I had a good experience of sneaking into a theater to see it years after it had come out. I grew up in a small town adjacent to an Indian reservation. The theater was *packed*. It wasn't a fancy theater – almost like a big box, but it was dark and packed with all of these Native Americans. (laughs) It was the first time I had seen a horror movie like that, and it scared the living crap out of me. For me, the sequels have always been sort of lackluster. I like them and have a soft spot in my heart, and I'm glad they exist. They were all well-made. But when I was working on my take, I was definitely cribbing from the original *Halloween*, and maybe some of the first sequel. I didn't really pay attention to the other ones.

**Were you given any sort of mandate on what you could or couldn't do?**

No. What I heard was, '*We don't know what we're looking for, but we'll know when we see it.*' It had to take place in Haddonfield during Halloween but for the most part, they were pretty open. At one point, I heard Dimension just wanted to use the title. Like *Season of the Witch*, they just wanted to use [the] Halloween [holiday]. There weren't a lot of guidelines. They'd give you bullet points. '*We want it to feel like the original.*' They want it to *feel* that way, but they never said they wanted it to *be* that way. They wanted it to be scary. That was the thing that stuck out. Like, how do you make *Halloween* scary again?

**On that note, what are some of your own personal favorite horror remakes?**

I really did the like the *Texas Chainsaw Massacre* remake with Jessica Biel. It didn't do anything too new; it was just a more amped version, but I liked that one a lot. I wanted to like the *Friday the*

*13th* reboot, but I'll be honest with you, I'm not a big *Friday the 13th* fan. (laughs) They look like they were fun to make and would be fun to be part of, and I did do a pitch on one just because I thought it would be fun to write. I respected the Rob Zombie *Halloween* remakes. It's one of those things where I know it's not the original. A huge percentage of the movie is his own vision, which could've been a completely different movie. At the time I saw it, I didn't have much of a filter when it came to a threshold of brutality so whatever he could do, I was into. (laughs) Oh, the other remake that I thought was good over the original was *Mother's Day*! (laughs)

**Of course! Now, with your treatment, you never allow the audience to know what's coming next. The story is vaguely familiar yet completely new starting with that opening abduction. How important was it to make the changes that you did?**

It was important because I knew there were so many takes coming in. I really wanted to do something that was different and that hopefully no one else was thinking of. At the time, I thought, '*Well, I'm going to play within the same sandbox but I'm going to dump the sand out.*' I wanted to stay true to the concept while also creating something new that you could build from, instead of just tweaking little things here and there, like, '*Well, this is just* Halloween *again.*' There had been so many of those movies that, for me, it was about trying to find ideas that you could do something with later on, or characters that you could develop across a few more movies. I was always fascinated by the Clint Eastwood movie *Changeling* with Angelina Jolie. It's about a real murder that happened in California; the Chicken Coop Murders, where all these boys were abducted. Part of the movie is, Angelina Jolie's kid goes missing and she's trying to find him, and he may or may not have been a part of these Chicken Coop killings. I was fascinated by that and had always had the horrific thought of kids disappearing while trick-or-treating. I thought it was a good way into this movie, if you had Michael and his friend trick-or-treating and then being abducted. The sister Judith was still in this but in a different way where she'd be irresponsible. Basically, it was taking the Laurie dynamic of the original and making it the B-story. In a weird way, it's almost an origin story in the sense that if this movie had been made, Laurie would've been the star of the next one. The dynamics would've changed.

**I liked that this event sort of tore the Myers family apart in a different way with Judith being detached and Daniel blaming her for their kidnapping. The conversation between Rachel and Laurie reads like it would've been pretty powerful, too.**

I liked that conflict. I loved the kidnapping concept, and what this opening scene could've been. It doesn't come across this way on the page but with my ideas, it would've been about making it really scary and gut-wrenching – being responsible for watching and taking care of someone who drops out of thin air and then having to live with that remorse and regret for the rest of their lives. I was looking forward to writing all those scenes – and then the idea of the two boys who were kidnapped on Halloween night and what happened to them over the ten years they were missing. Something about that treatment is that some of the math is wrong. Like, it's ten years later and these boys were, what, seven or eight? That would make the two killers in their late teens. (laughs)

**Only gradually do we come to realize the main Shape is actually Sean Carver hence why he's going after Rachel rather than Laurie. Aside from changing things up, what was your rationale for incorporating two killers?**

I've always been fascinated by the idea of more than one killer. I had that idea with a *Friday the 13th* sequel, too. How could Jason be in so many spots at once? '*What if he has a brother?*' (laughs) I played with that here just because I wanted this first movie to be something that could lead into a second movie. Because everybody wanted franchises. That was the whole thing. '*We need franchise-able ideas! We need to make sure that we can make a new movie! Don't kill Michael!*' That was important to me in writing this.

**Here, Daniel Myers assumes much of the role that Dr. Loomis occupied in the original while Loomis is re-imagined as an advisor to the FBI. Why this change?**

I didn't want to use Loomis in the same way. I've had the idea for a Daniel-type character for a while and I thought, '*Well, maybe this character will work here.*' In the original film, I liked that

Loomis was sort of the guy who's pushing the narrative forward, when it came to warning people about Michael and trying to find him. I wanted to do that here, but I also wanted to make it as if he knew something more than he was telling. Again, it was a set-up for another movie while giving this one enough momentum to where it could be its own movie without all that other stuff. In this movie, Daniel's sort of the version of Loomis that he was in the original. Loomis was still a part of Smith's Grove but in this version, that's more of his backstory. He became more of a *Mindhunter* guy – a John Douglas-esque type that was able to go out and profile these people. The thing about treatments – especially this treatment – is that it was designed to offer, '*Here's what I'm thinking. Here's all the moving parts. If you guys are interested, maybe we can sit down and start talking about certain things, developing and fleshing it out.*'

The treatment is very dense. My writing is better now than it was then so if I were to do it again, I would've probably structured the whole a lot differently, and made it cleaner. The way the studios do it, anyway, is they have one of their minions read it and cherry-pick things. '*This is a cool idea. That's a cool idea.*' And if they like it, they might steal it if they don't want to hire you. (laughs) If there's a hundred takes being submitted by every writer in town, who's to say they haven't come up with the same idea? That was part of my motivation. '*There's no way they would've come up with this!*' (laughs) Or at least I didn't think. I had sketched notes like, '*Well, this is what this is now, but if I ever write the script, then maybe I'd flesh it out this way.*' It excited me. It was something that I knew I could write, something I would've been a fan of to see.

**I think Dustin and I were surprised by how much we liked it. Though it does seem like something the studios might be hesitant on pursuing.**

That's sort of the rub in some ways. It's like, you want to go in and give them something totally different while staying in familiar territory, something that would get them excited and motivated, like, '*Yeah, this is something! We're onto something here!*' But then there's the other thought where it's like, they'll say all this stuff but then they talk themselves out of it and want to go in a more conservative route. '*Oh, we want to give the fans what the fans want.*' Sometimes, the fans don't know what they want until they get it. They may speculate, like, '*There better be so-and-so in this movie or else I'm not watching it!*' I get it. It's that knee-jerk thing. '*Oh, Michael Keaton as Batman? No way!*' It was definitely a roll of the dice.

**In terms of masks, did you see them being the same or might that have changed as well?**

You know, that's a good question. I didn't get specific about it in the treatment because I thought that was a bigger decision. You've got to have the mask in some way, shape or form, but how do you get it in the movie if you're trying to reboot the thing? I always thought one of the ways to do something like that was with the paintball scene. I had described that they were all wearing masks of different styles and whatnot. Would the Shape mask be one of the masks that the paintballers were wearing? I never got specific about it because it felt like it was going to be a bigger conversation, if they wanted that to be a part of the new *Halloween* or not. You almost need it because it's so iconic. I mean, it could be different in some way. It's just one of those things where it felt like a bigger conversation, so I didn't bother trying to figure it out. Sometimes, people will get bogged down by one little detail in your treatment or script, so it's a real conversation you need to have. '*Where does he get the mask? Are we going to have the mask in the movie? Is it going to be a different mask? Oh, we gotta have the mask!*'

**Tell us about the significance of the Black River Killer.**

I think the Black River Killer is who I had in mind as being similar to the Chicken Coop Killer. He was abducting these young boys and getting inside their heads or maybe using them as devices – almost like it could've been a cult. I was a bit inspired by the Man in Black, to be honest. '*How do I take a nod from that and stitch it into this story?*' I hadn't completely figured it out. Basically, I put it out there and hopefully, that would've drummed up enough of a conversation. It might not have even been necessary. It could've been cut out of the movie if it were to get that far. My idea was that we would eventually come to figure out what that was all about. Maybe he's the Boy Scout master and Michael and Sean are the Boy Scouts. Maybe these boys are being groomed to cause harm, whatever agenda he had in mind. I was trying to imply that bigger things were going on while also keeping it small so that we didn't get too much information. The whole idea, to begin with, was to keep the killers mysterious so that they would be scary.

The idea was to imply that the boys were being trained or groomed – and who's to say they were the only ones? They're the only ones that we knew of that had come back to Haddonfield. But under what orders? Were they ordered to go back into town and do what they were doing? You know, maybe the Black River Killer had other boys of the same ilk in different towns doing the same thing. When you do these treatments, the big thing is that you're trying to keep everything distilled down to something that's relatively clean without a whole lot of moving parts. That's why it was important to keep some of the familiar stuff intact. When you give producers or execs too many questions to stew on, sometimes they'll stew on the wrong things and then you've shot yourself in the foot. I was trying to keep a balance between a new story with new characters, while at the same time, following a familiar path with familiar characters.

I thought it was interesting because I didn't know where it was going to go – the whole idea of someone being mysterious where you're not one-hundred percent sure how they fit into anything, if they fit into anything at all. Because I was completely okay with it being something unrelated, and sending Daniel and Loomis down this path where it's like, '*Well, are we on the right path?*' Once they make the discovery at the farm, I think it pretty much cements what went on there. They find the remains of several bodies and find one that still has blonde hair, implying that it's Sean. But when you later find out that it wasn't him, then it may not have been the same thing, or the right lead. It's one of those things that you put in the story and then see if it sticks.

**Going off this, is there a significance to the mysterious symbols that Daniel and Loomis find painted on the walls of Smith's Grove?**

In my head, I always felt that Sean and Michael went to Smith's Grove to hide out, which is why when the paintballers show up, they get taken out. I had always thought that the symbols meant something, like a secret language, but it was one of those seeds that you plant. I wasn't one-hundred percent sure what the end result would be. Sometimes, you plant seeds where you're not sure what they're going to grow into, but you have an idea that they will be connected. We call them conversation starters. '*Wait, tell us more about the Black River Killer. Tell us about the symbols. Tell us what happened in the ten years that the boys were under this guy's spell.*' At some point, it would've been explained, if the treatment had been developed any further. Maybe we'd find out more in the opening scene of the sequel – give you a hint of what these boys went through and then you'd cut to the present day and continue the story. I knew I wanted to do something more with it so by adding those elements, it gave me conversation starters and seeds to plant. '*Here's some ideas that can elevate the movie and take it in another place it's not known for,*' which is what seemed like was going on with the Man in Black in the earlier sequels.

**In terms of the abduction of Michael and Sean, in the treatment, you justify your changes, noting that the standard 'clinical mumbo jumbo' was boring for today's audiences. Could you elaborate on that?**

It wasn't necessarily boring per se, but I think what gets monotonous is just that we've been there and done that, with the analysis of the doctor sitting down and trying to get inside the head of Michael. We've already been down that road before. It was a matter of, '*Is there a way for us to just get away from that?*' Which is why with him being abducted, we don't know what happened during that time or what turned him into what he is. I think once you get too far inside the mind of what makes these people tick, then it sort of dilutes their effectiveness of being unpredictable and scary. I mean, *Mindhunter* does a great job of that approach because they interview all these serial killers to find out why they did what they did. That stuff's interesting but back then, there was no *Mindhunter*. So, when I wrote this, I thought, '*Why not just get rid of that kind of stuff?*' and make it more visceral, in a way, where the things we find out are unexplainable.

By using the abduction angle here, you just don't know what happened to them during all this time. Had I been fortunate to do a sequel, maybe we would've explored a bit more of that manipulation. You know, holding up pictures of the family. '*They abandoned you. They let you go. They never came looking for you. That means they never loved you,*' sort of conditioning their minds and probably even making them do things like killing other boys. '*This boy's been bad. He's not good for us. If he gets away, he's going to hurt us.*' Maybe the boys killed other boys as part of their conditioning or training, whatever they were put through to turn them into what they became. The imagery they find [at Smith's Grove], it's almost like a beacon to others. You know, there's so much weird cult-y type stuff like Waco and how he brainwashed all these people, and that's always what I thought about this Black River Killer character. There's a lot to mine from something like that.

It's been a long time since I read the treatment. When I did, I was like, '*Eh, this isn't terrible,*' but I can see why they probably didn't want to make it because it was a bit too outside the box for what they were comfortable with doing because they want to make money. They want to make a successful franchise. As much pussyfooting as they do when it comes to finding a take that works, they usually go back to what worked before. (laughs)

**The finale on the ferry reads like it would've been quite a spectacle. Upon re-reading your treatment, do you have any favorite moments?**

I definitely have a big thing for the ferry sequence. I've been trying to do ferry sequences in a couple of horror projects over the last several years. I grew up in Seattle and took the ferries a lot. One of my early jobs out of college was that I would drive and pick up medical samples. One of my routes was to hop on a ferry, take a thirty-minute ride, pick up samples, get back on the ferry and drive back to the hospital. Sometimes, you're waiting two hours for a ferry. All these cars are packed in this lot by the pier, and in rows, they load onto the ferry. A lot of people get out and walk around, especially if the ride is almost an hour, because you can go up top and get coffee or snacks. It's actually a beautiful experience if you ever get the opportunity. It's just neat. The islands are always cool, too, because they're small communities. No one's ever really done a horror movie on a ferry, at least that I know of, where you're sitting in your car and then go upstairs and you're just like, '*Man, this ferry is really long.*' If you were stuck on this thing, where would you go? How would you escape? With the cars down below, it's like this massive parking lot with no way out except going into the water.

I thought I hadn't seen this before and maybe this would be a cool thing to do in something like this. I could've had fun with Michael doing his thing in this setting. The fact that the kids were going to Port Townsend; some of the areas that I knew of [growing up] didn't celebrate Halloween. They were very conservative and religious, so the idea of celebrating a Pagan holiday isn't for them. (laughs) So, for kids who did want to celebrate Halloween, it was kind of edgy to go off and have their own little parties and what not. That was the inspiration behind that. '*Rachel doesn't want to celebrate Halloween because she hates it so let's go somewhere she won't be reminded of it.*' And of course, there it is on full display. (laughs) I liked the Port Townsend stuff because part of me felt like that was the most original stuff that I could bring to it. I liked the stuff with Daniel and Loomis, too. I like those type of characters and could imagine the banter being written for the two of them. Those are fun things to write, probably the things I liked best about it.

**Is there anything you'd do differently with your story today?**

That's a good question. Probably not. I mean, it was pretty much what I thought I could write and pitch in the room, if they wanted me to come in. If I could've done anything differently, I guess I would've positioned Laurie at the forefront of the story. In this version, she's sort of a secondary character while Rachel is the lead. I may have tried to maintain more of a balance with that and that could've easily happened if there had been more work on this, if they said, '*Hey, here's some notes. Make Laurie and Rachel more of a team.*' I probably would've killed Rachel, and in the last few minutes, maybe Laurie would've become the focal point. She's the face of *Halloween* when it comes to that, so by introducing this version, I think I would've balanced the two characters, giving Laurie more stuff to work with instead of just making her Rachel's friend.

**You mentioned that your treatment was a contender – out of a thousand pitches. Did you ever receive any feedback from Brad Fuller or anyone from Dimension?**

I believe I had heard that through my manager. Once I made the initial contact, I let my reps know that I was doing this, and they gave me their support. They try to keep you hopeful because they don't know what's going to happen. Their guess is as good as yours. I don't recall getting any feedback from Brad. He may have had someone else read and do coverage. In that situation, when you have so many people coming in with takes, it's not like Brad has the time to read all of them. Most producers don't read their own stuff. They just get coverage. '*You should read this. This is really cool.*' After that, they'll take the time to read, but for the most part, it's like, '*Oh, just put it on the stack. Here's the contender stack. Here's the non-contender stack.*' I didn't hear from Brad specifically, but I had heard that he liked it and it was a contender. That was the end of it. I never heard anything afterward, which was kind of a bummer. You always want some response. '*Oh, we loved it. Big fans. But it doesn't necessarily fit with the direction we're going in.*' But then you're like, '*Well, what direction are you going in because you just told me you don't know!*' (laughs)

**As we know, Platinum Dunes never had the chance to oversee a Halloween sequel. Do you know what exactly led to their exit?**

What I'd heard is that, ultimately, the guys at Platinum became frustrated. Like with anything Dimension was involved with, they were too hesitant to pull the trigger. It's like, '*Look, we just put all these takes on the material in front of you, and you guys just can't make up your minds about which one you want to pursue.*' Dimension was so flaky. It was such a revolving door company which is why I think a lot of things got held up. It seemed like there was a new VP every year, and they always promised to make movies. *Hellraiser* went through the same thing. I actually pitched on that as well. So, I think it was a butting heads situation. Finally, that's when the guys at Platinum Dunes were like, '*Okay, we're done. We're not going to waste any more of our time or resources trying to find a take for a movie that shouldn't be that difficult to make.*' By talking to Brad, I knew that he was frustrated, almost like he didn't believe they would ever actually get there. That's why I don't think there was ever a deal in place for an official announcement. It was all whispers and hearsay.

I actually resubmitted the treatment back when Blumhouse was taking pitches as well. For a while there, they didn't know what they were going to do. I knew Ryan Turek pretty well and I actually know Jason [Blum] as well, so it was a pretty easy way to say, '*Yeah, I did a treatment around the time Platinum Dunes was involved.*' I thought about coming up with something new. It always felt like a big waste of time because those guys usually go for the path of least resistance. It's like, '*Jesus, if I knew you guys were going to do the version you did, then yeah, I probably should've gone a different direction!*' (laughs) But everybody was thinking of a way to stand out from the crowd. When you go into these writing assignment bake-offs, everybody's coming up with the same stuff, so the challenge is separating yourself from the pack and coming up with something that no one else was thinking of.

**How do you think fans would've reacted to such a radical reboot of the series?**

I would hope they would see it as something new, as if somebody made an effort to try something new with the material instead of just giving audiences a paint-by-numbers retread of what's already been done before. As a fan myself, I wanted to try something different that I would've loved to have seen, while still honoring what we all loved about *Halloween* instead of just going with an easy, lazy take on it. Part of me thinks you can never make anyone happy. There would've been people that hated it and there would've been people who liked it as much as you guys did.

That's all you can ever ask for when you write this stuff. You're just never going to make people happy, so I basically wrote what I would've wanted to see.

## How would you envision a sequel to this?

I think Laurie would've been the lead and maybe the story went in a more traditional approach. To be honest, I didn't give it a lot of thought. I just knew I wanted Laurie as the lead, with Michael having just killed Judith at the end of the first treatment, which is a nod back to the original film's opening. He escapes, and Daniel and Loomis would be involved in tracking him down. With Sean Carver put to bed, maybe you'd open the sequel with some information about what happened to the boys during their time of abduction, shedding some light on the whole Black River Killer thing. Something I probably would've done was extract more information out of Loomis. He would've been an exposition device, relaying some information he's already compiled. We would've come to find that this isn't new to him. He's been aware of these situations, and maybe he hasn't been ready to present his findings. Some of it might've been hard to swallow.

Maybe Loomis had dealt with the Black River Killer in the past. Maybe he feels that could be the person that needs to be investigated. With Sean Carver dead, we would need Loomis to figure out who this Black River Killer is, to see if he's even connected to these boys – all in order to get to Michael, bring him in, go through the whole PTSD thing, if he has anything like that. There'd be a lot to unpack there. An angle like this might've even given you a goal, in that if you get Michael, maybe it would help with another situation. Maybe another abduction has occurred. That could've even been a component of this first treatment if it had been developed any further. Maybe another kid has been abducted on Halloween, so use that as an investigating situation to get you into the next story. Those are sort of my vague ideas.

## Have you seen the latest film? If so, what were your thoughts?

I enjoyed it the first time I watched it. I guess it's one of those movies that I never really need to see again. I can't put my finger on the pulse of it because I'd have to watch it again. Not that I hated it. I liked it, and thought it was okay. I thought there was some cool stuff in it. I thought there were some missed opportunities. I don't know what the sequels are going to be like. I thought it was well-made, but it wasn't my favorite. I didn't really buy the Jamie Lee Curtis thing that much, just some of the tonal stuff. I didn't really care about the granddaughter. I did like the PTSD element. It made sense that Laurie would be like that because she went through a pretty horrific thing, but there was a lot of stuff that earned that [in the sequels] that if you were to just bank on that movie as a sequel to the original *Halloween*, I don't know if it warranted that. I don't know. It feels like it only earns that because of everything we've seen before in the different movies.

**That said, do you think the series would still benefit from going a drastically different route?**

It's hard to say because what they have going right now is working for them. After all is said and done, if a drastic route approach to *Halloween* were taken, I think it could work. At some point, you have new audiences. You've got 12-year-olds who are getting to see these movies in ways that you couldn't when there were restrictions. Now, with VOD and all these other things, the younger kids are still getting their eyes on these kinds of movies. I think you have more leniency to reinvent things in ways that aren't so familiar because you have a new audience that is being reared on what movies are now, and at some point, they're going to want something new. It depends on what the idea is, too. But *Halloween*, the name itself is such that you can do a variation. *Season of the Witch* was the first time they tried to do something different with the title *Halloween* but without Michael Myers. After David Gordon Green is done with his movies, and whatever Blum is planning with the next trilogy of movies, I mean, what's it going to look like? Even in the one they just did; Michael Myers is an old man! He's in his sixties. (laughs) At some point, he's going to die. So, who's taking over? Who's going to be the next threat? Or are they just going to do a complete reboot, start from scratch and literally remake *Halloween* with new actors and just tell the same story again? I do feel that by doing that, it kind of takes the air out of the tire. But if you take *Halloween* out of the title and create a new take on the story, what is that? Is it another cool story that happens on Halloween and takes place in the same universe? I mean, there's so many options to try and figure it out. It's really a simple story at the end of the day. I mean, how complicated do you want to make it? (laughs)

It's really a loaded question because it gives you a lot to unpack in your head. Because you're not just thinking about the story itself and what the movies are, you're also thinking about the world that these movies are living in now, and the kinds of movies they are and where they fit with all the rest of the movies out there. When *Halloween* came out – even the sequels – there was a certain type of movie that was out at the time, a certain vibe. All the horror movies of the last ten to twenty years have gone through different tonal shifts from fun, laugh-out-loud gorefests to really intense, sweat-dripping-down-your-head movies. There's a lot of reinvention, a lot of experimentation, with Jordan Peele and what he's bringing to the picture. But if you look at Jordan Peele's movies, they're very *Halloween*-influenced in the style they're made. So, with TV and all of the content out there, it's like sensory overload. All of them are trying to take things to the next level or try different approaches in storytelling. I think anything's possible with *Halloween*, where you almost need to reinvent it, in some way, to keep it fresh and interesting, because if you keep remaking the same movies over and over again, in one way, shape or form, I don't know if they can stand the test of time, in the company these films are keeping.

Everybody is trying to outdo each other now with different takes and different visions. It almost feels like *Halloween* could easily suffer the fate of being very pedestrian in their approach to storytelling. But *Halloween* has a few things going for it. It's a name recognizable franchise with a lot of fans and it's like comfort food. (laughs) I don't know what *Halloween Kills* does. But with everybody looking super excited about it, hopefully that's a good thing. I would be very discouraged if I heard the opposite. But I don't know, it's a hard one to put your finger on because who knows where we'll be at in the world by then? The world is changing and has changed so much, it's affecting the output of content and what that's going to look like. Will people want the stuff that feels familiar? Or are they going to want new, fantastical versions of things? It's just really hard to think about right now because of the world we live in, and what entertainment as a whole is going to look like in the next years to come. Where does *Halloween* fit in all of that?

THE REBOOT TRILOGY

RISE OF THE BOOGEYMAN    THE WITCHING HOUR    FIRES OF SAMHAIN

The Night *Halloween* Came Home!

**Treatments by**
**Stef Hutchinson**

As mentioned in the previous chapter, the *Halloween* franchise had fallen into a narrative bind in the wake of Rob Zombie's *Halloween II*. The Weinsteins still had no desire to return to the *H20* continuity for a direct sequel to *Halloween: Resurrection*. And yet the new remake timeline seemed a dead end with the director's cut deaths of Laurie, Loomis, and Michael. There was just no clear direction as to what should happen next. As writer Stef Hutchinson saw it, that alone was the problem. The solution then was not to simply contrive a new sequel but to imbue the series with that missing sense of direction.

When we last left Hutchinson in late 2009, he had just submitted a draft of *Halloween 3D* to Trancas International Films. That script, like the *Halloween III* project itself, would ultimately go nowhere. Sadly, the *Halloween* comics that Hutchinson had also been nurturing along would abruptly cease publication this same year. This left the concluding issue of *The First Death of Laurie Strode* trilogy unpublished, much to the frustration of readers. As *Halloween*'s prospects dried up, the UK-based scribe turned his attention elsewhere in the genre. He would next direct select interviews for the documentaries *Never Sleep Again: The Elm Street Legacy* and *Scream: The Inside Story*. Hutchinson would also write comic sequels to Lamberto Bava's *Demons* and George Romero's *Day of the Dead*. He would return to *Halloween* in 2012 by providing liner notes to the expanded edition release of Alan Howarth's *Halloween 4* soundtrack. This is when he took notice of the franchise's lack of direction. As he saw it, the two best options for reviving *Halloween* were with either a standalone sequel in the original timeline or with another reboot, both options widely unprecedented in the genre.

It's important that we appropriately contextualize Hutchinson's realization within the cinematic climate of the time. The year is 2012 and horror isn't exactly flourishing at the box office. Ignoring cross-genre fare like *Dark Shadows* and *Underworld: Awakening*, the top horror grosser is *Paranormal Activity 4*. With a domestic haul of $53.9 million, this marks the lowest-grossing box office topper for the genre since 1996. By now, nearly all of the classic horror franchises had been rebooted. Rob Zombie's *Halloween*, while a success for the franchise, had trailed the box office hauls of other slasher remakes by tens of millions of dollars. No major slasher property had yet been rebooted *twice* in so few years. Nor were any franchises returning to their original continuities. The *Halloween* series had chased trends before, but there was just no trend to chase.

After mulling the state of the franchise, Hutchinson reasoned that *Halloween*'s best bet was to reinvent itself once again but with a focus on longform storytelling. If done correctly, this could potentially propel *Halloween* out of its slump and forward across multiple sequels. To this end, Hutchinson formulated story possibilities for a new trilogy of films. He would pen a full treatment for the first chapter entitled *Rise of the Boogeyman* and conceive rough outlines for the subsequent entries titled *The Witching Hour* and *Fires of Samhain*. While his proposed trilogy would tell a complete story, it would also leave the door open for future tales. It might seem like a no-brainer to plan out the franchise's future with a narrative roadmap, but this is just not how *Halloween* has ever operated, at least not until the Blumhouse trilogy. Circa 2012, it was a fresh idea.

"There's almost an irresponsibility with the *Halloween* movies," Hutchinson says. "Everyone wants to say '*Mine's the final one. That's it. I'm closing it off*'. But it's a franchise, so why would you ever do that? All you're doing is making it hard for the next person who comes along. I wanted to do the opposite. At the end of mine, I wanted there to be a massive blank canvas for anyone to add on what they want."

It's interesting to compare Hutchinson's reboot trilogy with Todd Farmer and Patrick Lussier's *Halloween 3.0*. On the surface, they bear some passing similarity. Both projects sprang to life within a year of each other. Hutchinson was pitching his ideas to Malek Akkad at Trancas International Films while Farmer and Lussier were working with Bob Weinstein at The Weinstein Company. Both pitches sought to reboot the franchise timeline but in very different ways. *Halloween 3.0* was arguably the safer proposal whereas Hutchinson's vision served as a major departure from *Halloween* as we then knew it. Overall, they're far more different than alike.

## PART ONE: RISE OF THE BOOGEYMAN

The first chapter of Hutchinson's trilogy opens in Haddonfield on October 31, 1984. Seventeen-year-old Debra Strode and her boyfriend Jake are babysitting five-year-old Sally. They receive a phone call from a hysterical woman named Jennifer begging them to leave the house because "the darkness is coming." Brushing this off as a prank, they ignore her warning. The house loses power and they're soon attacked by a young boy in a clown costume, who badly injures Debra before killing her boyfriend. Having also been tipped off by Jennifer, police arrive just in time to see the boy plunge his knife in young Sally's skull. (Main titles here.) Finding her to be highly disturbed, Jennifer is placed under the care of psychiatrist Sam Loomis. She attributes her foreknowledge of the night's attacks to a vision she saw while gazing through the veil separating life and death. Loomis, who considers this a delusion, seems utterly incapable of helping her. Jennifer will eventually commit suicide by self-immolating on the front lawn of Sally's home, which has been nicknamed "the Murder House" by locals.

> **Jennifer to Loomis:** "*I couldn't save them. You can't save anybody from these things, but I had to try. And now he's here. Do you know how many people they would sacrifice to keep the darkness away? The fires they'd set up on the hillside to burn women and children? The hills and the fields, they were drenched with rivers of blood – and it's going to happen again.*"

We then flash forward to October 29, 2015 in nearby Morton, Illinois. Loomis is now a family man with a supportive wife Maria and six-year-old son David. He's about to begin a new job at Smith's Grove Psychiatric Hospital in Russellville, but remains haunted by his previous failure to save Jennifer. Maria gives him a small present for good luck, a Zippo lighter engraved "SAM." In touring Smith's Grove, Loomis encounters the boy from the opening, whose identity was never confirmed. Unofficially referred to as "the Boogeyman," he's been largely catatonic for the past three decades. That doesn't stop him from spooking Loomis, however, who unknowingly drops his new lighter in the patient's cell. In his moment of terror, Loomis envisions quick flashes of a strange netherworld similar to what Jennifer described years before. That night, a deadly fire breaks out at Smith's Grove. To the staff's horror, the patients also experience a synchronized mass seizure, banging their heads against the walls until bloodied and unconscious. Amid the chaos, the Boogeyman escapes into the night.

Loomis is woken several hours later with news of the fire. While heading in to help, he stops to buy a pack of cigarettes and notices his lighter missing. Mentally retracing his steps, he reaches the alarming conclusion that he must've dropped it in the Boogeyman's cell. Upon learning of the slasher's escape, Loomis speeds toward Haddonfield, believing the Shape will return to his old stomping grounds. Elsewhere in Haddonfield, a pair of seventeen-year-olds – Annie Brackett and Laurie Strode – are discussing their Halloween plans. The ordinarily social Annie will be babysitting eight-year-old Kelly. In doing so, she'll be skipping a small Halloween party thrown by gal pal Tara, which promises booze, pills, and weed. Meanwhile, the socially awkward Laurie will be staying home with her mentally ill mother, whom we recognize as Debra from the opening.

Unfortunately, Laurie doesn't last until nightfall, instead encountering the Shape in her bedroom. In a ghastly kill, he quite literally cuts her like a pumpkin.

Across town, Sheriff Hall and Deputy Brackett are investigating a hardware store break-in where several masks were stolen among other items. Upon arriving in town, Loomis tries warning Debra Strode of the Shape's escape, but she responds with hysterics. He next visits the Murder House where he has a brief but terrifying encounter with the Shape. This quick visit ends with Brackett angrily arresting Loomis for upsetting Debra. ("I know who you are, Loomis. And I don't need to know you personally to know I don't like you at all.") Sheriff Hall believes Loomis' hunch to be worth checking out and joins him out on patrol, but not before ordering Brackett to remain at the station to cool down. As night falls on Haddonfield, the Shape attacks Tara and her friends, slaughtering them in grisly fashion.

Returning to his hotel room, Loomis tries sketching the netherworld from his earlier vision. He plays back one of his taped consultations sessions with Jennifer, focusing on her words as she speaks of the veil between worlds. Closing his eyes, Loomis finds himself standing in this netherworld – known here as the "Liminal." He's quickly attacked by the young boy from the opening, which jolts him back to reality. Just then, he receives a call from Smith's Grove. Staff have made an unsettling discovery within the Boogeyman's burned cell – the dead body of a nurse and a name written countless times in smeared blood. ("LOOMIS.") With this, a haunting laughter drowns out the call. Loomis tries another phone, but the laughter is inescapable – it's on every phone line. The veil separating the worlds has begun to tear apart. Alarmingly, this event causes ravens to fall from the sky in large numbers, dying instantly upon smashing into the ground.

Elsewhere, Sheriff Hall checks on Annie and Kelly just as the Shape attacks, wounding Annie. The girls manage to escape, though Hall is killed while defending them. Annie tries calling for help, but the phone lines are still overrun with laughter. With the veil thinning, Loomis manages to track Annie and Kelly by following their ethereal screams in the netherworld. (Though he physically walks in reality, he's experiencing visions from the Liminal.) The girls escape to Tara's home where they discover the mutilated corpses of Tara and her party friends. Concurrent with this, Debra discovers Laurie's corpse. Just before the laughter drowns her out, she hysterically phones Brackett, who sets out into the night. The Shape arrives at Tara's to terrorize the girls once more. Too injured to run any further, Annie helps Kelly escape to safety. Loomis arrives a moment later, but is unable to stop the Shape from slitting Annie's throat and vanishing into the night. Brackett rushes in to find Loomis cradling his dying daughter. Overcome with anger and sadness, he shoots Loomis in the chest. As Loomis lies gasping for air, he has one final horrifying vision from the Liminal. Too pained to speak, he silently mouths his wife's name.

Back in Morton, Maria Loomis waits by the phone, having been unable to reach her husband for hours. A police cruiser belonging to Deputy Brackett pulls into her driveway. Maria hears a knock and goes to answer it. Opening the door, she screams. The door slams shut and the house goes silent. ("Only the sounds of the wind and rustling leaves remain.")

## NOT YOUR FATHER'S HALLOWEEN

It was Wes Craven who famously said, "The first monster you have to scare the audience with is yourself." This could not be more appropriate for Stef Hutchinson and *Rise of the Boogeyman*. With the opening murders, Hutchinson would've immediately jolted the audience from their comfort zone. He once again breaks one of the unspoken rules of the slasher film – *you don't kill the kid*. It's a rule every *Halloween* has abided by thus far with the exception of *Season of the Witch* and perhaps *Halloween 2018*. In *Rise of the Boogeyman*'s opening moments, the young Shape murders Debra Strode's teenage boyfriend, which is nothing too shocking. Police arrive soon after and we're made to feel as though the danger has passed. That's when the adolescent Shape emerges from the darkness to bury his knife into five-year-old Sally's skull, killing her instantly. With this, Hutchinson has shattered the social contract between the filmmakers and the audience. If he'll break this rule so early on, there's no telling what he might do next. All bets are off. No one is safe.

And that's just the start. *Rise of the Boogeyman* stands as the most provocative and outside-the-box project you're going to read about in this book. It might honestly be too smartly written not only for this franchise, but the slasher sub-genre as well. *Rise* isn't a simple retelling of John Carpenter's *Halloween* – it's a complete reinvention from the ground up. Its screenwriter modifies not only the characters we've come to know but their relationships to one another. His story is one of supernatural and psychological terror. To state the obvious, this is not your father's *Halloween*.

So much has already been said about how the original *Halloween* worked because of its winning simplicity. That simplicity applied not only to the story but to the characters as well. The residents of that Haddonfield led normal lives in a town where the only gunshots you ever heard were to start the local track meet. Yet the same cannot be said of those in Hutchinson's story as he takes a decidedly different approach. These versions of the characters are all damaged in some way. Loomis is still recovering from the tragic suicide of the patient he couldn't save. Having been a friend of the dead woman, Brackett harbors a deep grudge against Loomis for his failure. Laurie isn't exactly carefree either, struggling to cope with her mother's paranoia and mental illness, both attributable to her encounter with the Shape decades before. Hutchinson clearly isn't interested in writing vanilla characters. These Haddonfield residents come with scars both physical and emotional. It all makes for a much more complex story.

As a storyteller, Hutchinson clearly relishes the opportunity to show you something familiar and then shatter your expectation of what will happen next. When the story opens with a knife-wielding boy dressed as a clown, we expect to see the teenage babysitter murdered. (We do NOT expect a five-year-old to die in her place.) When we meet Laurie Strode in the second act, we expect her to become the new main character. (We do NOT expect her to die several scenes later, before nightfall even.) When an armed Loomis rushes in to save Annie at film's end, we expect him to fire upon the Shape six times. (We do NOT expect Loomis to choke, allowing the Shape to slash Annie's throat.) When Brackett arrives a moment later, we expect him to grieve his daughter. (We do NOT expect him to shoot Loomis in the chest.) Hutchinson doesn't care how many times you've seen *Halloween*. He's not here to play into your preconceived notions – he's here to destroy them.

## ENTER THE LIMINAL

If we're being honest, it's a missed opportunity that the *Halloween* franchise has only ever tiptoed around its ties to the ancient festival of Samhain with throwaway references and nods. Aside from being namedropped in the second, third, and sixth installments, it's just never played that big of a role in the ongoing mythology. With his reboot trilogy, Hutchinson aimed to change that in a big way. His story doesn't just hint at a supernatural backstory – it fully embraces it. Samhain, of course, refers to the Gaelic festival commemorating the end of the harvest season and the beginning of winter. Celebrants would dance around huge bonfires, create alters to honor their dead, and partake in special feasts. It was during these festivals that ancient peoples believed the veil separating life and death grew thin, which allowed for some passage between the worlds. Samhain would later inspire the holiday we now know as Halloween.

In *Rise of the Boogeyman*, the world of the dead is known as "the Liminal." Hutchinson describes this as "a dark otherworld which exists on the other side of the veil, what seems to be the land of the unquiet spirits, the land of the dead." Per Merriam-Webster, a liminal refers to an intermediate or transitional state between places. In this case, it represents a gateway between our reality and the afterlife, a crossing over space. The word itself derives from the Latin root – limen – which means threshold, also an appropriate descriptor. The Liminal appears to be where this story's Boogeyman first originated and where he also summons his power from. (We might draw comparisons between this story's Liminal and the Upside-Down from *Stranger Things*. Of course, *Rise* predates *Stranger Things* by several years.)

Hutchinson shows us multiple visual representations of the Liminal throughout his story, though we won't grasp its full significance until closer to the ending. The opening scene finds Debra sketching it before she receives the disturbing phone call. (She teases little Sally, "This is where the monsters come from!") Loomis sees a quick flash of the Liminal when spooked by the Shape at Smith's Grove. He later sketches it at home, though he knows not why. Annie Brackett is shown to have painted multiple canvases of the portal in her home-studio. Hutchinson describes the Liminal as a terrifying landscape filled with blackened trees, twisted branches, bloody pathways, and the charred skulls of both humans and animals. This dark world is filled with grinning swede lanterns, which are an early and even creepier form of jack-o-lanterns carved from turnips and rutabagas.

**Jennifer to Loomis:** *"It's everything. It's the end and the beginning. Life and death itself. You see, the veil, whatever it is that keeps us from the other worlds, it's thinner on Halloween night. Things that shouldn't be here can come through. And they do - I watched it happen. […] Some of us can see it, Doctor Loomis. They used to call us witches. The babysitter saw it, that horrible place. She didn't even realize it. She didn't stare into it like I did. I couldn't look away and the Boogeyman crossed over. I could see where he would be, see the horrible things he wanted to do. He let me see just to taunt me."*

As revealed in her consultations, Jennifer was cursed with the ability to see into the Liminal, which allowed her to warn Debra of the Shape's approach. Loomis later focuses his mind on his own sketch of the gateway, which gives him the same cursed ability. He uses this new perception to track Annie and Kelly by their ethereal screams in an effort to find and help them. Tapping into the Liminal is something made easier by the fact that the veil is much thinner on Halloween. By night's end, the veil has begun to tear apart entirely, spilling evil into our world. We first see this manifested in the phone lines, which are filled with the endless laughter of a creepy clown toy.

Hutchinson doesn't go all-in on the Liminal concept in this first story. Rather, he introduces the idea and gives us a tease of what all it could entail. The second and third parts of his trilogy would've explored this dimension to a much greater extent. It's an intriguing thought that the Shape's evil would grow stronger as the veil between worlds thins, which seems to crescendo as Halloween night unfolds. This would eventually result in a period of time where the veil outright splits – spilling over so much evil and madness into our world. There's also the eerie effect the Liminal has on the natural world – causing ravens to fall from the sky.

## NEW LOOMIS

While *Halloween 2007* offered audiences a new spin on Michael Myers, it didn't change all that much with Sam Loomis. Sure, Malcolm McDowell's version wasn't quite as doom-prophesizing as Donald Pleasence's, but they were essentially the same role. In both the 1978 and 2007 films, Loomis is assigned by the court to be young Michael's psychiatrist in the wake of his horrific crime(s). Hutchinson foregoes this familiarity for a much different take on the character. As we find him in *Rise of the Boogeyman*, Loomis hasn't yet joined the staff of Smith's Grove Sanitarium. Nor has he met Michael Audrey Myers. Nor will he ever serve as the slasher's psychiatrist.

So how does he get tangled up in the story if not by being the Shape's court-appointed doctor? By providing psychiatric care to one of his victims. Loomis is assigned to care for Jennifer, the prophetic caller from the opening with the cursed ability to see into the Liminal. She's understandably haunted by the painful memory of that tragic night, of the little girl and young man she was unable to save with her intervention. Jennifer eventually succumbs to her demons by lighting herself on fire outside the "Murder House" where it all happened, ending her suffering and her life. Loomis' failure to save Jennifer is one he takes very personally. We gather that he still feels responsible for her death, even as he prepares to start a new job at Smith's Grove.

Not that Loomis and the Shape don't eventually cross paths – *they do*. In fact, Hutchinson gives us the treat of allowing us to eavesdrop on their first encounter inside Smith's Grove. Unlike in the 1978 and 2007 films, Loomis first meets the Shape as a grown man, not a boy. Entering into his cell, the already-nervous Loomis is badly startled by the silent slasher, even though he displays no outward aggression. It's here he unknowingly drops his lighter, which the Shape will later use to escape. Loomis is devastated upon the realization that he enabled the Boogeyman to break out of Smith's Grove. Given the countless lives at stake, he rushes to Haddonfield in an effort to recapture the escaped patient before bodies start to pile up. He doesn't know it yet, but he's already become a target of the monster he's now hunting. Smith's Grove staff find the escaped patient's cell in startling condition with Loomis' name having been written countless times on its walls... *in blood*.

In another departure from earlier depictions, this Loomis is a family man. (Pleasence's Loomis never mentions a wife or kids. McDowell's Loomis does mention several short-lived marriages, but no children.) He appears happily married to Maria with whom he has a son in young David. The new facet to the character is an important one as it means Loomis has something to lose – his loved ones. This makes him vulnerable in a way that previous versions of the character were not. (If the name David Loomis sounds familiar, it's because Hutchinson previously utilized the character in his *One Good Scare* comic.)

Even with these many changes, this Loomis remains an easy hero to root for. His backstory and circumstances may be different, but the energy is the same. He's not quite as infallible as the original Loomis was, but that only makes him more interesting. Would fans have been accepting of New Loomis? Assuming he came clad in a beige trench coat and white button-down, probably so. Who would Hutchinson have ideally cast in the role? He mentions Cillian Murphy, specifically how he looked as Dr. Jonathan Crane in Christopher Nolan's *The Dark Knight* trilogy.

(Random fun fact: This Loomis lives in Morton, Illinois, which is an actual place unlike Haddonfield. The Governor of Illinois officially proclaimed Morton the "Pumpkin Capital of the World" since, at one point, 85% of all canned pumpkin was processed there. This designation was given back in 1978, the same year the original *Halloween* first hit theaters. Morton also has an annual Pumpkin Festival to commemorate their claim to fame, which looks friggin' delightful. We hope to go someday.)

## A DIFFERENT SHAPE

The boldest change Hutchinson makes with *Rise of the Boogeyman* involves the Shape. It's fascinating to compare his revised take on the character with that of Rob Zombie's in the 2007 remake. Zombie humanized the slasher by giving him a tragic backstory involving bullying and domestic abuse. He also assigned the character a concrete motive by reinstating the sibling connection first introduced back in 1981's *Halloween II*. The rocker-turned-filmmaker never once refers to Michael Myers as "the Shape" in his screenwriting, a fact that epitomizes his overall approach to the role. Hutchinson, meanwhile, goes in the complete opposite direction. His efforts to *dehumanize* the Boogeyman are so extensive that he strips the Shape of his human identity altogether. That's right – there is no Michael Myers in this treatment! As far as we know, he's just a stabby child who materialized out of thin air on October 31, 1984. We're also never given anything even remotely resembling a motive for his violent acts. He truly is a Shape.

"If you look at most of John Carpenter's films, evil is the force that removes personality from an individual," Hutchinson says. "I find that fascinating, that idea of anonymous evil. People don't normally look into the subtext of Carpenter's work. They go for the obvious stuff. But he has this weird thing about evil stripping away identity. He does great with the idea of evil being an abstraction, but he doesn't overstate it. Look at *Assault on Precinct 13* – it's basically an army of Michaels. They're almost robotic. Then *The Fog*. Then look at *Halloween III* – while not directed by Carpenter, his touch is all over it, and there's another army of robot Michaels. You can see evil erasing identity again in *Prince of Darkness* and *Ghosts of Mars*. He does it time and time again."

Hutchinson's approach to the Shape signifies that he understands a hard truth about the character, that he's scariest when we don't know much about him. The more you reveal about his backstory or agenda, the less scary he becomes. It's therefore crucial to preserve the slasher's mystique as much as possible. It's no small accomplishment that *Rise of the Boogeyman* achieves this even while adding overtly supernatural qualities to the role. While the slasher's characterization is scaled way back, his aesthetic remains largely unchanged. *Rise* finds the adult Shape wearing an expressionless white mask and dark coveralls. Even so, he's written in such an ethereal manner that he's always in the shadows.

This version of the character also kills with a barbaric cruelty far above what we're used to, often striking enormous fear into his victims before they die. (It's almost as if he feeds on their fear. *Almost.*) Take the murder of one of Annie's party-going friends late in the story. The Shape could easily kill her quickly from behind, but he does not. He instead bashes in her teeth with a hammer, disorienting but not killing her. The Shape then stabs her hand to a kitchen counter, pinning her in place. Unable to escape, she's forced to watch on helplessly as her killer retrieves multiple blades from the cutlery drawer, which he'll stab into her one-by-one. By scene's end, the poor girl resembles a human pin-cushion in a grisly display.

It goes without saying that the original *Halloween* was chock-full of unforgettable moments involving the Shape. With his 2007 remake, Rob Zombie sought to recreate most of these right down to the exact shot composition. Boldly, Hutchinson never once tries recreating anything John Carpenter did with the 1978 original. Michael outside Laurie's classroom? Not here. Stalking the girls after school? Doesn't happen. Pretending to be Bob underneath a sheet? Also not here. Hutchinson instead focuses on creating new potentially iconic scares. He does sometimes toy with the existing iconography, however. Instead of having the Shape disguise himself with a bedsheet, Hutchinson cleverly envisions a victim trying to scare someone dressed this way. The Shape jumps out and stabs the prankster to death, which causes red stains to appear all over the white sheet during their struggle.

## PART TWO: THE WITCHING HOUR

While Hutchinson wrote a full treatment for *Rise of the Boogeyman*, he only devised preliminary outlines for the second and third chapters of the trilogy. These assorted pages give us but a brief and partial look at where the story might've gone next. Titled *The Witching Hour*, the second film was meant to be even darker than the first. Whereas *Rise* took place in suburbia with Haddonfield as the main backdrop, *The Witching Hour* shifts to metropolitan Chicago. This, of course, would make for a very different vibe. Recall that *Rise of the Boogeyman* ended with the Shape visiting Loomis' wife and young son late on Halloween night. This second story quickly establishes that Maria was killed and young David abducted, current whereabouts unknown. Given this devastating loss, you might conclude that the Shape has taken everything from Loomis.

# "He hasn't. He absolutely hasn't. Things can always get worse. Loomis can always fall further."

- Stef Hutchinson

*The Witching Hour* begins with Loomis hospitalized at Haddonfield Memorial Hospital. (It would seem a legal requirement that all second *Halloween*s begin here. See Rick Rosenthal's original *Halloween II,* Rob Zombie's *Halloween II*, and David Gordon Green's *Halloween Kills*.) A groggy Loomis wakes in his hospital bed after having been shot by Deputy Brackett. He suddenly hears the toy clown laughter from earlier outside his room and goes to investigate. At the end of the hallway, he sees his wife and son staring at him. Unaware of the danger they've encountered, he goes to them but is attacked by a child-sized Shape in a clown costume. Multiple child-Shapes appear before him and join in the attack. Back in his hospital bed, Loomis is jolted awake from this nightmare. Now in true reality, he's horrified to find the Shape standing at the foot of his bed holding the severed head of his wife. The slasher drops Maria's head on the bed and leaves.

The story would then jump ahead a year to just before Halloween. Loomis has begun to suffer emotional and mental breakdowns in the wake of his wife's murder and son's disappearance (although he believes his son to be dead). In a reversal of his traditional role, the doctor has now become the patient. He's recently turned to a therapist in Chicago to help him work through these feelings of intense grief. Additionally, Loomis has become the target of an aggressive journalist hoping to crack a big story by digging into his past and the incident at Smith's Grove.

Beyond these troubles, he's also become obsessed with further exploring the Liminal. Hutchinson would go on to explain that certain people can see the Liminal (Debra, Annie) while certain others can see into it (Jennifer, Loomis). Loomis has gone beyond this and actually entered it, and we learn that his links to it go back into his Russellville childhood, which is why he was drawn to Jennifer in the first place. The curse of this sixth sense is that the seer is never in danger of the evil that flows into our world. Rather, it's those around them that suffer. This would explain why the Shape goes after Maria and David and not Loomis himself. (Similarly, the Shape so easily murdered Laurie Strode because she wasn't among those who could see into the Liminal.)

As Hutchinson tells it, *The Witching Hour* would see things get considerably worse for Sam Loomis. While leaving a therapy session, he would spot the Shape in the hallway of his therapist's downtown high-rise. Chasing him into the adjoining office, he would make an unsettling discovery: the long dead body of his therapist's neighboring office tenant. Loomis would then notice a small hole in the wall that offers a voyeur's view of his therapist's office. With this, a grim realization sets in – the Shape has been eavesdropping on his therapy sessions for the past year. He knows Loomis' greatest fears and deepest secrets. The chase resumes and culminates up on the roof where the Boogeyman dangles Loomis over the edge by the throat. He doesn't kill him, however, for there is a worse fate in store.

Loomis has started hearing the voice of his son David, just as he heard the laughing clown in *Rise*. This gives him hope that he is somehow still out there and alive. As night falls over Chicago, Loomis pursues this voice into the Liminal, and makes a "gruesome and unsettling" discovery – the dead and supernaturally distorted body of his missing son. As Loomis loses control, the forces around him cause him to mentally experience his son's prior death at the Shape's hands. Spiritually crushed by this loss, he'll soon realize that his therapist has also betrayed him. It's in this highly emotional state that Loomis confronts and murders her, transforming him into that which he had previously hunted and despised – a killer. *The Witching Hour* ends just as it began with the visual of a dead woman's body floating down the Chicago River. It's only now that we realize this is the murdered therapist.

Given how much anguish and torture Hutchinson subjects his Loomis to, you'd be forgiven for thinking he had a serious vendetta against the character, but he doesn't. He's actually quite fond of the role, having featured Loomis extensively throughout his various *Halloween* comics.

Hutchinson explains that, in his reboot trilogy, Loomis is on a certain path. One of the most popular trajectories in modern storytelling is the hero's journey in which a character is called to action, has an adventure, emerges victorious, and returns home transformed for the better. That is obviously *NOT* the journey Loomis is on here. Hutchinson instead has his Loomis on a "nekyia," which is a term from ancient Greek literature. The Jungian reading of the "nekyia" describes it as a descent into hell, which is basically the complete opposite of a hero's journey. As evidenced here, Hutchinson's story concepts are thoroughly researched and steeped in psychological complexities.

"In many ways, he's the Shape's ultimate victim," Hutchinson told the *Dark Media* website. "The path of his life is formed as a response to the Shape's actions. It's a game in many ways, and Loomis, be it by guilt, fear, or duty, is bound to it. He's a very tragic character, and I can't help but be drawn to that. […] The thing that really stands out with Loomis is that he should be the voice of reason. He's a doctor – a man of science. However, something about the Shape has caused him to abandon all of his knowledge and replace it with a much more metaphysical stance. The Shape is beyond everything he has learned and it terrifies him. Loomis is important in establishing how the Shape crosses boundaries – science and magic, of life and death."

# "In the first story, Loomis is losing everyone around him. In the second story, he's losing himself."

- Stef Hutchinson

## PART THREE: FIRES OF SAMHAIN

With *Rise of the Boogeyman* unfolding in suburban Haddonfield and *The Witching Hour* in metropolitan Chicago, *Fires of Samhain* shifts location again – this time to the more rural Russellville. To communicate his vision for the fictional locale, Hutchinson invokes the opening credit montage from *Halloween 4*. ("Envision that place and you've got Russellville as I saw it.")

*Fires of Samhain* opens with a terrified Debra Strode in her home on October 27th, one year after *The Witching Hour*. The veil is thinner than ever - birds are already falling from the sky, and Debra's protective dogs are horrifically smashing their heads into the walls. The Shape murders Debra's police protection before burning her alive – very much like Alice Brackett at the end of Hutchinson's *Halloween 3D*.

We continue on Halloween and find Loomis living as a fugitive from the law since, after all, he did murder his own therapist in the last installment. Having grown up in Russellville, he returns here hoping to better understand his past and use that as a way to find the Shape. He immediately runs into Lee Brackett, who is now sheriff of Russellville. Unlike their last encounter in *Rise of the Boogeyman*, Brackett is sympathetic toward Loomis in this story and an ally of sorts. He's since come to realize that Loomis was only trying to save his daughter's life that Halloween night and that shooting him in the chest was probably the wrong move. In a goodwill gesture, Brackett returns Loomis' lighter from that story despite it still technically being evidence. As the last gift his wife gave him before her untimely death, and the flame that set the Shape free, the lighter carries a special significance. Speaking of Brackett, Hutchinson reveals that Annie did not die in *Rise of the Boogeyman* as previously thought. We now find her living in Russellville as a strong single mother, but also a bit of a loner.

Across the past year, Loomis has begun to suffer terrible visions of the Shape's murders before he commits them – not unlike Jamie Lloyd in *Halloween 5*. He's seen Debra's unexpected death, and now repeatedly sees Annie in these premonitions, leading him to believe she's in danger. The Shape is at his strongest and there is no need for those that 'see' him to remain alive. Loomis figures that saving Annie just might be his first step on the road to redemption.

As for the Shape, he's not done with Loomis yet. Having gone after his family in *Rise of the Boogeyman* and his sense of self in *The Witching Hour*, he'll now go after Loomis' past in Russellville. At Smith's Grove Sanitarium, the patients are again in mass seizure as the Liminal breaks through around them, controlling them with a shared purpose. Breaking into Smith's Grove using an ambulance, the Shape unleashes the entire patient population. Beholden to his influence, they rip apart bedsheets and pillowcases to form crude masks and escape into the night. This Shape-army then engages in a murder-spree across the town of Russellville, killing everyone they encounter and destroying the town and people Loomis once knew. The Shape then focuses his own hunt on Annie.

With the town under nightmarish attack, Brackett teams with Loomis in an effort to find the real Shape, though he dies saving Loomis from the patient hoarde. Elsewhere, Annie, and her child take refuge with other townsfolk in a large dance hall. These locals eventually figure out that Annie can see the Liminal in ways they cannot and deem her a witch, which she technically is. They're about to cast her out when the hoarde breaks into the dance hall, resulting in an all-out battle. Possessing mom-strength, Annie takes out several Shape-clones in defense of her little one.

She manages to wound the actual Shape for the first time, a wound which Loomis himself feels. It's here that Loomis has a startling epiphany. He realizes that, given how connected they've now become, he will need to die in order to stop the Shape. With this, Loomis becomes one with the Liminal and starts to see it as never before. In fact, he begins to gaze into alternate dimensions, each with their own unique Shape. In one dimension, *Halloween '78*'s Shape is breaking through a closet door to get Laurie Strode. In another dimension, it's *Halloween 4*'s Shape. In yet another, it's Rob Zombie's Shape attacking someone. Some dimensions contain Shapes we've never even seen before. From this, Loomis realizes that everyone has a Shape. This dimension's Boogeyman just happens to be his own.

Back in reality, Annie is now besieged from all sides as she fights off the real Shape. Using the lighter, Loomis sets himself on fire just as Jennifer did years before outside the "Murder House." Concurrent with his death, the swarm of mind-controlled Shapes slit their own throats all throughout the burning town of Russellville. The resulting blood flow is so extreme that the hills literally run red. The trilogy ends on Annie standing amid this massive-scale carnage.

We've seen dark takes on Dr. Loomis before (gestures to *Halloween 5*), but *Fires of Samhain* may be the darkest of all. He's now metaphysically connected to the Shape like never before and can even at times see through his eyes. (He's later alarmed to learn this is a two-way street.) Having lost his family and sense of self, Loomis is actually becoming more like the Shape every day. (Recall that he committed his first murder back in *The Witching Hour*.) The urge to indiscriminately kill grows stronger inside him in this part of the story, though he suppresses it. He's even compelled to murder the one person whom he's trying to save – Annie Brackett. For Loomis, the stakes could not be higher. Grim is the realization that he must sacrifice himself to end this mayhem. If he remains alive, he may become that very thing which he has hunted. The question then becomes – what is Loomis willing to lose and to what end? His life or soul? It's a much more sophisticated characterization than a simple slasher-chasing psychiatrist.

With this concluding chapter, Hutchinson delivers on the prophecy of Samhain as first laid out by Conal Cochran back in *Halloween III*. For those following along, he ingeniously laid the groundwork for this idea during Jennifer's consultations in *Rise of the Boogeyman*. Of course, Loomis brushes off any such talk as simply another part of her delusion, but Jennifer was on point. Similarly, Hutchinson first began demonstrating Samhain's disturbing effect on the natural world back in *Rise* with birds falling out of the sky. By *Fires of Samhain*, multiple species are suddenly dying where they stand in a mass fatality event. It's altogether *horrifying*. There's a dark richness to this narrative, which would've proven incredibly transformative for the overall *Halloween* franchise. Had this been made, the series would've no longer been about an escaped slasher stalking babysitters on Halloween night. Yes, that's still part of it, but there's something so much bigger at work – an ancient and unstoppable prophecy of evil.

**Jennifer in *Rise of the Boogeyman***: *"Do you know how many they would sacrifice to keep the darkness away? The fires they'd set up on the hillside to burn women and children? The hills and the fields, they were drenched with rivers of blood – and it's going to happen again."*

**Conal Cochran in *Halloween III***: *"The barriers would be down, you see, between the real and the unreal, and the dead might be looking in to sit by our fires of turf. Halloween – the festival of Samhain. The last great one took place three thousand years ago, when the hills ran red with the blood of animals and children."*

Most of the triumphs in this trilogy belong to the Shape, but *Fires of Samhain* does contain one for the audience with the surprise return of Annie Brackett. We last saw Annie in *Rise of the Boogeyman* bleeding to death in her father's arms in what seemed like her demise. Having apparently survived that injury, she's now the single mother of a young child. Previously a social butterfly, we find the character withdrawn and isolative in *Fires* due to the trauma she experienced years prior. (Coincidentally, the same thing happened to Rob Zombie's version of Annie Brackett in his *Halloween II*.) Tapping into her maternal instincts, Annie proves an able fighter, taking out multiple Shape-clones and holding her own against the actual slasher. The *most* interesting development with the character here is that she is, in fact, a witch of sorts. (Hutchinson also uses the term "seer.") While unable to fully gaze into the Liminal as Loomis does, Annie does experience visions of it, which was first alluded to back in *Rise* with her paintings. Her witchiness doesn't enable her to cast spells or broom-fly, but Annie does realize she can manipulate those around her to a degree. The surviving citizenry of Russellville discover her secret and determine her to be the target of the evil now attacking them. They subsequently cast her out into the night.

With the Shape, Hutchinson once again pushes the boundaries of how we define the character. His supernatural influence commands an entire hospital full of the mentally ill to join in his bloody attack on Russellville. Instead of having only one Shape on the loose, this story has dozens of Shapes running around in a sort-of army. The screenwriter likens this approach to John Carpenter's *Assault on Precinct 13*, which is honestly some top-shelf inspiration. Imagine the horrific-looking masks the patients of Smith's Grove might fashion from their bedsheets and pillowcases before breaking out of their confines. As with Annie's visions, this development was first teased back in Rise of the Boogeyman when Smith's Grove's patients began experiencing a synchronized mass seizure on Halloween night. In explaining this plot point, Hutchinson emphasizes the need for a careful approach to depicting the mentally ill as emotionless killers. It's not that they're murderous because they're mentally ill. They're murderous because they're being preyed upon and manipulated by an evil force. If anything, their mental illness makes them psychologically vulnerable to the Shape's powers. Being that the Shape-clones suicide concurrent with Loomis' self-immolation, they're as much victims in this story as anyone else, if not more so.

# "You don't have one Shape in this - you have one hundred of them."

- Stef Hutchinson

*Fires of Samhain* is packed with big ideas. The Shape destroying Loomis on every possible level. Loomis losing his sanity and even his identity. Annie being a witch. But the biggest arguably comes in its final moments when Hutchinson reveals the *Halloween* Multi-verse. Hutchinson obviously didn't invent the concept with his story, but he did utilize it several years before it was popularized on the small screen (CW's *Arrow*-verse) and the big screen (*Spider-Man: Into the Spider-Verse.*) No doubt, *Halloween* fans would've lost their minds upon seeing the Shapes of yesteryear cameo in *Fires of Samhain*. This moment comes just as Loomis sets fire to himself in an act of suicide. It's here that his mind melds into the Liminal, allowing him to see through to these other worlds. His takeaway is that there are countless Shapes out there in other universes, not that he has to defeat them. His only demon is Haddonfield's Boogeyman, whom he's finally figured out how to best. As Loomis dies a painful death, so does his tormentor and all his followers. Loomis may ultimately prevail over evil in the end, but it's difficult to call this a win for the character. He lost everything he had to lose – the last of which was his very life. By any measure, the poor guy suffered more than any other character in the entire franchise. But he also gave more.

Why end with the multi-verse? Hutchinson explains that it's not simply for the cool cameos. It's so much more than that. It's an effort to tie the multiple timelines of the franchise together in a meaningful way. The Multi-verse would serve to re-legitimatize earlier sequels that newer films have tried to erase from existence. There are now so many different factions of the fanbase with different concepts of what *Halloween* is or is not. As Hutchinson sees it, they're all perfectly valid even though they conflict with one another. Are you only a fan of the "Sister Trilogy?" Or do you prefer the Thorn storyline? Maybe you're a *Halloween: Resurrection* apologist. Or maybe you're only turned on by the Rob Zombie films. "Whatever your version of *Halloween* is, it's legitimate," Hutchinson says. "Don't let anyone tell you that your take is wrong."

As Hutchinson intended it, there would be another huge bonus to the multi-verse ending of his trilogy. By legitimizing *Halloween*'s multiple timelines as alternate universes, you could now more easily return to them in future sequels. Want to pick up the story from *Halloween 6* with Tommy, Kara, and Dr. Wynn? That's now do-able. Want to sequelize *Halloween H20* with John Tate avenging his mother's murder? Go for it. Want to return to the Zombie-verse sometime down the road? Hey, it's always an option. This move would've opened up the franchise in a big, big way. *Halloween* would no longer be about ignoring or re-writing its own past every few years, but instead embracing it.

"It's the most unselfish way of ending a *Halloween* movie," Hutchinson says. "You can make any movie you want from that point on. No one's boxed in by a certain concept. It frees everything up in a big way."

## WHY THEY WEREN'T MADE

There were ultimately several reasons why Stef Hutchinson's reboot trilogy never advanced through the development process. Foremost was that Miramax/Dimension simply weren't ready to remake *Halloween* quite so soon after the Rob Zombie efforts. Malek Akkad reportedly responded favorably, but his approval alone was not enough to force a script through the process.

Furthermore, *Rise of the Boogeyman* wasn't some one-off – it was but the opening chapter of a trilogy. To produce this first entry would mean committing to the second and third entries as well. This would constitute a sizable investment on the studio's part. Never in Dimension's twenty-one-year history had they theatrically committed to such longform storytelling. Not even Rob Zombie could convince the Weinsteins to take such a dive and he was then riding the success of *House of 1,000 Corpses* and *The Devil's Rejects*. (Recall that Zombie had originally wanted to split *Halloween 2007* into two films but was turned down.) Unfortunately, Hutchinson lacked the long resume of horror hits that would be required to convince Dimension of such an ambitious plan.

There was also the fact that there hadn't been anything like this trilogy ever before, which made it more of a risk. Tonally, it ventured into the supernatural along the lines of *Halloween III: Season of the Witch*, which wasn't exactly a template for box office success. "The only time you could've ever written the *Halloween* sequel you really wanted to is to have done it back before the big studios got involved," Hutchinson comments. "You'd need to have done it back in the late 80s when it was Moustapha Akkad in charge of everything. That was the time for it. Now, there's just too many people involved. The studios and test screenings will mangle whatever comes through. That's why we'll never get a pure *Halloween* movie ever again."

## "I imagine that the general response to Halloween II had made them very averse to any surrealism."
- Stef Hutchinson

**So it's 2012. The franchise is stalling out with no clear place to go. Why attempt this entirely new direction now — and why a trilogy?**

I think the years after 2009's *Halloween II* had left the franchise in a strange place that didn't point to a clear path forward. This wasn't the first time, and it struck me that after every film, there'd be this limbo period where they'd have to figure out a new direction. There was never any forward planning beyond the current film at hand, and it would either leave the next story snared by some very random narrative threads (*Halloween 5*) or end with a complete sense of narrative closure so there was seemingly nowhere left to go (*H20*).

I had a few ideas in the original timeline, but I already had most of that storyline – well, my take on it – fixed in my head with writing the comic books. I'd written for John Carpenter's Shape in those, and for Rob Zombie's Michael Myers in my *Halloween 3D* treatment. With that in mind, I toyed around with a one-off story that could take place in any continuity, with a very retro subtitle – *The Hunt for Michael Myers*. But as I progressed, I felt a strong urge to try something new. If you'd asked me my opinion a few years prior, I would have described even the *idea* of remaking *Halloween* as heresy. By this point, however, that lemonade had been pissed in, and I had an idea for a direction that I thought would work best with a fresh start.

In years of reading works about the genre, I'd noticed that so much of the theory written on it was from a psychoanalytical perspective – specifically Freudian. It's not surprising, because horror films generally lend themselves to such interpretations with wanton abandon. I started thinking about a more Jungian take on *Halloween* and its characters – something more metaphysical and esoteric, with vague ideas of archetypes, shared fears, and the collective unconsciousness. Just that simple move sideways helped to suggest a storyline that would, hopefully, expand the idea of what a *Halloween* film could be and open up the possibilities for the series. The previous remake had gone towards a 'real world' take, but I wanted this to be the opposite of that. I wanted an overtly supernatural tone, and to make use of the night itself. I didn't want this to be a story that just happens to be set on Halloween; it had to be an integral part of what would occur.

There's definitely a friction between the celebratory and capitalist nature of a modern Halloween night, and the archaic darkness that it is supposed to represent. We could argue that it's a time in which we can safely laugh at our fears, embodying them in rituals and costumed tradition. Inevitably, the darker forces are going to push back against this. We've seen this addressed in the series before, in the extremely prescient *Halloween III*, which had a similar feel to what I was aiming for in this trilogy, despite the Shape being the black hole at the center of it.

Cues to this approach came from dialogue in these previous films, too, namely from Loomis and Cochran in *Halloween II* and *Halloween III*. These characters deliver speeches that describe a very scary and apocalyptic vision of what Halloween *was*, and most terrifyingly, what it could be again – from the darkness of the unconscious mind, to fields that run red with blood, to the sacrifices of the insane and those deemed as 'witches'. The story, as it evolved, would tap into the scale hinted at in those words, and that's what led to it being mapped out as a trilogy.

The names were only placeholders, but the three chapters became *Rise of the Boogeyman*, *The Witching Hour*, and *The Fires of Samhain*. The awful first title in particular is not something I'd want to keep, but it's a fairly accurate summation of what we see. The first chapter is in Haddonfield, the second in Chicago, and the third in Russellville (envisioned here as a very rural setting, not unlike the opening credits of *Halloween 4*, rather than how I portrayed it in *Nightdance*). It wasn't a starting point to plan three films, but the level of transition in the narrative – from slasher film to cosmic horror – needed space for the journey to be convincing and tonally consistent. I had to start somewhere familiar to go somewhere new, while hopefully keeping true to the feel of a classic *Halloween* movie.

**While *Rise of the Boogeyman* pre-dates *Stranger Things*, the Liminal appears to bear some resemblance to the Upside Down, at least superficially. Are they more similar or different?**

I've only seen the first season of *Stranger Things*, and that was quite some time ago, so I'm not sure what the Upside Down actually *is* within the story at this point. I think that's a great name that they gave it. From an aesthetic point of view, I can see a similarity, but I think that's because we're both using obvious iconography to create a nightmarish 'other world,' and it works to keep the abstract elements simple.

Both places deliberately remind us of our own reality in sensory ways, but they're shrouded in darkness, too – like a thing in a bad dream that you can't quite remember. They're abject landscapes that have to come from within us and also be outside of us to evoke that feeling. While I envisioned the Liminal represented as a primal, charred forest, I imagined it having the feel of the painting *Isle of the Dead* by Arnold Böcklin.

The Liminal is probably vaguer, less literal than the Upside Down. It doesn't actually have a name in the context of the film itself at all – I only call it 'The Liminal' to clarify it in the script and story. It's an idea or perception as much as it is a place – something evil in the thrall of its own malevolent nature, a collective unconscious fed by fear.

**Your Dr. Loomis differs from earlier incarnations in that he truly is responsible for the Shape's escape from custody and subsequent murder spree. He was already feeling responsible for Jennifer's suicide, now he has this enormous burden to carry. Tell me about your decision to make Loomis the one who accidentally allows the slasher to escape by dropping his lighter.**

From a simple storytelling perspective, it makes Loomis a much more interesting character. He's got many layers of guilt, rather than just having the one that drives his character, and these push him in contradictory directions. His key flaw would be a known inability to listen to his inner warnings, making him someone who'd psychologically punish himself for his failures. There are real consequences to his mistakes, and the people close to him suffer greatly. I wanted Loomis to be my central protagonist this time, rather than Laurie Strode (although we do spend a lot of time with Annie Brackett). He'd be younger, more curious and naïve than the previous incarnations, but already troubled. I like damaged characters – the emotions are already heightened and it makes me feel for them more when things start to go bad (or worse).

When we meet him, he's oddly at the beginning of a redemptive phase. He has a shadow that haunts him, and he's finally learning to let it go. Unfortunately, the moment in the asylum when he decides to enter the Shape's room is the moment he destroys any progress he's made. He knows it's the wrong decision, but he still commits himself to it. The tumbling lighter is just a plot-facilitating metaphor for the choice he's made. When he looks into the Shape's face, he's suddenly glimpsing what he's about to unleash, and his fear brings these things into reality.

A deliberate Jungian element in the writing here, was the loose idea of the 'nekyia' – the descent inwards, a voyage into darkness – which is the psychological opposite of 'the hero's journey'. The protagonist becomes a character falling through hell, with no guarantee of any salvation or return. His guilt doesn't have an end-point, either. The Shape is still out there. He's still butchering innocent people. As such, there's never a point where Loomis can allow his own guilt to falter, because more people *will* die. This keeps him driving the narrative forward, even though he's never in any real control.

**You introduce Laurie Strode – only to kill her off soon after, before night has even fallen on Halloween. This shock recalls Marion Crane's sudden murder in *Psycho*. Tell me about that.**

It's a radical departure from *Halloween* as a franchise, but not so much from the 1978 original, I feel. If you take the original film on its own terms, and without the retcon of *Halloween II*, Laurie Strode was simply the first person who the Shape set eyes on. She left a key at his door, a symbolic gesture – Red Riding Hood inviting The Wolf into her world. She becomes the Shape's target purely by circumstance, not by bloodline. She's only afforded the 'special target' status by the plot mechanics of the sequel, and the decisions later in the franchise to bring her back repeatedly.

I never cared for the family angle and found it both limiting and diminishing (and I was surprised that this relationship formed a focal point of the 2007 remake). It makes the Shape less of a mythical force, and more of a guy with family issues. I needed to show that this interpretation was not going that route in any way, quite early and quite bluntly. All I did was shift Laurie's role from 'intended victim' to 'associate of intended victim'. As you know, in slasher films, that puts her in far more danger than being the main target! So here, she suffers the fate that befell her friends in previous continuities, just at the point we're getting to know her and feeling comfortable that she's our lead. For this moment, I could've created a new character, but I wanted *some* names to be in there that audiences already had an idea of. While these characters aren't identical to their other versions, they certainly evoke them and don't stray too far from prior interpretations. As the storyline went on, it would stretch further and further out from the *Halloween* basics, so I felt we needed these initial anchors of recognition.

Killing Laurie confirms that we're going down a very different journey in this story. There's a deliberate disruption of the familiar throughout the treatment, both acknowledging and playing on the audience's expectations. This scene is probably the bluntest example of that. It plays out like the original, creating the expectation of a surprise coming from one direction. We still get that moment, but then Laurie turns around, the Shape is *there* and it's over. She's savagely murdered, and we're heading into dark and uncharted territory.

**You go to great lengths to dehumanize the Shape, even stripping him of his human identity altogether. There's no Michael or Judith Myers, nor a Myers house. Tell me about that decision. Was it liberating as a storyteller to ditch that narrative baggage?**

Most of those elements are still there, but distilled down to even more archetypal forms. While there's no Myers house as such, there's still the equivalent – the 'place where bad things happened' still stains Haddonfield. It's deliberately less specific. All of this goes back to Carpenter's position that the Shape isn't so much a character, but a simple evil force. Everything about his presentation of the Shape supports that idea, from the anonymous visual design with its distorted mannequin sensibilities, to the murderous intent that absolutely cannot be reasoned with. You can see variations of this thinking throughout Carpenter's work – the villains are often faceless, devoid of their individual identity, yet very capable of committing horrible acts.

What contradicts it, and gives the Shape the potential of humanity, is the fact that he has a name. Over the sequels (and the remake), the name Michael Myers has become a portal to the human side of the Shape, and also a doorway to giving the audience his supposed motivations. I first saw *Halloween* on its first or second UK television airing. I had no knowledge of what the film was about, no idea of the Shape, of the mask or anything. As Laurie Strode saw the brief glimpses of her stalker, so did I. I only saw what she saw and knew what she knew for the most part, and this made the Shape all the more terrifying. Because he was such an unknown quantity and presence, I was unsettled throughout, and the whole experience burned its way into my psyche to the point where, almost forty years on, I'm talking about it to you now.

Sadly, it's almost impossible to discover the film in that way now. The image of the mask is omnipresent and has been integral to the advertising since *Halloween 4* and you can even buy Michael Myers socks now. The Shape is as much a pop culture icon as he is a boogeyman now, demystified into a thousand collectibles and diluted by endless memes.

Despite him being a purported blank, that's not truly the case. His presentation and behaviors have evolved over the series. Particularly in the first two films, for example, there's a psychosexual element to the Shape that we see in his frozen voyeurism and constant observance of the female form. This generally fades into the background from *Halloween 4* onwards – as the Shape became Michael Myers, he transitioned from 'movie serial killer' to 'movie slasher'. And these different takes have different expectations. You have Carpenter's ethereal and shadowy Shape, but you also have the iconic brute of *Halloween 4* onwards. You have the visceral and violent Michael Myers of the *Halloween* remake, but you also have the character humiliation that unfortunately comes with *Halloween Resurrection*.

I didn't want this version of the Shape to have any of those expectations or history. They sometimes felt like limitations on what the character could – and likely would – do. Occasional responses to the comic stories would say something on the line of '*but the Shape wouldn't do that*'. Well, he would, and indeed, he just did, and I'd happily point to any cinematic cues leading to the decision I made. However, it showed me how much people have their own fixed idea of what the Shape is and how they don't like to deviate from that.

None of the filmmakers after Carpenter really addressed this in any detail. Instead, we have to expect that this force of evil, that has stared at a wall for 15 years, has shown us all the possible behavior it's capable of, on a single night in Haddonfield. There's very little attempt to *expand* on Carpenter's ideas, and instead they are only mimicked which leads to the constant repetition of the sequels. We're given a very fixed definition to something supposedly 'a shape'.

I wanted to restore some of that uncertain nature that was present in my naïve first viewing of the original film, and for the Shape to be unknown in every quantity other than his evil. This would also give me the freedom to write him how I want – familiar in some ways, startling in others. It's also one of the reasons I specifically brought back other recognizable names, such as Laurie Strode, Sam Loomis, and Annie Brackett. Those names are familiar hooks, and having them there draws more attention to the Shape's anonymity. It emphasizes the uncertainty of the horror that is coming for them.

**Your *Rise* treatment doesn't just tell a self-contained story. You're world-building in that treatment, which is something no other *Halloween* has ever set out to do. Tell me about that.**

I think you could argue that the franchise has attempted this before, but unfortunately, that attempt was *Halloween 5*.

*Halloween 5* was probably the first time a *Halloween* sequel had been conceived solely as an episode in an ongoing saga, rather than something with its own self-contained and coherent story. As befits its gothic stylings, it's the 'penny dreadful' of the series. I like many aspects of the film (particularly the Loomis and Myers interactions, the cookie woman, and the '*Charlie, Charlie...*' moment), but it is a film that is utterly irresponsible in its world-building. It's throwing new things in there, bluntly in the narrative foreground, but with no actual plan for them. Instead, it's leaving its successor in a very difficult position. "Here's *stuff...*"

Alternatively, if you go back further, the original two films have these great dialogue flourishes which really establish the world of Haddonfield beyond the screen. The use of full names for off-screen characters – as if we should know them personally – really captures the sense of a living small town. I'm sure *Eddie Lee* is a really fun guy. Hearing about places with distinctive names – *The Lost River Drive-In* – subtly evokes your imagination to give a strong sense of place.

With the story I wanted to tell, world-building was a necessity beyond giving a sense of the culture and location's external life. This take on *Halloween* would have its own mythology (albeit a deliberately vague one) and I needed to create a world that could convincingly support this. I had a lot of elements in play and planned them all the way through individually, so I'd know how far in advance I'd need to set something up or introduce it.

It also goes back to what I was saying about leaving the franchise open for new installments. This wouldn't mean an incomplete storyline, far from it, but instead would leave behind a very realized universe (or several) with many places left to explore.

I'd learned a lot about this writing the comic books. Even writing *One Good Scare*, I had a feeling and a direction that I could see beyond its final page. I didn't know exactly where everything was going in a specific way initially, but I understood what characters and situations would unfold within the reality that was being shaped. I learned that world building isn't just adding supporting characters, setting up plot events and so on, but also establishing themes, motifs, and ideas organically – building a distinctive zeitgeist for your universe.

**Have you ever considered shaking off the *Halloween* elements and turning this into its own original story? So much of this is original, it would probably work as a standalone, right?**

I have thought about it, and if I do work any elements into something original, then they're more than likely going to be from the second and third chapters. The first story, even with my original material and mythology, is very much a story for the *Halloween* franchise. It's still the Shape, it's still Loomis, it's still the stalking of babysitters, it's still the falling leaves. Because the later parts are more radical in their departures, the first chapter would still have to feel familiar enough to not alienate an audience that has certain expectations.

When we reach the second and third chapters, the stories are structured differently, the locations change, including Chicago and rural Illinois, the supernatural comes into play more, and everything more or less explodes into something we haven't seen before – certainly not in a *Halloween* film. Much of that could be repurposed or sculpted into something new.

As to if I will ever do that – I don't know. I'd like to. I still have lots of other stories I'd like to tell that didn't start with something that existed already, though. I have enough noise in my head for this life and several after, which is a great thing. So, it's not so much if I think I can adapt it, but just if the time and opportunity should appear.

**I'm getting the sense that you love a story where evil triumphs. Why?**

I don't know if I necessarily *love* that type of story but it's true that I keep writing it. I hope to evoke an emotional response that is true to the story being told. Given the events that transpire within, it feels like I'd be cheating and betraying the suffering of the characters if I forced a happy ending. Life is an ongoing struggle even without having a masked murderer to worry about.

These are horror stories, first and foremost. It's the one narrative space in which you can experience, by proxy, things you would never want to in reality and things you quite rightly fear. No matter how traumatic a story is, by being the viewer, you're in a safe place, and you always have the choice to look away. If you stay, you can live through hell and then return to life as normal. In this sense, I feel a darker ending can often be cathartic. There's a rush that comes from experiencing a fictional shock, and it's frequently a giddy excitement that is the opposite of what has just been witnessed. Darker endings aren't always as final, either – they feel like cliff-hangers, and imply there's more out there, even if we're not going to be privy to it – and I think that can be an exciting feeling too.

Both the trilogy and the *Black Rose* storyline that formed the comics are exceptionally dark journeys. However, that's not to say that the conclusions they would finally reach would be the same. The type of story that I *do* love is the melancholic, tragic one. It's dark and it's sad, but there is an emotional release that thrives alongside it. I wouldn't say *Rise* is that type of story, but it's something at the forefront of *The First Death of Laurie Strode*, for example, particularly in the conclusion. I do like to have a little hope in my endings, despite what it seems. Even though my stories are generally fatalistic, I'm of the thinking that if there's just that one star in a really black sky, it will shine brighter. While those fragments of light won't survive the night, they are there forever, and their beauty doesn't diminish when the morning comes and they're hidden away.

***Fires of Samhain* ends with Loomis seeing into the *Halloween* Multi-verse, which is a wild and fascinating concept. Tell me about that!**

*Halloween* as a franchise is interesting in that it has *deliberately* broken its own canon and timeline on multiple occasions. The retcon tendencies start with the sister twist of *Halloween II*, escalating to *H20* stating "those other films didn't happen". Then, we have a remake. As such, there are a lot of stories that hover in the *Halloween* ether that are forever unfinished, even within the final released films. I was often asked when writing the comic books about bringing back the Thorn concept and the bloodline storylines from the middle trilogy. I didn't do that, primarily because I didn't want to, and secondly because I struggle to imagine these sequels existing in the same world as 1978's *Halloween*. Their basic realities feel too different (I'd argue *Halloween III* is closer in feel to the original two than *Halloween 4* is, in this respect), and that's before we even begin to tackle the narrative changes.

The next comic due to be published was *The Mark of Thorn*, and that would have addressed these problems somewhat by providing two different realities within. The first, set in the comic and *H20* timeline, would be the story of a modern day Tommy Doyle. He would be a comic creator, and the second storyline, written and illustrated by him, would be an alternative version of the Thorn storyline, intended as some form of catharsis.

The two storylines inevitably converge and things get quite horrible in both realities, as you might expect. However, there was a key scene I had planned towards the end, in which it is discovered that Tommy has changed his storyline, to save the life of one character that had died in his reality. As long as that story existed and as long as she was alive in his fiction, so too would the character remain alive in the minds of those that read about her. It led to an open-ended conclusion that basically said, '*Halloween is what you imagine it to be.*' The characters you care about are still out there – but inevitably so is the monster.

It's not central to the trilogy narrative, but it's a moment that organically rises throughout and fits into the finale. The Liminal provides a gateway to endless expressions of the same fears throughout different worlds. When Loomis becomes one with the dimension in his attempt to destroy the Shape, he realizes this, like Samhain, is a ritual that plays out time and time again and always results in bloodshed as a demand of Halloween night itself. Each Shape is a manifestation of the same abject evil that will *always* be there in every world, even our own. This goes back to my original intent of expanding the canvas. As well as acknowledging everything that had gone before, it would hopefully allow for countless new interpretations of the franchise.

**What kind of feedback did you get?**

Very little, really! Admittedly, only the first chapter was submitted. Malek liked it and thought it to be particularly well thought out, but along the way, the studio had decided they didn't want to go the remake route, so that was that. I don't think they wanted to drop what they had already, and thought it was likely too soon to remake *Halloween* again. They seemingly wanted a way back that didn't commit to anything creatively risky. I imagine that the general response to [Rob Zombie's] *Halloween II* had made them very averse to any surrealism.

I'm happy with the whole storyline, but it would require audiences to have fairly open minds towards what has become a very closed idea. It's a big ask - and possibly an unfair one - before you even come to discuss whether it's even good or not. Look at how unfairly maligned *Halloween III* was upon its release.

The problem with a script – be it for a film or for a comic book - is that it's a blueprint, rather than a finished piece in itself. So, if it doesn't get beyond the stage where my part is done, it never reaches anybody else. At least having the outlines presented here means people get an idea of these stories. There are a lot of different ideas and material in these pitches, particularly after Loomis first hunts the Shape in Haddonfield – so maybe one day these moments will find their way out into the world as part of something new.

# HALLOWEEN
# ASYLUM

Evil cannot be contained.

Screenplay by
**Josh Stolberg & Pete Goldfinger**

## "God help us all."

So ends Matt Venne's forsaken *Halloween: Asylum* script. Sadly, this smartly-written follow-up to *Halloween: Resurrection* was never developed beyond a first draft. Though Venne received positive feedback from studio suits, he was never given any notes to incorporate into a second pass. This likely owed to the fact the Weinstein brothers were in the process of breaking away from The Walt Disney Company, a split that was publicly announced two months after Venne's submission. If this tumultuous divorce didn't throw *Asylum 2005* into development hell, then the cinematic rise of rocker-turned-filmmaker Rob Zombie surely did. His film *The Devil's Rejects* – a sequel to his own *House of 1,000 Corpses* – would hit theaters six months later to surprisingly strong box office and critical acclaim. This made the rocker a much sought-after horror director within the industry. The Weinsteins moved quickly to attach Zombie to a project by offering him a stab at remaking *Halloween*, which he accepted. The following June, Zombie was announced as the producer, writer, and director of this latest *Halloween*. With this announcement, Venne's *Asylum* was certifiably dead.

Flash forward two films and eight long years later to January 2013. The *Halloween* franchise was once again lacking a clear direction to go in. Having helmed two polarizing but modestly successful entries, Rob Zombie had decided to step away from *Halloween* for good. As he informed *SciFiNow.co.uk* that month, "I don't think they are doing anything with *Halloween* at the moment. That is the last thing that I heard – and I'm definitely not directing it if they ever do go ahead with a third movie." In light of the project's period of development hell, executives within The Weinstein Company held differing views on whether to continue the Zombie saga, return to the original continuity, or remake *Halloween* once again. After a failed attempt to embark on a sequel co-produced by Platinum Dunes, Dimension VP of Production Matthew Signer began meeting with potential new writers once more. Among these hopefuls were scribes Josh Stolberg and Pete Goldfinger. (If Stolberg's name sounds familiar, it's because he unsuccessfully pitched a *Halloween/Hellraiser* crossover to Moustapha Akkad back in 2002.)

Together, Stolberg and Goldfinger had co-written the successful horror revamps *Sorority Row* and *Piranha 3D*, released in 2009 and 2010, respectively. (They would later helm two installments of the *Saw* franchise, 2017's *Jigsaw* and 2021's *Spiral: From the Book of Saw*.) A longtime *Halloween* fan, Stolberg was excited to pitch several new concepts alongside his writing partner. Signer liked this duo's ideas enough to set up a follow-up meeting with Malek Akkad, whom the writers would also need to impress. And while Akkad didn't particularly like their ideas, he did respond well to them as writers. Concurrently, Dimension was in the process of finding a hired gun to re-write an older *Halloween* script that they felt had promise. The script in question was Matt Venne's *Halloween: Asylum*.

Recall that Venne had been one of the many writers brought forward to pitch Dimension on a Platinum Dunes-produced *Halloween* circa 2012. While the studio was ultimately shy on following through with that co-production, Venne's original *Asylum* script very much remained on the company's radar. The reasoning? Lore tells us that Bob Weinstein had taken a great liking to helming a *Halloween* set almost entirely within the walls of Smith's Grove Sanitarium, with Venne's script continuously serving as a blueprint for how such a story might've been enacted. Thus, the studio dusted off *Asylum 2005* and, after disagreements with the original writer, began toiling away at a revision.

To this end, writers Josh Stolberg and Pete Goldfinger were contacted once more in summer 2013 – some months after their initial pitch – and were presented with *Halloween: Asylum* to revise. Both men read the script and agreed on its strong potential. They then offered some preliminary notes on how it might be improved upon, notes to which Signer and Akkad both responded positively to. With that, the eleventh *Halloween* finally had another team of writers attached. Stolberg and Goldfinger were officially hired to re-write Venne's work.

## THE STORY

*Asylum 2013* opens on Halloween night in Covington, Indiana. A group of fun-loving teens – including seventeen-year-old Bethany – are trespassing at a remote farmhouse believed to be the birthplace of Michael Myers. As it turns out, the slasher is currently living here and murders all but Bethany, who manages a narrow escape. The story then shifts to Smith's Grove Sanitarium this same night. Here we meet the fame-chasing Dr. Cushing along with several grad students – the smart and likable Callie, her promiscuous bestie Stephanie, and hopeless nerd Brenner. Sanitarium staff witness a news report of Bethany's brush with the Shape, which prompts a massive manhunt. Cushing tells police Michael will head for either the Myers house, the Strode house, or Smith's Grove. Callie believes differently, predicting that he will go after Bethany to finish his kill.

Stephanie bails on giving Callie a ride home, forcing her to accept a ride from Wyatt, visiting a brother to one of her patients. Upon discussing the situation, they agree to drive to Covington to warn Bethany that Michael may still come after her. Wyatt jokes about this being a strange first date. After discerning Bethany's home address, the pair arrive to find the Shape in mid-attack. Callie calls 911 as she and Wyatt rush in to help. The Shape kills Bethany, knocks Wyatt unconscious, and is about to murder Callie when police arrive in full force. They quickly put a bullet in the slasher's kneecap before launching a merciless baton assault. Eerily, the Shape never takes his eyes off Callie, even while being beaten senseless.

We then jump ahead two years to October 30th, 2015. Callie is now engaged to Wyatt and she remains an intern at Smith's Grove Sanitarium alongside Stephanie and Brenner. The asylum is once again home to Michael Myers, who has been sentenced to death for his crimes. Unfortunately, the governor has ordered a ban on all executions beginning November 1st. State officials have announced their decision not to execute Michael prior to the ban, resulting in considerable public outcry. Smith's Grove director Edward Phelps is especially eager to carry out the death sentence, which he believes will boost his upcoming bid for the governorship. The issue, however, is that all current executions require authorization from the sitting governor. Against the advice of Security Supervisor James Ensor and District Attorney Danielle Hawthorne, Phelps decides to execute Michael on October 31st at Smith's Grove without authorization. He's backed by Dr. Cushing, who plans to extract Michael's brain for scientific research. A former warden, Phelps quietly imports an electric chair from a federal facility. To prevent news of Michael's execution from leaking out, he orders a facility lockdown and jams all cellphone signals.

The guards taunt and torture the Shape prior to his execution, even flaunting his old mask in front of him. They strap him into the chair and place a black hood overtop his face. At 11:59 PM – one minute before the governor's ban takes effect – the switch is engaged. However, the execution goes awry, and the Shape breaks free from the chair. The reason being for this escape is that he's now supernaturally empowered by the enormous jolts of electricity. He murders

the attending guards and several witnesses, regaining his classic mask in the process. Security Supervisor Ensor and intern Brenner are also soon murdered. Rather than call for outside help, Director Phelps decides to personally hunt down and execute the Shape within Smith's Grove, which is still under lockdown. The escaped slasher confronts Dr. Cushing, who begs for his life to no avail. ("It's after midnight, Michael! They can't execute you anymore! It's going to be okay!") Grabbing the skull-saw intended for his own autopsy, the Shape murders Cushing in gory fashion.

Phelps and District Attorney Hawthorne trick Callie and Stephanie into going into the facility's basement, known as "Homicide Hall," by insisting there's a tunnel through which they can escape. Their actual plan is to use the girls as bait to lure the Shape, whom they'll follow after and kill. This plan goes poorly, resulting in the hospital's most dangerous patients escaping their underground cells. They initially try to overpower Michael, who slashes through them all – and Phelps – with horrifying ease. Retreating into the Hall of Records, Callie finds an audiotape of an old therapy session between Dr. Loomis and a young Michael. Playing it works as an effective distraction, allowing her to strike. A nasty fight ensues, resulting in the deaths of Stephanie and Wyatt, the latter of whom snuck into the facility hoping to save his fiancée. Callie ultimately prevails after seriously wounding her adversary multiple times. Authorities move in and recapture Michael, ultimately returning him to his old room. At Wyatt's funeral, a mourner comments on Michael's fate: "It's just a shame the deadline's passed.  Now, maybe...he'll never die." The final shot is of Michael sitting quietly in his cell. (Script: "Michael is home.")

## A DARKER HALLOWEEN

If there were ever a contest for the darkest unmade *Halloween* sequel, *Asylum 2013* would be a strong contender. That's not an aspersion on the material but merely an observation. Not only is the Shape at his most brutal in this story, but the "good guys" aren't all that good. The administrators and staff of Smith's Grove Sanitarium – whom we'll detail in a bit – range from dangerously self-interested to pure human garbage. That makes this script's many kill scenes, which are written in horrifyingly bloody detail, somewhat of a macabre pleasure to read through. Some fans have criticized Rob Zombie's *Halloween* for being overly bleak, but even that version of Smith's Grove had good-natured types like Dr. Loomis and Ismael Cruz hanging around. There are no such characters in this story. The only remotely likable character is final girl Callie – and we have a front row seat as the Shape takes everything from her but her life.

Just how similar is Stolberg/Goldfinger's script to Matt Venne's original? Not all that similar, it turns out. These screenplays feature radically different twists and turns with starkly different characters. (Recall how something similar happened on *Halloween 666* where the re-written material was virtually unrecognizable from the original work.) *Asylum 2013* only shares the most basic story overlay with its predecessor: The Shape is apprehended by police while chasing a victim that got away. He's re-incarcerated at Smith's Grove Sanitarium and tried for his crimes. Sentenced to death, the slasher's execution goes horribly wrong, after which he goes on a rampage throughout the hospital. Almost every other detail differs between the two drafts – including the endings. The only character that appears in both stories is the Shape himself. Would Venne have still received screenwriting credit for his original draft? Possibly not, though he might've gotten a "Story by" nod. It's the kind of situation that the Writer's Guild Arbitration was made for.

As different as they are, the two *Asylum* drafts do share several similar moments. One of these includes a special cameo from beyond the grave. In *Asylum 2005*, Lucy Garrety discovers a taped therapy session between young Michael and Dr. Loomis in the old Hall of Records, which she plays to distract the Shape. Hearing his own adolescent voice again stuns him long enough for her to gain the upper hand, albeit briefly. This same moment happens in *Asylum 2013* with Callie, though it unfolds differently. Michael is again "mesmerized" by the tape, even dropping his weapon as he stares transfixed. The playback slows as the machine's battery dies, however, causing their voices to become distorted and almost demonic. Loomis repeatedly asks the boy why he killed his sister. Adult Michael listens intently, "as if wanting to know the answer himself." Callie throws the tape player to the floor and, rather than attacking her, the Shape reaches down to retrieve it. She takes this opportunity to attack, driving antique surgical clamps through the back of his neck, which protrude out through his throat. (*Jesus.*) On the whole, such shared moments are few and far between.

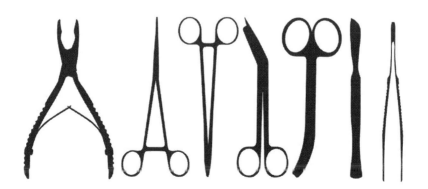

Whereas *Asylum 2005* was clearly written as a potential *Halloween 9*, it's not immediately evident which continuity *Asylum 2013* fits into. Stolberg and Goldfinger walk a fine line with their narrative in that it doesn't overtly reference any specific timeline. It could be a sequel to *Halloween: Resurrection* or it could just as easily be a follow-up to Rob Zombie's *Halloween II*, which was released four years prior. This ambiguity may be by design. As a standalone tale, it's self-contained enough to not require its viewers to have seen any other *Halloween* films to enjoy it. The opening scenes leading up to Michael's apprehension feel like part of the John Carpenter timeline. Yet the material at Smith's Grove reeks of the Rob Zombie era.

Venne's *Asylum* notably ended with the Shape having escaped custody on Halloween morning, leaving the door open for an immediate sequel set that evening. *Asylum 2013* alternately ends with the slasher re-incarcerated at Smith's Grove. He's even returned to his old room, which has been left untouched since his 1978 escape. This makes *Asylum 2013* one of the few proposed *Halloween* sequels that ends with the Shape in police custody. (And unlike *Halloween 5*, no one shows up to free him this time.) As the script's final page puts it, "Michael is home." That phrasing feels like a play on the original *Halloween*'s iconic tagline – "The Night He Came Home." Oddly enough, Smith's Grove probably does feel like home for Michael to an extent. Consider that he spent far more time incarcerated there than he ever did living at 45 Lampkin Lane.

The irony of *Asylum 2013* is that – while it ends with Michael being caught – it doesn't boast a happy ending. There is *nothing* happy in this entire script, which envisions one of the most brutal and mean-spirited *Halloweens* of all time. The entire cast dies except for final girl Callie but consider all she loses along the way. Her fiancé, her best friend, her schoolmates, and her professor are all dead. Her years studying at Smith's Grove are likely for naught, which leaves her academic career in a bind. She'll never know peace again, unable to forget that the Shape knows who she is and specifically targeted her on this night of unholy hell.

## THE BIRTHPLACE OF EVIL

By this late point in the saga, most fans probably feel as though they know the relevant details of Michael Myers' early life. Raised in Haddonfield by a seemingly normal family, something snaps within the boy at age six, which leads him to murder his older sister in cold blood. Original *Halloween* filmmakers John Carpenter and Debra Hill intentionally avoided overexplaining the circumstances of this original murder, never so much as hinting at a motive or reasoning. *That*, they would argue, is what makes it scary – that a normal person could become evil without warning. But what if there were previously unknown details that foreshadowed his transformation into the Shape? Stolberg and Goldfinger try adding new pieces to the original mythology in *Asylum 2013* that suggest Michael may have been evil from the start. The implications of this development change Carpenter and Hill's vision considerably.

*Asylum 2013*'s opening sequence finds a group of teenagers en route to a rundown farmhouse in rural Indiana roughly two hours from the Illinois state line. (In a modern but still nice touch, a pop-punk version of the Chordettes' "Mr. Sandman" would've been heard on the radio.) Mark, our storyteller, informs his friends that they've arrived at the true birthplace of Michael Myers. ("What? You thought it was in Haddonfield?") Per his story, Michael's family did live in Haddonfield, but he wasn't actually born there. Mark tells that Edith Myers and young daughter Judith were out for a drive in the country when their car suddenly flipped into a ditch, cause unknown. The impact of the crash caused Edith's water to break despite her only being seven months pregnant with Michael. Mother and daughter manage to pull themselves from the ditch and crawl to this very farmhouse. Hoping to find a phone with which to call a doctor, they instead find the house empty.

> **Mark:** *Edith went into labor right there. Pushed a bloody and premature baby out on the front porch as little Judy pounded on the front door. The little girl was crying. Mom was crying. Do you know who wasn't crying? (beat for effect) Michael. [...] He just lay there. In the pool of his mother's blood. Happy.*

Now that is *some* development! Not only does it suggest Michael was prematurely delivered, which might've cursed him with developmental issues, but that he was also a blood-loving psycho from his first moments out of the womb. If we accept this notion, that he was born evil and thus pre-destined to become a slasher, then we must reject the original Carpenter/Hill approach. Michael can't suddenly snap in October 1963 if he was evil from the start. That may seem like sacrilege, but the series has tried this before. *Halloween 6* suggested Michael killed Judith under influence from Thorn. Rob Zombie's remake alternately tried to blame psychosocial and socioeconomic factors. Even the original *Halloween*'s official novelization theorized that Michael's evil was part of a curse passed down from his ancient ancestors.

Aside from expanding on the Shape's origin, this development also provides a spooky new locale for *Asylum 2013*'s opening. Why not just have the adventurous teens visit the Myers house instead? Well, in the wake of *Resurrection,* that location was largely played out. (Not to mention, it might not be the most covert place to hide after that film's events.) It would seem as though the writers needed a new home for Michael to haunt and a remote farmhouse certainly fit the bill. The teens eventually realize they've stumbled upon the Shape's current residence, after which he slaughters all but one of them. One benefit to the farmhouse backdrop is that with no neighbors within walking distance, the Shape's victims have nowhere to run but into the dark night.

## UNSAVORY TYPES

For reasons unknown, the staff of Smith's Grove Sanitarium have never been depicted in a favorable light in this series. They're either shown as being grossly negligent (*Halloween*), as harboring an evil Druid cult (*Halloween 6*), or as depraved redneck rapists (*Halloween 2007*). The same is true in the lost sequels. Matt Venne's *Asylum* saw Smith's Grove morphed into a hybrid sanitarium-penitentiary, which made for a much grittier atmosphere. In this new *Asylum* draft, the facility is back to being a psychiatric hospital. Yet i's now run by a bunch of self-serving assholes. As a result, we wouldn't feel too badly watching the Shape slash his way through the staff. Seriously, these are not good people.

In this story, Smith's Grove is run by Director Edward Phelps. A former prison warden, Phelps is planning a bid for governor next year and feels that overseeing Michael's execution would be a serious notch in his political belt. In his self-centered worldview, the current governor's upcoming execution ban is but a ruse to keep Phelps from boosting his own electability. Stepping outside the law, Phelps decides to perform the execution in secret at Smith's Grove and imports an antique electric chair from his former employer. ("I am going to be the man who executed Michael Myers.") Of course, this impromptu execution goes horribly wrong, resulting in a massive loss of life. It just goes to show what can happen when you do the right thing (executing Michael) for the wrong reason (political gain). Despite the mounting kill count, Phelps refuses to call for outside help to stop the Shape out of fear he might be held criminally responsible for all the hell that's transpired. ("It would really be a shame if we all go down for this when the solution to our problem is wandering out there right now, just needing one bullet to the head.") Fortunately, the director meets a fitting end in the final act courtesy of the Shape. After being beaten senseless, the slasher jams a live smoke grenade into Phelps' chest cavity. Smoke billows from the dying administrator's mouth, nose, and ears.

Of course, Phelps doesn't operate in a vacuum. He's repeatedly egged on by District Attorney Danielle Hawthorne, who may see a place for herself in his bid for the governor's seat. Hawthorne goes along with every step of the unauthorized execution. She's also the first to insist they can't call in the feds to help stop Michael due to their own culpability. Like Phelps, she eventually meets a fitting end. Unlike Phelps, however, that end doesn't come at the hands of the Shape, but at the hands of a killer she'd convicted on a triple-homicide years before. ("You should know the truth. It was only a *double* homicide, but we can change that right now.") This makes Hawthorne the only role in the story murdered by someone other than the Shape.

That brings us to Dr. Cushing, who manages one of the wards and also the grad student program. (It's difficult to imagine this role wasn't named for Hammer legend Peter Cushing, whom John Carpenter originally approached to play Dr. Loomis in *Halloween*.) Cushing is a mad scientist-type every bit as self-serving as Phelps and Hawthorne. Upon learning of the Shape's attack in Covington, he presents himself to police as the preeminent expert on all things Michael Myers, which he is not. ("You want to catch Michael?" Cushing intones dramatically. "Then I suggest you join me in Haddonfield.") Of course, his predictions on the slasher's whereabouts prove false. We later see Cushing obtaining unauthorized tissue samples from the Shape's brain in order to test for a potential serial killer gene. Without proper authorization, he's unable to perform a full craniotomy and instead extracts the samples by inserting a large syringe into the Shape's eye-socket. (It's a stomach-churning moment. Even his assistant vomits.) Somewhat eerily, the heavily-restrained slasher never reacts to the pain of the procedure. Like Hawthorne, Cushing is more than willing to go along with Phelps' unlawful execution as he's been promised a chance to dissect the slasher's brain. At first glance, you might be tempted to equate this draft's Dr. Cushing with *Asylum 2005*'s Dr. Craine, but they're very different characters. Craine was a generally good man and a selfless hero, none of which applies to Cushing. Appropriately, the Shape murders Cushing using tools intended for his own dissection later that night.

Then there are the various guards, all apparent graduates of the Noel Kluggs School of Assholery. One guard steals the Shape's mask from evidence and teases him with it. ("Still trying to figure out whether to piss on it or sell it on eBay. Some sicko'd pay a lot of money to whack off to it.") Another officer known as the "Hick Guard" is tasked with shaving the slasher's head, which is standard protocol before going into the electric chair. The hick intentionally nicks the Shape's scalp with the razor, though he doesn't react. Hoping to get a rise, the guard then carves out a large chunk of his subject's head. (Script: "Again, no reaction from Michael... which, for the first time, freaks the Hick Guard out.") Then we have the "Sadistic Guard," who taunts Michael with the fact that so many people wanted to throw the switch that they had to draw straws. ("I won! You know what that means? I'm the one who gets to fry you up. *Bzzzzzzz!*") Not that Michael deserves compassion per se, but this doesn't seem like the right level of reverence for putting someone to death.

## A NEW FIXATION

In the original *Halloween*, the Shape fixates on seventeen-year-old Laurie Strode seemingly at random, stalking her throughout the day and evening. This arguably represents *Halloween* at its *most* pure – the ultimate boogeyman stalking an everyday babysitter. We can theorize endlessly as to why he chose her, but we'll never truly know. It ultimately remains a mystery within the context of that first entry. (We're ignoring *Halloween II*'s sibling twist here, of course.) The subsequent films would introduce numerous final girls in the tradition of Laurie Strode, but none ever having the same kind of connection with the Shape. The slasher would stick mostly to blood relatives and their peer groups in these follow-ups, but not here. With final girl Callie, *Asylum 2013* returns to the simplicity of the original film. Callie isn't related to Michael nor does she tresspass on his family home. No, the Shape *chooses* her as his new obsession just as he chose Laurie.

Callie first encounters the Shape with Wyatt while trying to save Bethany in the opening sequence. The slasher swiftly renders Wyatt unconscious before murdering Bethany in gruesome fashion. He starts to approach Callie, but is intercepted by police, who shoot, tase, and beat him to the ground. While relieved by this last-minute rescue, she remains unsettled. Police officers physically subdue the Shape, though they're unable to break his chilling gaze. In spite of the ongoing assault, his eyes remain fixed solely on Callie. (Script: "He raises his head, and no amount of beating can get him to drop it. He just stares out directly at Callie.") In this moment, we glean that she isn't just another victim that got away. For whatever reason, Callie is special to him.

This fact becomes even more evident as the story progresses. Two years forward, Callie and Stephanie are present as Dr. Cushing extracts tissue samples from the Shape's eye socket. Concerned about the effect seeing Callie again might have on their patient, Cushing instructs her to watch from behind one-way glass. She remains silent during the procedure and no one acknowledges her presence, yet Michael still turns and stares directly at her through the glass. Alarmed, she hurriedly exits the viewing room. Something similar happens just before his execution. Led through the hallway while wearing a thick black hood, the Shape stops walking and stares in Callie's direction. He turns his head to follow her movement despite having zero visibility through the hood. Cushing theorizes that it may be related to smell.

> **Dr. Cushing:** *Young ladies tend to incite our subject. In many ways, Michael is an animal. Do you know that a male wolf can smell a female wolf's menstruation from a half a mile away? And you, Callie, you are the last female he's seen. In two years. You can't be here.*

Callie and Michael later share what we might call a *Halloween H20* moment. While chasing after Stephanie, he notices Callie watching in horror from behind a windowed security door. Suddenly losing all interest in Stephanie, the Shape walks over to the door. Slasher and final girl lock eyes for a tense beat. (Think back to *H20*'s face-to-face sibling reunion.) The moment soon passes, and he punches through the thick glass. Callie manages to get away, but not before her attacker grabs a fistful of hair, which he pockets into a makeshift trick-or-treat bag. (We'll touch on that shortly.)

Curiously, the Shape's fixation on Callie is exclusive to the *Asylum 2013* draft. Looking back on Venne's *Asylum 2005*, we see no such obsession with nurse Lucy Garrety. In that iteration of the story, Lucy simply had the misfortune of working on the same night as Michael's execution. Yes, he did travel to her home in the finale, but that was only to exact a bit of revenge. He does the same with Bethany in this story's opening. Even so, Callie remains in a different category. (The screenplay refers to her as "his true purpose.")

## THE SUPER SHAPE

With regard to its depiction of the Shape, *Asylum 2013* is a mixed bag. In one sense, Stolberg and Goldfinger return the character to its roots by playing up his penchant for macabre theatricality. (This is something the sequels often ignore.) Yet in another sense, the screenwriters risk their standing with the audience by supernaturally transforming Michael into a "Super Shape." At any rate, this story finds the slasher just as merciless and depraved as he's ever been. Take the opening in Covington, Indiana. He throws one teen under the tire of a truck stuck in the mud. The spinning tire rips his face off and then his entire head. (Script: "The SFX of a cantaloupe being thrown into a wood chipper as his MUSH HEAD comes out the other side.") Moments later, the Shape chases an injured Bethany. He stabs his knife into her leg with such force that it pins her to the ground. He then stabs into her skull so deeply that he struggles to retrieve his blade. In a darkly humorous visual, he has to plant one foot on her skull just to gain enough leverage to extract it.

One detail that sets the Shape apart from his slasher brethren is that he's often creative and even playful with his handiwork. Whether it's staging Annie Brackett's corpse with Judith's tombstone in *Halloween* or carving Officer Francis' head like a jack-o-lantern in *Halloween 2018*, Michael enjoys curating his kills in creative ways. Stolberg and Goldfinger take this to a sick new level in *Asylum 2013* by having him go trick-or-treating around Smith's Grove... sort of. For his goodie bag, Michael peels off the bloodied black hood that melted onto his face during the electrocution sequence. If that wasn't nauseating enough, he goes around filling it not with candy but with small trophies of his victims from throughout the night. (A finger here, some hair there, perhaps a tooth.) It's as though – even fifty years later – the Shape is still that little boy in the clown costume enjoying a night of trick-or-treating.

It's interesting to note that, at this story's outset, Michael Myers is widely believed to be dead. Obviously, he's not. He's just off the radar, living as though a ghost at his birth site in Covington. It stands to reason that, at a certain point, he would need to leave Haddonfield, Illinois due to having become so infamous there. Even if the Myers house hadn't burned down, it would likely have become overrun with curious tourists and true crime aficionados. In another early scene, Stephanie wanders into Michael's old room at Smith's Grove and is unnerved to find that it's remained unchanged since his escape years prior. Turning to Dr. Cushing, she asks, "Why do they keep it like this? Michael is dead." Patting her leg, Cushing flatly responds: "Yeah, I read that too," as though he's hopeful Michael might one day turn back up.

Visually, the Shape appears much like how he did in *Asylum 2005* with a white restraint mask before opting for his usual getup. (Script: "We don't see Michael's face, but we do catch GLIMPSES of SCARS and BURNS. Gruesome.") If *Asylum 2013* missteps with the character at all, it's in his superhuman depiction after the electrocution sequence. This may honestly be a bridge too far. As already mentioned, Michael emerges from the electric chair supercharged with heightened strength. It's an unexpected development that surprises even him. Shortly after, he goes to open a locked door and accidentally pulls the entire handle off with "miraculous ease." Confused, he stares down at the metal handle before single-handedly crushing it. In the writers' defense, this idea was directly handed down from Bob Weinstein, who wanted to see an even more superpowered Shape than we have here. Fortunately, Stolberg and Goldfinger incorporate the suggestion with tremendous restraint, never fully exploiting an arguably hammy concept. The most impressive display of his newfound strength comes during his trek through Homicide Hall near story's end. Hoping to stall her attacker, Callie releases the hospital's most dangerous inmates, who immediately surround the Shape. ("Brother, you are in the wrong place at the wrong time.") Michael makes shockingly quick work of the murderous mob in a graphic kill sequence. As the script puts it, "We've never seen Michael like this before."

## WHY IT WASN'T MADE

Stolberg and Goldfinger received positive marks upon submitting their draft. They were then given notes on how to improve upon it. Yet it would seem that these notes are what would actually prevent this second iteration of *Halloween: Asylum* from reaching theater screens. It should be restated that the idea of the "Super Shape" – his supernatural abilities and all – did not hail from the writers' original concept. These elements were mandated by Bob Weinstein, who ideated a bold new vision for the Shape, which the writers were apprehensive towards. Somewhere in development, this approach must've lost whatever luster it once had. It seems reasonable to think this approach may have gone against the interests of Malek Akkad, who might've preferred starting back at square one rather than follow through with the Stolberg/Goldfinger draft in its latest form.

Despite dismissing this duo's script, we'll come to find that both Dimension and Trancas still wished to utilize the setting Smith's Grove (and by extension, Matt Venne's original draft) as the basis of the eleventh *Halloween*, which nicely leads us into the next unmade sequel. However, it should be noted that Stolberg and Goldfinger weren't the only writers brought on for this revision assignment. Another team brought to Dimension's attention during this time was that of Andrew Dabb and Adam Glass. Aside from their work in the comic industry, this duo is perhaps best remembered for their work as writers and producers on the CBS series *Supernatural.*

As Glass tells it, "I was asked by The Weinstein Company to write *Halloween* after delivering for them on some other scripts. These jobs were always fast and furious. Quick money. Most of them for the Weinsteins was just getting a script so they could keep their option on the material, so it was all a legal step. Honestly, I think it was a re-write. But we did a page one and just tried to ground it and make it production-friendly. And that was it. Never heard anything again. Five weeks and done." Though he doesn't recall whose script he was revising, the writer revealed that his script was most likely developed somewhere between 2014 and 2015, which would occur just after the timeframe of Stolberg and Goldfinger's involvement, just as Dimension was pushing for the asylum angle once more.

"I love the *Halloween* franchise but because of the situation, I knew this was only a gig," Glass went on to say. "Andrew and I wrote our best version, which honestly I can barely remember. Something about a prison break. Or asylum break. It was never going to be made because it was just a step for the Weinsteins to keep the option. They did this all the time." Prior to their exit, Glass met with Malek Akkad, whom he found "a nice guy. It was obvious he wanted this [*Halloween*] out of the Weinsteins so he could go do it the way he wanted [...] [Malek] gave me a bottle before I left of the whiskey we were drinking. He made it. It was called A Writer's Tear." (How fitting!)

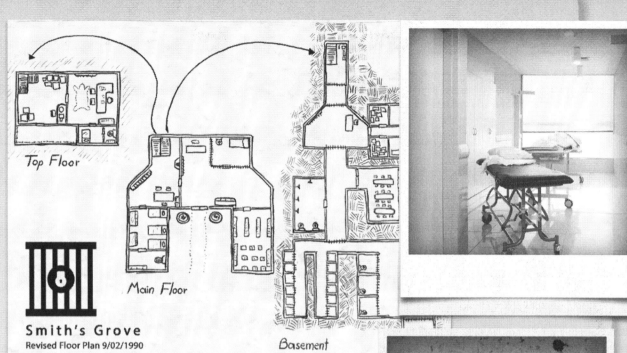

**Top Floor**

**Main Floor**

**Basement**

## Smith's Grove
Revised Floor Plan 9/02/1990

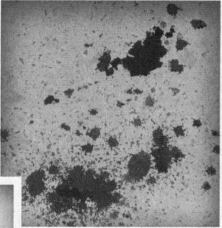

**ILLINOIS DEPARTMENT OF CORRECTIONS**

BURTON MERCER
OFFICER

KL5-4777
(312) ███-████

**Ten years after pitching *Michael vs Pinhead*, you and Pete Goldfinger are now attached to *Halloween: Asylum*. How did you come to be involved this time?**

Pete and I had had a general meeting with Matthew Signer, one of Bob Weinstein's executives, in early 2013, and we pitched a few random ideas about a new sequel to *Halloween*. As you do in general meetings, they weren't fully fleshed out ideas, but he liked one of them and he set up a meeting for us to pitch the idea to Malek in the summer of 2013. I honestly don't even remember what the idea was. But we heard back from Matthew that Malek didn't respond to our idea, but he liked our enthusiasm. Later that year, they decided that they wanted to rework a script that was written to follow *Halloween: Resurrection*. It was called *Halloween: Asylum* and was written by Matt Venne. Malek and Matthew and the other exec there – Keith Levine – reached out to Pete and I and asked if we were interested. And, well, it wasn't a difficult decision because I was *dying* to work on a *Halloween* movie. We gave some notes and were eventually hired to do the rewrite. They had decided that they wanted to "retreat from the brutality" of Rob's films and they wanted to throwback to a more Carpenter vibe.

**Hypothetically, *Halloween: Asylum* would've been the first *Halloween* after the Rob Zombie films. What were your thoughts on where the franchise had gone thus far?**

I really liked what Rob did. They were fucking violent and angry and tried to dig deep into the psychology of Michael Myers. It's funny because I've hung out with Rob a dozen times over the past few years. He directed Pete's wife [Jennifer Jostyn] in *House of 1,000 Corpses* and he's very different from the way you might think. He's really this gentle, thoughtful guy. Yes, he's clearly a little demented but in the best possible way. And he has an encyclopedic knowledge of horror. I liked what he did.

**How'd you feel about using Matt Venne's script as a blueprint?**

Pete and I really loved what Matt did with his script, but it was dated. Hell, I think it opened with Busta Rhymes, and after speaking with him about taking over the writing duties, it was clear that he was ready to have someone else take a crack at the material. I always try to reach out to previous writers when I'm working on a rewrite because it's nice to hear from them what they think works and doesn't work. They were in the trenches with the material and usually have good insight. Matt was particularly cool about having us brought in, and I tried to keep him in the loop as things progressed. As a matter of fact, we even chatted on the phone when [*Halloween 2018*] went to arbitration because we were all in the chain of title. Interestingly, later in the process, I discovered that they might have hired another writer to work on a different script simultaneously to ours, but I don't actually know for sure. A buddy of mine who follows tracking boards found a listing for a *Halloween III 3D* listed, with a logline under wraps that was supposed to be directed by Patrick Lussier, who was the editor of *H20*. I don't know if anything ever came of that, but I was surprised to hear about it when I was told about the secret project.

**Did you have any goals in tackling this revision?**

Pete and I set out to make a bit of a throwback film. The first act is most definitely a mash-up of the original *Halloween* vibe and *Halloween H20*. My personal favorite part in our script was a simple scene on the front porch of the farmhouse where Michael Myers was born, where we describe his birth. The kids see a faded-out stain of blood on the wooded porch and one of the characters – soon to die – describes how Michael was born premature and how his mother and sister were crying but Michael wasn't. And we had a few fun kills. The idea for the film was all Matt Venne. We were just playing in the sandbox. And that first act, to me, is my favorite part of the script. But, it's a first draft so it's most definitely flawed. People forget that by the time they've seen a film, the scripts have gone through dozens and dozens of drafts, so looking at our script is sort of like taking a Polaroid photograph and then showing it before it's developed. There is a hazy image, but it needs to develop more to be ready to show.

**You mentioned liking the Rob Zombie films but wanting to go in a direction more "OG *Halloween*-meets-*H20*." That said, what timeline would you say your *Asylum* operates under?**

Yes, we loved Rob's films. But they were clearly Rob's films. And that gritty, uncompromising Zombie aesthetic isn't really our *Halloween* aesthetic. I have a more romanticized feeling about the *Halloween* franchise. Our story was always supposed to be outside Rob's films. So, timeline, it was post-*Resurrection*, although I think we were careful not to get into the timeline too much. Some franchises, like Marvel, are all about continuity and a continuation. Then, there are franchises like James Bond and *Alien* where the films have a very different vibe. We saw ours living here. Like *Bumblebee* in the *Transformers* franchise. Or *Rogue One* in the *Star Wars* universe.

**As opposed to your initial meeting with Moustapha, you were now working with Malek. Did the two differ in their approach to *Halloween*?**

Working with Malek was great. He has a lot of love for the franchise. I mean, he grew up with it. We talked a lot about his father and the evolution of *Halloween*. He was much more open to taking things in new directions and wasn't tied to the mythology in the same way that I found Moustapha to be. Overall, I really liked him.

**A big part of your *Asylum* story focuses on the pending abolishment of the death penalty in Illinois. Was this strictly a story element or is there a social commentary here?**

A lot of that was because as we were doing research, we learned that the death penalty had recently been repealed in Illinois, I think a couple of years before we started writing the script. When we found this, we decided it might make a great ticking clock for the story and for the execution of Michael Myers. Any way to ground your story is going to help you, especially when you're dealing with a story like this. Both Pete and I probably lean toward "anti-death-penalty" but I'd be lying if I said that the social commentary factored in here. It was a decision made primarily for storytelling purposes. If shit's not working properly, wouldn't it be nice if they were *forced* to go through with the execution because of timing? There was more opportunity for things to go sideways. And as a writer, you're always looking for things to go sideways.

**You create a new backstory for the Shape by telling of his birth in Covington, Indiana. Why move the action from Haddonfield to Covington? Is there a personal connection there?**

Again, this was for storytelling. We knew we wanted to start with a big act one massacre, and felt that if we did it in Haddonfield, we'd have to readdress Laurie and all the other stuff that comes with Haddonfield. And that just wasn't this story. I might be wrong, but I don't think anyone established Michael's birthplace before, so we felt like it was fair game. We made sure to say that he was from Haddonfield, and that the birth took place because of a car accident. We liked the idea of Michael being born into chaos and pain. And we loved the idea that he came out not crying.

**You populate the staff of Smith's Grove with some really unsavory characters from doctors to security guards. Everyone seems to have their own self-centered agenda. What led you to take this approach?**

Going back to your question about "social commentary," this was done with more purpose than the death penalty story point. I think the demonization of people in prison is troublesome, and while I don't deny that there are probably very kind wardens and prison guards, I think there is a systemic problem with our prison system. The way that we're turning prisons into a profit industry is disturbing. It helped that we needed bodies to fill the body bags.

**Your script has an audio cameo by Dr. Loomis via an old therapy session tape. Why was it important to bring his voice back to the series, even if only briefly?**

I'm not sure which draft of the script we sent you, but the idea we wanted to play with was that it was Loomis' voice that triggers Michael. And we use it as a plot point to move action. Also, his voice is *so* iconic to the franchise. It felt like wish-fulfillment for us to have him heard in our film.

**Your Shape has a playful side, not unlike the Shape in Carpenter's original. He has a trick-or-treat bag (his bloodied electrocution hood), which he uses to store little mementos from each victim. Where'd you get this macabre idea from? (It's chilling!)**

Thanks! Yes, we really wanted to bring back a little of that Nick Castle playfulness. That head turn looking up at the body he's pinned to the wall? We wanted to continue that vibe. Which, again, was a step away from the recent *Halloween* films that Rob directed, which we were coming in after. Pete has a really funny story about doing the Universal Studios Halloween tour *with* Rob in the house that he designed (Pete's wife was one of the stars of *House of 1,000 Corpses*), and, the way Pete tells it, he was *horrified* at all of these gruesome, real autopsy videos that Rob used in the maze – and when they stepped out of the maze, Pete asks him about the videos, and Rob smiles and says, '*I know, isn't that funny?*'

**Your script ends with Michael back in his old cell at Smith's Grove rather than out wandering free. Why this incarcerated ending? Was there any pressure to leave it more open-ended so as to set up another sequel?**

We weren't purposely trying to set up a sequel. That might have been a note from Harvey Weinstein or Malek Akkad or someone from Dimension. We knew going in that this was a one-and-done for us. It had always been a dream to write a *Halloween* movie, and not many people can say they did and got paid for it. I guess anyone can write their own movie if they want. Ours just happened at the wrong time – at the end of the Weinstein/*Halloween* era. We may have also been trying to make it easier for the next writer. Because there always is one.

**What was the reaction to your draft?**

We received great feedback after the first draft. And I was pretty excited about it. It's always a balancing act, especially rewriting a script that's been in the system for a while. There are so many cooks in the kitchen. I felt that we kept the parts of Matt's original draft that worked, and retooled stuff that we were excited about. But at the end of the day, Bob Weinstein decided that he wanted something different. We were contracted to two drafts of the script, so we were on board to get notes and go another round. And while we disagreed with the direction that Bob wanted to take the script, he was the one writing the check, so we gave it a shot. He wanted more of a "hook" to the film and decided that it would be fun if, after Michael was electrocuted, he became sort of *super-Michael*. That he'd be able to do things he wasn't previously able to do. I remember, specifically, one of the notes from him was the idea that he wanted Michael to jump up toward the ceiling and through a skylight, landing on the roof. Basically, he wanted us to give Michael super-strength.

We did our best to make the adjustment, but at the end of the day, I think the script was hurt by it. Who knows? If we had continued to work on the script past two drafts, maybe we would have found the right balance. But the second draft we delivered, with that big change, just didn't work. You know, one of the things that I love about Michael is that he is human. He's a monster. He's evil. But he's a dude. He's not Freddy or Uber Jason. And I think making that change was the poison pill that killed the momentum on the project. Or maybe we just blew it. I don't know. We'll never know for sure. But that was it for us. We were done. Somewhere along the way, Weinstein lost the rights to *Halloween* and the rest is history. But no matter what, I got paid to write kill scenes for Michael Myers. I'll never forget that. Fucking awesome.

# HALLOWEEN
## *RETURNS*

In 1978, Michael Myers escaped custody.
Tonight, he'll do it again.

**Screenplay by**
**Marcus Dunstan & Patrick Melton**

Updates on *Halloween* had been relatively nonexistent throughout 2013, the year of the franchise's 35th anniversary. Though Josh Stolberg and Pete Goldfinger had cultivated a revision of Matt Venne's *Halloween: Asylum*, their involvement had not been made public at the time. Neither had that of Adam Glass and Andrew Dabb. Thus, fans had little to go on in terms of a new film. The year 2014 marked five years since Rob Zombie's *Halloween II* had sharply divided audiences. In the time since, multiple passes at a *Halloween 3D* had failed. Release dates were set and then missed. A collaboration with Platinum Dunes fell through. The franchise was kept afloat only with an admittedly impressive "Complete Collection" Blu-ray set released by Scream Factory. But as far as another film was concerned, news was pretty much zilch. It seemed the online fanbase had collectively grown either impatient waiting for the next film or given up hope entirely. Purists, on the other hand, seemed satisfied just to receive yet another transfer of the original movie. (On that note, just *where* are the *Halloween 5* deleted scenes?!)

Any impatience from the fanbase was likely shared by Malek Akkad, who still strived to develop another sequel, despite Dimension Films' uncertainty on when or how to proceed. Though previous attempts at revising *Halloween: Asylum* proved futile, Bob Weinstein continued to advocate for either a return to Smith's Grove or utilizing a prison as the main locale. Several months after the dismissal of Stolberg and Goldfinger, news of the latest *Halloween* began to percolate on the web once more. On April 30th, *Bloody-Disgusting* reported news of yet another *Halloween 3D* in the works from sources at the Cannes Film Festival. While it wasn't immediately clear whether this iteration would utilize the script by Patrick Lussier and Todd Farmer, it was at least a glimmer of hope.

Even more promising, actress Scout Taylor-Compton took to Twitter that very same day to seemingly confirm the *Bloody-Disgusting* report: "No more secrets. Can't wait to jump back into Laurie Strode's mindset." Such a remark may have been a bit premature as it isn't known just how involved the actress was during these calls. Two days later, however, Trancas International officially announced that the latest sequel was in active development. To support this, a working logo was posted on the official *Halloween* website featuring the title *Halloween 3*, which would've suggested a follow-up to the Rob Zombie films.

The following month, *Collider.com* further inquired about the status of the project when speaking with Malek Akkad. Once again referring to the developing sequel as *Halloween 3*, the producer stated, "I can't talk about it too much right now, but it will definitely keep elements and bring in new elements. Because the last one [*Halloween II*] got a little dark, I really want to bring it back to the classic Friday night horror film that people will really like." Details of the project remained shrouded in mystery as updates became fewer and fewer. The October 2014 reports of a screenplay titled *Halloween: The Next Chapter* were refuted by Trancas not long after.

Hopeful news finally arrived on February 9th, 2015, when *The Hollywood Reporter* unofficially announced that the next *Halloween* was to be written by Patrick Melton and Marcus Dunstan with the latter also directing. Melton and Dunstan were then best-known for having co-written *Feast* for Dimension, along with the fourth, fifth, sixth, and seventh entries in the popular *Saw* franchise. (Melton and Dunstan also wrote *Piranha 3DD*, the sequel to *Piranha 3D*, which was written by previous *Halloween* hopefuls Josh Stolberg and Pete Goldfinger.) The duo's involvement was finally confirmed on June 15th when Dimension announced the greenlight on what was to be *Halloween Returns*. Shooting was expected to begin not long after.

Melton and Dunstan's new storyline had managed to win the approval of Malek Akkad, whom they found an agreeable collaborator. Their story would not continue in the continuity of the remake timeline, but instead carve out its own path. Widely referred to as a "recalibration" of the franchise, *Halloween Returns* billed itself as a direct sequel to John Carpenter's original and would therefore serve as an alternate *Halloween II*. Despite this, *Shock Till You Drop* exclusively reported that original *Halloween II* character Gary Hunt would appear in a major role.

*"Halloween Returns" will pit a new group of Haddonfield youngsters against Myers. The now 18-year-old child of one of Myers' victims plays a central role along with the child of a cop who has long been obsessed with Myers' case, even putting it before his own daughter. Myers is now on Death Row and the two kids with their own personal vendettas against the killer sneak in to watch his execution. But when things go awry and Myers escapes, the pair, along with their friends, find themselves in the firing line."*

As a franchise recalibration, *Halloween Returns* is an utterly fascinating tale from its very first page. Having seen 1981's *Halloween II*, we feel as though we already know what happens to Michael Myers after Loomis shoots him off the balcony in *Halloween* – he goes to Haddonfield Memorial to find his sister, right? Not so in this story, which veers in an entirely new direction involving none of the protagonists from the original film. Melton and Dunstan deserve high marks for introducing an all-new ensemble of characters and immediately giving us reasons to care about them. Their story has faint vibes of the original *Nightmare on Elm Street* in that the younger generation is suffering for the sins of the parents. The Shape's return here is but a violent echo of the past.

In a rare interview with Darnell Weeks ("TheMyersFan25"), Dunstan revealed that he and his writing partner hoped their story would stand on its own, likening it to *Aliens* – a film he didn't initially realize was a sequel upon first viewing. Having worked on the highly-serialized *Saw* films, Dunstan further expressed hope that *Halloween Returns* would be rewarding as a complete experience – not simply another sequel wedged between predecessors and follow-ups.

## THE STORY

*Halloween Returns* begins where the original *Halloween* ended with the Shape having just been shot six times by Dr. Loomis. Escaping that encounter, the injured slasher continues to stalk Haddonfield's streets. He attacks a teenager named Karen, who seeks refuge at the home of Deputy Gary Hunt. The deputy's wife lets Karen inside and dials 911, though the Shape soon forces his way in. He attacks both women, killing Mrs. Hunt in front of her eight-year-old son Noah. Karen manages another escape, though a large knife now protrudes from her back. The Shape follows her outside but is immediately apprehended by Deputy Hunt and Dr. Paul Rogers of Smith's Grove. Rogers begs Michael to stop as he's "killed everyone." With this, the Shape surrenders and is taken into custody. Dr. Rogers testifies in court that Michael Myers is sane enough to be tried for his crimes and must be put to death.

Ten years later, we find the Shape on death row at the Warren County Correctional Center, his execution scheduled for the day before Halloween. Rogers' teenage daughter Sofia has begun to date a now teenaged Noah Hunt, who desperately wants to watch the demise of his mother's killer. Sofia and Noah sneak into the prison for the midnight execution and unwittingly catch the the Shape's attention from the audience. Sheriff Hunt, still angry and blaming Rogers for Michael's original escape, is also in attendance. Officials utilize an unconventional drug mixture to execute the slasher, which fails to do so and instead spikes his adrenaline. This enables the Shape to break free and slaughter a handful of guards and attendees. Meanwhile, a raging storm cuts power to the facility and causes a utility room to catch fire. The Shape escapes federal custody amid the widespread pandemonium, though prison officials believe him to have died in the blaze.

Without a body, Hunt and Rogers refuse to believe the initial reports of Michael's death. With Halloween now in full swing, the two men begrudgingly team up to find him. Elsewhere, the Shape murders the owner of a novelty store and acquires a new white mask while doing so. Hunt and Rogers discover a stolen police cruiser near the prison with Rogers' name entered into the address database. He calls home just in time to hear his wife being attacked by the escaped slasher. Arriving moments later, Rogers' wife dies in his arms. He and Hunt soon make a startling realization – that their children were both at the execution and are now likely targets. With the sun setting on Halloween night, Hunt and Rogers race to find their kids before the Shape does. They eventually arrive at the youth's party destination, an old farmhouse adjacent to Farmer John's Haunted Pumpkin Patch. By the time the fathers arrive, Sofia and Noah's friends are all dead.

Inside the farmhouse, the Shape murders Sheriff Hunt, setting the structure ablaze in the process. Rogers rushes inside and distracts his former patient so that Sofia and Noah, both injured, can escape. Rogers remains inside to taunt the slasher as police arrive and surround the property. Through the billowing smoke, police spot the Shape running from the house, blade in hand. They open fire and the figure drops to the ground. This turns out to be a diversion, however. Police unmask the slasher to find Rogers – his tongue split, and a giant glass shard impaled through his palm. The true Shape has escaped into the night once more, but not before inscribing a message in blood on a farmhouse wall: "This town will never be safe again."

In a post-credit scene, a hospitalized Rogers recounts the ordeal to an unspecified colleague, who comments: "You speak of Michael Myers as if he were just a man. He's not a man, Dr. Rogers. He never was. He's purely... and simply... *evil*." This is revealed to be Dr. Sam Loomis. Cut to black.

# A RECALIBRATION

*Halloween Returns* may be among the strangest endeavors in this book for its efforts to once again rewrite the timeline. It not only positions itself as an alternate *Halloween II* by picking up from *Halloween*'s ending, but it then ventures into *Halloween 4* territory with a time jump set ten years later. Yet in true recalibrated form, *Halloween Returns* appears to operate as if the original *Halloween* took place in 2005. This new timeline asks a bold question – what if Laurie Strode and Dr. Loomis weren't all that important to the Shape's story? Every follow-up to the original has thus far banked on the crucial importance of these two characters, but *Returns* does not. What if Laurie's connection to the Shape ended after the first movie? What if they weren't siblings? What if Dr. Loomis wasn't Michael's only doctor and didn't devote his entire life to keeping him locked up? The answers to these questions – that's the world *Halloween Returns* takes place in. Laurie and Loomis never make an appearance – not even in flashback – nor are they ever mentioned by name. The latter does appear in a post-credit scene, but it frankly adds little to the proceedings.

Even stranger than Laurie and Loomis' absence is the introduction of two new main protagonists who were minor characters in the original *Halloween II*, which no longer exists in this timeline. Stepping in for an also absent Sheriff Brackett is Deputy Gary Hunt, played by Hunter von Leer in the 1981 sequel. Filling the void left by Dr. Loomis is Dr. Paul Rogers, a fellow psychiatrist at Smith's Grove Sanitarium. Rogers was never seen onscreen in *Halloween II*, but he was mentioned in dialogue by Marion Chambers. ("Dr. Rogers is just afraid this could jeopardize our whole rehabilitation program.") The *Returns* script retcons that Michael Myers has been under Rogers' care – not Loomis' – since his original admission to Smith's Grove at the age of six.

This story's time jump allows the writers to depict the long-term effects of trauma and survivor's guilt, both things *Halloween H20* thoroughly tackled years before. While Laurie Strode would seem the best survivor to revisit ten years on, the actress behind the role was unlikely to return. (Not to mention, it would've been difficult making the fifty-seven-year-old Curtis look both seventeen and twenty-seven again.) To make up for Laurie's absence, we're introduced to the teenaged Karen, another target of the Shape's first killing spree whom we'll later revisit ten years down the road. Some fans have mistakenly interpreted Karen as a retooled version of Laurie Strode, but this is incorrect – they are separate characters. While Laurie is never mentioned by name, she is alluded to during a news report. ("A teenage girl and man, believed to be the suspect's doctor, were found just minutes ago in the upstairs hallway of a Haddonfield residence.")

Karen is a horribly tortured soul, possibly even more so than Laurie. Her wounds this night are also far worse – she takes a butcher's knife to the back before tumbling off a second-story balcony. She makes an agonizing attempt to crawl away even with the blade still in her back. These wounds are nothing compared to the haunting guilt she'll have to live with, however. In escaping her first brush with the Shape, Karen runs to the home of Deputy Hunt. Finding only his wife and children, she takes refuge inside, tragically unaware that her attacker has followed after. Karen will ultimately survive this second attack, though Mrs. Hunt will not. In coming here, Karen has unintentionally caused the death of Deputy Hunt's wife, mother of two. Even worse, her eight-year-old son, Noah, witnesses the murder.

It's not hard to draw comparisons between *Halloween Returns* and the later-produced *Halloween 2018*. Spiritually, these movies have quite a lot in common. (This was, in fact, the last lost sequel developed before the creation of the Blumhouse trilogy.) That isn't to suggest David Gordon Green and company ripped anyone off, just that these projects had similar intentions. For starters, they both reset their timelines to ignore all prior sequels. *Halloween 2018* was also originally written to open with a continuation of *Halloween*'s ending just as *Returns* does. Deputies Hunt and Hawkins are similar for both having peacefully apprehended the Shape back in 1978. That they didn't simply kill him instead is a decision they've come to deeply regret. There's also an identical scare in both scripts. In *Returns*, we follow Hunt as he searches a farmhouse for the Shape. Spotting the slasher out of the corner of his eye, he fires his shotgun. The slug hits only a mirror, which shatters. Hunt was actually looking at the Shape's reflection, who is lurking elsewhere in the room. (Recall that Laurie does this exact thing in the 2018 film.)

## THE OPENING SEQUENCE

Whereas the original *Halloween II* gently eased audiences back into the story with three minutes of recap, *Halloween Returns* gets right down to business with its very first shot. This script opens with an unspecified point-of-view perspective, which we soon realize belongs to the Shape. We find him flat on his back looking up at the Doyle's balcony, which he's just fallen from. Not wanting to give Loomis time to reload, the injured slasher quickly flees onto the street. It's interesting to envision this scene as written into the *Returns* script. We've actually already seen this exact moment play out, just not from this angle. (This all happens concurrent with Laurie and Loomis' "It was the boogeyman," exchange.) You have to wonder if general audiences would've been able to recognize this as a continuation of *Halloween*'s ending with so few clues given. Laurie and Loomis are absent. There are no gunshots. We don't see the slasher fall. We're not even told what year this is, just that it's Halloween night. To the uninitiated, it almost looks as if the Shape was taking a nap in someone's backyard.

Melton and Dunstan intended for the audience to experience the opening sequence entirely from the Shape's point-of-view, which would've required an ambitious feat of camerawork. This, of course, would recall the iconic opening shot from Carpenter's *Halloween* in which we see young Michael murder his older sister in first-person. There is an important distinction between the two, however. *Halloween*'s opening POV had an extremely limited range of vision once Michael donned his clown mask, forcing us to watch through the eyeholes of the mask. Melton and Dunstan wrote for their opening POV shot to ditch the eyehole matte, allowing the image to fill the entire frame. This strongly evokes a similar eyehole-less POV from early in *Halloween II* in which the Shape wanders Haddonfield's back alleys after being shot by Dr. Loomis.

In *Halloween*'s opening, the camera holds on Michael's POV until he's unmasked by his father in the front yard, at which point we cut to a reverse shot of the boy's emotionless face. The camera then slowly cranes up to a wide shot of Michael, his parents, and the house at 45 Lampkin Lane. *Returns* pays homage to this by doing something similar albeit different. As written, the camera holds on the Shape's POV until he's unmasked by Dr. Rogers outside the Hunt residence. Instead of cutting to Michael's face, the camera cuts to a reversal of Carpenter's reverse, alternately showing us the back of Michael's head. (*Returns* will make a priority out of not showing the adult slasher's face.) The camera then cranes up to show Michael, Dr. Rogers, and a growing swarm of police officers with their weapons drawn.

Like *Halloween II*, *Returns* picks up directly from the original film's ending, but there is an issue with the timeline. As already mentioned, we open with the Shape having just fallen from the Doyle's second-floor balcony. It's here we notice the nearby screams of Karen, who is somehow already stabbed and crying out for help. When could the Shape have possibly attacked her? He's been inside the Doyle house after Laurie for a period of time. If he attacked Karen before then, why isn't she farther away by now? The Shape follows after her to finish the job, which sets this story in motion. A newscaster does later mention there being "reports of at least five violent attacks tonight by the escaped mental patient." We only know of three from *Halloween* (Annie, Bob, Lynda), so that does leave room for Karen's attack – but when?

The opening also gives us our first glimpse of Dr. Rogers, who begs Michael to cease his assault. ("Michael, stop! They will kill you! There is nowhere left to go. Everyone is dead. You've killed everyone. Please stop. There's nothing left. It's over. Let me help you.") This dialogue strongly recalls the workprint ending to Rob Zombie's *Halloween* in which Malcolm McDowell's Loomis begs Michael to release Laurie from his grasp. It also more faintly recalls Donald Pleasence's Loomis appealing to the Shape's humanity in *Halloween 5*. It's always intriguing anytime someone tries to reason with the boogeyman. The results do vary, but they're almost never good.

## THE OLDER GENERATION

In a bit of revisionist history, *Halloween Returns* charges that Sheriff Brackett and Dr. Loomis weren't the only sheriff/doctor team out looking for Michael Myers. Per this story, Deputy Hunt and Dr. Rogers were also out searching – just elsewhere. While Brackett and Loomis eventually split up, neither manage to apprehend the escaped slasher. Hunt and Rogers do manage to arrest their suspect and do so without firing a single shot – something both men will come to regret.

It's clear from the start whom Rogers is meant to represent in this story, which is a nice touch as Loomis has been sorely missed since his last appearance in *Halloween 6*. Given this intent, the character works well. Much like his predecessor, Rogers has no shortage of quotable lines about his patient being evil incarnate. ("All those years we thought we were watching him. But no. He was watching us. Every move. Patiently waiting. One night, we blinked, and he was gone.") There are some important differences between the two, however. Whereas Loomis was largely depicted as being a loner (at the personal request of Donald Pleasence, no less), Rogers is shown to be a family man with a wife and daughter. That makes him far more vulnerable than Loomis ever was. Further like his predecessor, Rogers is obsessed with keeping his star patient locked away. This has apparently caused problems at home as his duties as a husband and father have taken a back seat to his obsession. The true extent of Rogers' absence is revealed when daughter Sofia shares that her Princeton admission essay was about growing up second to a notorious mass murderer. *Ouch.*

In the first two *Halloween* films, Brackett repeatedly blames Loomis for his patient's escape from Smith's Grove. ("You let him out. His own goddamn doctor.") This is categorically untrue, however, as Michael had already escaped by the time Loomis and Marion Chambers arrived for his transfer. Per *Halloween Returns*, there *is* someone to blame for Michael's breakout – Dr. Rogers himself. Not only was Rogers the last person to see the incarcerated slasher at Smith's Grove, it was through his open office window that Michael escaped. This much-publicized fact has made Rogers' persona non grata in Haddonfield. It's also forced his wife and daughter to live with the public shame of his grave error. Knowing he can never fully atone for his mistake, Rogers spends a decade ensuring that his patient receives the death penalty.

> **Dr. Rogers:** *I don't believe in Capital punishment. Never have. People are reactive. Emotional. Easily affected by circumstance or environment. So, I've never believed that no one is unreachable... beyond rehabilitation, incapable of change. (beat) Except you. Ten years behind these bars... I've seen nothing. No remorse. No regret. No pain. Nothing. I wonder if there is anything left inside you... or if there was ever a soul at all. Michael, what you did... was... not human. You destroyed lives. Families. You don't belong here... amongst the living. (finding words) So, that's why I testified. That's why I put you here. And your death will bring closure...and a hopefully, just a bit of peace. Goodbye, Michael.*

With Rogers filling the Loomis vacancy, it's Deputy Hunt who steps into Brackett's shoes. Hunt is understandably devastated following his wife's murder in the opening and never fully recovers. Nor does he forgive Rogers for allowing Michael to escape in the first place. The time jump finds Hunt promoted to sheriff and now living in nearby Warren County. (It's briefly mentioned that Brackett is still sheriff in Livingston County where Haddonfield is located, though he does not appear in this story.) Now an alcoholic, Hunt has grown emotionally distant from everyone, even his children. His own deputies are forced to restrain him upon seeing Rogers again on the day of Michael's execution. ("You got real nerve showing your face in this town today! I warned you!")

Of course, the execution goes awry and Michael escapes. This forces Hunt and Rogers to work together once again in what is an incredibly tense partnership. Having been witness to the Shape's first massacre, they know what's at stake if they don't recapture the slasher. Unfortunately, history soon tragically repeats itself as the Shape murders Rogers' wife while he's on the phone with her. While Hunt remains bitter about his own wife's murder, this is nothing he would ever wish on anyone, not even the man he blames for her death. The script finds Hunt frozen in silence as he watches Rogers' wife die in his arms, which all-too-vividly recalls his own trauma a decade earlier. This would've easily ranked among the most somber moments in the franchise.

## THE YOUNGER GENERATION

One major theme running throughout *Halloween Returns* involves children paying for the sins of their fathers. The story's new final girl is Sofia Rogers, teenaged daughter to the psychiatrist whose infamous blunder allowed Michael to escape Smith's Grove in the first place. Sofia has lived for years with the stigma of being her father's daughter. Worse than that, she's grown deeply resentful of him for always being Michael Myers' psychiatrist first and a father second. In fact, this painful topic is the subject of her admission essay to college – what it's like taking a lifelong backseat to the nation's most notorious serial killer. Given how much she's had to endure over the years, Sofia feels entitled to have a seat at the Shape's execution, a request her father denies. Unwilling to accept his decision, she steals his security badge and attends anyway.

As unlikely as it would seem, Sofia's boyfriend is Noah Hunt, teenaged son of the deputy-turned-sheriff. At only eight years old, Noah witnessed the Shape murder his mother in their home on Halloween night. The emotional devastation of this loss would be conveyed through an image seen during the opening credit montage of young Noah holding his mother's photo at a candlelight vigil. (So rarely do mainstream horror films touch on the brutal pain of losing a loved one.) Ten years later, Noah emotionally manipulates Sofia into sneaking him into the Shape's execution, believing this will finally bring him closure. Fully embarking on her boyfriend's guilt trip, she agrees to sneak him inside. Of course, seeing his mother's killer writhe in excruciating pain does nothing to heal his wounds. Noah suffers a panic attack and is forced to leave the room.

**Noah:** *My mom is dead, is that right? A dozen people were murdered in Haddonfield because your dad didn't do his job, is that right? I'm asking you for a simple favor... and you don't think you owe me that? […] He killed my mom. Right in front of me. I see it every time I close my eyes. Over and over. That knife... that mask... all the blood... […] Please help me, Sofia. I don't want to see my mom die anymore.*

Sneaking into the execution comes with its own unintended consequence for the rebellious teens. As the Shape looks out into the viewing audience of the chamber, he spots Sofia and does exactly what he always does – he fixates on her. Why Sofia? What special quality does she possess? Does he somehow know she is Rogers' daughter? Does she remind him of someone? We don't know. But by attending the execution, Sofia places a bullseye on her own head.

Sofia and Noah are both backed by several friends, all of whom accompany them to the farmhouse in the final act. Sofia brings along Brie and Ashley while Noah brings pals Bear and Fog. This stereotypical lot exist solely to serve as slasher fodder near story's end.

## WINKS & NODS

In yet another similarity to *Halloween 2018*, the *Returns* script features numerous references to previous films in the franchise. These make for rich fan service and firmly establish Dunstan and Melton as true-blue series aficionados. Surprisingly, the majority of these nods are toward *Halloween III: Season of the Witch*. For starters, the screenwriters resurrect Harry Grimbridge, who died in that sequel's opening moments when visited by a robot assassin. In this story, Grimbridge runs Haddonfield's premiere mask shop – *Silver Shamrock Novelties!* (How fitting since he also owned a mask shop in *Halloween III*.) Located in the town square, Silver Shamrock's storefront window prominently displays a trio of familiar masks – a skull, a pumpkin, and a witch. Grimbridge also has a display offering replicas of the Shape's white mask, which Deputy Hunt finds distasteful. ("Don't get on me. Take it up with Cochran and his golden rule. '*Sell what the kids want*.' And today, that's what they want. (with a shrug) Happy Halloween.") While Cochran never appears in *Returns*, it is fun to have such a direct reference to him as though the worlds of *Halloween* and *Halloween III* had somehow merged!

Sadly, just as in the 1982 sequel, this Grimbridge does not live to see November 1st as he's decapitated by the Shape early on Halloween night. There is one final nod to *Halloween III* just before his death. While closing up shop, he overhears an annoying commercial on TV. Sure enough, it's the old Silver Shamrock jingle wishing viewers a "Happy, Happy Halloween." Grimbridge grumbles and switches to the news, which is reporting on the previous night's sanitarium fire.

*Returns* later tips its hat to the first *Halloween* with the location of its finale. Think back to the 1978 original when Dr. Loomis is trying to find Judith Myers' grave in Haddonfield Cemetery. The caretaker rambles on about the last tragic occurrence in Haddonfield, which involved Charley Bowles doing something horrible to his family. ("[He] went out into the garage and got a hacksaw, then came back into the house, kissed his wife and two children goodbye, and then proceeded to...") Melton and Dunstan set their story's climactic end inside the abandoned Bowles farmhouse, which is located next to Farmer John's Haunted Pumpkin Patch. (This set piece would seem to recall *Halloween 5*'s Tower Farm.) Noah and Sofia's friends decide this would be a great spot for Halloween night shenanigans. Unfortunately for them, the Shape reaches the same conclusion. At one point, Noah's little brother tries telling the Bowles legend, but he's cut off right where the caretaker was in *Halloween*. (Will we *ever* learn what old Charley did with that hacksaw?)

The finale also references *Halloween II* in creepy fashion. At one point, the Shape attacks Sofia and Brie as they try to escape the farmhouse in Noah's truck. Turning the keys, the radio blares to life playing "Mr. Sandman" by The Chordettes. The slasher breaks through the driver's window and grabs the keys, killing the engine. The lights and radio remain on, but the sound is warbled. A distorted, creepy-sounding version of *Halloween II*'s opening tune plays as Sofia and Brie fight for their lives.

In addition to the *Halloween* references, the screenwriters also pack in nods to the films of John Carpenter. The most obvious of these involve the character Fog, who seems to be named after Carpenter's 1980 chiller *The Fog*. In another tribute, Halloween night finds Noah's little brother tuned into a broadcast of Carpenter's remake of *The Thing*. (Recall that in Carpenter's *Halloween*, Tommy and Lindsey were watching the original *The Thing From Another World* from 1951.) The screenwriters specifically mention showing the infamous chest fibrillation scene in which Doc Copper's arms are bitten off by the monster.

## YOU CAN'T KILL THE BOOGEYMAN

*Halloween Returns* presents a depiction of the Shape largely in step with the original 1978 film. He's not overtly superhuman in his strength or ability to withstand damage. He is, however, a trickster and also intent on spreading fear rather than just killing. The screenplay's prologue lets us bear witness to something we've never before seen – the peaceful apprehension of Michael Myers by police. But why does the Shape go down without a fight? Was he tricked by Rogers' assertion that he's "killed everyone?" Or is he too injured to go on? Or is this an act self-preservation knowing he won't survive the hailstorm of bullets about to strike him? Or is he somehow disarmed by being unmasked? These are all interesting possibilities to consider. Ultimately, Melton and Dunstan leave it for the audience to decide.

The opening title sequence plays overtop footage and images from Michael's trial and sentencing. It's here we ascertain that he is suspected of murdering twelve people upon escape from Smith's Grove. But wait, we only saw him kill four people in *Halloween* – the Phelps Garage mechanic, Bob, Annie, and Lynda. He murders Mrs. Hunt in *Returns'* opening moments, but that's still only five people. *Who are the other six?* Did Michael murder any staff or fellow patients before leaving the sanitarium? Are there other victims he killed prior to Laurie's friends? Does this count include Lester the dog? Or the one he ate at home? Six victims – that's quite a discrepancy.

Had this script been made, we would likely still be talking about its hellacious execution sequence, which ends with the Shape still very much alive and roaming free. We've seen this tried several times before. In *Asylum 2005*, the Shape swapped duds with a guard whom authorities mistakenly execute via electric chair. In *Asylum 2013*, it was Michael himself in the chair, though the voltage supernaturally empowered him to become a sort-of "Super Shape." In *Halloween Returns*, prison officials have switched over to using lethal injection for executions. The drugs required for this have become increasingly difficult to procure, leading staff to substitute alternatives. Dr. Rogers is seriously concerned over the potential side effects of this unproven cocktail, though he's ignored by his superiors.

Scheduled for the night before Halloween, the Shape's execution is attended by surviving victims and the families of those who didn't survive. This includes Karen from the opening, who now requires a cane to walk due to injuries sustained. Somewhat appropriately, a storm rages outside the facility as visitors arrive. Unfortunately, Rogers' concerns over the drug mixture will soon prove well-founded. Michael violently jerks against his restraints as the drugs take hold,

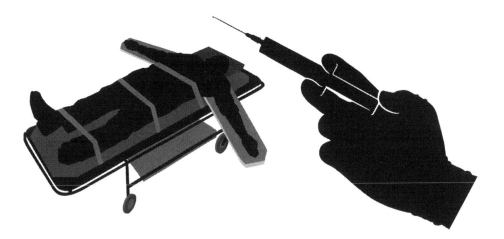

gasping for air as his heart rate soars. Thunder cracks wildly outside, the storm growing stronger as the condemned slasher writhes. Instead of killing the Shape, the drugs majorly spike his adrenaline. He breaks free concurrent with the storm knocking out the power. Plunged into darkness with the freed slasher, the audience panics. The Shape murders Karen along with the attending staff before vanishing. Rogers and Hunt attempt to chase after but are unsuccessful. An explosion soon rocks the facility, possibly caused by the storm. This creates even more pandemonium to aid in the killer's escape. It's an altogether gloriously choreographed sequence of abject hell.

While the Shape goes unmasked for much of this story, the screenwriters note that we are *never* to see his naked face. He will later acquire a new white mask at Silver Shamrock Novelties in Haddonfield. (Yes, that technically means he's wearing a Silver Shamrock mask!) After murdering Grimbridge, the slasher notices several boys egging the closed storefront. One boy peers into the darkened window and comes face to face with the Shape. Startled, he backs away just as Michael tosses the storeowner's severed head out into the street. The terrified youth scream and scatter.

If there's one part of the Shape's depiction here that might seem uncharacteristic, it's the threat he scrawls in blood on the farmhouse wall during the story's final moments. ("This town will never be safe again.") While the Shape has finger-painted things in blood before, they're usually only words. ("Sister" in *Halloween*'s television cut and "Samhain" in *Halloween II*.) This threat would mark the character's most fully composed communication since first going silent in 1963. Even stranger is that the Bowles farmhouse isn't in Haddonfield, but Russellville. So... we're to assume the Shape has some new stomping grounds then? Or is he more of a roamer? Does this mean he's done with Haddonfield? These are things at least worth considering.

## THE FINALE

The final act unfolds entirely at the Bowles farmhouse, which functions as Russellville's de facto Myers house. (Speaking of which, we sadly never visit the house on Lampkin Lane in this story.) It's here at the farmhouse that the partying teens incur the Shape's wrath across several memorable kill sequences. The first of these unfolds in a corn maze adjacent to the farmhouse. Ashley leads Fog on a drunken striptease-turned-chase throughout the maze, both unaware that the Shape is hiding just around the corner. The slasher stabs his knife up through Fog's chin, lifting him off the ground until they're eye-to-eye. Sofia and Brie hear Ashley's screams from inside the farmhouse a moment later but dismiss them as the couple likely having a wild sex romp.

Brie is attacked soon after while taking selfies in the darkened house, blissfully unaware of the danger approaching from behind. It's only upon reviewing the photos a moment later that she notices the Shape's white mask lurking in the darkness. By this point, it's far too late. The Shape stabs a pitchfork into Brie's back, which protrudes through her torso and even stabs the phone in her hand. She will ultimately survive these wounds and survive to the end.

Hunt and Rogers arrive at the farmhouse mid-massacre. Knowing their children's lives are at stake, they jointly agree to shoot first and ask questions later. (They're smartly not looking to arrest the slasher this time.) Prior to their arrival, Hunt gives Rogers a revolver with a nine-round cylinder and instructs him to pull the trigger until he's either out of bullets or their enemy is dead. (Nine shots! Because as Dr. Loomis will attest, six just aren't enough.)

Sofia discovers the bodies of her friends outside and looks back to the farmhouse. She sees Bear and Noah upstairs, dangerously unaware that the Shape is waiting downstairs. She frantically calls Bear's phone and attempts to safely guide them through the old house without encountering the stalking slasher. (There's just no way this scene isn't an homage to Sara and Deckard in *Halloween: Resurrection*.) They soon encounter the Shape, who savagely slashes Bear's eyes out before *burying his boot* into the boy's chest. Noah is slashed as well but saved when Deputy Hunt rushes into the house. He angrily confronts the monster who murdered his wife, but sadly loses the fight. ("I'll be waiting for you in hell. *I'll be waiting.*") Their struggle knocks over a candle, which slowly engulfs the house in flames. With Hunt dead, the Shape turns his attention back to Sofia and Noah. Rogers now rushes in and tries to distract the slasher with taunts.

> **Dr. Rogers:** "*I'm the one you want. (breaking) You killed my wife. You want to kill my daughter. But I'm the one who locked you in that cage all those years. I'm the one who filled you with drugs. I'm the one who condemned you to death. (beat) Me. It was my decision. I'm the one you want. I'm the one who tried to kill you! Me! I'm the one you want! Kill me, Michael! FINISH WHAT YOU STARTED! COME ON, MICHAEL! KILL ME! (growling) KILL ME! KILL ME!!! KILL ME!!!*"

Rogers' plan works and the Shape turns to approach him, allowing Sofia and Noah to escape to the authorities arriving outside. Pleased that his plan worked, Hunt drops the act. ("They've got you, Michael. They've got you surrounded. You're caught.") Angered at this turn of events, the script has the Shape charging his former doctor – "almost running at this point." The scene ends with the Shape using Rogers as a diversion to escape. Having slashed his tongue, given him his mask, and stabbed a glass shard through his hand – Michael has created a red herring. In the chaos, police fail to realize the Shape isn't wearing his trademark jumpsuit and open fire. Several bullets strike Rogers, but he somehow survives.

Police approach the burning farmhouse and find the slasher's message: "This town will never be safe again." As they look on in horror, the blood itself begins to sizzle. Reunited with his daughter, a distraught Rogers mumbles, "He doesn't just want to kill me and you... he wants to kill everyone." As Michael disappears into the woods outside the farmhouse, the script reads: "The Shape is back. FADE TO BLACK. THE END"

By this point in the series, stealthily swapping places with other people has become something like a hobby for the Shape. He did it with Dr. Wynn in *Halloween 6* and again with a paramedic in *Halloween H20*. (Recall that he tried this twice in the unproduced *Asylum 2005* script.) His blood-scrawled threat on the farmhouse wall promises that this is, in fact, not the end but a new beginning. The story's final scene, a post-credits tag in Rogers' hospital room, reintroduces Dr. Loomis to the story with one of his most iconic lines. Describing him as being in his forties and looking like "Gary Oldman with the eyes of a chopping block," this was clearly going to be a new take on the old character.

## WHY IT WASN'T MADE

*Halloween Returns* was originally set to begin filming in Louisiana one month after being announced in June 2015, though cameras never rolled on the project. While the sequel did enter into pre-production, its first day of filming was pushed back several times. The filmmakers went so far as to cast several lead roles and audition multiple performers for the new Shape. Dunstan spoke publicly of wanting to cast Gillian Jacobs of *Community* fame in a lead role. Cinematographer Brandon Trost, returning from Rob Zombie's *Halloween II*, was invited to join the production and accepted. Dunstan spoke publicly of the project still happening as late as September 2015. Unfortunately, behind the scenes drama at the studio level would soon derail the sequel altogether.

In late October, Malek Akkad officially confirmed that *Halloween Returns* had been scrapped. Speaking to the *Daily Dead*: "Unfortunately, things happen in Hollywood where you have issues with studios and different variables. We've had to take a step back and now we're trying to refigure this beast that is the new *Halloween*. So, there is a bit of a delay with this sequel now." He went on to further say, "This new *Halloween* isn't going to be quite what has been announced and what people are expecting, so we're making some changes there as well." It appears that Dunstan and Melton's *Halloween Returns* had once again been the source of creative strife between Trancas and Dimension, thus leading its dissolution. The producer cited issues with Dimension regarding the general direction of the film, thus leading to its postponement and later dissolution. Far more shocking news was just around the corner.

On December 28, 2015, *Bloody-Disgusting* reported that Dimension Films had lost the rights to *Halloween*, thus ending its twenty-year reign over the franchise. This bit of unconfirmed news surprised even fans, with the site's Brad Miska calling the scoop "an exclusive so shocking that I can't even believe I'm reporting on it." As difficult as it was to imagine a *Halloween* that didn't begin with the familiar Dimension logo, this news turned out to be *very* true. The reason for the Weinsteins' loss can presumably be attributed to the long-gestating process of developing another sequel – a lapse of *six years*, no less. (It would be yet another almost three years before *Halloween 2018* would grace theater screens – the longest delay between sequels as of yet.)

With this, the franchise rights reverted back to Miramax, which had once housed the series when that company was under the Weinsteins' oversight. But this was no longer the same Miramax. This Miramax had remained at Disney while Bob and Harvey took the Dimension label to their newly formed Weinstein Company. As previously mentioned, Disney/Miramax had sub-leased the *Halloween* rights to Weinstein/Dimension in a deal that had several conditions, one of which involved yearly payments to Miramax regardless of whether a new film was produced. Another condition was that Dimension continue producing sequels to prevent the franchise from stagnating. Having been five years since the last *Halloween* movie, Dimension had missed their contractual deadline and been granted several extensions on the license, all of which they continued to miss. This was fertile legal ground for Miramax to take back the series.

In the decade since the formation of The Weinstein Company, Miramax had changed hands several times. Disney first sold the studio to Filmyard Holdings in 2010 for over $660 million. At the deal's conclusion, Filmyard came into possession of Miramax's back library of more than seven-hundred films, which included the studio's already-produced *Halloween* efforts. Miramax would change hands again in 2015 when Filmyard sold their interest to beIN Media Group. If Malek Akkad was going to develop a new *Halloween* sequel, it was going to be alongside Miramax's new owners.

Before the fall of Harvey Weinstein in 2017, neither he nor brother Bob ever commented on what the loss of *Halloween* meant to their now defunct company. A cursory look at their filmography in the 2010s will show that the Dimension label had gradually fallen to the wayside, far overshadowed by the output of Platinum Dunes and Blumhouse. For Dimension, long-stalled reboots like *Scream 4* and *Scary Movie 5* did only respectable if not slightly disappointing business. Tentpoles like *Piranha 3DD* and *Sin City: A Dame to Kill For* were outright disasters. (Can you believe the former was the *only* film Dimension released in 2012?) Compare the profitability of the two previous *Halloween*s to their Dimension brethren, and the Weinsteins' fumbling to produce a follow-up seems all the more perplexing. It was their only franchise left that could've reliably yielded decent profits. Quite frankly, all aborted concepts for the eleventh *Halloween* would've made for worthwhile chapters in the saga and yet these opportunities were missed. The consequences for such, on the Weinstein side of things, would then seem fairly just.

In October 2018, Akkad voiced his frustration to *Daily Dead*. "There have been several stops and starts, and this was at a previous distribution company, and for whatever reason, it would just come down to some sort of silliness." Expanding on this, the producer touched upon another issue that may have kept *Halloween Returns* from coming to fruition. "I can tell you [Dimension] wanted the last one to be shot in Serbia, for example, and I refused to go to Serbia. This is the most Americana horror franchise set in the Midwest and I don't know if they know what Halloween is in Serbia. So, little things like that just kept impeding our progress, and next thing you know, seven years have gone by." Note that Serbia was just one of several Eastern European countries in which it was cost efficient to shoot films; Romania being another frequently used by Dimension.

While disappointed, news of the studio's loss of *Halloween* didn't halt the careers of Dunstan and Melton. They would go on to 2016's *The Neighbor* and 2019's *Scary Stories to Tell in the Dark*. Currently, they're attached to helm the sixth installment in the *Final Destination* franchise, which, Death-willing, will come to fruition soon.

"We had been working with a bunch of writers where we got close, but then we brought in Marcus and Patrick and worked closely with them. We found that we all were very much on the same level of what we wanted to do, in spite of the fact that the studio wasn't necessarily in agreement."

- Malek Akkad, Daily Dead

# Epilogue:
# Let It Burn

Prior to re-acquiring the *Halloween* franchise, Miramax had seriously slowed in its filmmaking output – to the point where it was largely considered a library company, in fact. For the first time in its history, the studio would not release any films in 2012, a regrettable feat it repeated the following year. Yet in 2014, Miramax bosses publicly affirmed the company's desire to resume production efforts. To this end, producer Zanne Devine was hired in January of that year as executive vice president. Under her leadership, the studio would return to the box office with just one immediate film offering – Robert Rodriguez's *Sin City: A Dame to Kill For*. Unfortunately, this comeback was anything but triumphant as this sequel failed to even recoup its production budget. Undeterred by this failure, Devine immediately set her sights on exploiting the company's vast library of film properties, which could be tapped for sequels, theatre productions and television series. Among her first such projects was overseeing the television adaptation of *From Dusk Till Dawn*, which ran for three seasons on the El Rey network.

In May 2015, Devine hired executive David Thwaites as vice president of film. Upon his arrival at Miramax, Thwaites began scouring its library for titles to exploit. In doing so, he noticed that the studio was then negotiating with Dimension to grant yet another extension of the *Halloween* license – despite Dimension not having done anything with the property in several years. Feeling that *Halloween* would fare better at Miramax, Thwaites convinced Devine to take back the franchise. In his *Taking Shape* interview, he commented that his bosses were initially skeptical of this move and questioned the value of *Halloween* as an ongoing franchise. Believing in the property's potential, Thwaites insisted and ultimately prevailed in December 2015, as Dimension finally lost the rights. Thwaites' initial hope was to oversee a direct sequel to the 1978 original – one that would ignore the numerous and sometimes conflicting developments of the existing sequels. In reviving the franchise, his first move was to connect with Malek Akkad.

"Malek had been bounced around a lot by Dimension over the years," Thwaites said in his interview. "He had gone through a lot of starts and stops with them over different scripts. They were always telling him, '*We're gonna make a new movie soon. We're gonna rush it into production.*'

There was a lot of effort to try and retain those rights at Dimension, often with scripts that just weren't ready. I know there were numerous writers who were really excited about being a part of it and put in a lot of hard work. We never engaged with any of them on our *Halloween*. Those scripts had originated at Dimension and we needed a completely clean copyright on our film."

Concurrent to this, Malek Akkad – now free from the constraints of working with the Weinsteins – had already been exploring new iterations of the franchise with different writers. Among these were Todd Farmer and Patrick Lussier, who had previously written *Halloween 3D* and *Halloween 3.0*. As Farmer tells us in his interview, "[Malek] had wanted to do a soft reboot and start from scratch. *'I want this to be the sort of thing where if you watched it, it could be cut right out of the newspapers as a real serial killer – that no part of this feels like a slasher movie.'* [Patrick and I] came up with a pitch that was Michael Myers right out of high school, and we loved it."

After assuring Akkad that Miramax did not intend to bullshit him with years of fruitless development, David Thwaites then reached out to Jason Blum of Blumhouse Productions. The exec sought to gauge Blum's interest in co-producing the new *Halloween* alongside Trancas and Miramax. (Oddly enough, Blum first learned the movie business during a several year stint at Miramax under the abusive mentorship of Harvey Weinstein. As the CEO of his own namesake company, such days were long behind him.) Now a horror heavyweight, Blum had in recent years established several popular franchises through Blumhouse, most notably *Paranormal Activity, Insidious, Sinister,* and *The Purge*. Blum responded enthusiastically to the prospect, but on one occasion – they had to secure the involvement of original *Halloween* writer/director John Carpenter. This would be a Herculean task, but one he agreed to personally take on.

By all accounts, Carpenter was perceived to be a tough egg to crack where the *Halloween* franchise was concerned. He'd spent a lifetime sharply criticizing its sequels, many of which he claimed to have never even seen. He'd also had several attempts at re-joining the franchise rebuffed by producers, studio execs, and even himself, notably on *Halloween 4, Halloween 6,* and *Halloween H20*. Even so, Carpenter agreed to hear Blum's proposal. According to the studio exec, he made a fifteen-minute pitch for the project, which seemed to have little effect on the master of horror. In recalling his pitch to the *Daily Dead* website, Blum became quite blunt in a last-ditch effort. "I said, *'John, they're going to make this movie with or without us. I'm not doing it without you, so if you don't do it, I'm not doing it. But they're still going to do it. We may as well join the party instead of letting them do it alone.'*" Amazingly, this plea won over Carpenter.

Marking his first involvement with the series in nearly thirty years, John Carpenter officially joined the new *Halloween* as producer and creative consultant. With Carpenter onboard, Jason Blum likewise joined as well. On May 23, 2016, a small group of journalists were invited to a screening room at Blumhouse HQ for an unspecified announcement. Blum opened the press conference by first introducing Miramax's Zanne Devine and David Thwaites. He then brought out Trancas' Malek Akkad, which tipped off many in the audience as to the nature of the announcement. The most unexpected guest, however, was Carpenter himself. This group of five then officially announced their plans to resurrect the *Halloween* franchise together. Details were few, though the enthusiasm was palpable. The group also shared that Universal Pictures would be distributing the project, marking their first involvement with the series since *Halloween III: Season of the Witch*.

Speaking of the project, Carpenter told reporters, "We're probably going to go back to the original traditions that we started with early on. It's kind of gone astray a little bit. I thought maybe the remakes went off somewhere that I didn't want 'em to go. Michael Myers is not a character. He is a force of nature. He is not a person. He is part supernatural, part human. He's like the wind. He's an evil wind. When you start straying away from that and you get into explaining, you're lost. So hopefully we can guide it back in that direction."

While the newest *Halloween* had been officially announced, it was still a long way from reaching theater screens. It lacked many a crucial thing, namely writers, a director, and a release date. Rampant speculation on who might write and helm the sequel began within hours of its announcement with two filmmakers emerging as frontrunners, both admitted fans of the series. It was *Bloody-Disgusting* who first broke word that Mike Flanagan was among the leading candidates to write and/or direct. Having then helmed *Hush* and *Ouija: Origin of Evil*, both for Blumhouse, Flanagan made good sense as a contender. Unfortunately, by his own admission, he was unable to come up with a strong enough premise to justify making a new movie. After having been passed over for *Halloween*, Flanagan went on to write and direct several critically acclaimed projects including *Gerald's Game*, *The Haunting of Hill House*, and *Doctor Sleep*. He would later discuss his brief time on the project with the same site that broke news of his involvement.

"I tried to come up with a take for a minute when Blumhouse got *Halloween*," Flanagan told *Bloody-Disgusting*. "The answer to that is, I would've done *Hush*. I'm glad that I didn't and so glad it did not come to me because the only note that I had scribbled over three days of brainstorming was '*Dr. Loomis as a woman?*' That's as far as I got on *Halloween*. They made the right call in not trusting the franchise to me. [...] In a lot of ways, *Hush* was my riff on the beautiful, simplicity, silence, tension, suspense that *Halloween* is. All of my love for Carpenter's film is poured into that. If *Hush* didn't exist, and I was doing *Halloween*, it would look a lot like *Hush*."

Another leading candidate was Adam Wingard, fresh off the 2016 *Blair Witch* reboot. Prior to that, he'd directed such acclaimed chillers as *You're Next* and the Netflix original *Death Note*. His 2014 effort *The Guest* was a self-proclaimed love letter to *Halloween* and featured a Carpenter-esque score along with overt references to *Halloween III* and *Halloween 4*. Fans took notice when Wingard began tweeting images from the *Halloween* films on the same day as Blumhouse's announcement, one of which Jason Blum "liked." Wingard would later tell *The Movie Crypt* podcast, "I actually got an email, in confidence, where John Carpenter basically gave them the thumbs up for me. I walked away from it like, I just got everything I wanted out of this job, you know. Like I just want approval from dad. I walked away like, '*This is about as good as it gets.*'"

Miramax, Blumhouse, and Trancas would spend the rest of 2016 fielding pitches from prospective filmmakers. Finding a concept worthy of meriting Carpenter's return proved a difficult task, however. "We haven't landed on an approach," Jason Blum told *Cinema Blend* in October. "We thought we had a filmmaker and an approach, and we don't. We're talking to a handful of people about it – all of them have different ideas. I don't believe in coming up with an idea and telling a filmmaker what to do. So, we have three to five different people we're talking with, and all of them have a different idea about what it should be."

On February 9, 2017, Blumhouse finally announced that the new *Halloween* would be scripted by the writing team of Jeff Fradley, Danny McBride, and David Gordon Green with the latter also directing. In a sense, these three were unconventional choices given their largely comedic backgrounds. These three weren't hired on the basis of those credits, however, but on the degree to which they impressed Carpenter, Blum, and Akkad with their approach to the material. As Green saw it, there were two distinct directions they could take the project in. The first would've gone the nostalgia route and featured the return of Laurie Strode, which was obviously dependent upon the unlikely return of Jamie Lee Curtis. The second approach would've re-envisioned the Shape's formative years at Smith's Grove, which the Rob Zombie remake had sort-of already done. (These approaches were likened to *Star Wars: The Force Awakens* and *Batman Begins*, respectively.)

Green initially struggled to score a meeting with Curtis to discuss the project. Upon doing so, the actress was skeptical about returning to the series she had already said goodbye to. Green e-mailed her the screenplay later that day. The following morning, she phoned the director to pledge her participation. An announcement was made on September 15, 2017, heralding the return of *Halloween*'s original "scream queen." The project's stars had aligned – truly.

The momentous return of Carpenter and Curtis helped propel Blumhouse's *Halloween* out of development and into production, thus ending a long string of "lost sequels." The project would film across January and February of 2018 with reshoots occurring in June. Universal would release the sequel in mid-October to massive success. The Blumhouse production marked the second biggest October opening of all time and also the second biggest horror opener. It would earn an astounding worldwide box office haul of $255 million, more than the previous nine follow-ups combined. Critically, *Halloween 2018* holds a 79% "Fresh" rating on *Rotten Tomatoes*, making it the second highest-rated series entry beyond the original.

For the first time in series history, *Halloween* has a solid narrative direction. For the first time in series history, the filmmakers are *returning* with the goal of continuing the franchise, not ending it. And for the first time in series history, its surviving creator and star are returning not because they feel pressured to (à la *Halloween II*), but because they want to. You could easily argue that there's never been a better time to be a *Halloween* fan. We have not one but *two* sequels in the pipeline – *Halloween Kills* and *Halloween Ends*, which are set to release in back-to-back years. These sequels won't be haphazardly rushed to capitalize on the success of the 2018 film. Instead, they will be a thoughtful and well-planned conclusion to this new Laurie Strode tetralogy.

As weird as it still seems for *Halloween* to not be at Dimension Films, it's probably for the best. The majority of lost sequels in this book – all but four – occurred during the studio's twenty-odd year tenure with the series. And if we're being honest, Dimension's five *Halloween* efforts were a mixed bag both critically and financially. From Malek Akkad and Jason Blum to David Gordon Green and John Carpenter, the series is in better hands now. And so that's where we'll leave you... waiting patiently for the Shape to escape the burning basement of Laurie Strode's fortified home. Meanwhile, the franchise fires continue to burn bright. In the immortal words of *Halloween*'s iconic heroine, "Let it burn!"

LAURIE STRODE & THE SHAPE
WILL RETURN IN

# HALLOWEEN KILLS
## &
# HALLOWEEN ENDS

# APPENDIX:
# Film Summary Guide

Was it Rosenberg's *Halloween 666* where Dr. Loomis became a patient at Smith's Grove Sanitarium? Or was that the Belateche/Guterman script? Hmmm...

Let's not even pretend that keeping the minute details of twenty-four lost sequels straight is an easy task. *It's not* - and we should know. To aid in your digestion of this lengthy tome, here's an easy summary guide to the twenty-four unmade projects covered. If you happen to see a lost sequel that catches your interest, feel free to skip ahead to it. While our book is ordered chronologically, it was written in such a way that you can move around and still understand what's going on.

Happy Reading.

## HALLOWEEN 4 - THE ETCHISON DRAFT (page 38)

Ten years later, the Shape returns to Haddonfield amid a ban on Halloween. Former victims Tommy Doyle and Lindsey Wallace – now teenagers – take on the reborn slasher, whose newfound powers leave no trace of his former humanity.

## HALLOWEEN 4 - THE KENNEY/MEDINA DRAFT (page 62)

Despite being submerged in Lake Michigan, the slasher is back to terrorize Laurie Strode, now a successful photographer in Chicago. Suffering from nightmares and amnesia, Laurie is treated by Dr. Loomis. Meanwhile, Killer Mike murders a rock star and assumes his fashion sense.

## HALLOWEEN 4 - THE BITTERMAN DRAFT (page 88)

Dr. Loomis renews his hunt for Killer Mike, who once more has escaped custody in search of Amanda Hatch, his recently orphaned niece. Dangerously naïve, Amanda hopes to form a relationship with her slasher uncle. Loomis and Sheriff Brackett re-team to keep the child safe.

## HALLOWEEN 5: THE KILLER INSIDE ME (page 106)

Picking up from Halloween 4, a frightened Jamie Lloyd discovers newfound powers while also battling her own bloodlust. She and Rachel continue to flee the Shape. A wrathful Dr. Loomis isn't far behind, firmly believing Michael's niece must be destroyed.

## HALLOWEEN 666: THE ORIGIN (page 144)

A reporter travels to Haddonfield for a story on Michael Myers – only to discover she and her subject share much closer ties than previously known. Meanwhile, outcast Tommy Doyle uses virtual reality to learn a mysterious netherworld portal exists under Judith Myers' grave.

**HALLOWEEN 666: THE ORIGIN OF MICHAEL MYERS** (page 178)

A new family moves into the Myers house, prompting the return of the Shape. Elsewhere, Tommy Doyle and Dr. Loomis theorize on how to vanquish the slasher, which involves a mysterious portal in Judith Myers' old closet that opens each Halloween.

**HALLOWEEN 7: TWO FACES OF EVIL** (page 212)

It appears the Shape is up to his old tricks again when a babysitter is murdered, only for police to realize the slasher is actually incarcerated. They then suspect a shady magician with a Myers obsession. The real Shape soon escapes, forcing detectives to hunt for two identical killers.

**HELLRAISER: HELLOWEEN** (page 238)

Michael Myers is revealed to have long been possessed by Sam Hain, an escaped demon from Hell. With Pinhead and the Cenobites intent on recapturing the demon, a furious battle unfolds on Earth and in Hell, trapping survivors from both franchises in the middle.

**HALLOWEEN IN HELL: MICHAEL VS PINHEAD** (page 238)

In pursuit of his niece Jamie, the Shape slaughters *Hellraiser* heroine Kirsty Cotton. This angers Pinhead and the Cenobites, who swear revenge against the slasher. Their battle unfolds first on Earth, then in Hell. Meanwhile, Jamie teams with a sketchy horror expert to defeat both evils.

**HALLOWEEN H25** (page 266)

One year after *Resurrection*, Freddie Harris is set to debut a documentary on the Shape, who has secretly been kept alive in a govt. research lab, which he escapes. Meanwhile, franchise survivors converge in Haddonfield for the doc's premiere, which the Shape crashes in bloody fashion.

## HALLOWEEN: RETRIBUTION (page 280)

A blizzard strands several teens at the shuttered Smith's Grove Sanitarium on Halloween night. Unbeknownst to them, the Shape now calls this home. When police refuse to help, John Tate and Leigh Brackett team up to rescue the teens and destroy their common enemy.

## HALLOWEEN: HADDONFIELD (page 304)

A cash-strapped Haddonfield now embraces Halloween with a tacky festival celebrating Michael Myers. Dr. Jason Loomis, son of the late Sam Loomis, arrives in town to warn against such a celebration, but it's too late. The Shape has already returned to express his extreme disapproval.

## HALLOWEEN: ASYLUM '04 (page 304)

Jason Loomis has since gone to work for Smith's Grove in hopes of preventing the next Michael Myers. A storm knocks out power, triggering a lockdown while also releasing the patients. Jason must now survive a dangerously-ill Shape-imitator who's targeted him as part of his delusion.

## HALLOWEEN: ASYLUM '05 (page 326)

Picking up from *Resurrection*, the Shape murders Freddie Harris, but is soon caught and arrested. Upon trial, he's found guilty and sentenced to death by electric chair. This execution goes horribly wrong, however, resulting in the slasher being released inside Smith's Grove State Penitentiary.

## HALLOWEEN: THE MISSING YEARS (page 356)

This prequel-sequel examines young Michael Myers' initial incarceration at Smith's Grove Sanitarium while also picking up from *Halloween II*'s ending. Badly burned, the Shape returns to a recently shuttered Smith's Grove where he doesn't take kindly to teenaged tresspassers.

## HALLOWEEN 3D - THE FARMER/LUSSIER DRAFT (page 392)

Michael Myers returns one year after the events of Rob Zombie's *Halloween II* to rescue his sister from a psychiatric hospital. Internally, Laurie struggles over whether to join or reject her brother. Meanwhile, survivors of last year's carnage plot revenge on Laurie and Michael for their crimes.

## HALLOWEEN 3D - THE HUTCHINSON DRAFT (page 432)

In the aftermath of Rob Zombie's *Halloween II*, a grieving Lee Brackett burns down the Myers house and moves to Langdon, Illinois. This brings Michael Myers out of hiding to exact revenge on the retired sheriff, who devises a plan to kill his enemy using a local teenager as bait.

## HALLOWEEN 3.0 (page 456)

This reboot re-imagines the first *Halloween*'s ending. Instead of escaping into the night, the Shape is taken down by a SWAT team led by Dr. Loomis. The slasher escapes federal custody a year later hoping to recruit Laurie Strode to join him in his muderous crusade. Loomis again chases after.

## PLATINUM DUNES' HALLOWEEN (page 474)

In this total re-imagining, Michael Myers is abducted as a child along with another boy. When he seemingly resurfaces years later as an adult slasher, it's up to his detective-brother to find and stop him with the help of FBI consultant Sam Loomis. But things are not what they seem...

## REBOOT TRILOGY: RISE OF THE BOOGEYMAN (page 502)

In this supernatural spin on *Halloween*, a deadly slasher without an identity escapes from a mental hospital to once again torment Haddonfield, Illinois. When Dr. Sam Loomis commits to tracking down the escaped killer, he discovers that an ancient and otherwordly evil is at work.

## REBOOT TRILOGY: THE WITCHING HOUR (page 502)

With his wife and son murdered, Loomis spirals into madness and seeks out therapy for himself. Meanwhile, the Shape continues to torment him as Halloween once again grows near. Loomis is eventually transformed into that which he's hunted – a killer.

## REBOOT TRILOGY: FIRES OF SAMHAIN (page 502)

In an effort to destroy Loomis' past, the Shape psychically commands an army of mentally-ill patients to murder the residents of Russellville. Elsewhere, Loomis crosses into the barrier between reality and the afterlife. Here, he finally learns the secret to defeating the evil of the Shape.

## HALLOWEEN: ASYLUM '13 (page 534)

The Shape is finally caught and arrested during his latest holiday slaughter. Sentenced to death, his execution by electric chair fails to kill him. Instead, the chair's powerful jolt empowers him with superhuman strength. Staff struggle to lock down the facility in the wake of the slasher's escape.

## HALLOWEEN RETURNS (page 556)

In this alternate *Halloween II*, the Shape is arrested by police after attacking Laurie Strode in 1978 and sentenced to death. The execution goes awry and the slasher escapes. He then targets the teenaged children of the doctor and deputy responsible for his apprehension years earlier.

# A Note on Sources

While most of the research for *Taking Shape II* encompassed treatments, screenplays, and filmmaker interviews, the authors also turned to outside sources for help in sorting out the franchise timeline. These works are cited throughout the text itself, though a handful merit special mention here. So much of our research owed to the online archives of terrific websites like *Bloody-Disgusting, Fangoria, Dread Central, Shock Till You Drop, Creature-Corner, The Daily Dead*, and, of course, the official *HalloweenMovies.com*.

# Author Bios

Dustin McNeill                    Travis Mullins

**Dustin McNeill** is the author of six books released through Harker Press. A lifelong genre fan, he gets his kicks obsessing over old horror movies. Dustin published his first foray into film journalism in 2014 with *Phantasm Exhumed*, which *Rue Morgue* called "a perfect prelude to the Tall Man's return." His subsequent works include *Slash of the Titans: The Road to Freddy vs Jason*, *Further Exhumed: The Strange Case of Phantasm Ravager*, and *Adventures in Amity: Tales From the Jaws Ride*. He has also written for *HorrorHound Magazine* and *DVD Active*. Dustin lives in Greensboro, North Carolina with his wife and two children. Sadly, he still brags about having once made a meme that both Jamie Lee Curtis and Rob Zombie re-tweeted.

**Travis Mullins** is an occasional journalist, having written for *Dread Central* since 2017. In this role, he has interviewed a plethora of talent, ranging from Jerry O'Connell to Fairuza Balk, as well as scoring the first-ever interviews from *Halloween* alumni Sandy Johnson and Wendy Wessberg. In 2018, he assisted with Scream Factory's Collector's Edition release of *Texas Chainsaw Massacre: The Next Generation*. As a youngster, Travis wrote his own version of *Halloween 9*, one that might've featured Gwen Stefani's "The Sweet Escape" as the closing credits song. (He will never be so close to this franchise again.) The *Taking Shape* duology marks his first print publications. He currently lives in the Orlando, Florida area.

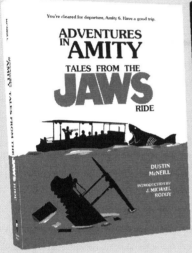 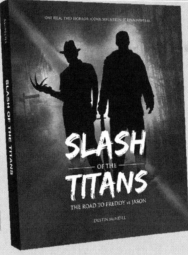 

"This house is sacred to him.
He has all of his memories here, his rage..."
- Dr. Loomis, Halloween 6

It's always Halloween at the **Myers House NC**, a stunning replica of the iconic
home at 45 Lampkin Lane located in Hillsborough, North Carolina.  Built
by fan Kenny Caperton in 2008, the **Myers House NC** has been featured in
various shows and movies to become a filming location in its own right.

To learn more, visit **MyersHouseNC.com.**
(Photo courtesy Kenny Caperton)

# CARVED
## IN KIN

Pumpkin artisans **Robert Kriess** and **Natalie Tomaszewski** are carving up custom jack-o-lanterns for every fandom. Being made of foam means they last forever!

To see more and order your own, visit

# http://Facebook.com/CarvedInKin

# Acknowledgements

Highest Thanks to **Natalie Tomaszewski** for editing this even bigger beast!

Very Special Thanks to **George Todoroff** for carving up another awesome cover!

Special Thanks to **Michael Ryan Assip** for sharing his Dennis Etchison interview!

Thanks to **PL Boucher** for the Prop Art assist!

Dustin would again like to thank coffee, elixir of the gods. He would also like to thank his wife, Lindsay, for her support and patience while this second book took shape.

Travis would like to thank his friends, family, interview subjects, and all that have supported him during this exhausting yet profoundly amazing personal endeavor.

The authors would like to jointly thank:

Dudi Appleton, Roger Avary, Irving Belateche, David Bergantino, Shem Bitterman, Sean Clark, Ben Collins, Tim Day, Carl V. Dupré, Todd Farmer, Ryan Freimann, Rob Galluzo, Adam Glass, Lawrence Guterman, Robert Harders, Joe Harris, Stef Hutchinson, Patrick Lussier, Anthony Masi, Marc Allyn Medina, Scott Milam, Dave Parker, Matthew Patrick, Nick Phillips, Phil Rosenberg, Scott Spiegel, John Squires, Josh Stolberg, John Sullivan, Matt Taff, Steve VanMeter, Matt Venne, Jake Wade Wall, Robert Zappia

Printed in Great Britain
by Amazon